T0213621

Lecture Notes in Computer Science　10337

Commenced Publication in 1973
Founding and Former Series Editors:
Gerhard Goos, Juris Hartmanis, and Jan van Leeuwen

More information about this series at http://www.springer.com/series/7407

José Manuel Ferrández Vicente
José Ramón Álvarez-Sánchez
Félix de la Paz López · Javier Toledo Moreo
Hojjat Adeli (Eds.)

Natural and Artificial Computation for Biomedicine and Neuroscience

International Work-Conference on the Interplay
Between Natural and Artificial Computation, IWINAC 2017
Corunna, Spain, June 19–23, 2017
Proceedings, Part I

 Springer

Editors
José Manuel Ferrández Vicente
Departamento de Electrónica, Tecnología
  de Computadoras y Proyectos
Universidad Politécnica de Cartagena
Cartagena
Spain

José Ramón Álvarez-Sánchez
Departamento de Inteligencia Articial
Universidad Nacional de Educación
  a Distancia
Madrid
Spain

Félix de la Paz López
Departamento de Inteligencia Articial
Universidad Nacional de Educación
  a Distancia
Madrid
Spain

Javier Toledo Moreo
Departamento de Electrónica, Tecnología
  de Computadoras y Proyectos
Universidad Politécnica de Cartagena
Cartagena
Spain

Hojjat Adeli
The Ohio State University
Columbus, OH
USA

ISSN 0302-9743   ISSN 1611-3349 (electronic)
Lecture Notes in Computer Science
ISBN 978-3-319-59739-3   ISBN 978-3-319-59740-9 (eBook)
DOI 10.1007/978-3-319-59740-9

Library of Congress Control Number: 2017942994

LNCS Sublibrary: SL1 – Theoretical Computer Science and General Issues

Printed on acid-free paper

This Springer imprint is published by Springer Nature
The registered company is Springer International Publishing AG
The registered company address is: Gewerbestrasse 11, 6330 Cham, Switzerland

Preface

The hybridization between social sciences and social behaviors with robotics, neurobiology and computing, ethics and neuroprosthetics, cognitive sciences and neurocomputing, neurophysiology and marketing will give rise to new concepts and tools that can be applied to information and communication technology (ICT) systems, as well as to natural science fields. Through IWINAC we provide a forum in which research in different fields can converge to create new computational paradigms that are on the frontier between neural sciences and information technologies.

As a multidisciplinary forum, IWINAC is open to any established institutions and research laboratories actively working in the field of this interplay. But beyond achieving cooperation between different research realms, we wish to actively encourage cooperation with the private sector, particularly small and medium-sized enterprises (SMEs), as a way of bridging the gap between frontier science and societal impact, and young researchers in order to promote this scientific field.

In this edition, there were four main themes highlighting the conference topics: affective computing, signal processing and machine learning applied to biomedical and neuroscience applications, deep learning and big data, and biomedical applications.

Traditionally, when ICT research has been performed in relation to the human brain, the focus has been on the cognitive brain. Primary research in computer science, engineering, psychology, and neuroscience has been aimed at developing devices that recognize human affects and emotions. In computer science, affective computing is a branch of the study and development of artificial intelligence that deals with the design of systems and devices that can recognize, interpret, and process human emotions. It is an interdisciplinary field spanning computer sciences, psychology, and cognitive science.

Emotion recognition refers to the problem of inferring the significance of human expressions of different emotions. This inference is natural for human observers but is a non-trivial problem for machines. The data gathered on the cues humans use to perceive emotions in others may be used in machine-learning techniques. Emotional speech processing recognizes the user's emotional state by analyzing speech patterns. EEG analysis may also detect human emotions by studying the positive and negative peaks located in specific areas around 450 ms after stimulus induction. Another area within affective computing is the design of computational devices proposed to exhibit either innate emotional capabilities or that are capable of convincingly simulating emotions. Robots may be used for embodying personality traits that induce desired emotions in humans and behave in an appropriate manner when recognizing human emotional state. Neuroprosthetics may be used for treating emotional disorders by electrical stimulation of certain specific areas in the thalamus or other neural centers.

The increasing spread of in vivo imaging technologies, such as magnetic resonance imaging (MRI), diffusion tensor imaging (DTI), functional MRI (fMRI), single photon emission computed tomography (SPECT), positron emission tomography (PET) and other non-invasive techniques such as electroencephalography (EEG) or magnetoencephalography (MEG), have meant a breakthrough in the diagnosis of several pathologies, such as Alzheimer's disease, Parkinson's disease, etc. Today, signal processing and machine learning methods are crucial as supporting tools for a better understanding of diseases. In this way, signal processing and machine learning applied to biomedical and neuroscience applications became an emergent and disruptive field of research.

Deep learning has presented a breakthrough in the artificial intelligence community. The best performances attained so far in many fields, such as computer vision or natural language processing, have been overtaken by these novel paradigms to a point that only ten years ago was pure science fiction. In addition, this technology has been open sourced by the main artificial intelligence (AI) companies, thereby and hence making it quite straightforward to design, train, and integrate deep-learning based systems. Moreover, the amount of data available every day is not only enormous, but, growing at an exponential rate over the past few years, there has been an increasing interest in using machine-learning methods to analyze and visualize massive data generated from very different sources and with many different features: social networks, surveillance systems, smart cities, medical diagnosis, business, cyberphysical systems, or media digital data. This special session is designed to serve researchers and developers to publish original, innovative, and state-of-the art machine-learning algorithms and architectures to analyze and visualize large amounts of data.

Finally, biomedical applications are essential in IWINAC meetings. For instance, brain–computer interfaces (BCI) implement a new paradigm in communication networks, namely, brain area networks. In this paradigm, our brain inputs data (external stimuli), performs multiple media-access control by means of cognitive tasks (selective attention), processes the information (perception), makes a decision (cognition) and, eventually, transmits data back to the source (by means of a BCI), thus closing the communication loop. Image understanding is a research area involving both feature extraction and object identification within images from a scene, and a posterior treatment of this information in order to establish relationships between these objects with a specific goal. In biomedical and industrial scenarios, the main purpose of this discipline is, given a visual problem, to manage all aspects of prior knowledge, from study start-up and initiation through data collection, quality control, expert independent interpretation, to design and development of systems involving image processing capable of tackling these tasks. These areas are clear examples of innovative applications in biology or medicine.

The wider view of the computational paradigm gives us more elbow room to accommodate the results of the interplay between nature and computation. The IWINAC forum thus becomes a methodological approximation (set of intentions, questions, experiments, models, algorithms, mechanisms, explanation procedures, and engineering and computational methods) to the natural and artificial perspectives of the mind embodiment problem, both in humans and in artifacts. This is the philosophy that prevails at IWINAC meetings, the "interplay" movement between the natural and the artificial, facing this same problem every two years. This synergistic approach will permit us not only to build new computational systems based on the natural measurable phenomena, but also to understand many of the observable behaviors inherent to natural systems.

The difficulty of building bridges between natural and artificial computation was one of the main motivations for the organization of IWINAC 2017. The IWINAC 2017 proceedings contain the works selected by the Scientific Committee from nearly 200 submissions, after the review process. The first volume, entitled *Natural and Artificial Computation for Biomedicine and Neuroscience*, includes all the contributions mainly related to the methodological, conceptual, formal, and experimental developments in the fields of neural sciences and health. The second volume, entitled *Biomedical Applications Based on Natural and Artificial Computing*, contains the papers related to bioinspired programming strategies and all the contributions related to computational solutions to engineering problems in different application domains.

An event of the nature of IWINAC 2017 could not be organized without the collaboration of a group of institutions and people whom we would like to thank, starting with UNED and Universidad Politécnica de Cartagena. The collaboration of the Universidade da Coruña was crucial, as was the efficient work of the local Organizing Committee, chair by Richard Duro with the close collaboration of José Santos and their colleagues José Antonio Becerra Permuy, Francisco Bellas Bouza, Abraham Prieto, Fernando López Peña, Álvaro Deibe Díaz, and Blanca Priego. In addition to our universities, we received financial support from the Spanish CYTED, Red Nacional en Computación Natural y Artificial, Programa de Grupos de Excelencia de la Fundación Séneca and from Apliquem Microones 21 s.l.

We want to express our gratitude to our invited speakers Prof. Hojjat Adeli (Ohio State University, USA), Prof. Manuel Graña (Universidad del País Vasco, Spain), Prof. Martin Greschner (Carl von Ossietzky Universit of Oldenburg, Germany), and Prof. Gusz Eiben (Vrije Universiteit Amsterdam, The Netherlands) for accepting our invitation and for their magnificent plenary talks.

We would also like to thank the authors for their interest in our call for papers and their effort in preparing the papers, condition sine qua non for these proceedings. We thank the Scientific and Organizing Committees, in particular the members of these committees who acted as effective and efficient referees and as promoters and managers of pre-organized sessions and workshops on autonomous and relevant topics under the IWINAC global scope.

Our sincere gratitude also goes to Springer and especially to Alfred Hofmann and his team, Anna Kramer, Elke Werner, and Christine Reiss, for the continuous receptivity, help, and collaboration in all our joint editorial ventures on the interplay between neuroscience and computation.

Finally, we want to express our special thanks to Viajes Hispania, our technical secretariat, and to Chari García and Beatriz Baeza, for making this meeting possible and for arranging all the details that comprise the organization of this kind of event.

We would like to dedicate these two volumes of the IWINAC proceedings to Professor Mira. In 2018, it will have been 10 years without him, without his inquiring spirit. We miss him greatly.

June 2017

José Manuel Ferrández Vicente
José Ramón Álvarez-Sánchez
Félix de la Paz López
Javier Toledo Moreo
Hojjat Adeli

Organization

General Chairman

José Manuel Ferrández Vicente, Spain

Organizing Committee

José Ramón Álvarez-Sánchez, Spain
Félix de la Paz López, Spain
Javier Toledo Moreo, Spain

Honorary Chairs

Hojjat Adeli, USA
Rodolfo Llinás, USA
Zhou Changjiu, Singapore

Local Organizing Committee

Richard Duro Fernández, Spain
José Santos Reyes, Spain
José Antonio Becerra Permuy, Spain
Francisco Bellas Bouza, Spain

Abraham Prieto, Spain
Fernando López Peña, Spain
Álvaro Deibe Díaz, Spain
Blanca Priego, Spain

Invited Speakers

Hojjat Adeli, USA
Manuel Graña, Spain

Martin Greschner, Germany
Gusz Eiben, The Netherlands

Field Editors

Juan Carlos Burguillo Rial, Spain
Alfredo Cuesta Infante, Spain
Adriana Dapena, Spain
Antonio Fernández-Caballero, Spain
Jose García-Rodríguez, Spain
Juan Manuel Górriz, Spain
Javier de Lope Asiain, Spain
Miguel Angel López Gordo, Spain

Dario Maravall Gomez-Allende, Spain
Arturo Martínez-Rodrigo, Spain
Jesus Minguillón, Spain
Juan José Pantrigo, Spain
Blanca Priego, Spain
Javier Ramirez, Spain
Jose Santos Reyes, Spain

International Scientific Committee

Antonio R. Anaya, Spain
Diego Andina, Spain
Manuel Arias Calleja, Spain
José M. Azorín, Spain
Margarita Bachiller Mayoral, Spain
Emilia I. Barakova, Netherlands
Francisco Bellas, Spain
Guido Bologna, Italy
Enrique J. Carmona Suarez, Spain
José Carlos Castillo, Spain
Sung-Bae Cho, Korea
Carlos Colodro Conde, Spain
Ricardo Contreras, Chile
Luis Correia, Portugal
Jose Manuel Cuadra Troncoso, Spain
Richard J. Duro, Spain
Paulo Félix Lamas, Spain
Miguel A. Fernandez-Graciani, Spain
Francisco J. Garrigos Guerrero, Spain
Elena Gaudioso, Spain
Pedro Gomez Vilda, Spain
Manuel Graña, Spain
Roberto Iglesias, Spain
Joost N. Kok, Netherlands
Markus Lappe, Germany
Emilio Leton Molina, Spain
Maria Teresa Lopez Bonal, Spain
Manuel Luque, Spain
Francisco Martínez Álvarez, Spain

Jose Javier Martinez-Alvarez, Spain
Oscar Martinez Mozos, Spain
Rafael Martinez Tomas, Spain
Sergio Miguel-Tomé, Spain
Jose Manuel Molina Lopez, Spain
Miguel Angel Patricio Guisado, Spain
Francisco Peláez, Brazil
Francisco Pelayo, Spain
David Pérez Lizán, Spain
Maria Pinninghoff, Chile
Alberto de Ramón Fernández, Spain
Mariano Rincon Zamorano, Spain
José C. Riquelme, Spain
Camino Rodriguez Vela, Spain
Daniel Ruiz Fernández, Spain
Ramon Ruiz Merino, Spain
Jose M Sabater-Navarro, Spain
Diego Salas-Gonzalez, Spain
Angel Sanchez, Spain
Eduardo Sánchez Vila, Spain
Luis M Sarro, Spain
Andreas Schierwagen, Germany
Antonio J. Tallón-Ballesteros, Spain
Rafael Toledo-Moreo, Spain
Jan Treur, Netherlands
Ramiro Varela Arias, Spain
Carlos Vazquez Regueiro, Spain
Hujun Yin, UK

Contents – Part I

Natural Computing in Bioinformatics

Physiological Computing in Affective Smart Environments

Emotions

Signal Processing and Machine Learning Applied to Biomedical and Neuroscience Applications

Contents – Part II

Human Robot Interaction

Deep Learning

Machine Learning Applied to Big Data Analysis

Computational Intelligence in Data Coding and Transmission

Applications

Theoretical Neural Computation

Robot's and Human's Self: A Computational Perspective

Ángel de la Encarnación García Baños[(✉)]

GUIA Research Group, Escuela de Ingeniería de Sistemas y Computación,
Universidad del Valle, Cali, Colombia
angel.garcia@correounivalle.edu.co,
http://eisc.univalle.edu.co/

Abstract. A hypothesis on how the robot's self might emerge in the future will be set in this paper, as this could help us understand how it worked on humans. Since here, a sound computational explanation about some aspects of consciousness will be offered; as physical, chemical and psychological ones lack power to do so. This explanation involves neural modules that forecast each other and a computational fixed point that emerges from there. In this paper, the self is proposed as an emergent fixed point caused by a loop in the scope of prediction functions inside the brain.

Keywords: Consciousness · Self · Artificial Intelligence · Forecast · Fixed point

1 Introduction

It has often been said that the highest aim for Artificial Intelligence is the creation of consciousness in machines. Even when there are already machines that plan, solve non-mathematical problems, process and produce natural language and other jaw-dropping feats, some scholars claim that for a machine (computer or robot) to be truly intelligent, it has to display features of consciousness such as awareness of its own self and qualia. Nevertheless, human knowledge has been unable to explain consciousness. Even though many theories of consciousness have been proposed, a general consensus has not been reached. The reason for this was indicated by Chalmers [1]: trying to explain consciousness by describing chemical reactions or physical low-level processes, as the famous 40 Hz hypothesis proposed by Crick [2], is like trying to find the beauty of Van Gogh's "Wheatfield with Crows" by examining the pigments used in the painting. Simply stated, it is not the correct level of abstraction.

A low level physical process like the 40 Hz oscillation is, naturally, involved in the perception of a unified subjective experience, but it is impossible to argue that the 40 Hz oscillation originates consciousness by itself. Conversely, many electronic devices that oscillate at this frequency can be built without hope

© Springer International Publishing AG 2017
J.M. Ferrández Vicente et al. (Eds.): IWINAC 2017, Part I, LNCS 10337, pp. 3–9, 2017.
DOI: 10.1007/978-3-319-59740-9_1

to observe any kind of consciousness. 40 Hz oscillation can be an indicator, a measure, or a by-product of consciousness but not a cause.

Then, one might wonder, what level of abstraction may be suitable for the task at hand? Which kind of processes can construct and explain consciousness if they are not physical or chemical? Psychological processes might be an alternative, yet psychology today is mostly experimental and descriptive, and has failed to achieve causal explanations for the phenomena it studies. The only fields of knowledge that have achieved causal power and such a level of abstraction are mathematics and computing (the latter being, in fact, a branch of mathematics). It seems reasonable to assume, thus, that an explanation and representation of consciousness must be something related to information fluxes or feedback loops carried out inside the brain. That is to say, the explanation must be structural, not physical or chemical. The current paper offers an explanation of consciousness from this structural perspective framed as computational functionalism.

Although explaining consciousness has been an elusive goal, remarkable progress has been made in order to understand it in recent years. From all previous works, this paper will focus on a few which, in the author's opinion, seem to point out the right path, mainly due to philosopher Daniel Dennett [4–6] and engineers Hawkins [9] and Kurzweil [11].

According to these authors, for any entity to be considered conscious it must display all of the following:

- Environment awareness: the entity can sense its surroundings, looking for dangerous or beneficial events, reacting to these perceptions and having memories about past similar events.
- The self: the entity can identify itself as distinct from its environment and, apparently, can also govern its body and exercise free will.
- Self-awareness: the entity is able to think about its internal states.
- Qualia: the entity experiences internal subjective states that cannot be compared to their equivalents in the brains of other similar entities.
- Subjective feeling: this is the hard problem of consciousness.

A sound explanation of consciousness should address all these features. The first one is very simple, nowadays, and it can be easily explained as a computing process that maintains internal models, segmenting and representing the behavior of objects in the real world, something like Google's TensorFlow software [13] which recognizes cats in videos. Thus, the rest of this paper will concentrate only on the self and self-awareness. Qualia and subjective feeling will not be discussed here neither additional features like sensory integration, attention focus and others. By the way, focusing on only one object at the time is a capability that implies a contractive function on consciousness as it will be seen later.

2   The Brain as a Prediction Tool

Artificial Intelligence has been defined in many impractical ways, i.e. the science of making machines do things that would require intelligence if done by men as said by Marvin Minsky (quoted by [14, p. 20]). Yet, from an evolutionary point of view, there is a more operational definition: all entity behavior aimed to its own survival and reproduction. There are several levels of intelligence, of course, and the mere fact of being alive is the first of them. Consciousness appears in the highest levels. In this line of reasoning, the main task an entity must accomplish is to forecast its environment to be warned from dangers and alert to opportunities as soon as possible. The second task may be to modify the environment to make its own life easier. However, modifying the environment also requires forecasting all possible outcomes from a given set of potential actions. Internal simulators have been proposed theoretically in Popperian creatures by Dennett [4, p. 88]), in order to test predictions and select the best one. Thus, it can be argued that forecasting is essential to intelligence.

Many other functionalities, if not all, usually ascribed to an intelligent being can be interpreted in terms of forecasting (i.e. classifying, clustering, designing, manipulating, and so on).

A neurobiological discovery supports this idea [3]. There are some neural structures into the neocortex, named cortical columns, whose main function is to forecast. Each structure has six layers of neurons arranged in such a manner as to recognize spatial and temporal patterns, to learn the patterns, to find causal relationships between them and to predict the continuation of a sequence when it begins (as Hawkins [9, p. 60] and Kurzweil [11] point out). At its high level, the brain contains many of these predictive neural modules that receive inputs from other modules, some of which are related to sensory and neuromotor information and others to internal information. As there are about 2×10^8 modules, the existence of closed loops within these modules is almost unavoidable. In other words, it would be natural to think that at some point, these modules will end up trying to predict themselves.

3 Fixed Points

In mathematics, if you have a continuous contractive function that maps into itself in a bounded and closed set $X : \forall x \in X, f(x) \in X$, it can be shown that it has at least one fixed point x_F defined as $f(x_F) = x_F$ [16].

Fixed points also exist in computing: when a function is applied repetitively over its own results, as long as special conditions are met, it may happen that some isolated points emerge asymptotically as overall result as the iteration process unfolds [15].

Consider the following example: a car is traveling from city A to city B along a road. It leaves A at 8:00 am and arrives to B at 11:00 am. Some days later, it makes the reverse travel at the same times, i.e. departing B at 8:00 am and reaching A at 11:00 am. Instantaneous speed in both journeys may vary unpredictably. It can be high, low, zero or even negative (due to traffic lights, traffic jams or even if the driver has to go back to pick something that has been forgotten). Despite not knowing the exact ranges of speed, it can be demonstrated that there is some point along the road where the car passes in both trips at the same time of the day. This is a fixed point. You cannot determine where that point on the road is, neither the time of the day when it happens. But mathematics can prove the existence of at least one fixed point (there could be more).

Consider another more intriguing example: a person has an open box with a pile of sheets of paper. The person takes the paper atop, crumples it (without cutting) and throws it again over the pile. It can be demonstrated that at least one point of this sheet remains in the same vertical state as it was before being crumpled.

These are excruciating problems for the layman. Despite the arbitrary complexity of the trip or the crumpled paper, it can be demonstrated that in both a point remains the same. For most people these are unbelievable statements. The surprise generated from this fact can last for long even if a cursory explanation is given. This perplexity can only be eliminated when knowing all the intricacies of the mathematical demonstration process. It is a well-known fact that fixed points generate perplexity in humans.

4   Making the Self and Self-awareness Emerge

Let us now think of a sophisticated but unconscious robot. This hypothetical robot is somewhat aware of its environment since it can identify isolated objects, it can control its body, and it has a primitive instinct to survive (assuming it was built by an evolutionary algorithm). Because it lacks consciousness, its body is only another piece of its environment as stated by [9, p. 134]. The robot has also forecast algorithms, similar to those proposed by [8,9] or [11].

In its attempt to survive, this robot would forecast all surrounding objects, sometimes successfully, sometimes not so, but the learning algorithms will help it improve its responses. However, it would be impossible for it to predict accurately all objects in all situations. There are often unexpected behaviors in all objects, in all but one. At that point, the robot has made an extraordinary discovery: there is one object that is 100% predictable, the self. Incidentally, this is a fixed point that comes out when a forecasting functionality of a robot is applied over a set of items including the robot itself. Without knowing when or in which part of the brain of the robot it will emerge, its emergence will naturally take place.

Because of this, when talking about consciousness, perplexity can be expected. Double perplexity, in fact, as the main product of consciousness is a fixed point and, simultaneously, I am that fixed point.

A proof of the existence of the fixed point is hard to show, if not impossible. It can be signaled its soundness because neural forecasting space is in some way contractive, but not continuous. Its existence is very probable but not guaranteed, and this could be the case of some mental illness due to several fixed points or the absence of any inside the brain.

The expectations over the self are always fulfilled. This does not happen as a result of the self ruling over the brain, but as a result of the privileged information the forecasting mechanism has about the self. I can know what I am about to do, since my motor neurons can be interrogated to forecast my behavior. Obviously, this information is not available from any other external object.

According to psychologist Nicholas Humphrey, cited by [12, p. 158], evolution pushes organisms to gain consciousness so later this can be used to observe and understand other beings. Without denying the strength of this claim, the opposite can also be proposed: while playing social roles trying to understand others, a special object emerges -the self- and since this very moment self-awareness emerges too, thereby resulting in a circular causality.

5   Discussion and Related Work

Edelman [7] also offers a cornerstone for this paper. In his work, neural feedback loops were described as consciousness-related. He empathized on low level neural feedback loops (reentrant maps as he labeled them). The forecast nature of the main process was not mentioned because he considered recognition as the main function of the brain, instead of prediction, which is the perspective in this paper.

Closed loops of neurons under certain conditions (positive feedback) usually produce quasi-periodic oscillations due to their non-linear nature (chaotic paths with strange attractors). Neural electric activity carried out at this level does not make a solid argument for consciousness. As previously stated, high level concepts are required. The prediction module feedback loop can be traced down to these reentrant maps, for sure, but without the high level prediction concept, it is impossible to sustain any claims about the self.

Closed loops are built by high level prediction modules, in a way that resembles a stochastic Boolean network model proposed by Kauffman [10], differing on the use of prediction modules instead of Boolean gates. In the brain, all these prediction modules are implemented by neurons. On the other hand, in robots, they could be carried out by other kind of algorithms (artificial neurons, genetic algorithms, bayesian reasoning among others).

This is not to say that as fixed points cause perplexity, and consciousness causes perplexity too, then consciousness is a fixed point. The point being made is that due to the modular-predictive architecture of the brain, it is highly likely that a closed loop appears (self-awareness) causing a fixed point to emerge (the self); then, the subjective experience of self-awareness is the same as the one caused by the recognition of a fixed point. To be certain, this argument does not offer a cause-effect explanation of self-awareness subjective experience, but it does offer an alternative to understand the way we perceive it.

It is worth noting that fixed points are not the same as attractor points. In one of the previous examples, the car does not get trapped while it gets to a fixed point. Rather, the car goes along seamlessly. Likewise, the brain does not get stuck when attention is directed to the self. Indeed, after this point, attention can wander to other things.

6 Conclusions

In this paper, the following points have been made:

When an evolutionary being, human or robot (i.e. with its own motivations and capabilities to conduct optimization processes) is endowed with forecast algorithms that try to predict all its internal states (some derived from sensorial inputs, some derived from neuromotor outputs, and some completely internal) a special internal object arises because is 100% predictable, namely, the self.

The self exists as a fixed point. However, it is not the cause of a forecasting closed loop, but rather its product. And free will does not reside in the self. If freedom exists, it is the whole brain that exercises it, not the self. As any other fixed point, the self is associated to perplexity.

Self-awareness exists. However it is not related to magic. Its mystery arises from the potentially infinite loops it generates. A computer in a closed loop can linger on for an infinite number of times but, luckily, the brain gets bored soon and stops the loop after two or three iterations avoiding getting trapped forever. However, this leads to the paradox of the homunculus inside the homunculus, at a figurative level, while leading to the self examining of the self, at a more abstract level. Potentially infinite loops arise rendering self-awareness mysterious. If the researcher attention does not concentrate on these loops, the mystery fades.

From an engineering point of view, only one forecasting closed loop is enough to generate the self and the self-awareness inside the brain of a futuristic robot. It should not be forgotten, though, that the human brain is a very complex structure with richer capabilities. There must be many loops at several description levels, running in parallel and with some acting as inputs or metaphors for others. This loop entanglement creates our conscious rich experience.

References

1. Chalmers, D.J.: Facing up to the problem of consciousness. J. Conscious. Stud. **2**(3), 200–219 (1995)
2. Crick, F., Koch, C.: Towards a neurobiological theory of consciousness. Semin. Neurosci. **2**, 263–275 (1990)
3. DeFelipe, J., Markram, H., Rockland, K.S.: The neocortical column. Front. Neuroanat. **6**(22) (2012). doi:10.3389/fnana.2012.00022
4. Dennett, D.: Consciousness Explained. Penguin Books, London (1991)
5. Dennett, D.: Kinds of Minds - Toward an Understanding of Consciousness. Basic Books, New York (1996)
6. Dennet, D.: Freedom Evolves. Penguin Books, New York (2003)
7. Edelman, G.M.: Bright Air, Brilliant Fire - On the Matter of the Mind. BasicBooks, New York (1992)
8. Google: TensorFlow. https://www.tensorflow.org/
9. Hawkins, J., Blakeslee, S.: On Intelligence. Henry Holt and Co. LLC, New York (2004)
10. Kauffman, S.A.: The Origins of Order. Oxford University Press, New York (1993)
11. Kurzweil, R.: How to Create a Mind - The Secret of Human Thought Revealed. Duckworth Overlook, London (2013)

12. Lewin, R.: Complexity - Life at the Edge of Chaos. MacMillan Publishing Company, New York (1992)
13. Le, Q.V., et al.: Building high-level features using large scale unsupervised learning. In: The 29th International Conference on Machine Learning Conference Proceedings, Edinburgh, pp. 127–137 (2012)
14. Whitby, B.: Reflections on Artificial Intelligence. Intellect Books, Exeter (1996)
15. Wikipedia: Banach contractive maps. https://en.wikipedia.org/wiki/Banach_fixed-point_theorem
16. Wikipedia: Brouwer fixed-point theorem. https://en.wikipedia.org/wiki/Brouwer_fixed-point_theorem

A Neurologically Inspired Network Model for Graziano's Attention Schema Theory for Consciousness

Erik van den Boogaard$^{(\boxtimes)}$, Jan Treur, and Maxim Turpijn

Behavioural Informatics Group, Vrije Universiteit Amsterdam,
Amsterdam, Netherlands
evandenboogaard@hotmail.com, j.treur@vu.nl, maxim.turpijn@gmail.com

Abstract. This paper describes a network-oriented model based on the neuroscientist Graziano's Attention Schema Theory for consciousness. This theory describes an *attention schema* as an internal model of the attention process supporting the control of attention, similar to how our mind uses a *body schema* as an internal model of the body to control its movements. The Attention Schema Theory comes with a number of testable predictions. After designing a neurologically inspired temporal-causal network model for the Attention schema Theory, a few simulations were conducted to verify some of these predictions. One prediction is that a noticeable attention control deficit occurs when using attention without awareness. Another is that a noticeable attention control deficit occurs when using only bottom-up influence (from the sensory representations) without any top-down influence (for example, from goal or control states). The presented model is illustrated by a scenario where a hunter imagines (using internal simulation) a prey which he wants to attend to and catch, but shortly after he or she imagines a predator which he then wants to attend to and avoid. The outcomes of the simulations support the predictions that were made.

1 Introduction

Understanding and modeling consciousness has been a challenge since a long time. Several theories have been put forward over time, often with involvement of neuroscientists or at least essential knowledge from neuroscience; see, for example, [1,2,5,6,11–13] to name just a few. Some of the themes that often recur in such theories are:

- A winner takes it all competition between unconscious processes in order to achieve a selection of what is to reach consciousness; e.g., [1,2,6]
- Internal simulation of the own mental and bodily processes, other persons' mental and bodily processes, and other external processes; e.g., [5,7,11–13]
- By becoming conscious certain aspects are more explicitly presented to (other parts of) the brain and thus become more accessible to the brain; e.g. [1,2,6]
- The relation between attention and consciousness; e.g., [16]

© Springer International Publishing AG 2017
J.M. Ferrández Vicente et al. (Eds.): IWINAC 2017, Part I, LNCS 10337, pp. 10–21, 2017.
DOI: 10.1007/978-3-319-59740-9_2

– The extent to which consciousness fulfils a functional role in behaviour, or instead is only an epiphenomenon

A recent theory which addresses the above five themes is the Attention Schema Theory for consciousness of the neuroscientist Graziano; see, for example, [8–10,23]. It is claimed that this theory explains the brain basis of subjective awareness in a mechanistic and scientifically testable manner. The theory starts with attention which is a process by which signals compete for the brain's limited computing resources. This internal competition is partly under bottom-up influence of sensory representations and partly under top-down control of other mental states such as goal states or control states. According to this theory the top-down control of attention is improved when the brain has access to an (simplified) internal model of attention itself that can be used for internal simulation of the attention process. The brain therefore constructs a schematic model of the process of attention, called the *Attention Schema*. This is similar to the brain's construct of a schematic model of the body, the *Body Schema*, with its role in body movements. The presence of this internal model for attention leads a brain to concluding that it has a subjective experience.

An advantage of the Attention Schema Theory is that it explains how we can be aware of both internal and external events. The brain can apply attention to many types of information including external sensory information and internal information about, for example, affective and cognitive states. If awareness is based on a model of attention, then this model will pertain to the same domains of information to which attention pertains. A further advantage of this theory is that it has a neurological basis and provides testable predictions. If awareness is based on an internal model of attention, used to help control attention (see Fig. 1), then without awareness, attention should still be possible but could show deficits in control.

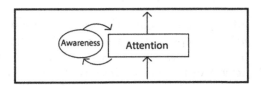

Fig. 1. Awareness as an internal model of attention supporting control of attention

This paper introduces a neurologically inspired computational model for the Attention Schema Theory. The model was designed by a Network-Oriented Modeling approach based on temporal-causal networks [19,20], taking into account causal relations assumed in the Attention Schema Theory. The model addresses all of the five themes mentioned above. It has been used to perform simulation experiments and it was verified by mathematical analysis. Model parameters such as connection weights, update speed factors, and steepness, threshold were estimated to fulfil the requirements that reflect the expected internal behavioural patterns based on the Attention Schema Theory.

2   The Neurologically Inspired Network Model

In this section, the Network-Oriented Modeling approach used is briefly introduced, and the conceptual and numerical representation of the developed network model are described. The Network-Oriented Modeling approach based on temporal-causal networks described in more detail in [19,20] is a generic and declarative dynamic modeling approach based on networks of causal relations. Dynamics is addressed by incorporating a continuous time dimension. This temporal dimension enables modelling by networks that inherently contain cycles, such as networks modeling mental or brain processes, or social interaction processes, and also enables to address the timing of the processes in a differentiated manner. The modeling perspective covers (adaptive) recurrent neural network models and (adaptive) social network models. It is more generic than each of these methods in the sense that a much wider variety of modeling elements are provided, enabling the modeling of many types of dynamical systems, as described by many examples in [19] and confirmed by a formal analysis in [22].

The Network-Oriented Modeling approach is supported by dedicated modeling environments (e.g., in Matlab, or in Pyhon) that can be used to model at a conceptual level. The obtained temporal-causal network models are based on states and connections between them; they can be represented at two levels: by a conceptual representation and by a numerical representation. A conceptual representation of a temporal-causal network model can have a (labeled) graphical form with (states as nodes and connections as edges) or a matrix form (with states on the axes and connections in the cells). More specifically, the following three model parameters define a temporal-causal network, and are part of a conceptual representation of such a network model:

- **connection weight** $\omega_{X,Y}$ Each connection from a state X to a state Y has a *connection weight* $\omega_{X,Y}$ representing the strength of the connection, often between 0 and 1, but sometimes also below 0 (negative effect).
- **combination function** $\mathbf{c}_Y(..)$ For each state Y (a reference to) a *combination function* $\mathbf{c}_Y(..)$ to aggregate the causal impacts of other states on state Y. This can be a standard function from a library (e.g., a scaled sum or logistic function) or an own-defined function.
- **speed factor** η_Y For each state Y a *speed factor* η_Y is used to represent how fast a state is changing upon causal impact, usually in the [0, 1] interval.

Each state Y is assumed to have an (activation) level in the [0, 1] interval that varies over time, indicated in the numerical representation by a real number $Y(t)$. Combination functions can have different forms. The applicability of a specific combination rule may depend much on the type of application addressed, and even on the type of states within an application. Therefore, for the Network-Oriented Modeling approach based on temporal-causal networks a number of standard combination functions are available as options and a number of relevant properties of such combination functions have been identified; e.g., see [19], Chap. 2, Table 2.10. Some of these standard combination functions are scaled sum, max, min, and simple and advanced logistic sum functions. These options cover elements from different existing approaches, varying from approaches based on neural networks to approaches considered for social network modeling, or reasoning with uncertainty or vagueness.

A *conceptual representation* of the designed network model is shown in Fig. 2. The legend shown in Table 1 explains the different states in the model. Nodes outside the box called *Mind* represent external states. For the scenario considered here the model only incorporates two different stimuli; it represents a situation where a human hunter first spots a prey and then is confronted with a predator. This should result in a shift of attention from the prey to the predator and eventually result in the hunter fleeing from the predator instead of going after the prey. An arrow between two nodes means that there is a temporal-causal relation from one state to the pointed state. Such a relation means that one state has either an strengthening (positive connection weight) or a suppressing (negative connection weight) effect on the other state.

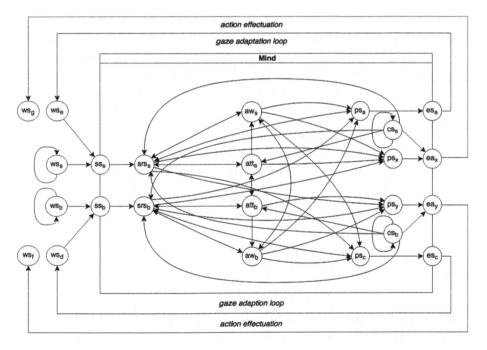

Fig. 2. A graphical conceptual representation of the temporal-causal network model

In the hunter and prey scenario, the external world states ws_s and ws_b respectively represent the prey and predator. The world states ws_e and ws_d represent the output of the *gaze adaptation loop*, which leads to control of the sensor states ss_s and ss_b. This can be interpreted as directing and sharpening of the senses (for example, eyes or ears), as a result of focusing of the attention. The world states ws_f and ws_g represent approaching or distancing behavior with regard to the prey and predator, modelled as *action effectuation*. Specific attention and awareness states were modelled for prey (att_s and aw_s) and predator (att_b and aw_b). These states are affected via both top-down and bottom-up influences. The bottom-up influences occur via the sensory input, which leads to a sensory representation which in turn affect attention and awareness for that input. Top-down influence comes from two control states: cs_s for the prey and cs_b for the predator; for example this can relate to goals.

Besides bottom-up and top-down influence there is also a mutually suppressing effect. For example, a high value of the attention state att_b for the predator will have a suppressing (inhibiting) effect on the attention state att_s for the prey, and conversely. Similarly the awareness states aw_b and aw_s mutually suppress each other. This can work as a winner takes it all competition, in order to obtain a single attention and awareness focus.

Also action execution states are included in the model, with their corresponding preparation states. These can perform gaze adaptation by the *gaze adaptation loop* and actual execution of actions (e.g., escape from the predator) by the *action effectuation loop*. But the preparation states (without activating the corresponding execution states) also play an important role in internal simulation. Internal simulation takes place by using internal *as-if loops* as a kind of shortcuts for the gaze adaptation loop and the action effectuation loop. These as-if loops are modeled by direct (predictive) connections from preparation states to the sensory representation states of the effects of the prepared actions. Via these internal as-if loops, so-called *simulated action and perception chains* are generated [11–13], through which the preparation states directly affect the sensory representation states of the action effects, instead of through the external loop via action execution, action effectuation, and sensing.

The conceptual representation of the model can be transformed into a numerical representation in a systematic manner. The *impact* of state X_i on state Y at time point t can be determined by multiplying the state value $X_i(t)$ of each state X_i ($i = 1, 2, .., k$) with impact on Y by the weight $\omega_{X_i,Y}$ of the connection from X_i to Y:

$$\mathbf{impact}_{X_i,Y}(t) = \omega_{X_i,Y}\, X(t) \qquad (1)$$

The aggregated impact is a combination of multiple impact values $V_{X_i,Y} = \mathbf{impact}_{X_i,Y}(t)$ for the states X_i and is calculated using combination function $\mathbf{c}_Y(..)$:

$$\mathbf{aggimpact}_Y = \mathbf{c}_Y(V_{X_1,Y}, \ldots, V_{X_k,Y}) = \mathbf{c}_Y(\omega_{X_1,Y}X_1, \ldots, \omega_{X_k,Y}X_k) \qquad (2)$$

Table 1. Legend of the state labels in the model

ws_s	World state for prey	ps_a	Preparation state for action a
ws_b	World state for predator	ps_c	Preparation state for action c
ss_s	Sensor state for prey	ps_x	Preparation state for action x
ss_b	Sensor state for predator	ps_y	Preparation state for action y
srs_s	Sensory representation state for prey	es_a	Execution state for action a
srs_b	Sensory representation state for predator	es_c	Execution state for action c
aw_s	Awareness state for prey	ea_x	Execution of action x
aw_b	Awareness state for predator	ea_y	Execution of action y
att_s	Attention state for prey	ws_d	World state for d
att_b	Attention state for predator	ws_e	World state for e
cs_s	Control state for prey	ws_f	World state for f
cs_b	Control state for predator	ws_g	World state for g

The speed of the influence of $\mathbf{aggimpact}_Y(t)$ on Y depends on the speed factors η_Y. Thus the following *difference* and *differential* equations are obtained for each state Y:

$$
\begin{aligned}
T(t + \Delta t) &= Y(t) + \eta_Y \left[\mathbf{aggimpact}_Y(t) - Y(t)\right] \Delta t \\
&= Y(t) + \eta_Y \left[\mathbf{c}_T\left(\omega_{X_1,Y} X_1(t), \ldots, \omega_{X_k,Y} X_k(t)\right) - Y(t)\right] \Delta t \quad (3) \\
dY(t)/dt &= \eta_Y \left[\mathbf{c}_T\left(\omega_{X_1,Y} X_1(t), \ldots, \omega_{X_k,Y} X_k(t)\right) - Y(t)\right]
\end{aligned}
$$

The current model consists of 24 states and about 50 connections. Note that not all connections are active during a specific scenario, for example, as discussed in the next section. For the combination functions for the control states in the presented model the *identity function* $\mathbf{id}(..)$ was used:

$$
\mathbf{c}_Y(V) = \mathbf{id}(V) = V \quad (4)
$$

The identity function was used here as in the scenario illustrated here the control states have only a single impact, from themselves. The other states use the *scaled sum combination function* $\mathbf{ssum}\lambda(\ldots)$ with scaling factor λ:

$$
\mathbf{c}_Y(V_1, .., V_k) = \mathbf{ssum}_\lambda(V_1, .., Vk) = (V_1 + .. + V_k)/\lambda \quad (5)
$$

To avoid negative state values a prevention is applied: if the outcome of $(V_1 + .. + V_k)/\lambda$ is negative, the value 0 is taken for $\mathbf{ssum}_\lambda(V_1, .., V_k)$ instead; so in fact the following is used: $\mathbf{ssum}_\lambda(V_1, .., V_k) = \max(0, (V_1 + .. + V_k)/\lambda)$. This is important for cases in which negative connection weights are involved to model suppression. Note that in the Network-Oriented Modeling approach followed, also alternative combination functions can be used, for example logistic sum functions. A change of combination function is similar to and as simple as a change of a parameter value.

3   Simulation Experiments

Several scenarios were simulated, based on the literature on the Attention Schema Theory, with a hunter first hunting for a spotted prey and later fleeing from a spotted predator. Figure 3 shows an internal simulation scenario. In this scenario the external stimuli (ws_s and ws_b) are inactive and the internal states are triggered internally by the control states (cs_s and cs_b). All parameter values of this example simulation can be found in the Appendix.

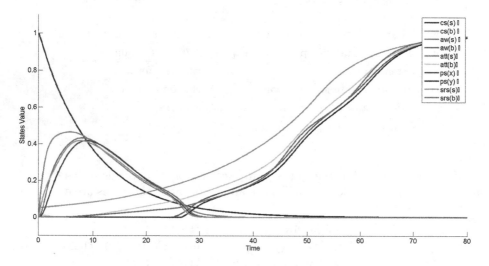

Fig. 3. Example simulation: internal simulation

The hunter first visualizes (constructs a mental image of) a prey and attention to it and then visualizes a predator and attention to it. This will cause a shift in (simulated) attention from the prey to the predator. For this scenario, the attention state att_s for the prey initially increases, which also leads to an increase in awareness state aw_s of the prey. As soon as the predator is visualized, the attention shifts from the prey to the predator which is shown as a *decrease* in the activation level of the attention state att_s for the prey and an *increase* in the level of the attention state att_b for the predator. This effect also occurs for the awareness states aw_s and aw_b for prey and predator. The sensory representation states and preparation states for action execution also follow the same trend, but no action is executed, because as it only concerns internal simulation, these states are suppressed by the control states.

4   Verification by Mathematical Analysis

In order to verify the model a general method for verification of temporal-causal networks was followed. It is based on substitution of values from a simulation in stationary point equations; see [21] or [19] Chap. 12. A state Y has a *stationary point* at time point t if $dY(t)/dt = 0$. A stationary point is usually a local maximum or a local minimum. Using the simulations by the model, several stationary points can be found. Using the difference or differential Eq. (3) mentioned earlier and a scaled sum combination function it can be deduced that a state Y has a stationary point at t if and only if:

$$\textbf{aggimpact}_Y(t) = Y(t)$$
$$\textbf{c}_Y\left(\omega_{X_1,Y}X_1(t), \ldots, \omega_{X_k,Y}X_k(t)\right) = Y(t) \tag{6}$$
$$\left(\omega_{X_1,Y}X_1(t) + \cdots + \omega_{X_k,Y}X_k(t)\right)/\lambda = Y(t)$$

Three stationary points were selected:

1. a local maximum for state att_s (attention for the prey)
2. a local minimum for state ps_y (preparation state *before* attention shifts from prey to predator)
3. a local minimum for state srs_s (sensory representation state *after* attention shifts from prey to predator)

According to this verification method, the model is verified by using for each of the stationary points mentioned above the state values from the simulation and substituting them into the equation above (6). As an example, the equation expressing that att_s is stationary at time t is as follows:

$$\textbf{aggimpact}_{\textbf{att}_s}(t) = att_s(t)$$
$$\max\left(0, \left(\omega_{\textbf{cs}_s,\textbf{att}_s}cs_s(t) + \omega_{\textbf{srs}_s,\textbf{att}_s}srs_s(t) + \omega_{\textbf{att}_b,\textbf{att}_s}att_b(t)\right)/\lambda\right) \tag{7}$$
$$= att_s(t)$$

In the simulation results shown in Fig. 3 a maximum for state att_s is found at $t = 5.8$. For att_s, the scaling factor is $\lambda = 1.7$. This provides the equation

$$\max\left(0, \left(\omega_{\textbf{cs}_s,\textbf{att}_s}cs_s(5.8) + \omega_{\textbf{srs}_s,\textbf{att}_s}srs_s(5.8) + \omega_{\textbf{att}_b,\textbf{att}_s}att_b(5)\right)/1.7\right) \tag{8}$$
$$= att_s(5.8)$$

From the simulation data it was found that the state value for att_s at this time point is 0.4651, while the state value for cs_s is 0.5639 at $t = 5.8$, srs_s had a state value of 0.3954, and att_b had a state value of 0. The weight $\omega_{\textbf{cs}_s,\textbf{att},s}$ was 0.7, the weight $\omega_{\textbf{srs}_s,\textbf{att},s}$ was 1 and the weight $\omega_{\textbf{att}_b,\textbf{att},s}$ was -0.1. Substituting these values into the equation above (7) results in the following

$$\max(0, (0.7 * 0.5639 + 1 * 0.3954 - 0.1 * 0)/1.7) = 0.4651$$
$$0.4648 = 0.4651$$

So the equation for this stationary point holds with an accuracy <0.001. Next stationary points verified are a minimum for ps_y that can be found at $t = 20$ and a minimum for srs_s found at $t = 60$. The same method was used as above and this resulted in the following equations:

$$\max(0, (\omega_{\textbf{aw}_b,\textbf{ps}_y}aw_b(20) + \omega_{\textbf{srs}_s,\textbf{ps}_y}srs_s(20) + \omega_{\textbf{att}_b,\textbf{ps}_y}att_b(20) +$$
$$\omega_{\textbf{srs}_b,\textbf{ps}_y}srs_b(20))/\lambda) = ps_y(20) \tag{9}$$

Substitution of the values provides

$$\max(0, (1 * 0 - 1 * 0.1932 + 0 * 0.0596 + 1 * 0.0343)/2) = 0$$
$$\max(0, -0.0794) = 0$$
$$0 = 0$$

So, the equation for this stationary point holds with accuracy 0. Finally

$$\max(0, (\omega_{ss_s,srs_s} ss_s(60) + \omega_{cs_s,srs_s} cs_s(60) + \omega_{aw_s,srs_s} aw_s(60) \\ + \omega_{att_s,srs_s} att_s(60) + \omega_{ps_a,srs_s} ps_a(60)\omega_{cs_b,srs_s} cs_b(60))/\lambda) = srs_s(60) \tag{10}$$

Substitution provides:

$$\max(0, (1 * 0.0017 + 1 * 0.0024 + 1 * 0 + 1 * 0 + 1 * 0 - 3 * 0.8503)/5) = 0$$
$$\max(0, -0.5094) = 0$$
$$0 = 0$$

The equation for this stationary point also holds with a very small accuracy 0. These verification results provide some evidence that the implemented model is correct.

5   Discussion

The presented neurologically inspired temporal-causal network model, designed following the Network-Oreinted Modeling approacvh put forward in [19,20], is based on the Attention Schema Theory for consciousness recently developed by neuroscientist Michael S.A. Graziano and others; e.g. [8–10,23]. The model was illustrated for a relatively simple scenario in which an attention shift takes place in relation to two different stimuli. For reasons of presentation the incorporated model of attention was kept simple. However, the network model can also incorporate a more complex model for attention involving multiple stimuli, for example, as described in [4].

A number of conclusions can be drawn from the different simulation experiments that have been performed using the developed model, among which the one shown in Sect. 3. These simulation experiments show a functional role of awareness in evolutionary perspective as theorized by, for example, [6]. Given the temporal-causal loop between attention and awareness, it turns out that the impact on attention grows faster and higher than without this loop being active. Based on the results of simulation scenarios such as the one shown in Fig. 3, support was found for a positive effect of visualizing a scenario by internal simulation to the flow of attention and awareness. With an amplifying effect of the (bottom-up) sensory representation states, the effect on both attention and awareness is prolonged with an amplifying effect on attention to the predator which may lead to a faster response to the occurrence of the predator, because a preparation state threshold is exceeded sooner. This suggests a potential faster response to, for example, an encounter with a predator or prey which implies an increased survival chance and therefore an evolutionary advantage. So, it seems that the developed model based on the Attention Schema Theory, connects well to some theories about the functional role of awareness; see also [23]. These theories also provide an answer to the question of whether or not subjective awareness serves a useful purpose or whether it is merely an epiphenomenon with no clear purpose. This suggests that an attention schema may be of great utility, at least, in the top-down control of attention.

Future research can be done to test the model more extensively, by simulating more scenarios, in relation to claims made in literature such as [8–10,23]. Although these scenarios at the time of writing were not all tested yet, it is however likely that the model will also work with these scenario's, because they mostly largely rely on the same internal connections and patterns generated by them. The following additional example scenarios are some of the relevant ones:

1. *Simulation with external stimuli* of a prey and a predator.
   Based on previous results with the model using control states to trigger internal simulation (visualization) of stimuli (prey and predator), similar results using real world external stimuli (world states for prey and predator) can be expected. The only real difference is that in this case the sensory representation states are activated by the sensor states instead of by the control states; the rest of the processes will be similar.
2. Simulation with external stimuli (visible prey and predator) and external reactions (eye gaze, approaching, fleeing) using *attention without awareness*
   In this scenario first the hunter attends to the prey which he does *not* become aware of (achieved by disconnecting those parts of the model), and soon after the predator comes into sight his attention shifts from the prey to the predator and there is no shift in awareness from the prey to the predator. It can be predicted that the attention level - *without* awareness - will not rise as fast and as high as *with* awareness, as there are less causal impacts on the attention states; see also [23]. If this indeed is the case, then this confirms that awareness can play a crucial role in attention such that *without* awareness a reaction to spotting a prey or a predator may be too late or even absent which leads to an increased existential risk for the hunter.
3. A *mirroring scenario* where an individual spots another hunter reacting to a prey and a predator.
   In this case the trigger is not from internal control states or from external stimuli concerning prey or predator, but from external stimuli concerning observation of another hunter addressing prey and predator. By way of modeling a mirroring mechanism, the sensory representations corresponding to these observations are connected to the own preparation states (with mirror function) as if the hunter him or herself would be in the situation. These preparation states trigger the whole internal simulation process (mental imagination) as shown in Sect. 3. Based on the results of the presented model, for this case similar results can be expected compared to the case of using real external stimuli (for prey and predator) for the hunter him or herself. In addition, a self-other distinction control state can be incorporated, so that the hunter is able to know that in this case it is not his or her own process

that is internally simulated but somebody else's. This is a basis for generating empathy with somebody else: having and feeling the same mental states, but at the same time knowing that they are relating to states of somebody else; e.g., [18]. This scenario relates to an angle on consciousness as related to social interaction; see also [9], Chap. 10 on more elaboration on the relation of the Attention Schema Theory to social theories of consciousness, and [14] to how this may relate to attributing awareness to somebody else.

Appendix   Parameter Values Used in the Example Simulation Shown in Sect. 3

states and connections	1 ws_a	2 ws_b	3 ss_a	4 ss_b	5 srs_a	6 srs_b	7 aw_a	8 aw_b	9 att_a	10 att_b	11 ps_a	12 ps_c	13 ps_x	14 ps_y	15 es_a	16 es_c	17 cs_a	18 ea_x	19 cs_b	20 ea_y	21 ws_d	22 ws_e	23 ws_f	24 ws_g
1 ws_a	0.9	0	0	0	0	0	0	0	0	0	0	0	0	0	0	0	0	0	0	0	0	0	0	0
2 ws_b	0	1.5	0	0	0	0	0	0	0	0	0	0	0	0	0	0	0	0	0	0	0	0	0	0
3 ss_a	0	0	0	0	1	0	0	0	0	0	0	0	0	0	0	0	0	0	0	0	0	0	0	0
4 ss_b	0	0	0	0	0	1	0	0	0	0	0	0	0	0	0	0	0	0	0	0	0	0	0	0
5 srs_a	0	0	0	0	0	0	1	0	1	0	1	-1	1	-1	0	0	0	0	0	0	0	0	0	0
6 srs_b	0	0	0	0	0	0	0	1	0	1	-1	1	-1	1	0	0	0	0	0	0	0	0	0	0
7 aw_a	0	0	0	0	0	0	0	-1	0	0	1	1	1	0	0	0	0	0	0	0	0	0	0	0
8 aw_b	0	0	0	0	0	1	-1	0	0	0	1	1	0	1	0	0	0	0	0	0	0	0	0	0
9 att_a	0	0	0	0	1	0	1	0	0	-0.1	0	0	0	0	0	0	0	0	0	0	0	0	0	0
10 att_b	0	0	0	0	0	1	0	1	-0.1	0	0	0	0	0	0	0	0	0	0	0	0	0	0	0
11 ps_a	0	0	0	0	1	0	0	0	0	0	0	0	0	0	1	0	0	0	0	0	0	0	0	0
12 ps_c	0	0	0	0	0	1	0	0	0	0	0	0	0	0	0	1	0	0	0	0	0	0	0	0
13 ps_x	0	0	0	0	0	0	0	0	0	0	0	0	0	0	0	0	1	0	0	0	0	0	0	0
14 ps_y	0	0	0	0	0	0	0	0	0	0	0	0	0	0	0	0	0	0	1	0	0	0	0	0
15 es_a	0	0	0	0	0	0	0	0	0	0	0	0	0	0	0	0	0	0	0	0	1	0	0	0
16 es_c	0	0	0	0	0	0	0	0	0	0	0	0	0	0	0	0	0	0	0	0	0	1	0	0
17 cs_a	0	0	0	0	1	-0.1	0	0	0	0.7	0	0	0	0	0	0	0	-2	-1	0	0	0	0	0
18 ea_x	0	0	0	0	0	0	0	0	0	0	0	0	0	0	0	0	0	0	0	0	0	0	0	1
19 cs_b	0	0	0	0	-3	1	0	0	0	0.7	0	0	0	0	0	0	0	0	1.5	-1	0	0	0	0
20 ea_y	0	0	0	0	0	0	0	0	0	0	0	0	0	0	0	0	0	0	0	0	0	1	0	0
21 ws_d	0	0	0	1	0	0	0	0	0	0	0	0	0	0	0	0	0	0	0	0	0	0	0	0
22 ws_e	0	0	1	0	0	0	0	0	0	0	0	0	0	0	0	0	0	0	0	0	0	0	0	0
23 ws_f	0	0	0	0	0	0	0	0	0	0	0	0	0	0	0	0	0	0	0	0	0	0	0	0
24 ws_g	0	0	0	0	0	0	0	0	0	0	0	0	0	0	0	0	0	0	0	0	0	0	0	0

speed factors

0.3	0.3	1	1	1	1	1	1	1	1	1	1	1	1	0.1	0.1	0.1	0.1	0.1	0.1	0.1	0.1	0	0

initial values

0	0	0	0	0	0	0	0	0	0	0	0	0	0	0	0	0	1	0	0.05	0	0	0	0

combination functions

	1	2	3	4	5	6	7	8	9	10	11	12	13	14	15	16	17	18	19	20	21	22	23	24
id(.)	0	0	0	0	0	0	0	0	0	0	0	0	0	0	0	0	1	0	1	0	0	0	1	1
ssum(..)	0	0	0	0	1	1	1	1	1	1	0	0	1	1	0	0	0	0	0	0	0	0	0	0
factor λ	0	0	0	0	5	5	2	2	1.7	1.7	0	0	2	2	0	0	0	0	0	0	0	0	0	0
slogistic(..)	1	1	0	0	0	0	0	0	0	0	0	0	0	0	0	0	0	0	0	0	0	0	0	0
steepness σ	10	10	0	0	0	0	0	0	0	0	0	0	0	0	0	0	0	0	0	0	0	0	0	0
threshold τ	0.6	0.368	0	0	0	0	0	0	0	0	0	0	0	0	0	0	0	0	0	0	0	0	0	0
alogistic(..)	0	0	1	1	0	0	0	0	0	0	1	1	0	0	1	1	0	1	0	1	1	1	0	0
steepness σ	0	0	10	10	0	0	0	0	0	0	10	10	0	0	10	10	0	10	0	10	10	10	0	0
threshold τ	0	0	0.5	0.5	0	0	0	0	0	0	0.5	0.5	0	0	0.5	0.5	0	0.5	0	0.5	0.5	0.5	0	0

References

1. Baars, B.J.: In the Theater of Consciousness: The Workspace of the Mind. Oxford University Press, Oxford (1997)

2. Baars, B.J.: The conscious access hypothesis: origins and recent evidence. Trends Cogn. Sci. **6**, 47–52 (2002)
3. Bosse, T., Jonker, C.M., Treur, J.: Formalisation of Damasio's theory of emotion, feeling and core consciousness. Conscious. Cogn. **17**, 94–113 (2008)
4. Bosse, T., van Maanen, P.-P., Treur, J.: Simulation and formal analysis of visual attention. Web Intell. Agent Syst. **7**, 89–105 (2009)
5. Damasio, A.R.: The Feeling of What Happens. Body and Emotion in the Making of Consciousness. Harcourt Brace, New York (1999)
6. Dennett, D.C.: Consciousness Explained. Little Brown, Boston (1991)
7. Goldman, A.I.: Simulating Minds: The Philosophy, Psychology, and Neuroscience of Mindreading. Oxford University Press, New York (2006)
8. Graziano, M.S.A., Webb, T.W.: The attention schema theory: a mechanistic account of subjective awareness. Front. Psychol. **6**, 1–11 (2015)
9. Graziano, M.S.A.: Consciousness and the Social Brain. Oxford University Press, New York (2013)
10. Graziano, M.S.A., Webb, T.W.: A mechanistic theory of consciousness. Int. J. Mach. Conscious. **6**, 163–176 (2014)
11. Hesslow, G.: Will neuroscience explain conscious-ness? J. Theoret. Biol. **171**, 29–39 (1994)
12. Hesslow, G.: Conscious thought as simulation of behaviour and perception. Trends Cogn. Sci. **6**, 242–247 (2002)
13. Hesslow, G.: The current status of the simulation theory of cognition. Brain Res. **1428**, 71–79 (2012)
14. Kelly, Y.T., Webb, T.W., Meier, J.D., Arcaro, M.J., Graziano, M.S.A.: Attributing awareness to oneself and to others. In: Proceedings of the National Academy of Sciences, U.S.A., vol. 111, pp. 5012–5017 (2014)
15. Kim, J.: Philosophy of Mind. Westview Press, Boulder (1996)
16. Koch, C., Tsuchiya, N.: Attention and consciousness: two distinct brain processes. Trends Cogn. Sci. **11**, 16–22 (2007)
17. Port, R.F., van Gelder, T.: Mind as Motion: Explorations in the Dynamics of Cognition. MIT Press, Cambridge (1995)
18. Singer, T., Leiberg, S.: Sharing the emotions of others: the neural bases of empathy. In: Gazzaniga, M.S. (ed.), pp. 973–986. MIT Press (2009)
19. Treur, J.: Network-Oriented Modeling: Addressing Complexity of Cognitive, Affective and Social Interactions. Springer, Heidelberg (2016)
20. Treur, J.: Dynamic modeling based on a temporal-causal network modeling approach. Biologically Inspired Cogn. Architectures **16**, 131–168 (2016)
21. Treur, J.: Verification of temporal-causal network models by mathematical analysis. Vietnam J. Comput. Sci. **3**, 207–221 (2016)
22. Treur, J.: On the applicability of network-oriented modeling based on temporal-causal networks: why network models do not just model networks. J. Inf. Telecommun. **1**, 23–40 (2017)
23. Webb, T.W., Kean, H.H., Graziano, M.S.A.: Effects of awareness on the control of attention. J. Cogn. Neurosci. **28**(6), 842–885 (2016)

Multilevel Darwinist Brain: Context Nodes in a Network Memory Inspired Long Term Memory

Richard J. Duro$^{(\boxtimes)}$, Jose A. Becerra, Juan Monroy, and Luis Calvo

Integrated Group for Engineering Research,
Universidade da Coruña, A Coruña, Spain
{richard,ronin,juan.monroy,luis.calvo}@udc.es

Abstract. The Multilevel Darwinist Brain (MDB) is a cognitive architecture aimed at providing autonomous and self-motivated life-long learning capabilities for robots. This paper deals with a new structure and implementation for the long term memory (LTM) in MDB based on Fuster's concept of Network memory and on the introduction of a new type of node or cognit called Context Node (Cnode). The idea of Network memory as proposed here, provides a path to hierarchically and progressively relate LTM knowledge elements, allowing for a developmental approach to learning that permits very efficient experience based responses from the robot. We include a simple, albeit quite illustrative, example of the application of these ideas using a real Baxter robot.

Keywords: Cognitive architecture · Long term memory · Network memory

1 Introduction

From a Psychological or Cognitivist perspective, "a cognitive architecture is a broadly-scoped domain-generic computational cognitive model, capturing the essential structure and process of the mind, to be used for broad, multiple-level, multiple-domain analysis of behavior." [1]. Thus, we can consider it a generic computational model, a basic operational mechanism that is not specific to any particular task or domain. It is only when knowledge is introduced or acquired that it can carry out tasks in particular domains. As indicated by Vernon, a cognitive architecture establishes the structure and organization of a cognitive system through the definition of the modules that make it up and their relationships as well as the way knowledge is acquired, represented, and acted upon, including the types of memories used to store it [2].

An artificial cognitive architecture is always based on a set of assumptions and views of the designer. Most designers take inspiration from the only reference that is available, that is, natural cognitive architectures and, in particular, from their assumptions on how the one that is closest to them (the human one) operates.

© Springer International Publishing AG 2017
J.M. Ferrández Vicente et al. (Eds.): IWINAC 2017, Part I, LNCS 10337, pp. 22–31, 2017.
DOI: 10.1007/978-3-319-59740-9_3

Natural cognitive architectures, however, were not designed the way they are, they are the result of a very long evolutionary process of the species and reflect the interactions of the evolutionarily changing hardware (bodies, organs, sensors, etc...) with different sets of environments. The result is a mixture of knowledge and structures present at birth (phylogenetically coded knowledge) that include a set of capabilities that allow the modification of the knowledge content (and maybe even some of the structures) in order to adapt to the particular environments and situations the organism faces (ontogenetically acquired knowledge).

In any case, the final function of a cognitive architecture is to provide a means for a motivated system (a system that has goals) to choose actions that allow those goals to be fulfilled. Thus, appropriately deciding on what actions to choose each instant of time is what a cognitive architecture is about. These decision processes almost always revolve around two main concepts: prospection and experience.

Prospection has to do with the prediction and evaluation of future states so that the system can select among the potential actions or policies as a function of the expected achievement of its goals. It requires performing predictions into the future, usually carried out by models (forward models, world models, internal models), and evaluations of the predicted states by means of value functions.

On the other hand experience has to do with relationships the system has found among its knowledge components (models, policies, perceptual classes, etc.) when it was successful at achieving a goal (or, in some cases, even unsuccessful). These relationships allow the system to directly choose an action or policy if it can determine the context it is in, that is, if it can determine in which world it is operating, what its goal is and what is its current perception. Through these previously observed relationships it can directly activate the action or policy that produced a successful result in a previous instance of the same or a similar context.

Both of these decision making approaches require of a long term memory where the system can store knowledge elements that it has learnt (models, policies, perceptual classes, value functions, etc.), but more importantly, where it can store the experience based relationships among these knowledge elements. Long term memory is critical for addressing lifelong learning and cognition [3]. However, most authors have paid very little attention to this system except as a passive storage container for knowledge. A computer architecture like analogy of the mind has been the predominant paradigm in this regards: memory as a hard disk. Thus, human memory is usually described as a storage system organized by content with discrete encoding, storage, and retrieval functions [3].

However, authors such as [3,4] argue that to achieve properties such as adaptivity, flexibility and robustness, biological system memories are a distributed and active component of cognition which in embodied agents should be situated within the perception–action cycle of adaptive behavior. Consequently, memory is proposed as the central component of any cognitive architecture. Furthermore, authors like Oberauer [6] or Fuster [4] do not even adhere to the classical division of memory into two separate subsystems: Short Term Memory (STM) and Long Term Memory (LTM). They take STM as the currently activated parts of LTM. Anyway, whatever the view, the most relevant mechanisms for life-long cognition are those related to LTM and its operation.

In particular, in Fuster's view [5], memory consists of the modulation of synaptic contacts within distributed networks of interconnected cortical cells. Memory is achieved through the potentiation or inhibition of synaptic links between neural aggregates as a response to perceptual or other types of activations. These activation patterns supported by the connections between neural populations that are acquired through experience is what he calls memory networks or cognits [4]. A consequence of this model is that memories can be taken as distributed throughout large areas of the associative cortex, with nodes corresponding to neural aggregates with particular processing functions that are linked through synaptic links that connect them, much in the same way as graphs. It follows that in this view memory shares the same neurons and networks used by perception, defining perception as object classification by means of the activation of the networks that represent these concepts in memory.

From a computational perspective, this approach is similar to that of traditional semantic networks, as considered for instance in ACT-R [7]. However, autonomously acquired network memories that grow directly from the perceptual apparatus of the system all the way to the executive part of the cognitive structure without any explicit foreignly imposed symbolic structure does not suffer from the problems of classical symbolic approaches with respect, for instance, to grounding. In this line, Wood indicates that the storage of semantic information is a property of the memory system as embedded in the wider cognitive architecture [3] and not something that is explicitly encoded. In fact, these ideas become very important in architectures such as the one we are working on, which aim at exploiting development as a facilitator of life-long learning. In this case, LTM becomes one of the most important parts of the architecture as it is where the knowledge the system has acquired, and upon which it must developmentally construct new knowledge, is stored.

This paper is concerned with presenting our current advances in the introduction of the concept of network memory within the LTM structure of the Multilevel Darwinist Brain cognitive architecture. In particular, it deals with the introduction of the concept of Context Nodes and the initial experiments carried out to demonstrate their effectivity. Thus, Sect. 2 is devoted to a brief introduction of the Multilevel Darwinist Brain. The network memory based LTM structure that has been constructed is described in Sect. 3. An example of its use in a real robot is presented in Sect. 4. Finally, some conclusions and outlooks are provided in Sect. 5.

2   Cognitive Architecture and Multilevel Darwinist Brain

A robot must be able to obtain enough utility from an initially not completely known world in order to survive for as long as possible (in other words, its utility level must not drop below a certain threshold for as long as possible). As indicated in the introduction, a cognitive mechanism is the structure that allows for this in an open-ended manner in a closed loop between the system and the world. Thus, in a cognitive mechanism, knowledge is exploited to lead the robots towards Goals (points or areas in state space that provide utility).

The Multilevel Darwinist Brain (MDB) is a cognitive architecture for real time robotics. When designing the MDB, the idea was to create a computationally effective structure that provided the required cognitive functionality. We were not looking to produce a biologically plausible, but rather a biologically inspired architecture. MDB follows a developmental approach and its operation revolves around 4 basic types of elements:

- Models: prediction structures in the form of forward models and satisfaction models (value functions in reinforcement learning terms) that are usually instantiated as Artificial Neural Networks. They conform the declarative knowledge acquired through interaction with the world. MDB relies on evolutionary algorithms for model learning,
- Policy or Behavior: a policy is a decision structure that needs to be learnt and that provides the action to be applied in time t from the sensorial input in t.
- Episodes: real world samples that are obtained from the robot sensors and actuators after applying an action. Typically, within the MDB these episodes are made up of the sensorial information plus the applied action in time t and the sensorial information including sensed rewards or satisfaction derived from the execution of the action in time $t + 1$. These episodes are used as targets for model learning.
- Memories: two main kinds of memory elements were considered in the first implementations of the MDB: Short-Term (STM) and Long-Term (LTM)
  - The STM is made up of a model memory, which contains models and behaviors that are relevant to the current task, and an episodic buffer (EB) that stores the last episodes experienced by the robot. The EB has a very limited capacity according to the temporal nature of the STM.
  - The LTM is made up the models that have been consolidated due to their significance and reliability, and the consolidated behaviors.

The full details of the operation of the MDB can be found in [8]. However, as a short summary, we have to say that the MDB interacts with its environment by performing actions, these produce new perceptions and rewards (which, in any case, are also perceptions) that are stored together in the episodic memory as episodes. The elements in the episodic memory are used as ground truth, that is, as the information obtained from reality to determine the fitness of evolving populations of models by testing them over the episodic memory instances. These populations are evolved just for a few generations for every interaction with the environment (we do not want the models to converge to a particular content of the small episodic memory, but rather to slowly converge to the series of episodic memories it is being exposed to). The best current models are selected and used in order to evaluate possible policies that are being generated in a second evolutionary process. This is achieved through a prospective process that determines the new state a policy would lead to (using forward or world models) and provides a satisfaction or reward value for this state (using the satisfaction model or value function). The best policy is chosen and it is used to select the next action to apply to the environment. This policy will be active until a new policy that improves on it is provided by the MDB. Those models and policies that are successful and are applied to the real world are copied to LTM for their preservation and possible reuse. It is how LTM is constructed and managed that is the subject of the work we are presenting here.

3   Network Memory Based Long Term Memory

The MDB tries to fulfill a robot's goals by means of an appropriate choice of actions or policies to carry out in order to survive in the long term. To this end, apart from random selection, a robot has mainly two possible mechanisms for choosing actions or policies: Experience or Prospection.

In this paper we are going to concentrate on the issues surrounding experience based action selection (EBAS), as the prospection based case has been considered before [8]. To this end, we are going to expand the basic LTM structure of the traditional MDB in order to accommodate the relationship structure that would be necessary for EBAS through the introduction of a series of concepts inspired by the memory network ideas proposed by Fuster [5].

By experience based decision we mean that as the system interacts with the world it can relate a state S_i and a policy or action that was successful (even though initially the policy could have been chosen at random) and save this relationship in some type of memory so that the policy can be reused when the same state arises. In general, this is a bit more complex, as the validity of a policy to produce a result given an initial state (its repeatability) also depends on the result we want (the goal) and on the world we are in (we assume the world includes the agent), as different worlds may work differently. It is not the same to walk on solid ground than on ice, for instance. In general, the world we are in can be identified by knowing which forward model is successful at predicting it or, alternatively, by having a particular sensor that helps identify worlds. Thus, we must relate the state (S_i) or its representation (R_n), the goal (G_k) or its related value function (V_k), the policy (π_r) and the successful forward model (FM_j) and when the tuple $\{S_i, FM_j, G_k\}$ is found again, then the system can infer that applying policy π_r, should lead to a successful result.

The need of experience based decision making of having context dependent mechanisms available to recover information from LTM as well as the need of later memory consolidation processes to have access some type of neighborhood structure of LTM contents so that similarities can be detected and generalizations made, has driven us to create a new LTM structure that goes beyond the simple storage of knowledge elements of the MDB (individual policies, perception classes, forward models, value functions) that were successful. To this end, and following the principles stated by Wood [3] and Fuster [4], we started in [9] by directly introducing experience modulated activating or inhibitory connections between the different knowledge elements present in the LTM (they are usually neural groups represented as ANNs). These connections were strengthened when those instances of the elements co-occurred, that is, when they were chosen to carry out a decision process in the robot leading to the final instantiated behavior. The resulting structure they generated was a graph where the connections are the edges and the knowledge elements of the architecture stored in the LTM are the nodes (see Fig. 1(a)).

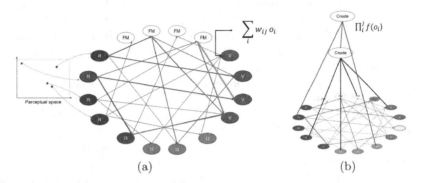

$$\sum_i w_{ij} o_i \qquad \Pi_i^j f(o_i)$$

(a)   (b)

Fig. 1. Memory network based approaches in the MDB LTM: (a) direct activation and inhibition, (b) including context nodes.

The operation of this first approach could be described by considering that when a new perception (P_s) is presented to the agent, its represention class (R_n) is activated, activating whatever links it has to forward models, policies or value functions. This activation is propagated through the graph, either until the policy level is reached, in the case of a strictly tree like structure, or until some type of convergence, time limit or attractor is reached in the case of considering all of the possible cycles and feedback connections in the graph. The activation pattern will determine what elements are related through experience to the perceptual state and how strongly they are related to it. Thus, the policy with the highest activation can be chosen for direct application in urgent cases (strictly experience based approach) and/or a subset of all the elements in the architecture consisting of those with the highest activations can be selected and used in order to evaluate policies through deliberative processes in a prospective manner when considering both experience and prospection.

As indicated before, a long term learning process occurs through the permanent modification of the edge weights through co–occurrence. A consequence of this is that the connectivity structure that arises tends to define in what contexts an element is activated. That is, elements with similar connectivity vectors will tend to be activated in similar contexts or situations. Therefore, the connectivity matrix itself can be used to establish some order or neighborhood structure for the different elements in the LTM. Elements with connectivity vectors that are similar can be considered similar. Independently of whether the nodes themselves present any structural similarity, they respond to the same contexts.

However, as the number of worlds and tasks the architecture is faced with grows, this simple connectivity structure becomes quite difficult to maintain. It tends to drift depending on the sequence in which the system is faced with the worlds or goals it has to work with and on how long it is presented with each combination (which in real systems cannot be predicted). Thus, the connectivity matrix is quite local in time and tends to forget co–ocurrence relationships related to world–goal combinations it has not seen in a while or even get stuck in connectivities related to combinations it has seen for too long or that are simpler. This is mainly due to the fact that the activation of a node is given by a function over a summation of its inputs (activations of the nodes leading to it that go through weighed edges) and the training is achieved by increasing and decreasing the weights in the edges.

To address this issue, we propose here to delegate the task of relating elements in a more permanent way to a new type of knowledge element that is added to the previously presented LTM structure, a relational node we have called "context node" or Cnode for short (see Fig. 1(b) for a depiction of the LTM structure with Cnodes). A context node is a node that is created when the co–occurrence of a series of elements within the LTM leads to a relevant event. All the elements that co–occur are linked to the newly created Cnode through weighed connections. Initially, relevant events are taken as events in which a reward is achieved, but any other type of event could be considered. Basically, the idea is that whenever a reward is obtained, it is not a bad idea to remember in a relatively permanent manner the context in which this occurred. Cnodes become active when the product of their inputs surpass a threshold (in a binary case, when this product is not zero).

In the case of continuous domains, the connections leading from the sensing apparatus of the system to a Cnode are filtered for each dimension of state space. This means that each dimension of the state or perceptual space that is linked to the Cnode is connected to it through a filtering function (a Gaussian, for instance) that determines the value interval of that particular dimension (variable) that is relevant for the Cnode decision. Any value of that variable that is outside the corresponding interval will lead to a zero in that link and, as Cnodes are product units, to a zero total input to the Cnode. These intervals for the filtering functions are learnt through interaction with the world. Initially, they will be very narrow and given by the first perceptual (state) point that led to a reward for that particular world, goal and policy but as more states lead to rewards for the same context in terms of world, goal and policy, these filters will become less narrow and will correspond to wider multipoint areas in state space. Summarizing, Cnodes represent memories of relevant events that are related in LTM. Thus, in cases were we consider only a finite number of world–goal combinations (domain-task combinations), once the cognitive architecture has identified all the contexts (world, goal, state space area, policy) that lead to relevant events by interaction of the sytem with the world, it will have Cnodes for each one of them. Thus it will be able to directly choose or activate appropriate policy (series of actions) in order to obtain a reward or reproduce the relevant event in any case where this is possible.

4   Application Example

In order to demonstrate the operation and capabilities of the approach introduced above, we present a very simple experiment using the Baxter Robot. The setup is shown in any of the images of Fig. 3. A Baxter robot sees, using its camera, a workspace where there are two containers, one with a round hole and one with a square hole. There are also two objects, a cube and a cylinder, with colored lights on top (red and blue). The cube fits in the square hole and the cylinder in the round one. The Baxter robot can grab any of the two objects and it can move them anywhere within its reach, including putting them in one of the holes. However, the robot perceptual system only detects the colored light on top of each object, it does not detect shape. This implies that the only way the robot has to distinguish one shape from the other is through the colored light on it.

Using this basic setup, we have constructed an experiment that involves two types of worlds and two types of tasks (as defined by their goals). In one world, cylinders have a red light on top and cubes a blue light. In the other world, the light assignment is inverted (cylinders are blue and cubes red). Regarding the goals, there are two possible situations: reward is obtained when a hole (the screen in the scene indicates which hole) is full with the correct shape or reward is obtained when all the holes are empty. The initial state may involve one of the holes having the wrong object in it, which implies taking it out before being able to put the other one in.

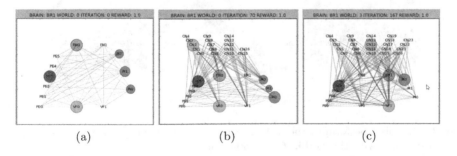

(a)   (b)   (c)

Fig. 2. Three states of the LTM during the interaction with the world.

Thus, as this is a very simple experiment, we can know in advance all the possible combinations of things that should lead to the creation of Cnodes, that is, all of the relevant events. In terms of goals and worlds, we have four combinations. For each of these cases, there are six relevant situations, leading to a total of 24 Cnodes that should be obtained through interaction with the different worlds with different goals. We assume that the robot will not be interacting continuously with any world (they will change randomly) and that its goal will change after a random number of interactions. This implies that, in fact, the robot will have to learn to achieve the maximum reward concurrently in the four situations.

Figure 2 displays a sequence of views of the robot LTM. One at the beginning of the process, where there are no Cnodes, one after 70 interactions with the different worlds and one after 167 interactions. At the beginning, the robot is performing a trial and error process. It is making mistakes that allow it to find the relevant events. After 70 interactions with the world, the robot has already learnt some Cnodes, and when the associated situations arise, the robot chooses the right policy directly. Exploration is only taking place with regards to the ones it has not learnt yet. It is easy to see that after 167 interactions, the robot has learnt all of the possible relevant events in the environment and, thus, when faced with any state in any of the four world-goal combinations, it directly chooses the optimal policy. It is very important to note here that this process was quite efficient and did not take very long. Figure 3 shows four snapshots of the robot doing one of the tasks.

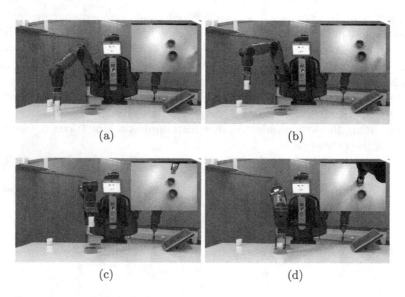

Fig. 3. The robot performing the task of introducing a cube in the square hole in after 170 interactions with the world. (Color figure online)

5   Conclusions

In this paper we have presented a new implementation of the long term memory of the Multilevel Darwinist Brain cognitive architecture. This new implementation is based on the ideas of Fuster's memory networks, which establish a graph-like connection structure among the knowledge components stored in LTM (models, policies, perceptual classes, goals,...). In the implementation presented here we have introduced a new type of node called Context Node, or Cnode, which provides for the establishment of product–like activations that permit the long term storage of context relationships. The combination of this type of connectivity together with the basic direct connection among components that provide a summation type activation function allow for the categorization of the context space into classes corresponding to the relevant events the robot must associate in order to be able to achieve rewards in the environment it is faced with. These ideas were tested over a simple experiment using a real Baxter robot and the results were very promising.

Acknowledgements. This work has been partially funded by the EU's H2020 research programme grant No 640891 (DREAM) as well as by the Xunta de Galicia and the European Regional Development Funds grant redTEIC network (ED341D R2016/012).

References

1. Sun, R.: The importance of cognitive architectures: An analysis based on CLARION. Journal of Experimental & Theoretical Artificial Intelligence. **19–2**, 159–193 (2007)
2. Vernon, D.: Artificial cognitive systems: A primer. MIT Press (2014)
3. Wood, R., Baxter, P., Belpaeme, T.: A review of long-term memory in natural and synthetic systems. Adaptive Behavior **20–2**, 81–103 (2012)
4. Fuster, J.: Cortex and memory: emergence of a new paradigm. J. Cogn. Neurosci. **2111**, 20472072 (2009)
5. Fuster, J.: Network memory. Trends Neurosci. **20–10**, 451–459 (1997)
6. Oberauer, K.: Access to information in working memory: Exploring the focus of attention. J. Exp. Psychol. Learn. Mem. Cogn. **28–3**, 411–421 (2002)
7. Anderson, J.R., Reiser, B.J.: Production systems and the ACT-R theory. Mind readings: Introductory selections on cognitive science,59–76 (1998)
8. Bellas, F., Duro, R.J., Faiña, A., Souto, D.: Multilevel Darwinist Brain (MDB): Artificial evolution in a cognitive architecture for real robots. IEEE Trans. Auton. Ment. Dev. **2**, 340–354 (2010)
9. Duro, R.J., Becerra, J.A., Monroy, J., Caamano, P.: Considering Memory Networks in the LTM Structure of the Multilevel Darwinist Brain. Proceedings of the 2016 on Genetic and Evolutionary Computation Conference Companion, 1057–1060 (2016)

Motivational Engine for Cognitive Robotics in Non-static Tasks

Rodrigo Salgado, Abraham Prieto, Francisco Bellas$^{(\boxtimes)}$, and Richard J. Duro

Integrated Group for Engineering Research, Universidade da Coruña,
15403 Ferrol, Spain
{rodrigo.salgado,abprieto,francisco.bellas,richard}@udc.es
http://www.gii.udc.es

Abstract. This work proposes a new method to model the extrinsic motivation of a cognitive architecture based on the discovery of *separable utility regions* (SUR), which reduce the complexity of the standard value functions typically used. Those regions exhibit a correlation between the expected utility and the response of one sensor of the robot. Once they are discovered, the evaluation of the candidate states is only based on the changes of one sensor, which provides a strong independence from noise or dynamism in the utility models. A non-static variation of the classical collect-a-ball scenario was used to test the mechanism in order to generate and define the certainty maps associated to those SURs. Preliminary results show a good response of the technique and a clear improvement in performance when this is associated to a restructuring mechanism for the utility model, which, in this case, corresponds to the creation and chaining of sub-goals.

Keywords: Motivational system · Extrinsic motivation · Cognitive robotics

1 Introduction

The motivational system of a cognitive robot is in charge of the evaluation of the candidate states according to a set of innate and learned motivations [1,2]. From this evaluation, the robot selects the action that must be applied in the environment to reach a goal state. As a consequence, the motivational system guides the cognitive development, from learning to operation. The most remarkable approaches in this line [3] distinguish between two main types of motivations: intrinsic and extrinsic. Intrinsic motivations can be assimilated to innate motivations, those obtained by evolution in animals or humans, and they are involved in exploring the state space to promote learning without requiring the presence of an explicit goal. Intrinsic motivations have been widely analyzed in reinforcement learning [4] and cognitive robotics [5], and their ultimate goal is to improve autonomous knowledge and skill acquisition. On the other hand, extrinsic motivations drive the robot towards reaching a goal state where a reward can be

© Springer International Publishing AG 2017
J.M. Ferrández Vicente et al. (Eds.): IWINAC 2017, Part I, LNCS 10337, pp. 32–42, 2017.
DOI: 10.1007/978-3-319-59740-9_4

obtained based on the current knowledge. Typically, extrinsic motivations have also been provided by the designer, creating, again, a sort of innate motivation [6,7]. This approach can be useful from a practical point of view if we aim to have a robot that can solve a set of predefined tasks in a controlled fashion.

However, following a more general and cognitivist perspective, extrinsic motivations should be autonomously acquired during development [8,9]. Thus, the robot may start its operation with just a set of predefined sensors and intrinsic motivations, as commented above. When some sensorial states are reached, the robot receives a reward, which defines a goal and, as a consequence, a new extrinsic motivation emerges guiding the robot operation towards fulfilling such motivation. Many other extrinsic motivations can appear during robot development, and the motivational system must handle them efficiently. From a practical point of view, this approach means that the robot is able to learn any goal (any task) if an appropriate reward is provided, for instance, by an external teacher.

As part of the EU's H2020 DREAM project (www.robotsthatdream.eu), we have proposed a new motivational system called MotivEn (Motivational Engine) based on the previous framework. Thus, MotivEn considers a cognitive robot as an open-ended system that operates guided by autonomously learned extrinsic motivations, but containing a set of innate intrinsic motivations required to foster robot development in the most reliable way. MotivEn has been tested in a collect-a-ball experiment in simulation [10] and with a real robot [11], providing successful results in the autonomous acquisition of new goals and sub-goals in static tasks. In this paper, we present a new version of the MotivEn motivational system improved to operate in *non-static* cases, that is, in more realistic tasks where the sensorial path to reach the goal state can change between episodes.

2   Motivational Engine

In order to formalize the MotivEn framework, some basic definitions are required:

- *Sensorial state (S):* an array of sensorial values in a given instant of time. It should be noted that MotivEn operates in continuous domains.
- *Action (A):* set of values provided to the robot actuators
- *Reward (R):* scalar value that can be measured by the robot which defines its goal. The robot aims to maximize the reward it achieves during its lifetime.
- *Utility function (UF):* function that assigns a reward to the sensorial states. It is out of the control of the robot and depends on the problem nature.
- *Episode (E):* sample of the real world response to the robot actions.

$$episode = [S(t), A(t), S(t+1), R(t+1)]$$

- *Trace (T):* discretized trajectory of episodes that finish with a reward
- *Episodic buffer (EB):* memory element that stores the last episodes experienced by the robot. The EB has a predefined limited capacity

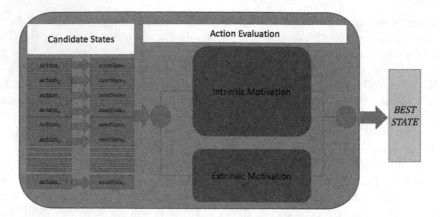

Fig. 1. MotivEn state evaluation based on intrinsic and extrinsic motivations

– *Value Function (VF):* function representing the expectancy-value (V), that is, the assessment of the cognitive system on how probable it is that it will get a reward starting from that point modulated by the amount of the expected reward. It is a useful internal representation of the utility function:

$$V(t+1) = VF(S(t+1))$$

The expectancy-value (hereafter value) at a state space point containing a reward is the value of the reward. At any other point with no reward, it will be a value that is smaller than the reward and which is assigned by the motivational system to provide information to the robot and thus allow it to reach the reward by following state space paths of increasing value.

The original version of MotivEn [11] was based on the motivational model shown in Fig. 1. We assume that there is a cognitive architecture that selects a set of candidate actions and provides a set of candidate sensorial states that must be evaluated by the motivational system in a given instant of time. The combination of intrinsic and extrinsic motivations must be correctly handled in order to choose the most appropriate sensorial state, with the final objective of guiding the robot towards the completion of its tasks. In a first approach, we have defined two types of intrinsic motivations (IM) [11]. The *Blind IM* guides the robot behavior towards the discovery of unvisited sensorial states and operates as an explorative intrinsic process. The *Certainty-based IM* is devoted with guiding the robot to improve the VF, that is, it enhances learning to increase VF reliability. On the other hand, the *Extrinsic Motivation* is a single component based on the current VF model which aims to maximize the utility function. However, since modeling the utility function can require more than one VF due to its complexity or some other learning limitations (trace length, memory size...), MotivEn is endowed with a sub-goal creation mechanism to divide VF into simpler sub-VFs, including a sub-VF combination mechanism [11].

As commented in the introduction, this initial MotivEn approach was highly successful in static environments [10], but in the case of more complex scenarios it was not possible to obtain a reliable VF model. To solve it, we have developed an improved Extrinsic Motivation component for the MotivEn, which will be described in the following section.

3   Extrinsic Motivation for Non-static Tasks

To provide an extrinsic motivational value for a sensorial state, apart from the one provided by the VF, we introduce a second method based on the concept of *separable utility regions (SUR)*. These represent subspaces of the sensorial space where the expected utility and the value of one sensor are correlated, this is, the VF corresponding to that region would be a one dimensional and monotonic function. The identification of SURs in the state space provides a fast and simple way of implicitly defining VFs. SURs are defined by the sensor which is correlated, the tendency of the correlation (increasing or decreasing in a first approach) and the region where they are active. Therefore, all the effort is focused on correctly finding regions where one of the possible correlations (2 x number of sensors) is active and there is no need to model any explicit utility model. In a way, the use of SURs to estimate the utility function constitutes an orthogonal linearization of the model. In this work, we have developed an algorithm that is continuously searching for tendencies in the sensor values as a way to find possible SURs. This algorithm operates concurrently with the VF learning that was used in the previous version of MotivEn [11], so we now have two extrinsic criteria to evaluate the sensorial states. As a first approach, the VF will only be used if no SUR can be detected.

Before presenting how SURs have been implemented in MotivEn, a definition of the regions where they are active (certainty areas) must be carried out.

3.1   Certainty

Our extrinsic motivation model considers the fact that the reliability of the value provided by the VF is not uniform, neither in time nor in (state) space. In the first stages of learning, there are a small number of traces that can be used to learn the VF, so its reliability remains low. Also, in regions that are far away from those where the goal was found, the VF is not reliable either. Hence, the extrinsic motivation requires a measurement that indicates the validity of the VF in those points. Similarly, the definition of SURs also requires information to indicate where they are active and how reliable that activation is. To this end, we have defined a *certainty function* which associates, for each sensorial state, a certainty (reliability) value. This function works mainly as a density map based on the visited past states that are stored as traces in the episodic buffer (EB), assuming that if a new state is close to an old state, the information we acquired from the old state could be used to extrapolate information to the new one [11].

To create the certainty maps, the system must handle three types of traces:

- Positive Traces (p-traces): created when a goal is reached while the robot is acting in a existing certainty area under the influence of its extrinsic motivation.
- Negative Traces (n-traces): created when a robot fails to reach a goal under the influence of the extrinsic motivation in its associated certainty area.
- Weak Positive Traces (w-traces): created when a goal is reached but the robot was not executing actions guided by its extrinsic motivation (for instance, the robot reached a goal by exploring an unknown part of the environment).

On the one hand, p-traces will have a positive weight on the density certainty value, while n-traces will have a negative one. On the other hand, we consider w-traces as positive traces that are not as reliable as proper p-traces, because the robot was not taking into account its extrinsic motivation directly to reach the goal, so the information obtained may not be consistent. W-traces will have less influence on the certainty value and their presence in the system will be temporal, however very important to the initial steps of the creation of certainty maps. The area of influence of each type of trace (p, n or w-traces) varies with time. The addition of p-traces expands the certainty area, while the addition of n-traces reduces it. It starts being wider, covering most of the state space, and it gradually converges towards a range which is correlated with the variance of the available trace points.

The following mathematical model defines the implementation used for the creation of certainty maps. First, of all, we provide some basic definitions:

- $T \equiv \{t_1, t_2, t_3, t_4, \ldots\}$ is the set of trace points (episodes) that will be used to define the certainty map. Each point is defined by n components (n sensors), $t_j \equiv \{c_1^j, c_2^j, c_3^j, \ldots, c_n^j\}$.
- $d_j^m = \max_i \left| c_m^j - c_m^i \right|$ is the maximum distance, for the m-th dimension, between the j-th trace point and the rest of the trace points in T.
- $D^m \equiv \{d_1^m, d_2^m, d_3^m, \ldots, d_n^m\}$ is the set of the maximum distances for all the points in T.
- $De_y^m = perc_y(D^m)$ is the y-effective distance in dimension m, being $perc_y(X)$ the percentile y over the set X.
- N_T is the number of traces available. $N_T = N_{ht} + C_f * N_{st}$: sum of p-traces and c_f times w-traces.
- L_m^{sup} and L_m^{inf} is the superior and inferior limits of the m-th sensor.
- $D_r = \min_j \{ \left| c_m^j - L_m^{sup} \right|, \left| c_m^j - L_m^{sup} \right| \}$ is the minimum distance to the m-th sensor limits.
- p is the point of coordinates $\{p_1, p_2, \ldots, p_n\}$ in the state space for which the certainty is to be computed.
- $h_m^j = \left| p_m - c_m^j \right|$ is the distance in the m-th dimension between the j-th trace point and any point p.

Thus, we can define H_{lim} as the limit distance in dimension m from which the traces quickly decrease their effect on the state space. It is calculated as:

$$H_{lim} = \begin{cases} \dfrac{De_{100}^m + (Dr^m - De_{100}^m) * K^{N_T - 1}}{2}, & Dr^m > De_{100}^m \\ \dfrac{De_{100}^m}{2}, & Dr^m > else \end{cases}$$

with $K = 0.05^{\frac{1}{N_{T5\%}-1}}$ and $N_{T5\%}$ being the number of traces to reduce the feasible distance to $1.05De_{100}^m$ ($N_{T5\%} = 4$ by default), and with $De_{100}^m \equiv max(D^m)$. Based on this limit, the effective distance in the m-th dimension between the j-th trace point and any point p, hn_j^n, is calculated using the following expression:

$$hn_j^n = \begin{cases} h_m^j, & h_m^j < c_eH_{lim} \\ c_eH_{lim} + (h_m^j - c_eH_{lim}) * M, & else \end{cases}$$

Finally, the weight, W_j of a trace point t_j in any point p is calculated as follows:

$$W_j = \frac{norm_t(\{hn_j^1, hn_j^2, \ldots, hn_j^n\}))}{L_m^{sup} - L_m^{inf}}$$

Combining the weights of p-traces, n-traces (Z_j) and w-traces, (W_j^*), the certainty value for a point p is given by:

$$C = max\left(0, \tanh\left(c_p * \left(\Sigma_T W_j + c_w * W_j^* - c_a Z_j\right)\right)\right)$$

with c_w and c_a being the weighing factors for n- and w-traces regarding p-traces.

3.2 Separable Utility Regions (SUR)

The idea behind the SURs is to model the expected utility by chaining regions which require of movements in the search space associated to increasing or decreasing a specific sensor value in order to reach the goal. This way, the implicit value function proposed will be very simple, this is, the action that most increments/decrements the sensor value will get a higher evaluation. As mentioned, the learning process in this case relies on the determination of what SUR is active each moment and in what direction (incremental or decremental). MotivEn will initially consider all possible SURs and will try to find traces that support them. As new traces are included in the episodic memory, some of the SURs are deactivated and some others are reinforced. This way, the suitable SUR will be finally activated in each point in the state space.

Under this approach, the robot can be in three situations according to its current action-selection criterion:

1. If one SUR is active, the state evaluation follows that sensor as long as it can until it reaches a goal.
2. If there no SUR is active but there are reliable SURs associated to the current state (certainty value higher than 0) the robot randomly selects a SUR among those with positive certainty and activates it, then all possible candidate states are evaluated according to that sensor response.
3. In any other case, the states are evaluated using the blind IM.

A tendency trace will be an ordered list of perceptual states s_t for which a specific sensor value is increased/decreased with respect to s_{t-1}. So, after a goal achievement, a robot with n sensors, will create m tendency traces being $m \leq n$.

As these tendency traces are created depending on the increase or decrease of a sensor value, both situations cannot be possible for the same sensor. In addition, some sensors could present a constant value, so no tendency trace would be created for them. If the goal was achieved while a sensor tendency was active, its relative tendency trace would be an s-trace, and the remaining $m - 1$ would be w-traces. These tendency traces would have different lengths depending on when the tendency is broken.

3.3 Sub-goals

The certainty area is now limited to a state subspace that is close (depending on the trace length limitation) to the goal. This way, a large part of the state space would be outside the certainty area. To complete the Extrinsic Motivation model, we must be able to combine different certainty areas with their own extrinsic evaluation structures. This way, we create the concept of sub-goal in this new representation. As obtaining a reward would be considered the goal of the robot, and associated to this the traces will be created, now reaching a certainty area will be considered a sub-goal, and the traces for reaching it would be linked to a new extrinsic evaluator in a hierarchical way.

4 Experimental Results

The simulated experiment that has been used to test the new MotivEn implementation is shown in Fig. 2, and it is based on the collect-a-ball experiment originally proposed by Ollion and Doncieux [12]. The scenario is divided into two parts by a wall. The robot is placed in the left part, where it can sense a blue box and an green button. In the right side there is a red ball that, initially, cannot be perceived by the robot. The robot is able to move on this environment and to reach the different objects. Hitting the button makes the wall open, allowing the robot to see the ball. Whenever the robot reaches the ball, it automatically picks it up. Also, when the robot reaches the box carrying the ball, the ball is dropped into the box and the robot receives a reward. This event triggers a reset of the scenario and all the elements (button, box, ball and robot) are placed in a random location, creating this way a non-static version of this experiment.

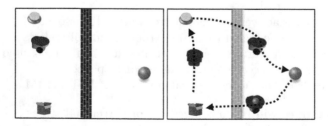

Fig. 2. Collect-a-ball scenario with a typical execution trace followed by the robot (Color figure online)

The robot has three sensors: distance to the green button (g), distance to the red ball (r) and distance to the blue box (b). When it cannot see the ball, the sensor returns the maximum distance it can measure. As for the actions (a), the robot can change its orientation by an angle between $-90°$ and $90°$, with a constant linear speed. Consequently, the sensorial state is given by a vector (g,r,b).

This experiment implies that the robot has to learn a complex and ordered behavior. In order to achieve a reward it will first have to reach the button, then go and pick the ball, so that it can finally go to the box, drop it, and receive the reward. Initially, the robot has no idea of where the reward is or of how to reach it. It will thus have to discover the reward and associate it to a point in its state space. The fact that the different elements in the scenario can be located anywhere produces that the utility model may show inconsistencies (dynamism) from one run to the next. Therefore, it provides an interesting scenario to test whether the extrinsic motivation model benefits from using SURs.

In order to understand how MotivEn creates the certainty model associated to all SURs, Fig. 3 displays the final state of the certainty regions for all available SURs at the end of the learning process in an exemple execution of this experiment. The first three rows show the active certainty regions for the first goal of the scenario (reaching the box while carrying the ball: distance zero to

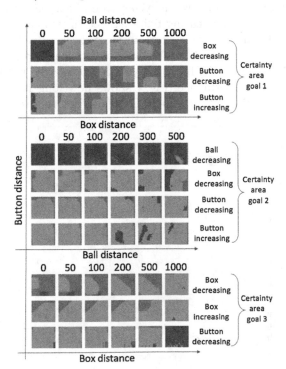

Fig. 3. Activation of the SURs for the different sub-goals. Representation of the certainty values of the SURs. Blue, violet and red represent, positive, zero and negative values of certainty respectively (Color figure online)

ball and box). Box, button and ball distances are represented in the x axis, y axis (in each graph) and column (discretized into 6 ball distances). Each row represents one SUR. Blue areas represent regions with positive certainty, violet indicates zero certainty and red indicates negative certainty. In the first goal, only three SURs generated traces and most of them are concentrated in the box distance decreasing SUR, as expected. More in detail, only when ball distance is zero is the box distance decreasing SUR active, for any value of box and button distance, this is, when carrying the ball follow the direction which minimizes box distance. Sometimes, when the robot is carrying the ball (ball distance = 0) close to the box, increasing the distance to the button can lead to fortuitously (robot located between button and box) reaching the box. Thus, we can also find active regions in the button distance increasing SUR for ball distance = 0 and box distance $\simeq 0$. Several button decreasing traces were also created but negative traces overcome positive ones removing any active area. As a result, the active (blue) area in this set of SURs (ball and box distances = 0: reaching the box while carrying the ball) becomes a goal for the next set of SURs.

The next four rows indicate the SURs which received traces to reach the second goal. In this case the ball, button and box sensors are represented by X, Y and columns in order to better visualize the active areas. The most populated SUR is the one which corresponds to decreasing the ball distance and the whole state space is active. Therefore, when trying to find the ball, wherever you are in the state space aim for decreasing ball distance (if you can see the ball: ball distance < 1000). Finally, the third certainty sets seek to *see* the ball and the active region created corresponds to the button distance decreasing SUR and to ball distance = 1000 (reach the button if you do not see the ball).

Regarding general performance, Fig. 4 shows how long it takes to find the goal in a typical run of 8000 iterations. Each red dot represents the iteration

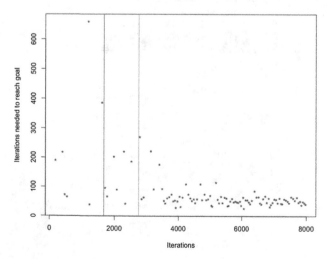

Fig. 4. Evolution of the time to reach the goal as the SURs are learnt and activated. Green and blue lines indicate the creation of first and second sub-goals. (Color figure online)

when the main goal was reached (ball to the box). The Y axis represents how many iterations it took for the robot to find the goal in each run. The green vertical line indicates the creation of the first sub-goal (find the ball). The blue vertical line indicates the creation of the second sub-goal (press the button). The figure shows how the time to reach the goal gradually decreases and that the creation of sub-goals is associated with that reduction. Shortly, after the creation of the second sub-goal, the system learns the last certainty area and converges to a stable performance in finding the goal.

5 Conclusions

An improved version of the MotivEn motivational system for cognitive robots designed to operate in non-static tasks has been presented. It is based on the identification of *separable utility regions*, which constitutes a simple and fast way of implicitly defining Value Functions. To provide a first indication of the usefulness of SURs, we have tested them in a non-static version of the collect-a-ball experiment, showing the potential of the proposed method, which allowed us to solve this task in a more general and autonomous fashion.

Acknowledgments. This work has been partially funded by the EU's H2020 research and innovation programme under grant agreement No. 640891 (DREAM project) and by the Xunta de Galicia and redTEIC network (ED341D R2016/012).

References

1. Cangelosi, A., Schlesinger, M.: Developmental Robotics: From Babies to Robots. MIT Press, Cambridge (2015)
2. Ryan, R., Deci, E.: Intrinsic and extrinsic motivations: classic definitions and new directions. Contemp. Educ. Psychol. **25**, 54–67 (2000)
3. Baldassarre, G., Mirolli, M.: Intrinsically motivated learning systems: an overview. In: Baldassarre, G., Mirolli, M. (eds.) Intrinsically Motivated Learning in Natural and Artificial Systems, pp. 1–14. Springer, Heidelberg (2013)
4. Singh, S., Lewis, R.L., Barto, A.G., Sorg, J.: Intrinsically motivated reinforcement learning: an evolutionary perspective. IEEE Trans. Auton. Mental Dev. **2**(2), 70–82 (2010)
5. Oudeyer, P.Y., Kaplan, F., Hafner, V.V.: Intrinsic motivation systems for autonomous mental development. IEEE Trans. Evol. Comput. **11**(2), 265–286 (2007)
6. Di Nocera, D., Finzi, A., Rossi, S., Staffa, M.: The role of intrinsic motivations in attention allocation and shifting. Front. Psychol. **5**, 273 (2014)
7. Bellas, F., Duro, R.J., Faiña, A., Souto, D.: MDB: artificial evolution in a cognitive architecture for real robots. IEEE Trans. Auton. Mental Dev. **2**, 340–354 (2010)
8. Nguyen, S.M., Baranes, A., Oudeyer, P.Y.: Bootstrapping intrinsically motivated learning with human demonstration. In: Proceedings of ICDL 2011, pp. 1–8 (2011)
9. Huang, X., Weng, J.: Inherent value systems for autonomous mental development. Int. J. Humanoid Robot. **4**, 407–433 (2007)

10. Salgado, R., Prieto, A., Bellas, F., Duro, R.J.: Improving extrinsically motivated developmental robots through intrinsic motivations. In: Proceedings of ICDL 2016 (2016)
11. Salgado, R., Prieto, A., Bellas, F., Calvo-Varela, L., Duro, R.J.: Motivational engine with autonomous sub-goal identification for the Multilevel Darwinist Brain. Biologically Inspired Cogn. Architectures **17**, 1–11 (2016)
12. Ollion, C., Doncieux, S.: Why and how to measure exploration in behavioral space. In: Proceedings of GECCO 2011, pp. 267–294 (2011)

Models

Execution of Written Tasks
by a Biologically-Inspired Artificial Brain

Sebastian Narvaez[✉], Angel Garcia, and Raul Ernesto Gutierrez

Universidad del Valle, Cali, Colombia
{sebastian.narvaez,angel.garcia,raul.gutierrez}@correounivalle.edu.co

Abstract. Communicating with machines in the same way we do with other people has been a long-time goal in computer science. One of its many advantages would be the ability to give instructions to our computers without the need of learning how to use specific software or programming languages. Since we're dealing with human language, it would make sense to use a model of the human brain to build a system with such capabilities. In this work, the Hierarchical Temporal Memory algorithms are explored and evaluated as a biologically inspired tool capable of working with natural language. It's proposed that task execution can be achieved by training the algorithms to map certain sentences with keywords that correspond to the tasks. Different encoders are tested, that translate words into a proper representation for the algorithms. The configuration of algorithms and encoders with the highest success rate is able to correctly map up to 90% of the sentences from a custom training set. The behaviour of the success rates does not vary greatly between different subsets of the training set, suggesting that the learning system is able to find patterns and make inferences about missing data.

Keywords: Hierarchical Temporal Memory · Natural language processing · Neural networks · Task execution · Language understanding

1 Introduction

Imagine you're a student of arts. You have to build a 3D model due tomorrow. But you spent last night with your friends, having some drinks and a lot of fun. Noon has already passed, yet you're just getting up, really tired. And now you'll have to learn how to use that confusing software your teacher likes? No way! You turn on your laptop. Could this software be compatible with your favourite task execution program? "Create a sphere", you say to the mic, and a sphere appears floating in the screen. Way to go! You won't need to learn commands specific to this new software, you'll just use the concepts you're already familiar with!

Of course, not everything is parties and procrastination. A software with such capabilities could, for example, improve the life quality of people who don't have easy access to computers. They'd be able to immediately take advantage

© Springer International Publishing AG 2017
J.M. Ferrández Vicente et al. (Eds.): IWINAC 2017, Part I, LNCS 10337, pp. 45–52, 2017.
DOI: 10.1007/978-3-319-59740-9_5

of resources that are freely available in the Internet, like homemade technology or environmental advice.

Language understanding has been tackled from different perspectives. Models built on top of semantic databases, like wordnet [5], can solve problems such as Word Sense Disambiguation [6]. Deep learning techniques have recently provided some of the most accurate results in many areas, like speech generation [4], and are used by important companies in their natural language processing tasks.

The Hierarchical Temporal Memory (HTM) theory is an attempt to reverse-engineer the human cortex [2]. As a recent technology, not much studies have been made to evaluate its potential for Natural Language Processing. Notably, the cortical.io start-up has developed a framework based on the HTM theory principles that identify and take advantage of semantic relations between words in a given context [11].

In this work, we'll experiment with the biologically-inspired HTM theory by building a task execution system that receives instructions in natural language. Such system was implemented in an open-source software called HTM-TEUL[1], which uses the official HTM algorithms implementation, Nupic [8]. Now let's take a look at the parts it was built upon.

2   The Training Set

In order to avoid bias toward the vocabulary of a specific person, the data used to feed the learning system was collected by posting a Google Sheets document in social networks. In the post, people were requested to write the different ways they would ask an agent to execute certain tasks. The resulting data contained sentences in both Spanish and English and was reviewed by a human in order to filter out duplicated or inappropriate sentences. Nothing wrong was found in this process, so it was kept intact. A copy of such data can be found in the HTM-TEUL github repository.

Four subsets were built, that were then subdivided in pairs of training data (used to train the models) and test data (used to evaluate the models) as follows: (1) Both the 'Total' training and test sets have all the sentences. (2) The 'Partial' training set is comprised of a random selection of 80% of the sentences, leaving the other 20% for the 'Partial' test set. (3) For the 'Spanish' sets, the 80/20% ratio is maintained, but only sentences in Spanish are taken into account. (4) The same goes for the 'English' sets, but applied for the sentences in English.

3   The Virtual World

The Virtual World is merely an interface element where users can visually identify the task being executed after they input a sentence. It was conceived as a grid of 5×5 where a cartoonish character [2], who executes the tasks, lives in. The possible tasks are (1) move to the left, (2) move to the right, (3) move upwards, (4) move downwards, (5) pick up an object, and (6) dance.

---

[1] DOI:https://zenodo.org/badge/latestdoi/45553850.
[2] The ant *Ectatomma ruidum*.

4   The Encoders

Our sensory organs are constantly translating stimuli from the real world into sets of active neurons that hold semantic meaning [9]. These sets have the form of Sparse Distributed Representations (SDRs), which means that the information is held across multiple neurons, and that the relative number of active neurons at any given time is low. SDRs have a number of desired properties that contribute to scalability, robustness and generalization [1].

HTM systems also work with SDRs, and *encoders* are in charge of generating them from raw data [9]. Building an encoder capable of extracting semantic features from words is not an easy task. As the scope of this work was to experiment with the HTM theory and evaluate its capabilities in text processing, three fairly simple encoders were used.

The sparsity and length of the encoded outputs comply with the recommendations given in [9]. At any rate, the collected data didn't have any source of noise or randomness, which are one of the main reasons for those recommendations. You may look for use examples of the encoders in the HTM-TEUL's github repository.

4.1   Custom Category Encoder (CCE)

The first encoder is a modified version of the Nupic's Category Encoder. As its name implies, it treats every new input (words or tasks, in our case) as a different category, semantically isolated from all the other known inputs. The modifications allow you to specify a number of extra slots for yet unknown categories, so new inputs can get a unique representation. The length of the output arrays depend on the number of words and tasks of the training set being used. The sparsity varied from approximately 0.77% to 12.5%.

4.2   Totally Random Encoder (TRE)

The TRE assigns a unique random sequence of bits to every new word, though two completely different inputs may have overlapping bits. This goes explicitly against the recommendations given in [9], but it was included for comparison purposes. For this work, the output arrays have a length of 1024 with 204 active bits, resulting in a sparsity of approximately 20%.

4.3   Randomized Letter Encoder (RLE)

This encoder has two parts. First, each letter of the word is encoded using a Category Encoder. Then a random sequence is appended at the end, in order to prevent errors from homonyms. In this work, 3 active bits per letter were used for the first part and an array of length 600 with 60 random active bits for the second. As there are 26 letters in the English alphabet and the words in the training data varies from 1 to 20 letters, the sparsity of the encoded output ranges from approximately 5% to 30%.

5   The HTM Models

The HTM theory include two main algorithms: The Spatial Pooler (SP), which finds spatial patterns between the inputs and create SDRs, and the Temporal Memory (TM), that learns and predicts the sequences in which the inputs are fed [2]. For this work, let's call 'HTM models' to a set of instances of such algorithms, interconnected (the output of one is the input of another) in a specific way.

The HTM models developed for this experiment, depicted in Fig. 1, receive input from two sensors: One for the words and the other for the tasks. When training, the models are fed with inputs from both sensors. Then, to evaluate them, only words are fed, and their predictions about the corresponding tasks are recorded. The evaluation metric used is the percentage of successful predictions.

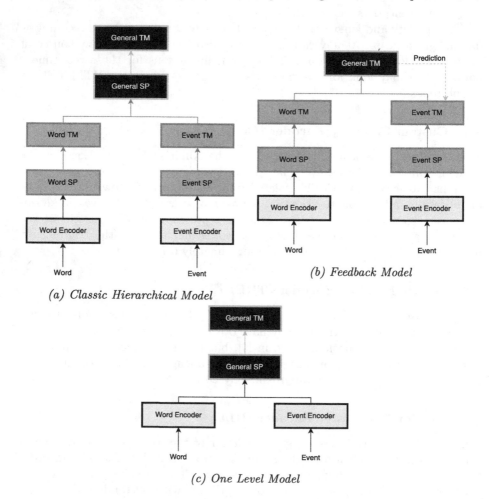

(a) Classic Hierarchical Model

(b) Feedback Model

(c) One Level Model

Fig. 1. HTM models structures

5.1   Classic Hierarchical Model

In the neocortex, neurons are arranged in regions, which are connected in a hierarchical fashion. This allows noise reduction and reuse of already-learned patterns in order to build more abstract concepts upon them [2]. The Classical Hierarchical Model is based on this idea.

Inputs from the two sensors are received separately in a lower region. The 'Word TM' learns the order in which the words must go to form a sentence, while the 'Event TM' learns the possible sequences of tasks. The higher region is fed first with the outputs of the 'Word TM' and then with those of the 'Event TM'. Note that the HTM theory doesn't describe how to accomplish a hierarchy yet. This implementation has no biological foundations.

5.2   Feedback Model

As the Classic Hierarchical model, the Feedback Model processes the inputs from the two sensors independently in the first region. However, the OR operation is applied to the outputs of the TMs so a single representation of the whole sentence (or tasks sequence) is passed to the next region.

In other words, the higher region processes sequences of two elements: A sentence and its corresponding tasks sequence. Then it's prediction about the tasks sequence that follows a sentence is passed down to the 'Event TM' to bias its own predictions. This mechanism is believed to provide lower regions in the Neocortex with a glance of the general world so they can situate the input they're processing in a context [2].

Contrary to the Classic Hierarchical Model, the Classifier is fed with the output of the 'Event TM' rather than with those of the 'General TM'. This is because the 'General TM' in this case only holds a representation of the whole tasks sequences, which would make it difficult to tell apart individual tasks.

5.3   One Level Model

This is a simplification of the Classic Hierarchical Model. It skips the first region so the encoded data is fed directly into a general SP and TM.

6   The Classifier

The Classifier extracts human-readable data back from the HTM system's memory. The Nupic's CLA Classifier can determine the most likely value that will appear in the next n steps. It was modified for this work, so it only considers the tasks for its predictions.

7 Parameters Selection

The SP and TM algorithms can be tunned trough various parameters. Nupic's tool 'Swarming' explores different values in the parameter space and picks the ones that it considers appropriate for the specific case. However, Swarming was designed for streaming data (like the hourly measure of a building's temperature) and is not well suited for the data collected in this work. Therefore, an evolutionary algorithm was used for this task. It's worth noting that the parameters found by an evolutionary algorithm are not necessarily the best.

8 Results and Discussion

Results, depicted in Fig. 2[3], were consistent across the data subsets. This shows the system's flexibility and robustness, given that the subsets contained different languages and the sentences used to train the models were different from the one used to test them.

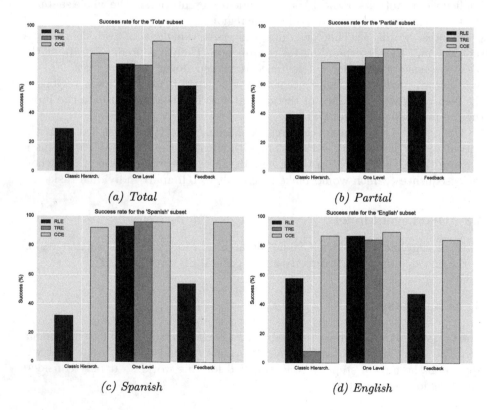

Fig. 2. Results for the different subsets of the collected data

---

[3] The graphs were created with the matplotlib [3] and seaborn [10] visualization tools.

The system was also able to map partial sentences with the corresponding tasks, which proves its capacity to extract patterns from the data. For example, when the word "arriba" (Up) was introduced, it was mapped to the *move upwards* task, even though it was not present in the training set as a full sentence.

The same random seed (420) was used in all the tests, but the scores didn't went high for the randomness-based encoders. In fact, the best scores were invariably obtained by the Category Encoder, followed by the Randomized Letter Encoder in almost all cases. These results are surprising in the sense that the RLE was the only encoder that produced representations partly based on semantic meaning. A possible weak point are homonyms, but there are none in the collected data. The random bits could have lowered the success rates.

As for the models, One Level obtained the best success rates. The fact that there's no official support for hierarchies in Nupic [7] could have influenced these results. Hierarchy is supposed to boost robustness [2], but this effect wasn't strong enough to justify the loss of information generated by going from one region to another.

9   Conclusions and Future Work

The HTM algorithms' flexibility allow to experiment with different kinds of data and connections between them. Thanks to this, anyone can attempt to implement characteristics that are core to the HTM theory but for which there's no algorithmic description yet (like hierarchy and feedback).

The experiments demonstrated that there's potential in HTM systems for NLP. An advantage with respect to traditional methods is that there's no need for a big corpus annotated by professionals. In fact, anyone could participate in the data collection. However, this comes with the cost of having to build an encoder that captures semantic meaning. In this work, the simple Category Encoder did the job, but would it be sufficient for a larger, more complex data set?

Aside from prediction, another strong point of HTM systems is anomaly detection. Using existing corpus annotated at grammatical and syntactic levels, the task execution system could make use of such features to detect poorly-written sentences. Furthermore, with the appropriate encoders, a system that combines inputs from different sensors (like images, sounds and text) and create relationships between them could be built on top of the HTM algorithms.

References

1. Ahmad, S., Hawkins, J.: Properties of sparse distributed representations and their application to hierarchical temporal memory. arXiv preprint arXiv:1503.07469 (2015)
2. Hawkins, J., Ahmad, S., Dubinsky, D.: Hierarchical temporal memory, including HTM cortical learning algorithms. Technical report, Numenta (2011). http://numenta.com/learn/hierarchical-temporal-memory-white-paper.html

3. Hunter, J.D.: Matplotlib: a 2D graphics environment. Comput. Sci. Eng. **9**(3), 90–95 (2007)
4. Ling, Z.-H., Kang, S., Zen, H., Senior, A., Schuster, M., Qian, X.-J., Meng, H., Deng, L.: Deep learning for acoustic modeling in parametric speech generation: a systematic review of existing techniques and future trends. IEEE Sig. Process. Mag. **32**, 35–52 (2015)
5. Miller, G.A.: Wordnet: a lexical database for English. Commun. ACM **38**(11), 39–41 (1995)
6. Morato, J., Marzal, M.Á., Llórens, J., Moreiro, J.: Wordnet applications. In: Global Wordnet Conference, vol. 2, pp. 270–278 (2004)
7. Numenta. Nupic faq. http://numenta.org/faq/, September 2016
8. Numenta. Nupic v0.4.5. https://github.com/numenta/nupic/tree/0.4.5, February 2016. http://dx.doi.org/10.5281/zenodo.45225
9. Purdy, S.: Encoding data for HTM systems. arXiv preprint arXiv:1602.05925 (2016)
10. Waskom, M., Botvinnik, O., Drewokane, Hobson, P., Halchenko, Y., Lukauskas, S., Warmenhoven, J., Cole, J.B., Hoyer, S., Vanderplas, J., Gkunter, Villalba, S., Quintero, E., Martin, M., Miles, A., Meyer, K., Augspurger, T., Yarkoni, T., Bachant, P., Evans, C., Fitzgerald, C., Nagy, T., Ziegler, E., Megies, T., Wehner, D., St-Jean, S., Coelho, L.P., Hitz, G., Lee, A., Rocher, L.: seaborn: v0.7.0, January 2016. Zenodo. http://doi.org/10.5281/zenodo.45133
11. De Sousa Webber, F.E.: Semantic folding theory. Technical report, Cortical.io (2015). http://www.cortical.io/static/downloads/semantic-folding-theory-white-paper.pdf

A Cognitive Architecture Framework for Critical Situation Awareness Systems

Felipe Fernandez[1], Angel Sanchez[2]([⊠]), Jose F. Velez[2], and Belen Moreno[2]

[1] ETSIINF, Universidad Politecnica de Madrid, Madrid, Spain
felipefernandez@fi.upm.es
[2] UETSII, Universidad Rey Juan Carlos, Madrid, Spain
angel.sanchez@urjc.es
https://www.fi.upm.es/

Abstract. Goal-oriented human-machine situation-awareness systems focus on the challenges related to perception of the elements of an environment and their state, within a time-space window, the comprehension of their meaning and the estimation of their state in the future. Present computer-supported situation awareness systems provide real-time information fusion from different sources, basic data analysis and recognition, and presentation of the corresponding data using some augmented reality principles. However, a still open research challenge is to develop advanced supervisory systems, platforms and frameworks that support higher-level cognitive activities, integrate domain specific associated knowledge, learning capabilities and decision support. To address these challenges, a novel cognitive architecture framework is presented in this paper, which emphasizes the role of the Associated Reality as a new cognitive layer to improve the perception, understanding and prediction of the corresponding cognitive agent. As a proof of concept, a particular application for railways safety is shown, which uses data fusion and a semantic video infrastructure.

Keywords: Knowledge modelling · Cognitive architectures · Situation awareness · Human-machine interactive systems · Safety systems · Semantic video analysis

1 Introduction

Goal-oriented human-machine situation-awareness interactive systems are crucial in many decision-making activities and associated control processes in real-time environments, such as driving vehicles or trains, monitoring nuclear power plants, or supervising manufacturing systems, or in sectors such plant automation, intelligent transportation systems, civil construction, homeland security, cyber security or healthcare.

A common cognitive problem in these critical real time systems is the necessity of managing the corresponding environment and context information in a

© Springer International Publishing AG 2017
J.M. Ferrández Vicente et al. (Eds.): IWINAC 2017, Part I, LNCS 10337, pp. 53–62, 2017.
DOI: 10.1007/978-3-319-59740-9_6

suitable way. The involved *Situation Awareness* (SA) systems focus on the challenges related to three basic cognitive layers (Endsley 1995 Model of SA) [1]: 1. Perception (observation) of the elements of a particular environment and their state, within a time-space volume (window), 2. Comprehension (understanding) of their meaning and 3. Projection (prediction-estimation) of their state in the future.

Robust computer-aided situation awareness systems, in semiautonomous or autonomous scenarios, are crucial for managing the involved critical real-time process, including surveillance, security, safety and emergency fields, command and control centres, human-machine interactive systems and alarm management frameworks.

In general, the evolving relationship between humans, technology and machines is a crucial factor pointed out by Gartner's Hype Cycle [2]. Particularly the corresponding situation-awareness cognitive systems need to tightly share knowledge and goals with the involved teams in order to be really useful for the corresponding services.

In the corresponding supervisory systems and involved cognitive architectures, the following information levels are usually considered [3,4]: 1. Reality-world 2. Perception 3. Situation comprehension 4. Future estimation 5. Decision 6. Action. Present computer-supported situation awareness systems provide real-time information fusion from different sources, basic data analysis and recognition, and presentation of the corresponding data using some augmented reality principles [5–9]. However, a still open research challenge in situation awareness and alarm management fields is to develop integrated goal-oriented supervisory systems, platforms and frameworks that support higher-level semantic cognitive activities, integrate context and historical knowledge, learning capabilities and robust decision support.

From a cognitive perspective, the main situation awareness challenges of safety, security and emergency monitoring systems lay in integrating timestamped data fusion techniques, data semantic analysis, alarms and events statistics, and expert rules knowledge. To also address context and content aware problems [10], to extract meaning and relevance, and to have a deep understanding of the systems of interest, a novel cognitive architecture framework is presented in this paper, which emphasizes the role of *associated reality as new cognitive layer* to really improve perception, understanding and prediction of the involved human-machine interactive systems.

Additionally, in this paper a particular system architecture and application developed for railway safety, which uses a semantic video framework and sensor data fusion, is also shown. The corresponding software has been implemented in C++ using OpenCV libraries, to analyse, visualize and verify the safety state, manage warnings and alarms, and generate historical and statistic records of trains. The considered approach focuses on the *interplay between humans and machines* in SA systems, and between the corresponding perception, understanding, and semantic and reasoning elements.

The paper is organized as follows. In Sect. 2, we discuss some cognitive architecture concepts applied to situation awareness systems, and introduce the associated reality cognitive layer for human-machine systems. In Sect. 3, we describe a general cognitive architecture framework for situation awareness which includes the associated reality layer. Section 4 describes a specific data fusion and semantic video architecture for situation awareness, specifically designed for railways safety applications. Section 5 summarizes a railway safety application we have developed using the previous framework. Finally, Sect. 6 discusses the conclusions and further research.

2 Associated Reality Cognitive Layer

In this paper we borrow some general concepts from systems architecture description, standard IEEE 42010 [11], to define and categorize some cognitive aspects of the situation awareness model considered. The purpose of this architectural approach is to improve the definition and abstraction levels of the corresponding cognitive elements.

A *cognitive architecture* refers to a theory about the structure of the human mind, and analogous computer cognitive layers and cognitive agents. The main purpose of a goal-oriented architecture is the understanding, and description, of the main elements of the system of interest from a particular point of view. A cognitive architecture should include data, information, knowledge and suitable techniques used to perceive, interpret, and analyse a system from the corresponding viewpoint.

A *cognitive layer* of a collaborative architecture contains information (more specifically: data, information and knowledge) and suitable processes to carry out the involved goals. When we try to develop machine cognitive layers for situation awareness, to emulate or improve human brain capabilities, usually we have to provide them with similar information and techniques to reach the corresponding goals. A cognitive layer usually incorporates different cognitive agents.

A *cognitive agent* can be considered as an active RT architect that constructs dynamic goal-oriented views of the system-of-interest and integrates these views within the general description using cognitive models and schemas, and general cognitive processes. This paper introduces the concept of Associated Reality (see Fig. 1) as an additional *cognitive layer* (architectural view) that enriches the real world with *related semantic information and data for enhancing the capabilities of a goal-oriented cognitive agent*, which can be considered as a generalization of the concept of Augmented Reality layer for HMI's [12].

A goal-oriented *Associated Reality* (AsR) cognitive layer (cognitive-copilot or expert layer), for human-machine interactive systems, *modelizes, combines and stores direct or indirect related real-time information from multiples sources, from a particular viewpoint*. This cognitive layer can include: system characteristics, state, mode and context, semantic information and historical data, models,

Fig. 1. Example of an Associated Reality (AsR) layer that provides a semantic goal-oriented associative layer between the world and a goal-oriented cognitive agent (Source: https://goo.gl/images/zSMTuY)

and simulation and estimation methods. Analogous knowledge associative structures are also prevalent in natural cognitive systems: especially in brain cortex of the humans and other mammals.

For developing goal-oriented AsR cognitive layers, it is also necessary to have flexible and hierarchical visualization tools to improve the corresponding processes.

The conception of the AsR cognitive layer proposed in this paper, for situation awareness system was partially inspired by Hawkin's model [13]: *"memory-prediction framework of intelligence"*, which points out the strong relation among intelligence, continuous predictions and associated stored semantic knowledge. Analogous prediction ideas: "prediction is the ultimate function of the brain", were also emphasized by the neurophysiologist Llinas [14].

The AsR cognitive layer can significantly *improve the observability, controllability and situation awareness* of the system of interest. It implies a human-machine sharing of the considered goals and objectives, and a continuous vigilance and alertness for extracting relevant information and drawing inferences and conclusions. The involved cognitive agents should perceive, analyse and associate the available information about the system and its environment to improve their knowledge and make better decisions in the future.

Following Endslay's approach [1,3,4] and explicitly adding the association phase, an AsR cognitive layer for situation awareness can be decomposed into the following four basic layers (sublayers), with different feedback loops in the corresponding processes: *1. Perception of the elements and state space of a particular environment. 2. Comprehension-fusion of their meaning. 3. Association of the involved information. 4. Prediction-estimation of their state in the future.*

Using the JDL Data-Information Fusion's model [15] for situation awareness systems, cognitive layers can also be categorized into the following five levels: 0. Signal 1. Object. 2. Situation. 3. Impact. 4. Process improvement.

A goal-oriented AsR cognitive layer of an object (JDL Level 1) can includes the following timestamped attributes:

$$Table = (Time, Object - type, Object - name, (Object - attributes), (Object - related - information))$$

Example. For a particular train safety application, the corresponding historical AsR cognitive layer, and the involved timestamped database, can include the following object-attributes = (thermometer, GPS, odometer, tachometer, gyroscope, Doppler radar...) and object-related-information = (GSM-R data, GPRS-R data, command & control information, railway incidents information, and present 4G LTE external cloud information or future extended 5G connections and associated cloud services).

3   A Cognitive Architecture for Situation Awareness

Figure 2 depicts an associated reality architecture for situation awareness. Its main elements of are:

$$AsR = (Specification, \ Control, \ Management, \ AsR \ cognitive \ layer, \ Decision, \ Actions)$$

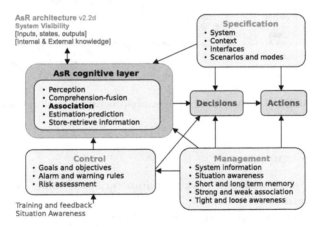

Fig. 2. AsR architecture. Situation awareness architecture with an associated reality layer.

Following the system architecture guideline IEEE 42010 [11], we include in the diagram the main elements and relations of the corresponding cognitive system. The main innovation aspect of this cognitive architecture framework is the AsR cognitive layer, which contains an active cognitive agents for situation awareness with associative knowledge. This structure basically emulates some associative properties of human brain for situation awareness activities.

The AsR cognitive layer provides the basis to perceive (capture), comprehend (analyze) and associate (relate) the corresponding semantic information, make estimations (predictions), and also store and retrieve the corresponding historical database.

4 A Situation Awareness Architecture for Railways Safety

This section presents a particular AsR cognitive architecture for critical situation awareness, specifically designed for train safety applications, which uses semantic-video and data-fusion processes (AsR.SVDF). Figure 3 depicts its main architecture components. This cognitive redundant architecture uses the associated reality layer, and it is based on a continuous vigilant semantic video, sensors, GPS, RFID balises and cloud agents. The main components of this architecture are:

$$AsR - SVDF = (I1, I2, I3, I4, FT\ SV, DF, HMI, HDB, AsR.SVDF\_Plan\ \&\ Scheduler)$$

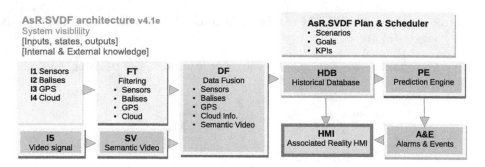

Fig. 3. AsR.SVDF model. SA system architecture for railway safety.

Main System Components

I1. System and environmental sensors: odometer, tachometer, accelerometer, gyroscope, thermometer, etc.

I2. Balises, transponders or RFID beacons placed between the rails of the railway.

I3. GPS module and antenna.

I4. External RT cloud connection with low latency. It provides additional information for the situation awareness process: context, environment and system information.

I5. Video signal input. It provides the visual perception of the environment.

FT. Filtering of sensors signals, GPS, balise and cloud information.

SV. Semantic Video. It analyzes the input video information, and detects objects and situations of interest (markerless detection).

DF. Data Fusion. It combines all available information, and stores the fusion results and complementary information in XML format.

HDB. Timestamped Historical Fusion Database of system and environment variables.

HMI. Associated reality HMI. It shows annotated and symbolic information of alarms & events, and relevant related information for the development and operations.

PE. Prediction-estimation Engine. Estimation model uses the present data and previous system state to estimate the state in the near future state. The train position estimation is basically based on a dead reckoning procedure (using previously determined position and integrating the speed over the elapsed time). GPS, balises and video information optimize the position references.

A&E. Alarms and Events Management. A&E's are triggered using A&E Rule Database, according to the detected scenario and context. A&E conditions and Rule Database can be modified by the corresponding Command & Control cloud service. The timestamp A&E's triggered are stored in the historical A&E Database.

AsR.SVDF Plan and Scheduler. It manages the complete process according to scenarios, goals, objectives, and key performance indicators (KPI's) considered.

Main Design and Operational Principles

- *Design principle:* In AsR-SVDF architecture, the associated reality layer contains HDB, A&E, PE and HMI modules.
- *Design principle:* Reliability of an AsR-SVDF situation awareness system depends on the semantic video analysis and robustness of the data fusion (redundancy).
- *Design principle:* The Quality Management and KPI's of an AsR-SVDF system depend on the monitoring of historical fusion database and historical A&E database.
- *Design principle:* The semantic video drastically reduces the necessary storage resources and the ulterior analysis computation (economy).
- *Operational principle:* Situation awareness can be improved by controlling and monitoring the trip-plan data and the statistic parameters of previous trips derived from the corresponding historical database (copilot knowledge).
- *Operational principle:* System reliability, availability and robustness depend on the maintenance plan and continuous improvement process (CIP) defined.

Example of a Record of the Historical Database

A simplified timestamped sample of the historical database is:

$$Sample = (Date : 26.05.2016; Time : 13 : 25; TrafficSign : Max90;$$
$$Speed : 80.4\,Km/h; TripDistance : 146.3\,Km)$$

This register stores the traffic sign detected, present train speed and present trip distance derived from the redundant data fusion-association available data and prediction. The present trip distance or position of the train can be dynamically estimated from different redundant sources: GPS, radar, odometer, tachometer integration, RFID balises (marker-based references) and video specified railway objects (markerless references) that sequentially correspond to particular travelling distances of the railway. Traffic signs and others significant elements are sequentially detected with a video camera on the machine train through an intelligent video analysis (IVA). The corresponding data fusion and data association allow estimating the train position based on sensors and sources available, train state and railway conditions.

Example of a Situation Awareness Alarm Rule

A simplified register example of an Alarm & Event Rule Database for a train is:

$$Register = (Train : 00151; Rule : 8.1; Weather : normal; Begin : 143\,Km; End : 147\,Km;$$

$$Type : Alarm; Variable : Speed; Min : 0\,Km/h, Max : 90\,Km/h; AlertMessage : Reducespeed)$$

The corresponding A&E Rule Database specifies the speed constraints based on weather conditions and distance intervals. In operation, the triggered timestamp A&E's are stored in the historical A&E Database. Notice that in the associative situation awareness architecture considered, the train speed and position can be estimated in many different direct or indirect ways, which is essential for the reliability of the alarm system. This redundant structure provides much more robustness to diverse scenarios, even with a partially damaged or sensor degraded system. This way, the machine cognitive behaviour emulates the remarkable robust cognitive behaviour of many survival animals of our natural ecosystems. Next section, presents a practical demonstration of a railways situation awareness system which uses the considered AsR framework.

5   A Situation Awareness Application for Railways Safety

Severe accidents in railway systems are often based on the loss of situational awareness of engine drivers and rail traffic operators, due to different factors: distraction, fatigue, violation of procedures, etc. [16]. For example: Santiago de Compostela's derailment occurred on 24.07.2013 at 20:44 CET in Alvia Talgo high-speed train with an ASFA-ERTMS hybrid management system [17]. This accident was initially originated by a loss of situation awareness of the engine driver, with the consequences of 80 deaths and 152 injuries (Fig. 4). Further investigation of train's data recorder, revealed that the train was travelling at 179 Km/h instead the posted speed limit of 80 Km/h.

The involved tracks of the accident were equipped with Eurobalises ERTMS-ETCS Level 1 [17], which provide relevant information regarding the track ahead of the train, e.g. track conditions, maximum speed, and maximum distance allowed to travel with the corresponding balise. If the driver exceed this maximum speed, the train shall be slowed down automatically, but the corresponding Alvia trains had compatibility problems with ERTMS, and were not conveniently configured for using the Eurobalises.

To prevent this kind of railway accidents, we have developed an AsR-SVDF situation awareness demonstration platform (Fig. 5). The RT platform will be able to analyse and detect the railway traffic signs and associated data, generate an annotated reality video with the suitable information, store the time-stamped semantic video in the corresponding historical database, and compute the rule-based alarms and events module.

Fig. 4. Derailment in Alvia high-speed train (source: spanishnewstoday.com).

Fig. 5. Particular view of the application graphical user interface of AsR.SVDF system.

6   Conclusions

This paper has presented a general cognitive architecture framework to empower the development of novel situation awareness systems based on the *associated reality layer*. This approach emphasizes the role of this active cognitive layer *as a copilot or personal assistant for machine cognitive agents*, which contains and models related information of the system and its environment for enhancing the corresponding process. To improve real railway safety systems, a particular situation awareness architecture was defined, with redundant data fusion and a semantic video schema, to manage the corresponding A&E system. This alarm framework supports simple and flexible declarative rule style for building situation awareness systems and services. A particular demonstration prototype, to improve the railway safety, was also presented to practically show some capabilities of the approach. In the future we plan to extend the AsR cognitive layer defined and develop more applications with different scenarios and contexts.

Acknowledgments. This work was funded by the Spanish Ministry of Economy and Competitiveness under grant number TIN2014-57458-R.

References

1. Endsley, M.R.: Towards a theory of situation awareness in dynamic systems. Hum. Factors **37**(1), 32–64 (1995)
2. Gartner, Inc.: Hype Cycle for Emerging Technologies (2013)
3. Endsley, M.R.: Bringing cognitive engineering to the information fusion problem: creating systems that understand situations. In: Plenary Presentation to IEEE 14th International Conference Information Fusion (2011)
4. Endsley, M.R., Jones, D.G.: Designing for Situation Awareness: An Approach to Human-Cantered Design. Taylor & Francis, Oxford (2012)
5. Nowak, C., Lambert, D.: The semantic challenge for situation assessments. In: IEEE 8th International Conference on Information Fusion, Los Alamitos, July 2005
6. Baader, F., Bauer, A., Baumgartner, P., Cregan, A., Gabaldon, A., Ji, K., Lee, K., Rajaratnam, D., Schwitter, R.: A novel architecture for situation awareness systems. In: Giese, M., Waaler, A. (eds.) TABLEAUX 2009. LNCS, vol. 5607, pp. 77–92. Springer, Heidelberg (2009). doi:10.1007/978-3-642-02716-1_7
7. Kokar, M.M., Matheus, C.J., Baclawski, K.: Ontology-based situation awareness. Inf. Fusion **10**(1), 83–98 (2009)
8. Kokar, M.M., Endsley, M.R.: Situation awareness and cognitive modelling. In: IEEE Intelligent Systems, Cyber-Physical-Social Systems, pp. 2–7, May-June 2012
9. Ulicny, B., et al.: Augmenting the analyst via situation-dependent reasoning with trust-annotated facts. In: Proceedings of 2011 IEEE International Multi-Disciplinary Conference Cognitive Methods in Situation Awareness and Decision Support, pp. 17–24. IEEE (2011)
10. Laing, C., Vickers, P.: Context informed intelligent information infrastructures for better situational awareness. In: International Conference on Cyber Situational Awareness, Data Analytics and Assessment (CyberSA), 8–9 June 2015
11. ISO/IEC/IEEE 42010: Systems and software engineering. Architecture description (2011)
12. Lukosch, S., et al.: Providing information on the spot: using augmented reality for situational awareness in the security domain. Comput. Support. Coop. Work **24**(6), 613–664 (2015)
13. Hawkins, J.: On Intelligence. St. Martin's Griffin, New York (2004)
14. Llinas, R.: I of the Vortex: From Neurons to Self. The MIT Press, Cambridge (2001)
15. Steinberg, A.N., et al.: Revisions to the JDL data fusion model. In: Proceedings of the SPIE. Sensor Fusion: Architectures, Algorithms and Applications, pp. 430–441 (1999)
16. Fischer, K.: Railway Situation Awareness Project, Swiss Federal Railways, Institute Humans in Complex Systems (2011). http://www.fhnw.ch/aps/miks
17. European Railway Agency: ERTMS. Supporting Documents (2016). http://www.era.europa.eu/Core-Activities/ERTMS/Pages/List-of-supporting-documents.aspx

A Conductance-Based Neuronal Network Model for Color Coding in the Primate Foveal Retina

Pablo Martínez-Cañada[1,2]($\boxtimes$), Christian Morillas[1,2], and Francisco Pelayo[1,2]

[1] Department of Computer Architecture and Technology,
University of Granada, Granada, Spain
{pablomc,cmg,fpelayo}@ugr.es
[2] Centro de Investigación en Tecnologías de la Información y de las
Comunicaciones (CITIC), University of Granada, Granada, Spain

Abstract. Descriptive models of the retina have been essential to understand how retinal neurons convert visual stimuli into a neural response. With recent advancements of neuroimaging techniques, availability of an increasing amount of physiological data and current computational capabilities, we now have powerful resources for developing biologically more realistic models of the brain. In this work, we implemented a two-dimensional network model of the primate retina that uses conductance-based neurons. The model aims to provide neuroscientists who work in visual areas beyond the retina with a realistic retinal model whose parameters have been carefully tuned based on data from the primate fovea and whose response at every stage of the model adequately reproduces neuronal behavior. We exhaustively benchmarked the model against well-established visual stimuli, showing spatial and temporal responses of the model neurons to light flashes, which can be disk- or ring-shaped, and to sine-wave gratings of varying spatial frequency. The model describes the red-green and blue-yellow color opponency of retinal cells that connect to parvocellular and koniocellular cells in the Lateral Geniculate Nucleus (LGN), respectively. The model was implemented in the widely used neural simulation tool NEST and the code has been released as open source software.

Keywords: Primate retina model · Conductance-based neuronal network · Parvocellular pathway · Koniocellular pathway · Red-green color opponency · Blue-yellow color opponency · NEST simulation

1 Introduction

The majority of retina models basically fall into two categories. The first one consists of descriptive or phenomenological models [3,8,31], which are filter functions that convert input visual stimuli into some neuronal response, commonly recorded from ganglion cells. While they involve just a few parameters whose values are easily calculated from experiments, these models retain only some gross features of the retina and it is hard to construct a qualitative interpretation of

© Springer International Publishing AG 2017
J.M. Ferrández Vicente et al. (Eds.): IWINAC 2017, Part I, LNCS 10337, pp. 63–74, 2017.
DOI: 10.1007/978-3-319-59740-9_7

the retinal network behavior. The second category, known as mechanistic models [11,27], attempts to incorporate known morphological and physiological data of the system. The challenge to construct them lies in finding precise values of all their parameters, provided also that some of them cannot be reliably acquired. Model neurons are formulated in terms of differential equations, whose numerical resolution entails a considerable increase of the computational load. There are also hybrid models that combine descriptive filters in some stages of their circuit, where the response can be approximated by a linear function, with more detailed neuron models in those other stages that exhibit nonlinear responses [20,21,34].

While descriptive models have proven to be successful in explaining the general properties of the visual system, improvement of computational technologies and neuroimaging techniques allows implementation of large-scale biophysical models that can facilitate the understanding of its structural and dynamic complexity [13,14]. However, there are two key limiting factors that continue to hinder the development of biophysical models of the primate retina. One of them is the scarcity of physiological data from primates. The second factor is the lack of standardized neuron models for neurons that communicate via graded potentials instead of spikes, as happens with retinal neurons. Moreover, existing biophysical models of the primate retina [12,23] are not exhaustively benchmarked against well-established visual stimuli.

To address these challenges, we implemented a two-dimensional network model of the primate retina built on conductance-based neurons. We show spatial and temporal responses of the model neurons to well-known visual stimuli, e.g., light flashes and sine-wave gratings of varying spatial frequency. Simulated response at every stage of the model was correlated with published physiological data. The circuit model was implemented in NEST v2.11 [26] and the code has been released as open source software [9].

2   Methods

2.1   Overview of the Network Model

The model is organized in two-dimensional grids of retinal cells synaptically connected as shown in the schematic of Fig. 1A. Each layer is scaled to span a patch of 2 deg × 2 deg in the foveal visual field of the primate retina and contains 40×40 neurons. The network is driven by the three different types of cones, S, M and L types, which correspond to short-, medium- and long-wavelength light respectively. Response of cones was implemented according to van Hateren's model of primate cones [10] with linear cone-horizontal cell feedback (Fig. 1B). We chose the same generic parameter values given in Table 1 of the reference [10], with the exception of parameter g_s, which was 0.5 instead of 8.81 to slightly increase the overshoot of the response with a stimulus onset.

All remaining retinal cells (horizontal cells, bipolar cells, amacrine cells and ganglion cells) are implemented as single passive compartments [11,12]. The membrane potential dynamics are given by:

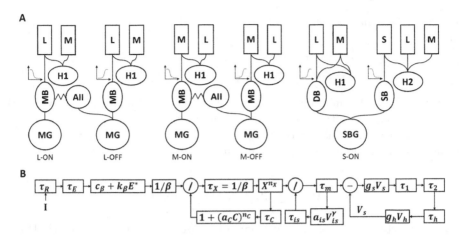

Fig. 1. A: Schematic of the circuit model including the different neuron types and connections in the five color opponent pathways: L-ON, L-OFF, M-ON, M-OFF and S-ON. L, M and S are the different types of cones. H1 and H2 are horizontal cells. While H1 type horizontal cells tend to avoid S-cones, H2 cells innervate all types of cones indiscriminately. The different types of bipolar cells are: midget bipolar cell (MB), diffuse bipolar cell (DB) and S-ON bipolar cell (SB). The two types of ganglion cells are: midget ganglion cell (MG) and small bistratified ganglion cell (SBG). ON bipolar cells excite AII macrine cells through gap junctions and, in turn, AII amacrine cells inhibit both OFF bipolar cells and OFF ganglion cells. The different activation functions of the synapse cone-bipolar cell are shown in the insets. B: Model of response of the cone cells consisting of a nonlinearity cascaded with two divisive feedback loops and a subtractive feedback loop [10]. The output of this model, the membrane potential of cones, V_s, is connected with horizontal cells and bipolar cells.

$$\frac{dV_m(t)}{dt} = -g_L\frac{V_m(t) - E_L}{C_m} - \frac{I_{in}(t)}{C_m} + \frac{I_e}{C_m} \tag{1}$$

where $V_m(t)$ is the membrane potential of the neuron, g_L the leak conductance, E_L the leak reversal potential, C_m the capacity of the membrane and I_e a constant external input current. Ganglion cells also include integrate-and-fire dynamics based on a threshold potential, V_{th}, and a refractory period, t_{ref}. $I_{in}(t)$ represents either incoming synaptic currents or gap junction currents. In horizontal cells, bipolar cells and ganglion cells, $I_{in}(t)$ is the sum of excitatory and inhibitory synaptic currents:

$$I_{in}(t) = \sum_{i=1}^{N} w_i g_i(t)(V_m(t) - E_{ex}) + \sum_{j=1}^{M} w_j g_j(t)(V_m(t) - E_{in}) \tag{2}$$

w_i, w_j are synaptic weights and E_{ex}, E_{in} are the reversal potentials for the N excitatory synapses and the M inhibitory synapses respectively. $g_i(t)$ and $g_j(t)$ are the synaptic activation functions of the neuron. Synaptic activation functions are modeled as a direct function of some presynaptic activity measure. In the simplest case, synaptic interactions are described by an instantaneous sigmoid function [7, 28, 33]:

$$g_i(t) = \frac{1}{1 + e^{-(V_{pre_i}(t) - \theta_{syn})/k_{syn}}} \tag{3}$$

where $V_{pre_i}(t)$ is the membrane potential of the neuron i and θ_{syn} and k_{syn} are parameters used to customize the sigmoid function.

By contrast, in amacrine cells, $I_{in}(t)$ is the sum of gap junction currents through electrical synapses with a constant gap junction conductance (g_{gap}):

$$I_{in}(t) = \sum_{i=1}^{N} g_{gap}(V_m(t) - V_{pre_i}(t)) \tag{4}$$

Photoreceptors release only one type of neurotransmitter, glutamate. However, bipolar cells react to this stimulus with two different responses, ON-center and OFF-center responses [24, 29]. While OFF bipolar cells have ionotropic receptors that maintain light-activated hyperpolarizations of photoreceptors, ON bipolar cells have instead metabotropic receptors that produce a sign reversal at the photoreceptor-ON bipolar cell synapse. Ionotropic glutamate receptors are positively coupled to the synaptic cation channel of OFF bipolar cells, which is opened with an increase of glutamate. On the contrary, ON bipolar cells are negatively coupled to the synaptic cation channel and glutamate acts essentially as an inhibitory transmitter, closing the cation channel.

To simulate the activation function of this cation channel based on the cone membrane potential ($V_{cone}(t)$), we used a sigmoid function whose exponent is negative for OFF bipolar cells (standard sigmoid) and positive for ON bipolar cells (inverted sigmoid):

$$g_{OFF}(t) = \frac{1}{1 + e^{-(V_{cone}(t) - \theta_{syn})/k_{syn}}} \tag{5}$$

$$g_{ON}(t) = \frac{1}{1 + e^{(V_{cone}(t) - \theta_{syn})/k_{syn}}} \tag{6}$$

In the synapse horizontal cell-bipolar cell, although both bipolar cell types express the same ionotropic GABA receptors, GABA release from horizontal cells can evoke opposite responses. One evidence suggests that GABA evokes opposite responses if chloride equilibrium potentials of the synaptic chloride channel in the two bipolar cell types are on opposite sides of the bipolar cell's resting potential [32]. In our model, ON bipolar cells receive excitatory synapses from horizontal cells, which have a positive reversal potential taking as a reference the bipolar cell's resting potential, and OFF bipolar cells receive inhibitory synapses, which have a negative reversal potential.

Among all types of amacrine cells, the model includes only the AII amacrine cell since it is the most studied amacrine cell and the most numerous type in the mammalian retina [18, 22]. The AII amacrine cell is a narrow-field, bistratified

Table 1. Parameter values of neuron models.

	C_m(pF)	g_L(nS)	E_L(mV)	E_{ex}(mV)	E_{in}(mV)	θ_{syn}(mV)	k_{syn}	g_{gap}(nS)
Horizontal cell	100	10	-60	0	-	-50	3	-
ON bipolar cell	100	10	-54	0	-70	-35	3	-
OFF bipolar cell	100	10	-45	0	-70	-35	3	-
AII amacrine cell	100	10	-60	-	-	-55	3	10
Ganglion cell	100	10	-62	0	-70	-	-	-

cell that is connected through gap junctions with ON bipolar cells and synaptically innervate OFF cone bipolar terminals and OFF ganglion cell dendrites. The AII amacrine cell plays an essential role in the circuit for rod-mediated (scotopic) vision. However, it is shown that the AII amacrine functionality also extends to cone-mediated (photopic) vision [6,19]. Under cone-driven conditions, ON cone bipolar cells excite AII amacrine cells through gap junctions and, in turn, AII amacrince cells release inhibitory neurotransmitters onto OFF bipolar cells and OFF ganglion cells. Thus, the AII amacrine network produces crossover inhibition from the ON pathway.

Parameter values of neuron models were chosen as generic as possible (see, for example, values of C_m, g_L, E_{ex} and E_{in} in Table 1). The leak reversal potential, E_L, was adjusted in horizontal cells and bipolar cells to force a resting potential in the dark of about -45 mV, as observed experimentally [1,28], and in amacrine cells for a resting potential of about -65 mV. For ganglion cells, we chose values of the leak reversal potential and the threshold potential, V_{th}, to keep the cell constantly depolarized, resulting in a spontaneous firing rate of about 40 spikes/s. Values of the synaptic activation functions, θ_{syn} and k_{syn}, were set to force a synaptic threshold below resting potential [28].

Synaptic connections were made using the NEST Topology module [25]. In the description of connections shown in Table 2, every cell to the left of the arrow connects to all nodes to the right within a circular mask of radius R_s and with a delay τ_s. Weights of synaptic connections are generated according to a Gaussian distribution of standard deviation σ_s. The sum of the weights of all incoming synapses is equal to the total weight W_s.

The value of σ_s in the red-green vertical pathway, formed by L and M cones, midget bipolar cells, amacrine cells and midget ganglion cells, corresponds to the radius of the receptive-field center of P cells [4]. The surround of the receptive field is accounted for by horizontal cells. Diffuse bipolar cells contact multiple cones so that their value of σ_s is larger than the receptive field center of P cells but still smaller than the σ_s of horizontal cells. To create the spatially coextensive receptive field of the blue-yellow pathway [5], the value of σ_s of S-ON bipolar cells is the same as that of diffuse bipolar cells. To approximate experimental results [5], both values are set to $0.05°$.

Values of synaptic weights were calibrated to reproduce the features of neuronal activity of the primate retina but always keeping W_s between 1 and 10 nS.

Table 2. Parameter values of synaptic connections.

	R_s(deg)	W_s(nS)	σ_s(deg)	τ_s(ms)
L-Cone → L-ON MB	0.09	3	0.03	1
L-Cone → L-OFF MB	0.09	2.5	0.03	1
L-Cone → DB	0.15	1	0.05	1
S-Cone → SB	0.15	3	0.05	1
L-Cone → H1	0.3	2	0.1	1
L-Cone → H2	0.3	1	0.1	1
S-Cone → H2	0.3	2	0.1	1
H1 → L-ON MB	0.3	2	0.1	5
H1 → L-OFF MB	0.3	−3	0.1	5
H2 → SB	0.3	2	0.1	5
H1 → DB	0.3	−2	0.1	5
AII → L-OFF MB	0.09	−2	0.03	1
AII → L-OFF MG	0.09	−2	0.03	1
L-ON MB → L-ON MG	0.09	10	0.03	1
L-OFF MB → L-ON MG	0.09	10	0.03	1
DB → SBG	0.09	5	0.03	1
SB → SBG	0.09	5	0.03	1

To reproduce the delayed response of the surround, which is measured, on average, between 5 and 15 ms [15], a delay of 5 ms was given to the connection from horizontal cells to bipolar cells.

3   Results

3.1   Red-Green Pathway

In Fig. 2, we show model responses to a flashing spot of radius 0.5° situated in the center of the grid and covering the whole receptive field of the center neuron. By using a white spot (Fig. 2A) we aim to depict some general spatial properties of the network. The effect of the center-surround antagonism in bipolar cells clearly emerged during the time interval the spot was ON, from 500 to 750 ms. ON bipolar cells at the edge of the spot receive less inhibition from the surround and, thus, showed a marked increase of the response compared to center bipolar cells. The response of OFF bipolar cells at the edge of the spot showed a similar behavior but of opposite sign, resulting in a significant drop below the spontaneous firing. Similar responses were seen for a black spot (Fig. 2B) but with the time windows swapped.

Temporal dynamics of membrane potentials are shown in Fig. 2C. White spots evoked strong depolarizations in ON cells during the stimulus onset, followed by a rebound inhibition for the stimulus offset. Dark stimuli evoked

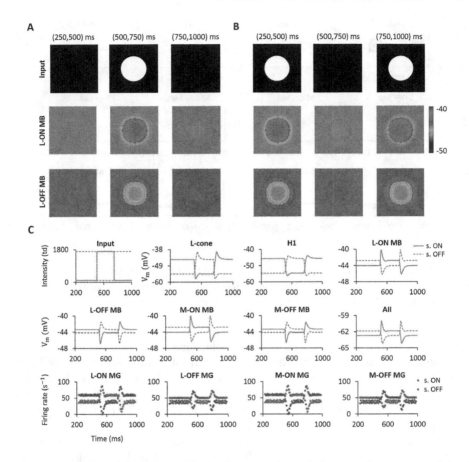

Fig. 2. Time-averaged topographical representation of the membrane potential of L-ON and L-OFF midget bipolar cells to white flashing spots of radius 0.5° (A and B). The intensity of the spots is 1600 trolands (td) and they are superimposed on a spatially uniform background of 100 td. The three time windows at the top are used for averaging the membrane potentials. C: Responses of cells situated in the center of the different neuron grids to the stimulus shown in A (s. ON) and to the stimulus shown in B (s. OFF).

responses of the opposite sign, i.e., pronounced hyperpolarization followed by rebound excitation. This response pattern corresponds to the well-known mechanism of push-pull, inherent to all neurons in the first stages of the visual system. After the overshoot of the response with the stimulus onset, inhibition is able to partially counterbalance the initial excitation within the receptive field and the membrane potential returned close to the resting potential (or spontaneous rate for ganglion cells). The same analysis applies for OFF cells but taking into account that the responses are now of opposite sign.

In the following experiment, we used spots and annuli in order to favor either the center or the surround mechanisms of the receptive field [2] (see

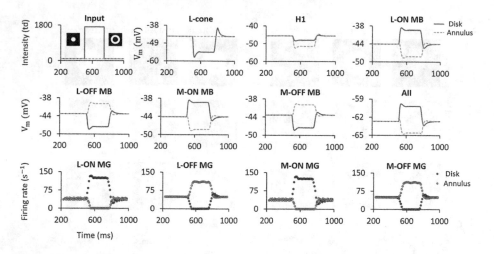

Fig. 3. Responses of cells situated in the center of the different neuron grids to a white disk of radius 0.09° and a white annulus with inner and outer radii of 0.09 and 0.5° respectively. Stimuli are flashed from 500 to 750 ms.

Fig. 3). Notice that, as a consequence of isolating one of the two mechanisms, the response did not return to the resting potential after the initial overshoot. The center response, activated by the disk stimulus, showed a peak 35 ms after the stimulus onset. The peak of the surround response, activated by the annulus stimulus, was delayed by approximately 10–15 ms with respect to the center response [2].

We simulated spatial frequency responses for luminance, chromatic and cone-isolating gratings (Fig. 4) and our results are correlated with physiological measures [17]. Firstly, for Fig. 4A, the mosaic of cones that describes the spatial distribution of the different cone types in the fovea is spatially uniform, such as the one used so far. One important aspect shown here is how chromatic and luminance signals were multiplexed in low and high spatial frequencies respectively by midget cells in the retina. Thus, the spatial frequency tuning curve with a chromatic grating was low-pass and with a luminance grating was band-pass. The response to the luminance grating showed also a peak at about 3 cpd, as shown for the cell in Fig. 4B of reference [17]. The spatial frequency tuning curves for L- and M-cone-isolating gratings showed different high-frequency cutoffs, a feature consistent with the spatial structure of the receptive field. The response modulation to M- and L-cone-isolating gratings was 180° out of phase as long as the response to the M-cone-isolating grating was nonzero.

However, the response to the L-cone-isolating grating was slightly band-pass, as a consequence of the mixed input of L and M cones we chose for the H1 horizontal cell, prioritizing morphological studies of the primate retina. The majority of cells measured in [17] showed marked low-pass responses though. We thus next asked the question of whether the spatial distribution of the mosaic of cones could influence the response to the L-cone-isolating grating. In Fig. 4B and C, a more

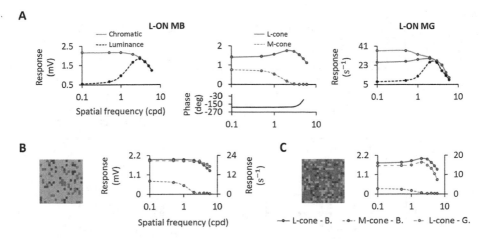

Fig. 4. A: Spatial frequency curves of center cells for luminance, chromatic gratings and gratings isolating a receptive field cone class (L-cone and M-cone). Sine-wave gratings are drifted at 2 Hz, with a mean luminance level of 1000 td and a contrast of 0.8. The response amplitude corresponds to the first harmonic computed based on Fourier analysis of either the membrane potential or the firing rate. The mosaic of the different cone types is spatially uniform. B: Spatial frequency curves of a cell situated in the center of a retina region with a high density of M-cones. Cones are randomly placed according to an uniform distribution with the following probabilities: 30% of L-cones, 60% of M-cones and 10% of S-cones. C: Spatial frequency curves of a cell situated in a region of the retina with a high density of L-cones. Probabilities are now: 60% of L-cones, 30% of M-cones and 10% of S-cones. L-cone-B. and M-cone-B. are the responses of the midget bipolar cell to the L- and M-cone-isolating gratings. L-cone-G. is the response of the midget ganglion cell to the L-cone-isolating grating.

realistic scenario is presented, in which we randomly situated the different cone types in the grid. We used two different sets of probabilities to simulate either a region of the retina rich in M-cones (Fig. 4B) or a region with a high density of L-cones (Fig. 4C). As expected, the spatial frequency curve for the mosaic in Fig. 4B was low-pass as a result of the considerable degree of cone-specific input to the surround of the receptive field.

3.2   Blue-Yellow Pathway

To study the receptive-field structure of retinal cells in the blue-yellow pathway we used cone-isolating stimuli that modulate either S cones or L and M cones independently [5] (Fig. 5). The small bistratified ganglion cell receives S-ON excitatory input from the S-ON bipolar cell and LM-OFF excitatory input from the diffuse bipolar cell. The response pattern of the small bistratified ganglion cell in Fig. 5A correspond to a distinct blue-ON/yellow-OFF opponent cell type.

Receptive fields were further analyzed with drifting sinusoidally modulated gratings that varied in spatial frequency (Fig. 5B). Focusing on the small bistratified ganglion cell, it is shown that both the S and LM spatial frequency

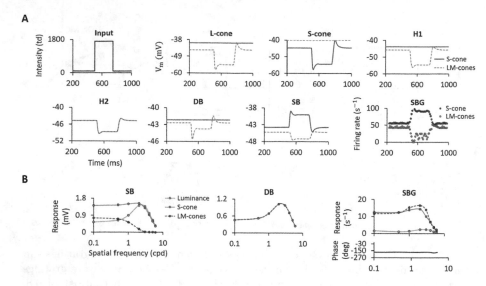

Fig. 5. A: Responses of center cells to a 0.5° spot. B: Spatial frequency curves for an uniform cone mosaic.

responses have similar spatial tuning, as a result of the spatially coextensive receptive fields of S-ON and diffuse bipolar cells [5]. These curves were mainly low-pass although a small band-pass resonance peak is observed at 3 cpd that stem from the receptive field surrounds of S-ON and diffuse bipolar cells. Note that the response to the luminance grating is bandpass and it is greatly attenuated. Parameters of the model were chosen to produce similar S and LM spatial frequency responses rather than a more prominent response to the luminance grating as observed in other studies [30].

4   Conclusion

We have implemented a conductance-based retina model that incorporates key aspects of the neuroanatomical organization of the primate foveal retina [16]. Most of the parameters correspond to physiological magnitudes that can be measured experimentally. The model aims to provide a coherent account of the response of red-green and blue-yellow color opponent cell types. We have exhaustively benchmarked the model against well-established visual stimuli, showing spatial and temporal responses of the model neurons to light flashes, which can be disk- or ring-shaped, and to sine-wave gratings of varying spatial frequency. By providing a reliable model within which a broad range of neuronal interactions can be examined at several different levels, the model offers a powerful platform for further investigations in visual areas beyond the retina, focusing on color-coding in the primate visual pathway.

Acknowledgments. This work was supported by the Spanish National Grant TIN2016-81041-R and the research project P11-TIC-7983 of Junta of Andalucia (Spain), co-financed by the European Regional Development Fund (ERDF). P. Martínez-Cañada was supported by the PhD scholarship FPU13/01487, awarded by the Government of Spain, FPU program.

References

1. Arman, A.C., Sampath, A.P.: Dark-adapted response threshold of OFF ganglion cells is not set by OFF bipolar cells in the mouse retina. J. Neurophysiol. **107**(10), 2649–2659 (2012)
2. Benardete, E.A., Kaplan, E.: The receptive field of the primate P retinal ganglion cell, i: linear dynamics. Vis. Neurosci. **14**(01), 169–185 (1997)
3. Berry, M.J., Brivanlou, I.H., Jordan, T.A., Meister, M.: Anticipation of moving stimuli by the retina. Nature **398**(6725), 334–338 (1999)
4. Croner, L.J., Kaplan, E.: Receptive fields of P and M ganglion cells across the primate retina. Vis. Res. **35**(1), 7–24 (1995)
5. Crook, J.D., Davenport, C.M., Peterson, B.B., Packer, O.S., Detwiler, P.B., Dacey, D.M.: Parallel ON and OFF cone bipolar inputs establish spatially coextensive receptive field structure of blue-yellow ganglion cells in primate retina. J. Neurosci. **29**(26), 8372–8387 (2009)
6. Demb, J.B., Singer, J.H.: Intrinsic properties and functional circuitry of the AII amacrine cell. Vis. Neurosci. **29**(01), 51–60 (2012)
7. Destexhe, A., Mainen, Z.F., Sejnowski, T.J., et al.: Synaptic currents, neuromodulation, and kinetic models. Handb. Brain Theory Neural Netw. **66**, 617–648 (1995)
8. Enroth-Cugell, C., Robson, J.G.: The contrast sensitivity of retinal ganglion cells of the cat. J. Physiol. **187**(3), 517–552 (1966)
9. Github: code repository. https://github.com/pablomc88
10. van Hateren, H.: A cellular and molecular model of response kinetics and adaptation in primate cones and horizontal cells. J. Vis. **5**(4), 5–5 (2005)
11. Hennig, M.H., Funke, K., Wörgötter, F.: The influence of different retinal subcircuits on the nonlinearity of ganglion cell behavior. J. Neurosci. **22**(19), 8726–8738 (2002)
12. Hennig, M.H., Wörgötter, F.: Effects of fixational eye movements on retinal ganglion cell responses: a modelling study. Front. Comput. Neurosci. **1**, 1–12 (2007)
13. Hill, S., Tononi, G.: Modeling sleep and wakefulness in the thalamocortical system. J. Neurophysiol. **93**(3), 1671–1698 (2005)
14. Izhikevich, E.M., Edelman, G.M.: Large-scale model of mammalian thalamocortical systems. Proc. Nat. Acad. Sci. **105**(9), 3593–3598 (2008)
15. Kaplan, E., Benardete, E.: The dynamics of primate retinal ganglion cells. Prog. Brain Res. **134**, 17–34 (2001)
16. Kolb, H., Fernandez, E., Nelson, R., Jones, B.W.: Webvision: The Organization of the Retina and Visual System. National Library of Medicine, Bethesda (2011). Copyright
17. Lee, B.B., Shapley, R.M., Hawken, M.J., Sun, H.: Spatial distributions of cone inputs to cells of the parvocellular pathway investigated with cone-isolating gratings. JOSA A **29**(2), A223–A232 (2012)
18. MacNeil, M.A., Masland, R.H.: Extreme diversity among amacrine cells: implications for function. Neuron **20**(5), 971–982 (1998)

19. Manookin, M.B., Beaudoin, D.L., Ernst, Z.R., Flagel, L.J., Demb, J.B.: Disinhibition combines with excitation to extend the operating range of the OFF visual pathway in daylight. J. Neurosci. **28**(16), 4136–4150 (2008)

20. Martínez-Cañada, P., Morillas, C., Pino, B., Ros, E., Pelayo, F.: A computational framework for realistic retina modeling. Int. J. Neural Syst. **26**(07), 1650030 (2016)

21. Martínez-Cañada, P., Morillas, C., Pino, B., Pelayo, F.: Towards a generic simulation tool of retina models. In: Ferrández Vicente, J.M., Álvarez-Sánchez, J.R., de la Paz López, F., Toledo-Moreo, F.J., Adeli, H. (eds.) IWINAC 2015. LNCS, vol. 9107, pp. 47–57. Springer, Cham (2015). doi:10.1007/978-3-319-18914-7_6

22. Masland, R.H.: The fundamental plan of the retina. Nat. Neurosci. **4**(9), 877–886 (2001)

23. Momiji, H., Hankins, M.W., Bharath, A.A., Kennard, C.: A numerical study of red-green colour opponent properties in the primate retina. Eur. J. Neurosci. **25**(4), 1155–1165 (2007)

24. Nawy, S., Jahr, C.E.: Suppression by glutamate of cGMP-activated conductance in retinal bipolar cells. Nature **346**(6281), 269 (1990)

25. Plesser, H.E., Austvoll, K.: Specification and generation of structured neuronal network models with the NEST topology module. BMC Neurosci. **10**(suppl 1), P56 (2009)

26. Plesser, H.E., Diesmann, M., Gewaltig, M.O., Morrison, A.: NEST: the Neural Simulation Tool. In: Jaeger, D., Jung, R. (eds.) Encyclopedia of Computational Neuroscience. Springer, Heidelberg (2015). www.springerreference.com/docs/html/chapterdbid/348323.html

27. Publio, R., Oliveira, R.F., Roque, A.C.: A computational study on the role of gap junctions and rod Ih conductance in the enhancement of the dynamic range of the retina. PLoS ONE **4**(9), e6970 (2009)

28. Smith, R.G.: Simulation of an anatomically defined local circuit: the cone-horizontal cell network in cat retina. Vis. Neurosci. **12**(03), 545–561 (1995)

29. Snellman, J., Kaur, T., Shen, Y., Nawy, S.: Regulation of ON bipolar cell activity. Prog. Retinal Eye Res. **27**(4), 450–463 (2008)

30. Tailby, C., Szmajda, B., Buzas, P., Lee, B., Martin, P.: Transmission of blue (S) cone signals through the primate lateral geniculate nucleus. J. Physiol. **586**(24), 5947–5967 (2008)

31. Tranchina, D., Gordon, J., Shapley, R.: Retinal light adaptation-evidence for a feedback mechanism. Nature **310**(5975), 314–316 (1984)

32. Vardi, N., Zhang, L.L., Payne, J.A., Sterling, P.: Evidence that different cation chloride cotransporters in retinal neurons allow opposite responses to GABA. J. Neurosci. **20**(20), 7657–7663 (2000)

33. Wang, X.J., Rinzel, J.: Alternating and synchronous rhythms in reciprocally inhibitory model neurons. Neural Comput. **4**(1), 84–97 (1992)

34. Wohrer, A., Kornprobst, P.: Virtual retina: a biological retina model and simulator, with contrast gain control. J. Comput. Neurosci. **26**(2), 219–249 (2009)

Simulative Models to Understand Numerical Cognition

Michela Ponticorvo[✉], Onofrio Gigliotta, and Orazio Miglino

Department of Humanistic Studies, University of Naples "Federico II",
Naples, Italy
{michela.ponticorvo,onofrio.gigliotta,orazio.miglino}@unina.it

Abstract. This paper starts from summarizing different methods to study numerical cognition, from comparative to developmental, from experimental to simulative. Then the focus moves to different kinds of simulative models that are introduced together with the example of a simulative model applied to numerical representation and midpoint calculation: Midpoint. This software allows to study relevant bias in humans, such as the number interval position effect. Together with a detailed description of the software and the underlying model, some results are reported.

Keywords: Simulative models · Numerical cognition · Bisection of number intervals · NIPE effect · Developmental studies

1 Introduction

The human beings have extraordinary numerical abilities and have reached a very high sophistication in tools to work with numbers. But humans are not the only species who can rely on some sort of numerical ability. From insects [1] to primates [9] it is possible to find many interesting example of numerical competence.

In the last years, the research in this field has become more intense and many different approaches have been employed. In what follows a summary of the different methods to study numbers is reported.

2 Methods to Study Numerical Cognition

Different methods can be used to understand the origins, the mechanisms and the bias of numerical and mathematical cognition. Each method is able to reply to specific questions.

Additional materials: More details about the model and the related code can be provided to whom is interested by emailing the authors Onofrio Gigliotta, Orazio Miglino or Michela Ponticorvo.

J.M. Ferrández Vicente et al. (Eds.): IWINAC 2017, Part I, LNCS 10337, pp. 75–84, 2017.
DOI: 10.1007/978-3-319-59740-9_8

It is possible to run *comparative* studies on different animal species to understand if there are common mechanisms. In this vein, the Approximate Number System (ANS) has been identified [7,8]: a cognitive system that supports the estimation of the magnitude of a group with more than four elements without relying on language or symbols, together with the parallel individuation system, or object tracking system for smaller magnitudes.

A great bulk of research is devoted to *developmental* studies. In this case the children, starting from newborn are tested to verify their numerical skills. In this case, the goal is to understand when and how numerical abilities are born, if education has an effect on them and, if so, how it affects the starting endowement.

Interesting insights may also come from the study of brain-damaged patients in *neuropsychological* studies. Studying these subjects, it is possible to verify if specific brain damages produce specific effects on numerical performance, what is preserved, what ability is more likely to be lost. Comparative and developmental studies rely on behavioural methods and use relevant experimental procedures, for example free choice, training, habituation procedures, cross-modal studies for human children and adults; laboratory and free environment observation for animals. Moreover for human beings it is possible to ask precise mathematical questions, often very simple, and record the replies. Experimenters can ask the participant to reply as soon as possible in order to avoid that they use tips or procedured learnt along the formal education pathway.

It is also possible to run *genetic* studies understanding if there is inheritance of specific disturbs such as dyscalculia, for example in monozygotic or dizygotic twins.

Understanding the structural and functional basis for numerical abilities is made possible also by *neuro-physiological* studies. In this kind of studies, neuro-imagining is used to get information on the brain areas that are involved in numerical processing and under which condition they activate. Thanks to these studies it was possible to identify a cerebral substrate connected to human ability in arithmetics: the intraparietal sulcus that systematically activates in all number tasks [2]. Neuro-physiological studies can be used also in a comparative way, to verify if there are analogous areas in different species, phylogenetically close or far. This methodology has led to relevant results: for example, the seminal work by Nieder and Miller [13], they analyzed both behavioral and neuronal representations of numerosity in the prefrontal cortex of rhesus monkeys and the data clearly indicated a nonlinearly compressed scaling of numerical information, according to the Weber-Fechner law for psychophysical magnitudes.

The last, but not least, approach we would like to introduce is *modelling*. In this case models can be conceived to explain the general functioning of numerical mechanisms or bias.Some models are meant to explain behavioural data, some others to replicate neural dynamics: All these models can be roughly divided in three groups:

a. Abstract models based on data
b. Biologically plausibles models relying on artificial neural networks
c. Embodied models with robots

The first kind of models is represented by the triple-code model by Dehaene et al. [3]. In this model, starting from the evidence on number representations in animals, infants, normal and gifted adults, and brain-lesioned patients, a synthesis is traced as a triple-code model, assuming that numbers are mentally manipulated in an arabic, verbal or analogical magnitude code depending on the requested mental operation.

An example of the second kind of models is offered by the models that try to reproduce brain mechanism in artificial neural networks. In Stoianov and Zorzi [19], it is shown that visual numerosity emerges as a statistical property of images in 'deep networks' that learn a hierarchical generative model of the sensory input. The third kind of models tries to replicate not only the neural networks dynamics, but also how they are related to input that can be selected in the environment. This case is well-represented by Di Ferdinando et al. [4]: a series of simulations involving neural networks that learned to perform their task by self-organizing their internal connections and controlling artificial agents with an orienting eye and an arm. Another meaningful example comes from Gigliotta et al. [6] that trained artificial embodied neurorobotic agents equipped with a pan/tilt camera, provided with different neural and motor capabilities, to solve a well-known neuropsychological test: the cancellation task. As often, the neural computationa is not enough to clarify how cognition emerges, it is useful to use the modelling approach where the importance of the body is adequately recognized.

In the context of numerical cognition, an embodied computational model can be an interesting way to approach cognitive issues [11, 16]. Artificial models, in fact, offer the possibility to produce an artifact that can be anoverated in the list of species to be studied and compared. If comparative sciences are a precious source for insights about cognition, artificial models can give further insights in reproducing a certain phenomenon.

The scientific challenge is building a new artificial species with its own specific features. These artificial networks can reproduce phenomena at various levels: behavioural, physiological, neural with different granularity from the single neuron to whole structures. This approach has been already used in modelling neuropsychological phenomena, [20] linking these phenomena with neural representation as well as organisms interaction with the environment [12].

This approach has produced interesting results in the case of geometric cognition, that relying on lenghts and angles estimation can be considered as part of mathematical abilities. In Ponticorvo and Miglino [10, 15] the primacy and the modularity of geometric information are put to test with embodied artificial robots governed by neural networks and evolved with genetic algorithms. The data indicate that environmental exposition to different spatial information during a learning/adaptive history can produce agents with no modular neurocognitive systems that are able to process different types of spatial information and display various orientation behaviors.

We will now describe an artificial model to explain the NIPE effect, an example of the second type of this models applied to numerical cognition.

3   The NIPE Effect

When healthy adults provide estimates of a number interval midpoint, error biases vary as a function of the interval length and, length being equal, as a function of the position occupied by the interval within tens (i.e. Number Interval Position Effect) [5]. When 7-unit and 5-unit intervals are positioned at the beginning of tens, subjective midpoints are shifted toward values higher than true midpoints. When the same intervals are positioned at the end of tens, subjective midpoints are shifted toward values lower than true midpoints. With 3-unit intervals a progressively increasing negative bias is found the more intervals are placed at the end of tens. This bias has been observed consistently in healthy adults, right-brain damaged patients and children.

To understand the functional origins of this phenomenon an artificial model was conceived.

3.1   The Task

As illustrated in the previous section, one method of study of numerical cognition is to propose simple arithmetics questions to human participants, demanding an immediate reply. This way, participants cannot rely on their formal education and related tips and procedures.

One such task foresees that participants have to identify the natural number that divides equally a numerical series that is delimited by two natural numbers: a bisection task.

For example, if we consider the series of the first natural ten (1–10), the partecipant can be asked to identify the middle number between 3 (lower bound) and 7 (upper bound) or between 4 (lower bound) and 6 (upper bound) and so on. As the first natural ten includes even and odd numbers, this task takes different forms: the limits may have an even or odd sum. The odd sum permits two solutions.

For example, the middle number between 1 and 8 can be 4 or 5. To reply indicating a natural number, the participant must choose the number that is closer to the lower bound, rounding down, or the upper, rounding up. For this reason, it is preferred to propose the task form with even sum.

This task has been used in neuropsychological literature, applying the traditional bisection task, used for investigating spatial neglect [17] to the study of numerical representation. It has been administered to healthy adults right-brain damaged patients [5] and children [18].

3.2   The Model

Let us now describe in detail the artificial model for number encoding. This is a simulative artificial model based on artificial neural networks dynamics, as explained above. The starting point for this model is represented by two principles about neural mechanisms that, along the years, have been confirmed many times by empirical findings:

a. Natural numbers neural coding: basic numbers in a certain notation are coded in an amodal way by distinct neural groups. In other words, if we consider the decimal notation, there is a neural group whose activation is more probable when the number 1 is presented regardless of the presentation form, another one for number 2 and so on up to 10.
b. Neural accumulation mechanisms: neural elaboration takes place by energy transfer between neural groups and arrives to its conclusion when some neural group accumulates a certain energy level.

In this model we adopt an approach which considers nodes as made up by group of neurons; it is a functional representation of brain areas, rather than a single-cell simulation. As hinted above, in order to understand which are the functional bases of the NIPE, a simple model consisting of two modules was imagined.

The first module represents how number are encoded in the artificial system whereas the second module is computes the midpoint for each interval. To focus the investigation on number representation, the second module is a perfect calculator whose output correctly bisects the interval received as input. Number representations have been modeled through percolation networks. Typically, a percolation network is a system of interconnected nodes in which information (or metaphorically a liquid) injected into an input node can percolate to nearby connected nodes. Figure 1 presents the percolation networks used to encode integer number from 1 to 9. Information is given in input to nodes (in yellow in Fig. 1) and it percolates, in all-or-none fashion, to one of the nearby 5 nodes (including itself). This percolation happens according to a discrete probability density function that, in the network, is translated into the connection weights between nodes.

In case of a perfect representation, for example, the probability of the activation to percolate to nearby nodes would be 0 as depicted in Fig. 2. In this case the bisection error would be 0. This means that when the magnitude or the number 1 is presented only the corresponding group of neurons becomes active.

In order to model number interval bisection for different limits of intervals, the activation was spread through the dedicated percolation network for one step, then active nodes are used to compute the midpoint and the related error. This computing is just the exact calculation of the mean of the active nodes. Figure 3 illustrates how step by step error and midpoint are computed for a single run for 1–3 interval bisection.

4   The Software Simulator: Midpoint

The above described model was implemented into an application developed in C# and called Midpoint.

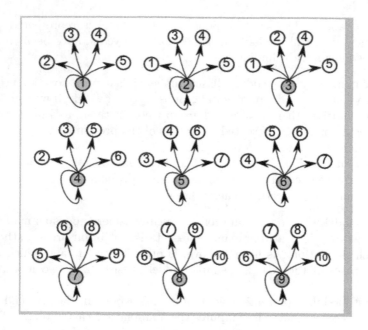

Fig. 1. Percolation networks (Color figure online)

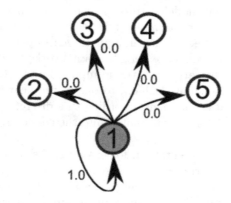

Fig. 2. Perfect encoding of number 1, activation does not percolates to nearby nodes but is retained to the input node

Midpoint can be used to run simulation of numerical bisection task in a percolation network. It can be used also by people with little background in informatics because it has a user-friendly interface. In this interface, represented in Fig. 4 every number is represented as a node and it is possible to set the connection weights to the nearby nodes.

These connection weights in the percolation network correspond to the statistical probability that an activation is transmitted from one node to another

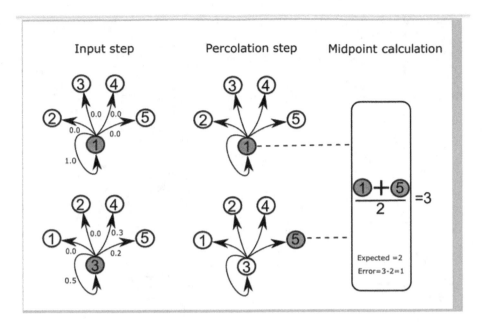

Fig. 3. Step by step process of computing error and midpoint. The interval is 1–3 interval. At step one, nodes are activated only for node 1 and 3. After a one step percolation, computed according to a discrete density probability function (probabilities to percolate are reported beside connection arrows), active nodes are used to compute midpoint and error

node. A set of 9 sliders allows users to easily set connections for each node representing numbers from 1 to 9. To each slider, the probability, multiplied by 100, is pictured.

Resulting curves are displayed beneath the sliders panel. Each time a slider is modified, Midpoint runs a new experiment by administering to the percolation model 3-, 5- and 7-unit intervals for 10,000 times. Collected bisection errors are then displayed through three graphs in the main window of the application.

To run new experiments it is possible to select *Experiment* where *Run and save* option allows to save the average performance of 10,000 artificial subjects for each interval described above. Data are saved in *datFile* that can be imported in calculation sheets or software for data analysis.

The sliders indicate the probability that the number that is selected with the radio button under *select input number code* is encoded as another number for the effect of percolation. Every pattern of curves can be saved from the menu *File* in a file .data. Some initial sets are already available and can be modified so as to see the outcomes on error. Every time a slider is modified, the simulations are run and graphics are updated.

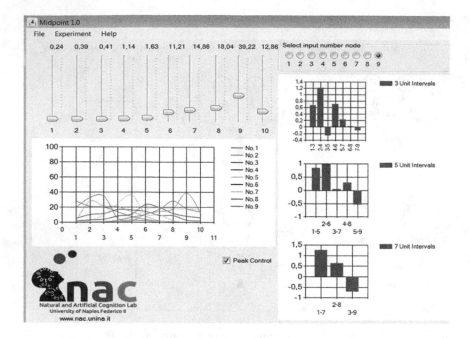

Fig. 4. Midpoint user interface with the slider to modify connection weights

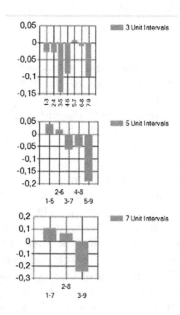

Fig. 5. Data from the midpoint simulator for different intervals

4.1   Results

The Midpoint simulator has been used to replicate the data observed in adults and children [5,18], confirming the indications from a previous mode [14]. The model, if the percolation model is arranged so as to replicate the compressed scaling of numerical information found in primate prefrontal cortex [13], replicates the patterns observed in human adults and children (Fig. 5). The artificial model commits a systematic error, shows a bias, that is consistent with the NIPE effect: the closer one boundary of the interval is to the border of a ten, the more the midpoint is shifted. This is particularly evident for 5 unit intervals and 7 unit intervals.

These results show that a model which relies exclusively on percolation, energy transfer and accumulation, can account for the bias observed in human beings reproducing the NIPE effect.

5   Conclusions and Future Directions

In this paper we have reviewed different methods to study spatial cognition and focused out attention on simulative methods. Moreover, an example of artificial model to explain numerical bias has been illustrated. This model indicates that the mental number line does not represents numbers in a spatial guise and the arithmetics module can, at least in principle, work on energy transfer rather than on number spatial representation. It is possible to affirm that in humans or other species this is the mechanism that actually underlies number encoding and representation, but it is a proof that the spatial representation of numbers is not necessary to explain the data.

The NIPE effect can mirror the logarithmic central representation of numerical magnitudo that is independent from school education and that is shared by non-human species too. This opens the way to new questions: which is the connection between space and number? Are these two core knowlegde connected more strictly than others? Does this link have implication for number education?

To go on searching in this direction, an embodied model will be implemented to better understand which are the links between space and number in a simple embodied agent, such as a mobile robots. On a complementary side, an extended model of the described one will be conceived with different layers, able to reproduce not only the behavioural side of NIPE effect but also the corresponding neural circuitry, as discussed in neurophysiological and neuropsychological literature.

References

1. Chittka, L., Geiger, K.: Can honey bees count landmarks? Anim. Behav. **49**(1), 159–164 (1995)
2. Dehaene, S.: Varieties of numerical abilities. Cognition **44**(1), 1–42 (1992)
3. Dehaene, S., Molko, N., Cohen, L., Wilson, A.J.: Arithmetic and the brain. Curr. Opin. Neurobiol. **14**(2), 218–224 (2004)

4. Di Ferdinando, A., Parisi, D., Bartolomeo, P.: Modeling orienting behavior and its disorders with "ecological" neural networks. J. Cogn. Neurosci. **19**(6), 1033–1049 (2007)
5. Doricchi, F., Merola, S., Aiello, M., Guariglia, P., Bruschini, M., Gevers, W., Tomaiuolo, F.: Spatial orienting biases in the decimal numeral system. Curr. Biol. **19**(8), 682–687 (2009)
6. Gigliotta, O., Bartolomeo, P., Miglino, O.: Approaching neuropsychological tasks through adaptive neurorobots. Connect. Sci. **27**(2), 153–163 (2015)
7. Gilmore, C., Attridge, N., Inglis, M.: Measuring the approximate number system. Q. J. Exp. Psychol. **64**(11), 2099–2109 (2011)
8. Halberda, J., Feigenson, L.: Developmental change in the acuity of the "Number Sense": the approximate number system in 3-, 4-, 5-, and 6-year-olds and adults. Dev. Psychol. **44**(5), 1457 (2008)
9. Matsuzawa, T.: Use of numbers by a chimpanzee. Nature **315**(6014), 57–59 (1985)
10. Miglino, O., Ponticorvo, M.: Place cognition as an example of situated cognition: a study with evolved agents. Cogn. Process. **10**(2), 250–252 (2009)
11. Miglino, O., Ponticorvo, M. Exploring the roots of (spatial) cognition in artificial and natural organisms. The evolutionary robotics approach. Horiz. Evol. Robot., 93–123 (2014)
12. Miglino, O., Ponticorvo, M., Bartolomeo, P.: Place cognition and active perception: a study with evolved robots. Connect. Sci. **21**(1), 3–14 (2009)
13. Nieder, A., Miller, E.K.: Coding of cognitive magnitude: compressed scaling of numerical information in the primate prefrontal cortex. Neuron **37**(1), 149–157 (2003)
14. Ponticorvo, M., Rotondaro, F., Doricchi, F., Miglino, O.: A neural model of number interval position effect (NIPE) in children. In: Ferrández Vicente, J.M., Álvarez-Sánchez, J.R., de la Paz López, F., Toledo-Moreo, F.J., Adeli, H. (eds.) IWINAC 2015. LNCS, vol. 9107, pp. 9–18. Springer, Cham (2015). doi:10.1007/978-3-319-18914-7_2
15. Ponticorvo, M., Miglino, O.: Encoding geometric and non-geometric information: a study with evolved agents. Anim. Cogn. **13**(1), 157 (2010)
16. Ponticorvo, M., Walker, R., Miglino, O. Evolutionary robotics as a tool to investigate spatial cognition in artificial and natural systems. Artif. Cogn. Syst., 210–237(2007)
17. Reuter-Lorenz, P.A., Posner, M.I.: Components of neglect from right-hemisphere damage: an analysis of line bisection. Neuropsychologia **28**(4), 327–333 (1990)
18. Rotondaro, F., Gazzellini, S., Peris, M., Doricchi, F.: Number interval bisection and number to position performance. In: Poster presented at the European Workshop Cognitive Neuroscience, Bressanone, Italy (2012)
19. Stoianov, I., Zorzi, M.: Emergence of a 'visual number sense' in hierarchical generative models. Nat. Neurosci. **15**(2), 194–196 (2012)
20. Urbanski, M., Angeli, V., Bourlon, C., Cristinzio, C., Ponticorvo, M., Rastelli, F., Bartolomeo, P.: Negligence spatiale unilaterale: une consequence dramatique mais souvent negligee des lesions de l'hemisphere droit. Rev. Neurologique **163**(3), 305–322 (2007)

Restoration Model for Attenuated Low Spatial Frequencies in the Retinal Output

Adrián Arias[1]([✉]), Eduardo Sánchez[1], and Luis Martínez[2]

[1] Grupo de Sistemas Inteligentes (GSI),
Centro Singular de Investigación en Tecnologías de la Información (CITIUS),
Univ. de Santiago de Compostela, Santiago de Compostela, Spain
[2] Instituto de Neurociencias de Alicante, CSIC-Univ. Miguel Hernández,
Alicante, Spain

Abstract. The difference of Gaussian model predicts that the retinal computation reduces the spatial correlation of the natural images by attenuating the range of low spatial frequencies. However, our cognitive system is able to discriminate two images with the same high frequency information but different low frequency content. This study is focused on answering how the visual system could restore from the retinal output those original information.

Keywords: Retinal ganglion cells · Difference of Gaussians · Lateral geniculate nucleus · Restoration model · Dual-band filter · Stop-band filter · Notch-band filter

1 Introduction

Theoretical neuroscientist and electrophysiologist of the visual system have been on the hunt of a suggested efficient coding hypothesis first coined by Barlow [1] that arose around the birth of information theory [11]. This hypothesis mostly focused on the encoding process for efficiently transmitting the sensory information to the brain but too little attention has been paid to the decoding process. In this context, it has been claim that one of the roles of the retina within the visual systems is to spatially decorrelate the redundant information that a natural scene contains [1]. That means roughly to remove the low spatial frequencies of an image. However, our cognition system tells us that we can discriminate two images with the same content of high frequencies but different low frequencies or mean values (Fig. 1). It may suggest that the removed information should be restored at some point of the visual pathway.

2 Methods

2.1 DoG Model

The difference of Gaussians (DoG) model [10] has been used in electrophysiology experiments to characterize the contrast sensitivity behavior of several neurons

© Springer International Publishing AG 2017
J.M. Ferrández Vicente et al. (Eds.): IWINAC 2017, Part I, LNCS 10337, pp. 85–94, 2017.
DOI: 10.1007/978-3-319-59740-9_9

Fig. 1. Intuitive view of the restoration process. In: image with same spatial frequency but different mean value (left vs right). RGC: retinal output. LGNi: internueron output. LGNr: relay cell output. Profiles: evolution of each signal along the middle cross section of the image. Simulated with optimal parameters ($\sigma_c = 1.75, r_\sigma = 2.1, r_v = 0.95, K_i = 1/DC, r_i = 3.6$)

in the visual system when they are stimulated with drifting sinusoidal gratings of different spatial frequencies. In this study, we used this model to implement computational simulations of retinal ganglion cells (RGC) spatial filters. The model consists in a difference of two Gaussian functions: a positive narrower Gaussian which represents the excitatory center receptive field behavior and a negative wider one which represents the inhibitory surround.

$$F_{DoG}(r) = k_c e^{-r^2/\sigma_c^2} - k_s e^{-r^2/\sigma_s^2} \text{ with } k_c > k_s, \ \sigma_s > \sigma_c \tag{1}$$

It requires four parameters: the amplitude of each Gaussian (k_c, k_s) and the sigma of each Gaussian (σ_c, σ_s). However, in the results we used equivalently another four parameters: the center sigma (σ_c), sigma ratio ($r_\sigma = \sigma_s/\sigma_c$), volume ratio ($r_v = k_s \sigma_s^2/k_c \sigma_c^2$) and a constraint which forces the filter to fulfill the requirement of unity maximum gain ($Gain_{Max} = 1$).

2.2   Restoration Model

Within the framework of restoration, we can say that a DoG filter degrades specially the low frequencies of an input signal and here we introduce a simple computation to restore them. Although, in this study, we consider that the best candidate to implement this restoration algorithm is the LGN, it could also be implemented by some other neuronal structure along the visual pathway.

The restoration model takes the output of a DoG filter (RGC, Fig. 2) and adds to this signal an estimate of the local mean signal (LGNi, Fig. 2). Strikingly, this estimate can be computed by applying a normalized Gaussian filter to the output of the DoG filter and then multiplying the result by a scaling factor. We identify the scaling factor as the LGNi gain (K_i) and the sigma of the new Gaussian (2) as the LGNi sigma (σ_i). However, we think more appropriate to express this sigma parameter as the ratio between the LGNi sigma and the RGC surround sigma ($r_i = \sigma_i/\sigma_s$).

$$F_{G_i}(r) = \frac{1}{\pi \sigma_i^2} e^{-r^2/\sigma_i^2} \tag{2}$$

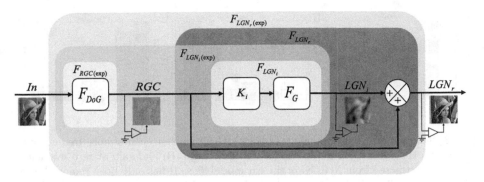

Fig. 2. Control block diagram of the restoration model. The operational amplifier symbols indicate the places where electrophysiology experiments can register the activity while the sub-blocks indicate a possible block simplification. Those simplifications that are noted with the "exp" subscript can be easily determined by electrophysiology but the remaining ones require registering simultaneously a RGC and the LGN neurons which it projects.

If we represent the restoration algorithm as a control block diagram (Fig. 2) we can identify two types of transfer functions. The outer ones which are calculated by dividing the output signals by the input signal and the inner ones which are determined by dividing the output signals by the output of the RGC (top equations, Fig. 5). The convenience of this classification is that outer transfer functions can be reported in electrophysiology experiments and that is the reason why we labeled with an "exp" subscript. Meanwhile, the inner transfer functions are quite difficult to report by experiments because it is too difficult to register simultaneously a RGC and the two types of neurons of the thalamus to which it projects: local interneuron the (LGNi) and relay cell (LGNr). Thus, this modeling framework has the potential to predict these inner transfer functions.

3   Results

3.1   The parameters of a RGC filter

Among the complete parameter space of the DoG model, we are interested in assessing the subset that it is implemented by the RGC. Therefore, taking into account experimental studies, we can notice that eccentricity changes do not affect systematically the sigma ratio and the volume ratio [2]; however center sigma increases with eccentricity. That means that sigma center is roughly independent for the other parameters. Therefore, in the simulation it is enough to compute the results for one single value of center sigma without loss of generality.

On the contrary, the values of sigma ratio and volume ratio reported in retina experiments show that these parameters can take any value but within a restricted range (Fig. 3). Even more interesting, if we use these experimental data to compute the gain at zero frequency (DC), we can observe that although it can

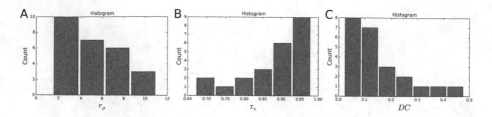

Fig. 3. The parameterization values of the DoG filters that occurs more frequency in the retina. Histograms of sigma ratio (A), volume ratio (B) and gain at zero frequency (C). Data extracted from X-RGC in the cat model [5,8]. It has only been removed from the data an outlier which presents a high sigma ratio ($r_\sigma = 23$).

takes values up to 50% of the maximum gain, the most common values rarely exceed the 20%. Thus, among the complete parameter space we can identified the DoG filters that can be more biologically plausible (start marked, Fig. 4A) based on electrophysiology data (Fig. 3).

3.2   LGNi Gain: The Scaling Factor

The main goal of the LGNi in our restoration model is to estimate the lower frequency components of the original input by means of the RGC signal. Although this estimator would be able to restore that component, it could be out of scale. Thus, it is essential to multiply this signal by a scaling factor (K_i, Fig. 2) to put the signal in an acceptable scale. Besides that, as we said above, the DoG filter attenuates the zero frequency of the original signal and as a consequence, we think that a reasonable value for this scaling factor should be the inverse of this attenuation ($K_i = 1/DC$). Notice that this scaling factor depends on the DoG filter used.

3.3   LGNi Extension

There is a lack of experimental data to determine the ratio between the extension of the receptive field of a RGC and the extension of the LGNi to which it projects (r_i, Sect. 2.2). In the absence of this information, we computed the restoration model for different values of this unknown ratio (Fig. 4B) for each DoG filter within its complete parameter space (Fig. 4A). Then, we calculate the mean square error (MSE) between the LGNr output and the original input, as well as the saturation percentage of the LGNr signal. Our results suggest that as this ratio increases, the saturation always decreases, while the MSE exhibits a minimum value (downward triangle marker, Fig. 4B). That means that there is an optimal value for this ratio which restores the original image better than others. An even more striking observation is that the restoration results that exhibit the lower minimum MSE were computed with the biological plausible

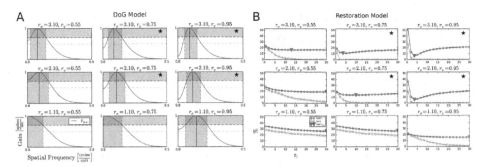

Fig. 4. (A) Parameter space of the DoG model in the spatial frequency domain for a fix value of center sigma ($\sigma_c = 1.75$) while sigma ratio changes vertically and volume ratio horizontally. It has been marked with a star those DoG filters that belong to the parameterization subset of RGC (see Fig. 3). (B) Parameter space of the restoration model. Every single plot shows the MSE and saturation results (circles and squares, respectively) for a fix DoG parameterization (same arrangement as in A) while the LGNi sigma ratio (r_i) changes through the x-axis. It has been marked the minimum MSE value for each plot (downward triangle).

DoG filters (star marked, Fig. 4B). Specially, the lowest minimum MSE occurs for high values of volume ratio where a high attenuation of the zero frequency takes place ($DC \leq 0.2$). In turn, high volume ratio values present the highest probability of occurrence in the RGC circuitry (Fig. 3B). Taking all of this into account, we can state that the optimal value of the extension of a LGNi is roughly three times and a half greater than the extension of a RGC receptive field ($r_i = 3.6$) for those RGC that occur more frequently in the retina. In addition, it is important to mention that in this simulation (Fig. 4B) we use the image of Lena as the input signal to compute LGNr output; however similar results were obtained with other natural images (not shown). Thus, the performance of our restoration model is input independence.

3.4 The Family of LGN Filters

For the sake of clarity, the following results were generated with a fix DoG filter ($\sigma_c = 1.75, r_\sigma = 2.1, r_v = 0.95$) which belongs to the subset of the RGC filters that occurs more frequency in the retina (Fig. 3A and B). Once the DoG filter is set, we computed both, the experimental and inner transfer functions of the restoration model (Fig. 5) for different values around the optimal LGNi sigma ratio (around downward triangle marker, Fig. 4B).

Our simulations illustrate that, the $F_{LGNi(exp)}$ changes its behavior from a DoG-like filter to a Gaussian-like filter as the LGNi sigma increased (first column in Fig. 5). However, both behaviors are focused on letting pass the low frequencies and both present a unity gain at zero frequency. On the other hand,

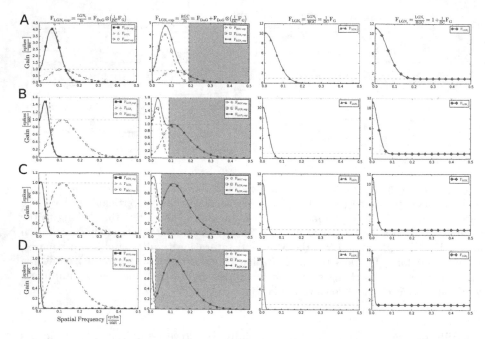

Fig. 5. Transfer functions computed with a fixed RGC filter ($\sigma_c = 1.75, r_\sigma = 2.1, r_v = 0.95$) but different LGNi sigma ratios ($A : r_i = 1, B : r_i = 2.25, C : r_i = 3.6, D : r_i = 8$)

the $F_{LGNr(exp)}$ shows signs of a more elaborate behavior. In fact, we can classify it into three categories. $F_{LGNr(exp)}$ type 1 behaves as a DoG-like filter (second column, Fig. 5A) taking place for LGNi sigma values that roughly equals the surround sigma of the RGC ($r_i = 1$). $F_{LGNr(exp)}$ type 2 seems to perform a dual-band pass filter (second column, Fig. 5B) with one of its band pass filers with an evident higher maximum gain which is shifted towards low frequencies. This filter occurs for LGNi sigma values about twice the surround sigma ($r_i = 2.25$). Finally, $F_{LGNr(exp)}$ type 3 can be considered that it is formed by a sum of a low-pass filter and a band-pass filter (second column, Fig. 5C and D) and it arises for greater values of LGNi sigma ($r_i \geq 3.6$). The most interesting feature of this filter type is a remarkable stop band or even notch band interval which is shifted towards low frequencies.

On the contrary, inner filters are easier to describe because both are based on the same Gaussian (F_{G_i}, see Sect. 2.2). As the results suggest, F_{LGNi} is devoted to amplify low frequencies with a gain well above the unity. Moreover, the upper cutoff frequency of this filter shifts towards lower frequencies when LGNi sigma increases (third column, Fig. 5). Finally, F_{LGNr} is also focused on amplifying low frequencies but additionally it allows passing the remaining frequencies with a unity gain (fourth column, Fig. 5).

3.5   The LGN Coding

In this section, it is shown how the restoration model restores a natural image through the RGC output. In this case, we use the same RGC filter that has been used in other sections which belongs to the type of filters which occurs more frequency in the retina. Once the DoG filter is fixed, we determined the LGNi and LGNr outputs (Fig. 6) for different values around the optimal LGNi sigma ratio as has been done previously (see Sect. 3.4).

When LGNi sigma ratio equals one ($r_i = 1$, Fig. 6A), the LGN images seem to be burned for both brights and darks. In fact, the histogram presents two high peaks in both the right and left sides indicating that the outputs are suffering of saturation. Although subjectively the outputs seem to recover the low frequencies of the original image, the truth is that the amplitude spectrum slopes of the LGNi and LGNr outputs ($\alpha = -0.84$ and $\alpha = -0.83$, respectively) are more flattened than the slope of the input image ($\alpha = -1.39$). That reveals the DoG-like behavior of these filters (first and second column, Fig. 5A).

If we set the LGNi sigma ratio around two ($r_i = 2.25$, Fig. 6B), the LGNi image seems slightly blurred while LGNr image looks quite similar as the input image but it also seems as if some psychophysical aspect had been enhanced. The histograms of both LGN outputs show a stretching in its dynamic range but the LGNr output slightly saturates in the side of darks. As a consequence, the histogram flattened and in turn the entropy subtly increased. The results also show that, the slopes values of both LGN outputs are quite closed to the original input; they just have to be a little bit bigger to restore completely the low frequency component. It is also worth mentioning that the amplitude spectrum of the outputs presents a section where is higher than the input. That section match with the range of frequencies around which the maximum filter gain takes place (second column, Fig. 5B). This is probably the cause of the psychophysical enhancement that has been reported.

In accordance with the minimum MSE criterion, if we look at the results of the optima LGNi sigma ratio ($r_i = 3.6$, Fig. 6C), we can report that the LGNi image is also quite blurred. Meanwhile, LGNr image looks almost equal the input image but it also presents another enhancement feature that can be described as a vaguely glossy effect. In line with this, the profile signal of the LGNi output nicely matches with a local mean signal estimator (see Methods, Sect. 2.2) while the profile of the LGNr output almost matches perfectly with the original image. Besides, both LGN output histograms are very similar as the input one, as well as its statistical indexes. Likewise, the amplitude spectrum slopes are almost equal as the input one, especially the slope of the LGNr output. In this case, there is a section of the LGNr amplitude spectrum that is lower than the input around the range of frequencies that match with the stop-band range of the filter (second column, Fig. 5C) and that could be the cause of the glossy effect.

Finally, if LGNi sigma ratio is greater than its optimal ($r_i = 8$, Fig. 6D), the LGNi image is evidently blurred while the LGNr image presents a stronger glossy effect. The profile signals and the histograms of both LGN outputs are further away in resembling the original ones. Again the most remarkable feature

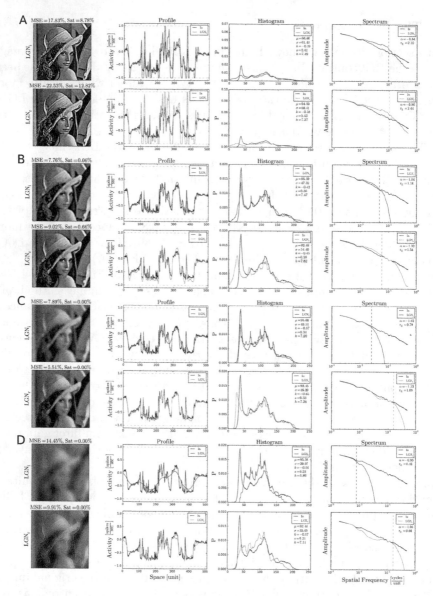

Fig. 6. LGN outputs computed with a fix DoG filter ($\sigma_c = 1.75, r_\sigma = 2.1, r_v = 0.95$) but for different LGNi sigma ratios ($A : r_i = 1$, $B : r_i = 2.25$, $C : r_i = 3.60$, $D : r_i = 8$). For each LGNi sigma ratio it is shown the plots for the LGNi output image (top rows) and for the LGNr output image (bottom rows). The profile plots illustrate the evolution of each signal along the middle section of the image. The histogram plots represent the probability density function of the image signals. Notice that these plots include related statistical indexes: the mean (μ), standard deviation (σ), kurtosis (k), skewness (s) and entropy (h). The amplitude spectrum plots represent in a log-log scale the average amplitude spectrum among all spatial frequency directions. In these plots are included the slope index of the spectrum (α) and the energy ratio index (r_E, not covered in the text).

is that the LGNr amplitude spectrum falls above the input spectrum around the frequencies where the stop-band of the filter occurs (second column, 5D) and that is related for sure with the strong glossy effect.

4 Discussion

Our restoration model fits pretty well with the description of the putative push-pull circuitry of the LGN [6]. In fact, our RGC output resembles the push while our LGNi output can stand for the pull component. Another reported feature is that the pull receptive field is larger than the push [6] and that is in line with our results which suggest that an acceptable restoration is only possible for LGNi sigma values 2–4 times greater than RGC surround sigma (Sect. 3.3). Although the local interneuron is inhibitory in a conventional synaptic sense [15], functionally operates as a desinhibition or net excitation when its excitatory drive decreased. This is precisely the case of the LGN circuitry where these interneurons prefer to contact relay cells with the reverse center sing [6]. Therefore, adding our LGNi output to the RGC output is accordance with the suggested circuitry (Fig. 2). Moreover, we conducted simulations (not shown) splitting the RGC output into On-Off components by a rectification non-linearity. In this context, the On-LGNr output was computed by adding the On-RGC signal and subtracting the Off-LGNi signal which in turn was driven by Off-RGC outputs. In that simulations we also obtain similar restoration results of those presented here.

On the other hand, the transfer functions obtained in our results (Sect. 3.4, Fig. 5) are also in accordance with most common spatial frequency tuning responses registered in electrophysiology experiment in the LGN. That is truth at least for the DoG-like and Gaussian-like behavior of the $F_{LGNi(exp)}$ and the DoG-like behavior of the $F_{LGNr(exp)}$ type 1. However, the dual-band behaviour of the $F_{LGNr(exp)}$ type 2 and the stop-band or notch-band behavior of the $F_{LGNr(exp)}$ type 3 are rarely reported in the thalamus [12]. Despite this, in recent studies these unexpected behaviors were reported in the LGN of unanesthetized rats [13,14]. Taking that and our results, it could be suggested that anesthesia could affect the transmission of the information from the local interneuron to the relay cell. Thus, if this transmission fails, the most likely scenario is that the spatial frequency tuning functions reported in electrophysiology only show the DoG-like and Gaussian-like behaviors. Another potential experimental bias is the stimulus used to obtain the spatial frequency tuning function. Indeed, if the stimulus size only covers the classical receptive field of the relay cells, the results are not going to reflect the local interneuron contribution within the circuitry. Thus, our results suggest that the stimulus used in electrophysiology should be much greater than the classical receptive field of thalamus relay cells to see this unexpected behavior [13].

Moreover, dual-band and notch-band filters were reported in other electrophysiology experiments. The notch behavior was observed in M-cone driven RGC [3,7] in the context of color processing. Meanwhile, in other study, both behaviors emerged in the RGC as a degenerative disease progresses [9]. In addition, notch-band filters were also present in temporal modulation transfer functions in the visual thalamus [4]. Even more striking is that, the reported notch effect only was present for those stimulus that extended beyond the classical receptive field [4]. These studies lead us to think that our model could be useful to fit quantitatively experimental data when the DoG model fails. Specially in those cases in which a crossover inhibition take place [15]. Thus, the presented model is a great candidate to be the building block for a new canonical computation of the brain.

References

1. Barlow, H.B.: Possible principles underlying the transformation of sensory messages. In: Sensory Communication, pp. 217–234 (1961)
2. Croner, L.J., Kaplan, E.: Receptive fields of P and M ganglion cells across the primate retina. Vis. Res. **35**(1), 7–24 (1995)
3. Crook, J.D., Manookin, M.B., Packer, O.S., Dacey, D.M.: Horizontal cell feedback without cone type-selective inhibition mediates 'red-green' color opponency in midget ganglion cells of the primate retina. J. Neurosci. **31**(5), 1762–1772 (2011)
4. Dhruv, N.T., Tailby, C., Sokol, S.H., Majaj, N.J., Lennie, P.: Nonlinear signal summation in magnocellular neurons of the macaque lateral geniculate nucleus. J. Neurophysiol. **102**(3), 1921–1929 (2009)
5. Enroth-Cugell, C., Robson, J.G.: The contrast sensitivity of retinal ganglion cells of the cat. J. Physiol. **187**, 517–523 (1966)
6. Hirsch, J.A., Wang, X., Sommer, F.T., Martinez, L.M.: How inhibitory circuits in the thalamus serve vision. Ann. Rev. Neurosci. **8**(38), 309–329 (2015)
7. Lee, B.B., Shapley, R.M., Hawken, M.J., Sun, H.: Spatial distributions of cone inputs to cells of the parvocellular pathway investigated with cone-isolating gratings. J. Opt. Soc. Am. A Opt. Image Sci. Vis. **29**(2), A223–A232 (2012)
8. Linsenmeier, R.A., Frishman, L.J., Jakiela, H.G., Enroth-Cugell, C.: Receptive field properties of x and y cells in the cat retina derived from contrast sensitivity measurements. Vis. Res. **22**(9), 1173–1183 (1982)
9. Pu, M., Xu, L., Zhang, H.: Visual response properties of retinal ganglion cells in the royal college of surgeons dystrophic rat. Invest. Ophthalmol. Vis. Sci. **47**(8), 3579–3585 (2006)
10. Rodieck, R.W.: Quantitative analysis of cat retinal ganglion cell response to visual stimuli. Vis. Res. **5**, 583–601 (1965)
11. Shannon, C.E.: Mathematical theory of communication. Bell Syst. Tech. J. **27**, 379–423, 623–656 (1948)
12. Solomon, S.G., Tailby, C., Cheong, S.K., Camp, A.J.: Linear and nonlinear contributions to the visual sensitivity of neurons in primate lateral geniculate nucleus. J. Neurophysiol. **104**(4), 1884–1898 (2010)
13. Sriram, B., Reinagel, P.: Strong surround antagonism in the dLGN of the awake rat. arXiv:1204.3683 [q-bio.NC] (2012)
14. Sriram, B., Meier, P.M., Reinagel, P.: Temporal and spatial tuning of dorsal lateral geniculate nucleus neurons in unanesthetized rats. J. Neurophysiol. **115**(5), 2658–2671 (2016)
15. Werblin, F.S.: Six different roles for crossover inhibition in the retina: correcting the nonlinearities of synaptic transmission. Vis. Neurosci. **27**(1–2), 1–8 (2010)

Assessment and Comparison of Evolutionary Algorithms for Tuning a Bio-Inspired Retinal Model

Rubén Crespo-Cano[1(✉)], Antonio Martínez-Álvarez[1], Sergio Cuenca-Asensi[1], and Eduardo Fernández[2]

[1] Department of Computer Technology, University of Alicante, Alicante, Spain
rcrespocano@gmail.com, {amartinez,sergio}@dtic.ua.es
[2] Institute of Bioengineering and CIBER BBN, University Miguel Hernández, Alicante, Spain
e.fernandez@umh.es

Abstract. One of the basic questions in neuroscience is how visual information is encoded in the retina. To design artificial retinal systems it is essential to emulate the mammalian retinal behaviour as well as possible. Furthermore, this is a question of primary interest in the design of an artificial neuroprosthesis where it is necessary to mimic the retina as much as possible. This work selects the best algorithm from a set of well-known evolutionary algorithms to perform a reliable tuning of a retinal model. The proposed design scheme optimizes various parameters belonging to different domains (that is, spatio-temporal filtering and neuromorphic encoding) to compare the biological and the simulated registers. Five algorithms have been tested: three different Genetic Algorithms (SPEA2, NSGA-II and NSGA-III), a Particle Swarm Optimization algorithm and a Differential Evolution algorithm. Their performances have been compared by using the hypervolume indicator.

Keywords: Retinal modelling · Evolutionary algorithms · Evolutionary search · Multiobjective optimization · SPEA-2 · NSGA-II · NSGA-III · Particle Swarm Optimization · Differential Evolution

1 Introduction

The vertebrate retina is formed by three layers of nerve cell bodies and two layers of synapses. The first layer contains the rod and cone cells, the second layer contains the horizontal, bipolar and amacrine cells, and the third layer is composed by ganglion cells and displaced amacrine cells. Between these three layers there are two neuropils where synaptic contacts occur. The first one is the outer plexiform layer (OPL) where the rods and cones connect with bipolar and horizontal cells. The second one is the inner plexiform layer (IPL) where the bipolar cells connect to ganglion cells, in addition to interacting different varieties of horizontally and vertically directed amacrine cells with the ganglion cells too [1].

© Springer International Publishing AG 2017
J.M. Ferrández Vicente et al. (Eds.): IWINAC 2017, Part I, LNCS 10337, pp. 95–104, 2017.
DOI: 10.1007/978-3-319-59740-9_10

The development of cortical prostheses capable of eliciting visual percepts in profoundly blind people involves to mimic the retinal behaviour in a real-time manner. The produced signals should be as similar as possible to the output signals of the vertebrate retina. The basic processing blocks of the bio-inspired retinal model under study are shown in Fig. 1.

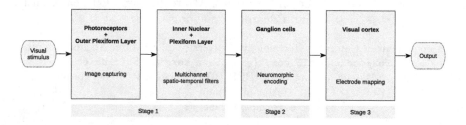

Fig. 1. Functional processing blocks of the bio-inspired retinal model under study.

Mathematically, the first stage of the model (Fig. 1) consists of a weighted combination of different spatio-temporal filters over the captured images. The second stage carries out the neuromorphic encoding. Finally, in the third stage takes place the electrode mapping that addresses the output from the second stage to the appropriate electrodes. Each processing block from the retinal model has many parameters candidates to be adjusted, most of which are real numbers. Thus, the process of fine tuning these parameters represents a difficult problem to be addressed. To overcome this problem, we present an extension of our previous works [2,3], where a proposal to use an automatic evolutionary multiobjective strategy was presented. In this paper, we carry out a comparative study between different strategies of the Evolutionary Computation field to compare which of them can be used to adjust a retinal model more efficiently.

In the remainder of this paper, we first present a review of some of the most widely used algorithms to solve multiobjective optimization problems. Thereafter, in Sect. 3, we present the materials and methods used on this study. After that, we present the experiments and the results of the study. Finally, conclusions of this study are drawn in Sect. 5.

2   Multiobjective Evolutionary Algorithms

On nature, the ever-ubiquitous optimization problems usually have more than a single objective or criterion to be satisfied so that they are actually multiobjective problems. In these problems, the goal is to find or approximate the set of Pareto-optimal solutions. Multiobjective evolutionary algorithms (MOEAs) are one type of stochastic search heuristics that are appropriate for multiobjective optimization problems because of their capacity of computing a set of trade-off solutions in one run. Details of the most popular and used methods, i.e. Genetic

Algorithm (GA), Particle Swarm Optimization (PSO), and Differential Evolution (DE), can be found below, where we describe these approaches in brief. For more details, readers are encouraged to refer to the original studies.

2.1 Genetic Algorithms

GA is a search heuristic where the natural selection process is imitated through three genetic operators: selection, crossover, and mutation [4,5]. The solutions are represented as chromosomes and all of them make up the population. The better chromosomes are selected to become parents to produce new offspring, where the individuals with better fitness are selected with higher probabilities. To avoid that the diversity of the population may decline, the mutation operator is used to inject diversity into the population. Hereafter, some of the most widely used algorithms are described.

The nondominated sorting genetic algorithm II (NSGA-II) was presented by Deb et al. [6] as a fast nondominated sorting approach with $O(M \times N^2)$ computational complexity (where M is the number of objectives and N is the population size). Here, the individuals of population are sorted in different fronts according to the concept of Pareto dominance. The highest rank is assigned to the individuals of the first front, the second highest rank to the individuals of the second front, and so on.

The Strength Pareto Evolutionary Algorithm (SPEA2) is a genetic algorithm for approximating the Pareto-optimal set for multiobjective optimization problems [7]. Besides the population, SPEA2 uses an external archive with a predefined size to store all nondominated population members. On the matting selection stage, the individuals are selected from the union of population and archive through binary tournaments. Straightaway, the recombination and mutation stages are performed. At the end, the population is replaced by the offspring population.

Optimization problems with four or more objectives should be defined as many-objective problems. The existing EMO algorithms may have trouble for solving this type of optimization problems such as having a large fraction of non-dominated individuals in the population or evaluating the diversity measure with computationally expensive procedures. Deb and Jain suggested a reference-point based many-objective nondominated sorting genetic algorithm (NSGA-III) for handling many-objective optimization problems [8] where the maintenance of diversity between population members is managed by using a number of well-spread reference points. Results show that the NSGA-III approach had been able to successfully find a well-converged and well-diversified set of solutions in all test problems.

2.2 Particle Swarm Optimization

Particle Swarm Optimization (PSO) is a population-based heuristic search and optimization technique of nonlinear functions, that is based on simplified animal social behaviours such as fish schooling or bird flocking [9]. The initial step of the PSO algorithm is the random initialization of a population of individuals (called particles) in the search space, but unlike other algorithms, there is no recombination of genetic material between particles during the search. The algorithm finds the global best solution by adapting the direction of each particle toward its own best location and toward the best particle of the entire swarm at each generation.

The original scheme of the strategy needs to be modified for solving multiobjective optimization problems. Several modifications of the PSO algorithm have been published and a superb state-of-the-art of them has been published by Reyes-Sierra and Coello [10]. In this work, we have used an external archive to store the nondominated solutions which were found, working as leaders when the positions of the particles of the swarm have to be updated.

2.3 Differential Evolution

Differential Evolution (DE) is an Evolutionary Algorithm published by Storn and Price in 1995 to solve optimization problems [11]. DE is a population-based procedure where the recombination and mutation operators are used to generate new solutions. The basic operation is the mutation process where a new descendant is created based on differences between pairs of solutions combined with the candidate solution. The population size is maintained by using a replacement mechanism where the newly generated descendant competes only against its corresponding parent and replaces it if the descendant has a higher fitness value. This is an important advantage because any improvement applies to the whole population without having to wait until the end of the iteration.

As with PSO, the original scheme of the strategy needs to be modified for solving multiobjective optimization problems. Several modifications of the DE algorithm have been published and an excellent state-of-the-art of them has been published by Mezura-Montes et al. [12]. In this work, we have used the approach proposed by Robič and Filipič called Differential Evolution for Multi-Objective Optimization (DEMO) [13], in particular, the *"DE/rand/1/bin"* variant.

3 Material and Methods

3.1 Electrophysiological Recordings

As we want to assess the reliability of the simulated bio-inspired retinal models, we have used biological data to compare them and for effectiveness evaluation. The biological recordings from populations of retinal ganglion cells (RGCs) where obtained from wild-type adults mice. Briefly, after enucleation of the eye, the retinas were carefully removed and mounted on an agar plate ganglion cell side up. After that, extracellular RGCs recordings were carried out by using a 100 multi-electrode-array (MEA), and were stimulated with two different visual stimuli. Several repetitions of a 700 ms flash were displayed followed by darkness for 2300 ms to classify the ganglion cells. Afterward, the biological retinas were stimulated with $250\,\mu$m wide white bars crossing a black screen at 0.5 & 1 Hz in 8 orthogonal directions. All experimental procedures were carried out in accordance with the ARVO and European Communities Council Directives (86/609/ECC) for the use of laboratory animals. For a more detailed description of the procedure of obtaining extracellular recordings, the interested reader is referred to [2].

3.2   Comparison of MOEAs

The aim of multiobjective optimization is to find a set of best compromise solutions which cannot be improved according to one objective without deteriorating the others. Because of the complex nature of most real-life problems, only an approximation to such an optimal set can be obtained. To assess the performance of different search heuristics, their resulting sets of best solutions have to be compared. For this purpose, unary quality measures are usually applied. Among these, one of the most relevant in this context is the hypervolume (HV) indicator [14,15] because it is a quality indicator in the evolutionary multiobjective optimization field which allows the comparison between different search heuristics due to its favorable properties. It measures the volume of the dominated section of the objective space and is of exceptional interest because of possessing the highly desirable feature of strict Pareto compliance. HV is simply defined as the volume of the objective space enclosed by the set of Pareto-optimal solutions and a predefined reference point.

Because of the exact Pareto-optimal surface is unknown, we have rejected the inverted generational distance (IGD) [16] as a single metric to compare the performance of different EAs. For this reason, we have chosen the HV indicator as a performance metric, because it has the property that when a solution set is better than another one in terms of Pareto dominance, the HV indicator value of the former is higher than the one of the later.

4   Experiments and Results

Biological registers were used as golden patterns for tuning our retinal model by means of five different EA approaches (SPEA2, NSGA-II, NSGA-III, PSO and DE). Next, a one by one comparison were carried out between the resulting models. Biological retinas were stimulated with $250\,\mu$m wide white bars crossing a black screen at 0.5 Hz and 1 Hz. Four pairs (eight moving bars) of stimuli were used: $0°$, $45°$, $90°$, $135°$, $180°$, $225°$, $270°$ and $315°$.

The algorithms were implemented according to their description in the literature. Parameter settings suggested in their original studies have been used for each algorithm. Any effort in finding the best parameter setting has been made, leaving this task for a future study. On all test problems, 100 generations were simulated per optimization run, the probabilities of crossover and mutation were fixed (0.4 and 0.05, respectively). The population size N was fixed to 40 individuals. In PSO experiments, the parameters ϕ_1 and ϕ_2 where fixed both to

2.05. In DE experiments, the parameter F was fixed to 1. For each algorithm, identical population and archive sizes were used.

Four fitness functions were selected to compare real and simulated electrophysiological recordings and also to test the behaviour of the proposed MOEAs strategy. The electrophysiological recordings coming from the experimental setup are comprised of a raster and peristimulus time histogram (PSTH) data for each isolated RGC, which are the same type of data produced by our retinal simulator. For the purpose of comparing PSTH data, Kullback-Leibler Divergence (PSTH-KLD) is introduced to measure the quality of the PSTH response, due to is widely used to compare probability distributions or histograms. The interspike interval histogram (ISIH) data of each RGC has been compared by using the same method (ISIH-KLD). To compare the firing rate we have used the absolute difference (FRAD). Additionally, for the purpose of rebuild the receptive fields of the populations of RGCs, we have used the method proposed by Díaz-Tahoces et al. [17]. At last, to compare these receptive fields we have used the absolute difference (RFAD).

As in all multiobjective problems with more than 3 objectives, the visualization of the results is very difficult. The more objectives the problem have, the more difficulty for a decision-maker to choose a preferred solution will be. Therefore, as a preliminary analysis, graphs from Fig. 2 show the Pareto front solutions minimizing the values for all metrics at the same time for one experiment run. Data are represented for pairs of criteria. In a general view, all Pareto-optimal solutions are similar. We cannot say that one of the EAs is much worse or better that the others if we only compare the metrics paired up. Both NSGA-III and PSO present Pareto fronts with more solutions than the rest of EAs in most cases. For example, in Fig. 2(a) the resulting Pareto front of the SPEA2 algorithm contains 34 individuals while the NSGA-III algorithm contains 46 individuals and the PSO algorithm contains 52 individuals. In Fig. 2(f) the NSGA-III algorithm outperforms the rest of EAs with 21 individuals. In Fig. 2(d) the PSO experiment obtains better results than the other EAs due to its well-spread Pareto front that dominates the other Pareto fronts clearly. To summarize, if we compare the metrics by pairs, maybe there is not a big difference between all the EAs but NSGA-III and PSO appear to be the best search heuristics for this experiment.

Considering that we want to compare stochastic search heuristics, in order to avoid the influence of random efects altogether 10 independent runs were performed per EA. Figure 3 shows the mean hypervolume of these 10 experiment runs at their last generation. Here, to visualize the data distribution of the HV samples, a violin plot has been used [18], which is a combination of a box plot and kernel density plot. Results obtained by DE and NSGA-II are very similar due presumably to the selected selection algorithm in DE for maintain the population size. SPEA2 results are very similar to DE and NSGA-II too, but they are more spread out. The worst results have been obtained with the NSGA-III algorithm. Finally, we could see that the best result is produced by the PSO algorithm. We have to remark that we are showing the HV distribution obtained in the last

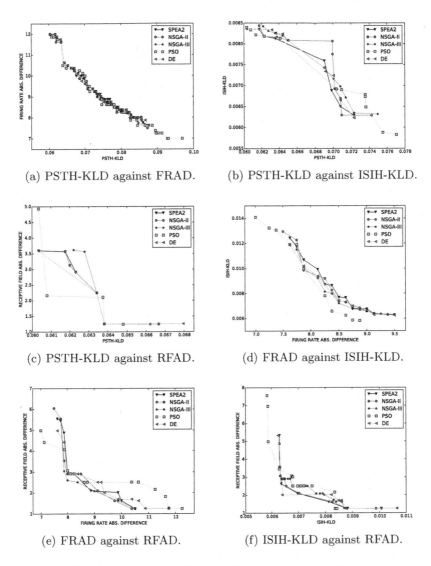

Fig. 2. Pareto-optimal sets facing each pairs of criteria.

generation and these values does not necessarily have to be the highest values obtained because no algorithm is optimizing the HV explicitly.

Figure 4 shows the average of the hypervolume indicator for each EA throughout 100 generations. No EA from those presented here is optimizing the hypervolume indicator directly as well as other algorithms like Hype [19], therefore, the fact that HV values can decrease during the search should not surprise us. As can be noted from the above chart, the best results are obtained with the PSO search heuristic. On the other hand, NSGA-III seems to be the worst approach

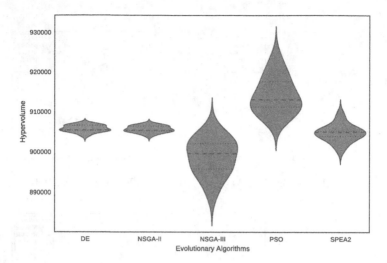

Fig. 3. Distribution of the hypervolume quality indicator for 10 independent runs.

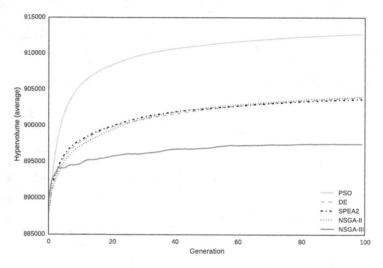

Fig. 4. Course of the averaged hypervolume indicator values for selected algorithms over time.

for adjusting the retinal model presented on Fig. 1 since the HV average is worse than the rest.

Statistical hypothesis tests have to be applied to validate the HV results of different executions. In our case, we performed a Kruskal-Wallis test [20] to determine if the algorithms have yield statistically significant different results or not, or, in other words, if they were produced by the same probability distribution or not. A significance level, α, of 0.05 was used for the test. The p-value was equal to 1.21e−7 and therefore, we can assert that the results are not the same, i.e. a significant difference does exist.

5   Conclusions

A comparison of some of the best known and used MOEAs for tuning a retinal model has been presented. The main contribution of our work is two-fold. First, the quality of the evaluated retinal models are compared with biological extracellular recordings from mice by means of four proposed metrics, which allows us to obtain a more accurate models. Secondly, we have proposed several different search heuristics to carry out a fine tuning of some of the parameters of a retinal model. Furthermore, we have selected the hypervolume as a quality indicator to compare different search heuristics. We have demonstrate through the Kruskal-Wallis that a significant difference does exist between the analysed MOEAs. Finally, we conclude that for this multiobjective problem the PSO algorithm is better than the others due to the hypervolume achieved is higher than the rest.

Our ultimate goal is to apply the search heuristics presented here to studies carried out in humans, as it would allow us to select well optimized retinal models.

References

1. Kolb, H., Fernandez, E., Nelson, R.: Webvision: the organization of the retina and visual system. University of Utah Health Sciences Center, Salt Lake City, UT. https://www.ncbi.nlm.nih.gov/books/NBK11530/
2. Martínez-Álvarez, A., Crespo-Cano, R., Díaz-Tahoces, A., Cuenca-Asensi, S., Ferrández Vicente, J.M., Fernández, E.: Automatic tuning of a retina model for a cortical visual neuroprosthesis using a multi-objective optimization genetic algorithm. Int. J. Neural Syst. **26**(07), 1650021 (2016)
3. Crespo-Cano, R., Martínez-Álvarez, A., Díaz-Tahoces, A., Cuenca-Asensi, S., Ferrández, J.M., Fernández, E.: On the automatic tuning of a retina model by using a multi-objective optimization genetic algorithm. In: Ferrández Vicente, J.M., Álvarez-Sánchez, J.R., de la Paz López, F., Toledo-Moreo, F.J., Adeli, H. (eds.) IWINAC 2015. LNCS, vol. 9107, pp. 108–118. Springer, Cham (2015). doi:10.1007/978-3-319-18914-7_12
4. Holland, J.H.: Adaptation in Natural and Artificial Systems: An Introductory Analysis with Applications to Biology, Control and Artificial Intelligence. MIT Press, Cambridge (1992)
5. Goldberg, D.E.: Genetic Algorithms in Search, Optimization and Machine Learning, 1st edn. Addison-Wesley Longman Publishing Co. Inc., Boston (1989)
6. Deb, K., Pratap, A., Agarwal, S., Meyarivan, T.: A fast and elitist multiobjective genetic algorithm: NSGA-II. IEEE Trans. Evol. Comput. **6**(2), 182–197 (2002)
7. Zitzler, E., Laumanns, M., Thiele, L., et al.: SPEA2: improving the strength Pareto evolutionary algorithm. In: Eurogen, vol. 3242, pp. 95–100 (2001)

8. Deb, K., Jain, H.: An evolutionary many-objective optimization algorithm using reference-point-based nondominated sorting approach, part I: Solving problems with box constraints. IEEE Trans. Evol. Comput. **18**(4), 577–601 (2014)
9. Kennedy, J.: Particle swarm optimization. In: Sammut, C., Webb, G.I. (eds.) Encyclopedia of Machine Learning, pp. 760–766. Springer, Heidelberg (2011)
10. Reyes-Sierra, M., Coello, C.C.: Multi-objective particle swarm optimizers: a survey of the state-of-the-art. Int. J. Comput. Intell. Res. **2**(3), 287–308 (2006)
11. Storn, R., Price, K.: Differential Evolution-A Simple and Efficient Adaptive Scheme for Global Optimization Over Continuous Spaces, vol. 3. ICSI, Berkeley (1995)
12. Mezura-Montes, E., Reyes-Sierra, M., Coello, C.A.C.: Multi-objective optimization using differential evolution: a survey of the state-of-the-art. In: Chakraborty, U.K. (ed.) Advances in Differential Evolution, pp. 173–196. Springer, Heidelberg (2008)
13. Robič, T., Filipič, B.: DEMO: differential evolution for multiobjective optimization. In: Coello Coello, C.A., Hernández Aguirre, A., Zitzler, E. (eds.) EMO 2005. LNCS, vol. 3410, pp. 520–533. Springer, Heidelberg (2005). doi:10.1007/978-3-540-31880-4_36
14. Zitzler, E., Thiele, L.: Multiobjective optimization using evolutionary algorithms— a comparative case study. In: Eiben, A.E., Bäck, T., Schoenauer, M., Schwefel, H.-P. (eds.) PPSN 1998. LNCS, vol. 1498, pp. 292–301. Springer, Heidelberg (1998). doi:10.1007/BFb0056872
15. Zitzler, E., Thiele, L.: Multiobjective evolutionary algorithms: a comparative case study and the strength Pareto approach. IEEE Trans. Evol. Comput. **3**(4), 257–271 (1999)
16. Van Veldhuizen, D.A., Lamont, G.B.: Multiobjective evolutionary algorithm research: a history and analysis, Technical report. Citeseer (1998)
17. Díaz-Tahoces, A., Martínez-Álvarez, A., García-Moll, A., Humphreys, L., Bolea, J.Á., Fernández, E.: Towards the reconstruction of moving images by populations of retinal ganglion cells. In: Ferrández Vicente, J.M., Álvarez-Sánchez, J.R., de la Paz López, F., Toledo-Moreo, F.J., Adeli, H. (eds.) IWINAC 2015. LNCS, vol. 9107, pp. 220–227. Springer, Cham (2015). doi:10.1007/978-3-319-18914-7_23
18. Hintze, J.L., Nelson, R.D.: Violin plots: a box plot-density trace synergism. Am. Stat. **52**(2), 181 (1998). doi:10.2307/2685478
19. Bader, J., Zitzler, E.: HypE: an algorithm for fast hypervolume-based many-objective optimization. Evol. Comput. **19**(1), 45–76 (2011)
20. Kruskal, W.H., Wallis, W.A.: Use of ranks in one-criterion variance analysis. J. Am. Stat. Assoc. **47**(260), 583 (1952). doi:10.2307/2280779

Natural Computing in Bioinformatics

Efficient Localization in Edge Detection by Adapting Artical Bee Colony (ABC) Algorithm

Jaime Vásquez F., Ricardo Contreras A.$^{(\boxtimes)}$, and M. Angélica Pinninghoff J.

Department of Computer Science, University of Concepción, Concepción, Chile
{javasquezf,rcontrer,mpinning}@udec.cl

Abstract. The problem of edge detection considers two stages: localization and identification, where localization is the search of pixels in an image and identification is the process of deciding if a pixel belongs, or not, to an edge. The Canny edge detector has an effective identification involving the analysis of every pixel that belongs to an image. On the other side, artificial bee colony (ABC) algorithm simulates the foraging behavior of honey bees, doing an efficient search of food sources. In this proposal, ABC algorithm and Canny are integrated to create ABC-ED, an efficient edge detector algorithm, that does not require to analyze all the pixels of an image to detect its edges. The dataset BSDS500 was used for experimentation, and results show that it is not necessary to analyze every pixel in the image to detect the same edges detected when using Canny.

Keywords: ABC-ED · ABC algorithm · Edge detection · Canny edge detector

1 Introduction

In artificial vision and in image processing, edge detection deals with the localization and identification of significant gray level variations in a digital image. Localization refers to the search of points at a particular location in a grid of pixels. Identification refers to the process of deciding if a particular pixel belongs (or not) to an edge.

In image processing, an important number of edge detector have been proposed, exhibiting differences in terms of mathematic and algorithmic properties [6]. One of the standard edge detection methods is proposed by Canny [5], that offers a very effective pixel identification and analyzes every pixel in the image. In Canny, the first step is to smooth the image by using a Gaussian filter, then the gradient magnitude and direction is computed; the third step is for thinning edges through non-maximum suppression and, finally, it is applied a double thresholding process and edge tracking by hysteresis.

Artificial Bee Colony algorithm (ABC), is a swarm intelligence algorithm that simulates the natural foraging behavior of honey bees, which have a good balance

© Springer International Publishing AG 2017
J.M. Ferrández Vicente et al. (Eds.): IWINAC 2017, Part I, LNCS 10337, pp. 107–114, 2017.
DOI: 10.1007/978-3-319-59740-9_11

between exploitation and exploration and use communication mechanisms as the waggle dance to search optimally new and better food sources [3,9]. The term swarm is used to refer to any restrained collection of interacting individuals.

ABC has been adapted for various problems in the area of image processing, in particular, in edge detection. In [4], ABC was adapted for edge enhancement to improve visual perception of blurred images. In [11], ABC was used to generate Cellular Neural Networks (CNNs) cloning templates. In [12], ABC was used to develop a method for edge detection without mask operator to compute the fitness of a pixel. In [13], a hybrid model of saliency-based visual attention and ABC was developed to narrow the searching region of an image with the purpose of an unmanned combat air vehicle (UCAV) be able to recognize targets in complex noisy environments.

We propose in this work to combine an effective identification mechanism as Canny, with an efficient search mechanism, as the ABC algorithm, to show that it is possible to develop an efficient edge detector algorithm for digital images, called ABC-ED (Artificial Bee Colony - Edge Detector).

This article is structured as follows, the first section is the present introduction, the second section describes the design of the ABC-ED model, the third section shows the results obtained and the final section shows the conclusions and future work.

2   ABC-ED Model

The main steps and parameters of the ABC-ED model are described in Algorithm 1. The algorithm considers two stages. The first stage is the integration of ABC with the first two steps of Canny procedure, which involves until the end of the main loop of the algorithm. The second stage is the application of the next three steps of Canny, but only for the food sources created on the first phase, i.e., it is not necessary to take into account every pixel as Canny does.

A pixel of an image is a possible food source. The algorithm works only with food sources which have a *fitness* greater or equal than μ_{min}, in other words, μ_{min} is the minimum threshold value for classifying a pixel as a food source. This condition considerably improves the algorithm efficiency in resources management, amount of *fitness computation* or *pixels analysis* and execution time. Every *fitness* computation is activated only once, at the moment of the food source creation, applying a Gaussian filter to the neighborhood and computing the gradient magnitude for the central pixel by using Sobel.

The Moore neighborhood is used for considering the eight neighbors around every food source.

The parameters of the algorithm are as follows: IM is the input image matrix; μ_{min} and μ_{max} are the same thresholds parameters used by Canny; SN, MCN and $limit$ are the same parameters used in ABC algorithm, with the exception that $limit \in [0,8]$ is the maximum number of trials to consider a food source exhausted and not abandoned; $\varepsilon \in [0,100]$, controls the search by selecting to explore between a randomly generated new food source and an inactive or abandoned food source.

Algorithm 1. Pseudo-algorithm ABC-ED. Main steps.

Input: Image and set parameters.
 1: IM : input image (I) matrix.
 2: μ_{min} : minimum threshold value to classify a pixel as food source.
 3: μ_{max} : maximum threshold value to classify a food source as weak edge.
 4: SN : amount of food sources.
 5: MCN : maximum cycle number.
 6: $limit$: maximum number of trials for exhausting a food source.
 7: ε : value to control the search by exploration.
Output: OM: image binarized after hysteresis.
 8: **procedure** ABC-ED( )
 9:    INITIALIZATION( );
10:    $cycle \leftarrow 0$;
11:    **while** $cycle < MCN \wedge SN > 0$ **do**
12:        EMPLOYED-BEES-PHASE( );
13:        CALCULATE-PROBABILITIES( );
14:        ONLOOKER-BEES-PHASE( );
15:        SCOUT-BEES-PHASE( );
16:        $cycle \leftarrow cycle + 1$;
17:    **end while**
18:    NON-MAXIMUM-SUPPRESSION( );
19:    DOUBLE-THRESHOLD( );
20:    HYSTERESIS( );
21: **end procedure**

In order to represent and manage the possible states of a food source in the first phase, four disjoint sets are defined as follows: AFS are the active food sources, every source is associated only with one employed bee at the same time; IFS are the inactive or abandoned food sources, these ones were active but were replaced by a neighbor through greedy selection; EFS are the exhausted food sources, given that their neighborhood have been analyzed.

In order to represent and manage the food sources in the second stage, $FSP2$ set is created in the first stage. When a food source is created, it is added to $FSP2$, and hence, $FSP2 = AFS \cup IFS \cup EFS$.

Additionally, the set RP is defined for storing all the rejected pixels founded in the execution that are not food sources, having a gradient magnitude lower than μ_{min}, in order to avoid to compute a magnitude more than once.

In the following, there is a more detailed description for the different components of the algorithm presented in Sect. 2.

In **Initialization**, a population of SN food sources is created by doing a random search, and adding every food source to AFS. Every checked pixel that is not a food source is added to a special list (rejected pixels) for not to consider them in future computations.

In **Employed Bees Phase**, for each food source in AFS, the procedure is as follows. A candidate neighbor is chosen through greedy selection and it is marked. This is doing randomly on the neighbors of the food source that are still not marked.

The greedy selection in ABC-ED is not the same as in ABC. In this algorithm, the selection condition to replace an actual food source is that its neighbor must have its *fitness* greater or equal to μ_{min}, i.e., it is a food source and it does not belong to AFS or EFS. Then, if the condition is satisfied, the neighbor replaces the actual food source and it is added to AFS, and the replaced food source is added to IFS, or to EFS if it is exhausted. Otherwise, the trials counter of the current food source (limit) is increased in one unit.

In **Calculate Probabilities**, for each food source in AFS, the algorithm proceed as follows. The probability $p(f_k)$ of a food source f_k is computed using expression (1), thus creating an AVL Roulette wheel selection using the self-balancing binary search tree AVL [1], in order to search a food source based on its probability efficiently. It represents the waggle dance of bees.

$$p(f_k) = \frac{fit(f_k)}{\sum\limits_{k=1}^{SN} fit(f_k)} \tag{1}$$

In **Onlooker Bees Phase**, SN food sources are chosen stochastically using the AVL Roulette. For each food source chosen, it must be checked if it is not exhausted, given that it could have been exhausted on the employed bees phase and it can be chosen more than once in the same phase of the cycle. Then, the algorithm proceeds as the employed bees phase already described.

In **Scout Bees Phase**, for each food source in AFS, it is checked if it is exhausted to replace it. If it is exhausted, the food source is removed from AFS and then added to EFS and the replacement mechanism is chosen between *New Random Exploration* and *Inactive Food Source*. The parameter ε is used to chose the replacement mechanism, where $\varepsilon = 100$ indicates replacement mechanism is *New Random Exploration* and $\varepsilon = 0$, indicates that the replacement mechanism is *Inactive Food Source*; $\varepsilon \in]0, 100[$, indicates the probability of selecting *New Random Exploration* as the replacement mechanism.

In the *New Random Exploration* mechanism, the new food source is added to AFS. In the *Inactive Food Source* mechanism, the replacing food source is removed from IFS and then added to AFS.

When the first stage of the algorithm is finished, the second stage is activated. The set $FSP2$ is used to proceed with edge thinning by using non-maximum suppression, double threshold and edge tracking through hysteresis, analogous to Canny. The difference is that it considers only the food sources created and not all the pixels of the image (as in Canny). Thus, ABC-ED is probably more efficient. The food sources suppressed by edge thinning need to be removed from $FSP2$.

It is important to notice that the algorithm can be adapted to every mask filter operator for identification and *fitness* computation. It only changes the precision of identification, and it is possible to use other kernel filter. If it is not necessary edge thinning, double threshold and hysteresis, the second phase of the algorithm can be omitted, but it always remains the characteristic of the algorithm that makes unnecessary to analyze all the pixels of an image to detect edges.

3   Results

The performance is measured, as the percentage of pixels that needs to be analyzed to achieve the same results obtained by Canny, and a comparison with the corresponding ground truth images is realized.

For experimentation it was used the dataset BSDS500 [2] (The Berkeley Segmentation Dataset and Benchmark) that contains 2696 segmented images with its corresponding ground truth image. For each image, four automatic threshold methods were used to compute the threshold values μ_{min} and μ_{max}, which are: Mean [7], Median, Matlab[1] and Otsu [10]. In the average, the threshold values computed for the different methods are similar, except for Matlab which obtains significantly lower values.

The metric to evaluate the algorithm performance is *pixels analysis*, defined as how many *fitness* computations have been made; *Hamming Distance (HD)* [8], adapted to get the difference between two binarized matrices of same size, thus defining a HD percentage as the difference between the image obtained by using the algorithm and one of the following: the image obtained by using Canny, or the corresponding ground truth image.

The algorithm parameters used are as follows: $SN = \sqrt{m*n}$ (amount of food sources), the square root of the number of pixels of the input image; $MCN = 1000$ (maximum cycles number). $limit = 8$.

Table 1 shows the percentage range of pixels analyzed (FG), for the set of considered images. *Amount* refers to the number of output images (for every original image, there are four testing images, considering the four threshold computations). *Fit* represents the fitness average percentage for those images, μ_{min} and μ_{max} are average threshold values, and $\overline{HD\,GT}$ is the average difference percentage between the output image and the corresponding ground truth image. MCN represents the number of necessary cycles for detecting the 100% of edges detected by Canny.

The results for FG percentage $\in\,]26,\,95[$ contains less than 70 output images which are, therefore, omitted.

Table 1 shows two interesting output groups. The first one considers a pixels analysis up to 25% of the total of pixels for the image, and the second one is the group that considers a pixels analysis ranging from 96% to 100% of pixels for the complete image. Comparing both output concentrations, in the first one the proposed algorithm output presents an average difference with the ground truth lower than the second one, less average cycles are necessary and lower average

---

[1] Given by the function *edge* using Canny on Matlab.

Table 1. Summary table of all outputs results of the algorithm.

Amount	FG	$\overline{Fit}$	$\overline{\mu_{min}}$	$\overline{\mu_{max}}$	$\overline{MCN}$	$\overline{HDGT}$
3,224	15	12.27	26	58	82	1.03
1,079	20	16.94	15	30	122	1.54
518	25	21.89	24	44	131	1.79
5,312	100	99.94	35	74	151	2.01

threshold values are obtained. Hence, the algorithm has an edge identification precise, but for a reduced number of *pixels analysis*.

Figure 1 shows a sample of four images processed by the algorithm. The first column shows the input image, the second column shows image obtained after processing, and the third column shows the corresponding ground truth image. Additionally first two rows correspond to images that require no more than 15% of pixels analysis; the third and fourth row correspond to images requiring a pixels analysis above 95%, for every image.

The reason for the difference of pixels that is necessary to analyze, lies on the images characteristics. If edges are homogeneously distributed on the complete image, the proposed algorithm behaves as a classical Canny algorithm but, if edges are grouped into regions that do not cover all the image, the performance of the proposed algorithm is clearly improved.

4 Conclusions and Future Work

This work presents the integration of ABC algorithm and Canny, to create the algorithm ABC-ED with the purpose of reducing the pixels analysis work on a specific image, to detect their edges. The dataset BSDS500, containing 2696 images, was used for experimentation in order to analyze the proposed performance. The algorithm obtained the best average results using the automatic threshold method Otsu.

Due to the fact that the algorithm integrates the Canny edge identification, it detects every edge that Canny algorithm detects.

The algorithm performs better with images bounded to specific regions than with images with homogeneously distributed edges, due the combination of local and global search of the ABC algorithm.

A remarkable issue is that the proposed algorithm obtains results that differs from ground truth values, in the average, in no more than 2.01%.

As future work, there are some issues that can be addressed: scout bees phase by demand, i.e., to activate this phase only when a food source is exhausted; to analyze the possibility of a complete local analysis of neighborhood at the moment of a food source creation to suppress immediately rejected pixels positions; experiment with a lower size of the population SN, keeping a proportion

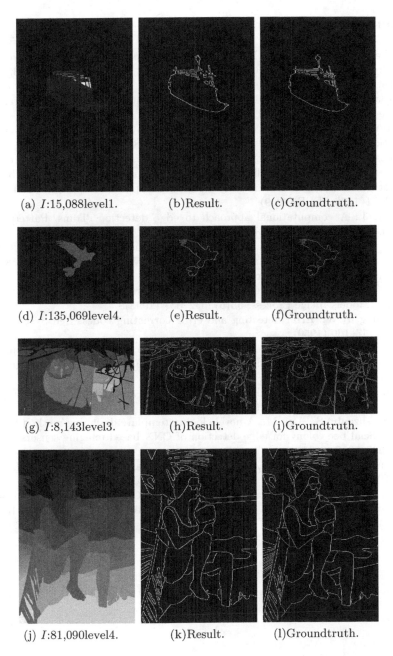

(a) I:15,088level1.   (b)Result.   (c)Groundtruth.

(d) I:135,069level4.   (e)Result.   (f)Groundtruth.

(g) I:8,143level3.   (h)Result.   (i)Groundtruth.

(j) I:81,090level4.   (k)Result.   (l)Groundtruth.

Fig. 1. ABC-ED samples.

with the input image size; greater integration with Canny, moving the edge thinning to the first phase of the algorithm in order to suppress food sources that later would be eliminated.

References

1. Adelson-Velsky, G., Landis, E. An algorithm for the organization of information. In: Proceedings of the USSR Academy of Sciences, vol. 3, pp. 1259–1263. Soviet Math. Doklady (1962)
2. Arbelaez, P., Maire, M., Fowlkes, C., Malik, J.: Contour detection and hierarchical image segmentation. IEEE TPAMI **33**(5), 898–916 (2011)
3. Basturk, B., Karaboga, D.: An artificial bee colony (abc) algorithm for numeric function optimization. IEEE Swarm Intell. Symp. **8**, 687–697 (2006)
4. Benala, T.R., Jampala, S.D., Villa, S.H., Konathala, B. A novel approach to image edge enhancement using artificial bee colony optimization algorithm for hybridized smoothening filters. In: Nature and Biologically Inspired Computing, NaBIC 2009, pp. 1071–1076. IEEE (2009)
5. Canny, J.: A computational approach to edge detection. Trans. Pattern Anal. Mach. Intell. **6**, 679–698 (1986)
6. Ziou, D., Tabbone, S., et al.: Edge detection techniques - An overview. Pattern Recogn. Image Anal. C/C Raspoznavaniye Obrazov I Analiz Izobrazhenii **8**, 537–559 (1998). Nauka/Interperiodica Publishing
7. Glasbey, C.A.: An analysis of histogram-based thresholding algorithms. CVGIP. Graph. Models Image Process. **55**(6), 532–537 (1993)
8. Hamming, R.W.: Error detecting and error correcting codes. Bell Syst. Tech. J. **29**(2), 147–160 (1950)
9. Karaboga, D. An idea based on honey bee swarm for numerical optimization. Technical report-tr06, Erciyes University, Engineering Faculty, Computer Engineering Department (2005)
10. Otsu, N.: A threshold selection method from gray-level histograms. IEEE Trans. Systems Man Cybern. **9**(1), 62–66 (1979)
11. Parmaksuzoglu, S., Alci, M.: A novel cloning template designing method by using an artificial bee colony for edge detection of CNN based imaging sensors. Sensors **11**, 5337–5359 (2011)
12. Yigibasi, E., Baykan, N.: Edge detection using artificial bee colony algorithm (ABC). Int. J. Inf. Electron. Eng. **3**(6), 634–638 (2013)
13. Deng, Y., Duan, H.: Biological edge detection for UCAV via improved artificial bee colony and visual attention. Aircr. Eng. Aerosp. Technol. Int. J. **86**(2), 138–146 (2014)

Electric Vehicle Charging Scheduling Using an Artificial Bee Colony Algorithm

Jorge García-Álvarez, Miguel A. González$^{(\boxtimes)}$, Camino R. Vela, and Ramiro Varela

Department of Computer Science, University of Oviedo, Gijón, Spain
jgarcia-alvarez@outlook.com, {mig,crvela,ramiro}@uniovi.es

Abstract. In this paper we face a scheduling problem that consists in charging a set of electric vehicles such that the total tardiness is minimized. Building an efficient schedule is difficult due to some physical constraints of the charging station, such as a maximum contracted power and a maximum imbalance between the lines of the three-phase electric feeder. We propose an artificial bee colony metaheuristic specifically designed to solve this problem. Its performance is analyzed and compared against the state of the art, obtaining competitive results and outperforming previous approaches.

Keywords: Electric vehicle · Charging strategy · Scheduling · Artificial bee colony · Metaheuristic

1 Introduction

Electric vehicles (EVs) are increasingly important nowadays for several reasons, including economical and environmental ones. However, this emerging technology requires new infrastructures, for example specialized charging stations. Additionally, these charging stations must solve a scheduling problem when deciding which EVs to charge and when they are going to start charging, due to the high charging time batteries of the EVs. This scheduling problem is very important because ideally we have to avoid peak demand in order to balance the electrical needs, while at the same time meeting the requirements of the users and also taking into account the physical constraints of the charging station. In fact, there is an increasing interest in the literature for this type of scheduling problems [4,11]. Each particular charging station has his own set of constraints and objectives, and so the number of proposed methods is very large.

The problem tackled in this paper is described in [3,6] and [7] and it comes from a charging station where we have to schedule the charging of a set of EVs. Each vehicle has a due date, which is the expected time that the user is going to take the vehicle away. We should schedule the charging in such a way that the total tardiness is minimized.

The complexity of building an efficient schedule that fulfills all constraints suggests the use of metaheuristics, because exact algorithms are efficient in small

© Springer International Publishing AG 2017
J.M. Ferrández Vicente et al. (Eds.): IWINAC 2017, Part I, LNCS 10337, pp. 115–124, 2017.
DOI: 10.1007/978-3-319-59740-9_12

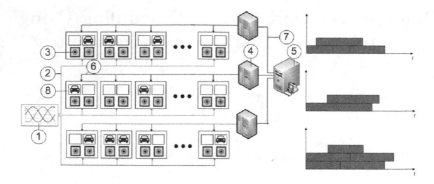

Fig. 1. Components of the charging station: (1) power source, (2) three-phase electric power, (3) charging points, (4) masters, (5) server with database, (6) communication RS 485, (7) communication TCP/IP, (8) slaves. The Gantt Chart shows the charging interval of the vehicles.

instances but they usually behave poorly in real-world sized instances. Different metaheuristics are used in the literature for similar problems, as ant-based swarm algorithms [13] or particle swarm optimization [14]. In our work we are adapting the artificial bee colony algorithm, which is a recent evolutionary metaheuristic. In the experimental study we analyze and compare it with previous approaches.

The remainder of this paper is organized as follows: in Sect. 2 we present the characteristics of the charging station and define the problem. In Sect. 3 we describe the proposed artificial bee colony algorithm, whereas in Sect. 4 we report the results of the experimental study. Finally, Sect. 5 summarizes the contributions of this paper and proposes some ideas for future work.

2   Problem Definition

The charging station we deal with has 180 charging points that are feeded by a three-phase power source (60 charging points in each line). Figure 1 shows the main components of the charging station. The interested reader is referred to [12] for more details. When a vehicle arrives to the station, its user has to input the charging time and a due date, which is the expected time that he/she is going to take the vehicle away. The control system must schedule the charging of all vehicles so that the total tardiness is minimized and all constraints are fulfilled. First, the contracted power is limited, and hence there are a maximum of N vehicles that can charge at the same time in any given line. Moreover, due to economical and electro-technical reasons, the power used by the three lines should be balanced at any given time. An added difficulty is that each vehicle user is the owner of a particular space in the charging station, feeded by a particular line, and so maintaining the balance between the lines is harder because we cannot assign the most appropriate line for each vehicle. Additionally, as soon as a vehicle starts charging, it cannot be disconnected until its charging ends. Following [3], we consider the static and dynamic versions of this problem.

2.1   The Static Problem

The static problem is not realistic, as it assumes that all arrival times, charging times and due dates of all vehicles are known in advance. However, it is indeed very interesting, for example, for assessing the quality of a schedule for the dynamic problem.

We have three lines $L_i, 1 \leq i \leq 3$ with n_i charging points each. Each line L_i receives M_i vehicles, denoted by $v_{i1}, \ldots, v_{iM_i}$. The data we have for each vehicle is its arrival time $t_{ij} \geq 0$, charging time $p_{ij} > 0$ and due date $d_{ij} \geq t_{ij} + p_{ij}$, that is the time at which its user is expected to take the vehicle away.

The objective is to create a feasible schedule, i.e. to decide the starting time st_{ij} for the charging of each vehicle v_{ij} $1 \leq i \leq 3, 1 \leq j \leq M_i$. The schedule must fulfill the following constraints in order to be feasible:

$$\forall v_{ij}, \quad st_{ij} \geq t_{ij} \tag{1}$$

$$\forall v_{ij}, \quad C_{ij} = st_{ij} + p_{ij} \tag{2}$$

$$\max N_i(t) \leq N, \quad t \geq 0; 1 \leq i \leq 3 \tag{3}$$

$$\max \left(\frac{|N_i(t) - N_j(t)|}{N} \right) \leq \Delta, \quad t \geq 0; 1 \leq i, j \leq 3 \tag{4}$$

Equation 1 forbids that vehicles can start charging before their arrival time. Equation 2 ensures that vehicles can not be disconnected until they finish their charging (C_{ij} is the ending time of the charge of v_{ij}). Equation 3 represents the maximum number N of active charging points at the same time in any given line ($N_i(t)$ denotes how many active charging points are in line L_i at time t). Finally, Eq. 4 details the maximum imbalance between lines by means of a parameter Δ. Figure 2 shows an example of a feasible schedule for an instance with 180 vehicles. Furthermore, we want to minimize the total tardiness objective function, defined as:

$$\sum_{i=1}^{3} \sum_{j=1}^{M_i} \max(0, C_{ij} - d_{ij}) \tag{5}$$

2.2   The Dynamic Problem

The dynamic problem is more realistic because we do not know in advance the due dates, charging and arrival times of the vehicles. It can be modelled as a sequence $P_1, P_2, \ldots, P_n$ of instances, each composed by some vehicles that are already charging but have not yet finished and some vehicles that have arrived to the station but are not yet charging. For them we know its charging time p_{ij} and its due date d_{ij}. Again, we have to obtain a feasible schedule that minimizes the total tardiness. To do that, we have to assign a starting time st_{ij} for charging all vehicles that are in the station but are not yet charging such that all constraints from the static problem are satisfied.

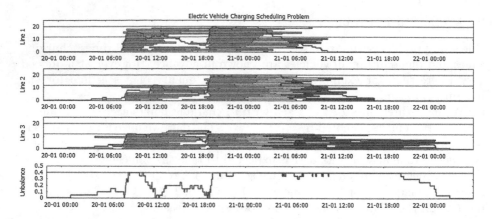

Fig. 2. Example of a feasible schedule, showing in green the charging interval of vehicles without tardiness, and in yellow and red the vehicles that end their charging after their due date. The red portion indicates the interval after the corresponding due date. The bottom graph indicates the maximum imbalance level at each time point. (Color figure online)

In the charging station, at each time point T_k the server checks if any new vehicle has arrived since the time point $T_{k-1} = T_k - \Delta T$. If some vehicle has arrived then a new instance P_k is created and solved and we apply its solution, otherwise the current solution remains valid until the next time point. Notice that, as soon as a vehicle starts charging, its st_{ij} cannot be further modified, but it can be modified in different P_k instances while it does not start charging. The time interval ΔT is set at two minutes in order to not overload the server.

3   Artificial Bee Colony Algorithm

The Artificial Bee Colony algorithm (ABC) is a relatively new swarm population-based metaheuristic algorithm introduced in [8], inspired by the intelligent foraging behaviour of honey bees. The method mimics the search for food of three types of foraging bees: employed, onlooker and scout bees. ABC is often used to solve scheduling problems because of its effectiveness and its good balance between diversification and intensification. A review of its fundamentals and some applications can be found in [9].

The ABC proposed in this paper starts by creating SN initial solutions or food sources. Then, the population iterates over a number of cycles. In each cycle several steps are performed: employed bee phase, onlooker bee phase and scout bee phase. The termination criterion is satisfied when the best solution is not improved for a consecutive number of cycles, or also if we find a solution with zero tardiness. In the following subsections we describe the main features and the different steps of our ABC algorithm.

3.1 Food Source Representation and Evaluation

We have codified the solutions as permutations of vehicles. Each solution has an associated variable *num_trials*, that represents how many consecutive times we tried to improve it without any success.

To evaluate a food source, our scheduler algorithm creates a schedule S from a permutation V by sequentially scheduling all vehicles of V choosing for them the earliest possible starting time such that all the constraints defined in Sect. 2 are met with respect to the vehicles previously scheduled.

3.2 Initial Population

We propose to combine two dispatching rules with some random food sources to create an initial population with good quality and diversity. In particular we create one third of the food sources with each technique.

The first dispatching rule is the Due Date Rule (DDR), which sorts all vehicles in increasing order of its due date d_{ij}. The second dispatching rule is the Latest Starting Time (LST), which sorts all vehicles in increasing order of its latest starting time, defined as $lst_{ij} = d_{ij} - p_{ij}$.

Both rules are deterministic, so we follow the approach proposed in [3] to create diverse food sources. To add the next vehicle to the permutation V, we sort the vehicles not yet added to V using the corresponding dispatching rule and then we perform a tournament selection. Therefore, we randomly select a number t_{size} of vehicles and we add to V the best of them according to the ordering given by the dispatching rule. This parameter t_{size} is relevant because if it is too large the generated food sources may be too similar, whereas if too small the food sources will be almost random.

Evidently, all created solutions are initialized with $num\_trials = 0$.

3.3 Employed Bee Phase

Employed bees search for new and better food sources within the neighborhood of the food source in their memory. In our approach, new food sources are found by applying a crossover operator between each food source and a selected outstanding food source.

First of all, we select the food source that will be combined with all the food sources in the population. In principle it will be the best solution found so far in the search. However, if that solution has already been selected for this role in previous cycles, then we select the food source in the population with the largest value of *num_trials* such that it was never chosen for this role. Therefore, it is necessary to maintain a list of solutions that were already chosen as "common parents" in previous cycles. This method improves diversity, as new solutions are always created with different parents in successive cycles of the algorithm.

Then, each food source in the population is combined with the selected food source, generating two new offspring solutions. We select the best of these new solutions (according to its fitness value) and, if it is better than the original food source, it is substituted by the new solution and its *num_trials* value is set to zero (i.e. the employed bee saves it in its memory). Otherwise the original food source remains intact and *num_trials* is increased in one unit.

In this paper we consider two different crossover operators. The first one, which is specially designed for this problem, is the Starting-time Based Crossover (SBX), initially proposed in [3]. It randomly selects a time t_0 and creates the first offspring O_1 with all vehicles of the first parent P_1 such that they start charging before t_0 and it is completed with the remaining vehicles of the second parent P_2 in the same order as they appear. The second offspring O_2 is created similarly. The second crossover operator is the well-known Partially-Mapped Crossover (PMX), originally proposed in [5]. We consider a third possibility: to randomly select between SBX and PMX each time a combination is made. In Sect. 4 we report some experiments to compare these crossover methods.

3.4   Onlooker Bee Phase

Employed bees share their information with onlooker bees waiting in the hive. Then, onlooker bees probabilistically choose their food sources depending on the information and they look for better neighboring food sources. In our proposal, for each solution i in the population we calculate a probability value that depends on the tardiness of each solution: $prob_i = (1/tard_i)/(\sum_{j=1}^{SN} 1/tard_j)$.

Notice that divisions by zero are not possible because our algorithm ends as soon as a solution with zero tardiness is found. This is the probability that the improvement procedure described in Algorithm 1 is applied to that solution. That procedure randomly selects up to the 10% of the vehicles in the permutation V. For each selected vehicle, it checks if its tardiness is zero or positive. When it is zero, it means that this vehicle could possibly be delayed, and therefore we try to swap it with all the vehicles from its position (v_i) until the end of the permutation (v_n) until we find a solution that improves the current solution. When the tardiness is positive we swap the vehicle (v_i) with the previous vehicles until the first position is reached (v_0). In any case, as soon as an improved solution is found, the procedure ends, replacing the old food source with the new one and setting its *num_trials* value to zero. Otherwise, if we cannot find a better solution using the described procedure, the original solution remains and we increase its *num_trials* value by one unit.

3.5   Scout Bee Phase

When the solution of an employed bee cannot be improved through a number of trials (denoted as *limit*), that bee becomes a scout bee, abandons its solution and randomly searches for a new solution. This may happen if the abandoned food source was initially poor, or also if have been made poor by exploitation.

To implement this phase in our algorithm, we simply check the *num_trials* value of all solutions in the population, and any solution with *num_trials* $\geq$ *limit* is substituted for a newly created random solution, with value *num_trials* $= 0$.

Algorithm 1. The improvement applied by the onlooker bees

Input A solution S
  $chosen\_vehicles \leftarrow 0$;
  while $chosen\_vehicles < 10\%$ of problem size **do**
    Select one vehicle v_i randomly;
    if tardiness of $v_i = 0$ **then**
      for v_j between v_i and v_n **do**
        Create a solution S' by swapping v_i and v_j in S;
        if S' is better than S **then return** the new solution S'; **end if**
      end for
    else
      for v_j between v_i and v_0 **do**
        Create a solution S' by swapping v_i and v_j in S;
        if S' is better than S **then return** the new solution S'; **end if**
      end for
    end if
    $chosen\_vehicles \leftarrow chosen\_vehicles + 1$;
  end while
  return The current solution S;

4   Experimental Results

In this section we report the results of an experimental study designed to evaluate our approach and compare it with the state of the art in this problem: the dispatching rule method proposed in [7] and the genetic algorithm of [3].

We are using the first scenario of the benchmark described in [7], with 720 instances grouped in 24 sets of 30 instances. Each set is characterized by a tuple (type, N, Δ). We consider three values for N: 20, 30 and 40, and four values for Δ: 0.2, 0.4, 0.6 and 0.8. There are two types of instances: in type 1 instances the vehicle arrivals are balanced, as one third of the vehicles arrive to each line, whereas type 2 instances are unbalanced, and 60% of vehicles arrive to line 1, 30% to line 2 and 10% to line 3, so it is expected that type 2 instances are harder to solve, due to the difficulty to maintain the maximum imbalance constraint.

Our *ABC* method is implemented in C++ in a single thread and target machine is a Xeon E5520 running Linux (SL 6.0). We run our method 30 times in order to obtain statistically significant results, due to its stochastic nature.

Table 1. Comparison between combination operators in a set of 24 instances. We report average tardiness in hours of 30 executions, grouped by instance type.

Ins	Static			Dynamic		
	SBX	*PMX*	*SBX-PMX*	*SBX*	*PMX*	*SBX-PMX*
Type 1	55.59	57.89	**54.78**	71.72	73.10	**71.68**
Type 2	1091.14	1120.28	**1090.79**	1115.03	1132.15	**1114.77**

Table 2. Comparison with the state of the art. Each value represents the sum of the tardiness (in hours) of the 30 instances of each group. **Bold** numbers indicate the best value for each version of the problem.

N	Δ	Static problem		Dynamic problem		
		GA [3]	ABC	EVS [7]	GA [3]	ABC
Type 1 instances						
20	0.2	5442.3	**5331.7**	8386.3	7141.6	**7027.9**
20	0.4	2680.1	**2586.1**	4120.4	3976.7	**3898.1**
20	0.6	2299.7	**2258.2**	3670.6	3568.8	**3558.0**
20	0.8	2238.7	**2200.4**	3590.9	**3501.9**	3509.1
30	0.2	996.9	**771.9**	1959.3	**1411.7**	1445.7
30	0.4	92.1	**76.8**	421.2	374.7	**366.6**
30	0.6	50.0	**34.9**	347.9	318.9	**317.7**
30	0.8	49.2	**34.1**	347.6	316.8	**316.4**
40	0.2	364.1	**238.6**	735.0	**511.0**	545.2
40	0.4	0.4	**0.0**	14.0	**6.4**	7.8
40	0.6	**0.0**	**0.0**	3.4	3.4	3.4
40	0.8	**0.0**	**0.0**	3.4	3.4	3.4
Averages		1184.5	**1127.7**	1966.7	1761.3	**1749.9**
Type 2 instances						
20	0.2	124380.0	**123409.0**	128185.0	124599.3	**124168.0**
20	0.4	45263.1	**44152.7**	46319.3	45461.3	**45183.9**
20	0.6	21205.6	**20597.0**	22966.8	22074.6	**21847.7**
20	0.8	13031.0	**12734.1**	14573.1	14337.1	**14212.1**
30	0.2	71129.0	**69954.3**	72860.8	71462.5	**70942.6**
30	0.4	20629.5	**20097.6**	21479.9	21321.0	**21150.5**
30	0.6	7188.0	**7033.0**	8088.9	8006.8	**7923.0**
30	0.8	3607.7	**3536.4**	4486.3	4407.8	**4391.0**
40	0.2	45216.0	**44146.7**	46135.4	45455.4	**45192.6**
40	0.4	10010.6	**9775.7**	10869.3	10799.0	**10669.2**
40	0.6	2916.8	**2855.7**	3599.1	3517.8	**3515.1**
40	0.8	922.8	**876.3**	1635.5	**1568.8**	1574.9
Averages		30458.3	**29930.7**	31766.6	31084.3	**30897.5**

For all experiments we have chosen a population size SN of 200 food sources, we have set $limit = 100$, and the stopping condition is defined as 25 consecutive cycles without improving the best solution found so far. Using this parameter setting, the convergence pattern is adequate and the computational time is comparable to other methods of the state of the art.

We have made some experiments to select the combination operator. We have considered three possibilities: always using the SBX operator, always using

PMX, or randomly choosing between SBX and PMX each time a combination is made. For this comparison we do not use the full benchmark, but only 24 instances: the first one for each combination of parameters. Table 1 reports the results of these experiments, where we can see that the best option in both the static and dynamic problems is to randomly select between the two operators, probably because of the increased diversity of the generated solutions.

Table 2 reports the results of the experiments in the full benchmark. For the static problem we show the tardiness values reported in [3] (denoted by GA) as well as those obtained by our ABC algorithm, whereas for the dynamic problem we show the tardiness values reported in [7] (denoted by EVS), in [3] and also our results. As expected, the results in the static problem are better than those of the dynamic problem, which means that the methods are able to exploit the extra information. Moreover, it can be seen that our method is able to outperform previous approaches in both the static and dynamic problems.

We have run statistical tests to check if the improvement is significant. As proposed in [2], as we have multiple-problem analysis, we should use non-parametric tests. We start with a Shapiro-Wilk test that confirms the non-normality of our data. Afterwards we launch paired Wilcoxon signed rank tests to compare the average results in all instances. In both the static and dynamic problems, p-values lower than 2.2e-16 confirm that the differences in these instances are statistically significant and we can conclude that ABC is better than GA and EVS.

The computational time that ABC requires to solve a subproblem in a dynamic instance is 0.32 s in average, or 3.68 s in the worst case. These times are much smaller than two minutes (see Sect. 2.2), so ABC could be used in a real scenario. The average time required by GA is slightly higher, being 0.45 s per subproblem, whereas the EVS approach is much faster, as expected in a simpler dispatching rule approach. Regarding the static problem, ABC requires 84 seconds in average against the 93 s required by GA.

5   Conclusions

In this paper we have dealt with the problem of scheduling the charging of a set of EVs in a charging station. To this end, we have proposed an artificial bee colony metaheuristic specifically tailored for our problem. In the experimental results we have seen that our approach performs significantly better than previous approaches for the problem, probably because of the good balance between intensification and diversification in the search.

There are many possibilities for future work, although the most interesting one is probably to consider more realistic energy models. For example considering that the energy cost may be variable depending on the time of day, as for example in [10], or maybe that the vehicles can be charged at a non constant rate, as modelled in [1]. Clearly, if we want to minimize energy costs as well as total tardiness, we face a multi-objective optimization problem and so the metaheuristics should be modified accordingly.

Acknowledgments. This research has been supported by the Spanish Government under grant TIN2016-79190-R.

References

1. Gan, L., Topcu, U., Low, S.: Optimal decentralized protocol for electric vehicle charging. IEEE Trans. Power Syst. **28**(2), 940–951 (2013)
2. García, S., Fernández, A., Luengo, J., Herrera, F.: Advanced nonparametric tests for multiple comparisons in the design of experiments in computational intelligence and data mining: Experimental analysis of power. Inf. Sci. **180**, 2044–2064 (2010)
3. García-Álvarez, J., González, M., Vela, C.: A genetic algorithm for scheduling electric vehicle charging. In: Proceedings of the Genetic and Evolutionay Computation Conference (GECCO 2015), pp. 393–400 (2015)
4. García-Villalobos, J., Zamora, I., San Martín, J., Asensio, F., Aperribay, V.: Plug-in electric vehicles in electric distribution networks: a review of smart charging approaches. Renew. Sustain. Energy Rev. **38**, 717–731 (2014)
5. Goldberg, D.E., Lingle, R.: Alleles, loci, and the traveling salesman problem. In: Proceedings of the First International Conference on Genetic Algorithms and Their Application, pp. 154–159. L. Erlbaum Associates Inc., Hillsdale (1985)
6. Hernandez-Arauzo, A., Puente, J., Gonzalez, M.A., Varela, R., Sedano, J.: Dynamic scheduling of electric vehicle charging under limited power and phase balance constraints. In: Proceedings of the 7th Scheduling and Planning Applications Workshop (SPARK 2013), pp. 1–8 (2013)
7. Hernandez-Arauzo, A., Puente, J., Varela, R., Sedano, J.: Electric vehicle charging under power and balance constraints as dynamic scheduling. Comput. Ind. Eng. **85**, 306–315 (2015)
8. Karaboga, D.: An idea based on honey bee swarm for numerical optimization. Technical report, Technical report-tr06, Erciyes University, Engineering Faculty, Computer Engineering Department (2005)
9. Karaboga, D., Gorkemli, B., Ozturk, C., Karaboga, N.: A comprehensive survey: artificial bee colony (ABC) algorithm and applications. Artif. Intell. Rev. **42**(1), 21–57 (2014)
10. Ma, C., Rautiainen, J., Dahlhaus, D., Lakshman, A., Toebermann, J.C., Braun, M.: Online optimal charging strategy for electric vehicles. Energy Procedia **73**, 173–181 (2015)
11. Rahman, I., Vasant, P., Singh, B., Abdullah-Al-Wadud, M., Adnan, N.: Review of recent trends in optimization techniques for plug-in hybrid, and electric vehicle charging infrastructures. Renew. Sustain. Energy Rev. **58**, 1039–1047 (2016)
12. Sedano, J., Portal, M., Hernández-Arauzo, A., Villar, J.R., Puente, J., Varela, R.: Intelligent system for electric vehicle charging: design and operation. DYNA **88**(6), 644–651 (2013)
13. Xu, S., Feng, D., Yan, Z., Zhang, L., Li, N., Jing, L., Wang, J.: Ant-based swarm algorithm for charging coordination of electric vehicles. Int. J. Distrib. Sensor Netw. **2013**, 13 (2013). Article ID 268942
14. Yang, J., He, L., Fu, S.: An improved PSO-based charging strategy of electric vehicles in electrical distribution grid. Appl. Energy **128**, 82–92 (2014)

Protein Folding Modeling with Neural Cellular Automata Using the Face-Centered Cubic Model

Daniel Varela and José Santos[✉]

Computer Science Department, University of A Coruña, A Coruña, Spain
{daniel.varela,jose.santos}@udc.es

Abstract. We have modeled the protein folding process with cellular automata using the Face-Centered Cubic lattice model. An artificial neural network implements a cellular automaton-like scheme that defines the moves of each of the amino acids of the protein chain and through several time iterations until a folded protein is obtained. Differential Evolution was used to evolve these neural cellular automata, which take the information for defining the folding process from the energy space considered in the lattice model. Different proteins were used for testing the process, comparing the results of the folded structures against other methods of direct prediction of the final folded conformation.

1 Introduction

The importance of the knowledge of the native structure of a protein comes from the fact that the native structure is related to its biological function. The experimental determination of the native conformation (e.g. using X-ray crystallography or NMR spectroscopy) is difficult and time-consuming. As a result, the output of experimentally determined protein structures lags behind the output of protein sequences (result of genome sequencing projects), and the computational prediction of protein structure remains a "holy grail" of computational biology. In the *ab-initio* modeling, considering only the information of the protein primary structure (sequence of amino acids), there is an ample research performed on the direct prediction of the final folded conformation using simplified protein models or even detailed atomic models. For the search of the final folded conformation the general assumption is that the native structure of a protein is its minimum free energy conformation.

Typical approaches to *ab-initio* prediction simplify the complexity of the interactions and the nature of the amino acids. For example, lattice models assume that the amino acids are located in the sites of a lattice, whereas the off-lattice models do not impose such a restriction. But even in this last case, simplifications can be considered, like the low-resolution model employed by the Rosetta environment [13], which considers only the atoms of the backbone protein chain whereas uses a pseudo-atom for the representation of the amino acid residues. In this protein prediction problem many authors have been working on

© Springer International Publishing AG 2017
J.M. Ferrández Vicente et al. (Eds.): IWINAC 2017, Part I, LNCS 10337, pp. 125–134, 2017.
DOI: 10.1007/978-3-319-59740-9_13

the use of search methods, especially evolutionary algorithms [22], for determining the final conformation using lattice models like the HP model [5,10,14,21]. Other authors have used other natural computing algorithms [22] like ant optimization algorithms [19]. Fewer works have used evolutionary computing with off-lattice models [9].

However, most of the research work has ignored the temporal folding process to obtain the final folded conformation. This is different to the direct prediction of the final folded conformation since the dynamic process of interaction of the different amino acids has to be considered in order to model how the protein chain folds through time to obtain the final folded conformation. We have modeled this temporal process as an emergent and dynamic process using the classical tool of cellular automata (CA), tool employed in Artificial Life to study and characterize, for example, the emergent behavior property.

There is a very limited research in the modeling of the dynamic folding. Krasnogor et al. [8] used CA and Lindenmayer systems to try to define the folding process in 2D lattices, with a very limited success. The problem with their work is that they evolved CA rules to obtain the folding of particular proteins, without taking into consideration the specific amino acids the CA rule set is being applied to. Calabretta et al. [2] tried to establish the tertiary structure modeling the folding process through evolved matrices of attraction forces of the 20 amino acids in an off-lattice model. They tested the methodology only with a short fragment of crambin (13 amino acids). Danks et al. [4] used a stochastic Lindenmayer system to model protein folding with knowledge-based rewriting rules (that alter the torsion angles), where the states used by the rules took into account the probabilities of the amino acids to be in a particular secondary structure state (like helixes or sheets). Although local structure preference can be seen to emerge for some residues in a protein sequence, the resulting structures did not converge to a preferred global compact conformation.

In previous works we have used CA to model protein folding using the basic HP model [5], with the 2D square [15] and the 3D cubic lattices [16]. In the present work we extend the methodology to a more complex lattice model, the Face-Centered Cubic (FCC) lattice model [3], which allows a more detailed protein conformation representation. The next section details the methods used for the modeling: The FCC model, the neural-CA that provides the folding and the evolutionary algorithm (Differential Evolution) used to evolve such neural-CA. The results section expounds the experiments whereas the last section highlights the main conclusions obtained.

2   Methods

2.1   Hydrophobic-Polar Energy and Face-Centered Cubic Models

Most lattice models, like the HP model [5], use a reduced alphabet of amino acids based on the recognition that hydrophobic interactions are a dominant force in protein folding, and that the binary pattern of hydrophobic and polar residues is a major determinant of the folding. In the HP model [5] (H representing hydrophobic residues and P polar residues), the elements of the chain can be of two types: H (amino acids Gly, Ala, Pro, Val, Leu, Ile, Met, Phe, Tyr, Trp) and P (Ser, Thr, Cys, Asn, Gln, Lys, His, Arg, Asp, Glu). The protein sequence is embedded in a lattice that discretizes the space conformation, lattice that can exhibit different topologies such as 2D square or triangular, and 3D cubic or diamond topologies. Moreover, the total energy of a conformation based on the HP model becomes the sum of pairwise contacts on the lattice as shown in the Equation:

$$E = \sum_{i<j-1} c_{ij} \cdot e_{ij} \tag{1}$$

where $c_{ij} = 1$ if amino acids i and j are non-consecutive neighbors on the protein sequence and are neighbors (or in contact) on the lattice, otherwise 0; The term e_{ij} depends on the type of amino acids: $e_{ij} = -1$ if ith and jth amino acids are hydrophobic (H), otherwise 0. Therefore, the minimization of the energy E in Eq. 1 is equivalent to the maximization of the number of non-consecutive HH contacts.

With this basic categorization of the 20 amino acids and this hydrophobic-polar energy model, the 3D FCC lattice has the highest average density compared to other lattices like the cubic or the body-centered cubic [3]. In this FCC model, atoms are located in the center and in the middle of the edges of the cubic unit cell, as it is shown in Fig. 1. As a result, each lattice point has 12 neighbors with 12 basis vectors that are labeled as follows:

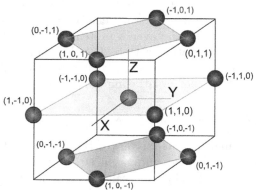

Fig. 1. FCC lattice

FR: $(-1, 0, -1)$	FL: $(1, 0, -1)$	BR: $(-1, 0, 1)$	BL: $(1, 0, 1)$
FU: $(0, -1, -1)$	FD: $(0, 1, -1)$	BU: $(0, -1, 1)$	BD: $(0, 1, 1)$
RU: $(-1, -1, 0)$	RD: $(-1, 1, 0)$	LU: $(1, -1, 0)$	LD: $(1, 1, 0)$

Therefore, a protein conformation, using this model, is a sequence of adjacent points with every amino acid position on the lattice. It will be a valid conformation if the sum of the coordinates of each point is even and it consists of a self-avoiding walk: that is, for all i ≠ j: pi ≠ pj (there are not two amino acids in the same lattice position). Two points p = (x, y, z) and q = (x', y', z') are adjacent in the lattice if and only if $|x - x'| \leq 1, |y - y'| \leq 1, |x - x'| \leq 1$ and $|x - x'| + |y - y'| + |z - z'| = 2$.

The research performed on the protein prediction problem (PSP) with this model is not as ample as with the simplest HP model. For example, Dotu et al. [6] used a Large Neighborhood Search (LNS) for the PSP problem with this

FCC model. Their algorithm starts with a tabu-search, whose solution is then improved by a combination of constraint programming and LNS. Shatabda et al. [17] presented a memory-based local search using the HP energy model and the FCC lattice, employing the local search of Dotu et al. [6]. The idea consists of memorizing local minima and then avoiding their neighborhood, which improved the performance and energy levels of the local search algorithm.

There also works using evolutionary algorithms. For instance, Rashid et al. [12] described a hybrid search framework that embeds a tabu-based local search within a population based genetic algorithm. Shatabda et al. [18] defined an efficient and non-isomorphic encoding for protein structures, which allows the efficient twin conformations removal of the genetic population and Tsay and Su [20] hybridized an evolutionary algorithm with three different local search methods, including lattice rotation for crossover.

Using other methodologies, the constraint-based protein structure approach (CPSP) by Backofen and Will [1] is one of the methods that produces the best results on the FCC model and it is commonly used for comparison purposes. The CPSP approach produces optimal structures by computing maximally compact sets of points known as hydrophobic cores (sets of H-monomers without any chain connectivity that depends only on the number of H-monomers) which can be precalculated. Given a protein sequence S, the approach searches the list of H-cores compatible with S. The H-monomers of S are constrained to the H-core positions and it success in a structure with global minimal energy given sufficient (possibly exponential) computation time [6].

2.2 Neural Cellular Automata

A cellular automaton defines the moves of the amino acids in the FCC lattice and this cellular automaton is implemented by a simple feed-forward neural network. Therefore, we call the structure that provides the folding as a neural cellular automaton (neural-CA) since the ANN implements the rule set of a classical CA.

The ANN is applied to each amino acid i of the protein chain sequentially, beginning from the second amino acid until the penultimate amino acid (the first move between the first and the second amino acids is fixed). The ANN selects the move to apply between amino acid i and $i + 1$ of the chain.

The inputs to the ANN are determined by the energy changes that would occur if the different moves were applied between amino acid i and $i + 1$. For each input, an energy difference is calculated between the current protein conformation and the conformation modified at those amino acid positions with the corresponding moves of the FCC model {FR, FL, BR, BL, FU, FD, BU, BD, RU, RD, LU, LD}. The energy calculations take into account the HH contacts (value -1) as in the basic HP model (Eq. 1) as well as the HP or PH contacts (value 0.1). The inclusion of the latter repulsive values, as in the HP Functional Model [7], allows a better discrimination between conformations with the same number of HH contacts, as well as a better detailed information of the energy landscape in protein conformations with very few H amino acids.

Therefore, there are 12 ANN inputs that correspond with the energy changes (positive, 0 or negative) when each of the moves are considered. Those increases/decreases correspond with the energy after the move with respect to the energy of the current conformation. Moreover, these changes are normalized in the range $[-1,1]$. This input information provides a partial view of the energy landscape to the ANN and can be associated with the central element and its neighborhood states in a classical CA.

In addition, for the energy calculation, only the close amino acids to the central amino acid i are considered, using the Euclidean distance with a given radius. That is, the possible HH or HP/PH contacts are those that occur between amino acids within a sphere centered on the amino acid i lattice site. Note that this is one of the central ideas of cellular automata that take into account only the state information of the neighborhood of a cell site to change that cell state.

The ANN has a hidden layer of nodes and an output layer with 12 outputs that correspond with each of the 12 possible moves. An optimized (evolved) ANN can decide the best appropriate move in each situation or state in order to provide an optimal final folded conformation. The standard sigmoid function is used as transfer function of the ANN nodes. The ANN node with the highest activation value determines the move to apply in each situation.

The same ANN is applied to all the amino acids and in different temporal steps, beginning with an unfolded conformation. A folding step means that the ANN is applied sequentially to

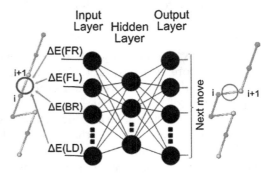

Fig. 2. Neural-CA scheme: The ANN is applied to each of the amino acids (i) of the protein chain to decide its next move (between i and $i + 1$). The inputs of the ANN are determined by the consequences of the possible moves in the amino acid the ANN is applied to. The same process is applied sequentially to all the amino acids and in different temporal steps until the final protein folded conformation is obtained.

the amino acids of the protein chain. Therefore, the process of the neural-CA is the same of classical CA, since the same ANN is applied iteratively to all the sites (amino acids) of the lattice to obtain the emergent behavior, the protein folded conformation in our case, and the neural-CA takes into account only the local information in each site or amino acid. The main difference is that in our application the information comes from the dynamic energy landscape instead of the definitions of site states obtained from spatial information of the lattice.

2.3   Differential Evolution

Differential Evolution [11] is a population-based search method. DE creates new candidate solutions by combining existing ones according to a simple formula

Algorithm 1. Differential Evolution Algorithm.

Initialize the population randomly
repeat
   for all individual x in the population **do**
      Let $x_1, x_2, x_3 \in$ population, randomly obtained $\{x_1, x_2, x_3, x$ different from each other$\}$
      Let $R \in \{1, ..., n\}$, randomly obtained $\{$n is the dimension of the search space$\}$
      for $i = 1$ *to* n **do**
         Pick $r_i \in U(0, 1)$ uniformly from the open range (0,1).
         if $(i = R) \vee (r_i < CR)$ **then**
            $y_i \leftarrow x_{1i} + F(x_{2i} - x_{3i})$
         else
            $y_i = x_i$
         end if
      end for$\{y = [y_1, y_2...y_n]$ is a new generated candidate individual$\}$
      if $f(y) \leq f(x)$ **then**
         Replace individual x by y
      end if
   end for
until termination criterion is met
return $z \in$ population $\backslash \forall t \in$ population, $f(z) \leq f(t)$

of vector crossover and mutation, and then keeping whichever candidate solution has the best score or fitness on the optimization problem at hand. The central idea of the algorithm is the use of difference vectors for generating perturbations in a population of vectors. This algorithm is specially suited for optimization problems where possible solutions are defined by a real-valued vector. The basic DE algorithm is summarized in the pseudo-code of Algorithm 1.

Differential Evolution needs a reduced number of parameters to define its implementation. Apart from the population size, the parameters are F or differential weight and CR or crossover probability. The weight factor F (usually in $[0, 2]$) is applied over the vector resulting from the difference between pairs of vectors (x_2 and x_3). CR is the probability of crossing over a given vector of the population (target vector x) and a "donor" vector created from the weighted difference of two vectors ($x_1 + F(x_2 - x_3)$). The "binomial" crossover (specified in Algorithm 1) was used for defining the value of the "trial" vector (y) in each vector component or position i. The index R guarantees that at least one of the parameters (genes) will be changed in the generation of the trial solution.

Finally, the selection operator maintains constant the population size. The fitness of the trial vector ($f(y)$) and the target vector ($f(x)$) are compared to select the one that survives in the next generation. Thus, the fitness of the best solution of the population is improved or remains the same through generations.

By combining different mutation and crossover operators various schemes have been designed. The usual variants or schemes of DE choose the base vector x_1 randomly (variant $DE/rand/1/bin$, where 1 denotes the number of differences involved in the construction of the mutant or donor vector and bin denotes the crossover type) or as the individual with the best fitness found up to the moment (x_{best}) (variant $DE/best/1/bin$). The fundamental idea of the algorithm is to adapt the step length ($F(x_2 - x_3)$) intrinsically along the evolutionary process. At the beginning of generations the step length is large, because individuals are far away from each other. As the evolution goes on, the population converges and the step length becomes smaller and smaller, providing this way an automatic balance in the search.

In our application DE is used for optimizing a neural-CA that provides the folding of a protein. Since a neural-CA is implemented with a simple feed-forward ANN, the individuals of the population encode the ANN weights. The fitness of a neural-CA is defined by the final energy of the final conformation, considering the HH contacts, as well as the HP/PH contacts, of the final protein conformation. That is, it is the same definition for the calculation of the energy changes that are inputs to the ANN, but considering only the final folded conformation and without any restriction of neighborhood centered on a particular amino acid.

3   Results

The evolutionary methodology was applied to optimize the neural cellular automata that provide the folding conformations with the FCC lattice restrictions and with several benchmark proteins commonly used with the FCC lattice. The DE setup is: population size of 500 individuals, with standard values for the crossover probability ($CR = 0.9$) and the weight factor ($F = 0.6$). The $DE/rand/1/bin$ scheme (commented in Sect. 2.3, which provides the lowest selective pressure), was used in 95% of cases to define a donor vector, whereas the $DE/best/1/bin$ scheme was used in the 5% of the cases. A maximum number of fitness evaluations (5000000) is set for all the evolutionary runs.

Regarding the ANN implementation, the ANN weights are directly encoded in the genetic population in the range [−1,1]. The same range is used when decoding the values for each ANN, since this range allows saturating the nodes using the standard sigmoid function as transfer function of the ANN nodes. The configuration of the number of nodes in each ANN layer is 12:8:12, trying to provide a trade-off between generalization and memorization. Finally, a radius of 3 was used for the calculation of energy contacts centered on the amino acid the ANN is applied to (Sect. 2.2).

Figure 3 includes an example of the folding provided by an evolved neural-CA for a protein benchmark with an optimum number of 18 HH contacts. The evolved neural-CA completes the process in 3 steps. The last snapshot corresponds to the optimized conformation with the H central core with the 18 HH contacts. In this example, in the folding process, the evolved neural-CA selected in 55% of cases the moves that correspond with the greedy moves, that is, those that provide the best improvement of local energy.

Table 1 summarizes results in terms of comparison of HH contacts obtained by the evolved neural cellular automata and other methods with different benchmark sequences. These sequences are detailed in different works like [20]. For each sequence its number of amino acids (L) is shown. The "neural-CA column" specifies the number of HH contacts provided by the best individual in different runs (10) of the evolutionary algorithm, together with the average number of HH contacts of such best solutions (neural-CA) in the different runs (between parentheses). The other columns specify the best values of HH contacts with different methods reported by the authors. We included the best algorithms in the

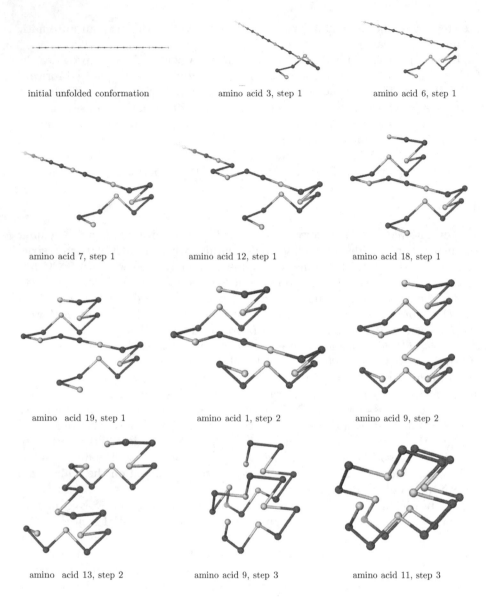

initial unfolded conformation   amino acid 3, step 1   amino acid 6, step 1

amino acid 7, step 1   amino acid 12, step 1   amino acid 18, step 1

amino acid 19, step 1   amino acid 1, step 2   amino acid 9, step 2

amino acid 13, step 2   amino acid 9, step 3   amino acid 11, step 3

Fig. 3. Different temporal steps in the folding process with protein sequence HPPH-PPHPPHPPHPPHPPHPPH. The neural-CA was applied to define the move between the amino acid specified in the caption and the next one.

prediction of the final folded conformation, such as the CSSP algorithm, using constraint programming [1], and solutions based on genetic algorithms [12,20]. These works do not report the maximum number of fitness evaluations used for obtaining the results. These results indicate that the best number of HH contacts using direct prediction methods can also be obtained with the neural-CA methodology with short sequences, while the neural-CA results degrade, in terms of HH contacts, with sequence length in comparison with the direct prediction methods.

Table 1. Comparison of results with benchmark sequences.

Seq	L	neural-CA	CPSP [1]	Tsay - Su [20]	Rashid et al. [12]
S1	20	23 (22.6)	23	23	-
S2	24	22 (20.0)	23	23	-
S3	25	17 (15.7)	17	17	-
S4	36	36 (34.1)	38	38	-
S5	48	60 (53.1)	74	74	-
S6	50	55 (44.8)	73	73	-
H1	48	60 (52.7)	69	69	69
H2	48	51 (45.9)	69	69	69
H3	48	59 (49.6)	72	72	72

4 Conclusions

We used neural cellular automata to model protein folding with the FCC lattice model. On the contrary to the ample research performed on the direct prediction of the final folded conformation, the neural-CA method provides an alternative approach to tackle the PSP problem, since it models protein folding through time to iteratively obtain the native folded conformation. For the improvement of results, in terms of maximum number of HH contacts, the next work should be focused on a better discrimination of the energy landscape to define the state in each situation and to test the generalization capability of an evolved/trained neural-CA with a protein or proteins in other different proteins.

Acknowledgments. This work was funded by the Ministry of Economy and Competitiveness of Spain (project TIN2013-40981-R) and Xunta de Galicia (project GPC ED431B 2016/035).

References

1. Backofen, R., Will, S.: A constraint-based approach to fast and exact structure prediction in three-dimensional protein models. Constraints **11**(1), 5–30 (2006)
2. Calabretta, R., Nolfi, S., Parisi, D.: An artificial life model for predicting the tertiary structure of unknown proteins that emulates the folding process. In: Morán, F., Moreno, A., Merelo, J.J., Chacón, P. (eds.) ECAL 1995. LNCS, vol. 929, pp. 862–875. Springer, Heidelberg (1995). doi:10.1007/3-540-59496-5_349
3. Conway, J.H., Sloane, N.J.A.: Sphere Packings, Lattices and Groups. Springer, New York (1998)
4. Danks, G., Stepney, S., Caves, L.: Protein folding with stochastic L-systems. In: Proceedings of the Artificial Life XI, pp. 150–157 (2008)

5. Dill, K.A.: Dominant forces in protein folding. Biochemestry **29**, 7133–7155 (1990)
6. Dotu, I., Cebrián, M., Van Hentenryck, P.V., Clote, P.: On lattice protein structure prediction revisited. IEEE/ACM Trans. Comput. Biol. Bioinform. **8**(6), 1620–1632 (2011)
7. Hirst, J.D.: The evolutionary landscape of functional model proteins. Protein Eng. **12**(9), 721–726 (1999)
8. Krasnogor, N., Terrazas, G., Pelta, D.A., Ochoa, G.: A critical view of the evolutionary design of self-assembling systems. In: Talbi, E.-G., Liardet, P., Collet, P., Lutton, E., Schoenauer, M. (eds.) EA 2005. LNCS, vol. 3871, pp. 179–188. Springer, Heidelberg (2006). doi:10.1007/11740698_16
9. Olson, B., De-Jong, K., Shehu, A.: Off-lattice protein structure prediction with homologous crossover. In: Proceedings Conference on Genetic and evolutionary computation - GECCO 2013, pp. 287–294 (2013)
10. Patton, W.P., Punch, W.F., Goldman, E.: A standard genetic algorithm approach to native protein conformation prediction. In: Proceedings of 6th International Conference on Genetic Algorithms, pp. 574–581 (1995)
11. Price, K.V., Storn, R.M., Lampinen, J.A.: Differential Evolution. A Practical Approach to Global Optimization. Natural Computing Series. Springer, Heidelberg (2005)
12. Rashid, M.A., Hoque, M.T., Newton, M.A.H., Pham, D.N., Sattar, A.: A new genetic algorithm for simplified protein structure prediction. In: Thielscher, M., Zhang, D. (eds.) AI 2012. LNCS, vol. 7691, pp. 107–119. Springer, Heidelberg (2012). doi:10.1007/978-3-642-35101-3_10
13. Rosetta system. http://www.rosettacommons.org
14. Santos, J., Diéguez, M.: Differential evolution for protein structure prediction using the HP model. In: Ferrández, J.M., Álvarez Sánchez, J.R., Paz, F., Toledo, F.J. (eds.) IWINAC 2011 Part I. LNCS, vol. 6686, pp. 323–333. Springer, Heidelberg (2011). doi:10.1007/978-3-642-21344-1_34
15. Santos, J., Villot, P., Diéguez, M.: Cellular automata for modeling protein folding using the HP model. In: Proceedings IEEE Congress on Evolutionary Computation - IEEE-CEC, pp. 1586–1593 (2013)
16. Santos, J., Villot, P., Diéguez, M.: Emergent protein folding modeled with evolved neural cellular automata using the 3D HP model. J. Comput. Biol. **21**(11), 823–845 (2014)
17. Shatabda, S., Newton, M.H., Pham, D.N., Sattar, A.: Memory-based local search for simplified protein structure prediction. In: Proceedings of the ACM Conference on Bioinformatics, Computational Biology and Biomedicine - BCB 2012, pp. 345–352 (2012)
18. Shatabda, S., Newton, M.H., Rashid, M.A., Sattar, A.: An efficient encoding for simplified protein structure prediction using genetic algorithms. In Proceedings of the IEEE Congress on Evolutionary Computation - IEEE-CEC 2013, pp. 1217–1224 (2013)
19. Shmygelska, A., Hoos, H.H.: An ant colony optimisation algorithm for the 2D and 3D hydrophobic polar protein folding problem. Bioinformatics **6**, 30 (2005)
20. Tsay, J.-J., Su, S.-C.: An effective evolutionary algorithm for protein folding on 3D FCC HP model by lattice rotation and generalized move sets. Proteome Sci. **11**(1), S19 (2013)
21. Unger, R., Moult, J.: Genetic algorithms for protein folding simulations. J. Mol. Biol. **231**(1), 75–81 (1993)
22. Zhao, X.: Advances on protein folding simulations based on the lattice HP models with natural computing. Appl. Soft Comput. **8**, 1029–1040 (2008)

A Memetic Algorithm for Due-Date Satisfaction in Fuzzy Job Shop Scheduling

Juan José Palacios[1]([✉]), Camino R. Vela[1], Inés González-Rodríguez[2], and Jorge Puente[1]

[1] Department of Computer Science, University of Oviedo, Oviedo, Spain
{palaciosjuan,crvela,puente}@uniovi.es
[2] Department of Mathematics, Statistics and Computing, University of Cantabria, Santander, Spain
ines.gonzalez@unican.es,
http://di002.edv.uniovi.es/iscop

Abstract. We consider the job shop scheduling problem with fuzzy sets modelling uncertain durations and flexible due dates. With the goal of maximising due-date satisfaction, we propose a memetic algorithm that combines intensification and diversification by integrating local search in a genetic algorithm. Experimental results illustrate the synergy between both components of the algorithm as well as its potential to provide good solutions.

1 Introduction

Traditionally, it has been assumed that scheduling problems are static and certain: all activities and their durations are precisely known in advance and do not change as the solution is being executed. However, for many real-world scheduling problems design variables are subject to perturbations or changes, causing optimal solutions to the original problem to be of little or no use in practice. It is also common to handle all constraints as sharp, while in some cases there is certain flexibility and some constraints are better expressed in terms of preference, so it is possible to satisfy them to a certain degree.

A source of changes in scheduling problems is uncertainty in activity durations. Within the great diversity of approaches dealing with this kind of uncertainty, fuzzy sets and possibility theory provide an interesting framework, with a tradeoff between the expressive power of probability and its associated computational complexity and knowledge demands. Additionally, fuzzy sets can be used to model flexibility or gradeness in certain management constraints such as due dates [4].

The variant of job shop scheduling problem with fuzzy durations and, optionally, fuzzy due dates, is called fuzzy job shop [1]. Most contributions in the literature concentrate on minimising the project's makespan, but some authors have tackled the problem of maximising due-date satisfaction, either on its own or in a multiobjective setting, combined with makespan.

© Springer International Publishing AG 2017
J.M. Ferrández Vicente et al. (Eds.): IWINAC 2017, Part I, LNCS 10337, pp. 135–145, 2017.
DOI: 10.1007/978-3-319-59740-9_14

In this paper, we intend to advance in the study of the fuzzy job shop scheduling problem, and in particular, in a metaheuristic method to maximise due-date satisfaction when uncertain task durations and flexible due dates are fuzzy sets.

2   The Fuzzy Job Shop Problem

The classical *job shop scheduling problem*, also denoted *JSP*, consists in scheduling a set of jobs $\{J_1, \ldots, J_n\}$ on a set $\{M_1, \ldots, M_m\}$ of physical resources or machines, subject to a set of constraints. There are *precedence constraints*, so each job J_i, $i = 1, \ldots, n$, consists of m tasks $\{\theta_{i1}, \ldots, \theta_{im}\}$ to be sequentially scheduled. Also, there are *capacity constraints*, whereby each task θ_{ij} requires the uninterrupted and exclusive use of one of the machines for its whole processing time. Additionally, each job J_i may have a due date d_i by which it is desirable that the job be completed. A solution to this problem is a schedule, i.e. an allocation of starting times for each task, which, besides being *feasible* (in the sense that all precedence and resource constraints hold), is *optimal* according to some criterion, in our case, maximal due-date satisfaction.

2.1   Fuzzy Durations and Flexible Due Dates

In real-life applications, it is difficult, if not impossible, to foresee in advance the exact time it will take to process a task. It is reasonable however to have some knowledge (albeit uncertain) about the duration, possibly based on previous experience. The crudest representation of such uncertain knowledge would be a human-originated confidence interval and, if some values appear to be more plausible than others, then a natural extension is a fuzzy interval or fuzzy number. The simplest model is a *triangular fuzzy number* or *TFN*, denoted $\widehat{a} = (a^1, a^2, a^3)$, given by an interval $[a^1, a^3]$ of possible values and a modal value $a^2 \in [a^1, a^3]$, so its membership function takes the following triangular shape:

$$\mu_{\widehat{a}}(x) = \begin{cases} \frac{x - a^1}{a^2 - a^1} & : a^1 \leq x \leq a^2 \\ \frac{x - a^3}{a^2 - a^3} & : a^2 < x \leq a^3 \\ 0 & : x < a^1 \text{ or } a^3 < x \end{cases} \tag{1}$$

Triangular fuzzy numbers (or, more generally, fuzzy intervals) are widely used in scheduling as a model for uncertain processing times [1,4,12].

In the job shop, we essentially need two operations on fuzzy numbers, the sum and the maximum. These are usually defined by extending the corresponding operations on real numbers. The resulting addition is pretty straightforward, so for any pair of TFNs $\widehat{a}$ and $\widehat{b}$ we have $\widehat{a} + \widehat{b} = (a^1 + b^1, a^2 + b^2, a^3 + b^3)$. Unfortunately, computing the extended maximum is not that simple and the set of TFNs is not even closed under this operation. Hence, it is common in the fuzzy scheduling literature to approximate the maximum of two TFNs as $\max(\widehat{a}, \widehat{b}) \approx (\max\{a^1, b^1\}, \max\{a^2, b^2\}, \max\{a^3, b^3\})$. Besides its extended use, several arguments can be given in favour of this approximation (cf. [12]).

Fuzzy sets can also be used to model flexible due dates. Consider the case where there is a preferred delivery date d^1, but some delay may be allowed until a later date d^2. Satisfying the due date constraint thus becomes a matter of degree, our degree of satisfaction that the job is finished on a certain date. A fuzzy set $\tilde{d} = (d^1, d^2)$ can be used to model such gradual satisfaction level with a decreasing membership function:

$$\mu_{\tilde{d}}(x) = \begin{cases} 1 & : x \leq d^1 \\ \frac{x-d^2}{d^1-d^2} & : d^1 < x \leq d^2 \\ 0 & : d^2 < x \end{cases} \tag{2}$$

This expresses a flexible threshold "less than", representing the satisfaction level $sat(t) = \mu_{\tilde{d}}(t)$ for the ending date t of the job [4].

When the job's completion time is no longer a real number t but a TFN $\hat{c}$, the degree to which $\hat{c}$ satisfies the due-date constraint $\tilde{d}$ may be measured using the *agreement index* [15]:

$$AI(\hat{c}, \tilde{d}) = \frac{area(\tilde{d} \cap \hat{c})}{area(\hat{c})} \tag{3}$$

where $area(\tilde{d} \cap \hat{c})$ and $area(\hat{c})$ denote the areas under the membership functions of $(\tilde{d} \cap \hat{c})$ and $\hat{c}$ respectively. This essentially measures the degree to which $\hat{c}$ is contained in $\tilde{d}$ following the standard definition of degree of subsethood. $AI(\hat{c}, \tilde{d})$ ranges between 0, when the due date is not satisfied at all, and 1, when the due date is fully satisfied.

2.2   Fuzzy Schedules

To determine a solution for a fuzzy JSP, it is necessary to establish partial task processing orders on all machines. These can be represented by a linear processing order π. A schedule (starting and completion times of all tasks) may be easily computed based on π. For every task x with processing time $\hat{p}_x$, let $PM_x(\pi)$ and $SM_x(\pi)$ denote the tasks preceding and succeeding x in the machine sequence provided by π, and let PJ_x and SJ_x denote respectively the predecessor and successor tasks of x in the job sequence. Then the starting time $\hat{s}_x(\pi)$ and completion time $\hat{c}_x(\pi)$ of x according to π are two TFNs given by:

$$\hat{s}_x(\pi) = \max(\hat{s}_{PJ_x} + \hat{p}_{PJ_x}, \hat{s}_{PM_x(\pi)} + \hat{p}_{PM_x(\pi)}), \tag{4}$$

$$\hat{c}_x(\pi) = \hat{s}_x(\pi) + \hat{p}_x(\pi). \tag{5}$$

The completion time of each job J_i, denoted $\hat{c}_i(\pi)$, is the completion time of the last task in that job. If there is no possible confusion regarding the processing order, we may simplify notation by writing $\hat{s}_x$, $\hat{c}_x$ and $\hat{c}_i$.

The resulting schedule is fuzzy in the sense that the starting and completion times of all tasks are fuzzy intervals, interpreted as possibility distributions on the values that the times may take. However, notice that the task processing ordering π that determines the schedule is deterministic; there is no uncertainty regarding the order in which tasks are to be processed.

Having built a schedule from π, we can now evaluate the degree of satisfaction of due dates. Indeed, the agreement index $AI_i(\widehat{c}_i(\pi), \widetilde{d}_i)$ as defined in (3), denoted AI_i for short, measures to what degree is each job's flexible due date $\widetilde{d}_i$ satisfied in this schedule, $i = 1, \ldots, n$. The overall value of due-date satisfaction for the schedule is then obtained by aggregating the individual AI_i values for $i = 1, \ldots, n$. Two main approaches for aggregation can be found in the literature: the minimum agreement index $AI_{min} = \min_{i=1,\ldots,n} AI_i$, and the average agreement index $AI_{avg} = \frac{1}{n} \sum_{i=1,\ldots,n} AI_i$. The minimum corresponds to the classical approach of fuzzy decision making, while the average provides an alternative for which the compensation property holds. Both aggregated indices need to be maximised.

The resulting job shop problem, with fuzzy processing times and fuzzy due dates, and where the objective is to maximise the aggregated agreement index AI_{agg} (where AI_{agg} can be AI_{avg} or AI_{min}) can be denoted $J|\widehat{p}_i, \widetilde{d}_i|AI_{agg}$ according to the three-field notation from [7].

3   A Memetic Algorithm to Maximise AI_{agg}

Hybrid algorithms, combining genetic algorithms with local search methods, have proved to be very powerful in different optimisation problems. The reason is their ability to integrate the intensification provided by the local search with the diversification provided by the population-based algorithm. In particular, some state-of-the-art methods for different variants of fuzzy job shop are hybrids of this kind [11,12]. This motivates our proposal of a memetic algorithm, combining a genetic component with local search.

3.1   Genetic Component

For the genetic component of our algorithm, solutions are codified into chromosomes as permutations with repetitions [2]. Each permutation represents a feasible task processing order π by identifying each operation θ_{ij} with j-th occurrence of index i in the permutation. For example, in a problem with three jobs and three machines, sequence $(1,3,2,2,3,1,1,3,2)$ represents the task ordering $\pi = (\theta_{11}, \theta_{31}, \theta_{21}, \theta_{22}, \theta_{32}, \theta_{12}, \theta_{13}, \theta_{33}, \theta_{23})$. For fitness evaluation, chromosomes are decoded into schedules using an insertion schedule generation scheme as proposed in [13] and the resulting AI_{agg} is taken as fitness value.

The algorithm starts from a random population. It then iterates until $maxIter$ consecutive iterations pass without any improvement in the best solution found so far. At each iteration a new generation is built from the previous one by applying the genetic operators of selection, recombination and replacement. In the selection phase all chromosomes are randomly paired, and then each pair is mated to obtain two offspring by applying crossover and mutation with a certain probability. Two individuals are then selected using tournament from each pair of parents and their two offspring to pass onto the next generation. In order to keep diversity, when possible the replacement strategy selects two individuals with different fitness values. For recombination, two classical operators are used: JOX crossover [9] and insertion mutation.

3.2 Local Search Component

This component follows a typical local search schema: starting from a given solution, at each step it selects a promising element from a neighbourhood structure to replace the current solution, until a stopping criterion is met. In our case, we use a simple hill climbing, where the local search moves to the first neighbour improving the objective value of the current solution. The search stops when it reaches a solution without improving neighbours. This strategy is very fast compared to other local search strategies, making it appealing for large neighbourhoods.

For the deterministic JSP several local search methods have been proposed where neighbours are generated by selecting (according to some criterion) two tasks that are sequentially scheduled in a machine and changing their relative order. This is equivalent to reversing an arc in a graph G representing a solution. In this graph, nodes correspond to tasks and directed arcs, weighted with the processing time of the task in the origin, represent immediate precedence between the two tasks either in the job or the machine. Another node, representing the start of the project is added and connected with zero weight to the first task in each job. Also, depending on the objective function, there is a single end node to which the last task of each job is (e.g. for the makespan minimisation) or there is an end node per job (this is the case of some objective functions considering due dates) [3].

The same approach is extended for the fuzzy JSP with makespan minimisation in [6]. To select arcs to be reversed, the solution graph G (with fuzzy arc weights) is decomposed in three parallel graphs G^j, $j = 1, 2, 3$, with identical topology but such that arcs are weighted with the j-th component of the processing time of the task corresponding to the source node. This allows to define critical paths in G as those paths from the start to the end that are critical (in the usual deterministic sense) in any of the parallel graphs G^j. Arcs to be reversed are then chosen from the set of arcs in a critical path that correspond to machine precedence. Neighbours thus generated are shown to be feasible solutions. It is also shown that reversing any non-critical arc cannot possibly lead to a solution with shorter critical paths and, hence, better makespan.

Based on these ideas, we propose two different neighbourhood structures, one for each aggregation of agreement indices. In the case of AI_{avg}, for its value to increase in a neighbouring solution it must be the case that at least one of the agreement indices AI_i improves. This implies reducing the completion time $\hat{c}_i(\pi)$ of that job or, equivalently, reducing the length of the longest path from the start node to the end node of job J_i in the solution graph. Therefore, we consider that a path is critical for job J_i if and only if it is a longest path from the start node to the last node of job J_i in any of the parallel graphs G^j. Notice that there might be more than one critical path for each job. Let CP_i denote the set of critical paths for job J_i, $i = 1, \ldots, n$. An improvement in $\widehat{c}_i(\pi)$ (and hence AI_{avg}) can only be obtained by reversing machine arcs belonging to one of the paths in CP_i, $i = 1, \ldots, n$. Furthermore, since $AI_i \leq 1$ for $i = 1, \ldots, n$, reducing the completion time of a job such that $AI_i = 1$ cannot improve AI_{avg} either. Therefore, the neighbourhood $\mathcal{N}_{AI_{avg}}$ is obtained by reversing machine arcs that belong to a critical path in the set $\{CP_i : AI_i < 1, 1 \leq i \leq n\}$.

In the case that the objective function is AI_{min}, a smaller neighbourhood structure can be considered. Indeed, for the minimum aggregation, reducing the completion time $\widehat{c}_i(\pi)$ of any job such that $AI_i > AI_{min}$ does not improve the objective function. Therefore we obtain a neighbourhood $\mathcal{N}_{AI_{min}} \subset \mathcal{N}_{AI_{avg}}$ by reversing an arc if and only if that arc is in a critical path in the set $\{CP_i : AI_i = AI_{min} < 1, 1 \leq i \leq n\}$.

In summary, the local search component consists in a simple hill climbing procedure using one of the neighbourhood structures $\mathcal{N}_{AI_{avg}}$ or $\mathcal{N}_{AI_{min}}$, depending on the objective function considered. This results in quite a fast local search procedure which is applied to all the individuals that are evaluated by the genetic algorithm.

4   Experimental Results

To provide an empirical evaluation of the proposed memetic algorithm, called MA hereafter, we perform a series of experiments with a C++ implementation running on a PC with Xeon processor at 2,2 Ghz and 24 Gb RAM with Linux (SL 6.0.1). The parameter values (obtained after a parametric analysis not reported here due to lack of space) are population size 100, crossover and mutation probability 1.0 and 0.05 respectively and $maxIter = 25$ as stopping criterion. In all cases, results correspond to 30 runs of MA. We evaluate solutions in terms of $1 - AI_{agg}$ for both $AI_{agg} = AI_{min}$ and $AI_{agg} = AI_{avg}$, representing the distance between the obtained overall due date satisfaction (measured with AI_{agg}) and the ideal situation where all due dates are fully satisfied. This ideal value of 1 provides an upper bound for solution performance, but if due dates are too tight it may occur that this upper bound is actually unattainable.

In a first set of experiments, we compare MA with two methods from the literature which, to our knowledge, conform the state-of-the-art. The first method is a genetic algorithm, denoted SMGA, proposed in [15] to optimise AI_{min}. It was tested on two new instances widely used in the literature thereafter (see the review [12]): S6.4 of size 6×6 and S10.4 of 10×10. On these instances, SMGA compared favourably to an alternative simulated annealing method SMSA. A second approach is a random key genetic algorithm (RKGA) from [8], also maximising AI_{min}. Both RKGA and the author's own implementation of SMGA were tested on a total of 10 instances: S6.4 and S10.4 above, 6 more instances from the literature and 2 new ones. We find 3 instances of size 6×6, denoted S6.1-3, and 3 of size 10×10, S10.1-3, originally proposed for a multiobjective approach in [14]. The two new instances of size 15×10, denoted Lei01 and Lei02 [12], are meant to provide more challenging scenarios. It must be noted that the results reported in [8] correspond to a different approximation for the maximum of fuzzy numbers which may lead to smaller completion times (cf. [12]). Figure 1 shows the performance of all three algorithms—SMGA, RKGA and MA using AI_{min} as objective function—on this test bed of 10 instances. The comparison is made in terms of average values of $1 - AI_{min}$ across all runs of MA and RKGA (30 and 20 respectively) and the best average value for SMGA between the two values reported in [8,15].

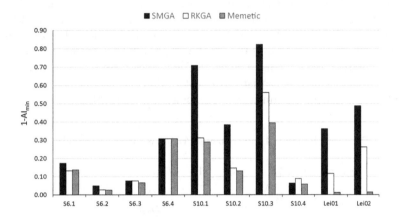

Fig. 1. Comparison with algorithms SMGA and RKGA maximising AI_{min}.

We can appreciate that differences among methods are almost negligible in small instances (S6). In fact, MA obtains the same AI_{min} value on all runs, which suggests that this value is very close to or is actually the optimum for these instances. For the larger instances S10.1-4 and Lei01-02, we can see that MA yields the best results. While improvement with respect to the other methods is small on instances S10.1 and S10.2, on S10.3 MA is 29.6% better in average values than RKGA and on S10.4 it is 34.6% better than RKGA and 7.9% better than SMGA. Differences grow on the largest instances: for instances Lei01 and Lei02, the results obtained by MA are respectively 89.9% and 94.8% better than RKGA. Moreover, the obtained average difference is close to 0, which shows the potential of MA to solve these instances.

Additionally, we consider another method that maximises AI_{min}, proposed in [5]. In a multiobjective setting, a lexicographic genetic algorithm is proposed to optimise makespan, AI_{min}, and AI_{avg} and tested on five instances, obtained by fuzzifying well-known deterministic instances: FT06 (6×6), La11, La12, La13 and La14 (20×5). The proposed method always obtains full due-date satisfaction on all instances, with $AI_{min} = AI_{avg} = 1$. For the sake of completeness, we have run our method on these instances, first optimising AI_{min} and then AI_{avg}. In both cases, the obtained results reach the optimal value for all instances.

A second set of experiments is conducted on a set of more challenging instances from [10]. These are obtained from 12 well-known benchmark problems for deterministic job shop which are considered hard to solve: FT10 (size 10×10), FT20 (20×5), La21, La24, La25 (15×10), La27, La29 (20×10), La38, La40 (15×15), and ABZ7, ABZ8, ABZ9 (20×15). The deterministic processing times from the original instances have been transformed into symmetric TFNs so the original duration is the modal value, and flexible due dates have been introduced. We refer the interested reader to [10] and references therein for further information on the fuzzification process.

The results obtained on each benchmark instance when the objective function is AI_{avg} are summarised in Table 1. After a first column containing the name of the instance, the second and third columns contain the value for the best solution and the average and standard deviation (the latter between brackets) of $1 - AI_{avg}$ across the 30 runs. The fourth and fifth columns are analogous, but measuring overall due-date satisfaction with $AI_{agg} = AI_{min}$. Finally, the last column shows the average runtime in seconds across the 30 runs.

Table 1. Results obtained using AI_{avg} as objective function.

Instance	$1 - AI_{avg}$		$1 - AI_{min}$		Runtime
	Best	Avg	Best	Avg	
ABZ7	0.335	0.355 (0.018)	1.000	1.000 (0.000)	132.9
ABZ8	0.312	0.333 (0.012)	1.000	1.000 (0.000)	128.0
ABZ9	0.300	0.325 (0.015)	1.000	1.000 (0.000)	199.1
FT10	0.243	0.246 (0.008)	1.000	1.000 (0.000)	5.4
FT20	0.701	0.714 (0.010)	1.000	1.000 (0.000)	9.3
La21	0.358	0.381 (0.010)	1.000	1.000 (0.000)	23.9
La24	0.334	0.362 (0.015)	1.000	1.000 (0.000)	23.2
La25	0.319	0.342 (0.010)	1.000	1.000 (0.000)	25.7
La27	0.501	0.536 (0.021)	1.000	1.000 (0.000)	68.4
La29	0.457	0.479 (0.018)	1.000	1.000 (0.000)	58.3
La38	0.156	0.167 (0.007)	1.000	1.000 (0.000)	48.8
La40	0.116	0.137 (0.013)	1.000	1.000 (0.000)	56.6

Since MA is run using AI_{avg} as objective value, the most relevant data are those in the second and third columns. We can appreciate that the distance to full due-date satisfaction varies significantly across the different instances, ranging from less than 0.2 in instances La38 and La40 to an extreme value of 0.714 in instance FT20. We believe this is related to the method used in [10] to generate due-date values. For FT20, with many jobs but just a few tasks per job, due dates are very tight and there is little flexibility to schedule the tasks of every job in such a way that due dates are met. On the other hand, for instances like La38 and La40, where both the number of jobs and tasks per job is large, due dates result less rigid so the obtained satisfaction values are much closer to the upper bound.

The fourth and fifth column of Table 1 illustrate how AI_{min} turns out to be too restrictive as aggregation method on this set of instances: even for those solutions with an average agreement index AI_{avg} relatively close the upper bound, at least one of the due dates cannot be satisfied, resulting in $AI_{min} = 0$. This is due to the difficulty of the proposed instances, with very tight due dates that make it very unlikely to find a solution such that $AI_{min} > 0$. Indeed, when running MA on this test bed using AI_{min} as fitness function, the error of the obtained solutions is always very close to 1 (1 in many instances). In fact, the initial population consists of random solutions for which $AI_{min} = 0$ in most cases, so there is no good solution to guide the algorithm to promising areas of the search space. On the other hand, using AI_{avg} as fitness value, the initial population already contains many individuals with fitness greater than 0, allowing MA to converge.

In a final set of experiments, we assess if both components of our memetic algorithm MA are actually contributing to the obtained results. To this end, the genetic component, GA, and the local search, LS, are run independently on the second set of more challenging instances. For a fairer comparison, LS is run as a multi-start local search with as many restarts as the average number of evaluations performed by MA on each instance. Analogously, GA is run with the same setup as MA for as long as the latter takes to converge. Due to the issues we have outlined regarding the optimisation of AI_{min} in the harder set of test instances, we take AI_{avg} as objective function in all cases. The multi-start local search starting from random solutions obtains the worst results, not only in performance, Fig. 2, but also in runtime which is 44% larger than MA. On the other hand, GA performs much better than the local search. Still, we can appreciate a synergy effect when combining both strategies, with MA obtaining much better results in the same running time than GA. This shows that MA benefits from the exploration of GA and also from the intensification of LS.

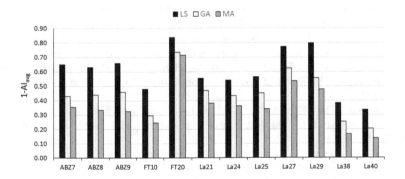

Fig. 2. Performance of the different components of MA

5   Conclusions

We have tackled the job shop scheduling problem with uncertain durations and flexible due dates modelled as fuzzy numbers. We have proposed a memetic algorithm, combining a genetic algorithm with a purpose-built local search. Experimental results compare favourably with the state-of-the-art methods, showing the potential of the proposed method.

Acknowledgements. This research has been supported by the Spanish Government under research grant TIN2016-79190-R.

References

1. Abdullah, S., Abdolrazzagh-Nezhad, M.: Fuzzy job-shop scheduling problems: a review. Inf. Sci. **278**, 380–407 (2014)
2. Bierwirth, C.: A generalized permutation approach to job shop scheduling with genetic algorithms. OR Spectr. **17**, 87–92 (1995)
3. Błażewicz, J., Domschke, W., Pesch, E.: The job shop scheduling problem: conventional and new solution techniques. Eur. J. Oper. Res. **93**, 1–33 (1996)
4. Dubois, D., Fargier, H., Fortemps, P.: Fuzzy scheduling: modelling flexible constraints vs. coping with incomplete knowledge. Eur. J. Oper. Res. **147**, 231–252 (2003)
5. González-Rodríguez, I., Puente, J., Vela, C.R.: A multiobjective approach to fuzzy job shop problem using genetic algorithms. In: Borrajo, D., Castillo, L., Corchado, J.M. (eds.) CAEPIA 2007. LNCS (LNAI), vol. 4788, pp. 80–89. Springer, Heidelberg (2007). doi:10.1007/978-3-540-75271-4_9
6. González Rodríguez, I., Vela, C.R., Puente, J., Varela, R.: A new local search for the job shop problem with uncertain durations. In: Proceedings of the ICAPS-2008, pp. 124–131. AAAI Press (2008)
7. Graham, R., Lawler, E., Lenstra, J., Kan, A.R.: Optimization and approximation in deterministic sequencing and scheduling: a survey. Ann. Discret. Math. **4**, 287–326 (1979)
8. Lei, D.: Solving fuzzy job shop scheduling problems using random key genetic algorithm. Int. J. Adv. Manuf. Technol. **49**, 253–262 (2010)
9. Ono, I., Yamamura, M., Kobayashi, S.: A genetic algorithm for job-shop scheduling problems using job-based order crossover. In: Proceedings of IEEE International Conference on Evolutionary Computation, pp. 547–552. IEEE (1996)
10. Palacios, J.J., Derbel, B.: On maintaining diversity in MOEA/D: application to a biobjective combinatorial FJSP. In: Proceedings of GECCO 2015, pp. 719–726. ACM (2015)
11. Palacios, J.J., González, M.A., Vela, C.R., González-Rodríguez, I., Puente, J.: Genetic tabu search for the fuzzy flexible job shop problem. Comput. Oper. Res. **54**, 74–89 (2015)
12. Palacios, J.J., Puente, J., Vela, C.R., González-Rodríguez, I.: Benchmarks for fuzzy job shop problems. Inf. Sci. **329**, 736–752 (2016)
13. Palacios, J.J., Vela, C.R., González-Rodríguez, I., Puente, J.: Schedule generation schemes for job shop problems with fuzziness. In: Schaub, T., Friedrich, G., O'Sullivan, B. (eds.) Proceedings of ECAI 2014, pp. 687–692. IOS Press, Amsterdam (2014)

14. Sakawa, M., Kubota, R.: Fuzzy programming for multiobjective job shop scheduling with fuzzy processing time and fuzzy duedate through genetic algorithms. Eur. J. Oper. Res. **120**, 393–407 (2000)
15. Sakawa, M., Mori, T.: An efficient genetic algorithm for job-shop scheduling problems with fuzzy processing time and fuzzy duedate. Comput. Ind. Eng. **36**, 325–341 (1999)

Indicator-Based Evolutionary Level Set Approximation: Mixed Mutation Strategy and Extended Analysis

Lai-Yee Liu[1], Vitor Basto-Fernandes[2,3]([✉]), Iryna Yevseyeva[4], Joost Kok[1], and Michael Emmerich[1]

[1] Leiden Institute of Advanced Computer Science, Leiden University,
Niels Bohrweg 1, 2333 CA Leiden, The Netherlands
emmerich@liacs.nl
[2] Instituto Universitário de Lisboa (ISCTE-IUL), University Institute of Lisbon,
ISTAR-IUL, Av. das Forças Armadas, 1649-026 Lisboa, Portugal
vmbfs@iscte.pt
[3] School of Technology and Management, Computer Science and Communications
Research Centre, Polytechnic Institute of Leiria, 2411-901 Leiria, Portugal
[4] Faculty of Technology, De Montfort University,
Gateway House 5.33, The Gateway, Leicester LE1 9BH, UK

Abstract. The aim of evolutionary level set approximation is to find a finite representation of a level set of a given black box function. The problem of level set approximation plays a vital role in solving problems, for instance in fault detection in water distribution systems, engineering design, parameter identification in gene regulatory networks, and in drug discovery. The goal is to create algorithms that quickly converge to feasible solutions and then achieve a good coverage of the level set. The population based search scheme of evolutionary algorithms makes this type of algorithms well suited to target such problems. In this paper, the focus is on continuous black box functions and we propose a challenging benchmark for this problem domain and propose dual mutation strategies, that balance between global exploration and local refinement. Moreover, the article investigates the role of different indicators for measuring the coverage of the level set approximation. The results are promising and show that even for difficult problems in moderate dimension the proposed evolutionary level set approximation algorithm (ELSA) can serve as a versatile and robust meta-heuristic.

1 Introduction

The problem of black box level set approximation is to find all inputs (arguments) of a function that give rise to an observed or targeted output. In general, we demand the output to be within a range or below a threshold $\epsilon \in \mathbb{R}$ and we aim to approximate the set. Given a black box objective function $f : S \to \mathbb{R}$, with $S \subset \mathbb{R}^d$, we search for the set $L(f \leq \epsilon)$ which is defined as:

$$L(f \leq \epsilon) := \{\mathbf{x} \in S \mid f(\mathbf{x}) \leq \epsilon\} \tag{1}$$

© Springer International Publishing AG 2017
J.M. Ferrández Vicente et al. (Eds.): IWINAC 2017, Part I, LNCS 10337, pp. 146–159, 2017.
DOI: 10.1007/978-3-319-59740-9_15

In the following we assume that $\mathbf{x}$ is taken from a compact domain S. More specifically, we will in the following look at problems where the input variables are constrained by box constraints:

$$S = [\mathbf{x}_1^{min}, \mathbf{x}_1^{max}] \times \cdots \times [\mathbf{x}_d^{min}, \mathbf{x}_d^{max}]$$

Problems of level set approximation occur in various disciplines of science and engineering.

- Fault Detection and Model-Based Diagnosis: The problem could be to find all possible source locations of a contamination given a model of a water distribution system [ZR07].
- Parameter Identification: Find all parameters of a system's model that can explain an observed behavior. The behavior can, for instance, be given by gene activation time series and it is used to find unknown reaction rates (propensities) in a gene regulatory network model [NE15].
- Design Engineering: Find all possible designs that comply with a prescribed behavior. For instance, different designs of building shapes that are compliant with maximum stress and with energy efficiency demands could be searched for [PCWB00, ZR07].
- *De Novo* Drug Discovery: Represent the space of molecular compounds that have chemical properties within a prescribed range. See for instance [vdB13]. Moreover, different low energy configurations and positions of molecules could be searched for in molecular docking problems.

This paper contributes to the development of a robust evolutionary algorithm for black box level set approximation. The steady-state algorithm ELSA (Evolutionary Level Set Approximation) [EDK13] is tested on a broader range of problems including for the first time problems in more than two dimensions. To test the ELSA approach, we construct a set of nonlinear test problems that cover a wide range of properties and we study the geometry of the solution sets. We also study a dual mutation operator that can help to better identify disconnected components of level sets.

The paper is structured as follows: After discussing related work in Sect. 2, we describe the ELSA algorithm in Sect. 3. After this a set of benchmark problems is introduced in Sect. 4 and we summarize experimental studies on the robustness and precision of selected algorithm variants in Sect. 5. Finally, Sect. 6 concludes the paper with a summary of main results and outlook to future studies in this research line.

2   Related Work

Level set approximation has received some attention in numerical analysis [Set99], where it is usually used for solving explicitly given problems and not for black box formulation, but so-far little attention has been paid to targeting black box problems and population-based search heuristics for solving them.

In practice, the use of complex simulation codes for function evaluations has increased the need for such black box enabled techniques.

As opposed to the often discussed problem of black box optimization, in level set approximation we are not in the first place interested in optimal solutions, but rather in solutions that satisfy certain criteria. The underlying assumption can be that the system's measurements are not exact and a minimization of, for instance, the deviation from the desired target could exclude possible explanations or solutions. A closely related question, related to level set approximation, is to find all solutions that are within a certain tolerance range close to the globally optimal solution [ZR07]. Moreover, approximating Pareto fronts in multi-objective optimization has much in common with level set approximation, as in both cases a set that satisfies certain conditions should be covered. However, in multi-objective optimization, the Pareto dominance relation is considered for qualification of whether a point belongs to the set to be covered relative to the position of other points in the objective space. Still, many principles of multi-objective algorithm design such as the use of indicators, population-based methods, and exploration/exploitation handling, are also of interest in the design of evolutionary level set approximation [EBN05].

A closely related work is *diversity optimization*, a term used by Ulrich and Thiele [UT11]. The idea of their algorithm NOAH is to find diverse sets of optimal or near optimal solutions. The algorithm NOAH lowers the threshold level gradually while evolving a population of points w.r.t. the maximization of diversity. In particular, the Solow-Polasky diversity metric [SPB93] was chosen in this context, which has several favorable theoretical properties but also requires the choice of a correlation parameter in its definition. Similar to ELSA, NOAH follows an indicator-based steady-state selection scheme, but it differs in the range of diversity indicators to be applied and in the way infeasible solutions are treated. Whereas ELSA uses augmentation, a kind of smooth penalization of infeasible solutions, in NOAH different phases of the algorithm are defined in which the constraints are gradually tightened. However, this scheme requires setting of many parameters which makes benchmarking of NOAH difficult. In our work, we use the Solow-Polasky metric, similar to NOAH. Hence ELSA can be considered as a very similar algorithm or variant of NOAH.

As opposed to diversity maximization, level set approximation seeks to find a representation of the level set. This should be expressed in the performance assessment. It has been argued in [EDK13] that if a set in $\mathbb{R}^d$ is approximated by a maximally diverse set, then the solution sets tend to distribute along the boundary of the level set. This would imply larger distances between solutions of the level set and gaps in the interior. In contrast, the problem of representing the level set well would rather imply closeness of the approximation set to the targeted set in the sense of minimal Hausdorff distance, meaning that all points in the targeted set should be as close as possible to (some) points in the approximation set, and vice versa, all points in the approximation set should be as close as possible to (some) points in the target set. Unfortunately, the first criterion cannot be assessed if the target set is not yet known. It is therefore, inevitable to use proxy indicators to assess the performance of an approximation set within the algorithm. Several such proxy indicators, including the Solow-Polasky indicator, have been discussed in [EDK13].

3   Evolutionary Level Set Approximation (ELSA)

ELSA is a relatively novel, simple in design, evolutionary algorithm (EA) for level set approximation. It is guided by quality indicators (QIs) that rate the fitness of a population. ELSA is a $(\mu + 1)$-EA (or steady-state EA), which means that ELSA creates one child per generation and only one solution cannot survive to the next generation. Steady-state selection is commonly adopted by indicator-based EAs (IBEAs) to circumvent computationally expensive subset selection problems [EBN05].

3.1   Quality Indicators for Level Set Approximation

A quality indicator (QI) assigns a single value to a level set approximation, that is a finite set $A \subset S$. It should consider how many points of the level set have been found and how well they are distributed. In [EDK13] a detailed discussion is provided and here we will only summarize the most important definitions. A quality indicator is monotonous, if it grows with the number of points in the feasible set. It should also reward a good coverage of the level set. Indicators which fulfill these properties are the Augmented Average Distance (ADI$^+$), Augmented Solow-Polasky (SP$^+$), and three types of Augmented Gap indicators (GI$^+$): Augmented Min-Max Diversity (GI$_N^+$), Augmented Arithmetic Mean (GI$_\Sigma^+$), and Augmented Geometric Mean (GI$_\Pi^+$). In this study, only the GI_Π^+ and the SP$^+$ indicator are used, as the ADI$^+$ indicator is computationally expensive and the other augmented gap indicators had several disadvantages that were highlighted in [EDK13]. The SP indicator is defined in [SPB93] and measures the number of species in a population. This indicator has a θ parameter that scales the distance matrix and $\theta = 10$ is recommended [UBT10]. Let $D(x, Y)$ denote the (Euclidean) distance of x to the closest point in a set Y. The Geometric Mean is defined as $GI_\Pi = \prod_{p \in A}^{n} D(p, A \setminus \{p\})$, with A being the approximation set that is made up of all solutions x combined. In level set optimization, we only measure the diversity of the feasible subset and subtract a penalty for all infeasible points that growth proportionally with the distance to the threshold ϵ. By this, each indicator can be extended to an augmented indicator which in turn can be used as a quality indicator: indicator$^+$ = indicator$(L \cap A)$ − penalty$(A \setminus L)$. For the Gap indicator we chose penalty$(X) = \sum_{x \in X} (\text{Diameter}(S) + (f(x) - \epsilon))$, where Diameter denotes the longest distance in S. For the SP indicator, the penalty reads penalty$(X) = \sum_{x \in X} (f(x) - \epsilon)$. By choosing these penalties, it is made sure that replacing an infeasible point in A by a feasible point always yields an improvement.

Algorithm 1. Indicator-Based Evolutionary Level Set Approximation (ELSA)

1: $P_0 \leftarrow$ init() {Initialize population}
2: $t \leftarrow 0$
3: **while** not terminate **do**
4:     $u \sim$ rand$(0, 1)$ {Draw uniform number between 0 and 1}
5:     **if** $u \leq \nu$ **then**
6:         $q \leftarrow$ mutate(P_t, σ) {create new child solution by mutation}
7:     **else**
8:         $q \leftarrow$ reinitialize(S) {create new child solution by random re-initialization}
9:     **end if**
10:     $P'_t \leftarrow P_t \cup \{q\}$
11:     $r = \arg\min_{p \in P'_t}(\Delta_{QI}(p, P'_t))$ {Select solution that least contributes to QI}
12:     $P_{t+1} \leftarrow P'_t \setminus \{r\}$
13:     $t \leftarrow t + 1$
14: **end while**
15: **return** P_t

3.2   Basic Algorithm

Algorithm 1 describes the steps of ELSA. P_t is the population of approximation set solutions in generation t. It contains the points that represent the level set. The first step in the main loop is to create the child $q \in S$, for instance by adding a small perturbation to a solution in P_t.

ELSA adopts a mixed mutation strategy, for a constant mutation probability, the algorithm either creates a child by randomly creating a new point in S (random reinitialization), or by adding a perturbation to a point in P_t (parent-based mutation). The perturbation is drawn from an i.i.d. multivariate normal distribution with a standard deviation of σ (step-size) and mean value of zero. The default pseudo-random number generator from MATLAB 11 was used in this work, both for the normal and for the uniform distribution. The decision of which mutation to use, is based on a random number itself. The parameter $\nu \in \{0, 1\}$ is the probability that a parent-based mutation is used, and $1 - \nu$ is the probability of random reinitialization. The reinitialization step is a simple means to prevent the algorithm getting trapped in a local optimum or to miss a component of the level set and the setting of ν and σ will be subject to further study in this paper. In the next step, P'_t denotes the temporary new population which includes solution r. To keep the population size constant, in step 11 and step 12, the least contributing individual in P'_t is identified and discarded from P'_t to form the new parent population P_{t+1}. The contribution of a point is decided by its Quality Indicator Contribution (QIC) which, for a given quality indicator (to be maximized) is defined as: $\Delta_{QI(p,A)} := QI(A) - QI(A \setminus \{p\})$. The algorithm is terminated when the number of evaluations exceeds a user-defined evaluation budget.

4   Benchmark Problems for ELSA

ELSA has only been tested on benchmark problems in two dimensions in previous research. Next we propose a set of benchmark problems for more than 2 dimensions. The benchmarks are divided into two categories: simple and complex shapes. Simple shapes refer to basic geometrical objects, such as generalizations of spheres. Simple shape benchmarks are Lamé, Ellipsoid, Hollow Sphere, and Double Sphere:

$$L_{Lam\acute{e}}(\boldsymbol{x}) = \left\{ \boldsymbol{x} \in [-3,3]^d \left| \sum_{i=1}^d \sqrt{\left|\frac{x_i}{3}\right|} - 1 \le 0 \right.\right\} \tag{2}$$

$$L_{Ellipsoid}(\boldsymbol{x}) = \left\{ \boldsymbol{x} \in [-3,3]^d \left| \sum_{i=1}^d \left(\frac{x_i}{c_i}\right)^2 - 1 \le 0 \right.\right\} \tag{3}$$

where $c = [1\ 2\ 2.5]$ for 3D, and $c = [1\ 2\ 2.5\ 1\ 2\ 2.5\ 1\ 2\ 2.5\ 1]$ for 10D

$$L_{Hollow}(\boldsymbol{x}) = \left\{ \boldsymbol{x} \in [-3,3]^d \left| \left| \sqrt{\sum_{i=1}^d x_i^2} - 1.5 \right| \le 0 \right.\right\} \tag{4}$$

$$L_{Double}(\boldsymbol{x}) = \left\{ \boldsymbol{x} \in [-3,3]^d \left| \left(\sqrt{\sum_{i=1}^d (x_i+1)^2} - 1 \right) \cdot \left(\sqrt{\sum_{i=1}^d (x_i-1)^2} - 1 \right) \le 0 \right.\right\} \tag{5}$$

Complex shapes refer to engineering relevant shapes described by functions more complex than those found in the simple shapes benchmark category. The shape functions used for the complex shape benchmarks are taken from mathematical functions in multimodal optimization problems. They are used to show the performance of the Indicator-Based Evolutionary Algorithms on more realistic landscapes in terms of practical test problems. The complex shape benchmarks are Branke's Multipeak [Bra98,Kru12], Rastrigin, Schaffer [Kru12], and Vincent [vdGSB08]:

$$f_{Branke's}(\boldsymbol{x}) = \frac{1}{d} \sum_{i=1}^d \left(1.3 - g(x_i) \right) \tag{6}$$

$$g(x_i) = \begin{cases} -(x_i+1)^2 + 1 & \text{if } -2 \le x_i < 0 \\ 1.3 \cdot 2^{-8|x_i-1|} & \text{if } 0 \le x_i \le 2 \\ 0 & \text{otherwise} \end{cases}$$

$$L_{Branke's}(\boldsymbol{x}) = \left\{ \boldsymbol{x} \in [-2,2]^d \left| f_{Branke's}(\boldsymbol{x}) \le 0.4 \right.\right\} \tag{7}$$

where this benchmark is not included as a level set benchmark for 10D

$$L_{Rastrigin}(\boldsymbol{x}) = \left\{ \boldsymbol{x} \in [-4.5,4.5]^d \left| 10d + \sum_{i=1}^d \left(x_i^2 - 10 \cdot \cos(2\pi x_i) \right) \le 29 \right.\right\} \tag{8}$$

$L_{Schaffer}(\boldsymbol{x})$

$$= \left\{ \boldsymbol{x} \in [-2.5, 2.5]^d \middle| \sum_{i=1}^{d-1} (x_i^2 + x_{i+1}^2)^{0.25} \cdot \left(\sin^2 \left(50 \cdot (x_i^2 + x_{i+1}^2)^{0.1} \right) + 1 \right) \leq 2 \right\} \quad (9)$$

$$L_{Vincent}(\boldsymbol{x}) = \left\{ \boldsymbol{x} \in [0.5, 5]^d \middle| -\frac{1}{d} \sum_{i=1}^{d} \sin \left(10 \cdot \ln(x_i) \right) \leq -0.8 \right\} \quad (10)$$

The difficulty of the level set benchmark depends on the level set shapes and their sizes. In general small objects are more difficult to locate, which leads to an increase in difficulty for the benchmark. The same applies for thin parts or acute angles in an object, which add a challenge when locally exploring a feasible component. If a level set has disjoint parts, it is expected that the algorithm should settle at least one solution on each disjoint part, unless the approximation set size is smaller than the amount of disjoint parts. Many of the chosen complex shape level sets have an exponential growth in the number of their disconnected component when increasing the dimensionality of the level set benchmark. Having large distances between the disjoint parts can serve as a way to test the global search capabilities of the algorithm. To this end, the difficulty of the level set benchmarks has been tailored according to the philosophy of the ELSA algorithm to not consider points in the exterior of the approximation set. Therefore, we avoid components of measure zero. The shape of the level sets can be seen in Fig. 1.

5   Experimental Analysis

The experiments with ELSA consist of two main parts: First part shows that implementing both global and local search is essential for black box level set benchmarks. The importance of mixed mutation strategy is measured by comparing different ν values for ELSA on 3D Ellipsoid and Vincent level set benchmark for two different σ step-sizes (results presented in Table 1); In the second part, the importance of choosing the right σ step-size is highlighted, this is seen from the experiments of ELSA on all benchmarks. These experiments show the robustness of ELSA with different σ step-sizes on 3D and 10D benchmarks (Tables 2 and 3, respectively), where ν is set to 0.5 (a recommended parameter value derived from the mixed mutation strategy experiments). Finally, Table 4 presents a comparison on the amount of evaluations to yield a population that solely consists of feasible solutions, with respect to different step-sizes, for 3D and 10D benchmarks. The Monte Carlo Search (MCS) is included as a reference algorithm configuration in all the experiments. ELSA can easily be transformed into the MCS approach by setting ν to 0 (σ is irrelevant as the algorithm never produce children through parent perturbation).

The evaluation budget for a single ELSA run is set to 10 K for all 3D level set benchmarks and 100 K for 10D benchmarks. Population size $\mu = 100$ is used for all experiments. Each configuration has been run 40 times. Several σ step-sizes are to be defined to use in ELSA. The generic form for the σ step-size is described below, where d is the dimension:

$$\sigma = \frac{\omega \cdot \text{mean}(\mathbf{x}^{max} - \mathbf{x}^{min})}{\sqrt{d}}$$

$\sqrt{d}$ is derived from the longest diagonal of an n-dimensional hypercube. The chosen ω values for the σ step-sizes are 1, 0.1, 0.01, and 0.001 (different magnitudes of 10). 3D Ellipsoid and 3D Vincent are used as the level set benchmarks to compare the results for mixed mutation strategy. They represent the core opposites of having a non-disjoint level set with Ellipsoid versus the multisegmented Vincent level set. The chosen ν values are 0, 0.25, 0.5, 0.75, and 1.

The following objectives are used for the comparison of the results:

- Diversity: The Quality Indicator value of the final population.
- Eval$_{Feasible}$: The amount of evaluations it takes to yield a population that solely consists of feasible solutions.
- Coverage of the final population on the level set determined by human observation.

Table 1 allows us to reason about the effect ν has in scenarios of small and big step-sizes, for single level set (Ellipsoid) and multiple level set (Vincent) problems. For the Ellipsoid problem with $\omega = 0.1$, we see that the higher the ν value the better the diversity yielded with GI_{Π}^{+} and SP^{+}. This behavior is mainly explained by the fact that Ellipsoid is a single level set problem. In Vincent problem with $\omega = 0.1$ both GI_{Π}^{+} and SP^{+} indicators show that intermedium values of ν (0.25 and 0.5) perform better than extreme ones such as 0 and 1 (best from worst for GI_{Π}^{+} and SP^{+}: 0.25, 0.5, 0, 0.75, 1, with $\nu = 1$ being significantly worse).

For $\omega = 0.01$, both GI_{Π}^{+} and SP^{+} indicators in the Ellipsoid problem also reveal that intermedium values of ν such as 0.5 and 0.75 perform better than extreme ones (GI_{Π}^{+} best to worst: 0.5, 0.75, 0.25, 0, 1; and SP: 0.75, 0.5, 0.25, 0, 1). A similar conclusion can be made for the Vincent problem with $\omega = 0.01$, intermedium values of 0.25 and 0.5 of ν allow for best GI_{Π}^{+} and SP^{+} results (best to worst, GI_{Π}^{+} and SP^{+}: 0.25, 0.5, 0, 0.75, 1).

Results from Table 1 show that the tuning/trade-off settings allowed by ELSA mixed mutation strategy, is essential for the exploration and exploitation of single and multiple level set problems. For the test on different values of ν it can be observed that higher values of ν have priority, in case of simple problems with connected level sets (Ellipsoid). On the contrary, a value of ν that lies between 0 and 1 should be chosen, if the level set is disconnected (Vincent). There is an optimal setting of ν which is in the middle between the two extremes. This makes sense, as in the multimodal case it is important to explore (find new components of the level set by reinitialization), but also one has to distribute points well in the found level set components (parent based mutation).

Table 1. The diversity of the final populations from ELSA with $\omega = 0.1$ and $\omega = 0.01$ for σ step-size and different ν values on selected 3D level set benchmarks.

		$\nu = 0$		$\nu = 0.25$		$\nu = 0.5$		$\nu = 0.75$		$\nu = 1$	
		mean	std	mean	std	mean	std	mean	std	mean	std
Ellipsoid ($\omega = 0.1$)	GI_Π^+	0.592	0.004	0.613	0.005	0.625	0.004	0.631	0.005	0.637	0.004
	SP^+	99.198	0.029	99.327	0.021	99.381	0.016	99.413	0.015	99.439	0.012
Vincent ($\omega = 0.1$)	GI_Π^+	0.518	0.015	0.532	0.013	0.525	0.016	0.485	0.021	0.355	0.030
	SP^+	98.736	0.243	98.953	0.125	98.920	0.202	98.665	0.379	94.613	2.098
Ellipsoid ($\omega = 0.01$)	GI_Π^+	0.592	0.004	0.637	0.006	0.647	0.005	0.641	0.007	0.504	0.050
	SP^+	99.198	0.029	99.444	0.022	99.498	0.016	99.510	0.017	99.091	0.411
Vincent ($\omega = 0.01$)	GI_Π^+	0.518	0.015	0.562	0.015	0.541	0.019	0.440	0.025	0.178	0.028
	SP^+	98.736	0.243	99.088	0.182	98.948	0.232	97.665	0.621	70.054	9.182

Experiment results in Table 2 show that ELSA is able to consistently find entirely feasible populations with high diversity on all 3D level set benchmarks for almost all the tested σ step-sizes. Even MCS can produce relatively good results with the exception of Lamé benchmark which proves to be too difficult to find feasible solutions with purely random search. The results from $\omega = 1$ resemble the results of MCS, thus it can be considered a too large step-size. ELSA with $\omega = 0.1$ and $\omega = 0.01$ are most successful at finding diverse approximation sets, where the results with $\omega = 0.1$ have noticeably better diversity in 3D Schaffer. Results from $w = 0.001$ however show a decline in diversity which indicates that this σ step-size is too small for the level set benchmarks. Similar patterns between the different step-sizes are reflected in the 10D level set benchmarks (See Table 3). Again, the configurations with $\omega = 0.1$ and $\omega = 0.01$ are observed to be most suited in general for these type of black-box level set benchmarks. However, the limitations of ELSA are revealed in higher dimensions as it struggles with finding an entirely feasible set for Lamé, Rastrigin and Schaffer regardless of σ step-size. MCS and ELSA with $\omega = 1$ are the most severe cases whereby they cannot even find any entirely feasible populations. For the other 10D benchmarks, ELSA with $\omega = 0.1$ or $\omega = 0.01$ find diverse populations where the results from Solow-Polasky on Ellipsoid and Hollow Sphere are near optimal in measurement.

Table 4 experiments compare 3D and 10D convergence to the level set, it shows that the setting of the step size parameter is crucial not only for finding sets with a good coverage, but also for finding the components of the level set. Step size settings are more critical in the high dimensional case and in the future work automatic adaptation of the step size should be developed.

Table 2. The diversity of the final populations from the tested algorithm configurations on the 3D level set benchmarks.

		MCS		$\omega = 1$		$\omega = 0.1$		$\omega = 0.01$		$\omega = 0.001$	
		mean	std	mean	std	mean	std	mean	std	mean	std
Lamé	GI_{Π}^+	−15.411	41.893	−6.820	23.989	0.326	0.006	0.284	0.015	0.121	0.022
	SP^+	68.961	2.642	67.740	2.609	86.442	0.448	85.503	1.103	57.155	4.318
Ellipsoid	GI_{Π}^+	0.592	0.004	0.593	0.006	0.625	0.004	0.647	0.005	0.594	0.007
	SP^+	99.198	0.029	99.192	0.035	99.381	0.016	99.498	0.016	99.170	0.045
Hollow	GI_{Π}^+	0.575	0.007	0.576	0.005	0.614	0.005	0.639	0.007	0.576	0.007
	SP^+	99.131	0.043	99.144	0.038	99.362	0.016	99.504	0.020	99.091	0.065
Double	GI_{Π}^+	0.413	0.006	0.413	0.007	0.463	0.003	0.464	0.007	0.396	0.010
	SP^+	95.128	0.203	95.049	0.203	96.709	0.077	97.059	0.107	94.230	0.468
Branke's	GI_{Π}^+	0.254	0.009	0.260	0.006	0.295	0.007	0.291	0.011	0.205	0.019
	SP^+	80.179	1.267	80.364	1.550	86.537	0.731	86.173	1.627	71.108	3.214
Rastrigin	GI_{Π}^+	1.549	0.014	1.552	0.019	1.506	0.023	1.563	0.025	1.493	0.022
	SP^+	100.000	0.000	100.000	0.000	100.000	0.000	100.000	0.000	100.000	0.000
Schaffer	GI_{Π}^+	0.302	0.016	0.307	0.012	0.395	0.005	0.302	0.016	0.190	0.032
	SP^+	84.973	1.839	84.918	1.991	93.275	0.434	86.424	1.767	71.024	4.023
Vincent	GI_{Π}^+	0.518	0.015	0.514	0.019	0.525	0.016	0.541	0.019	0.444	0.022
	SP^+	98.736	0.243	98.716	0.212	98.920	0.202	98.948	0.232	97.132	0.571

Table 3. The diversity of the final populations from the tested algorithm configurations on the 10D level set benchmarks.

		MCS		$\omega = 1$		$\omega = 0.1$		$\omega = 0.01$		$\omega = 0.001$	
		mean	std	mean	std	mean	std	mean	std	mean	std
Lamé	GI_{Π}^+	−2199.11	3.39	−2182.17	3.21	−1922.81	11.17	−1422.44	859.12	−2067.21	36.38
	SP^+	−301.53	3.79	−284.76	2.86	−32.02	1.43	−41.11	48.43	−174.82	31.63
Ellipsoid	GI_{Π}^+	−2027.30	15.73	−1980.68	26.12	1.663	0.014	1.242	0.076	0.177	0.045
	SP^+	−139.80	5.24	−104.30	7.35	100.000	0.000	100.000	0.000	27.434	14.023
Hollow	GI_{Π}^+	−1944.75	19.53	−1872.49	38.62	1.760	0.005	1.502	0.023	0.215	0.041
	SP^+	−68.39	4.55	−44.02	4.14	100.000	0.000	100.000	0.000	34.293	9.441
Double	GI_{Π}^+	−2586.90	12.45	−2467.93	17.08	0.966	0.032	0.945	0.008	−402.69	791.54
	SP^+	−692.29	15.41	−571.12	13.84	99.948	0.018	99.946	0.002	−0.89	39.49
Rastrigin	GI_{Π}^+	−7355.82	98.02	−7144.56	82.24	−3095.72	546.12	−2101.94	1743.26	−1985.23	1837.74
	SP^+	−4531.24	71.23	−4324.87	80.48	−600.63	286.13	−281.08	526.95	−494.81	672.37
Schaffer	GI_{Π}^+	−2439.64	8.68	−2403.24	9.41	−1743.84	41.45	−2118.51	95.64	−2114.59	70.52
	SP^+	−859.49	7.69	−824.42	9.42	−175.86	52.09	−526.95	123.59	−553.91	64.94
Vincent	GI_{Π}^+	−1210.98	56.09	−1174.72	62.49	0.943	0.102	0.726	0.112	0.218	0.029
	SP^+	9.88	3.63	13.87	3.56	99.933	0.041	98.281	2.331	51.121	9.313

Figure 1 represents the final populations of ELSA, generated with GI_{Π}^+ under the setting of $\nu = 0.5$ and $\omega = 0.1$, for 3D benchmarks of Lamé (a), Ellipsoid (b), Branke's Multipeak (c), Rastrigin (d), Schaffer (e) and Vincent (f). The populations are selected in a way that their measured diversity comes closest to the average diversity found over all runs. The populations from SP^+ have a

Table 4. Eval$_{Feasible}$ of the results from the tested algorithm configurations. Eval$_{Feasible}$ is calculated as the average of the results from GI$_{II}^{+}$ and SP^{+} combined. The "-" symbol marks a configuration that contains at least one population that does not solely consist of feasible solutions.

	3D										10D					
	MCS		$\omega=1$		$\omega=0.1$		$\omega=0.01$		$\omega=0.001$		$\omega=0.1$		$\omega=0.01$		$\omega=0.001$	
	mean	std	mean	std	mean	std	mean	std	mean	std	mean	std	mean	std	mean	std
Lamé	-	-	-	-	1067	113	911	137	957	238	-	-	-	-	-	-
Ellipsoid	1030	101	1044	93	468	40	454	49	456	49	3045	493	9022	2436	40474	17868
Hollow	1279	122	1252	119	539	46	492	46	488	60	2715	362	7852	2245	29867	12113
Double	2570	278	2542	255	686	68	622	75	642	100	4377	473	13679	3507	-	-
Branke's	4488	468	4105	419	969	89	764	109	758	127						
Rastrigin	1043	106	1062	93	710	66	465	44	453	42	-	-	-	-	-	-
Schaffer	6316	663	6247	586	1101	120	862	135	833	143	-	-	-	-	-	-
Vincent	2852	309	2843	283	1086	91	659	83	656	77	3152	534	2694	674	5946	2991

tendency for solutions to reside on the boundary of the level set which is not always a desired behavior when taking practical applications into account. While figures labeled with 1 (for example a1) represent 3D plots of the level sets, figures labeled with 2 represent a 2D projection of the 3D plots (for example a2). The level sets are depicted in light gray and are semi-transparent. In the 3D view, the RGB-value (converted into gray scale) of a solution maps to the (x_1, x_2, x_3)-coordinate of the solution with respect to the search space. In the orthographic view, gray scale coding is used to determine the location of the solution with respect to the x_3-axis.

By visual inspection of Fig. 1 we can state that the acute parts of Lamé are too challenging for ELSA to evenly distribute solutions over them. The populations are well-spread on simple shape benchmarks like Ellipsoid (while not depicted, it also holds for Hollow Sphere and Double Sphere). Branke's Multipeak has each level set component covered by solutions for both quality indicators, but the result from GI$_{II}^{+}$ does not balance the number of points evenly across the components. For Rastrigin the majority of the solutions are settled on the center raster-like structure, however ELSA is able to settle some solutions on the outer rim disjoint parts. 3D Schaffer has similarities to Lamé in terms of general shape and the same problems with ELSA are encountered, but ELSA manages to distribute solutions on the exterior parts to some degree despite the lack of connectivity. 3D Vincent has 64 disjoint level set parts and neither population can cover them all, although the overall diversity is good.

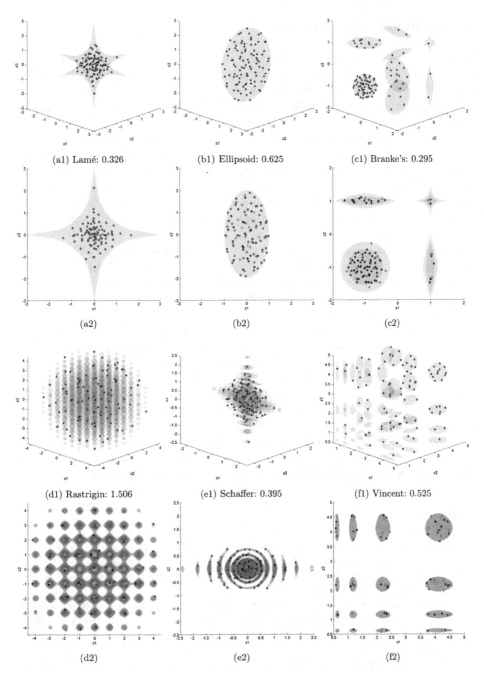

Fig. 1. Visualization of results on 3D benchmark achieved with GI_{Π}^{+} indicator.

6   Summary and Outlook

The current study shows that a mixed strategy of random reinitialization and parent-based mutation is preferable to using only one of these strategies, because it allows to explore and to refine at the same time, thereby minimizing the risk that a component of the level set is overlooked. This mixed strategy might be considered preferable, as we lose performance for the sake of reliability.

In contrast to previous work where only 2D problems were addressed, in our study ELSA performance is assessed for low (3D) and high dimensional level sets (10D). This study allowed to conclude that step size parameter is crucial (specially in higher dimensions) to get both good coverage and to find the components of the level set. Automatic adaptation of the step size (Self-adaptive σ) should be developed to adapt the algorithm parameters to problem specific properties.

Although ELSA has revealed very good performance in simple shape benchmarks such as Ellipsoid for low and high dimensions, there is still space for improvement in shapes with acute parts such as Lamé, Rastrigin and Schaffer, specially in high dimensions. To this end, new selection and cross-over operations can be designed for ELSA.

There are still some ways that can be tried to improve the performance of ELSA: The current version of ELSA does not utilize cross-over, that might help to improve the level set coverage (close gaps). However, it might also be disruptive, when applied to individuals from different components of the level set. Moreover, creating more than one children or introduction of mating selection could be beneficial for improving the quality of results, but would also significantly increase computational costs of an iteration.

In contrast to evolutionary algorithms AIS feature a variable population size and they also have some inherent mechanisms for diversity maintenance, which makes them a promising technique for level set approximation [CZ06].

References

[Bra98] Branke, J.: Creating robust solutions by means of evolutionary algorithms. In: Eiben, A.E., Bäck, T., Schoenauer, M., Schwefel, H.-P. (eds.) PPSN 1998. LNCS, vol. 1498, pp. 119–128. Springer, Heidelberg (1998). doi:10.1007/BFb0056855

[CZ06] Coelho, G.P., Von Zuben, F.J.: omni-aiNet: an immune-inspired approach for omni optimization. In: Bersini, H., Carneiro, J. (eds.) ICARIS 2006. LNCS, vol. 4163, pp. 294–308. Springer, Heidelberg (2006). doi:10.1007/11823940_23

[EBN05] Emmerich, M., Beume, N., Naujoks, B.: An EMO algorithm using the hypervolume measure as selection criterion. In: Coello Coello, C.A., Hernández Aguirre, A., Zitzler, E. (eds.) EMO 2005. LNCS, vol. 3410, pp. 62–76. Springer, Heidelberg (2005). doi:10.1007/978-3-540-31880-4_5

[EDK13] Emmerich, M.T.M., Deutz, A.H., Kruisselbrink, J.W.: On quality indicators for black-box level set approximation. In: Tantar, E., Tantar, A.-A., Bouvry, P., Del Moral, P., Legrand, P., Coello, C.A.C., Schütze, O. (eds.) EVOLVE-A Bridge Between Probability, pp. 157–185. Set Oriented Numerics and Evolutionary Computation. Springer, Heidelberg (2013)

[Kru12] Kruisselbrink, J.W.: Evolution strategies for robust optimization. Ph.D. thesis, Leiden Institute of Advanced Computer Science (LIACS), Faculty of Science, Leiden University (2012)

[NE15] Nezhinsky, A., Emmerich, M.T.M.: Parameter identification of stochastic gene regulation models by indicator-based evolutionary level set approximation. In: Proceedings of EVOLVE - A Bridge Between Probability, Set-Oriented Numerics, and Evolutionary Computation, Iasi, June 2015. Springer, Heidelberg (2015, in print)

[PCWB00] Parmee, I.C., Cvetković, D., Watson, A.H., Bonham, C.R.: Multiobjective satisfaction within an interactive evolutionary design environment. Evol. Comput. **8**(2), 197–222 (2000)

[Set99] Sethian, J.A.: Level Set Methods and Fast Marching Methods: Evolving Interfaces in Computational Geometry, Fluid Mechanics, Computer Vision, and Materials Science, vol. 3. Cambridge University Press, Cambridge (1999)

[SPB93] Solow, A., Polasky, S., Broadus, J.: On the measurement of biological diversity. J. Environ. Econ. Manag. **24**(1), 60–68 (1993)

[UBT10] Ulrich, T., Bader, J., Thiele, L.: Defining and optimizing indicator-based diversity measures in multiobjective search. In: Schaefer, R., Cotta, C., Kołodziej, J., Rudolph, G. (eds.) PPSN 2010. LNCS, vol. 6238, pp. 707–717. Springer, Heidelberg (2010). doi:10.1007/978-3-642-15844-5_71

[UT11] Ulrich, T., Thiele, L.: Maximizing population diversity in single-objective optimization. In: Proceedings of the 13th Annual Conference on Genetic and Evolutionary Computation, pp. 641–648. ACM (2011)

[vdB13] van der Burgh, B.: An evolutionary algorithm for finding diverse sets of molecules with user-defined properties. Technical report (2013)

[vdGSB08] van der Goes, V., Shir, O.M., Bäck, T.: Niche radius adaptation with asymmetric sharing. In: Rudolph, G., Jansen, T., Beume, N., Lucas, S., Poloni, C. (eds.) PPSN 2008. LNCS, vol. 5199, pp. 195–204. Springer, Heidelberg (2008). doi:10.1007/978-3-540-87700-4_20

[ZR07] Zechman, E.M., Ranjithan, R.S.: Generating alternatives using evolutionary algorithms for water resources and environmental management problems. J. Water Resour. Plan. Manag. **133**(2), 156–165 (2007)

Genetic Algorithm for Scheduling Charging Times of Electric Vehicles Subject to Time Dependent Power Availability

Carlos Mencía, María R. Sierra, Raúl Mencía, and Ramiro Varela[✉]

Department of Computer Science, University of Oviedo,
Campus of Gijón, 33204 Gijón, Spain
{menciacarlos,sierramaria,menciaraul,ramiro}@uniovi.es
http://www.di.uniovi.es/iscop

Abstract. The expected widespread adoption of electric vehicles (EVs) in the near future brings new challenges as for example that of scheduling the charging times under limited power and other technological constraints. In this paper, we tackle a scheduling problem derived from a EV charging model and control system recently proposed to organize the charging times of a large fleet of EVs. This problem may be formalized as that of scheduling a set of tasks with given processing times and due dates on a machine whose capacity varies over time. We first introduce a schedule builder and study its main properties. Then, we propose a genetic algorithm that exploits the schedule builder as decoding algorithm. Experimental results show the suitability of our approach.

Keywords: Scheduling · One machine sequencing · Electric vehicles charging · Genetic algorithm

1 Introduction

One machine sequencing problems are of great interest for the community of researchers and practitioners in scheduling. Sometimes, they appear as natural relaxations of more complex problems and so they are useful to obtain lower bounds [3]; while in other situations the resolution of some scheduling problem may be reduced to solve a number of instances of some one machine sequencing problem [2]. The later is the case of the problem considered in this paper in which a number of tasks must be scheduled on a single machine with capacity to process more than one task at a time, but whose capacity varies over time. This problem was introduced in [6] in the context of scheduling the charging times of a large fleet of Electric Vehicles (EVs).

The EV charging scheduling problem (EVCSP) considered in [6] is motivated by a charging station whose design is outlined in [10] to be installed in a community park where each user has his/her own space. Figure 1 shows the general structure and the main components of this charging station. Each space has a

© Springer International Publishing AG 2017
J.M. Ferrández Vicente et al. (Eds.): IWINAC 2017, Part I, LNCS 10337, pp. 160–169, 2017.
DOI: 10.1007/978-3-319-59740-9_16

charging point which is connected to one of the three lines of a three phase feeder. The system is controlled by a central server and a number of masters and slaves. Each slave takes control of two charging points and each master controls up to eight slaves in the same line. The control system registers events as EVs arrivals and sends activation/deactivation signals to the charging points in accordance with a schedule.

Due to the EVs arrivals being not known in advance, the EVCSP is dynamic and so that schedule must be calculated at different points over time. Furthermore, the physical characteristics and the operating mode of the charging station impose some restrictions to the EVCSP which make it really difficult to solve. In particular, the contracted power is limited and so it restricts the maximum number of EVs that may be charging (active) simultaneously in a line. Besides, the number of active EVs in the three lines must be similar to avoid an excessive imbalance among the three phases. Figure 2(a) shows a feasible schedule for the situation represented in Fig. 1; dark bars represent the EVs that are charging at time T_k and light bars represent EVs that are scheduled at a later time. In this example, the maximum number of active EVs in a line is 4 and the maximum difference in the number of active EVs in two lines is 2. For these reasons, none of the tasks 12 and 13 can be scheduled at T_k because if some of them were scheduled at this time, lines 2 and 3 would be imbalanced after completion of task 9.

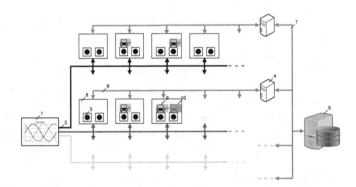

Fig. 1. General structure of the charging station. (1) Three-phase electric power 400v AC, (2) lines, (3) charging points Type 2/AC IEC 62196-2 with V2G communication interface ISO 15118, (4) masters, (5) server, (6) communication Rs 485, (7) communication TCP/IP, (8) slaves, (9) active vehicles, (10) inactive vehicles.

To solve the EVCSP, in [6] the authors proposed an algorithm which considers at each scheduling time the active EVs in each line (which cannot be rescheduled), the demanding EVs (which have not yet started to charge), the maximum number of active EVs in a line, N, and a profile of maximum load in each line $N_i(t), i = 1, 2, 3$, which is iteratively adapted to keep the imbalance among the lines under control. The objective is to schedule all the EVs in the three lines such that all the constraints are satisfied and the total tardiness, i.e.,

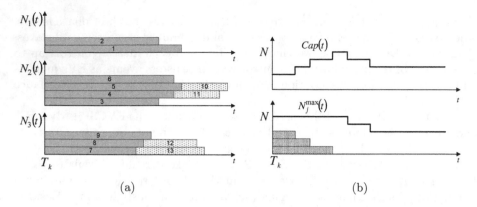

Fig. 2. (a) A feasible schedule for the problem in Fig. 1. Tasks 1–10 are the active EVs in lines 1, 2 and 3 at time T_k, while tasks 10–13 are the inactive EVs in lines 2 and 3, which are scheduled but not started to charge at time T_k. (b) Definition of the capacity of the machine $Cap(t)$ from the maximum profile $N_j(t)$ and the active EVs at time T_k.

the delay w.r.t. to the times the users want to take their EVs away, is minimized. If two of the obtained schedules are imbalanced at some time point, some of the maximum profiles $N_i(t)$ must be recalculated and a new schedule obtained for line i. The details of this process are given in [6].

Therefore, scheduling the EVs in each line, subject to the maximum load and taking into account the active EVs, may be viewed as the problem of scheduling a set of tasks on a machine with variable capacity over time. The calculation of the capacity of the machine from the active EVs and the maximum load profile is illustrated in Fig. 2(b). It is important to remark that the capacity of the machine is always a unimodal function. It is increasing at the beginning as long as the active EVs complete charging and decreasing towards the end due to the way the maximum profiles are updated. Furthermore, it finally gets stabilized at a value greater than 0, what guarantees that the scheduling problem is solvable.

This problem may be represented as $(1, Cap(t)||\sum T_i)$ in the conventional $(\alpha|\beta|\gamma)$ notation proposed in [5]. In [6] it was solved by means of the well-known *apparent tardiness cost* rule (ATC), which is usually exploited to solve scheduling problems with tardiness minimization. This is a simple priority rule that takes very low time and so it is suitable to be applied in a real time setting.

In this paper, we propose to solve this problem by means of a genetic algorithm. We first introduce a schedule builder, that allows for defining a search space to look for solutions to the problem. This schedule builder is exploited as decoder in the genetic algorithm. We conducted an experimental study, comparing the genetic algorithm with ATC and other priority rules. The results show that the genetic algorithm obtains (much) better solutions than any other method, at the cost of taking larger time; however this time is still low enough for the time requirementes of the EVCSP.

The remainder of the paper is organized as follows. In the next section we give a formal definition of the $(1, Cap(t)||\sum T_i)$ problem. Section 3 introduces a schedule builder for the problem and studies its main properties. In Sect. 4 we present the genetic algorithm designed to solve the problem. In Sect. 5 we report the results of the experimental study conducted to evaluate the proposed algorithm. Finally, in Sect. 6 we summarize the main conclusions and outline some ideas for future work.

2   Problem Definition

The $(1, Cap(t)|| \sum T_i)$ problem may be defined as follows. We are given a number of n jobs $\{1, \ldots, n\}$, all of them available at time $t = 0$, which have to be scheduled on a machine whose capacity varies over time such that $Cap(t) \geq 0, t \geq 0$, is the capacity of the machine in the interval $[t, t + 1)$. Job i has duration p_i and due date d_i. The goal is to allocate starting times $st_i, 1 \leq i \leq n$ to the jobs on the machine such that the following constraints are satisfied:

i. At any time $t \geq 0$ the number of jobs that are processed in parallel on the machine, $X(t)$, cannot exceed the capacity of the machine; i.e.,

$$X(t) \leq Cap(t). \tag{1}$$

ii. The processing of jobs on the machine cannot be preempted; i.e.,

$$C_i = st_i + p_i, \tag{2}$$

where C_i is the completion time of job i.

The objective function is the total tardiness, defined as:

$$\sum_{i=1,\ldots,n} \max(0, C_i - d_i) \tag{3}$$

which should be minimized.

In this paper, we consider that the capacity of the machine, $Cap(t)$, is a unimodal function, as this is always the case of the instances derived from the EV charging problem described in Sect. 1. In general, $Cap(t)$ is non decreasing for lower values of t until it reaches a maximum value and then it is non-increasing and gets stabilized at a value greater than 0. Figure 3 shows an example of two feasible schedules for a problem with 7 jobs and a machine with a capacity that varies between 2 and 5 over time. Due dates are not represented in the schedule. As we can observe, in both schedules $X(t) \leq Cap(t)$ for all $t \geq 0$.

One particular case of this problem is when the capacity of the machine is constant over time; i.e., $Cap(t) = P$. This is the problem considered in [7], which is denoted $(P|| \sum T_i)$ and proven to be NP-hard.

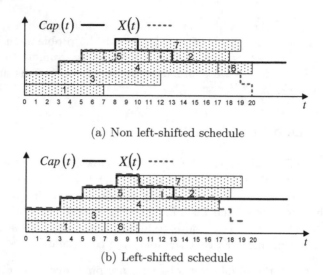

(a) Non left-shifted schedule

(b) Left-shifted schedule

Fig. 3. Two feasible schedules for an instance of the $(1, Cap(t) || \sum T_i)$ problem with 7 tasks and a machine with capacity varying between 2 and 5.

3   Schedule Builder

Schedule builders constitute an essential component for designing efficient scheduling algorithms. Also known as *schedule generation schemes*, these methods provide a way for computing and enumerating a subset of the feasible schedules, thus enabling the definition of a search space to look for solutions to the problem. We propose a schedule builder that produces all possible *left-shifted schedules* for a given problem instance, which can be formally defined as follows:

Definition 1 (Left-Shift Movement). *Let S be a feasible schedule, determined by starting times $st_1, st_2, ..., st_n$. A left-shift movement on job k is an operation that results in the feasible schedule S' with starting times $st'_1, st'_2, ..., st'_k, ..., st'_n$, such that $st'_k < st_k$ and $st'_i = st_i$ for $i \neq k$.*

Given a feasible schedule, a left-shift movement consists in scheduling a job earlier without altering the starting time of any other jobs, as long as the capacity constraints are satisfied. For example, we could apply a left-shift movement to job 6 in the schedule shown in Fig. 3(a) moving it earlier to time 7. This operation would result in the schedule shown in Fig. 3(b). The repeated application of left-shift movements until reaching a fixed point results in a left-shifted schedule:

Definition 2 (Left-Shifted Schedule). *Let S be a feasible schedule. S is said to be a left-shifted schedule if it does not admit any left-shift movement.*

Figure 3(b) is an example of a left-shifted schedule, since no job can be scheduled earlier without changing the starting time of some other job.

Algorithm 1. Schedule Builder

Data: A $(1, Cap(t)||\sum T_i)$ problem instance $\mathcal{P}$.
Result: A feasible schedule S for $\mathcal{P}$.
$US \leftarrow \{1, 2, ..., n\}$;
$X(t) \leftarrow 0; \forall t \geq 0$;
while $US \neq \emptyset$ **do**

> Non-deterministically pick job $u \in US$;
> Assign $st_u = min\{t'|\forall t$ with $t' \leq t < t' + p_u : X(t) < Cap(t)\}$;
> Update $X(t) \leftarrow X(t) + 1; \forall t$ with $st_u \leq t < st_u + p_u$;
> $US \leftarrow US - \{u\}$;

end
return *Feasible schedule $S = (st_1, st_2, ..., st_n)$;*

The proposed schedule builder is depicted in Algorithm 1. This method schedules one operation at a time, assigning it the earliest possible starting time so
that the total consumption does not exceed the capacity of the machine at any
instant. The algorithm maintains a set US with the *unscheduled* jobs that need
to be assigned a starting time, as well as the consumption $X(t)$ due to the jobs
scheduled so far. US is initialized with all the jobs, and $X(t)$ is initially set to
0 for all instants t in the scheduling horizon. Then, iteratively until all the jobs
have been scheduled, it selects one unscheduled job and assigns it the earliest
starting time so that the machine has enough capacity left during the processing
time of the job. After scheduling a job, US and $X(t)$ are updated accordingly.

Note that the selection of a job to be scheduled at each iteration is non-
deterministic. Regardless of this, we can guarantee that the application of
Algorithm 1 always results in a feasible left-shifted schedule. For example, the
sequence of choices $(1, 3, 4, 5, 6, 7, 2)$ would lead to building the schedule in
Fig. 3(b). It is easy to see that, since all the jobs are available at time 0, if
we consider all possible choices in this step we would obtain a search space characterized by the set of all left-shifted schedules. The schedule builder could also
be instantiated by using any priority rule or heuristic, or used as a decoder in a
genetic algorithm as we will see in the next section.

An important property of the search space defined by the schedule builder
is that it is *dominant*, i.e. it contains at least one optimal schedule for any
$(1, Cap(t)||\sum T_i)$ instance. This follows from the next result:

Proposition 1. *Let $\mathcal{S}^*$ be the set of all optimal schedules for a given
$(1, Cap(t)||\sum T_i)$ problem instance $\mathcal{P}$. There exists a left-shifted schedule $S \in \mathcal{S}*$.*

Proof. Let $S' \in \mathcal{S}^*$ be a non left-shifted optimal schedule. S' is not left-shifted,
so it admits a sequence of left-shift movements, each resulting in a feasible schedule $S'_1, ..., S'_k$, where S'_k is left-shifted. Since each left-shift operation schedules
earlier one job, leaving the other ones unaltered, the value of the total tardiness
$\sum_{i=1,...,n} max(0, C_i - d_i)$ cannot increase from one schedule to the next one in
the sequence. The resulting left-shifted schedule S'_k has the same total tardiness
than that of S', which is optimal. Therefore, $S'_k \in \mathcal{S}^*$.

Algorithm 2. Genetic Algorithm.

Data: A $(1, Cap(t) || \sum T_i)$ problem instance $\mathcal{P}$ and a set of parameters: crossover probability P_c, mutation probability P_m, number of generations #*gen* and population size #*popsize*.

Result: A feasible schedule for $\mathcal{P}$

Generate and evaluate the initial population $P(0)$;

for $t=1$ *to* #*gen-1* **do**

> **Selection:** organize the chromosomes in $P(t-1)$ into pairs at random;
> **Recombination:** mate each pair of chromosomes and mutate the two offsprings in accordance with P_c and P_m;
> **Evaluation:** evaluate the resulting chromosomes;
> **Replacement:** make a tournament selection among every two parents and their offsprings to complete $P(t)$;

end

return *the best schedule built so far*;

---

4 Genetic Algorithm for the $(1, Cap(t) || \sum T_i)$ Problem

Genetic algorithms (GAs) have been used to solve hard scheduling problems with notable success (some recent examples include [1, 8, 9]). In this section, we review the main components of the GA proposed in this work for the $(1, Cap(t) || \sum T_i)$ problem. Algorithm 2 shows its main structure: it is a generational genetic algorithm with random selection and replacement by tournament among parents and offsprings, which confers the GA an implicit form of elitism. We describe the main components of the GA:

Coding Schema. Individuals are defined each by a permutation of the jobs without repetition, i.e. a chromosome c is such that $c = (c_1, ..., c_n)$, where $c_i \in \{1, ..., n\}$ and $c_i \neq c_j$ for all $i \neq j$. Permutation-based encodings are common in scheduling, and allow for a number of effective genetic operators.

Crossover and Mutation. The GA uses the well-known *Order Crossover* operator (OX) [4]. Given two parents, an offspring inherits a sub-sequence (selected at random) in the same positions from the first parent and its other positions are filled in accordance with their relative order in the second parent. The second offspring is computed in the same way, but swapping the role of the parents. The mutation operator simply swaps two random elements in the chromosome.

Decoding Algorithm. The GA searches for an optimal solution in the search space defined by the schedule builder presented in Sect. 3. Given a chromosome, the decoder builds a schedule using Algorithm 1, scheduling jobs in the order they appear in the chromosome, i.e. at the *ith* iteration it schedules job c_i. For example, the chromosome $(1, 3, 4, 5, 6, 7, 2)$ would result in the schedule shown in Fig. 3(b). The chromosome $(3, 1, 4, 5, 6, 7, 2)$ would lead to the same schedule. So, the mapping is many-to-one. Once a schedule has been built, its total tardiness is taken as the fitness value of the corresponding chromosome.

5   Experimental Study

We have conducted an experimental study aimed at assessing the performance of the proposed GA and evaluating the quality of the solutions it obtains. To this aim, we implemented a prototype in Python 2.7, and ran a series of experiments on a Linux cluster.

For comparison purposes, our prototype also implements some well-known priority rules, often used in scheduling, such as *earliest due date* (EDD), *shortest processing time* (SPT), and *apparent tardiness cost* (ATC). These priority rules are integrated in Algorithm 1 and serve to select the job to be scheduled at each iteration (among the unscheduled ones): EDD picks the operation with the smallest due date, SPT selects the one with the least duration and ATC chooses the job j that maximizes the expression:

$$\Pi_j = \frac{1}{p_j} exp\left[\frac{-max(0, d_j - \Gamma(\alpha) - p_j)}{g\bar{p}}\right], \tag{4}$$

where $\Gamma(\alpha)$ denotes the earliest possible starting time among the unscheduled jobs, $\bar{p}$ refers to the average processing times of the jobs and g is a look-ahead parameter to be introduced by the user.

The experiments were carried out over 12 sets of instances, with the number of jobs $n \in \{15, 30, 45, 60\}$ and the maximum capacity of the machine $MC \in \{3, 5, 7\}$. For each configuration we generated 10 random instances, so we have 120 instances in all. The instances were built using uniform distributions: processing times $p_i \in [1, 100]$; for a job i its due date $d_i \in [p_i, max(p_i+2, \sum p_j/2)]$ the machine capacity is a unimodal function with each interval taking a duration in the range $[1, \sum p_j/MC]$. All the sampled values are integers.

Each instance was solved using EDD, SPT, ATC with parameter $g \in \{0.25, 0.5, 0.75, 1.0\}$, as was done in [6], and the GA with parameters $\#popsize = 250$, $\#gen = 300$, $Pc = 0.9$ and $Pm = 0.1$. It is important to remark that for GA, the initial population is generated at random.

Table 1. Summary of results. Error (in percentage) of the solutions returned by each method w.r.t. the best solutions known, averaged for groups of instances with the same number of jobs. Running times of GA are given in seconds.

n	EDD	SPT	ATC				GA		
			0.25	0.5	0.75	1.0	Best	Avg	Time
15	42.59	382.51	25.02	24.24	33.15	55.08	0.00	0.01	13.13
30	18.94	524.98	6.49	5.26	5.97	8.21	0.00	0.09	21.49
45	27.76	1146.33	11.84	13.27	12.65	23.31	0.00	0.85	30.22
60	36.28	3895.37	14.59	15.09	18.47	29.48	0.00	1.47	38.48
Avg	31.42	1526.90	14.40	14.37	17.80	29.02	0.00	0.60	25.83

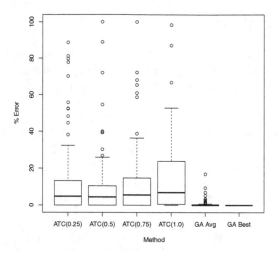

Fig. 4. Comparison of ATC and GA regarding the average error in percentage terms w.r.t. the best known solutions.

Table 1 compares the different approaches regarding the quality of the solutions computed. It shows the relative error in percentage terms of the cost of the solution returned by each approach w.r.t. to that of the best solution known for each problem instance. The results are averaged for groups of instances with the same number of jobs. The GA was run 10 times on each problem instance, and the best and average costs over the 10 runs are shown in the table, as well as the average solving time for one run (in seconds). As we can observe, for all the instances, the best known solution is given by the best solution found by GA over the 10 runs. Among the priority rules, the best method overall is ATC, with $g \in \{0.25, 0.5\}$; EDD is in average slightly worse than ATC in its worse configuration (with $g = 1.0$) and SPT performs very poorly. It is important to note that the reported errors for the priority rules are in general rather large, which means the GA finds (much) better solutions. Also, the average solutions of the GA over the 10 runs are in general very close to the best one, with an average improvement of one order of magnitude w.r.t. the best priority rule, in many cases being this improvement greater. Regarding running times, priority rules are clearly faster (taking negligible time), but the GA is quite efficient, taking less than 40 s for the largest instances. Also, note that the prototype was coded in Python, and an implementation in C or C++ would be expected to achieve very significant time reductions.

Figure 4 shows the errors achieved by ATC in its four configurations, and by GA. For the sake of clarity, the y-axis was limited to 100, although all the configurations of ATC included some values above this limit. This plot confirms the superiority of GA over ATC regarding the quality of the solutions computed.

6   Conclusions

In this paper we study the $(1, Cap(t) || \sum T_i)$ problem, which was recently proposed in the context of scheduling the charging times of a fleet of electric vehicles under time dependent power availability [6]. This problem consists in scheduling a set of jobs on a machine whose capacity varies over time. We propose a schedule builder which guarantees the possibility of finding an optimal solution to the problem. This schedule builder is then exploited by a genetic algorithm. The results from an experimental study show that the GA algorithm reaches high-quality solutions in short time.

A promising line for future research would be to investigate the heuristic generation of the initial population, enabling the genetic algorithm to reach better solutions and converge faster. Also, the development of local search methods for this problem seems a promising research avenue.

Acknowledgements. This research has been supported by the Spanish Government under research project TIN2016-79190-R.

References

1. Ahn, S., Lee, S., Bahn, H.: A smart elevator scheduler that considers dynamic changes of energy cost and user traffic. Integr. Comput.-Aided Eng. (on-line first) **24**(2), 187–202 (2017)
2. Balas, E., Simonetti, N., Vazacopoulos, A.: Job shop scheduling with setup times, deadlines and precedence constraints. J. Sched. **11**, 253–262 (2008)
3. Carlier, J.: The one-machine sequencing problem. Eur. J. Oper. Res. **11**, 42–47 (1982)
4. Davis, L.: Applying adaptive algorithms to epistatic domains. In: IJCAI, pp. 162–164 (1985). http://ijcai.org/Proceedings/85-1/Papers/029.pdf
5. Graham, R., Lawler, E., Lenstra, J., Kan, A.: Optimization and approximation in deterministic sequencing and scheduling: a survey. Ann. Discret. Math. **5**, 287–326 (1979)
6. Hernández-Arauzo, A., Puente, J., Varela, R., Sedano, J.: Electric vehicle charging under power and balance constraints as dynamic scheduling. Comput. Ind. Eng. **85**, 306–315 (2015)
7. Koulamas, C.: The total tardiness problem: review and extensions. Oper. Res. **42**, 1025–1041 (1994)
8. Kyriklidis, C., Dounias, G.: Evolutionary computation for resource leveling optimization in project management. Integr. Comput.-Aided Eng. **23**(2), 161–172 (2016)
9. Mencía, R., Sierra, M.R., Mencía, C., Varela, R.: Genetic algorithms for the scheduling problem with arbitrary precedence relations and skilled operators. Integr. Comput.-Aided Eng. **23**(3), 269–285 (2016)
10. Sedano, J., Portal, M., Hernández-Arauzo, A., Villar, J.R., Puente, J., Varela, R.: Intelligent system for electric vehicle charging: design and operation. DYNA **88**(6), 640–647 (2013)

Simulation of a Dynamic Prey-Predator Spatial Model Based on Cellular Automata Using the Behavior of the Metaheuristic African Buffalo Optimization

Boris Almonacid[✉]

Pontificia Universidad Católica de Valparaíso, Valparaíso, Chile
boris.almonacid.g@mail.pucv.cl
http://inf.ucv.cl/~balmonacid

Abstract. A dynamic population model of 2-dimensional lattice based on Cellular Automata and metaheuristics is used to simulate prey-predator behavior. The equations of movement from metaheuristics African Buffalo Optimization (ABO) are used for the behavior of the migration of predators. The simulations describes that a difference in the learning factors used by the ABO metaheuristic, increases the possibility of prey survival.

Keywords: Spatial dynamics · Cellular Automata · Swarm intelligence · African Buffalo Optimization · Animal Behavior · Simulation

1 Introduction

Models based on Cellular Automata [4,19] are a support tool because of their ability to be able to describe in detail the approximations of the increase or decrease of a species [5–8]. Being able to determine future scenarios entails being able to determine from another point of view, which land could be a priority to focus conservation resources [1–3,9]. These population simulation models should be simple in order to be treatable and be able to modify internal aspects quickly. To do this, the equations of motion of the ABO metaheuristic will be used in the dynamic simulation model.

African Buffalo Optimization (ABO) is a metaheuristic based on the behavior of the African buffalos [12,14]. There are several investigations using ABO. As a comparative study of ABO and randomized insertion algorithm for asymmetric Travelling Salesman's Problem (TSP) [15]. Numerical Function Optimization Solutions using the ABO [13]. Solving the TSP using the ABO [10,16]. ABO and the randomized insertion algorithm for the asymmetric TSP [11]. ABO for PID parameters tuning of Automatic Voltage Regulators [18]. ABO approach to the Design of PID Controller in Automatic Voltage Regulator System [17].

© Springer International Publishing AG 2017
J.M. Ferrández Vicente et al. (Eds.): IWINAC 2017, Part I, LNCS 10337, pp. 170–180, 2017.
DOI: 10.1007/978-3-319-59740-9_17

The scope of the research is perform a simulation of a Dynamic Prey-Predator Spatial Model based on Cellular Automata using the behavior of the metaheuristic African Buffalo Optimization. These contributions, to our knowledge, have not been reported yet.

This paper is organized in this way: In Sect. 2 the theory of Cellular Automata is revised. In Sect. 3 explains the African Buffalo Optimization algorithm. In Sect. 4 describes how to implement the Model Prey-Predator Dynamics via ABO. In Sect. 5 explains the experiments and discussion. Finally, in Sect. 6 concludes and provides guidelines for future work.

2   Cellular Automata

A Cellular Automaton (CA) is a type of model system of cellular objects that have the following characteristics:

– Cells (individuals) live on a grid of a finite number n of dimensions.
– Each cell in the grid has a state. The number of state possibilities is typically finite. For example, a cell can have two possibilities: 1 or 0, *on* or *off*, *alive* or *dead*.
– Each cell has a neighborhood. The neighborhood can be defined in different ways, but it is typically a list of adjacent cells.

2.1   Formal Definition

A cellular automaton is defined by the tuple $A = (d, Q, N, f)$, where:

– $d \in \mathbb{Z}^+$, is the d-dimension of the euclidean lattice $L \subseteq \mathbb{Z}^d$.
– $\mathbb{Q}$ is a finite set of states.
– N is a d-dimensional neighborhood vector $N = (n_1, n_2, \ldots, n_m)$, where each $n_i \in \mathbb{Z}^d$ and $n_i \neq n_j$.
– $f : \mathbb{Q}^m \rightarrow \mathbb{Q}$ is a local transition function that specifies the new state of a cell, taking into account the states of its neighbors.

A configuration of a d-dimensional cellular automaton is a function $c : \mathbb{Z}^d \rightarrow \mathbb{Q}$, that assigns a state to each cell in the lattice. The state of cell $n \in \mathbb{Z}^d$ at time t is given by $c^t(n)$, the set of all configurations is defined by $\mathbb{Q}^{\mathbb{Z}^d}$. The local transition function causes a global change in the configuration of the cellular automata. The configuration c is changed into configuration c', where for all $n \in \mathbb{Z}^d$: $c'(n) = f[c(n+n_1), c(n+n_2), \ldots, c(n+n_m)]$. The transformation $c \rightarrow c'$ is the global transition function of the cellular automaton, which is defined as $G : \mathbb{Q}^{\mathbb{Z}^d} \rightarrow \mathbb{Q}^{\mathbb{Z}^d}$.

In a 2-dimensional cellular automaton the Moore neighborhood is often used, it comprises the cell to evolve and its 8 nearest neighbors. It can be generalized as the d-dimensional M_r^d neighborhood defined as $M_r^d = \{n_i \in \mathbb{Z}^d | n_i = (n_{i1}, \ldots, n_{id}), n_{ij} \leq r\}$, where r is the radius of the neighborhood.

3   African Buffalo Optimization

African Buffalo Optimization (ABO) is a stochastic metaheuristic population algorithm. The ABO is inspired by the behavior of African buffalo, mainly in the migration of the herd. The migration of buffaloes has as main aim to find better lands for grazing. Finding good areas with lots of grass are considered as good solutions to solve an optimization problem. For this, they tend to follow the movement of the rainy seasons. To find good herbs the buffalo can be organized through two basic modes of communication: The "waaa" warning sound indicates the presence of hazards or lack of good grazing fields. It also allows animals to explore other places that may be more beneficial. The "maaa" alert sound is used to say a grazing area with a good benefit to the herd. It is also an indication that the animals continue to take advantage of the resources that are available.

3.1   African Buffalo Optimization Algorithm

The ABO steps are detailed in Algorithm 1.

Algorithm 1. African Buffalo Optimization algorithm

input : $N, \lambda, lp1, lp2$.
output: A solution.

1 Initialize the parameters: N, λ, $lp1$ and $lp2$.
2 Generate random and feasible solutions of N buffaloes in a search space.
3 **while** *the criterion of the term has not ended* **do**
4   **for** *all buffaloes* **do**
5   Update the buffaloes using the equation 1.
6   Update the location w_k using the equation 2.
7   **if** *the problem is minimization* **then**
8   **if** *fitness m_k < fitness $bpmax_k$* **then**
9   Update the $bpmax_k$.
10   **end**
11   **else**
12   **if** *fitness m_k > fitness $bpmax_k$* **then**
13   Update the $bpmax_k$.
14   **end**
15   **end**
16   **end**
17   Update $bgmax$ from the best solution obtained from $bpmax$ solutions.
18 **end**
19 Output the best solution.

The description of the parameters used in line 1 of the algorithm are described below:

- Number of buffaloes. Defined by the variable N.
- The Index k for the buffaloes, with k in $\{1, \ldots, N\}$.
- The lambda λ value with a domain in $[-1, 1]$, excluding the zero.
- The learning factors $lp1$ and $lp2$.

In the line 5, the Eq. 1 is used. The m_k variable represent the exploitation move. The $bgmax_k$ variable is the herd's best fitness. The $bpmax_k$ variable is the individual buffalo k best found location. Finally, the w_k variable represent the exploration move.

$$m_{k+1} = m_k + lp1(bgmax - w_k) + lp2(bpmax_k - w_k) \qquad (1)$$

In the line 6, the Eq. 2 represents when the location of buffalo k is update.

$$w_{k+1} = \frac{(w_k + m_k)}{\pm \lambda} \qquad (2)$$

4 Dynamic Prey-Predator Spatial Model via African Buffalo Optimization

The dynamic prey-predator model simulates as a theoretical population of prey and living predators [5]. For the model, the following concepts have been defined.

Lattice Definition: The lattice $L \subseteq \mathbb{Z}^2$ used has the shape of a torus. The values of allowed states for each cell is $\mathbb{Q} = \{0, 1, 2, 3\}$, where:

- 0 is an empty cell.
- 1 is a cell inhabited by a prey.
- 2 is a cell inhabited by a predator.
- 3 is a cell that containing a prey and a predator at the same.

Cellular Automata Definition: There are two types of Cellular Automata. Predators (buffaloes) and prey (grasslands). Predators are those who use the behavior of ABO metaheuristic. They have been designed in such a way to support an extra group of variables (see left Fig. 1). Prey are those that use the behavior determined by the prey-predator dynamic model rules (see right Fig. 1).

Season Definition: The model is composed of a life cycle that has the following stages or seasons (see Fig. 2).

Intraspecific competition. Preys die with a probability proportional to the number of individuals of the prey species surrounding them, this rule uses M_{rc}^d neighborhood. If $c^t(n) = 1$, the probability of death is given by $p(death) = \frac{\alpha y}{m}$, where α is the intraspecific competence factor, y is the number of preys in the neighborhood, and m is the number of neighbor ($m = |M_{rc}^d|$). The value of $bgmax$ is updated according to Eq. 2.

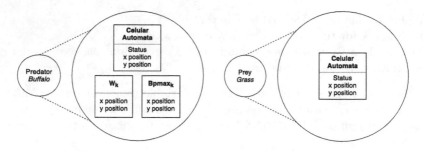

Fig. 1. Cellular Automata with African Buffalo Optimization.

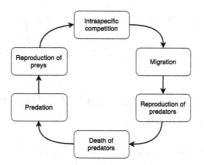

Fig. 2. Season - life cycle.

Migration. During this stage, the predators (buffalos) move within the space of the lattice according to their own experience and the experience of the herd. To perform the migration of a predator, the new position (x, y) is calculated according to Eqs. 3 and 4.

$$
\begin{aligned}
m(x)_{k+1} &= m(x)_k + lp1(bgmax(x) - w(x)_k) + lp2(bpmax(x)_k - w(x)_k) \\
w(x)_{k+1} &= \frac{(w(x)_k + m(x)_k)}{\lambda}
\end{aligned}
\tag{3}
$$

$$
\begin{aligned}
m(y)_{k+1} &= m(y)_k + lp1(bgmax(y) - w(y)_k) + lp2(bpmax(y)_k - w(y)_k) \\
w(y)_{k+1} &= \frac{(w(y)_k + m(y)_k)}{\lambda}
\end{aligned}
\tag{4}
$$

Finally, the value of $bgmax$ is updated according to Algorithm 2.

Reproduction of predators. At this stage, each predator creates new individuals at random within the neighborhood.

Death of predators. Predators that do not have a prey in a cell (Cellular Automata with state equal to 2), die from starvation.

Predation. Preys that share a cell with a predator die due to the predator's action (Cellular Automata with state equal to 3).

Reproduction of preys. At this stage, each prey creates new individuals at random within the neighborhood.

Algorithm 2. Calculate bgmax

---

    input : Predators.
    output: bgmax_x and bgmax_y.

1 Initialize the aux variables: $max\_number\_prey = 0, bgmax\_x = 0$ and
    $bgmax\_y = 0$.
2 Generate random and feasible solutions of N buffaloes in a search space.
3 **while** *the criterion of the term has not ended* **do**
4   **for** *all N predators (buffaloes)* **do**
5        $predator\_k \leftarrow$ get predator k in the lattice.
6        $number\_prey \leftarrow$ get number of neighbor of $predator\_k$ by Moore
7   Neighborhood.
8   **if** $max\_number\_prey < number_p rey$ **then**
9           $bgmax\_x \leftarrow$ Get x value of the $predator\_k$.
10           $bgmax\_y \leftarrow$ Get y value of the $predator\_k$.
11           $max\_number\_prey \leftarrow number\_prey$.
12   **end**
13   **end**
14 **end**

---

5   Experiments and Discussion

This section details the experiment performed and the observations found in the simulations.

Implementation: All simulation were coded in Java version 1.8.0_92 using IntelliJ IDEA 15 (15.0.6). For running the Dynamics Prey-Predator model we using Java(TM) SE Runtime Environment (build 1.8.0_92). The hardware features that have been run instances are a MacBook Pro computer (Retina, 13-inch, Late 2013), with an Intel Core i5 2,4 GHz, 4 GB RAM 1600 MHz DDR3. Running OS X El Capitan version 10.11.6 (15G1004).

Model Configuration: The experimental parameters using for the model are described in the Table 1.

Metaheuristic Configuration: The experimental parameters using for the ABO metaheuristic are described in the Table 2.

Table 1. Dynamic prey-predator model parameters

Prey	Value	Predator	Value
Initial density	1000	Initial density	5
Reproductive capacity	1	Reproductive capacity	3
Radius reproduction neighborhood	3	Radius reproduction neighborhood	1
Intraspecific competition coefficient	0.05	Radius update bgmax	1
Radius competition neighborhood	3		

Table 2. Metaheuristic parameters

Parameter	Case A	Case B	Case C	Case D	Case E
$lp1$	1	2	3	4	5
$lp2$	1	2	3	4	5
$lambda$	0.5	0.5	0.5	0.5	0.5

Simulation 1: This simulation uses the parameters of Table 1 and the parameters of Case E of Table 2. The Table 3 show the results for the simulation. Column ID is the identifier for each row. Column ID-S is the identifier for each season. Column ID-SS is the identifier for each step in the season. Column Name-SS Corresponds to the name of each step of the simulation. Column ID-M corresponds to the identifier for the migration (the simulation have five migration). Column N-Prey and N-Predator shows the number of predator in the lattice. Column N-S0, N-S1, N-S2 and N-S3, describes the number of the different types of states in the lattice.

Simulation 2 - Five Configurations: A set of simulations were carried out using the 5 cases of parameters described in Table 2. The Table 4 shows the initial amount of prey and predators. Subsequently, after 10 seasons have elapsed, the number of prey and predators has been extracted again. The results in general terms for cases A, B, C and D are that a low number of prey and a high population of predators. On the other hand, in the case E, a balance of dams and predators has been observed in the final stage of the simulation, even more prey has been obtained than predators. The important point of why this difference occurred is the value of the parameters of the ABO metaheuristic. The parameters that have given this behavior in case E are $lp1$ and $lp2$, both with the value 5.

Table 3. Simulation 1

ID	ID-S	ID-SS	Name-SS	ID-M	N-Prey	N-Pred	N-S0	N-S1	N-S2	N-S3
1	1	1	Intraspecific competition	-	710	5	1785	710	5	0
2	1	2	Migration	1	710	5	1789	706	1	4
3	1	3	Migration	2	710	5	1789	706	1	4
4	1	4	Migration	3	710	5	1789	706	1	4
5	1	5	Migration	4	710	5	1789	706	1	4
6	1	6	Migration	5	710	5	1789	706	1	4
7	1	7	Reproduction of predators	-	710	204	1648	648	142	62
8	1	8	Death of predators	-	710	121	1731	648	59	62
9	1	9	Predation	-	648	121	1731	648	121	0
10	1	10	Reproduction of preys	-	1422	121	957	1422	121	0
11	2	1	Intraspecific competition	-	1256	121	1123	1256	121	0
12	2	2	Migration	1	1256	121	1122	1257	112	9
13	2	3	Migration	2	1256	121	1122	1257	112	9
14	2	4	Migration	3	1256	121	1122	1257	112	9
15	2	5	Migration	4	1256	121	1122	1257	112	9
16	2	6	Migration	5	1256	121	1122	1257	112	9
17	2	7	Reproduction of predators	-	1256	402	960	1138	274	128
18	2	8	Death of predators	-	1256	266	1096	1138	138	128
19	2	9	Predation	-	1133	266	1096	1138	266	0
20	2	10	Reproduction of preys	-	1640	266	589	1645	266	0
21	3	1	Intraspecific competition	-	1507	266	722	1512	266	0
22	3	2	Migration	1	1507	266	722	1512	259	7
23	3	3	Migration	2	1507	266	722	1512	259	7
24	3	4	Migration	3	1507	266	722	1512	259	7
25	3	5	Migration	4	1507	266	722	1512	259	7
26	3	6	Migration	5	1507	266	722	1512	259	7
27	3	7	Reproduction of predators	-	1507	460	609	1431	372	88
28	3	8	Death of predators	-	1507	330	739	1431	242	88
29	3	9	Predation	-	1424	330	739	1431	330	0
30	3	10	Reproduction of preys	-	1782	330	381	1789	330	0
31	4	1	Intraspecific competition	-	1635	330	528	1642	330	0
32	4	2	Migration	1	1635	330	523	1647	327	3
33	4	3	Migration	2	1635	330	523	1647	327	3
34	4	4	Migration	3	1635	330	523	1647	327	3
35	4	5	Migration	4	1635	330	523	1647	327	3
36	4	6	Migration	5	1635	330	523	1647	327	3
37	4	7	Reproduction of predators	-	1635	475	424	1601	426	49
38	4	8	Death of predators	-	1635	365	534	1601	316	49
39	4	9	Predation	-	1592	365	534	1601	365	0
40	4	10	Reproduction of preys	-	1828	365	298	1837	365	0
41	5	1	Intraspecific competition	-	1684	365	442	1693	365	0
42	5	2	Migration	1	1684	365	440	1695	360	5
43	5	3	Migration	2	1684	365	440	1695	360	5
44	5	4	Migration	3	1684	365	440	1695	360	5
45	5	5	Migration	4	1684	365	440	1695	360	5
46	5	6	Migration	5	1684	365	440	1695	360	5
47	5	7	Reproduction of predators	-	1684	472	359	1669	441	31
48	5	8	Death of predators	-	1684	380	451	1669	349	31
49	5	9	Predation	-	1659	380	451	1669	380	0
50	5	10	Reproduction of preys	-	1848	380	262	1858	380	0

Table 4. Simulation 2 - five configurations

ID	Case	ID-Case	Star season						End season					
			N-Prey	N-Pred	S0	S1	S2	S4	N-Prey	N-Pred	S0	S1	S2	S3
1	A	1	674	5	1821	674	5	0	5	1366	1077	57	1366	0
2		2	664	5	1831	664	5	0	50	1374	952	174	1374	0
3		3	677	5	1818	677	5	0	28	1397	950	153	1397	0
4		4	676	5	1819	676	5	0	0	1375	1093	32	1375	0
5		5	674	5	1821	674	5	0	28	1381	977	142	1381	0
6		6	658	5	1837	658	5	0	3	1385	1065	50	1385	0
7		7	665	5	1830	665	5	0	0	1387	1062	51	1387	0
8		8	688	5	1807	688	5	0	54	1357	952	191	1357	0
9		9	660	5	1835	660	5	0	8	1380	1047	73	1380	0
10		10	689	5	1806	689	5	0	91	1357	906	237	1357	0
11	B	1	687	5	1808	687	5	0	226	1280	766	454	1280	0
12		2	682	5	1813	682	5	0	20	1363	1027	110	1363	0
13		3	667	5	1828	667	5	0	271	1288	709	503	1288	0
14		4	689	5	1806	689	5	0	0	1365	1101	34	1365	0
15		5	641	5	1854	641	5	0	0	1383	1060	57	1383	0
16		6	681	5	1814	681	5	0	0	1370	1088	42	1370	0
17		7	684	5	1811	684	5	0	65	1361	945	194	1361	0
18		8	677	5	1818	677	5	0	12	1396	1024	80	1396	0
19		9	680	5	1815	680	5	0	120	1323	842	335	1323	0
20		10	687	5	1808	687	5	0	35	1386	991	123	1386	0
21	C	1	670	5	1825	670	5	0	830	989	315	1196	989	0
22		2	653	5	1842	653	5	0	0	1365	1056	79	1365	0
23		3	662	5	1833	662	5	0	69	1378	895	227	1378	0
24		4	687	5	1808	687	5	0	5	1363	1057	80	1363	0
25		5	675	5	1820	675	5	0	92	1359	907	234	1359	0
26		6	676	5	1819	676	5	0	9	1388	1060	52	1388	0
27		7	677	5	1818	677	5	0	5	1409	1019	72	1409	0
28		8	645	5	1850	645	5	0	0	1363	1088	49	1363	0
29		9	671	5	1824	671	5	0	34	1328	1033	139	1328	0
30		10	664	5	1831	664	5	0	28	1390	982	128	1390	0
31	D	1	672	5	1823	672	5	0	10	1369	1027	104	1369	0
32		2	675	5	1820	675	5	0	544	1177	504	819	1177	0
33		3	694	5	1801	694	5	0	301	1258	683	559	1258	0
34		4	683	5	1812	683	5	0	40	1372	995	133	1372	0
35		5	644	5	1851	644	5	0	23	1377	991	132	1377	0
36		6	675	5	1820	675	5	0	1	1388	1057	55	1388	0
37		7	683	5	1812	683	5	0	2	1390	1063	47	1390	0
38		8	667	5	1828	667	5	0	7	1402	1030	68	1402	0
39		9	681	5	1814	681	5	0	4	1378	1055	67	1378	0
40		10	662	5	1833	662	5	0	2	1425	1029	46	1425	0
41	E	1	688	5	1807	688	5	0	1176	851	466	1183	851	0
42		2	674	5	1821	674	5	0	1768	494	229	1777	494	0
43		3	664	5	1831	664	5	0	265	1380	846	274	1380	0
44		4	678	5	1817	678	5	0	129	1465	900	135	1465	0
45		5	659	5	1836	659	5	0	404	1307	784	409	1307	0
46		6	690	5	1805	690	5	0	670	1165	659	676	1165	0
47		7	649	5	1846	649	5	0	71	1451	975	74	1451	0
48		8	652	5	1843	652	5	0	827	1053	619	828	1053	0
49		9	671	5	1824	671	5	0	104	1453	940	107	1453	0
50		10	663	5	1832	663	5	0	1548	637	295	1568	637	0

6   Conclusions

In this research we have considered simulations of a dynamic prey-predator model using the equations of movement of the ABO metaheuristic. The learning factors ($lp1$ and $lp2$) of ABO metaheuristics have been found to modify population density for both prey and predator. In discrete learning factors between 1 and 4 for $lp1$ and $lp2$, preys have to decrease and predators to increase their population. Instead with the learning factor $lp1$ with a value of 5, the preys and predators have a balance. As future research lines, dynamic learning factors can be implemented in the ABO. In addition to being able to integrate other metaheuristics in the dynamic prey-predator model. On the other hand, these models can be integrated in the area of biodiversity conservation. In which several cases of studies can be analyzed to determine new conservation areas.

Acknowledgements. Boris Almonacid is supported by Postgraduate Grant Pontificia Universidad Católica de Valparaíso, Chile (VRIEA 2016 and INF-PUCV 2015); by Animal Behavior Society, USA (Developing Nations Research Awards 2016) and by Ph.D (h.c) Sonia Alvarez, Chile. Also, we thank the anonymous reviewers for their constructive comments.

References

1. Deguignet, M., Juffe-Bignoli, D., Harrison, J., MacSharry, B., Burgess, N., Kingston, N.: United Nations List of Protected Areas. UNEP-WCMC, Cambridge (2014)
2. Hadley, M.: A practical ecology the man and the biosphere (MAB) programme. Sixty Years of Science at UNESCO, p. 260 (2006)
3. Ishwaran, N.: Science in intergovernmental environmental relations: 40 years of unesco's man and the biosphere (MAB) programme and its future. Environ. Dev. **1**(1), 91–101 (2012)
4. Kari, J.: Theory of cellular automata: a survey. Theoret. Comput. Sci. **334**(1–3), 3–33 (2005)
5. Martínez-Molina, M., Moreno-Armendáriz, M.A., Cruz-Cortés, N., Seck Tuoh Mora, J.C.: Modeling prey-predator dynamics via particle swarm optimization and cellular automata. In: Batyrshin, I., Sidorov, G. (eds.) MICAI 2011. LNCS, vol. 7095, pp. 189–200. Springer, Heidelberg (2011). doi:10.1007/978-3-642-25330-0_17
6. Molina, M.M., Moreno-Armendariz, M.A., Cruz-Cortes, N., Mora, J.C.S.T.: Prey-predator dynamics and swarm intelligence on a cellular automata model. Appl. Comput. Math **11**(2), 243–256 (2012)
7. Molina, M.M., Moreno-Armendáriz, M.A., Mora, J.C.S.T.: On the spatial dynamics and oscillatory behavior of a predator-prey model based on cellular automata and local particle swarm optimization. J. Theor. Biol. **336**, 173–184 (2013)
8. Molina, M.M., Moreno-Armendáriz, M.A., Mora, J.C.S.T.: Analyzing the spatial dynamics of a prey-predator lattice model with social behavior. Ecol. Complex. **22**, 192–202 (2015)
9. International Union for Conservation of Nature (IUCN): IUCN red list of threatened species. Version 2011.1 (2012)

10. Odili, J.B., Kahar, M.N.M., Noraziah, A.: Solving traveling salesman's problem using African buffalo optimization, honey bee mating optimization and Lin-Kerninghan algorithms. World Appl. Sci. J. **34**(7), 911–916 (2016)
11. Odili, J.B., Kahar, M.N.M., Noraziah, A., Odili, E.A.: African buffalo optimization and the randomized insertion algorithm for the asymmetric travelling salesman's problems. J. Theor. Appl. Inf. Technol. **87**(3), 356–364 (2016)
12. Odili, J.B., Kahar, M.N.M.: African buffalo optimization (ABO): a new meta-heuristic algorithm. J. Adv. Appl. Sci. **3**, 101–106 (2015)
13. Odili, J.B., Kahar, M.N.M.: Numerical function optimization solutions using the african buffalo optimization algorithm (ABO). Br. J. Math. Comput. Sci. **10**, 1–12 (2015)
14. Odili, J.B., Kahar, M.N.M., Anwar, S.: African buffalo optimization: a swarm-intelligence technique. Procedia Comput. Sci. **76**, 443–448 (2015)
15. Odili, J.B., Kahar, M.N.M., Anwar, S., Azrag, M.A.K.: A comparative study of African buffalo optimization and randomized insertion algorithm for asymmetric travelling salesman's problem. In: 2015 4th International Conference on Software Engineering and Computer Systems (ICSECS), pp. 90–95. IEEE (2015)
16. Odili, J.B., Mohmad Kahar, M.N.: Solving the traveling salesman's problem using the african buffalo optimization. Comput. Intell. Neurosci. **2016**, 3 (2016)
17. Odili, J.B., Nizam, M., Kahar, M.: African Buffalo Optimization Approach to the Design of PID Controller in Automatic Voltage Regulator System (2016)
18. Odili, J.B., Nizam, M., Kahar, M., Noraziah, A.: African Buffalo Optimization Algorithm for PID Parameters Tuning of Automatic Voltage Regulators (2016)
19. Wolfram, S., et al.: Theory and Applications of Cellular Automata, vol. 1. World Scientific, Singapore (1986)

Physiological Computing in Affective Smart Environments

An Innovative Tool to Create Neurofeedback Games for ADHD Treatment

Miguel A. Teruel[1], Elena Navarro[1,2(✉)], Dulce Romero[3], Mario García[1],
Antonio Fernández-Caballero[1,2], and Pascual González[1,2]

[1] Instituto de Investigación en Informática de Albacete,
Universidad de Castilla-La Mancha, 02071 Albacete, Spain
[2] Departamento de Sistemas Informáticos,
Universidad de Castilla-La Mancha, 02071 Albacete, Spain
Elena.Navarro@uclm.es
[3] Departamento de Psicología, Universidad de Castilla-La Mancha,
45600 Toledo, Spain

Abstract. One of the most frequent disorders in childhood is the attention-deficit/hyperactivity disorder (ADHD). The symptoms of ADHD are present in approximately 5% of children and adolescents with a strong over-representation of boys, irrespectively of their cultural background. There are different treatment approaches but conventional therapies and pharmacological proposals have proved to be insufficient to supply an effective rehabilitation in all cases. The most promising therapies make use of neurofeedback to train attention self-regulation in children with ADHD. In this paper, a new tool that enables therapists to design their own therapies by creating specific neurofeedback videogames adapted to each child is presented.

1 Introduction

One of the most frequent disorders in childhood is the Attention-Deficit /Hyperactivity Disorder (ADHD). This fact has facilitated to be the most deeply studied disorder [17]. Studies have focused on different aspects of ADHD along time, from the attention problem to the excessive motor activity or Hyperkinesia. Currently, most authors consider that ADHD reflexes an executive dysfunction, and, more specifically, controls the behavioral inhibition or executive attention [16]. Despite the high number of papers on ADHD many issues are still unsolved.

Hyperactive children tend to have slower reaction times when performing cognitive tasks that require quickness, showing problems to adjust their own motor response to the requested speed. In addition, hyperactive children devote less time to perform an activity than other children do, no matter whether the type of activity be cognitive, emotional or motor, showing performance problems for tasks of sustained attention and control of the interference. This problem is known as [12], *impulsivity*, that is characterized by an inappropriate use of time and speed, resulting in a premature style, lack of persistence and weakness in the control mechanisms. Moreover, it has also been observed that children who

© Springer International Publishing AG 2017
J.M. Ferrández Vicente et al. (Eds.): IWINAC 2017, Part I, LNCS 10337, pp. 183–192, 2017.
DOI: 10.1007/978-3-319-59740-9_18

have temperamental difficulties do not properly manage changes in their daily routines, showing a low frustration threshold and strong responses. All these difficulties are related to their problems of social interaction, rejection, and so on, which normally harms their social development.

ADHD is usually treated from three different perspectives: psychology, education and pharmacology. An important part of the psychological treatment focuses on family intervention, counseling and training for managing the difficulties related to this disorder. This is specially important because between 10–20% of cases with pharmacological treatment do not improve. This demonstrates the need for treatments different from drugs. This interest is highlighted by a recent survey [14] that identified 110 studies on non-pharmacological interventions in ADHD. Since 1980 this type of treatment has been centered on cognitive training, self-instruction programs and self-control to improve the behavior of the children in the classroom as well as their academic performance, as for instance [13]. In general, this type of treatment is preferred to a pharmacological one due to the reliability of the structure of the content and implementation methodology.

This paper focuses on non-pharmacological interventions in ADHD. We are particularly interested in the neurocognitive treatment for training attention and work memory, by using computerized tasks as well as biofeedback and neurofeedback. Specifically, this paper introduces a tool that can be used by specialists to design therapies for training the attention of children with ADHD. The rest of the paper is organized as follows. First, the related work is presented in Sect. 2. Then, the authoring tool and execution environment are presented in Sect. 3. Finally, the conclusions and future works are illustrated in Sect. 4.

2   Neurofeedback in ADHD Treatment

As stated by Pope et al. [11] humans have the capacity and inherent inclination to regulate their physiological processes. If they receive sufficient informative feedback, their body processes it in the right form. This capability is not only applied to neurofeedback but can also be found in other biofeedback training. But, for this aim, biofeedback training must take into account some specific requirements [6]: (1) the target physiological function must be monitored in real-time; (2) information about the function must be presented to the trainee so that the trainee perceives immediate changes in the parameter; and (3) the feedback information should also serve to motivate the trainee to be attentive to the training task.

Thus, biofeedback training consists in placing sensors on the patients' body to measure some biological activity and, through some computer output device (screen, audio or haptic devices) to show them what is going on inside their bodies. When patients are made aware of some specific changes in their physiological activity, they can learn to control some body functions that are usually outside their conscious control. In brainwave-based biofeedback or neurofeedback, training systems provide patients with real-time information about some brainwaves signals, showing them how well they are producing brainwave patterns that could be considered to be beneficial on their health.

Moreover, the immersion of this neurofeedback training in a game environment improves these treatments' effectiveness. The use of video game technology provides advantages over standard neurofeedback treatment in terms of both children' enjoyment and positive parent's perception, resulting in a lower attrition rate on the treatment [11]. One of the attractiveness of using games is the possibility to receive rewards as the user achieves some specific milestone. As noticed by Pigott et al. [10] "rewarding experiences lead to the release of neuromodulators (such as dopamine) that influence structural plasticity within the brain – so with sufficient repetition, the circuits and pathways whose activation leads to the reward are reinforced".

The use of neurofeedback in the treatment of ADHD is not new. This type of treatment has received "Level 1 Best Support" according to the American Academy of Pediatrics. This classification means that there have been studies with sufficient sample size indicating that neurofeedback treatment is safe for use with children. These treatments have also demonstrated effectiveness in reducing ADHD symptoms in children [9].

Although EEG-based Brain-Computer Interface (BCI) systems have been widely studied in research labs, these EEG recording devices are still too expensive for end-users and the costs of neurofeedback treatments are initially higher compared to traditional psychotherapy [10]. In addition, these devices use a lot of sensors so that the time needed to place the electrodes on the head scalp is a very time-consuming task. Recent advances in EEG technology have facilitated the development of cheaper and easier products, such as NeuroSky MindWave or Emotiv Epoc headset. Thus, among all the proposals that include neurofeedback in the treatment of ADHD, we have selected those which include a game environment and use a cheap EEG device (consumer BCI).

One of the first proposals that used a consumer BCI for treating ADHD was presented by Lim et al. [7]. In their study, they analyze the effects of a BCI-based attention training game system on 20 unmedicated ADHD children with significant inattentive symptoms. They use a BCI system consisting of a headband with dry-mounted EEG sensors (manufactured by Neurosky). Thanks to this device they obtain information about attentional activities. Their game combines the use of neurofeedback and some specific keys to control an avatar's movements. Participants need to achieve a concentration level in order to move the avatar; then they must press a key to make the avatar jump to collect the fruits that appear along the journey. The authors propose three difficulty levels. In the first one, the users only use their concentration level to move the avatar, and in the next levels they must combine their concentration for moving the avatar with the use of a specific key of the keyboard to catch some objects for achieving the game's goal. Their treatment consists of an 8-week training comprising 24 sessions followed by 3 once-monthly booster training sessions. Authors noticed significant positive effects on the treatment of ADHD symptoms.

Another proposal that makes use of a BCI device (MindWave) is that presented by Blandon et al. [2]. They created a video game for the sake of reinforcing four aspects related with ADHD: (i) waiting ability, (ii) planning ability,

(iii) ability to follow instructions and (iv) ability to achieve objectives. In this case, the BCI device is used to measure the child's attention level, which is used to control some aspects of the game. Thus, this video game is presented as a tool for sustained attention training in children with ADHD. To assess their proposal, 9 ADHD diagnosed children (between the ages of 5 and 12 years) played the video game in two 30-minutes sessions. The article concluded that there was an improvement in the game performance, reflecting an enhancement of the sustained attention skill during the game.

Although the devices used in the previous proposals could be appropriate for detecting neutral and attentive states of mind, their limited number of sensors (only measuring brainwaves on the forehead) does not allow controlling more complex states. Another commercial BCI device, namely the Epoc Emotiv, uses a set of electrodes placed with fixed arrangements based on the international 10–20 locations. This BCI device incorporates 14 different electrodes in addition to two reference ones (see Fig. 1). In spite of the fact that some studies indicate that the signal has a better Signal-to-Noise Ratio in a medical system than in the Emotiv Epoc device, in general, data provided by both systems are alike [3]. So, it is a good (and much cheaper) option for non-critical applications. There are studies that confirm that is possible to use this type of headset in a clinical context, where the usability of the device can positively influence the compliance of the subject [1]. Moreover, Mondéjar et al. [8] also noticed that this device enables being used during a long time. All these factors along with the fact of being wireless and very light makes it appropriate for children.

Thomas et al. [15] present a game that analyzes the user's attention while he controls the gameplay using an Emotiv EPOC. The player has to focus on and memorize a set of numbers displayed in a 3×3 matrix textbox. After that, he/she must correctly refill the matrix. The subject will only be able to refill the matrix if his/her attention level is higher than a specific threshold. For managing the system, his/her attention level is continuously analyzed, helping the user to regulate his/her concentration level. Although the authors present their game as adapted to ADHD children, they used five healthy subjects for the evaluation of the game. After three sessions an enhancement of performance in terms of attentions skills and memory power was observed.

Another proposal using the Emotiv Epoc device for cognitive training is presented by Benedetti et al. [1], which focus on adult subjects with an attention disorder. In this study, another capability of the Epoc device is exploited. The authors make use of the possibility of training the system to detect specific thoughts. Specifically, the user must train specific thoughts, that are then used by the engine to continually process the brainwaves and match them to the patterns of thought trained. The trained thoughts are related to imagined motor movements (Up, Down, Left and Right). Then, the user evokes a specific thought indicated on the screen at the beginning of the trial and that refers to the direction to which the user must move a cube. Upon exceeding the 65% intensity of the required brainwave pattern, a positive reinforcement visual stimulus appears. It is progressively extended until 100% intensity is reached.

After evaluating their system with a man who suffers from a frontal syndrome with medium–high severity character, including cognitive and behavioral disorders, they conclude that significant positive results were obtained regarding the subject's attention deficit. Although the evaluated proposals differ in terms of the device used and the brainwave signals analyzed, they have several common factors. First, they try to increase the attention of the patients by recording some brainwave activity, and showing a specific feedback that enables them to control the mental activity. Second, they integrate the therapy in a game environment in order to increase the patient's motivation. And finally, the designed game is the same for all users, just facilitating several difficulty levels. Although some proposals need a specific training phase for each participant, the game is not really tailored to each user. This contradicts Gingerich et al. claim [4] "for the individual with ADHD to receive appropriate evaluation and treatment an understanding of the effect of diversity variables must be carefully considered". Thus, therapists need to have the opportunity to apply some adaptations to improve the success of the therapies.

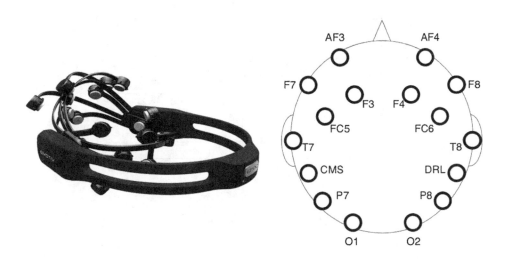

Fig. 1. Emotiv Epoc device and location of the electrodes.

3   Vi-SMARt-Neurofeedback: Creating ADHD Therapies Based in Neurofeedback Videogames

Vi-SMARt-Neurofeedback is a tool created to improve the treatment of ADHD children. Several experts in the treatment of this problem have collaborated in its design. We have designed this tool jointly with the experts for offering therapists a videogame that they can adapt to each patient. As the tool is designed for treating children, we have used a story customized to their age. Moreover, the "magic carpet" metaphor is used to improve the motivation and engagement of the children. Controlling the carpet movements with their mind could be seen as something magic making them feel as a "superman".

The proposed tool consists of two different parts. On the one hand, an authoring tool enables the therapist to design custom games for each patient (see Sect. 3.1). On the other hand, a therapy execution environment that is in charge of running the different games created by means of the authoring tool (see Sect. 3.2). In the following sections both of them are detailed.

3.1 Authoring Tool

One of the main components of the proposed system is the authoring tool. Therapists use it to create customized game configurations for each patient. The authoring tool provides a straightforward user interface to create such customized games. The tool has three tabs to edit players as well as game configurations and sequences among them for each player (see Fig. 2).

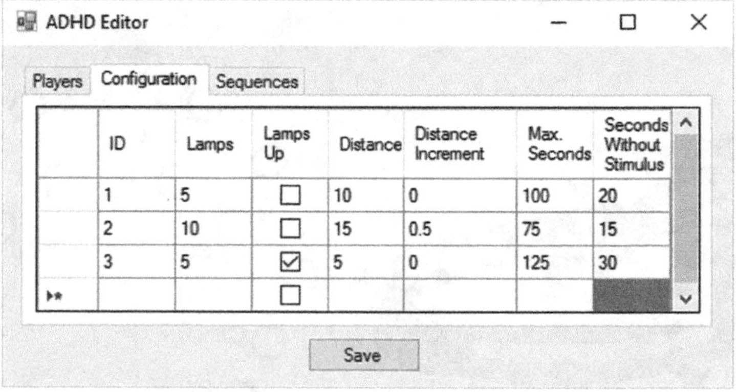

ID	Lamps	Lamps Up	Distance	Distance Increment	Max. Seconds	Seconds Without Stimulus
1	5	☐	10	0	100	20
2	10	☐	15	0.5	75	15
3	5	☑	5	0	125	30
▸*		☐				

Fig. 2. Exercise edition interface

In order to understand how the editor works, Fig. 3 shows the data model supported by the application.

The elements that the system manages are the following ones:

– *Player*: The systems stores the name of the players, as well as the initial configuration and the camera (point of view) each player will start the game with. Concretely, each player can play with the following cameras:
  - *Back fixed*: The camera will record the player's avatar from behind, without following it.
  - *Back following*: Similar to the previous one, but following the player's avatar.
  - *Lateral fixed*: The camera will record the game from the right side, remaining still (see Fig. 4).

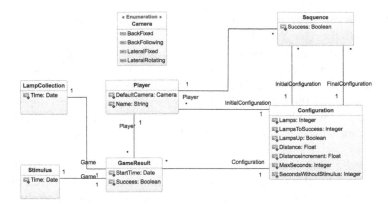

Fig. 3. System data model

Fig. 4. Child executing an exercise (color figure online)

- *Lateral rotating*: Similar to the previous one, but pivoting to face of the player's avatar.
- *Configuration*: This element is used to describe a game configuration considering:
  - *Lamps*: The number of lamps to be shown in the game.
  - *Lamps to success*: The number of lamps that the player needs to pick up in order to end the game successfully.
  - *Lamps up*: Whether or not the avatar will have to jump to pick up the lamps (see Sect. 3.2)
  - *Distance*: Distance in meters between each pair of lamps.
  - *Distance increment*: Distance to add to the original distance between two lamps according to $distance^{(1+increment)}$ For instance, if distance is set to 1, a distance increment of 0.5 will set the lamps in positions $1^{1.5}$, $2^{1.5}$, $3^{1.5}$...
  - *Max. Seconds*: Time that the player will have to pick up all the lamps.

- *Seconds without stimulus*: Time that the user can play without emitting any stimulus (see Sect. 3.2).
- *Sequence*: It determines the set of configurations to be played by a child. Hence, a sequence determines which configurations have to be activated depending on the current player, as well as which is the (*Initial Configuration*) and which will be the next configuration (*Final Configuration*) depending on the (*success*) while playing the initial configuration. If *Final Configuration* is not set, then whenever the (*Initial Configuration*) finishes, the game session will be over.
- *Game result*: This element stores the result of a child when playing game *configuration*. Furthermore, the game *start time*, as well as its result (*success*) are saved. Ir order to enable the therapist to perform a deeper analysis of the results, the time when the players picked up each lamp (*lamp collection*) and emitted each *stimuli* are also saved.

3.2   Therapy Execution Environment

Once the therapy authoring tool has been explained, this Section details the execution environment. In order to make this game engaging, it was decided to implement it by using Unity ([5]). First of all, the player has to train the Emotive Epoc software (see Fig. 5). This training consists in thinking of moving a training object forward and, optionally, up (if the therapist decides to put the game lamps in an upper position).

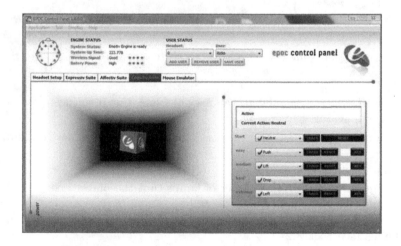

Fig. 5. Emotive Epoc training tool

When the Emotive Epoc device has been properly trained, the child can start to play. The game first shows a relaxing scene where the player only has to select his name, in order to load his configuration. Then, the game stage appears (see Fig. 4) loading the (*initial configuration*) defined.

The game rules are simple. The player only has to focus on moving forward (and optionally jumping). When the Emotive Epoc detects that the player has focused on one of the trained movements, it sends a signal to Unity to move the character forward or make it jump. It is worth noting that the game's user interface always shows the remaining time without receiving a stimulus (red and green bar), the remaining total time (sand clock) and the number of lamps picked up (bottom-right corner of Fig. 4). Moreover, the player can switch among the four cameras point of views by pressing keys from 1 to 4.

The player keeps on playing in the same level (*configuration*) until the total time or the time without stimulus is over, or every lamp on the level has been picked up (see Sect. 2). At that point, should the player have picked up the required lamps, the game will end successfully. In the opposite case, it ends unsuccessfully. Then, the execution environment checks if there is a new configuration for that player depending on the previous result. If so, a new game configuration is loaded and the game restarts with the new parameters. If not, the player is notified that the game is over and the execution environment will restart, thus enabling the same player or a new one to start another session.

4   Conclusions and Future Works

This paper has presented an authoring tool for the creation of neurofeedback videogames. This work is included as part of the Vi-SMARt research project, whose goal is the creation of rehabilitation environments that enable the therapist to define adapted therapies to each patient's specific impairments.

After having analyzed several previous proposals, we presented the Vi-SMARt-Neurofeedback tool for ADHD that enables therapists to create specific neurofeedback videogames. They can also define game sequences related with a specific therapy in order to control the evolution of its difficulty level. Moreover, the therapist can get information about the therapy execution of each particular patient. Although this tool has been designed with the collaboration of experts in the treatment of ADHD, our next task is to evaluate it in a controlled trial to analyze its effects in the treatment of ADHD patients.

Acknowledgements. This work was partially supported by Spanish Ministerio de Economía y Competitividad (MINECO)/FEDER EU under TIN2016-79100-R grant.

References

1. Benedetti, F., Catenacci Volpi, N., Parisi, L., Sartori, G.: Attention training with an easy–to–use brain computer interface. In: Shumaker, R., Lackey, S. (eds.) VAMR 2014. LNCS, vol. 8526, pp. 236–247. Springer, Cham (2014). doi:10.1007/978-3-319-07464-1_22

2. Blandón, D.Z., Muñoz, J.E., Lopez, D.S., Gallo, O.H.: Influence of a BCI neurofeedback videogame in children with ADHD. Quantifying the brain activity through an EEG signal processing dedicated toolbox. In: 2016 IEEE 11th Colombian Computing Conference (CCC), pp. 1–8. IEEE (2016)
3. Duvinage, M., Castermans, T., Petieau, M., Hoellinger, T., Cheron, G., Dutoit, T.: Performance of the Emotiv Epoc headset for P300-based applications. Biomed. Eng. Online **12**(1), 56 (2013)
4. Gingerich, K.J., Turnock, P., Litfin, J.K., Rosén, L.A.: Diversity and attention deficit hyperactivity disorder. J. Clin. Psychol. **54**(4), 415–426 (1998)
5. Hocking, J.: Unity in Action: Multiplatform Game Development in C# with Unity 5. Manning Publications, Greenwich (2015)
6. Kamiya, J.: Biofeedback and self-control: an Aldine reader on the regulation of bodily processes and consciousness. Aldine (1971)
7. Lim, C.G., Lee, T.S., Guan, C., Fung, D.S.S., Zhao, Y., Teng, S.S.W., Zhang, H., Krishnan, K.R.R.: A brain-computer interface based attention training program for treating attention deficit hyperactivity disorder. PLoS ONE **7**(10), e46692 (2012)
8. Mondéjar, T., Hervás, R., Johnson, E., Gutierrez, C., Latorre, J.M.: Correlation between videogame mechanics and executive functions through EEG analysis. J. Biomed. Inform. **63**, 131–140 (2016)
9. Nooner, K.B., Leaberry, K.D., Keith, J.R., Ogle, R.L.: Clinic outcome assessment of a brief course neurofeedback for childhood ADHD symptoms. J. Behav. Health Serv. Res. 1–9 (2016). doi:10.1007/s11414-016-9511-1
10. Pigott, H.E., Bodenhamer-Davis, E., Davis, R.E.: The evidence-base for neurofeedback as a reimbursable healthcare service to treat attention deficit/hyperactivity disorder. International Society for Neurofeedback and Research (2013). http://www.isnr.org/uploads/nfb-adhd.pdf
11. Pope, A.T., Stephens, C.L., Gilleade, K.: Biocybernetic adaptation as biofeedback training method. In: Fairclough, S.H., Gilleade, K. (eds.) Advances in Physiological Computing. HIS, pp. 91–115. Springer, London (2014). doi:10.1007/978-1-4471-6392-3_5
12. Rubia, K.: The dynamic approach to neurodevelopmental psychiatric disorders: use of fmri combined with neuropsychology to elucidate the dynamics of psychiatric disorders, exemplified in adhd and schizophrenia. Behav. Brain Res. **130**(1), 47–56 (2002)
13. Rubio, G., Navarro, E., Montero, F.: APADYT: a multimedia application for SEN learners. Multimedia Tools Appl. **71**(3), 1771–1802 (2014)
14. Satapathy, S., Choudhary, V., Sharma, R., Sagar, R.: Nonpharmacological interventions for children with attention deficit hyperactivity disorder in India: a comprehensive and comparative research update. Indian J. Psychol. Med. **38**(5), 376–385 (2016)
15. Thomas, K.P., Vinod, A., Guan, C.: Enhancement of attention and cognitive skills using EEG based neurofeedback game. In: 2013 6th International IEEE/EMBS Conference on Neural Engineering (NER), pp. 21–24. IEEE (2013)
16. Wagner, B.J.: Attention deficit hyperactivity disorder: current concepts and underlying mechanisms. J. Child Adolesc. Psychiatr. Nurs. **13**(3), 113–124 (2000)
17. Weiler, M.D., Bernstein, J.H., Bellinger, D.C., Waber, D.P.: Processing speed in children with attention deficit/hyperactivity disorder, inattentive type. Child Neuropsychol. **6**(3), 218–234 (2000)

Conditional Entropy Estimates for Distress Detection with EEG Signals

Beatriz García-Martínez[1]([⊠]), Arturo Martínez-Rodrigo[1],
Antonio Fernández-Caballero[2], Pascual González[2], and Raúl Alcaraz[1]

[1] Instituto de Tecnologías Audiovisuales,
Universidad de Castilla-La Mancha, 16071 Cuenca, Spain
beatriz.garcia58@alu.uclm.es
[2] Instituto de Investigación en Informática de Albacete,
Universidad de Castilla-La Mancha, 02071 Albacete, Spain

Abstract. Recently, distress has become a major problem in most advanced societies because of its negative side effects in physical and mental health. In this sense, the assessment of different physiological signals such as electroencephalogram (EEG) provides new insights about the body's reaction against distressful stimuli. Moreover, the non-linear and dynamic behaviour of the brain suggests the application of non-linear methodologies for EEG analysis. In this work, a symbolic technique called conditional entropy was applied for the assessment of 279 32-EEG channel segments of calm and distress emotional states. Results of all EEG electrodes were combined in a simple decision tree classifier, reporting a discriminatory power above 70%. Furthermore, a decreasing tendency of irregularity when changing from calm to distress conditions was observed for all EEG channels. The simplicity of this classification model allows an easy interpretation of the results, together with a possible implementation of the algorithm in a real-time monitoring system.

Keywords: EEG · Distress · Nonlinear analysis · Conditional entropy

1 Introduction

Nowadays, people living in developed countries are surrounded by countless physical, mental and social factors that might cause positive or negative stress [5,8,18]. Positive stress, also called *eustress*, helps to improve the concentration on a task, leading to a better performance. On the contrary, negative stress, or *distress*, is considered cause and consequence of failure and difficulties in a wide variety of daily situations. High levels of negative stress may also provoke such a mental blockage state that it becomes almost impossible to properly solve problems. As a result of that negative situation, psychological distress increases even more. In this sense, it is said that the subjectively perceived level of stress is usually higher than the actual externally-induced level [25]. Unexpected sudden stimuli provoke short-term distress, triggering a response to protect the integrity of the organism. The body secretes hormones like adrenaline and cortisol, and

© Springer International Publishing AG 2017
J.M. Ferrández Vicente et al. (Eds.): IWINAC 2017, Part I, LNCS 10337, pp. 193–202, 2017.
DOI: 10.1007/978-3-319-59740-9_19

blood pressure and bumping rate gets increased, preparing us for a *fight or flight* response [18]. This bodily reaction is acceptable in short periods of time. Nevertheless, the frenetic lifestyle of advanced societies creates an atmosphere of continuous negative stress.

As a consequence of long-term distress, physical and mental health can be severely affected. Disorders like anxiety, depression, cardiovascular diseases, irritable bowel syndrome or back pain might be caused or aggravated by distress [1,3,19,22]. For that reason, distress has become a major disorder in advanced countries in the last few years [9]. On the other hand, it is said that the contrary effects of distress on the body can also occur. More concretely, a calm emotional state decreases the levels of adrenaline and cortisol. The heart activity and blood pressure are also notably diminished. That high intercorrelation between calm and distress is the reason why these emotions are usually studied together [25].

Distress has been widely analysed in dozens of situations, such as stressful driving tests [10], surgical procedures [7], or control of levels of distress in ageing adults living alone at home [17]. In this sense, many works have assessed changes in different physiological signals of subjects under negative stress conditions. Having those bodily reactions perfectly defined, it would be possible to implement accurate real-time distress recognition algorithms. In this sense, the affective computing science [21] is focused on the development of affective human-machine interfaces able to detect different levels of distress and make decisions according to those measurements.

Although many physiological signals are studied for distress, electroencephalogram (EEG) recordings are especially interesting since brain signals represent the primary responses to any stimulus, while the rest of physiological variables are secondary effects of cerebral activity [12]. According to the literature, many studies of distress with EEG signals have been published. Most of those works are focused on EEG spectral features, especially in α (8–13 Hz) and β (14–29 Hz) bands. It is said that, during relaxation moments, spectral power in α band increases, while power in β is decreased. The contrary effects have been assessed under distress conditions, when α power decreases and β power increases [25]. In any case, frequency-based methodologies have reported inconsistencies in terms of inter-subject variability and changes in different frequency bands [26]. Recently, further research have depicted that neural processes follow a completely non-linear behaviour [4]. In this sense, it seems logical to apply non-linear analysis instead of traditional linear methodologies. Indeed, it has been demonstrated that non-linear techniques provide better results than frequency-based and other linear models for EEG analysis [27]. The aim of this work is to apply a predictability-based entropy metric, namely conditional entropy (CEn), for the assessment of EEG signals in order to determine how the brain works when a negative stress stimulus is perceived.

The remainder of this manuscript is structured as follows. Section 2 describes the main characteristics of the database analysed, together with the definition of CEn and the statistical analysis methodologies used. Section 3 shows the results obtained after the application of all analytical techniques. Finally, Sect. 4 discusses the results obtained, and presents some final conclusions.

2   Materials and Methods

2.1   Database

EEG recordings assessed in this work are contained in the Database for Emotion Analysis using Physiological Signals [13]. This publicly-available dataset provides EEG and other physiological variables from thirty-two participants (50% male, mean age 26.9 years). These signals where acquired during the visualisation of forty emotional video clips of one minute duration. After each video, subjects rated their levels of valence (pleasant or unpleasant) and arousal (excitement or calmness) by means of self-assessment manikins [20]. For acquisition of EEG recordings, 32 electrodes were located over the scalp at standard 10–20 system positions, and data were recorded with a sampling rate of 512 Hz. As preprocessing method, these data were down-sampled to 128 Hz and filtered using a bandpass filter between 3 and 45 Hz. Consequently, no further filtering was necessary to remove direct current and electrical power line. In addition, artefacts such as eye blinks and interferences from cardiac or muscular activity were eliminated using an independent component analysis. More information about this database is available in [13].

   Not all the samples in the database were analysed. Only segments from calm and distressed patients were chosen. The group of calm individuals contained samples with valence between 4 and 6, and arousal lower than 4. On the other hand, negative stress group was formed by segments with valence lower than 3 and arousal higher than 5. In total, 279 samples (146 calm and 133 distress) were assessed in this work.

2.2   Conditional Entropy

CEn is based on a symbolic representation of the amplitudes of the elements of the signal [24]. It has been especially proposed for the estimation of entropy in very short time series. The first step for CEn computation is the transformation of $x(n)$ into a positive valued signal $x_p(n)$ by the subtraction of its minimum value: $x_p(n) = x(n) - \min\{x(n)\}$. The full dynamic range of the time series, $\Gamma = \max\{x(n)\} - \min\{x(n)\}$, is then divided into ξ quantization levels. In addition, $x_p(n)$ is quantified with a resolution of Γ/ξ. The result is a symbolized signal $x_s(n)$ from the limited alphabet of symbols $\{0, 1, \ldots, \xi - 1\}$. Being N the length of window, the symbolized signal is then divided into $N - m + 1$ vectors of size m, $\mathbf{X}_{s,m}(i) = \{x_s(i), x_s(i+1), \ldots, x_s(i+m-1)\}$, which is a number in base ξ that corresponds to this decimal number:

$$\mathbf{X}_m(i) \rightarrow w_m(i) = x_s(i) \cdot \xi^0 + x_s(i+1) \cdot \xi^1 + \ldots x_s(i+m-1) \cdot \xi^{m-1} \quad (1)$$

   With this process, the time series is converted into a sequence of integer numbers $\{w_m(i)\}_{i=1,\ldots,N-m+1}$ that range from 0 to $N_m = \xi^m - 1$. Hence, the probability density function of w_m gives information about the distribution of the patterns $\mathbf{X}_m(i)$. Furthermore, the probability of the patterns is calculated as the relative frequency of $w_m(i)$, denoted by $p(w_m(i))$. This process is repeated for dimension $m-1$ and, finally, CEn is calculated as the difference in Shannon entropies for dimensions $m-1$ and m:

$$
\text{CEn}(m,\xi) = \sum_{k=1}^{N_{m-1}+1} p(w_{m-1}(k)) \cdot \ln\left(p(w_{m-1}(k))\right) - \sum_{k=1}^{N_m+1} p(w_m(k)) \cdot \ln\left(p(w_m(k))\right)
$$

$$(2)$$

where CEn is the representation of the amount of information given by the most recent sample of $x(n)$, knowing the previous $m-1$ samples. The maximum value of CEn is obtained when $x(n)$ is complex and unpredictable. On the contrary, CEn is zero when the past $m-1$ samples allow to accurately predict a new sample.

With the purpose of limiting the presence of single points, it is recommended that $N > \xi^{m-1}$ [23]. Moreover, the parameters of CEn computation for short data sequences are suggested to have small values [23]. In this work, $m = 2$, $\xi = 10$ and $N = 1280$ were chosen.

2.3 Statistical Analysis

Shapiro-Wilk and Levene tests were applied to check the normality and homoscedasticity of the distributions. As a result, values for each group are expressed as the mean $\pm$ standard deviation. In addition, a one-way ANOVA test was used to assess the statistical differences between calm and distress samples for each EEG channel. Only values of $\rho < 0.05$ were considered to be statistically significant. Furthermore, receiver operating characteristic curves (ROC) were applied to assess the discriminatory power of each channel in terms of sensitivity (Se), specificity (Sp) and accuracy (Acc). Sensitivity is the relation of positive values correctly classified, while specificity is the relation of negative values accurately identified. ROC curves are represented as Se against $1 - Sp$ at different thresholds to discern between calm and distress samples. The optimal threshold is chosen for each EEG channel as the one that provides the highest classification accuracy. Finally, all EEG channels were combined in a simple decision tree model to improve the global discrimination ability. The growth of the tree-based classifier was controlled, stopping when each node contained less than 20% of samples of a class. Gini index was also applied as a splitting criterion for each EEG channel [2].

3 Results

Almost all EEG channels in all brain regions presented relevant results. More concretely, frontal channel Fz showed the highest classification accuracy $Acc = 63.3\%$ ($Se = 70.1\%$, $Sp = 55.7\%$). Right fronto-central FC2 and right

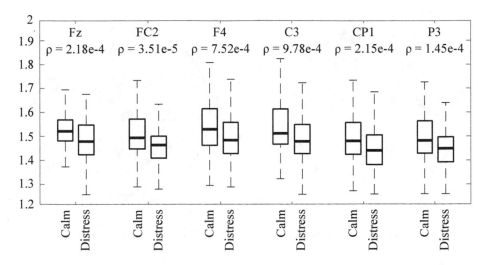

Fig. 1. Statistical significance and distribution of calm and distress CEn values for the most relevant EEG channels.

frontal F4 also reported discriminatory values 61% and 60.6%, respectively. Other relevant channels were left central C3 (59.5%), left centro-parietal CP1 (59.2%) and left parietal P3 (59.1%). The rest of EEG channels presented accuracy results ranging from 52% to 58%. Statistical significance values of the most relevant channels are shown in Fig. 1. Furthermore, distribution of calm and distress samples corresponding to the aforementioned channels are also depicted in that figure. As it can be observed, the mean value of CEn is higher for calm group than for distress samples in all cases. This decreasing tendency was reported by all 32 EEG channels.

In addition, Fig. 2 shows the mean value of CEn for all EEG locations analysed in this work. As it can be observed, calm samples present the highest CEn mean values along the lines between fronto-polar and temporal electrodes of both hemispheres. On the contrary, frontal channels F7 and F8, and fronto-central Fz, FC1 and FC2 do not show such a high level of complexity, despite being in the same brain lobes as those electrodes with larger values of CEn. The lowest unpredictability in this case can be found in parietal channel Pz. With respect to the group of distressed subjects, it can be seen that frontal electrodes Fp1, Fp2 and AF3 present almost the same CEn mean values than in calm group. Nevertheless, complexity in the rest of brain regions under distress conditions is notably lower than in the case of calm samples. This finding is in accordance with Fig. 1, in which mean CEn values were higher in calm samples than for distressed participants.

Differences of CEn mean values between calm and negative stress group were also computed, as shown in Fig. 3. It can be observed that the highest differences of complexity occur in right frontal and fronto-central regions (channels F4, FC2 and FC6), as well as in left centro-parietal and parietal areas (electrodes CP1 and

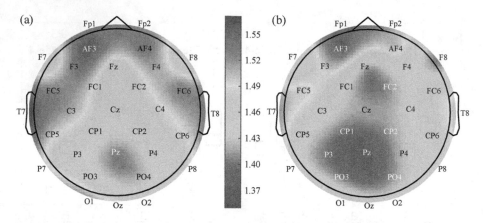

Fig. 2. Representation of mean values of CEn for all EEG channels in (a) calm group and (b) distress group.

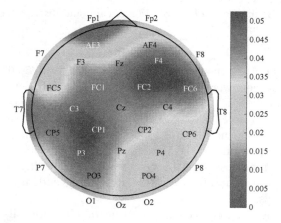

Fig. 3. Differences of mean CEn values in all EEG channels.

P3). These findings are in accordance with the most relevant channels in terms of classification accuracy results (see Fig. 1). On the other hand, as expected, left frontal channel Fp1 presents no difference of mean CEn value between calm and distress groups. Right parieto-occipital channel PO4 also reports a small difference in CEn mean value.

In order to improve the global discrimination ability of the model, a simple tree-based classifier was used. All EEG channels were introduced to this classification model. However, only channels Fz, T8 and Fp1 were finally selected, as depicted in Fig. 4. With this combination, the decision tree model reported a classification accuracy of 70.7% ($Se = 87.6\%$, $Sp = 51.6\%$). This discrimination result is an improvement of 7.4% with respect to the highest individual Acc of ROC analysis (63.3% in Fz).

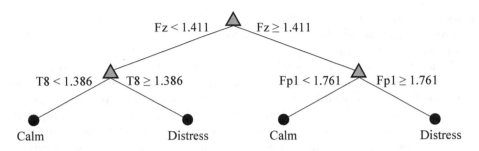

Fig. 4. Combination of all EEG channels in a decision tree classifier for an improvement of global accuracy.

4   Discussion and Conclusions

In the literature, a wide variety of works that are focused on the study of brain activity under different emotional states can be found [9,15,16]. Given the relevant statistical significance reported by many EEG channels in this work, CEn can be considered a suitable technique for distress recognition. Most of the electrodes in all brain regions presented an important discriminatory power between calm and distress stimuli. As observed in Fig. 1, right frontal and fronto-central electrodes, together with left central and parietal channels presented the highest discrimination ability. These results were in accordance with Fig. 3, in which the difference of complexity between calm and distress was especially relevant in right fronto-central and left centro-parietal areas.

In terms of predictability, Fig. 2 depicted that the mean value of CEn was higher for calm segments than for distress samples in all EEG channels. It means that the brain follows a more dynamic and unpredictable behaviour in a relaxed emotional state. On the other hand, brain responses elicited by negative stress stimuli present a more predictable performance than in euthymic (neither depressed nor highly elevated) moods. This decreasing tendency has been previously reported in other studies. For example, a reduction in fractal dimension in subjects dealing with distressful situations was assessed in [11].

Finally, the combination of all EEG channels in a decision tree-based classification model improved the global accuracy to 70.7%. It is worth noting that only electrodes Fz, T8 and Fp1 were chosen by the model shown in Fig. 4. Channel Fz was firstly selected because it provided the highest classification accuracy. Nevertheless, T8 and Fp1 did not report any relevant results in ROC analysis. The reason why those channels were selected is that they explain cases that Fz is not able to describe. In other words, T8 and Fp1 are complementary to Fz when discerning between calm and distress, despite not having a relevant discriminatory power individually. Having only three input channels in a small decision tree simplifies the clinical interpretation of the results. Previous studies reached higher values of classification accuracy than in this work. However, their classification models consisted of hundreds of input variables and complex statistical approaches, blurring any clinical interpretation of the results. The simple model applied in this study allows to easily know which brain areas help to an improvement of the global discriminatory ability between calm and distress samples.

In addition, it would be possible to implement this emotion recognition algorithm in a real-time monitoring device in future works. Different real-time systems have been implemented previously. For example, a human-machine interface able to recognise up to six different emotions in real-time has been proposed so far [14]. A music therapy site based on the assessment of EEG signals was then designed. Moreover, an on-line music player was created to select which music to display according to the user's feelings [14]. On the other hand, a method for adaptation of a game difficulty in terms of the user's emotions is also available [6]. For that purpose, EEG and peripheral signals were acquired to distinguish between three different emotional states [6]. In the case of this work, the algorithm could be applied for a real-time control of distress level in countless daily situations.

Acknowledgements. This work was partially supported by Spanish Ministerio de Economía, Industria y Competitividad, Agencia Estatal de Investigación (AEI)/ European Regional Development Fund under HA-SYMBIOSIS (TIN2015-72931-EXP), Vi-SMARt (TIN2016-79100-R) and EmoBioFeedback (DPI2016-80894-R) grants.

References

1. Bender, R.E., Alloy, L.B.: Life stress and kindling in bipolar disorder: review of the evidence and integration with emerging biopsychosocial theories. Clin. Psychol. Rev. **31**(3), 383–398 (2011)
2. Breiman, L.: Classification and Regression Trees. Wadsworth International Group, Belmont (1984)
3. Brzozowski, B., Mazur-Bialy, A., Pajdo, R., Kwiecien, S., Bilski, J., Zwolinska-Wcislo, M., Mach, T., Brzozowski, T.: Mechanisms by which stress affects the experimental and clinical inflammatory bowel disease (IBD): role of brain-gut axis. Curr. Neuropharmacol. **14**, 892–900 (2016)
4. Cao, Y., Cai, L., Wang, J., Wang, R., Yu, H., Cao, Y., Liu, J.: Characterization of complexity in the electroencephalograph activity of Alzheimer's disease based on fuzzy entropy. Chaos **25**(8), 083116 (2015)
5. Castillo, J.C., Castro-González, A., Fernández-Caballero, A., Latorre, J.M., Pastor, J.M., Fernández-Sotos, A., Salichs, M.A.: Software architecture for smart emotion recognition and regulation of the ageing adult. Cogn. Comput. **8**(2), 357–367 (2016)
6. Chanel, G., Rebetez, C., Bétrancourt, M., Pun, T.: Emotion assessment from physiological signals for adaptation of game difficulty. IEEE Trans. Syst. Man Cybern. Part A **41**(6), 1052–1063 (2011)
7. Duru, D.G., Duru, A.D., Barkana, D.E., Sanli, O., Ozkan, M.: Assessment of surgeon's stress level and alertness using EEG during laparoscopic simple nephrectomy. In: 2013 6th International IEEE/EMBS Conference on Neural Engineering (NER), pp. 452–455. IEEE (2013)
8. Fernández-Caballero, A., Martínez-Rodrigo, A., Pastor, J.M., Castillo, J.C., Lozano-Monasor, E., López, M.T., Zangróniz, R., Latorre, J.M., Fernández-Sotos, A.: Smart environment architecture for emotion recognition and regulation. J. Biomed. Inform. **64**, 55–73 (2016)

9. García-Martínez, B., Martínez-Rodrigo, A., Zangróniz, R., Pastor, J., Alcaraz, R.: Application of entropy-based metrics to identify emotional distress from electroencephalographic recordings. Entropy **18**(6), 221 (2016)
10. Healey, J., Picard, R.W.: Detecting stress during real-world driving tasks using physiological sensors. IEEE Trans. Intell. Transp. Syst. **6**(2), 156–166 (2005)
11. Hosseini, S.A., Naghibi-Sistani, M.B.: Classification of Emotional Stress Using Brain Activity. INTECH Open Access Publisher, Rijeka (2011)
12. Jenke, R., Peer, A., Buss, M.: Feature extraction and selection for emotion recognition from EEG. IEEE Trans. Affect. Comput. **5**(3), 327–339 (2014)
13. Koelstra, S., Mühl, C., Soleymani, M., Lee, J., Yazdani, A., Ebrahimi, T., Pun, T., Nijholt, A., Patras, I.: DEAP: a database for emotion analysis using physiological signals. IEEE Trans. Affect. Comput. **3**(1), 18–31 (2012)
14. Liu, Y., Sourina, O., Nguyen, M.K.: Real-time EEG-based emotion recognition and its applications. In: Gavrilova, M.L., Tan, C.J.K., Sourin, A., Sourina, O. (eds.) Transactions on Computational Science XII. LNCS, vol. 6670, pp. 256–277. Springer, Heidelberg (2011). doi:10.1007/978-3-642-22336-5_13
15. Martínez-Rodrigo, A., Alcaraz, R., García-Martínez, B., Zangróniz, R., Fernández-Caballero, A.: Non-lineal EEG modelling by using quadratic entropy for arousal level classification. In: Chen, Y.-W., Tanaka, S., Howlett, R.J., Jain, L.C. (eds.) Innovation in Medicine and Healthcare 2016. SIST, vol. 60, pp. 3–13. Springer, Cham (2016). doi:10.1007/978-3-319-39687-3_1
16. Martínez-Rodrigo, A., García-Martínez, B., Alcaraz, R., Pastor, J.M., Fernández-Caballero, A.: EEG mapping for arousal level quantification using dynamic quadratic entropy. In: Lindgren, H., De Paz, J.F., Novais, P., Fernández-Caballero, A., Yoe, H., Ramírez, A.J., Villarrubia, G. (eds.) ISAmI 2016. AISC, vol. 476, pp. 207–214. Springer, Cham (2016). doi:10.1007/978-3-319-40114-0_23
17. Martínez-Rodrigo, A., Zangróniz, R., Pastor, J.M., Fernández-Caballero, A.: Arousal level classification in the ageing adult by measuring electrodermal skin conductivity. In: Bravo, J., Hervás, R., Villarreal, V. (eds.) AmIHEALTH 2015. LNCS, vol. 9456, pp. 213–223. Springer, Cham (2015). doi:10.1007/978-3-319-26508-7_21
18. Minguillon, J., Lopez-Gordo, M.A., Pelayo, F.: Stress assessment by prefrontal relative gamma. Front. Comput. Neurosci. **10**(September), 1–9 (2016)
19. Mönnikes, H., Tebbe, J.J., Hildebrandt, M., Arck, P., Osmanoglou, E., Rose, M., Klapp, B., Wiedenmann, B., Heymann-Mönnikes, I.: Role of stress in functional gastrointestinal disorders. Evidence for stress-induced alterations in gastrointestinal motility and sensitivity. Dig. Dis. **19**(3), 201–211 (2001)
20. Morris, J.D.: Observations SAM: the self-assessment manikin - an efficient cross-cultural measurement of emotional response. J. Advert. Res. **35**(6), 63–68 (1995)
21. Picard, R.W.: Affective Computing. MIT Press, Cambridge (1995)
22. Pickering, T.G.: Mental stress as a causal factor in the development of hypertension and cardiovascular disease. Curr. Hypertens. Rep. **3**(3), 249–254 (2001)
23. Porta, A., Baselli, G., Liberati, D., Montano, N., Cogliati, C., Gnecchi-Ruscone, T., Malliani, A., Cerutti, S.: Measuring regularity by means of a corrected conditional entropy in sympathetic outflow. Biol. Cybern. **78**(1), 71–78 (1998)
24. Porta, A., Guzzetti, S., Montano, N., Furlan, R., Pagani, M., Malliani, A., Cerutti, S.: Entropy, entropy rate, and pattern classification as tools to typify complexity in short heart period variability series. IEEE Trans. Biomed. Eng. **48**(11), 1282–1291 (2001)
25. Reisman, S.: Measurement of physiological stress. In: Proceedings of the IEEE 1997 23rd Northeast Bioengineering Conference, pp. 21–23. IEEE, May 1997

26. Tran, Y., Thuraisingham, R., Wijesuriya, N., Nguyen, H., Craig, A.: Detecting neural changes during stress and fatigue effectively: a comparison of spectral analysis and sample entropy. In: 2007 3rd International IEEE/EMBS Conference on Neural Engineering, pp. 350–353. IEEE (2007)
27. Valenza, G., Lanata, A., Scilingo, E.P.: The role of nonlinear dynamics in affective valence and arousal recognition. IEEE Trans. Affect. Comput. **3**(2), 237–249 (2012)

Nonlinear Symbolic Assessment of Electroencephalographic Recordings for Negative Stress Recognition

Beatriz García-Martínez[1], Arturo Martínez-Rodrigo[1(✉)],
Antonio Fernández-Caballero[2],
José Moncho-Bogani[3], José Manuel Pastor[1], and Raúl Alcaraz[1]

[1] Instituto de Tecnologías Audiovisuales,
Universidad de Castilla-La Mancha, 16071 Cuenca, Spain
arturo.martinez@uclm.es
[2] Instituto de Investigación en Informática de Albacete,
Universidad de Castilla-La Mancha, 02071 Albacete, Spain
[3] Departamento de Ciencias Medicas,
Universidad de Castilla-La Mancha, 02071 Albacete, Spain

Abstract. Nowadays, electroencephalographic (EEG) recordings receive increasing attention in the field of emotions recognition with physiological variables. Moreover, the nonlinear nature of EEG signals suggests that nonlinear techniques could be more suitable than linear methodologies for the assessment of mental processes triggered under different emotions. One of the most relevant states is distress (the negative aspect of stress), because of its enormous influence in developed countries and its countless adverse effects in health. As a result, many researches have shown their interest in distress in the last few years. In the present study, a predictability-based entropy measure called amplitude-aware permutation entropy (AAPE) was applied to discern between calm and distress states. EEG signals from 32 channels were individually assessed to obtain the discriminatory ability of each single electrode. After that, only 2 out of 32 EEG channels were combined in a logistic regression model, reaching a global classification accuracy over 73%.

Keywords: Distress · EEG · Permutation entropy · Nonlinear analysis

1 Introduction

Emotions are complex psycho-physiological processes automatically generated as a reaction against externally-induced stimuli [13]. Emotions play a key role in countless daily situations like verbal and nonverbal communication, learning and rational decision-making [13]. Nevertheless, automatic systems cannot still interpret human feelings because of their lack of emotional intelligence [31]. Hence, human-machine interfaces (HMIs) are not able to properly decide which actions to execute according to the user's emotions [31]. In this sense, the aim

© Springer International Publishing AG 2017
J.M. Ferrández Vicente et al. (Eds.): IWINAC 2017, Part I, LNCS 10337, pp. 203–212, 2017.
DOI: 10.1007/978-3-319-59740-9_20

of the affective computing science is to endow those HMIs with emotional intelligence, enhancing their capability of recognising different moods and emotional states [27]. With this purpose, many automatic systems are based on the assessment of different physiological signals for emotions detection, being the electroencephalogram (EEG) one of the most relevant physiological variables.

EEG recordings have received increasing attention in the last years since they are a representation of the first impulse of the body against any external stimulus [17]. The rest of physiological signals are secondary processes produced by the autonomic nervous system as a result of the primary processes started in the brain [17]. In addition, the brain presents a nonlinear and dynamic nature at both cellular and global level [1,11]. Consequently, it has been demonstrated that nonlinear methodologies provide better results than traditional linear techniques in the assessment of mental disorders like Alzheimer [1,19,20], epilepsy [33] or depression [2]. Thus, this study aims to evaluate the results derived from the application of a nonlinear entropy metric for the recognition of different emotions in EEG signals. More concretely, a symbolic index called amplitude-aware permutation entropy (AAPE) will be computed for the recognition of negative stress and calm emotional states in EEG recordings.

Among the large number of emotions defined in the literature, negative stress (also called distress) has been chosen because of being one of the most relevant and influential in advanced societies [3,9]. Distress is defined as a change from a calm to an excitement state for the protection of self-integrity [9,15]. Long-time distress conditions might severely affect cerebral, immune and endocrine systems [4]. Thus, countless physical and mental diseases might be triggered or aggravated [8,10,25,28]. On the other hand, it has been verified that calm emotional conditions produce effects on the body that are contrary to the effects produced by negative stress [22,30,32]. A consequence, calm and distress emotional states are highly intercorrelated [29]. Thus in this work both emotions will be assessed in order to define the differences in brain's behaviour under calm and negative stress conditions.

In this manuscript, Sect. 2 presents a brief description of the database analysed, and defines the entropy index computed in this study. Statistical analysis techniques used are also described in Sect. 2. Results derived from the application of those methodologies are presented in Sect. 3 and discussed in Sect. 4, together with some final conclusions.

2 Materials and Methods

2.1 Database

Samples analysed in this study were selected from a publicly available dataset called Database for Emotion Analysis using Physiological Signals (DEAP) [18]. The experiment to create this database consisted of the visualization of forty one-minute length videoclips with emotional content. Meanwhile, EEG and other physiological signals of thirty-two subjects were acquired. For each video, participants rated their levels of valence (unpleasantness-pleasantness) and arousal (calmness-excitement) with self-assessment manikins (SAM) [26]. EEG recordings were acquired at a sampling rate of 512 Hz with 32 electrodes located over the scalp following the standard 10–20 system. The preprocessing method consisted of a downsampling to 128 Hz and the application of a band-pass filter between 3 and 45 Hz. Furthermore, an independent component analysis (ICA) was applied to eliminate artifacts such as eye blinks or interferences from cardiac or muscular activity. More information about the DEAP database can be found in [18].

Samples in the database covered the whole valence-arousal space. Nevertheless, only segments corresponding to calm and distress emotions were selected in this work. For this purpose, samples with arousal lower than 4 and valence between 4 and 6 were included in calm group. On the other hand, distress segments presented an arousal level higher than 5 and a valence level lower than 3. Thus, a total of 279 samples (146 in calm group and 133 in distress group) were analysed in this study.

2.2 Amplitude-Aware Permutation Entropy

In this work, a symbolic entropy measure was used to discern between calm and distress samples. The main characteristic of symbolic entropies is the assessment of ordinal sequences of symbols resulting from the transformation of a time series. The distribution of those symbols is quantified by means of Shannon's entropy (ShEn), thus the predictability of the time series is accurately estimated [5]. Symbolic entropies take into account the order of the symbols in a pattern, which is crucial for a proper assessment of the dynamics of a signal. In this study, a symbolic entropy called AAPE was computed for all EEG channels to detect negative stress states.

AAPE is a modification of permutation entropy (PE). This simple-concept estimate presents an easy method of parametrization, together with a high level of robustness against noise and a quick computation algorithm [7]. The calculation of PE starts with the association of each ordinal sequence with a vector $\mathbf{X}_m(i)$, considering that the sequence is the permutation $\kappa_i = \{r_0, r_1, \ldots, r_{m-1}\}$ of $\{0, 1, \ldots, m-1\}$ for which $x(i + r_0) \leq x(i + r_1) \leq \ldots \leq x(i + r_{m-2}) \leq x(i + r_{m-1})$. Vectors of length m are associated to $m!$ ordinal sequences or symbols π_k. For instance, the symbols of a vector of length $m = 2$ are $\pi_1 = \{0, 1\}$ and $\pi_2 = \{1, 0\}$. Those sequences have a probability of appearance in a signal that can be calculated as the relative frequency of the patterns, $p(\pi_k)$, within the $N - m + 1$ vectors of the time series. Finally, PE can be estimated as the ShEn of the $m!$ symbols π_k:

$$\mathrm{PE}(m) = -\sum_{k=1}^{m!} p(\pi_k) \ln p(\pi_k) \tag{1}$$

The presence of permutation sequences of a time series can provide valuable information about the underlying dynamics of the model under study. When the probability of appearance of all symbols is the same, then PE presents a maximum value of $\ln(m!)$. On the contrary, a minimum PE of 0 is obtained in the case of having a totally predictable time series with just one symbol.

In any case, results reported by PE only involve the order of the amplitudes, ignoring the value of those amplitudes. Hence, AAPE was defined to solve this deficiency [6]. AAPE is an entropy estimate that quantifies the symbols of a time series according to its changes of amplitude. In this sense, AAPE associates the histogram of probability appearance of each pattern with an amplitude-dependent value. In other words, each symbol presents a normalised value of relative probability [6]:

$$p(\pi_k) = p(\pi_k) + \left(\frac{A}{m} \sum_{i=1}^{m} |y_{t+(i-1)l}| + \frac{1-A}{m-1} \sum_{i=2}^{m} |y_{t+(i-1)l} - y_{t+(i-2)l}| \right), \quad (2)$$

In the previous equation, A is an adjustment coefficient regarding the average and differences between correlative samples of the signal, and l is a time delay. Then the probability of appearance of each symbol is normalised by the sum of all contributions:

$$p(\pi_k) = \frac{p(\pi_k)}{\sum_{t=1}^{N-m+1} \left(\frac{A}{m} \sum_{i=1}^{m} |y_{t+(i-1)l}| + \frac{1-A}{m-1} \sum_{i=2}^{m} |y_{t+(i-1)l} - y_{t+(i-2)l}| \right)} \quad (3)$$

The final step of AAPE computation is the same as for PE, the Shannon entropy of the $m!$ symbols π_k:

$$\text{AAPE}(m) = -\sum_{k=1}^{m!} p(\pi_k) \ln p(\pi_k). \quad (4)$$

2.3   Statistical Analysis

The normality and homoscedasticity of the distributions were checked with Shapiro-Wilk and Levene tests. Consequently, results obtained for each group are denoted as mean $\pm$ standard deviation. Then, a one-way ANOVA test was applied for the assessment of the statistical differences between samples of distress and calm in each EEG channel. Only significance values $\rho < 0.05$ were considered as significant. In addition, a ten-fold cross-validation approach was used to assess the discriminatory power of each channel. In each training step, that discriminatory ability was calculated by means of receiver operating characteristic curves (ROC). ROC curves are the representation of sensitivity (Se, relation of positives accurately classified) against 1-specificity (Sp, relation of negatives properly identified) at different thresholds. Classification accuracy (Acc) is the total rate of samples correctly identified. Then, the threshold chosen as the optimal is the one which provides the highest classification accuracy. The final value of classification accuracy is the average of the ten iterations of the ten-fold cross-validation model.

As a second analysis, all data were combined in order to find subsequent relationships between different brain regions. Nevertheless, not all EEG channels were included as input variables in the classification model. Instead, a feature selection method based on a forward stepwise technique was used. This approach starts with a reduced initial model that is then compared with larger models created by the addition of new terms from a multilinear system based on their statistical significance in a regression. At each step, the statistical significances of a model with and without a new term are compared to evaluate the possible contribution of that term to the classification procedure. Once all terms were chosen, they were included as input parameters in a logistic regression classification approach. Logistic regression is based on the determination of a binary dependent variable in terms of a set of independent or predictor variables, searching for the combination that best fits the relationship between both dependent and independent features.

3   Results

Different brain areas were activated in calm and distress conditions. Figure 1 shows the mean value of AAPE of all EEG channels for calm and distress groups. It can be seen that calm subjects (Fig. 1(a)) presented the highest levels of entropy mainly in frontal, temporal and left occipital regions. In contrast, central and parietal areas reported lower activity levels. With respect to distressed participants (Fig. 1(b)), it is observed that complexity in all EEG channels is notably lower than in the case of calm individuals. It was verified that this decreasing tendency was reported by all the EEG channels assessed in this study.

Moreover, the application of ROC analysis reported significant statistical values ($\rho < 0.05$) and high classification accuracies in many channels of all brain lobes. The highest discriminatory ability was reported by left parietal

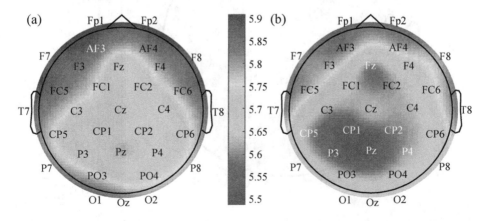

Fig. 1. Representation of mean values of AAPE for (a) calm and (b) distress groups of study.

channel P3, with a classification accuracy of 65.39%. Other channels like right frontal electrodes F8 and FC2, left parieto-occipital PO3 and left centro-parietal CP5 also reported high discriminatory results around 61%. Values of statistical significance ρ and ROC parameters (sensitivity, specificity and accuracy) of the aforementioned channels can be found in Table 1. Discriminatory results of the rest of electrodes were ranging from 55% to 60%.

Table 1. Statistical significance and ROC results for the most relevant channels of AAPE.

EEG channel	Significance value ρ	ROC results		
		Se (%)	Sp (%)	Acc (%)
P3	2.71×10^{-5}	78.83	50.05	65.39
F8	1.82×10^{-3}	71.56	50.84	61.84
FC2	1.34×10^{-3}	73.71	48.43	61.79
PO3	6.53×10^{-5}	58.49	64.82	61.46
CP5	5.31×10^{-4}	70.09	50.81	61.00

In addition, Fig. 2 shows the differences of AAPE mean level between calm and distress samples. According to ROC results reported in Table 1, the highest

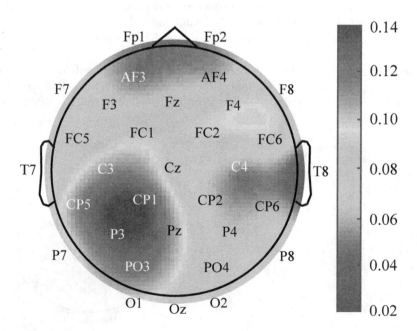

Fig. 2. Differences of mean values of AAPE between calm and distress segments for all EEG channels.

differences are mainly located in left parietal region, including channels P3, CP5 and PO3. These electrodes reported the highest discriminatory ability in ROC analysis. Moreover, right frontal hemisphere (channel P4) also presents a slightly higher difference of activation than the left frontal lobe. On the other hand, fronto-polar channels Fp1 and Fp2, right temporal T8 and right central C4 presented the smallest differences of mean level of AAPE between calm and distress samples.

Finally, all EEG channels were combined with the purpose of improving the global classification accuracy of this approach. With this purpose, a stepwise analysis was applied to reduce the number of channels included in the classifier. In this case, only parietal channels P3 and P4 were chosen and introduced as input variables in a logistic regression model. This combination reported a discriminatory ability of 73.75% (Se = 77.37%, Sp = 69.67%), thus improving the highest individual accuracy (channel P3) in more than 8%.

4   Discussion and Conclusions

Many works have tested the effectiveness on nonlinear methodologies for the assessment of EEG signals under different emotional states [14,23,24]. The relevant statistical significance values reported in this study suggest that AAPE is a suitable index for negative stress detection. Almost all brain areas presented electrodes with a considerable discriminatory power between distressful and relaxing stimuli. The highest discriminatory ability was located in electrodes of right frontal and fronto-central, left central and left parietal regions. Those findings were also obtained in Fig. 2, where right fronto-central and left centro-parietal regions reported relevant differences of predictability between calm and distress samples. On the other hand, Fig. 1 reported a higher mean value of AAPE for calm subjects than for distressed participants in all EEG electrodes, which means that the behaviour of the brain in calm is more dynamic and unpredictable than in distress situations. A similar decreasing tendency was reported by Hosseini *et al.*, declaring a reduction in fractal dimension in participants elicited with distressful stimuli [16].

In the present manuscript, a logistic regression model was applied to combine all EEG channels for an improvement of the discriminatory ability of each single electrode. After a stepwise analysis, only channels P3 and P4 were introduced in the model. Left parietal electrode P3 was firstly selected since it presented the highest discriminatory ability (Acc = 65.39%). Then, right parietal P4 was chosen because of complementing the information reported by P3, despite not presenting a relevant discriminatory power to discern between calm and distress emotional states. Finally, this logistic regression model provided a classification accuracy of 73.75%, which is an improvement of more than 8% with respect to the highest individual accuracy (channel P3). Furthermore, the simplicity of the classification model allows to easily interpret the results from a clinical point of view, since only 2 out of 32 channels are combined. In this sense, these new findings could be essential to enlarge our knowledge of the brain's behaviour under distress conditions.

Moreover, the implementation of this negative stress detection algorithm in real-time monitoring systems would be possible. In a previous study, Liu *et al.* [21] presented a human-machine interface prepared for the real-time recognition of six different emotions and a posterior control of a music player that automatically selected which music to play according to the user's emotional state. In other work, Chanel *et al.* [12] developed an algorithm of adaption of a game difficulty according to the user's feelings detected by means of EEG and other physiological signals. The algorithm presented in this study could also be implemented in a wide variety of systems for real-time control of distress levels in daily situations.

Acknowledgments. This work was partially supported by Spanish Ministerio de Economía, Industria y Competitividad, Agencia Estatal de Investigación (AEI)/European Regional Development Funder under HA-SYMBIOSIS (TIN2015-72931-EXP), Vi-SMARt (TIN2016-79100-R) and EmoBioFeedback (DPI2016-80894-R) grants.

References

1. Abásolo, D., Hornero, R., Gómez, C., García, M., López, M.: Analysis of EEG background activity in Alzheimer's disease patients with Lempel-Ziv complexity and central tendency measure. Med. Eng. Phys. **28**(4), 315–322 (2006)
2. Acharya, U.R., Sudarshan, V.K., Adeli, H., Santhosh, J., Koh, J.E.W., Puthankatti, S.D., Adeli, A.: A novel depression diagnosis index using nonlinear features in EEG signals. Eur. Neurol. **74**(1–2), 79–83 (2015)
3. Alberdi, A., Aztiria, A., Basarab, A.: Towards an automatic early stress recognition system for office environments based on multimodal measurements: a review. J. Biomed. Inform. **59**, 49–75 (2016)
4. Alonso, J., Romero, S., Ballester, M., Antonijoan, R., Mañanas, M.: Stress assessment based on EEG univariate features and functional connectivity measures. Physiol. Meas. **36**(7), 1351 (2015)
5. Amigó, J.M., Keller, K., Unakafova, V.A.: Ordinal symbolic analysis and its application to biomedical recordings. Philos. Trans. A Math. Phys. Eng. Sci. **373**(2034), 20140091 (2015)
6. Azami, H., Escudero, J.: Amplitude-aware permutation entropy: illustration in spike detection and signal segmentation. Comput. Methods Programs Biomed. **128**, 40–51 (2016)
7. Bandt, C., Pompe, B.: Permutation entropy: a natural complexity measure for time series. Phys. Rev. Lett. **88**(17), 174102 (2002)
8. Bender, R.E., Alloy, L.B.: Life stress and kindling in bipolar disorder: review of the evidence and integration with emerging biopsychosocial theories. Clin. Psychol. Rev. **31**(3), 383–398 (2011)
9. Bong, S.Z., Murugappan, M., Yaacob, S.: Methods and approaches on inferring human emotional stress changes through physiological signals: a review. IJMEI **5**(2), 152–162 (2013)
10. Brzozowski, B., Mazur-Bialy, A., Pajdo, R., Kwiecien, S., Bilski, J., Zwolinska-Wcislo, M., Mach, T., Brzozowski, T.: Mechanisms by which stress affects the experimental and clinical inflammatory bowel disease (IBD): role of brain-gut axis. Curr. Neuropharmacol. **14**, 892–900 (2016)

11. Cao, Y., Cai, L., Wang, J., Wang, R., Yu, H., Cao, Y., Liu, J.: Characterization of complexity in the electroencephalograph activity of Alzheimer's disease based on fuzzy entropy. Chaos **25**(8), 083116 (2015)
12. Chanel, G., Rebetez, C., Bétrancourt, M., Pun, T.: Emotion assessment from physiological signals for adaptation of game difficulty. IEEE Trans. Syst. Man Cybern. Part A **41**(6), 1052–1063 (2011)
13. Coan, J.A., Allen, J.J.B.: Handbook of Emotion Elicitation and Assessment. Oxford University Press, Oxford (2007)
14. García-Martínez, B., Martínez-Rodrigo, A., Zangróniz Cantabrana, R., Pastor García, J., Alcaraz, R.: Application of entropy-based metrics to identify emotional distress from electroencephalographic recordings. Entropy **18**(6), 221 (2016)
15. Healey, J., Picard, R.W.: Detecting stress during real-world driving tasks using physiological sensors. IEEE Trans. Intell. Transp. Syst. **6**(2), 156–166 (2005)
16. Hosseini, S.A., Naghibi-Sistani, M.B.: Classification of Emotional Stress Using Brain Activity. INTECH Open Access Publisher, Rijeka (2011)
17. Jenke, R., Peer, A., Buss, M.: Feature extraction and selection for emotion recognition from EEG. IEEE Trans. Affect. Comput. **5**(3), 327–339 (2014)
18. Koelstra, S., Mühl, C., Soleymani, M., Lee, J., Yazdani, A., Ebrahimi, T., Pun, T., Nijholt, A., Patras, I.: DEAP: a database for emotion analysis using physiological signals. IEEE Trans. Affect. Comput. **3**(1), 18–31 (2012)
19. Labate, D., Foresta, F., Morabito, G., Palamara, I., Morabito, F.C.: Entropic measures of EEG complexity in Alzheimer's disease through a multivariate multiscale approach. IEEE Sens. J. **13**(9), 3284–3292 (2013)
20. Lalonde, F., Gogtay, N., Giedd, J., Vydelingum, N., Brown, D., Tran, B.Q., Hsu, C., Hsu, M.K., Cha, J., Jenkins, J., et al.: Brain order disorder 2nd group report of f-EEG. In: SPIE Sensing Technology and Applications, p. 91180J. International Society for Optics and Photonics (2014)
21. Liu, Y., Sourina, O., Nguyen, M.K.: Real-time EEG-based emotion recognition and its applications. In: Gavrilova, M.L., Tan, C.J.K., Sourin, A., Sourina, O. (eds.) Transactions on Computational Science XII. LNCS, vol. 6670, pp. 256–277. Springer, Heidelberg (2011). doi:10.1007/978-3-642-22336-5_13
22. Manna, A., Raffone, A., Perrucci, M.G., Nardo, D., Ferretti, A., Tartaro, A., Londei, A., Gratta, C., Belardinelli, M.O., Romani, G.L.: Neural correlates of focused attention and cognitive monitoring in meditation. Brain Res. Bull. **82**(1–2), 46–56 (2010)
23. Martínez-Rodrigo, A., Alcaraz, R., García-Martínez, B., Zangróniz, R., Fernández-Caballero, A.: Non-lineal EEG modelling by using quadratic entropy for arousal level classification. In: Chen, Y.-W., Tanaka, S., Howlett, R.J., Jain, L.C. (eds.) Innovation in Medicine and Healthcare 2016. SIST, vol. 60, pp. 3–13. Springer, Cham (2016). doi:10.1007/978-3-319-39687-3_1
24. Martínez-Rodrigo, A., García-Martínez, B., Alcaraz, R., Pastor, J.M., Fernández-Caballero, A.: EEG mapping for arousal level quantification using dynamic quadratic entropy. In: Lindgren, H., De Paz, J.F., Novais, P., Fernández-Caballero, A., Yoe, H., Ramírez, A.J., Villarrubia, G. (eds.) ISAmI 2016. AISC, vol. 476, pp. 207–214. Springer, Cham (2016). doi:10.1007/978-3-319-40114-0_23
25. Mönnikes, H., Tebbe, J.J., Hildebrandt, M., Arck, P., Osmanoglou, E., Rose, M., Klapp, B., Wiedenmann, B., Heymann-Mönnikes, I.: Role of stress in functional gastrointestinal disorders. Evidence for stress-induced alterations in gastrointestinal motility and sensitivity. Dig. Dis. **19**(3), 201–211 (2001)
26. Morris, J.D.: Observations SAM: the self-assessment manikin - an efficient cross-cultural measurement of emotional response. J. Advert. Res. **35**(6), 63–68 (1995)

27. Picard, R.W.: Affective Computing. MIT Press, Cambridge (1995)
28. Pickering, T.G.: Mental stress as a causal factor in the development of hypertension and cardiovascular disease. Curr. Hypertens. Rep. **3**(3), 249–254 (2001)
29. Reisman, S.: Measurement of physiological stress. In: Proceedings of the IEEE 23rd Northeast, Bioengineering Conference, pp. 21–23. IEEE, May 1997
30. Rubia, K.: The neurobiology of meditation and its clinical effectiveness in psychiatric disorders. Biol. Psychol. **82**(1), 1–11 (2009)
31. Rukavina, S., Gruss, S., Hoffmann, H., Tan, J.W., Walter, S., Traue, H.C.: Affective computing and the impact of gender and age. PLoS ONE **11**(3), e0150584 (2016)
32. Vysata, O., Schätz, M., Kopal, J., Burian, J., Procházka, A., Jirí, K., Hort, J., Valis, M.: Non-linear EEG measures in meditation. J. Biomed. Sci. Eng. **7**(9), 731 (2014)
33. Xiang, J., Li, C., Li, H., Cao, R., Wang, B., Han, X., Chen, J.: The detection of epileptic seizure signals based on fuzzy entropy. J. Neurosci. Methods **243**, 18–25 (2015)

Recent Advances and Challenges in Nonlinear Characterization of Brain Dynamics for Automatic Recognition of Emotional States

Raúl Alcaraz, Beatriz García-Martínez,
Roberto Zangróniz, and Arturo Martínez-Rodrigo(✉)

Research Group in Electronic, Biomedical and Telecommunication Engineering,
University of Castilla-La Mancha, Cuenca, Spain
arturo.martinez@uclm.es

Abstract. Automatic recognition of emotions is an emerging field, because it plays a key role to improve current affective human-computer interactions. Although for that purpose a variety of linear methods have been applied to the electroencephalographic (EEG) recording, nonlinear analysis has recently revealed novel and more useful insights about the brain behavior under different emotional states. This work briefly reviews the main progresses in this context, also highlighting the main challenges that will have to be mandatory tackled in future.

Keywords: EEG · Emotion recognition · Nonlinear analysis

1 Introduction

From a psycho-physiological point of view, the emotions are mental processes characterized by a strong activity and high degree of hedonistic content [8]. Their study is highly interesting because they are present in a variety of daily human activities, including learning, verbal and nonverbal communication and rational decision-making processes [8]. Moreover, although recognition of emotions plays a key role in communication and interaction among people, nowadays automatic systems are not completely able to interpret human feelings [35]. This dysfunction often makes current human-machine interfaces (HMI's) unable to execute proper emotion-based actions [35]. Hence, more research is essential to improve affective computing systems, which are becoming increasingly applied to emerging fields such as medicine [28], digital society [38] or computer games [6].

A major problem to identify emotions is the lack of a standardized model for their definition [40]. In fact, several theories attempting to classify numerous emotional states can be found in the literature. Thus, Ekman firstly defined six basic emotions universally accepted, including happiness, surprise, sadness, fear, disgust and anger, their combination being also able to characterize more complex feelings [10]. However, nowadays the most widely used emotion classification model is the 2-dimension approach proposed by Russell [36]. This model

© Springer International Publishing AG 2017
J.M. Ferrández Vicente et al. (Eds.): IWINAC 2017, Part I, LNCS 10337, pp. 213–222, 2017.
DOI: 10.1007/978-3-319-59740-9_21

is based on how pleasant or unpleasant (valence) a stimulus is, as well as on its ability to produce excitement or calmness (arousal) on a normal subject. A wide range of emotions can then be defined depending on the combination of different levels of arousal and valence [36].

Another relevant problem dealing with emotions is that they are highly inter-correlated. Thus, subjects rarely describe isolated positive or negative feelings [8]. Additionally, a stimulus can trigger different emotions within several people, mainly depending on their mood, personality, disposition or motivation [8]. Hence, this high variability in expression of emotions makes their automatic identification highly complicated [40]. Nonetheless, some recent works have been able to discern among different emotional states from some physiological signals, like the electromyogram (EMG), the electrocardiogram (ECG), the electroen-cephalogram (EEG) and the electro-dermal activity (EDA) signal [40].

Given that the EEG signal is able to provide more information than other physiological variables, automatic recognition of emotions from this recording is currently receiving growing attention [17]. In fact, the emotional response to any external stimulus is firstly generated by the brain and, thereafter, distributed to the rest of biological systems [17]. Although the EEG signal has been character-ized both from linear and nonlinear points of view, more relevant insights have been provided by nonlinear analysis [40]. This is not surprising, since nonlinear-ity in the brain can be observed both at cellular and global levels. Precisely, the dynamical behavior of individual neurons is governed by threshold and satura-tion approaches [5]. Moreover, the brain function during sophisticated cognitive tasks is far from being completely stochastic [5]. Hence, the purpose of this work is to review the most recent advances released through the application of non-linear methods to the EEG recording in automatic identification of emotional states. The most relevant challenges in this context will also be remarked.

2   The EEG Recording and Its Typical Preprocessing

EEG signals measure brain electrical activity at many locations simultaneously by one electrode at each position on the human scalp. These recordings are electrical potentials acquired with respect to a reference electrode (usually placed at the earlobe). The number of electrodes depends on the application, normally ranging from 2 to 128 [39]. Nonetheless, to ensure reproducible measurements, as well as comparison among recordings from different subjects, a system limiting the number and location of electrodes has been internationally standardized, i.e. the 10–20 system [39]. Anyway, since every EEG signal presents an amplitude between -100 and $+100\,\mu$V, approximately, a previous preprocessing to reduce artifacts is required for further accurate characterization [21]. Briefly, different spatiotemporal filtering approaches are commonly used to remove baseline, high-frequency noise and power-line interference [39]. Moreover, most of technical artifacts (e.g., electrode-pops) and physiological ones (e.g., facial and ocular movements) are often reduced making use of independent component analysis (ICA) [32]. The resulting clean signal is then analyzed in terms of the nonlinear metrics that will be described below.

3   Nonlinear Characterization of Brain Time Series

The main goal of nonlinear time series analysis is to quantify a system complexity, which is related to the rate of intrinsic patterns hidden in the generated dynamics [11]. To date, a broad variety of indices, based on different mathematical foundations, can be found to measure different faces of the complexity of physiologically derived time series. These metrics can be grouped into five sets, according to the following subsections.

3.1   Quantification of Fractal Fluctuations

Time series dynamics can be explored through its correlation properties, or in other words, through its time ordering. To this respect, fractal analysis is an appropriate method to characterize complex time series by focusing on their time-evolutionary properties and correlation features. Thus, detrended fluctuation analysis (DFA) has been developed specifically to distinguish between intrinsic fluctuations generated by complex systems and those caused by external or environmental stimuli [30]. This method quantifies temporal organization of the fluctuations in a given non-stationary time series by a single scaling exponent α, which can be considered as a self-similarity parameter representing the long-range power-law correlation properties of the series. Another index widely used to quantify correlation properties of a time series is the Hurst exponent (HE). It is associated with the long-term statistical dependence of the series, thus assessing its statistical self-similarity and providing information of the recurrence rate of similar patterns at different scales [4].

The combination of these two metrics with other linear measures, such as spectral, bispectral and wavelet-based parameters, have revealed an interesting ability to track changes of six emotional states (i.e., happiness, sadness, fear, anger, surprise and disgust) over time in subjects with Parkinson's disease [42]. In a similar way, but dealing with healthy subjects, the combination of HE with other nonlinear characteristics, as well as with spectral and wavelet-based features, has also provided a high discriminant power around 90% between positive (valence > 5) and negative (valence < 5) emotional states [41]. In both works, nonlinear metrics have reported a slightly lower contribution than linear indices, but their role is still key to improve automatic identification of emotions [41,42].

Fractal dimension (FD) has also been proposed to analyze temporal ordering of time series [30]. In the literature numerous algorithms can be found to compute this parameter directly from the time series, such as those proposed by Katz, Petrosian and Higuchi [30]. Each method presents advantages and disadvantages and, thus, most of them have been considered to deal with physiological signals [30]. Regarding recognition of emotions, Hatamikia and Nasrabadi [13] have combined two of these FD measures with other two entropy-based metrics to discern emotional states from the four quadrants defined by the dimensions of valence and arousal (i.e., high valence and high arousal, high valence and low arousal, low valence and high arousal and, finally, low valence and low arousal). The accuracy reported in this work was around 70%. A similar discriminant ability has also been reported by Sourina and Liu [37], who have only used two FD estimates to discriminate among positive, negative and neutral emotional states. The combination of FD with other statistical and spectral features has also been useful to discern among four opposite emotions, such as pleasantness, happiness, fright and fear [23]. Moreover, in this work FD also showed a great stability to identify the same emotions from the same patients during successive days [23].

Despite these promising results, some physiological times series are extremely complex and exhibit a multifractal scaling behavior, thus requiring more than one scaling exponent to characterize inhomogeneous fluctuations derived from crossover timescales [30]. To consider this aspect, some recent works have studied the possibility of improving previous results in automatic recognition of emotions by analyzing multifractal DFA and FD indices [26,31]. To this respect, the combination of multifractal FD with other statistical and spectral features has provided a diagnostic accuracy around of 85% to discriminate among eight emotions, such as happy, surprised, satisfied, protected, angry, frightened, unconcerned, and sad [26]. A similar discriminant power has also been reported by several multifractal DFA features to discern between positive and negative emotional states [31]. As a consequence, nonlinear multifractal analysis can improve about 10% identification of several emotions, thus suggesting the need of further research in this line.

3.2   Quantification of Chaos Degree

The basic principle of chaos analysis is to transform properties of a time series into topological features of a geometrical object (attractor) embedded in a state/phase space. The concept of phase space reconstruction is essential in nonlinear analysis of dynamics. A valid phase space is any vector space where the state of a dynamical system can be unequivocally defined at any point [19]. The most used way to reconstruct full dynamics of a system from scalar time measurements is based on the embedding theorem, which states that one can "reconstruct" the attractor from the original time series and its time-delayed copies [19].

To characterize a reconstructed phase space, a variety of methods and algorithms are currently available. A widely used index is the correlation dimension (CD) [30], which assesses the attractor dimensionality, i.e., the organization of points in the phase space. It can be computed by first calculating the correlation sum of the time series, which is defined as the number of points in the phase space that are closer than a certain threshold r [19]. Then, CD is defined as the line fitting slope in the log-log plot of the correlation sum as a function of the threshold r.

Recently, several works have explored the capability of CD to gain new insights about the brain behavior under different emotional states. Indeed, Hoseingholizade et al. [14] have observed that CD decreases significantly in frontal, temporal and parietal EEG channels for emotional experiences both with negative and positive valences compared to rest states. According to the authors, these results suggest a more active involvement of these brain areas during emotional experience than rest [14]. On the other hand, Khalili and Moradi [20] have also proven that CD computed from EEG recordings is able to provide information related to subjects positively and negatively excited, as well as calm, beyond statistical features obtained from other peripherical signals, such as galvanic skin resistance, respiration, blood pressure and temperature.

Lyapunov exponents (LEs) are also habitually used to characterize the dynamics of the trajectories found in the phase space. These exponents quantify the exponential divergence or convergence of initially close trajectories, thus reflecting the amount of instability or predictability of the process. An m-dimensional dynamic system has m exponents, but in most of the applications it is sufficient to compute only the largest LE (LLE), which can be computed as follows. First, a starting point is selected in the reconstructed phase space and all the points closer than a predetermined distance, ϵ, are found. Then, average value of the distances between the trajectories of the initial point and their neighbors are calculated as the system evolves. The slope of the line obtained by plotting the logarithms of these average values versus time gives the LLE. To remove the dependence of calculated values on the starting point, the procedure is repeated for different starting points and the LLE is taken as the average.

This index has also been able to report statistically significant differences from brain dynamics recorded under several emotional states. To this respect, Acar et al. [1] have recently described notable differences in values of LLE computed for all brain regions from 20 subjects elicited to feel happiness, sadness and fear. Similarly, Natarajan et al. [29] have also noticed an increase in the predictability of some brain dynamics via LLE for healthy individuals under classic music and reflexologic stimulation. In this work, similar findings were also noticed making use of other nonlinear features such as CD, HE and some entropy-based metrics [29]. Nonetheless, it has to be remarked that numerous algorithms to characterize the attractor of time series have still not been tested in the context of emotion recognition, thus their analysis being a pending task. In this way, novel insights about the brain behavior under different affective states could be expected in future.

3.3 Quantification of Information Content

Symbolic analysis of time series involves the transformation of original data into a sequence of discrete symbols that are processed to extract useful information about the state of the system generating the process [30]. After the symbolization, words are constructed by collecting groups of symbols considering their temporal order. This process typically involves definition of a finite word-length template that can be moved along the symbol series one step at a time, thus each step revealing a new sequence.

Quantitative measures to estimate word sequence frequencies often include statistics, such as word frequency or transition probabilities between words. In this line, a metric widely used is the proposed by Lempel and Ziv [30], which is commonly referred to as Lempel-Ziv complexity (LZC). It provides a measure of complexity related to the number of distinct substrings and the rate of their occurrence along a given sequence, with larger values of LZC associated to more complex word sequences. This index has been recently used to discern among different emotional states, reporting a diagnostic accuracy about 80% [7]. This outcome is very interesting because, in contrast to most studies which require combinations of numerous markers with advanced classifiers to report a significant discriminant power [21], only a single index is considered in this case.

On the other hand, symbolized time series are also frequently characterized by computing their entropy, which evaluates the probability that different words occur [30]. In the context of emotion recognition, two different entropy estimates have only been used. Thus, Aravind et al. [2] have proposed the application of common Shannon entropy (ShEn) to the window-based symbolized γ band (30–45 Hz) for discerning among emotional states of excitement, happiness, sadness and hatred. A promising accuracy greater than 90% was observed in this study. Similarly, Li et al. [24] have analyzed the ability of permutation entropy computed from the EEG to discern between emotional states of excitement and fear, thus reaching a discriminant power around 80%. Despite that these results are highly interesting, developing new ways to symbolize brain time series and to quantify more accurately their underlying dynamics under different affective states are intriguing challenges yet.

3.4   Quantification of Irregularity

Approximate entropy (ApEn) is a well-known measure of time series irregularity. This index obtains a non-negative number, with larger values corresponding to more irregular data and smaller values corresponding to time series with more instances of recognizable features or patterns [19]. It is computed as the logarithmic likelihood that runs of patterns that are close (within a tolerance r) for length m continuous observations remain close (within the same tolerance r) on next incremental comparison. Although ApEn can be applied to relatively short time series, the amounts of data points have an influence on the obtained entropy estimates. This is due to the fact that the algorithm counts each sequence as matching itself to avoid the occurrence of $\ln(0)$ in the calculations. To avoid this bias, Sample entropy (SEn) has been proposed as an ApEn improvement by excluding self-matches, thus being less dependent of the length of data series [33]. Recently, a modification of SEn has been also proposed to make this index insensitive to the tolerance r. It is called quadratic SEn (QSEn) and is computed by adding the term '$\ln(2r)$' to SEn [22].

These indices have been widely analyzed in the context of emotion recognition. In fact, many works have proven their superior ability to other linear and nonlinear metrics to discern among different emotional states. Thus, QSEn has been revealed as the most promising single metric to identify negative stress in healthy individuals [12]. In this study, more than 270 samples from subjects appropriately stimulated with music videos were analyzed, the combination of QSEn values computed from left frontal and right parietal brain areas reporting an accuracy about 80% [12]. Although with a lower discriminant power, ApEn and SEn have also proven to be useful in discerning between calm and negatively stressed subjects [12,15], as well as among emotional states from the four quadrants defined by the dimensions of valence and arousal [18,34].

As previously mentioned, same physiological time series can exhibit different structures over multiple time scales [30]. To consider this aspect, a more robust regularity measure of time series is the named Multiscale entropy (MEn). This index is based on computing and averaging entropy estimates from different time scales, thus providing scale-independent values of regularity [9]. Several ways have been proposed to obtain different time scales. The most common approach consists of averaging different number of consecutive and non-overlapped samples. Li et al. [25] have used this algorithm to identify several emotional states with an accuracy around 70%. However, they have also reported an improvement in accuracy of about 12% by computing time scale through empirical mode decomposition of the original brain time series [25]. Thus, every preprocessed EEG channel was decomposed into intrinsic mode functions (IMFs) and SEn was computed on each one. This methodology has been also used by Zhang et al. [43] to reach a discriminant ability around 95% in the identification of emotions with high valence and high arousal, high valence and low arousal, low valence and high arousal and, finally, low valence and low arousal. In a very similar context, Mert and Akan [27] have shown that, in addition to SEn, ShEn also obtains accurate entropy estimates from IMFs. Nonetheless, since a broad variety of alternatives to compute MSEn has been proposed in last years [16], this index role in automatic recognition of emotions requires further investigation.

3.5 Quantification of Geometric Structure

A Recurrence plot (RP) is a visual representation of all the possible distances between the points constituting the phase space of a time series [19]. Whenever the distance between two points is below a certain threshold, there is a recurrence in the dynamics, i.e., the system visited multiple times a certain area of the phase space. This transformation is well-suited for the study of short nonstationary signals, nowadays existing many indices to characterize geometrically the resulting graph [19]. Nonetheless, four basic characteristics of a RP can be highlighted: isolated points (reflecting stochasticity in the signal), diagonal lines (index of determinism) and horizontal/vertical lines (reflecting local stationarity in the signal). The combination of these elements creates large-scale and small-scale patterns from which it is possible to compute many other features, mainly based on the quantification of number of points within each element.

Despite its potentiality, this tool has been poorly surveyed in the context of emotion recognition. To the best of our knowledge, only a study has considered RP analysis to discern between emotional states with high and low valences, high and low arousals and high and low likings, respectively [3]. In brief, 13 features were used to characterize the RP constructed from each EEG channel, including determinism, averaged diagonal length, entropy of the diagonal length and laminarity, among others. However, spatial information from the different brain areas was removed by averaging the features obtained for all the EEG channels.

Thus, accuracy values between 60 to 70% were only reported [3]. Overall, it is still possible to explore a long way regarding the application of RP analysis to automatic identification of emotional states.

4   Conclusions

The state of the art summarized in the present work suggests that the use of methods of nonlinear analysis can facilitate the understanding of the brain behavior under different emotional states by complementing the information reported by traditional linear techniques. However, only a few nonlinear tools have been considered to date in too limited studies, in terms of number of analyzed subjects and validation of results. Hence, further and more thorough research is still required to discover the true potential of nonlinear analysis of brain dynamics in automatic recognition of emotions.

Acknowledgments. This work was partially supported by Spanish Ministerio de Economía, Industria y Competitividad, Agencia Estatal de Investigación (AEI)/European Regional Development Funder under HA-SYMBIOSIS (TIN2015-72931-EXP), Vi-SMARt (TIN2016-79100-R) and EmoBioFeedback (DPI2016-80894-R) grants.

References

1. Acar, S., Saraoglu, H., Akar, A.: Feature extraction for EEG-based emotion prediction applications thorough chaotic analysis. In: Turkey National Biomedical Engineering Meeting (2015)
2. Aravind, E., Deepak, S., Sudheer, A.: EEG-based emotion recognition using statistical measures and auto-regressive modeling. In: International Conference on Computational Intelligence and Communication Technology, pp. 587–591 (2015)
3. Bahari, F., Janghorbani, A.: EEG-based emotion recognition using recurrence plot analysis and K-nearest neighbor classifier. In: Iranian Conference on Biomedical Engineering, pp. 228–233 (2013)
4. Blythe, D.A.J., Haufe, S., Müller, K.R., Nikulin, V.V.: The effect of linear mixing in the EEG on Hurst exponent estimation. Neuroimage **99**, 377–387 (2014)
5. Cao, Y., Cai, L., Wang, J., Wang, R., Yu, H., Cao, Y., Liu, J.: Characterization of complexity in the electroencephalograph activity of Alzheimer's disease based on fuzzy entropy. Chaos **25**(8), 083116 (2015)
6. Chanel, G., Rebetez, C., Bétrancourt, M., Pun, T.: Emotion assessment from physiological signals for adaptation of game difficulty. IEEE Trans. Syst. Man Cybern. Part A **41**(6), 1052–1063 (2011)
7. Chen, D., Han, N., Chen, J., Guo, H.: Novel algorithm for measuring the complexity of electroencephalographic signals in emotion recognition. J. Med. Imaging Health Inform. **7**(1), 203–2010 (2017)
8. Coan, J.A., Allen, J.J.B.: Handbook of Emotion Elicitation and Assessment. Oxford University Press, Oxford (2007)
9. Costa, M., Goldberger, A.L., Peng, C.K.: Multiscale entropy analysis of biological signals. Phys. Rev. E Stat. Nonlinear Soft Matter Phys. **71**(2 Pt 1), 021906 (2005)

10. Ekman, P.: An argument for basic emotions. Cogn. Emot. **6**(3–4), 169–200 (1992)
11. Faust, O., Bairy, M.G.: Nonlinear analysis of physiological signals: a review. J. Mech. Med. Biol. **12**(4), 124005 (2012)
12. García-Martínez, B., Martínez-Rodrigo, A., Zangróniz Cantabrana, R., Pastor García, J., Alcaraz, R.: Application of entropy-based metrics to identify emotional distress from electroencephalographic recordings. Entropy **18**(6), 221 (2016)
13. Hatamikia, S., Nasrabadi, A.: Recognition of emotional states induced by music videos based on nonlinear feature extraction and SOM classification. In: 21th Iranian Conference on Biomedical Engineering (ICBME), pp. 333–337. IEEE (2014)
14. Hoseingholizade, S., Golpaygani, M.R.H., Monfared, A.S.: Studying emotions through nonlinear processing of EEG. Procedia Soc. Behav. Sci. **32**, 163–169 (2012)
15. Hosseini, S.A., Khalilzadeh, M.A., Changiz, S.: Emotional stress recognition system for affective computing based on bio-signals. J. Biol. Syst. **18**, 101–114 (2010)
16. Humeau-Heurtier, A.: The multiscale entropy algorithm and its variants: a review. Entropy **17**, 3110–3123 (2015)
17. Jenke, R., Peer, A., Buss, M.: Feature extraction and selection for emotion recognition from EEG. IEEE Trans. Affect. Comput. **5**(3), 327–339 (2014)
18. Jie, X., Cao, R., Li, L.: Emotion recognition based on the sample entropy of EEG. Biomed. Mater. Eng. **24**(1), 1185–1192 (2014)
19. Kantz, H., Schreiber, T.: Nonlinear Time Series Analysis. Cambrigde University Press, Cambrigde (2003)
20. Khalili, Z., Moradi, M.: Emotion recognition system using brain and peripherical signals: using correlation dimension to improve the results of EEG. In: International Conference on Neural Networks, pp. 1571–1575 (2009)
21. Kim, M.K., Kim, M., Oh, E., Kim, S.P.: A review on the computational methods for emotional state estimation from the human EEG. Comput. Math. Methods Med. **2013**, 573734 (2013)
22. Lake, D.E., Moorman, J.R.: Accurate estimation of entropy in very short physiological time series: the problem of atrial fibrillation detection in implanted ventricular devices. Am. J. Physiol. Heart Circ. Physiol. **300**(1), H319–H325 (2011)
23. Land, Z., Sourina, O., Wang, L., Liu, Y.: Real-time EEG-based emotion monitoring using stable features. Vis. Comput. **32**, 347–358 (2016)
24. Li, X., Qi, X., Tian, Y., Sun, X., Fran, M., Cai, E.: Application of the feature extraction based on combination of permutation entropy and multi-fractal index to emotion recognition. Chin. High Tecnol. Lett. **26**(7), 617–624 (2016)
25. Li, X., Xie, J., Hou, Y., Wang, J.: An improved multiscale entropy algorithm and its performance analysis in extraction of emotion EEG features. Chin. High Tecnol. Lett. **25**(10), 865–870 (2015)
26. Liu, Y., Sourina, O.: EEG-based subject-dependent emotion recognition algorithm using fractal dimension. In: IEEE International Conference on Systems, Man and Cybernetics, pp. 3166–3171 (2014)
27. Mert, A., Akan, A.: Emotion recognition from EEG signals by using multivariate empirical mode decomposition. Pattern Anal. Appl. (2016)
28. Mitchell, A.J., Lord, K., Slattery, J., Grainger, L., Symonds, P.: How feasible is implementation of distress screening by cancer clinicians in routine clinical care? Cancer **118**(24), 6260–6269 (2012)
29. Natarajan, K., Acharya, U.R., Alias, F., Tiboleng, T., Puthusserypady, S.K.: Nonlinear analysis of EEG signals at different mental states. Biomed. Eng. Online **3**(1), 7 (2004)

30. Paraschiv-Ionescu, A., Buchser, E., Rutschmann, B., Aminian, K.: Nonlinear analysis of human physical activity patterns in health and disease. Phys. Rev. E Stat. Nonlinear Soft Matter Phys. **77**(21), 021913 (2008)
31. Paul, S., Mazumder, N., Ghosh, P., Tibarewala, D., Vimalarini, G.: EEG-based emotion recognition system using MFDFA as feature extractor. In: International Conference on Robotics, Automation, Control and Embedded Systems (2015)
32. Radüntz, T., Scouten, J., Hochmuth, O., Meffert, B.: EEG artifact elimination by extraction of ICA-component features using image processing algorithms. J. Neurosci. Methods **243**, 84–93 (2015)
33. Richman, J.S., Moorman, J.R.: Physiological time-series analysis using approximate entropy and sample entropy. Am. J. Physiol. Heart Circ. Physiol. **278**(6), H2039–H2049 (2000)
34. Rui, C., Li, L., Junjie, C.: Comparative study of approximate entropy and sample entropy in EEG data analysis. Biotechnol. Indian J. **7**(11), 493–498 (2013)
35. Rukavina, S., Gruss, S., Hoffmann, H., Tan, J.W., Walter, S., Traue, H.C.: Affective computing and the impact of gender and age. PLoS ONE **11**(3), e0150584 (2016)
36. Russell, J.A.: A circumplex model of affect. J. Pers. Soc. Psychol. **39**(6), 1161–1178 (1980)
37. Sourina, O., Liu, Y.: A fractal-based algorithm of emotion recognition from EEG using arousal-valence model. In: Proceeding of the International Conference on Bio-Inspired Systems and Signal Processing, pp. 209–214 (2011)
38. Tadic, B., Gligorijevic, V., Mitrovic, M., Suvakov, M.: Co-evolutionary mechanisms of emotional bursts in online social dynamics and networks. Entropy **15**(12), 5084–5120 (2013)
39. Tong, S., Thakor, N. (eds.): Quantitative EEG Analysis Methods and Clinical Applciations. Artech House, Norwood (2009)
40. Valenza, G., Lanata, A., Scilingo, E.P.: The role of nonlinear dynamics in affective valence and arousal recognition. IEEE Trans. Affect. Comput. **3**(2), 237–249 (2012)
41. Wang, X., Nie, D., Lu, B.: Emotional state classification from EEG data using machine learning approach. Neurocomputing **129**, 94–106 (2014)
42. Yuvaraj, R., Murugappan, M., Ibrahim, N.M., Sundaraj, K., Omar, M.I., Mohamad, K., Palaniappan, R.: Optimal set of EEG features for emotional state classification and trajectory visualization in Parkinson's disease. Int. J. Psychophysiol. **94**(3), 482–495 (2014)
43. Zhang, Y., Ji, X., Zhang, S.: An approach to EEG-based emotion recognition using combined feature extraction method. Neurosci. Lett. **633**, 152–157 (2016)

Towards Assistive Solutions for People with Central Vision Loss

Marina V. Sokolova[1,2](✉), Francisco J. Gómez[1], Jose Manuel Ortiz Egea[3],
Miguel Ángel Fernández[1], and Adoración Pérez Andrés[4]

[1] University of Castilla-La Mancha, Albacete, Spain
smv1999@mail.ru
[2] Southwest State University, Kursk, Russia
[3] University Hospital of Albacete, Albacete, Spain
[4] MARPE Opticos, Albacete, Spain

Abstract. The paper introduces a method of digital image processing for visually impaired people with central vision field loss. The method is based on image pixels relocation from the "blind zone" outside of its limits, and has been implemented within the CImagenMDI library. Transformed visual inputs are then used within the assistive tool with the aim to support a patient when performing everyday activities at work and home.

Keywords: Relocation · Visually impaired · AMD · Assistive solution

1 Introduction

World Health Organization, in the report about word blindness and visual impairments for 2014, estimated the number of visually impaired people in the world as 285 million, 39 million of which are blind and 246 million having low vision; 65% of people visually impaired, and 82% of all blind are 50 years and older [23].

A significant part of the visual impairments deal with people with central visual field loss (CFL). There are many sight diseases which may cause CFL, which include age related macular degeneration (AMD), glaucoma, diabetic retinopathy and cataract. Injuries can also result is CFL. The prevalence of CFL in Spain reaches 3–4% in people with an age equal to or greater than 65 years, and is increasing with age. As a consequence of the population aging, it has been estimated that the number of cases of AMD in Spain could reach 565,810 in 2025 [5].

Drastic decrease of visual acuity in most cases may result in scotoma and entire or partial losses of vision. In other words, patients are blind in some area of their visual field, i.e., they cannot use the foveal, the highest resolution part of the retina to explore visual scenes, as it is damaged.

Depending on the intensity of the loss of vision, scotomas can be divided into relative (areas where objects with lower luminescence cannot be seen but

© Springer International Publishing AG 2017
J.M. Ferrández Vicente et al. (Eds.): IWINAC 2017, Part I, LNCS 10337, pp. 223–232, 2017.
DOI: 10.1007/978-3-319-59740-9_22

those with the higher) and absolute (nothing is seen within the area) scotomas. Scotoma is surrounded by the area or reduced optical sensitivity depression.

However, patients with CFL are not blind, as they sight is partially damaged. For example, in case of central scotoma patients cannot see in a central part, and they try to adapt to this situation using reinforcing peripheral vision. These patients are very limited in carrying out their most essential everyday tasks. That means that in case necessary assistant tools are provided, patients can improve they perception of visual scenes and increase the number of everyday tasks they can do independently.

Unlike someone who is blind, a person with scotoma (central o peripheral) retains a part of her useful sight, although having "blind spots" or specific areas of their visual field where they cannot see. Because of that "partial" vision and because some part of the visual field perceives images, many patients intent to see with the not damaged areas of the eye. In this way, a patient use the peripheral part of the visual field, which has a lower visual acuity than the fovea [6]. As a result, visually impaired learn to use the eccentric vision through preferred retinal locus (PRL), which is formed in this case [19]. Eccentric viewing training is a time consuming process, and the results can be obtained in the long run.

In this paper we introduce a method for image transformation for people with CFL, which provides real-time personalized processing of visual inputs, and can be used within assistive wearable devices like smart glasses. The proposed method of image transformation can also be used with the aim to shorten the period of eccentric viewing training.

The paper is organized as follows. The Sect. 2 introduces the relation between the brain and the vision, and emphasize the importance of assistive solutions for the people with CFL. The Sect. 3 discuss the importance of the assistive tools for visually impaired. The Sect. 4 presents a method of scotoma zone relocation. Next, in the Sect. 5, the preliminary testing is introduced. The Sect. 6 discusses the proposed methods and its applications.

2   Vision and Brain

The appearance of a central cicatricial lesion in the retina, which causes a visual scotoma, results in the absence of neuronal potential stimulus inputs from the retinal photoreceptors to the retinotopically assigned regions of the occipital visual cortex. Animal studies have shown evidence of reorganization in mammalian adults for such experimentally induced central scotoma cortical areas [8]. However, it is still unknown if the reorganization occurs in the primary visual cortex $V1$ of patients with foveal lesion in AMD. It is also unknown if the adoption of a preferred retinal locus (PRL) corresponds to changes in the retinotopic mapping of $V1$ [21]. At this level, there are isolated published clinical cases that support the possibility of an improvement in visual quality by training a new PRL of fixation in healthy retina adjacent to the lesion [3].

Regarding occipital neuronal reorganization in patients with scarring foveal lesions (no entry in the first neuron), there are research works that support this possibility [3, 7, 21] and others that do not find occipital neuronal reorganization after foveal cicatricial lesion [1, 17]. All the spoken above is referred to the case of a dry cicatricial lesion and a training capacity of the healthy peripheral retina adjacent to the lesion.

The usage of advantages of digital image transformation for patients with foveal lesions would be a solution for this case. Enhanced visual inputs in accordance with individual requirements of a patient, would be used within supportive electronic aids or smart glasses previously to the PRL training procedure.

Therefore, this work initially aims to determine personalized scales of visual perception in patients with complete foveal lesions through a battery of digitally processed images. This knowledge makes grounds for the development of assistive systems for visually impaired people in the future.

Once this phase is defined, a second phase supposes the daily use of the electronic aids followed with monthly evaluations of perceived subjective visual acuity through collection of occipital brain potentials. This procedure is carried out using multifocal electroretinogram to check for neural reorganization in the optic pathway from the photoreceptors to V1 in Cortex occipital.

3   Assistive Solutions for People with Visual Impairements

Assistive technology for the patients with CFL facilitates carrying out their daily activities within the preferred environments. Visual impairment, as any other disability, affects the lifestyle of the people who suffer from it. In case of visual disability, this impact maybe even more sensitive, as vision is the main source of information for the brain.

Perception of visual scenes makes a patient to react agree with the received information. In case this information is not full or it is skewed, the response if the individual can be inadequate or even dangerous. Thus, people with CFL may appear not to see alarm signals or not be aware of potentially dangerous situations. For example, have twice the risk of falling, and four times or more probability to have a hip fracture [2, 13]. Basically, they also have difficulties on a communication level, and in working places, which affects they well-being, and can cause stress and depression [20]. As it is shown in [14], 50% of persons affected with AMD mention that they have certain difficulties while doing daily activities, 16.7% feels psychological pain of discomfort, and 50% confessed that their levels of anxiety and depression have increased. That alarming factors are especially notable within the youngest group of the test respondents. Indeed, in the one hand, visual impairment impedes collaboration with other persons, but, on the other hand, the same difficulties are met while visually impaired interact with other devices and environments. Figure 1 shows the principal benefits for visually impaired persons, which penetrate in all the spheres of their life.

In general, the benefits of the assistive technology for visually impaired persons would start with enabling their daily activities which include orientation, reading, going shopping, going in for sport, and making other activities at their work and leisure time. One of the daily activities that can be corrected is the

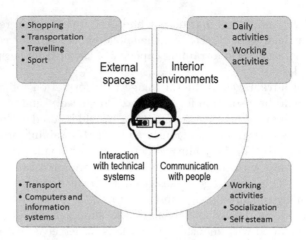

Fig. 1. Benefits of the assistive technology in everyday life

patient's perception of written text, independently if it is a book or an announcement in a shopping center or at the airport. In many cases like that, there is a need for image and video processing. It concentrates in particular on systems that use image and video processing for their transformation that can enable significant improvement of visual perception.

4   A Method of Scotoma Zone Relocation

Within the digital modification of the image, the new technologies enable a series of tools and software that can aid in the management and planning of aids to improve visual acuity through a healthy peripheral retina in patients with low visual acuity [22].

Digital image transformation makes it possible to enhance the input visual scene, allowing to a visually impaired person to perceive the image in a better way. There are many approached based on transformation of particular image characteristics, which include elevating its contrast levels [16], sharpening the edges [16,24], modifying its color and lighting parameters [11], magnifying [15], local image remapping [9], etc. Many claimed having achieved considerable feedbacks from the test participants. Nevertheless, to our opinion, there is still a way to improve the scene perception by a person with CFL. Even in case the image parameters are modified and adapted to the needs of patients, they still do not see a part of the image. They can find the missing element of a puzzle, but in this case they should move the eye, the head, or just guess about the possible answer.

A method of scotoma zone relocation which is presented in this paper, is based on the idea to relocate the image pixels from the "scotoma zone" (SZ) and made them visible to a subject. In more details the pixels from the SZ are moved outside of its limits. Figure 2 shows how the horizontal relocation

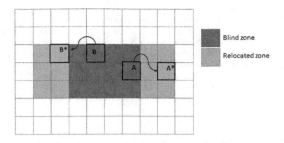

Fig. 2. Horizontal relocation.

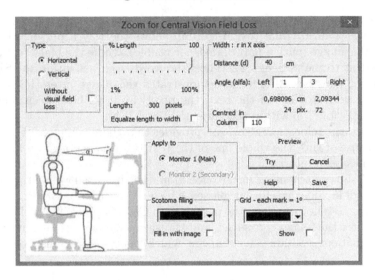

Fig. 3. The screenshot of the "Scotoma module"

is executed. Some points chosen for the example, A and B, are remapped into the points A^* and B^* outside of the SZ. This algorithm has been implemented within the CImagenMDI library.

CImagenMDI is a full and multifunctional C library for digital image processing [4]. It allows application of any generic filters, which are common for standard image processing [10,12]. The latest version 3.6 includes a "Scotoma module". This module provides a test maker with a set of tools to create personalized test images for any patient with CFL. Figure 3 shows a screenshot of the "Scotoma module".

The "Scotoma module" has been developed with the idea to allow precise and detailed configuration of the processed image. First, there is a geometrical localization of a scotoma and adjustment of its boundaries. Thus, the tab "Type" has two options: horizontal and vertical, which stand for the way of image relocated. If it is marked "Without visual camp loss" then the image is readjusted in such a way that non visual information is lost.

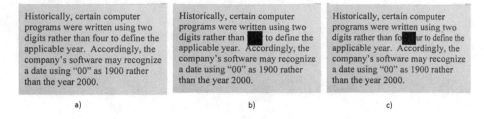

a)   b)   c)

Fig. 4. Scotoma zone relocation for the textual image

Figure 4 presents an example of horizontal SZ relocation for a textual input. Figure 4a shows an original text. Figure 4b shows the way a person with CFL perceives this image (with a part of text not visible), where the black rectangle is correspondent to the patient's SZ. Thus, the word "four" is within the SZ, and, hence, is not perceived. Figure 4c demonstrates the image after the proposed method has been applied to the text, the pixels from SZ have been relocated, and the word "four" is within the patient's visual field.

Moreover, the relocation algorithm provides that there is no loss of the visual camp. Because of this, the whole line of the text is visible, though an area equal to the SZ has been inserted.

Figure 5 shows a scheme of image relocation when it is used within the assistive tool. The tool includes intelligent glasses, which receive a visual input. A part of the input image is not visible to the patient with CFL, because it is occluded with scotoma. After the image is received, and transformed, the final output, which is shown to a patient, contains an subimage, which has been previously occluded.

Fig. 5. A general scheme for visual input relocation.

5   Preliminary Study

The purpose of the current study is to find digital solutions for assistive devices (smart-glasses) which would be integrated into their environments (home and working) and would help for people with CFL to be more independent within them. The software CImagenMDI, used in this study, first, process and generates images for the patient before the training. These images are used to obtain the best perceptive visual characteristics for every patient.

Before starting to use the assistive device, a patient with CFL should undergo two preliminary tests.

1. Visual acuity measurement with ETDRS and the patient with CFL should undergo the Pelli-Robson Contrast Sensitivity test (see Fig. 6a), which determines the ability to perceive slight changes in luminance between regions which are not separated by definite borders [18].
2. Exploration of scotoma size and functionality of the surrounding retina:
   - Microperimetry test (see Fig. 6b). This test is aimed to detect if there are pathologies affecting the macular area, and describe them. Moreover, the microperimetry test has additional abilities to record and control a fixation activity of a patient during the visual field measuring. This test is carried out with the equipment of TOPCON (Micro-meter Maia 2, Topcon) with grid 102 of 68 stimuli.
   - Automated visual field (see Fig. 7) (Zeiss Model Campus Zephyr Visual Field Analyzer 750) in model 30-2 and model 102 focused on fovea, to determine the actual size of perceptual visual field loss.

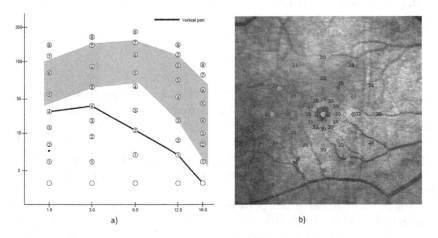

Fig. 6. Outcomes of the Pelli-Robson Contrast Sensitivity test and of the microperimetry test for a patient with scotoma in the right eye.

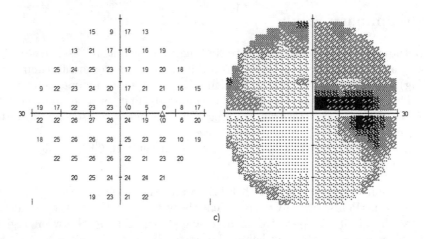

Fig. 7. Healthy automated visual field with central scotoma.

Subsequently in a second phase, once the image is individually adapted to the retinal lesion of a patient, occipital cortex wave through multifocal electroretinogram is registered in order to obtain data of a possible neural reorganization as some studies have found [3,7,20].

After obtaining and analyzing the results of the tests mentioned above, we obtain parameters that include information about the visual acuity of the patient, the location and morphology of the scotoma zone, and the sensitivity surrounding the retinal lesion. From there, the next task is with the help of CImagenMDI to prepare a customized battery of images appropriate to his injury, for each patient, and collect on a numerical scale his visual perception according to the digital modification of the image.

6   Discussion

This paper aims to introduce the method of scotoma zone relocation, and to lighten the ways how this method is going to be implemented within an assistive device for visually impaired. Though the project is on its beginning, a substantial part of the computational work is done. The presented method has been implemented and thoroughly tested within our research laboratory. Much work is still to be done, but at this point we can made some statements about the current state of the research.

Although mane research has been carried out in this area, out intention was to take into consideration limitations as well as achievements of the previous works. Thus, our method is focused on image remapping and its personalized adaptation for the needs of any concrete patient. Different types of visual inputs has been used in order to cover the maximum number of environments covered, though in this paper we concentrated in two types, which include images and texts as the most common inputs. Many researchers claimed that patients with

CFL confirmed that image modification algorithms such as equalization, contrast changes, etc., were better perceived. In this order our future modification of the method presented in this paper, would include these transformations as well.

Further development of the experiment supposes preparation of the personalized batteries of digitally transformed images with the proposed method. These images are given as the inputs for a person with CFL. The final testing suggests that test participants are wearing smart glasses with incorporated real time image enhancement.

Acknowledgements. This research was carried out within the PERVISION project, which has been supported by the Asociación de Innovaciones Tecnológicas en Oftalmología (AITO), Spain. We would also like to thank the Topcon® for the permission to use their equipment for the microperimetry test, as well as the Ophthalmology Department of the University Hospital of Albacete (SESCAM), and the members of the CRAB research group of the UCLM.

References

1. Baseler, H.A., Gouws, A., Haak, K.V., Racey, C., Crossland, M.D., Tufail, A., Rubin, G.S., Cornelissen, F.W., Morland, A.B.: Large-scale remapping of visual cortex is absent in adult humans with macular degeneration. Nat. Neurosci. **14**(5), 649–655 (2011)
2. Boptom, R.Q.I., Cumming, R.G., Mitchell, P., Attebo, K.: Visual impairment and falls in older adults: the Blue Mountains Eye Study. J. Am. Geriatr. Soc. **46**(1), 58–64 (1998)
3. Cheung, S.H., Legge, G.E.: Functional and cortical adaptations to central vision loss. Vis. Neurosci. **22**(2), 187–201 (2005)
4. https://www.dsi.uclm.es/personal/FcoGomez/CImagenMDI/CImagenMDI.html
5. Damian, J., Pastor, R., Armada, F., Arias, L.: Epidemiology of age-related macular degeneration. Situation in Spain. Aten. Prim. **38**(1), 51–57 (2006)
6. Deruaz, A., Whatham, A.R., Mermoud, C., Safran, A.B.: Reading with multiple preferred retinal loci: implications for training a more efficient reading strategy. Vis. Res. **42**(27), 2947–2957 (2002)
7. Dilks, D.D., Julian, J.B., Peli, E., Kanwisher, N.: Reorganization of visual processing in age-related macular degeneration depends on foveal loss. Optom. Vis. Sci. **91**(8), 199–206 (2014)
8. Haak, K.V., Morland, A.B., Engel, S.A.: Plasticity, and its limits, in adult human primary visual cortex. Multisens. Res. **28**(3–4), 297–307 (2015)
9. Farago, P., Barros, L., Cunha, G., Landau, L., Costa, R.M.: ATDV: an image transforming system. In: Sunderam, V.S., van Albada, G.D., Sloot, P.M.A., Dongarra, J.J. (eds.) ICCS 2005. LNCS, vol. 3514, pp. 727–734. Springer, Heidelberg (2005). doi:10.1007/11428831_90
10. Fernández-Caballero, A., Gómez, F.J., López-López, J.: Knowledge-based road traffic monitoring. In: Mira, J., Álvarez, J.R. (eds.) IWINAC 2007. LNCS, vol. 4528, pp. 182–191. Springer, Heidelberg (2007). doi:10.1007/978-3-540-73055-2_20
11. Gao, X.W., Loomes, M.: A new approach to image enhancement for the visually impaired. Electron. Imaging **20**, 1–7 (2016)

12. Gómez, F.J., Fernández-Caballero, A., López, M.T.: Tecnología .NET en Tratamiento Digital de Imágenes: Librería CImagen y aplicación CImagenMDI [in Spanish]. In: Advances en Informática Educativa, SIIE 2004, p. 134. Simposio Internacional de Informática Educativa, Cáceres (2004)
13. Klein, B.E., Klein, R., Lee, K.E., Cruickshanks, K.J.: Performance-based and self-assessed measures of visual function as related to history of falls, hip fractures, and measured gait time. The beaver dam eye study. Ophthalmology 105(1), 160–164 (1998)
14. Langelaan, M., Boer, M.R., Nispen, R.M., Wouters, B., Moll, A.C., Rens, G.H.: Impact of visual impairment on quality of life: a comparison with quality of life in the general population and with other chronic conditions. Ophthalmic Epidemiol. 14(3), 119–126 (2007)
15. Lawton, T.B.: Improved reading performance using individualized compensation filters for observers with losses in central vision. Ophthalmology 96(1), 115–126 (1989)
16. Leat, S.J., Omoruyi, G., Kennedy, A., Jernigan, E.: Generic and customised digital image enhancement filters for the visually impaired. Vis. Res. 45(15), 1991–2007 (2005)
17. Liu, T., Cheung, S.H., Schuchard, R.A., Glielmi, C.B., Hu, X., He, S., Legge, G.E.: Incomplete cortical reorganization in macular degeneration. Invest. Ophthalmol. Vis. Sci. 51(12), 6826–6834 (2010)
18. Mäntyjärvi, M., Laitinen, T.: Normal values for the Pelli-Robson contrast sensitivity test. J. Cataract Refract. Surg. 27(2), 261–266 (2001)
19. Morales, M.U., Saker, S., Amoaku, W.M.: Bilateral eccentric vision training on pseudovitelliform dystrophy with microperimetry biofeedback. BMJ case reports (2015)
20. Silverstone, B., Lang, M.A., Rosenthal, B., Faye, E.E. (eds.): The Lighthouse Handbook on Vision Impairment, Vision Rehabilitation: Two-Volume Set. Oxford University Press, Oxford (2000)
21. Schumacher, E.H., Jacko, J.A., Primo, S.A., Main, K.L., Moloney, K.P., Kinzel, E.N., Ginn, J.: Reorganization of visual processing is related to eccentric viewing in patients with macular degeneration. Restor. Neurol. Neurosci. 26(4–5), 391–402 (2008)
22. Virgili, G., Acosta, R., Grover, L.L., Bentley, S.A., Giacomelli, G.: Reading aids for adults with low vision. The Cochrane Library (2013)
23. WHO: Visual impairment and blindness. http://www.who.int/mediacentre/factsheets/fs282/en/. Accessed 18 Mar 2016
24. Wolffsohn, J.S., Mukhopadhyay, D., Rubinstein, M.: Image enhancement of real-time television to benefit the visually impaired. Am. J. Ophthalmol. 144(3), 436–440 (2007)

Performance of Predicting Surface Quality Model Using Softcomputing, a Comparative Study of Results

Víctor Flores[1](✉), Maritza Correa[2], and Yadira Quiñonez[3]

[1] Departamento de Ingeniería de Sistema y Computación,
Universidad Católica del Norte, Avda. Angamos 0610, Antofagsta, Chile
vflores@ucn.cl

[2] Facultad de Ingeniería, Departamento de Operaciones y Sistemas,
Universidad Autónoma de Occidente, Cali, Colombia
mcorrea@uao.edu.co

[3] Facultad de Informática Mazatlán, Universidad Autónoma de Sinaloa,
Av. Universidad y Leonismo Internacional S/N, Culiacán, Mexico
yadiraqui@uas.edu.mx

Abstract. This paper describes a comparative study of performance of two models predicting surface quality in high-speed milling (HSM) processes using two different machining centers. The models were created with experimental data obtained from two machine-tools with different characteristics, but using the same experimental model. In both cases, work pieces (probes) of the same material were machined (steel and aluminum probes) with cutting parameters and characteristics proper of production processes in industries such as aeronautics and automotive. The main objective of this study was to compare surface quality prediction models created in two machining centers to establish differences in outcomes and the possible causes of these differences. In addition, this paper deals with the validation of each model concerning surface quality obtained, along with comparing the quality of the models with other predictive surface quality models based on similar techniques.

Keywords: High-speed machining · High-speed milling · Softcomputing · Bayesian networks · Predictive models

1 Introduction

High-speed milling (HSM) is a technique used for producing industrial pieces using materials such as plastic or metal alloys. One of the reasons for using HSM is the high-quality surface finishing possible to get [13]. Currently, HSM is one of the processes producing the greatest economic impact on the metal making industry owing to the surface finishing influencing the functional behavior of a resulting piece, which is subjected to demanding friction conditions, sudden temperature changes, etc. [2,4].

© Springer International Publishing AG 2017
J.M. Ferrández Vicente et al. (Eds.): IWINAC 2017, Part I, LNCS 10337, pp. 233–242, 2017.
DOI: 10.1007/978-3-319-59740-9_23

The surface quality obtained with material removal techniques such as HSM greatly depends on experimental design (DOE) [18]. This must include several factors such as properties of the material to be milled, characteristics of the machining center, and the tool used. In the field of surface quality, there is a trend to use data management techniques such as Soft computing to obtain data for improving HSM quality outcomes using a given DOE. Soft computing techniques help identify factors influencing HSM and their most convenient values to achieve the best surface quality (Ra), minimizing associated costs such as instrument calibration, experimentation, intermediate or final quality measures, etc. [7].

Surface quality is frequently associated with texture or surface roughness; this can be calculated from several parameters [18]. In practice, Ra is the parameter most used for estimating the quality of a piece and may be quite easily measured [9] using, for example, profilometers. According to ISO standard 4288:1996, Ra values may be calculated with a equation, in [5] this procedure is described.

In addition, Ra has a great influence on other interesting factors for making metal pieces such as friction, electric and thermal resistance, and the appearance of a finished piece. In the same context, Ra is important because it contributes with ideas about the behavior of a surface in contact with others or dimensional warping [12]. In this way, the DOE and Ra are importants, since that the costs, machining time can be reduced [9,22]. Recently, studies as one presented in [1] introduce Artificial Intelligence techniques on DOE and pre-process designs, adding variables as power-consumption or results of previous experiences (learning) in order to achieve a automatic cutting parameters configuration.

1.1   Bayesian Models

A Bayesian network is a directed acyclical graph with nodes representing predictive variables and the class and arcs representing their relational conditions. Nodes may represent variables such as cutting parameters in a HSM process. So, given two variables X1, X2, an arc between X1 and X2 represents the conditional relation between X1 and X2 [10]. The acyclical graph contains the probabilistic distributions of the influences among variables P(X1, X2, ..., Xi, ..., Xn). This can be written as the product of local distributions of each node as follows [11]:

$$P(X_1, X_2, \ldots, X_n) = \prod_{k=1}^{k=n} X_1, X_2, \ldots X_n \tag{1}$$

The distribution of the conditional probability P(Xi) in Eq. 2 is determined by the set of parameters Parents(Xi). The Bayesian classifier selects the most probable classification P(Xi), given distribution values X1, X2, ... Xi, ..., Xn. The Bayesian classifier results from the Bayes theorem application (Friedman et al. 2005), which calculates the a posteriori probability P(Cj|Xi) from conditional probabilities P(Xi|Ck) and a priori probability P(Ck) as:

$$P(Xi) = \frac{P(Cj|Xi)}{\sum_{k=1}^{n} P(Ck)} \tag{2}$$

where: P(Cj|Xi) represents the a posteriori probability of Xi giving the class Cj. That is: giving the class Cj in the presence of the value Xi, the probability that sample Xi (with given characteristics) belong to a given class Cj. P(Cj) represents the a priori probability. This is the initial probability for a sample Xi to belong to a given class Cj, without Xi characteristic information.

The Bayesian classifier can be used to predict class or classify new or unknown instances of a class. In addition, the probabilities of Eq. (2) can be estimated from expert knowledge or training data, using predictive variables and class in the latter case [15]. There are several Bayesian classifiers for creating predictive models from data. This study uses the Tree Augmented Nave Bayes model (TAN), which is a variant of Nave Bayes model. TAN allows calculating conditional mutual data for each pair of predictive variables for a given class [6].

1.2 Related Studies

The use of Soft computing techniques to generate Ra predictive models has increased in the last few years. One of the reasons for this is the quality and accuracy of the estimation of a parameter such as Ra done with Soft computing techniques [3,14]. For example, in [8] a technique based on Artificial Neural Networks is proposed to optimize the selection of parameters participating in the process of mechanical cutting using steel Inconel 718. Other studies propose the use of Artificial Neural Networks to study the surface roughness on-line [22].

The Artificial Neuronal Networks are used also on [19] to studied the variables influence on final Ra where a milling process on aluminum alloys, variables as feed rate, milling deep or speed milling are been studied here. Other methods to Ra estimated based on Neuronal Artificial Networks are described on [17] using AISA1054 alloys or [7] that describe a Soft Computing experience to generate a Ra predictive model using neuro-fuzzy and artificial neuronal networks. To make this work, variables as milling speed or milling deep had been used.

2 Models Description

In this study, Bayesian networks were used to create probabilistic Ra prediction models in HSM by milling metal alloys. The models were created using data from two different machining centers, but only one experimental design (details in [6,9]). Two HSM geometries kinds had made here: slots and girth. Slots were made in the first essay and various geometries were conducted in the second one.

Essays were first conducted in a Kondia HS1000 machining center with 3 degrees of freedom equipped with a CNC Siemens 840D, maximum engine power of 17.5 KW, and maximum spindle speed of 24000 rpm. In the second essay, a machining center made by Nicolás Correa S.A., Versa model (variant 675004) with 5 degrees of freedom (hereinafter M-Versa) was used. This machining center is equipped with a CNC Heidenhain TNCi530, with maximum engine power of 50 KW and maximum spindle speed of 15000 rpm.

A Kistler dynamometric platform was used for collecting power data in axes x y, and z and a Kistler 5070 amplifier to improve signals. The signals collected were later registered with a data acquisition software (designed with Labview software tool) and installed in an industrial computer. The models were created with software Weka (http://www.cs.waikato.ac.nz/~ml/weka/index.html. Weka is a software licensed by GNU. It is implemented with Bayesian algorithms necessary to do this study).

2.1 Description of Experimention with Slots

To mill slots, $180 \times 100 \times 25$-mm F114 steel probes were used and 2–6 teeth Karnash tools (models 30.6455 and 30.6465) were used for milling the probes. Tools with different diameters were used in the experiments: 6, 8, 10, and 12 mm for each number of teeth. Slots were milled at different depths, varying the progress and spindle speed with the same tool to render several combinations of experiments (with increases of 25%, 50%, and 75%). Then, the essays were repeated for each tool. Table 1 shows values of variables in the essays.

To calculate Ra values, post-process measures were taken with a Karl Zeiss Handysurf profilometer, model E-35A. In the case of the Kondia machining center, experimentation rendered 625000 measures which were grouped in 250 cases from averaging roughness values, according to the experimentation objectives described in [6]. In the case of experimentation, the result was 1475 cases obtained in the same way.

To create the Ra predictive model with slots, a Bayesian model with 7 variables (6 predictive variables plus class Ra) were used. The variables associated with cutting conditions are: axial depth of cut (ap), feed rate (F), and spindle rotation speed (n). The variables associated with the tool are: number of teeth (z) and diameter (diam). Variable FT corresponds to the force resulting from measures in axes x, y, and z.

2.2 Slots Models Validation

Figure 1a and b illustrate the TAN structure learned from experimentation with slots in the Kondia HS1000 and M-Versa machining centers. Figure 1 also shows the causal arcs between predictive variables and the class.

The causal arcs in Fig. 1 represent the influence of physical relations between predictive variables and the class. The causal structure on Fig. 1a show the influence of variable rpm over diam, and the influence of variable diam on the rest of predictive variables. The rpm causal influence can be wear-machine attributed, losing all influence in M-Versa model. The networks in Fig. 1a show the influence of variable diam on the rest of the predictive variables in Kondia model, losing influence in M-Versa model.

The clear influence of variable F (feed rate) on the rest of the predictive variables is observed in the model of M-Versa machining center, while this influence

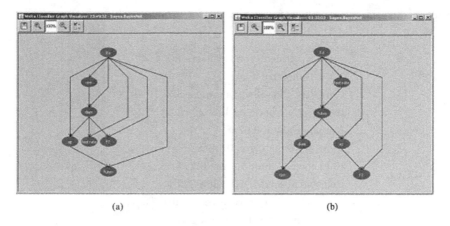

(a)   (b)

Fig. 1. TAN structure learned from slot experimentation.

does not exist in the model of the Kondia machining center. The causal structure on Fig. 1b show the influence of variable feed rate on the rest of predictive
variables, while this influence does not exist in the model of the Kondia.

Differences in the conditional relationships obtained may correspond to the
physical influence as vibrations of machines or other factors such power equipment, where the classification results are analyzed, they show interesting finds
respect to Bayes classifier blessing [20]. Tables 3 and 4 shows these results. The
Table 3 shows that 76.80% of cases are correctly classified instances (CCI) for
Kondia, while 72.74% are CCI for M-Versa (Table 4). The variation between
Kondia classification and M-Versa classification can be explained by the DOE
and Bayesian model were designed for Kondia.

2.3   Description of Experimentation with Islands and Pockets

To create cases with geometries (islands and pockets), aluminum pieces of 65–70
Brinell hardness and $170 \times 100 \times 25$ mm were milled. Milling was done with Sanvik
tools of 2 teeth and 8, 10, 12, 16, and 20-mm diameter at a maximum of 10-mm
depth of cut. Millings consisted of two types: pockets and islands. Pockets were
milled on 35-mm and 55-mm diameter circumferences, respectively, reaching 10-
mm depth.

Two types of geometries were designed for pockets: the first ones were
designed with 60-mm diameter pockets (pocket ++), milling the material at
a 0.5-mm axial depth of cut and a 10-mm radial depth of cut. The second ones
were designed with 35-mm diameter pockets (pocket +), milling the material at
a 1-mm axial depth of cut and a 5-mm radial depth of cut. To create the Ra
predictive model, an 8-variable Bayesian model (7 predictive variables and class
Ra) was used. The variables are feed rate (fz), tool diameter (diam), radial depth
of cut (ae), material hardness in Brinell (HB), geometry (geom) resulting from

Table 1. Stratification and confusion matrix for Kondia milling center with slots cutting

=== Stratified cross-validation ===
=== Summary ===
Correctly Classified Instances 192 76.80 %
Incorrectly Classified Instances 58 23.2%
Kappa statistic 0.6708
Mean absolute error 0.1392
Root mean squared error 0.2754
Relative absolute error 38.6323%
Root relative squared error 64.9107%
Total Number of Instances 250
=== Confusion Matrix ===
a, b, c, d, <– classified as
29 17 4 0 | a = Smooth
1 90 8 1 | b = Fine
0 11 33 6 | c = Semi-fine
0 1 9 40 | d = Medium

Table 2. Stratification and confusion matrix for Kondia milling center with slots cutting

=== Stratified cross-validation ===
=== Summary ===
Correctly Classified Instances 1073 72.74 %
Incorrectly Classified Instances 402 27.25%
Kappa statistic 0.465
Mean absolute error 0.1552
Root mean squared error 0.2827
Relative absolute error 59.8084%
Root relative squared error 78.5208%
Total Number of Instances 1475
=== Confusion Matrix ===
a, b, c, d, <– classified as
524 195 0 0 | a = Smooth
179 549 0 0 | b = Fine
27 1 0 0 | c = Semi-fine
0 0 0 0 | d = Medium

the combination of the characteristics of cut radio and curve, spindle rotation speed (n), and the resulting cutting force on the plane (Fxy) (Table 2).

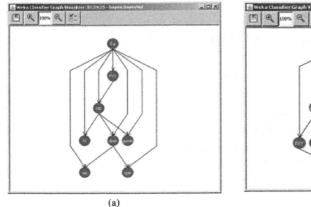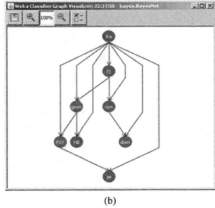

| (a) | (b) |

Fig. 2. TAN structure learned from islands and pockets experimentation.

2.4   Islands and Pockets Models Validation

Figures 2a and b illustrate the TAN structures learned from experimentation with islands and pockets. In the TAN network of the Konia model (Fig. 2a) the influence of variable Fxy on the other predictive variables can be observed; on the contrary, in the model obtained for the M-Versa center (Fig. 2b), the variable Fxy loses importance. In the two models, variable geom and variable hardness (HB) has reverse influences each other. This can indicates that the cutting geometry and material hardness relation of the workpiece to be machined must be taken into account in this type of milling.

In addition, the variations in conditional relations observed may correspond to the physical influence of the machining centers, although there are not enough data to interpret the phenomenon. It is sensed in this case being M-Versa a machining center stronger and better anchor (less vibration occurs), in add, on this case the relationship can be given by the type of material being cut.

Tables 3 and 4 summarize the classifications obtained. In the case of M-Versa, 96.09% cases were correctly classified, while in the case of Kondia, classification is quite significant (94.05%). The classification closest to this value is the one generated with the essays conducted in the Kondia machining center, thus supporting the good selection of predictive variables with respect to the class for this machine-tool.

Table 3. Stratification and confusion matrix for Kondia milling center with islands and pockets cutting

=== Stratified cross-validation ===
=== Summary ===
Correctly Classified Instances 1187 94.0571%
Incorrectly Classified Instances 75 5.9429%
Kappa statistic 0.9105
Mean absolute error 0.0381
Root mean squared error 0.1359
Relative absolute error 11.4089%
Root relative squared error 33.2712%
Total Number of Instances 1262
=== Confusion Matrix ===
a, b, c, d, <– classified as
492 15 0 3 | a = Smooth
50 324 0 0 | b = Fine
0 0 17 1 | c = Semi-fine
6 0 0 354 | d = Medium

Table 4. Stratification and confusion matrix for M-Versa milling center with islands and pockets cutting

=== Stratified cross-validation ===
=== Summary ===
Correctly Classified Instances 1575 96.0952%
Incorrectly Classified Instances 64 3.9048%
Kappa statistic 0.8454
Mean absolute error 0.0444
Root mean squared error 0.1781
Relative absolute error 18.2638%
Root relative squared error 51.0883%
Total Number of Instances 1639
=== Confusion Matrix ===
a, b, c, d, <– classified as
1364 43 0 0 | a = Smooth
21 211 0 0 | b = Fine
0 0 0 0 | c = Semi-fine
0 0 0 0 | d = Medium

3   Conclusion

The contribution of this study is mainly associated with the validation of an experimental design ad hoc for a machining center (Kondia) in another machine-tool with different characteristics. This validation is rather unusual in the domain of this industry because experimentation is rather costly. The models performance had been found during tests and analysis made on classifiers results.

This study proved that this experimental design can be applied in other machining centers with similar characteristics to Kondia center. That is the case of M-Versa, in which classification outcomes show accuracy higher than 70% correctly classified for slots cases and higher than 96% correctly classified for islands and pockets cases.

This allows to believe that the DOE and model designs are good quality for Ra estimation when machining center characteristics has been given. Another important contribution is that the models were created without considering the forces during milling as part of predictive variables, unlike previous studies. This makes the models rather independent of possible classification distortions, which may be caused by the different millings in the machining centers (e.g., spindle wear).

Acknowledgments. The authors want to thank the collaboration of Nicolás Correa S.A for the use of the M-Versa machining center made in the company, particularly thank Dr. Andrés Bustillo from Nicolás Correa S.A., who enabled experimentation in the company. The authors also thank the Centro de Automática y Robótica at CSIC (Spain), where the rest of the experimentation was made using Kondia machine-tool, as part of the team from Ghame group belonging to this center.

References

1. Ahmad, N., Janahiraman, T.V.: Modelling and prediction of surface roughness and power consumption using parallel extreme learning machine based particle swarm optimization. In: Cao, J., Mao, K., Cambria, E., Man, Z., Toh, K.-A. (eds.) Proceedings of ELM-2014 Volume 2. PALO, vol. 4, pp. 321–329. Springer, Cham (2015). doi:10.1007/978-3-319-14066-7_31

2. Altintas, Y., Weck, M.: Chatter stability of metal cutting and grinding. CIRP Ann. Manuf. Technol. **53**, 40–51 (2004)

3. Badu, S., Vinayagam, B.: Surface roughness prediction model using adaptive particle swarm optimization (APSO) algorithm. Intell. Fuzzy Syst. **28**, 345–360 (2015)

4. Benardos, P., Vosniakos, G.: Predicting surface roughness in machining: a review. Int. J. Mach. Tools Manuf. **43**, 833–844 (2003)

5. Correa, M., Bielza, C., Ramírez, M., Alique, J.R.: A Bayesian network model for surface roughness prediction in the machining process. Int. J. Syst. Sci. **39**, 1181–1192 (2008)

6. Correa, M., Bielza, C., Pamies-Teixeira, P.: Comparison of Bayesian networks and artificial neural networks for quality detection in a machining process. Expert Syst. Appl. **36**(3), 7270–7279 (2009)

7. D'Mello, G., Pai, S.: Prediction of surface roughness in high speed machining: a comparison. Proc. Int. J. Res. Eng. Technol. **1**, 519–525 (2014)

8. Ezugwua, E., Faderea, D., Onney, J., Bonney, J., Silva, R., Sales, W.: Modelling the correlation between cutting and process parameters in high-speed machining of Inconel 718 alloy using artificial neural network. Int. J. Mach. Tools Manuf. **45**, 1375–1385 (2005)

9. Flores, V., Correa, M., Alique, J.R.: Modelo Pre-Proceso de predicción de la Calidad Superficial en Fresado a Alta Velocidad basado en Soft Computing. Revista Iberoamericana de Automática e Informática Industrial RIAI **8**(1), 38–43 (2011)

10. Friedman, N., Geiger, D., Goldszmit, M.: Bayesian network classifiers. Mach. Learn. **29**, 131–161 (1997)

11. Hao, W., Zhu, X., Li, X.: Prediction of cutting force for self-propelled rotary tool using artificial neural network. J. Mater. Process. Technol. **180**, 23–29 (2006)

12. Izamshah, R., Yuhazri, M., Hadzley, M., Amran, M.: Effects of end mill helix angle on accuracy for machining thin-rib aerospace component. Appl. Mech. Mater. **315**, 773–777 (2013)

13. Jiang, B., He, T., Gu, Y., et al.: Method for recognizing wave dynamics damage in high-speed milling cutter. Int. J. Adv. Manuf. Technol. (2017). doi:10.1007/s00170-017-0128-1

14. Lela, B., Bajie, D., Jozié, S.: Regression analysis, support vector machines, and Bayesian neural network approaches to modelling surface roughness in face milling. Adv. Manuf. Technol. **42**, 1082–1089 (2009)

15. MacQueen, J.: Some methods for classification analysis of multivariate observations. In: Proceedings of the 5th Berkeley Symposium on Mathematical Statistics and Probability, pp. 281–297 (2003)

16. Shang, S., Li, J.: Tool wear and cutting forces variation in high-speed end-milling Ti-6Al-4V alloy. Int. J. Adv. Manuf. Technol. **46**, 69–78 (2010)

17. Ozel, T., Esteves, A., Davim, J.: Neural network process modelling for turning of steel parts using conventional and wiper inserts. Int. J. Mater. Prod. Technol. **35**, 246–258 (2009)

18. Ramírez-Cadena, M., Correa, M., Rodríguez-González, C., Alique, J.R.: Surface roughness modeling based on surface roughness feature concept for high speed machining. Am. Soc. Mech. Eng. Manuf. Eng. Div. **16**(1), 811–815 (2005)

19. Soleimanimehr, H., Nategh, M., Amini, S.: Modelling of surface roughness in vibration cutting by artificial neural network. Proc. World Acad. Sci. Eng. Technol. **40**, 386–390 (2009)

20. Stone, M.: Cross-validatory choice and assessment of statistical prediction. J. Roy. Stat. Soc. **36**, 111–147 (1974)

21. Zhou, L., Cheng, K.: Dynamic cutting process modelling and its impact on the generation of surface topography and texture in nano/micro cutting. In: Proceedings of IMechE-2009, vol. 233, pp. 247–266 (2009)

22. Zuperl, U., Cus, F.: Optimization of cutting conditions during cutting by using neural networks. Robot. Comput. Integr. Manuf. **19**, 189–199 (2003)

Emotions

Temporal Dynamics of Human Emotions: An Study Combining Images and Music

M.D. Grima Murcia[1,2]([✉]), Jennifer Sorinas[1], M.A. Lopez-Gordo[3],
Jose Manuel Ferrández[2], and Eduardo Fernández[1]([✉])

[1] Institute of Bioengineering, University Miguel Hernández and CIBER BBN,
Avenida de la Universidad, 03202 Elche, Spain
{maria.grima,e.fernandez}@umh.es
[2] Department of Electronics and Computer Technology,
University of Cartagena, Cartagena, Spain
[3] Department of Signal Theory, Communications and Networking,
University of Granada, 18071 Granada, Spain

Abstract. Much is currently being studied on emotions and their temporal and spatial location. In this framework it is important to considerer the temporal dynamics of affective responses and also the underlying brain activity. In this work we use electroencephalographic (EEG) recordings to investigate the neural activity of 13 human volunteers while looking standardized images (positive/negative). Furthermore the subjects were, at the same time, listening to pleasant or unpleasant music. Then we analyzed topographic changes in EEG activity in the time domain. When we compared positive images with positive music versus negative images with negative music we found a significant time window in the period of time 448–632 ms after the stimulus appears, with a clear right lateralization for negative stimuli and left lateralization for positive stimuli. By contrast when we compared positive images with negative music versus negative images with positive music, we found a delayed window compared to the previous case (592–618 ms) and the marked lateralization disappeared. These results demonstrate the feasibility and usefulness of this approach to explore the temporal dynamics of human emotions and could help to set the basis for future studies of music perception and emotions.

Keywords: EEG · Emotions · Music · IAPS

1 Introduction

The emotional interaction between humans and machines is one of the most important challenges in advanced human-machine interaction. One of the most important requisites in this field is to develop reliable emotion recognition systems, and for it we need to correctly identify emotions.

Some researchers support the notion of biphasic emotion, which states that emotion fundamentally stems from varying activation in centrally organized

© Springer International Publishing AG 2017
J.M. Ferrández Vicente et al. (Eds.): IWINAC 2017, Part I, LNCS 10337, pp. 245–253, 2017.
DOI: 10.1007/978-3-319-59740-9_24

appetitive and defensive motivational systems that have evolved to mediate the wide range of adaptive behaviors necessary for an organism struggling to survive in the physical world [1,2]. In this framework, neuroscientists have made great efforts to determine how the relationship between the stimulus input and the behavioral output is mediated though specific neural circuits that are highly organized [3].

The majority of studies in this area are based on techniques such as Positron Emission Tomography (PET) [4] or functional Magnetic Resonance Imaging (fMRI) [5] with exceptional spatial resolution but a very reduced temporal one (seconds). An alternative, which offers an excellent temporal resolution (in the range of milliseconds) is Electroencephalography (EEG).

In this study we investigated the temporal dynamics of neural activity associated to emotions (like/dislike) generated by looking at complex pictures derived from the International Affective Picture System (IAPS) [6] while the subjects listen to pleasant or unpleasant music. We used EEG to solve the problem of temporal resolution. We evaluated the correspondences between subjective emotional experiences induced by the pictures and then the role of the music in the resulting brain activity. Then we estimated the underlying neural places in which event-related potentials (ERPs) were generated and the tridimensional location of this locations was used for the assessment of changes in the activation of cortical networks involved in emotion processing.

Our results offer valuable information to better understand the temporal dynamics of emotions generated to visual and auditive stimuli and could be useful for the development of effective and reliable neural interfaces.

2 Methods

Participants

Thirteen persons participated in this study (mean age: 19.8; range: 19–38; seven men, six women). All of them were right handed with a laterality quotient of at least +0.4 (mean 0.7, SD: 0.2) on the Edinburgh Inventory [7].

All participants had no personal history of psychiatric or neurological disorder, alcohol or drug abuse, or current medication, and had normal or corrected to normal vision and audition. All were comprehensively informed about the details and the purpose of the study and gave their written consent for participation.

Visual and Auditory Stimuli

A set of standardized visual stimuli (80 pictures in total) was selected from the IAPS dataset [6]. These stimuli were validated in a previous study [8].

The images were divided into four groups, each one consisted of 20 images. Stimuli were presented in color, with equal contrast and luminance.

Pleasant music were two excerpts of joyful instrumental dance tunes: A. Dvorák, Slavonic Dance No. 8 in G Minor (Op. 46); J.S. Bach, Rejouissance (BWV 1069) and other fragments of music used previously in similar studies [9].

Unpleasant music were electronically manipulated (stimuli were processed using Cool Edit Pro software): For each pleasant stimulus, a new soundfile was created in which the original (pleasant) excerpt was recorded simultaneously with two pitches-shifted versions of the same excerpt, the pitch-shifted versions being one shade above and a return below the original pitch. Both pleasant and unpleasant versions of an excerpt, original and electronically manipulated, had the same dynamic outline, identical rhythmic structure, and identical melodic contour, rendering it impossible that simply the bottom-up processing of these stimulus dimensions already contributes to brain activation patterns when contrasting effects of pleasant and unpleasant stimuli.

Subjects were instructed to give each stimulus a score from 1 to 9 avoiding 5 depending on subjective taste (1: dislike; 9: like). Their verbal response was written.

Procedure

Figure 1 summarizes the serial configuration of the study. Each image was presented for 500 ms and was followed by a black screen lasting 3500 ms. The music started five seconds before the images started and finished five seconds later. The images appeared randomly and only once. The participants' task was to observe the images and rate the arousal and valence of its emotional experience. Pictures score ranged from 9 (very pleasant) to 1 (very unpleasant).

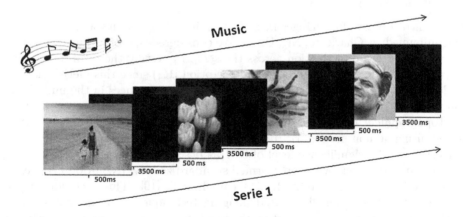

Fig. 1. Experimental scheme. The sequence of stimuli was presented in a random and continuous mode by using python software

Data Acquisition

The participants were seated in a comfortable position and asked to move as little as possible. Following the preparation phase, participants were instructed about the task. The pictures were presented through to a 21.5-inch computer screen to the subject in the dark.

We inculcated subjects to avoiding blinking during image exposure and trying to keep the gaze toward the monitor center. EEG data was continuously recorded by means of cap-mounted Ag-AgCl electrodes and a NeuroScan SynAmps EEG amplifier (Compumedics, Charlotte, NC, USA) from 64 locations according to the international 10/20 system (FP1, FPZ, FP2, AF3, GND, AF4, F7, F5, F3, F1, FZ, F2, F4, F6, F8, FT7, FC5, FC3, FC1, FCZ, FC2, FC4, FC6, FT8, T7, C5, C3, C1, CZ, C2, C4, C6, T8, REF, TP7, CP5, CP3, CP1, CPZ, CP2, CP4, CP6, TP8, P7, P5, P3, P1, PZ, P2, P4, P6, P8, PO7, PO5, PO3, POZ, PO4, PO6, PO8, CB1, O1, OZ, O2, CB2) [10]. The impedance of recording electrodes was examined for each subject prior to data collection and the thresholds were kept less 25 kΩ as recommended [11]. All the recordings were performed at a sampling rate of 1000 Hz. Data were re-referenced to a Common Average Reference (CAR) and EEG signals were filtered using a 0.5 Hz high-pass and low-pass 45 Hz filters. Electrical artifacts due to gesticulation and eye blinking were corrected using Principal Component Analysis (PCA) [12]. They were identified as signal levels above 75 µV in the 5 frontal electrodes (FP1, FPZ, FP2, AF3 and AF4). These electrodes were chosen because they are the most affected by potential unconscious movements. The time interval for artifact detection was within the interval (-200 ms, $+500$ ms) from stimulus onset.

The images were separated according to their valence (positive or negative) and the accompanying music (positive or negative).

Statistical Analyses

We studied topographic changes in EEG activity [13–16] with the help of Curry 7 (Compumedics, Charlotte, NC, USA). We considered the total time course and the whole pattern of activation across the scalp by testing the total field power from all electrodes (see for additional description [17]) since this method is able to detect not only variances in amplitude, but also differences in the underlying sources of activity.

Topographical differences in EEG activity between different images were tested using a non-parametric randomization test (Topographic ANOVA or TANOVA) and a significance level of 0.01 as described elsewhere [8,18].

On significant windows we performed standardized low resolution brain electromagnetic tomography (sLORETA) calculations [19]. This technique is an advanced low resolution distributed imaging technique for brain source localization that provides smooth and better localization for deep sources, with less localization errors but with low spatial resolution.

3   Results

Subjective Scores

The participants identified correctly the positive songs heard in each of the blocks, however, did not obtain very low scores for the unpleasant music (see Fig. 2). In fact, none was scored below five.

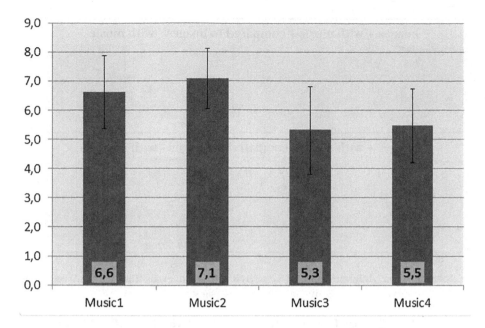

Fig. 2. Average score music for all volunteers. Music 1 and 2 correspond to the pleasant excerpts, while Music 3 and 4 correspond to unpleasant ones.

EEG

Upper Fig. 3 shows the main significant differences when we showed positive images (score 9 or 8) while the participants were listening to pleasant music regarding images with negative valence (score 1 or 2) presented simultaneously with negative music. We found a large significant time window between 448 ms to 632 ms (sig < 0.05). If the significant criteria is decreased to 0.01, the time window was reduced to 501–553 ms.

When the subjects were looking at positive images (score 9 or 8) while listening to negative music or looking at or negative images (score 1 or 2) while listening to positive music, there was also a large significant time window between 553 ms to 692 ms (sig < 0.05), see Fig. 3. When we decreased the significance to 0.01, the time window was also reduced to 592–618 ms.

sLoreta

Figure 4 shows the main results when we considered all possible source locations simultaneously applying standardized LORETA (sLORETA). We found a left lateralization when both the visual and auditory stimulus had positive valence whereas there was a clear right lateralization when both, visual and auditory stimuli were negative (Fig. 4). However, when we mixed positive images with negative sounds or viceversa there was not a clear laterality.

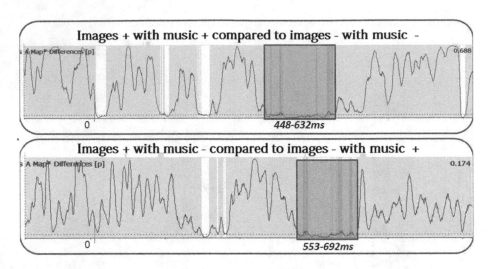

Fig. 3. Significant differences in EEG activity to each case. The vertical rectangle contains the interval with significant differences (sig < 0.05).

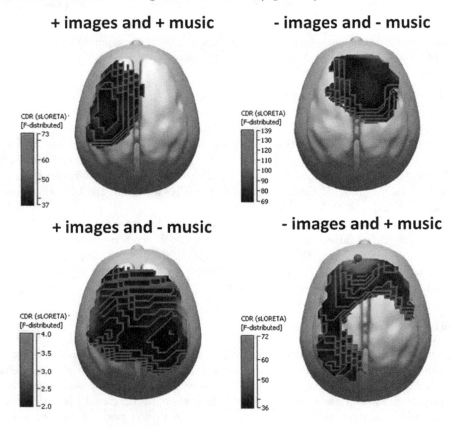

Fig. 4. Activation maps for sLoreta corresponding to a time window (sig < 0.01).

4   Discussion and Conclusion

Our results showed an increased activity in the left hemisphere for emotions with a positive valence whereas there was an increased activity in the right hemisphere for emotions with a negative valence. These results support our previous studies [8] and suggest that the visual emotional valence is reinforced when it coincides with the valence of the music. Furthermore these results agree with the valence hypothesis, which postulates a preferential engagement of the left hemisphere for positive emotions and of the right hemisphere for negative emotions [20, 21].

In addition we found a delay of a few milliseconds in the whole brain processing when images and music have different valences. Thus when both stimuli are not concordant, emotional processing takes more time.

Although more studies are still needed, our results demonstrate the feasibility and usefulness of presenting simultaneously visual and auditory information to explore the temporal dynamics of human emotions.

These results demonstrate the feasibility and usefulness of this approach to explore the temporal dynamics of human emotions and could help to set the basis for future studies of music perception and emotions. Furthermore this approach could be useful to better understand the role of specific brain regions and their relation to specific emotional or cognitive responses.

Acknowledgement. This work has been supported in part by the Spanish national research program (MAT2015-69967-C3-1), by a research grant of the Spanish Blind Organization (ONCE) by the Ministry of Education of Spain (FPU grant AP-2013/01842) and by Séneca Foundation - Agency of Science and Technology of the Region of Murcia.

References

1. Cacioppo, J.T., Berntson, G.G.: Relationship between attitudes and evaluative space: a critical review, with emphasis on the separability of positive and negative substrates. Psychol. Bull. **115**(3), 401–423 (1994). doi:10.1037/0033-2909.115.3. 401

2. Davidson, R.J., Ekman, P., Saron, C.D., Senulis, J.A., Friesen, W.V.: Approach-withdrawal and cerebral asymmetry: emotional expression and brain physiology. I. J. Pers. Soc. Psychol. **58**(2), 330–341 (1990). http://www.ncbi.nlm.nih.gov/pubmed/2319445

3. Fanselow, M.S.: Neural organization of the defensive behavior system responsible for fear. Psychon. Bull. Rev. **1**(4), 429–438 (1994). doi:10.3758/BF03210947. http://www.ncbi.nlm.nih.gov/pubmed/24203551

4. Royet, J.-P., Zald, D., Versace, R., Costes, N., Lavenne, F., Koenig, O., Gervais, R.: Emotional responses to pleasant and unpleasant olfactory, visual, and auditory stimuli: a positron emission tomography study. J. Neurosci. **20**(20), 7752–7759 (2000). http://www.jneurosci.org/ cgi/content/abstract/20/20/7752

5. Vink, M., Derks, J.M., Hoogendam, J.M., Hillegers, M., Kahn, R.S.: Functional differences in emotion processing during adolescence and early adulthood. NeuroImage **91**, 70–76 (2014). doi:10.1016/j.neuroimage.2014.01.035. http://www.ncbi.nlm.nih.gov/pubmed/24468408, http://linkinghub.elsevier.com/retrieve/pii/S1053811914000561
6. Lang, P., Bradley, M., Cuthbert, B.: International affective picture system (IAPS): technical manual and affective ratings. In: NIMH Center for the Study of Emotion and Attention, pp. 39–58 (1997). doi:10.1027/0269-8803/a000147, arXiv:0005-7916(93)E0016-Z, http://www.unifesp.br/dpsicobio/adap/instructions.pdf%5Cn, http://econtent.hogrefe.com/doi/abs/10.1027/0269-8803/a000147
7. Oldfield, R.: The assessment and analysis of handedness: the Edinburgh inventory. Neuropsychologia **9**(1), 97–113 (1971). doi:10.1016/0028-3932(71)90067-4. http://linkinghub.elsevier.com/retrieve/pii/0028393271900674
8. Murcia, M.D.G., Lopez-Gordo, M.A., Ortíz, M.J., Ferrández, J.M., Fernández, E.: Spatio-temporal dynamics of images with emotional bivalence. In: Ferrández Vicente, J.M., Álvarez-Sánchez, J.R., de la Paz López, F., Toledo-Moreo, F.J., Adeli, H. (eds.) IWINAC 2015. LNCS, vol. 9107, pp. 203–212. Springer, Cham (2015). doi:10.1007/978-3-319-18914-7_21. http://link.springer.com/10.1007/978-3-319-18914-7_21
9. Sammler, D., Grigutsch, M., Fritz, T., Koelsch, S.: Music and emotion: electrophysiological correlates of the processing of pleasant and unpleasant music. Psychophysiology **44**(2), 293–304 (2007). doi:10.1111/j.1469-8986.2007.00497.x. http://doi.wiley.com/10.1111/j.1469-8986.2007.00497.x
10. Klem, G.H., Lüders, H.O., Jasper, H.H., Elger, C.: The ten-twenty electrode system of the international federation. International federation of clinical neurophysiology. Electroencephalogr. Clin. Neurophysiol. **52**(Suppl.), 3–6 (1999). http://www.ncbi.nlm.nih.gov/pubmed/10590970
11. Ferree, T.C., Luu, P., Russell, G.S., Tucker, D.M.: Scalp electrode impedance, infection risk, and EEG data quality. Clin. Neurophysiol. **112**(3), 536–544 (2001). doi:10.1016/S1388-2457(00)00533-2
12. Meghdadi, A.H., Fazel-Rezai, R., Aghakhani, Y.: Detecting determinism in EEG signals using principal component analysis and surrogate data testing. In: 2006 International Conference of the IEEE Engineering in Medicine and Biology Society, pp. 6209–6212. IEEE (2006). doi:10.1109/IEMBS.2006.260679, http://www.ncbi.nlm.nih.gov/pubmed/17946363, http://ieeexplore.ieee.org/document/4463227/
13. Murray, M.M., Brunet, D., Michel, C.M.: Topographic ERP analyses: a step-by-step tutorial review. Brain Topogr. **20**(4), 249–264 (2008). doi:10.1007/s10548-008-0054-5. http://link.springer.com/10.1007/s10548-008-0054-5
14. Brunet, D., Murray, M.M., Michel, C.M.: Spatiotemporal analysis of multichannel EEG: CARTOOL. Comput. Intell. Neurosci. **2011**, 1–15 (2011). doi:10.1155/2011/813870
15. Martinovic, J., Jones, A., Christiansen, P., Rose, A.K., Hogarth, L., Field, M.: Electrophysiological responses to alcohol cues are not associated with Pavlovian-to-instrumental transfer in social drinkers. PLoS ONE **9**(4), e94605 (2014). doi:10.1371/journal.pone.0094605. http://dx.plos.org/10.1371/journal.pone.0094605
16. Laganaro, M., Valente, A., Perret, C.: Time course of word production in fast and slow speakers: a high density ERP topographic study. NeuroImage **59**(4), 3881–3888 (2012). doi:10.1016/j.neuroimage.2011.10.082. http://linkinghub.elsevier.com/retrieve/pii/S1053811911012523

17. Skrandies, W.: Global field power and topographic similarity. Brain Topogr. **3**(1), 137–141 (1990). http://www.ncbi.nlm.nih.gov/pubmed/2094301
18. Rosenblad, A., Manly, B.F.J.: Randomization, Bootstrap and Monte Carlo Methods in Biology, 3rd edn. Chapman & Hall/CRC, Boca Raton (2007) 455 p. ISBN: 1-58488-541-6, Comput. Stat. **24**(2), 371-372 (2009). doi:10.1007/s00180-009-0150-3
19. Pascual-Marqui, R.D.: Standardized low-resolution brain electromagnetic tomography (sLORETA): technical details. Methods Find. Exp. Clin. Pharmacol. **24**(Suppl D), 5–12 (2002). http://www.ncbi.nlm.nih.gov/pubmed/12575463
20. Costa, T., Cauda, F., Crini, M., Tatu, M.-K., Celeghin, A., de Gelder, B., Tamietto, M.: Temporal and spatial neural dynamics in the perception of basic emotions from complex scenes. Soc. Cogn. Affect. Neurosci. **9**(11), 1690-1703 (2014). doi:10.1093/scan/nst164. http://www.ncbi.nlm.nih.gov/pubmed/24214921, http://www.pubmedcentral.nih.gov/articlerender.fcgi?artid=PMC4221209, https://academic.oup.com/scan/article-lookup/doi/10.1093/scan/nst164
21. Fusar-Poli, P., Placentino, A., Carletti, F., Allen, P., Landi, P., Abbamonte, M., Barale, F., Perez, J., McGuire, P., Politi, P.L.: Laterality effect on emotional faces processing: ALE meta-analysis of evidence. Neurosci. Lett. **452**(3), 262–267 (2009). doi:10.1016/j.neulet.2009.01.065

Memory Effect in Expressed Emotions During Long Term Group Interactions

Roman Gorbunov, Emilia I. Barakova$^{(\boxtimes)}$, and Matthias Rauterberg

Department of Industrial Design, Technical University of Eindhoven,
Eindhoven, The Netherlands
e.i.barakova@tue.nl

Abstract. Long-term interactions in groups can be monitored through games in which the participants need to show their social preferences by making choice to help or to use egoistic game strategy. In this paper we analyse the facial expressions of a group of isolated individuals (astronauts) during repeated interactions in subsequent encounters in a game. The astronauts were taking part in the Mars-500 isolation experiment and their relations were influenced by the everyday interaction in this untypical environment, and monitored through the cooperative game. We analysed different statistical properties of the recorded emotional facial expressions of the astronauts, where emotions were determined by the FaceReader software. We found that there is a memory effect between the collective emotional expressions corresponding to subsequent experiments, separated by two weeks time period. This dependance suggest that it is possible to predict the development of interpersonal relations in groups of isolated individuals. In a broader perspective, this finding can inform the design of long-term interaction behavior of artificial agents.

1 Introduction

Measuring and analyzing the emotional states in long-term interactions is important for groups of individuals that need to engage in such interactions and especially if these interactions are in confined and isolated environments, such as submarines, arctic expeditions, and space ships. Healthy emotional states are as important for the success of the long-term missions and influence the interpersonal relations in the group.

The topic of measuring emotional behavior and interactions trough games gains an increasing interest [3, 13, 15]. Games provide semi-structured context for interaction between humans or between humans and agents. This is one among several reasons for using games as interaction medium between humans and agents [2, 4, 5, 15]. In addition, the use of games can increase the entertainment quality of the interaction, and can help to reveal relationships that are hidden in different contexts or even relationships that are subconscious.

The computer games could be a tool for measuring and establishing long-term relations since they may include many different aspects of real life interactions between people. In this case they can be used to understand and teach the

© Springer International Publishing AG 2017
J.M. Ferrández Vicente et al. (Eds.): IWINAC 2017, Part I, LNCS 10337, pp. 254–264, 2017.
DOI: 10.1007/978-3-319-59740-9_25

rules of collaboration and even create artificial agents that can function as a collaboration partner [2,15]. Many game designers are currently exploring the added value of cooperative strategies within their games [8] such as reaching a goal with limited resources. Gorbunov et al. [14,15] redesigned and tested a game which utilizes on collaborative patterns to induce cooperation within the game. The game was designed to be played multiple times - each time a player would choose to help or ask for a help expecting that next game the chosen partner may help back or request a help.

In this paper we show the analysis of the longitudinal game interactions through data from the Mars-500 isolation experiment. During this experiment six participants have been isolated for 520 days to simulate a flight to Mars. Every other week the participants played the game that was specially adapted from the existing Collored Trails game that is used in game theory and experimental economics to study cooperation and fairness. During the game sessions the crew members interacted with each other through a computer-based environment. To monitor emotional states in the group we use video records capturing facial expressions of the crew members during the game play. In this way, correlations between the events that occurred during game play and the coinciding facial expressions can be made. We need to mention that in this work we do not focus on the problem of facial expressions recognition. Instead, we utilize the progress in this field made by other researchers and companies by using commercially available software that can quantify facial expressions with good accuracy. This allows us to shift the focus from the problem of facial expressions recognition to the problem of interpretation of the time dependent facial expressions in a way that is relevant in the context of interpersonal relations and long-term effects of isolation. We discuss the general properties of the recorded data and the software that we used to automatically generate data describing the facial expressions of the participants. The main contribution of the paper is that we found memory effect observed for the collective emotional states, as revealed by the facial expressions, for the neighboring experiments separated by two weeks.

2 Background

2.1 Board Games for Long-Term Interaction

Several games have been used for monitoring and analysing collaborative behaviors of players. One example is Colored Trail game that has been designed to enable analyzing of the decision making strategies of multiple players in varying settings and complexity [16]. Different variations of the game have been used to study human-human and human-agent interactions [1,10–14,16–19,22,23]. The Colored Trail game resembles real life situations in which people have different goals and need some resources to reach these goals i.e., the resources can have different values to different players. A redistribution of the resources can be done if the players exchange resources (chips) so one or more players can came closer to the goal. If a player helped other player without having a benefit (because with any combination he/she would not have won this time) he can expect that in the next game the helped player will return the favor. Therefore, the game is interesting for analyzing long-term relationships since it contains both competitive and collaborative (social) components.

More specifically, the game is played on a rectangular board composed of colored squares (see Fig. 1).

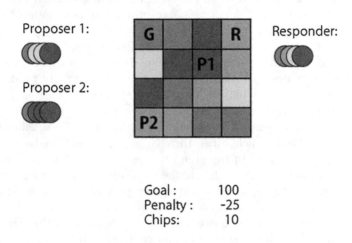

Proposer 1:

Proposer 2:

Responder:

Goal :   100
Penalty :   -25
Chips: 10

Fig. 1. Example of the colored trails game on the response phase. (Color figure online)

In the beginning of the game every player is placed on one of the colored squares of the board. Additionally to that one square is assigned to be the goal that should be reached by each player. Every player receives a set of colored chips which represent the resources of a player. The colors of the chips are taken from the same set as the colors of the board squares. Players can move on the board using their chips - a chip with a certain color will make possible one move to a neighbouring square with the corresponding to the chip color. The moves are restricted to horizontal or vertical moves to one of the neighboring squares. By making a step on the board a player irreversibly spends a chip. The goal of the player is to move as close as possible to the goal-square, spending a minimum of chips. Before making their moves players are allowed to exchange some of their chips with another player. Any exchange of chips is possible if both participants of the exchange agree to do this exchange. This redesigned version of the Colored Trails game is a redesign of the initial game that was proposed in Harvard university by Gal and colleagues [13] and is used in the game theory and experimental economics to study cooperation and fairness.

3   Analyzing Emotional States Caused by Interpersonal Relations

We assume that by measuring and analyzing emotional states of the group members caused by the natural development of their interpersonal relations and their emotional states are very tightly bound and influence each other. Healthy emotional states are as important for the success of the long-term missions as the interpersonal relations in the group. To monitor emotional states in the group we use video records capturing facial expressions of the crew members during the game play. In this way, correlations between the events that occurred during game play and the coinciding facial expressions can be made. We need to mention that in this work we do not focus on the problem of facial expression recognition. Instead, we utilize the progress in this field made by other researchers and companies by using commercially available software that can quantify facial expressions with good accuracy. This allows us to shift the focus from the problem of facial expressions recognition to the problem of interpretation of the time dependent facial expressions in a way that is relevant in the context of interpersonal relations and long-term effects of isolation.

3.1 Video Records from Mars-500

The video records of facial expressions were collected during the Mars-500 isolation experiment in which six participants were isolated for 520 days to simulate a flight to Mars. Every second week the participants had to interact with each other through a computer environment for approximately 30 min as a part of this experiment. During these sessions the participants were sitting in front of the computers performing different learning tasks supplied by the MECA software [20] and playing the CT game [16] with each other. The frontal video records of facial expressions were made by the cameras located on the participants' computers. To monitor emotional states in the group we applied correlation analysis between the events that occurred during game play and the coinciding facial expressions.

3.2 Face Reader

To extract facial expressions from the available video records we have used the FaceReader commercial software developed by VicarVision and Noldus Information Technology [6]. The FaceReader software can recognize facial expressions by distinguishing six basic emotions (plus neutral) with accuracy of 89% [6]. In particular, FaceReader recognizes happy, sad, angry, surprised, scared, disgusted and neutral components of the facial expressions. The system is built to correspond to Ekman and Friesen's theory of the Facial Action Coding System (FACS), that states that basic emotions correspond with facial models [7]. For an overview of the progress in the field of automatic facial expressions recognition see [9,21]. In the current study we have used FaceReader to generate components of the facial expression for every third frame of the video. It gives the time separations between the two neighboring data points (components of the facial expression) equal to 120 ms. By considering only every third frame we could reduce the computational time needed for the generation of the data describing facial expressions in a quantitative way, and the computational time required for the analysis of these data. By the chosen frame rate we still were able to get smooth dependencies describing the facial expressions.

3.3 Classification of Statistical Properties of the Data

The data generated by the FaceReader software can be considered as a set of real numbers depending on four variables: $v\,(c, u, e, f)$, where c indicates the component of the facial expression, u is used to indicate the participant, e is the index of the experiment and f is the frame index. The type of the facial expression can have one of the following seven values: "neutral", "happy", "sad", "angry", "surprised", "scared" and "disgusted". In our data from the Mars-500 experiment, the second argument (u) can have six different values, since we have six participants in this experiment. The third argument (e) is the index of the experimental session. Since we had 33 experiments, the index runs from one to 33. The separation between every experiment was two weeks except for experiments 18 and 19, which were separated by four weeks because of the simulation of a landing on Mars during which it was not possible for the crew members to play the game. The last argument (f) is the index of the frame in the given video.

The arguments present in the data can be classified based on their properties. First we distinguish between homogeneous and inhomogeneous variables. By homogeneous variables we understand those over which averaging makes sense. In our case all variables except the type of the facial expressions are homogeneous. It means that we can average facial expressions over users, for example, to calculate the average happiness of the crew. We can also average the facial expressions over different experiments to find how the happiness of a given user changes depending on the duration of the experiment. It is also possible to average a given component of the facial expressions over the frames of the video to find the average happiness of the given user in the given experiment. In contrast, we cannot average happiness and sadness because these properties have different meanings. However, the different components of the facial expressions can be combined in a way that is more sophisticated than averaging. For example, we could combine different components of the facial expressions in a way done by principal component analysis or independent component analysis, which could be helpful for identification of the most important or independent features. The variables can also be classified depending on whether they are subsequent or not. By subsequent variables we understand those variables for which a natural ordering of values exists. In the considered case the two variables, frame index and experiment index, are subsequent. These indexes can be ordered chronologically. In contrast, there is no preferred ordering of the components of the facial expressions and the users. We can group different values of a component of a facial expression if these values correspond to different values of a given homogeneous variable and to the same values of other variables. This procedure can be applied to several homogeneous variables at the same time. In this way we can get seven different properties. We will denote these measures by the removal of the arguments that were used for the grouping. Specifically, we get the following measures:

$$v(c, e, f) = \sum_u v(c, u, e, f),$$ (1)

$$v(c, u, f) = \sum_e v(c, u, e, f),$$ (2)

$$v(c, u, e) = \sum_f v(c, u, e, f),$$ (3)

$$v(c, u) = \sum_e \sum_f v(c, u, e, f),$$ (4)

$$v(c, e) = \sum_u \sum_f v(c, u, e, f),$$ (5)

$$v(c, f) = \sum_u \sum_e v(c, u, e, f),$$ (6)

$$v(c) = \sum_u \sum_e \sum_f v(c, u, e, f).$$ (7)

3.4   Averaging over Experiments

Averaging over users and experiments, i.e. the first two properties did not result in significant dependencies. We will give the results of averaging over the subsequent experiments, the third property $(v(c, u, e))$, since it relates to the memory effects. This property removes the dependency on the time frame, since we average over different frames from the same experiment. As a result we get different components of the facial expressions of different users as functions of the experiment index. These properties can be of particular interest since they potentially could capture a long-term effect of the isolation. For example, we could expect that the facial expressions of given users become more (or less) happy the more time they spent in isolation.

As an illustration, in Fig. 2 we show the dependence of three different components of the facial expressions (neutral, happy and sad) as functions of the experiment calculated for the one of the users.

With the black histograms we show the number of the available data points, divided by 10^5, as a function of the experiment number.

In Fig. 2 we cannot see any obvious dependence on the experiment number. However, we can see that some components of the facial expressions systematically increased for five experiments in a row. Since it is not obvious if there is some regularity in the considered dependencies, we have performed a quantitative estimation of this regularity. In particular, if a vector depends on a parameter, the distance between a pair of vectors decreases on average, if we decrease the difference between the pair of parameters corresponding to the two considered vectors. Therefore, we can use the average distance between the neighboring vectors as a measure of the regularity of the dependency of the vectors on a parameter. In our case the vector is composed of seven average components of the facial expressions and the parameter is the integer index of the experiment. To measure the similarity between a pair of seven dimensional

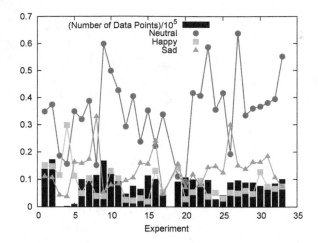

Fig. 2. Three different components of the facial expressions of an user through the evolution of the experiment

(7D) vectors we used the Euclidean distance. The average distance between the average values of the facial expressions corresponding to all available neighboring (subsequent) experiments has been calculated for all six users. Then we generated a new sequence of the 7D vectors just by shuffling the original sequence. If there was some dependence of the vectors on the experiments it was destroyed by shuffling. For the new sequence of the 7D vectors (average facial expressions) we have also calculated the distance between the neighboring vectors. This procedure has been repeated 10^4 times to determine in what percentage of cases the average distance between the neighboring vectors can be as small as, or even smaller than those calculated for the original ordering of the vectors.

This procedure has been performed for all six users and the following percentages have been found: 2.5%, 85.4%, 5.2%, 9.7%, 43.7% and 42.4%. These results indicate that the used measure of regularity calculated for the dependencies shown in Fig. 2 is very close to the values of the measure of regularity calculated for irregular sequences of vectors. Based on that, we can conclude that we have no solid reason to think that we are able to see some regular dependence of the average facial expressions on the experiments.

4   Dependency on Users

The fourth property $(v(c, u))$ removes the dependency on experiment and frame index. In other words, we get a property that depends only on the type of the component of the facial expressions and the user. In this way we can determine how happy or sad or angry a given group member was on average during the long-term isolation. This property can be used to characterize the person and his/her reaction in isolation. However, to study effect of isolation on the emotional state (facial expressions) we need to have video records for non-isolation conditions.

As a result of the considered averaging over the frames and experiments we get $6 \cdot 7 = 42$ values. These values are shown in Fig. 3.

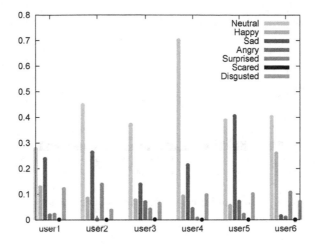

Fig. 3. Average values of seven different components of the facial expressions given for six participants of the Mars-500 experiment

4.1 Dependency on Subsequent Experiments

The fifth property $(v\,(c,e))$ is obtained by averaging over users and time frames. This property gives the combined emotional state of the crew as a function of the experiment index. For example, with this property we could see how the average happiness of the crew depends on the time (number of weeks) spent in isolation. This property is shown in Fig. 4. This figure is very similar to Fig. 2. The difference between Figs. 2 and 4 is that Fig. 4 shows the values averaged over all six users and Fig. 2 only shows values corresponding to user3. Moreover, in Fig. 4 we also show the "disgusted" component of the facial expression as a function of the experiment index. Like in the case of the separate considera- tion of the users we have performed a numerical estimation of the regularity of the dependency. For that we used the average distance between the neighboring vectors as a measure of the regularity. As a result we found that, after averag- ing over the users, the difference between the averaged facial expressions from neighboring experiments is, on average, smaller than the difference between the averaged facial expressions taken from two randomly chosen experiments. The probability that the difference between the neighboring experiments, in terms of the average facial expression, can be as small as it is, or even smaller, is equal to $8 \cdot 10^{-4}$. From this result we can conclude with high confidence that there is a relation (similarity) between the emotional states of the crew corresponding to the experiments separated by two-week time intervals. As a consequence, the averaged emotional state of the crew in a current experiment can be used as a predictor of the average emotional state that will be observed in two weeks. The sixth and seventh property did not show significant results.

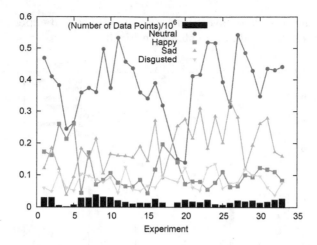

Fig. 4. Averaged (over frames and users) components of the facial expressions as functions of the experiment index

5   Discussion

In this paper we have proposed measures that can be used for analysis of the data generated by facial expressions recognition software in groups of people who are involved in interactions that can provoke emotional reactions. We used repeated cooperative (economic) games for monitoring the groups behavior, but also for provoking emotional reactions in the players. Fe proposed measures to find dependencies in the obtained data. Based on these measures we have found a statistically significant correlation between the average emotional states from two neighboring experiments separated by two weeks. This result means that there is a memory in the dynamics of the average emotional state of the crew so that two weeks cannot completely destroy the memory about the previous emotional state. This property of the dynamics of emotional states can potentially be used to predict emotional states of the group for the next few weeks.

The proposed method can be used for monitoring and predicting of the emotional state of group of isolated individuals. The method can also be used to design social agents. Previous findings of this research have been used for the design of social agents [14]. These agents were shown to outperform agents that do not utilize on the social behavioral strategy proposed in [14]. These design principles can be exploit for design of social strategies for long-term interactions between humans and virtual agents and in human-robot interaction.

References

1. Barakova, E.I., Gorbunov, R., Rauterberg, M.: Automatic interpretation of affective facial expressions in the context of interpersonal interaction. IEEE Trans. Hum.-Mach. Syst. **45**(4), 409–418 (2015)

2. Barakova, E.I., Bajracharya, P., Willemsen, M., Lourens, T., Huskens, B.: Long-term lego therapy with humanoid robot for children with ASD. Expert Syst. **32**(6), 698–709 (2015)
3. Barakova, E.I., Spink, A.S., Ruyter, B., Noldus, L.P.: Trends in measuring human behavior and interaction. Pers. Ubiquitous Comput. **17**(1), 1–2 (2013)
4. Castellano, G., Leite, I., Pereira, A., Martinho, C., Paiva, A., Mcowan, P.W.: Context-sensitive affect recognition for a robotic game companion. ACM Trans. Interact. Intell. Syst. **4**(2), 10:1–10:25 (2014)
5. Conati, C.: Probabilistic assessment of users emotions in educational games. Appl. Artif. Intell.: Int. J. **16**(7–8), 555–575 (2002)
6. Den Uyl, M.J., Van Kuilenburg, H.: The FaceReader: online facial expression recognition. In: Proceedings of Measuring Behavior, vol. 30, pp. 589–590. Citeseer (2005)
7. Ekman, P., Friesen, W.V.: Facial action coding system. In: Antropology of the Body (1977)
8. Seif El-Nasr, M., Aghabeigi, B., Milam, D., Erfani, M., Lameman, B., Maygoli, H., Mah, S.: Understanding and evaluating cooperative games. In: Proceedings of the 28th International Conference on Human Factors in Computing Systems, pp. 253–262 (2010)
9. Fasel, B., Luettin, J.: Automatic facial expression analysis: a survey. Pattern Recognit. **36**(1), 259–275 (2003)
10. Ficici, S.G., Pfeffer, A.: Modeling how humans reason about others with partial information. In: Proceedings of the 7th International Joint Conference on Autonomous Agents, Multiagent Systems, vol. 1, pp. 315–322 (2008)
11. Gal, Y., Pfeffer, A.: Predicting people's bidding behavior in negotiation. In: Proceedings of the 5th International Joint Conference on Autonomous Agents and Multiagent Systems, pp. 370–376 (2006)
12. Gal, Y., Pfeffer, A.: Modeling reciprocal behavior in human bilateral negotiation. In: Proceedings of the 22nd National Conference on Artificial Intelligence, vol. 1, pp. 815–820 (2007)
13. Gal, Y., Pfeffer, A., Marzo, F., Grosz, B.J.: Learning social preferences in games. In: Proceedings of the 19th National Conference on Artificial Intelligence, pp. 226–231 (2004)
14. Gorbunov, R., Barakova, E., Rauterberg, M.: Design of social agents. Neurocomputing **114**, 92–97 (2013)
15. Gorbunov, R., Barakova, E.I., R.M.C. Ahn, Rauterberg, M.: Monitoring interpersonal relationships through games with social dilemma, pp. 5–12 (2011)
16. Grosz, B.J., Kraus, S., Talman, S., Stossel, B., Havlin, M.: The influence of social dependencies on decision-making. initial investigations with a new game. In: Proceedings of the 3rd International Joint Conference on Autonomous Agents, Multiagent Systems, vol. 2, pp. 782–789 (2004)
17. Hennes, D., Tuyls, K.P., Neerincx, M.A., Rauterberg, G.W.M.: Micro-scale social network analysis for ultra-long space flights. In: The IJCAI 2009 Workshop on Artificial Intelligence in Space, Pasadena, California, USA (2009)
18. Kamar, E., Gal, Y., Grosz, B.: Incorporating helpful behavior into collaborative planning. In: Proceedings of the 8th International Conference on Autonomous Agents And Multiagent Systems, pp. 875–882 (2006)
19. Marzo, F., Gal, Y., Grosz, B.J., Pfeffer, A.: Social preferences in relational contexts. In: Proceedings of the 4th Conference in Collective Intentionality (2004)

20. Neerincx, M.A., Bos, A., Olmedo-Soler, A., Brauer, U., Breebaart, L., Smets, N., Lindenberg, J., Grant, T., Wolff, M.: The mission execution crew assistant: improving human-machine team resilience for long duration missions. In: Proceedings of the 59th International Astronautical Congress (IAC) (2008)
21. Pantic, M., Rothkrantz, L.J.M.: Automatic analysis of facial expressions: the state of the art. IEEE Trans. Pattern Anal. Mach. Intell. **22**(12), 1424–1445 (2000)
22. Talman, S., Gal, Y., Hadad, M., Kraus, S.: Adapting to agents' personalities in negotiation. In: Proceedings of the 4th International Joint Conference on Autonomous Agents And Multiagent Systems, pp. 383–389 (2005)
23. van Wissen, A., van Diggelen, J., Dignum, V.: The effects of cooperative agent behavior on human cooperativeness. In: Proceedings of the 8th International Conference on Autonomous Agents, Multiagent Systems, vol. 2, pp. 1179–1180 (2009)

Setting the Parameters for an Accurate EEG (Electroencephalography)-Based Emotion Recognition System

Jennifer Sorinas[1(✉)], M.D. Grima Murcia[1,2], Jesus Minguillon[3],
Francisco Sánchez-Ferrer[4], Mikel Val-Calvo[2], Jose Manuel Ferrández[2],
and Eduardo Fernández[1]

[1] Institute of Bioengineering, University Miguel Hernández and CIBER BBN,
Avenida de la Universidad, 03202 Elche, Spain
{jsorinas,e.fernandez}@umh.es
[2] Deparment of Electronics and Computer Technology,
University of Cartagena, Cartagena, Spain
[3] Department of Computer Architecture and Technology,
University of Granada, Granada, Spain
[4] Department of Pediatrics, "San Juan" University Clinical Hospital,
University Miguel Hernández, Alicante, Spain

Abstract. The development of a suitable EEG-based emotion recognition system has become a target in the last decades for BCI (Brain Computer Interface) applications. However, there are scarce algorithms and procedures for real time classification of emotions. In this work we introduce a new approach to select the appropriate parameters in order to build up a real-time emotion recognition system. We recorded the EEG-neural activity of 5 participants while they were looking and listening to an audiovisual database composed by positive and negative emotional video clips. We tested 11 different temporal window sizes, 6 ranges of frequency bands and 5 areas of interest located mainly on prefrontal and frontal brain regions. The most accurate time window segment was selected for each participant, giving us probable positive and negative emotional characteristic patterns, in terms of the most informative frequency-location pairs. Our preliminary results provide a reliable way to establish the more appropriate parameters to develop an accurate EEG-based emotion classifier in real-time.

Keywords: EEG · Emotions · Video database · BCI · Real-time

1 Introduction

The interest on human-machine interactions has been increasing due to the aim of improving users' experiences and also to the growing necessity of the BCI branch to be more accurate in their interaction with the patients. Therefore,

© Springer International Publishing AG 2017
J.M. Ferrández Vicente et al. (Eds.): IWINAC 2017, Part I, LNCS 10337, pp. 265–273, 2017.
DOI: 10.1007/978-3-319-59740-9_26

research in human emotion recognition systems has become an important target in this field. In the past decades, most of the studies have focused on using facial expressions and speech in order to identify human emotions [1]. However, both features are easy to fake or change consciously. For this reason, researchers explored new methods as physiological markers such as heart rate [2] and galvanic skin response [3]; and neuroimaging techniques, being the EEG the "gold standard" due to its millisecond temporal resolution [4].

Nowadays, the goal of the EEG-based emotion recognition research is to find a suitable system, which gives good enough results, to be implemented in real-time. In order to develop a system capable of recognize different emotions, some factors, such as the model of emotion, the stimulus and the classifier, must be specified, since the difficulty when comparing results among studies is due to differences in the selection of these parameters [5].

There are several methods to elicit emotions such as using pictures, sounds, odor and combinations of them [6]. But in the real world we have all the senses active at the same time, so the idea of stimulate only one of them is not a realistic approach for real-time emotion recognition. Behind this presumption, some authors began working with audiovisual stimuli resulting in the creation of audiovisual databases such as Database for Emotion Analysis using Physiological Signals (DEAP) [7], the Emotional Movie Database (EMDB) [8] or own-film selection [9]. However, these databases select considerable long extracts of movies at which the emotion is only present at some points of the plot, this fact make the classification difficult.

When studying emotions with the EEG technique, the target is the study of the spontaneous activity, i.e. the characteristic pattern of the different frequency bands for a specific stimulation. However, not all the EEG-bandwidths carry the relevant information for emotion recognition and not all channel locations participate in the same way on this process. For this reason, the correct electrode location and the appropriate frequency band of study must be set prior to any real-time classification. On the other hand, by using unsuitable window size, the emotion may be misclassified [5]. In this framework Candra et al. [10] develop a study in order to assess the effective window size using the dimensional model of emotion [11]. They concluded that the information regarding emotions in the EEG signal may be appropriately localized at around 3–12 s time segments. Unfortunately this range seems too wide for a real-time approach. Therefore, more efforts are still needed for efficient and automatic classification of EEG-based emotions.

In the present study, we used the biphasic model of emotion, which states that emotion vary the activation of the appetitive and defensive motivational systems that mediate the wide range of adaptive behaviors [12]. We elaborated a customized video-database able to provide sustained emotions during the whole video presentation and we classified each video-clip into positive or negative according with their emotional content. Moreover, due to the high inter-individual emotion experience variability, we used a subject-dependent model approach were the classifier must be trained for each participant. The main objective was to carry out a preliminary study in order to set the principal parameters for developing a real-time EEG-based emotion recognition system.

Our results are very encouraging and suggest that there are different bandwidth patterns at frontal regions when comparing positive and negative video clips. Furthermore, we also found that the best time window was slightly different for each volunteer what suggest the usefulness of developing customized procedures of real-time EEG-based emotion recognition systems.

2 Methods

Participants

5 voluntaries participated in the study (mean age: 24.02; range: 19–27; three men and two women). The participants were right handed with a laterality quotient of at least +0.4 (mean 0.9, SD: 0.2) on the Edinburgh Inventory [13]. None of them had personal history of psychiatric or neurological disorder, alcohol or drug abuse, or current medication, and they had normal or corrected to normal vision and audition. All participants were informed about the procedure and purpose of the study; they provided their written consent, approved by the Ethics Committee of the University Miguel Hernandez.

Stimulus

A total of 14 video clips were selected from the internet. Half of them with positive emotional content such as natural landscapes, comedy shows or cartoons; and the other seven with negative emotional content as for example excerpts from horror movies, violence scenes, dental surgery, etc. The audio content of the films met the requirement of been in the mother tongue of the participants (Spanish) or at least with instrumental non-verbal music. The video clips had durations between 43 and 180 s. All of the clips were extracted and edited using the Camtasia Studio 8 software.

Participants were instructed to seat comfortably while watching the clips. They were also instructed to not make abrupt movements and try to avoid blinking as far as possible. Films were presented continuously, preceded by a black screen lasting for 30 s. After viewing each clip, participants were asked to rate the emotional experience in terms of valence ranging from 9 (very pleasant) to 1 (very unpleasant). Video clips were presented in a random order, counterbalanced for each voluntary, by using python software.

Data Acquisition and Signal Preprocessing

We recorded EEG data through a cap-mounted 64 Ag-AgCl electrodes according to the International 10/20 System (FP1, FPZ, FP2, AF3, GND, AF4, F7, F5, F3, F1, FZ, F2, F4, F6, F8, FT7, FC5, FC3, FC1, FCZ, FC2, FC4, FC6, FT8, T7, C5, C3, C1, CZ, C2, C4, C6, T8, REF, TP7, CP5, CP3, CP1, CPZ, CP2,

CP4, CP6, TP8, P7, P5, P3, P1, PZ, P2, P4, P6, P8, PO7, PO5, PO3, POZ, PO4, PO6, PO8, CB1, O1, OZ, O2, CB2) [14], the data were amplified and registered by the NeuroScan SynAmps EEG amplifier (Compumedics, Charlotte, NC, USA). The electrode impedance for every electrode was kept under 25 kΩ as recommended [15]. All the data were acquired with a sampling rate of 1000 Hz. The recordings were re-referenced to a Common Average Reference (CAR) and EEG signals were filtered using a high-pass and low-pass filters, 0.5 Hz and 45 Hz respectively. This step was performed by means of the Curry 7 software (Compumedics, Charlotte, NC, USA). Artifact rejection were performed by removing the IC (independent components) corresponding to muscle noise (head movement and face gesticulation) and eye-blinking, selected by visual inspection, based on the Independent Component Analysis (ICA) [16] carried out with the MatLab toolbox EEGLAB [17].

Feature Extraction and Emotion Classification

The preprocessed EEG data corresponding to each video clip were segmented into different time windows ranging from 2 s (the smallest bandwidth period of interest), increasing by 1 s till reaching 12 s, which is the upper window size recommended for classifying emotions [10]; every segment was considered as a trial. In total, 11 sets of trials were extracted. Linear trends were removed. Each trial was z-scored so that they have zero mean and unit standard deviation. After that, a tapered cosine window (0.2 factor) was applied. For each trial, the power of 6 groups of frequency bands, Delta (1–3 Hz), Theta (4–7 Hz), Alfa (8–13), Beta1 (14–23 Hz), Beta2 (24–30 Hz) and Gamma (31–44 Hz), was estimated in every single channel. Although we have information from 64 channel location, at the present study we have just analyzed the prefrontal and frontal regions. The prefrontal and frontal channels were divided into 5 areas of interest, as represented in Fig. 1: Left-Prefrontal area (FP1, AF3); Right- Prefrontal area (FP2, AF4); Left-Frontal (F1, F3, F5, F7, FC1, FC3, FC5); Right-Frontal (F2, F4, F6, F8, FC2, FC4, FC6); and Frontal-midline (FPZ, FZ, FCZ).

The band power was estimated by using the Welch's method. The band power in every area of interest was used as a feature for classification. In total, 30 features were used. The features were normalized by using a 30-second baseline prior to the first stimulus. 50% of the video clips were utilized to train a Support Vector Machine (SVM) classifier. The remaining videos were classified into two classes, high-valence (positive) and low-valence (negative) emotion. Finally, the accuracy of the binary classification was computed for every group of frequency and area of interest.

3   Results

The classification process described previously was repeated for every subject with the 11 different sizes of window segments. We obtained the accuracies for every pair of frequency band – area of interest of every subject. Those pairs with

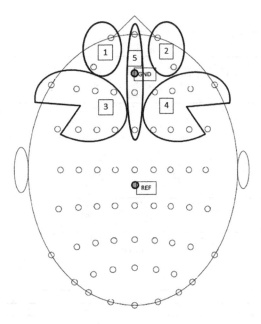

Fig. 1. Scheme of the 64 electrode positions across the scalp. The 5 grouped channels correspond to each of the areas of interest of study. (1. Left-Prefrontal area; 2. Right-Prefrontal area; 3. Left-Frontal; 4. Right-Frontal; 5. Frontal-midline. GND: ground channel. REF: reference channel).

a percentage of accuracy higher than a 70% were selected; the window size with the highest number of informative features was set as the more appropriate time trial-segmentation for each subject.

Once we had the appropriate size of window segment, we looked at those frequency bands – area of interest pairs with percentage of accuracy higher than 70% as being the most significant for the emotion classification into positive and negative valence. The selected time parameter and features for every subject are listed in Fig. 2.

We obtained, in general, good classification accuracies for subjects 2, 4 and 5. However the classifier failed when classifying the negative valence video clips. This result could be in line with the given subjective valence ratings of the subjects (Fig. 3). Thus almost all of the subjects rated correctly the positive valence video clips, but not the negative ones, which in some cases had scores above five.

For subjects 1 and 3 the classifier showed very good results for both positive and negative clips. Figure 4 shows the spatial distribution of the main informative frequencies of subject 1 with a 7 s window size. In this particular case the Beta2 bandwidth is lateralized toward the left hemisphere for positive emotional video clips and toward the right-hemisphere for negative emotional clips.

Subject 1

	POSITIVE			NEGATIVE				
Window size	7s			7s				
Frequency band	Beta2 Gamma	Beta2	Beta2	Beta1 Beta2 Gamma	Beta2 Gamma	Delta	Delta Beta2 Gamma	Delta Beta2 Gamma
Area of interest	Left Frontal	Right Frontal	Fontal Midline	Left Prefrontal	Right Prefrontal	Left Frontal	Right Frontal	Frontal Midline

Subject 2*

	POSITIVE	NEGATIVE		
Window size	All time segments	7s		
Frequency band	Beta1 Beta2 Gamma	Theta Alpha	Theta	Theta Alpha
Area of interest	All locations	Left Prefrontal	Right Prefrontal	Frontal Midline

Subject 3

	POSITIVE				NEGATIVE			
Window size	9s				9s			
Frequency band	Delta Beta1	Beta1	Alfa Gamma	Delta	Beta2 Gamma	Gamma	Delta	Delta
Area of interest	Left Prefrontal	Right Prefrontal	Right Frontal	Frontal Midline	Left Prefrontal	Right Prefrontal	Left Frontal	Right Frontal

Subject 4*

	POSITIVE	NEGATIVE	
Window size	All time segments	12s	
Frequency band	Delta Theta Alpha Gamma	Delta Beta1 Gamma	Delta Beta1 Gamma
Area of interest	All locations	Left Frontal	Right Frontal

Subject 5*

	POSITIVE					NEGATIVE	
Window size	6s					5s	
Frequency band	Delta Theta Beta2 Gamma	Theta Beta2 Gamma	Theta Alpha Beta1 Beta2 Gamma	Theta Beta1 Beta2 Gamma	Theta Beta1 Beta2 Gamma	Delta Beta1	Delta
Area of interest	Left Prefrontal	Right Prefrontal	Left Frontal	Right Frontal	Frontal Midline	Left Prefrontal	Frontal Midline

Fig. 2. Selected appropriate time segments for every subject and their most informative features based on frequency band – area of interest pairs, in front of the positive and negative emotional video clips. *Subjects for whom the classifier detects considerably better the positive valence clips than the negative ones.

Valence Subjective Ratings					
	Subject 1	Subject 2	Subject 3	Subject 4	Subject 5
Positive video clips	7 ± 0.82	8 ± 0.82	7 ± 0.82	6.71 ± 1.38	7.14 ± 1.46
Negative video clips	1.86 ± 1.07	3.71 ± 2.29	3.43 ± 1.9	5.28 ± 2.06	3.86 ± 2.34

Fig. 3. Mean subjective scores and standard deviation for the valence of the positive and negative emotional video clips.

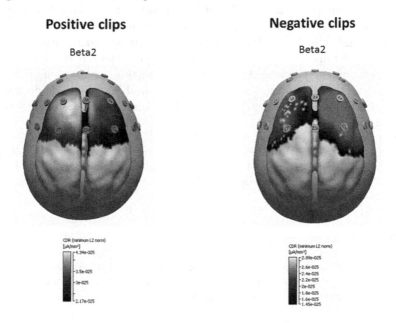

Fig. 4. Spatial distribution of the Beta2 frequency band for positive and negative video clips along the prefrontal and frontal electrodes. Images obtained with the help of Curry 7 software.

4   Discussion

Factors such as the model of emotion, the temporal window size for stimuli segmentation, the stimuli itself and the goal-directed electrode positioning and band frequency patterns are crucial parameters that must be specify to provide an efficient real-time classification of human emotions.

The results of this study, although very preliminary, suggest that there are different bandwidth patterns, specially at frontal regions when comparing positive and negative video clips. Furthermore, provide some insights for the selection of the appropriate time window and the most-informative channel locations and target frequency bands. Thus, the Beta2 bandwidth showed a preferential left hemispheric frontal lateralization for positive emotions whereas negative emotions were lateralized toward the right hemisphere. However, although our results showed a possible trend, it is too early to make conclusions, due to the small number of subjects and the problems encountered for classifying negative stimuli, fact that for some subjects our system failed to classify some negative stimuli. We believe that this failure could be due to the stimulation itself, considering that subjective valence score of such participants reflected a low-negative to neutral emotional experience.

Our results also emphasize that due to the high inter-subject variability, it is difficult to set global parameters and completely automatic real time classification algorithms that can be efficient for all subjects. Having said that, our main interest resides on finding the common characteristics that would allow the accurate and reliable classification between positive and negative emotions. However, we are fully aware that it is necessary to expand our studies, reconsidering some stimuli of our audiovisual database, increasing the sample size and finally, analyze the whole regions of the brain to find out the more appropriate electrode positioning for the analysis of the EEG signals driven by emotions.

Acknowledgement. This work has been supported in part by the Spanish National Research Program (MAT2015-69967-C3-1), by a research grant of the Spanish Blind Organization (ONCE), by the Ministry of Education of Spain (FPU grant AP-2013/01842) and by Séneca Foundation - Agency of Science and Technology of the Region of Murcia.

References

1. Ekman, P.: Facial expression and emotion. Am. Psychol. **48**(4), 384 (1993)
2. Appelhans, B.M., Luecken, L.J.: Heart rate variability as an index of regulated emotional responding. Rev. Gen. Psychol. **10**(3), 229–240 (2006). doi:10.1037/1089-2680.10.3.229
3. Khalfa, S., Isabelle, P., Jean-Pierre, B., Manon, R.: Event-related skin conductance responses to musical emotions in humans. Neurosci. Lett. **328**(2), 145–149 (2002). doi:10.1016/S0304-3940(02)00462-7
4. Mauss, I.B., Robinson, M.D.: Measures of emotion: a review. Cogn. Emot. **23**(2), 209–237 (2009). doi:10.1080/02699930802204677. http://www.tandfonline.com/doi/abs/10.1080/02699930802204677
5. Jatupaiboon, N., Pan-Ngum, S., Israsena, P., Chen, B.-W., Hsieh, S., Wu, C.-H.: Real-time EEG-based happiness detection system. Sci. World J. **2013** (2013). doi:10.1155/2013/618649. http://dx.doi.org/10.1155/2013/618649
6. Uhrig, M.K., Trautmann, N., Baumgärtner, U., Treede, R.-D., Henrich, F., Hiller, W., Marschall, S.: Emotion elicitation: a comparison of pictures and films. Front. Psychol. **7**, 180 (2016). doi:10.3389/fpsyg.2016.00180. http://dx.doi.org/10.3389/fpsyg.2016.00180
7. Soleymani, M., Member, S., Lee, J.-S.: DEAP: a database for emotion analysis using physiological signals. IEEE Trans. Affect. Comput. **3**(1), 18–31 (2012)
8. Carvalho, S., Leite, J., Galdo-Álvarez, S., Gonçalves, Ó.F.: The emotional movie database (EMDB): a self-report and psychophysiological study. Appl. Psychophysiol. Biofeedback **37**(4), 279–294 (2012). doi:10.1007/s10484-012-9201-6
9. Liu, Y.-J., Yu, M., Zhao, G., Song, J., Ge, Y., Shi, Y.: Real-time movie-induced discrete emotion recognition from EEG signals. IEEE Trans. Affect. Comput. **3045**(c), 1 (2017). doi:10.1109/TAFFC.2017.2660485. http://dx.doi.org/10.1109/TAFFC.2017.2660485

10. Candra, H., Yuwono, M., Chai, R., Handojoseno, A., Elamvazuthi, I., Nguyen, H.T., Su, S.: Investigation of window size in classification of EEG-emotion signal with wavelet entropy and support vector machine. In: Proceedings of the Annual International Conference of the IEEE Engineering in Medicine and Biology Society, EMBS 2015, pp. 7250–7253, November 2015. doi:10.1109/EMBC.2015.7320065
11. Russell, J.: A circumplex model of affect. J. Pers. Soc. Psychol. **39**, 1161–1178 (1980). doi:10.1037/h0077714
12. Davidson, R.J., Ekman, P., Saron, C.D., Senulis, J.A., Friesen, W.V.: Approach-withdrawal and cerebral asymmetry: emotional expression and brain physiology: I. J. Pers. Soc. Psychol. **58**, 330–341 (1990). doi:10.1037/0022-3514.58.2.330
13. Oldfield, R.C.: The assessment and analysis of handedness: the Edinburgh inventory. Neuropsychologia **9**(1), 97–113 (1971)
14. Klem, G.H., Lüders, H.O., Jasper, H.H., Elger, C.: The ten-twenty electrode system of the international federation. Electroencephalogr. Clin. Neurophysiol. **52**(Suppl.), 3–6 (1999)
15. Ferree, T.C., Luu, P., Russell, G.S., Tucker, D.M.: Scalp electrode impedance, infection risk, and EEG data quality. Clin. Neurophysiol. **112**(3), 536–544 (2001)
16. Jung, T.-P., Humphries, C., Lee, T.-W., Makeig, S., McKeown, M.J., Iragui, V., Sejnowski, T.J.: Extended ICA removes artifacts from electroencephalographic recordings. Adv. Neural Inf. Process. Syst. **10**, 894–900 (1998)
17. Delorme, A., Makeig, S.: EEGLAB: an open sorce toolbox for analysis of single-trial EEG dynamics including independent component anlaysis. J. Neurosci. Methods **134**, 9–21 (2004). doi:10.1016/j.jneumeth.2003.10.009

Exploring the Physiological Basis of Emotional HRI Using a BCI Interface

M. Val-Calvo[1,2], M.D. Grima-Murcia[1,3], J. Sorinas[3], J.R. Álvarez-Sánchez[2(✉)],
F. de la Paz Lopez[2], J.M. Ferrández-Vicente[1], and E. Fernandez-Jover[3]

[1] Dpto. Electrónica, Tecnología de Computadoras y Proyectos,
Univ. Politécnica de Cartagena, Cartagena, Spain
[2] Dpto. de Inteligencia Artificial, UNED, Madrid, Spain
jras@dia.uned.es
[3] Instituto de Bioingeniería, Univ. Miguel Hernández, Elche, Spain

Abstract. Emotional robots as therapist tools are the next frontier in care assistance, specially in the case of persons diagnosed with autism spectrum disorder (ASD). The current development in emotion estimation by robots is based mainly in face gestures, gaze attention, head position, etc., but that are exactly some areas where ASD patients have more difficulties to express their emotions. We consider that, in order to obtain a good interaction between robots and users, it is very important to have and accurate feedback of the emotional reaction detected during interaction, so we propose the merge between the emotional capabilities of actual robots and electroencephalogram tools to decrease the level of uncertainty of emotion state estimation.

Keywords: Human robot interface · Autism spectrum disorder · Socially assistive robotics · Electroencephalogram

1 Introduction

Emotional robots can open paths to research on new paradigms for the treatment of psychological disorders such as the autism spectrum disorder (ASD) [19]. In this paper, the focus is on the idea that robots, as therapist tools, may provide assistance through social interaction for children that suffer this disabilities.

ASD is known as a lifelong disability with no cure, including a wide range of symptoms. It is important to point the main general symptoms that define ASD, such as the deficit for communication, the incapabilities for understanding social cues, difficulties for social interaction as talking to each other as well as express their personal feelings [6]. Also, ASD patients suffer from the lack of eye contact, that is always related with their difficulties in joint attention [7,10]. Moreover, individuals diagnosed with ASD show repetitive patterns of behavior and they usually are extremely sensible to physical contact. These are the motivations that lead us to investigate an alternative to address their need for assistance.

© Springer International Publishing AG 2017
J.M. Ferrández Vicente et al. (Eds.): IWINAC 2017, Part I, LNCS 10337, pp. 274–285, 2017.
DOI: 10.1007/978-3-319-59740-9_27

Robots as therapy tools have been used in the last decade to improve social behaviors in ASD patients and to provide assistance through social interaction. In this way, a new field of research has been developed called socially assistive robotics (SAR) [6,8,9]. This new field, tries to solve some questions relative to the circumstances involving the interaction between patients and robots, such as, the effectiveness of robots for social assistance or how to model the behavior of these therapists robots.

Linking the need of support by ASD patients with this SAR systems, some researchers [1,2] have reported that the treatment in this new paradigm can increase the level of attention, improve their capacity for joint attention and the arising of spontaneous imitation. Researchers suggest that robots are considered socially as inanimate toys with some characteristics of social beings.

1.1 Emotional Robots

Since 90's, the research on social robots has been widely developed. Here we mention some of the best known socially intelligent robots. There is a great motivation behind the development of this type of robots, since there are a lot of possible applications. One of the best known motivation concerns giving assistance for children at hospitals due to the difficulties to provide socio-emotional support for patients during care [3]. There is a lack of attendance at hospitals so this high demand of social interaction can be covered by this new type of robots, as well as assistance for elderly people as a accompanier or assistance for handicapped people.

In this sense, it is worth noting The Huggable project [11]. They have demonstrated in [20] that a social interaction between child patients and robots are emotionally closer than between these child patients and a virtual character, reflecting the potential of such robots. The Huggable robot is covered with a teddy bear shape that permits a complete emotional experience for the children. This interesting project has been made in collaboration with the Boston Children's Hospital and the Northeastern University. The principal focus rely on the aim to mitigate the stress, the anxiety and pain of patient's through interactive games.

The second robot as a reference is Kismet, one of the first robot able to express feelings through its face expressions. It was developed by Cynthia Breazeal in early 90's. Its main capabilities include, expressiveness, visual and audio perception and proprioceptive control that enable him to focus the gaze direction to the source of stimulus. In that way, it is able to analyzing visual and auditory perceptions to interact in a natural way as a human being does. To close the loop in emotional interaction with humans, it can show different emotional states through its face gestures and tone of voice. As Breazeal and Scassellati suggest in [4], "the design of Kismet's motivation and behavior systems enable it to socially interact with a human while regulating the intensity of the interaction via expressive displays".

The third robot to mention is named Leonardo. This robot was built by the "personal robots group" of MIT and, attending the behavior and emotional responses of its caregivers, it can learn emotional meanings about new objects. Leo, as it is called by its developers, learns the names of new objects and, analyzing the gaze of its caregivers, it can detect where to focus its attention. Moreover, it is capable of detecting voice tones to appraisal its caregivers emotion and link it to the object that is learning about. Leo's memory is made affective, conforming and influencing Leo's reactions to the learned objects. In that way it can maintain such affective memories in a persistent way that permit to be evoked by re-presenting these objects.

The last mention goes to the PARO Therapeutic Robot developed by AIST, a leading Japanese industrial automation pioneer. PARO robot is being used in therapies for prevention of dementia. One of the last trends in USA for senile therapies implies the use of animals to improve the emotional relations of patients. In the last decade, some researchers have proposed the use of animal like robots to avoid some of the risks of working with real animals. As they suggest in [22], their main goal is to expect three effects:

– Psychological, e.g., relaxation, motivation.
– Physiological, e.g., improved vital signs.
– Social, e.g., stimulation of communication among inpatients and caregivers.

For our proposal, it is necessary to employ emotional robots that satisfy a series of principles of both software design and physical properties. This is important to develop a robot that fits the needs of the problem to deal with. We will therefore perform a brief description of the requirements for each aspect of the design.

The principles of software design are characterized by the need of the robot to interact with the patient in the most natural way and always under the treatment requirements. This implies a series of robot capabilities. The robot must be able to obtain information about both the environment and the patient's mood and behavior. On the one hand, the robot must detect the environment to move through it autonomously. On the other hand, it must evaluate the patient's mood and behavior, to generate the corresponding action, either initiating an interaction or requesting help from an external source. This second requirement is under the design paradigm called Human Robot Interaction (HRI) [5].

Under the HRI paradigm, the robot is expected to be able to model social interaction, which requires the robot to perceive and interpret human behavior. This is possible by detecting body and facial gestures and thus, monitor the activity of the patient, so that it is then possible to classify such activity and measure the feedback obtained in the interaction.

As for the physical properties, it is necessary for the robot to have a physical appearance that allows it to meet the expectations of the patient, and to enable the robot to perform the desired social interaction avoiding "the uncanny valley" as it was described in [21]. Much of the communication in social interaction is non-verbal, that is, much of the projected emotions depend on physical appearance. Therefore, the robot must project an amount of "humanness" while together projects an amount of "robotness", so that it does not create false expectations regarding its communicative capacities.

We consider that the Pepper robot (Fig. 1) from SoftBank Robotics possesses this set of characteristics, since externally it appears to be an intelligent social being, while maintaining a friendly robotic aspect. Pepper is based on a functional design approach, that is, its design is not made from the bioinspired perspective, except in its external aspect. Its core is a computer with limited operational and performance objectives that focuses on being able to effectively perform specific behavioral tasks.

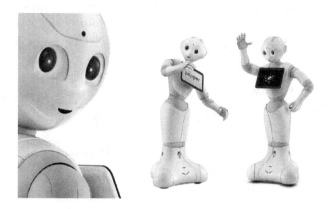

Fig. 1. Pepper robot from SoftBank robotics.

2   Detection of Emotions in EEG

We consider a classification of emotions in two states: positive and negative (biphasic emotion), which states that emotions fundamentally stems from varying activation in centrally organized appetitive and defensive motivational systems that have evolved to mediate the wide range of adaptive behaviors necessary for an organism struggling to survive in the physical world [18].

Emotion recognition through electroencephalogram (EEG) has a wide variety of practical applications. EEG is one tool that can directly measure brain activity and is the most effective way to measure neurons [12,13]. This activity, occurring simultaneously through the brain, involves a large number of neurons to generate minimum levels of electric potential enough to allow EEG record electrical signals. Electroencephalography records electrical brain activity on a millisecond time scale and thus permits temporal dynamics of brain function to be analyzed. There are five major brain waves distinguished by their different frequency bands (number of waves per second). These frequency bands from low to high frequencies, respectively, are called Delta (1–3 Hz), Theta (4–7 Hz), Alpha (8–13 Hz), Beta (14–30 Hz), and Gamma (31–50 Hz).

Most studies of the correlations between emotionally relevant stimuli and EEG features have adopted one of two approaches. One approach is to study the relationships between emotion and well-defined EEG features, such as frontal asymmetry in alpha activity [14], frontal midline theta [15], and the late positive potential (LPP) over central and posterior midline areas [16]. In contrast, the second approach has used machine learning methods to evaluate the relationships between emotion and classifiers that incorporate many EEG features (e.g., the powers in many frequency bands at many scalp locations)[17]. We have used the second method to classify the signal obtained by a portable EEG system.

When an emotional stimulus occurs, it is hard to predict which brain areas are supposed to be activated since this strongly depends on the memories the participant used to relive the emotion. Moreover, as the structures involved in recollection of events are deep in the brain and hard to precisely capture using EEG electrodes. We propose to realize a BCI system as shown in Fig. 2.

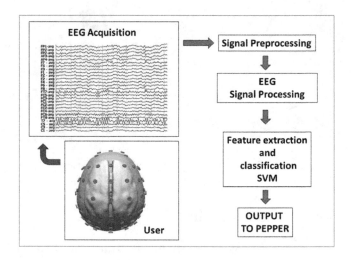

Fig. 2. Parts of a BCI.

EEG data was continuously recorded at a sampling rate of 1000 Hz from 64 locations (FP1, FPZ, FP2, AF3, GND, AF4, F7, F5, F3, F1, FZ, F2, F4, F6, F8, FT7, FC5, FC3, FC1, FCZ, FC2, FC4, FC6, FT8, T7, C5, C3, C1, CZ, C2, C4, C6, T8, REF, TP7, CP5, CP3, CP1, CPZ, CP2, CP4, CP6, TP8, P7, P5, P3, P1, PZ, P2, P4, P6, P8, PO7, PO5, PO3, POZ, PO4, PO6, PO8, CB1, O1, OZ, O2, CB2) using the international 10/20 system [8]. EEG was recorded via cap-mounted Ag-AgCl electrodes, with a 64-channel NeuroScan SynAmps EEG amplifier (Compumedics, Charlotte, NC, USA), but a less cumbersome device could be used (see Fig. 3). All the recordings were performed in a silent room with soft lighting. Signal processing was performed with the help of Curry 7 (Compumedics, Charlotte, NC, USA). Data were referenced to a Common Average Reference (CAR). EEG signals were filtered using a 45 Hz low-pass and a high-pass 0.5 Hz filters. Artifacts, such as flickers were filtered using Matlab software. The power features are obtained by first performing Fourier transform on the EEG signals and Support Vector Machine (SVM) as a classifier for each of the 64 channels. In this way, it is classified if the emotion is negative or positive and this information is sent to the robot.

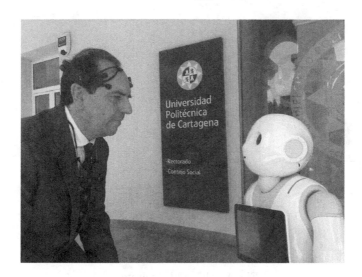

Fig. 3. Pepper interacting emotionally.

3   Emotional "engine" of the Pepper Robotic System

The emotional "engine" of the Pepper robot is based on the ALMood package [23]. This module is composed by several other modules that are integrated and coordinated through the ALExtractor module. In a simple way, ALMood module takes the information provided by the emotional extractor manager (ALExtractor) and from the user profile to provide the estimation of the instantaneous emotional state of the user. A simplified scheme is shown in the Fig. 4.

Through ALMood module, it is possible to subscribe to the ALGazeAnalysis, ALFaceCharacteristics, ALVoiceEmotionAnalysis and ALAudioDevice extractors. These extractors provide information relative to the emotional state of the human in front of the robot and also about the ambience sound level in the surroundings. All this information is dynamically triggered and adapted by the extractor manager depending on the events frequency of each extractor. The information provided is the emotional perception of people and the environment ambiance.

First, ALGazeAnalysis module, allows to analyze the direction of the gaze of a detected person, then it is possible to measure if the patient is looking at the robot by measuring the face orientation of the user. This module can also measure if the eyes are open or close. This module can calculate three different states of the user behavior relative to the robot: *Evasion, Attention, Diversion.*

Secondly, ALFaceCharacteristics module provides information relative to the face expression properties of the user and information about the smile. There are

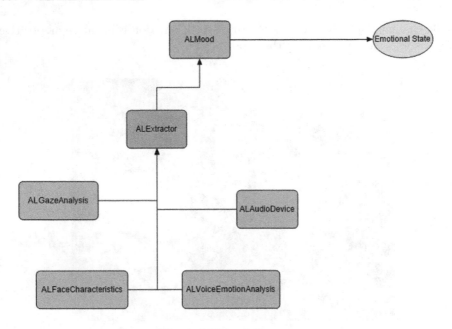

Fig. 4. ALMood diagram.

some traits in the face of each person that once measured can give information relative to the gender and age category. The module gives a measurement of the "smile degree" on a face, so it is capable of measure the difference between a faint smile and a frank smile. It also analyses facial expressions and tries to estimate whether a face is *neutral, happy, surprised, angry* or *sad*.

Another important module is ALVoiceEmotionAnalysis, which allows us to get relevant information about the acoustic voice emotion such as: *the utterance acoustic tone*, and *some linguistic semantics of speech*.

Finally, the module ALAudioDevice gets information from the ambience and calculates the general sound level, so that it return: *the energy level of noise*.

As a summary, for each user in front of the robot, structured data as shown in Listing 1.1 can be obtained simply by calling the method `currentPersonState()` in the ALMood API. It means that this library cannot get more emotions than these, but nevertheless, it allows us to play with the combinations of these emotions to perform a more realistic and complex mapping of user emotions.

4   Augmented Emotional Motor Capabilities

Some symptoms in ASD patients, like difficulties to express their personal feelings and lack of eye contact, could make the emotion state estimation of ALMood library to fail or to give inaccurate results, as it is based on face expressions, gaze direction, etc. Our proposal to make robots useful in ASD assistance is to

Listing 1.1. User data about emotional state.

```
PersonState =
{
    "valence" : { value, confidence },
    "attention" : { value, confidence },
    "bodyLanguageState" : { "ease" : { level, confidence } },
    "smile" : { value, confidence },

    "expressions" :
    {
        "calm" : { value, confidence },
        "anger" : { value, confidence },
        "joy" : { value, confidence },
        "sorrow" : { value, confidence },
        "laughter" : { value, confidence },
        "excitement" : { value, confidence },
        "surprise" : { value, confidence }
    }
}
```

enhance the data provided by Pepper with emotional information from EEG system. Also, the EEG record can provide some relevant information about the brain processes in ASD patients that can be useful for learning and getting a better understanding of this set of diseases. The diagram in Fig. 5 shows the design approach of our proposal.

The experiment consists in showing a series of videos to the patient through the tablet on the chest of the robot, in order to facilitate the information acquisition by Pepper, that must be in front of the patient to visualize the patient's face and gesture properties among other relevant data. The patient will carry the EEG portable brain computer interface, which will provide additional information to Pepper with the current emotional state. This information will be analyzed in real time and finally combined with the information obtained by the robot to improve the whole emotional detection capabilities of the robot. The main objective is to reduce the uncertainty of the information extracted by the robotic system.

In order to achieve the objective, the first approach is to focus in the "valence" field from the PersonState data provided by ALMood `currentPersonState()` method and to include a similar new field "EEGstate" with data from the EEG system, and finally to combine both fields to produce a new global field of mood or emotional reaction of patient. Therefore, our method consist in generating a combined structure with the information obtained in the whole system as is shown in Listing 1.2.

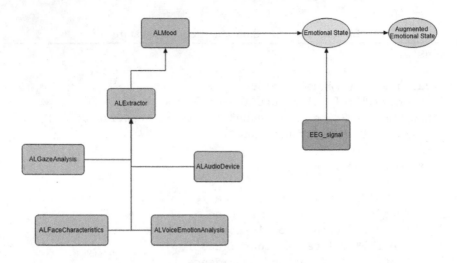

Fig. 5. Our proposal emotional "engine" diagram.

Listing 1.2. Augmented emotional "reaction" structure.

```
Reaction =
{
    "valence" : { value, confidence },
    "EEGstate" : { value, confidence },
    "global" : { value, confidence }
}
```

In this first approach, the value part of each field ("valence", "EEGstate" and "global") will be codified in the continuous range $[-1, 1]$, where value <0 maps to "negative" emotional reactions, value near zero is a "neutral" reaction, and value >0 means a "positive" reaction. The confidence part of the 3 fields will be codified in the continuous range $[0, 1]$ expressing the percentage of success (probability) while classifying the corresponding emotion state.

To compute the global emotional reaction from "valence" and "EEGstate" more relevance will be given to values depending on their higher corresponding confidence. We will define the following shorter notation: v is valence value, c_v is valence confidence, s is EEGstate value, c_s is EEGstate confidence, g is global value and c_g is global confidence. Then, the value of global reaction is

$$
g = \begin{cases} \dfrac{v + s}{2} & \text{if } c_v = 1 \text{ and } c_s = 1 \\[3ex] \dfrac{v \cdot (1 - c_s) + s \cdot (1 - c_v)}{(1 - c_s) + (1 - c_v)} & \text{otherwise} \end{cases}
\tag{1}
$$

and the corresponding global confidence is

$$c_g = 1 - \frac{1}{L}\left(\left(1 - \frac{c_v + c_s}{2}\right) \cdot (L - |v - s|) + |v - s|\right) \tag{2}$$

Equation 1 models the global value of emotional state by the weighted average between the valence value from robot and the EEGstate value, using as weights the corresponding probabilities estimated from confidences, $p_v = \frac{1}{L} \cdot \frac{1}{1-c_v}$ and $p_s = \frac{1}{L} \cdot \frac{1}{1-c_s}$, where $L = 2$ is the interval length (from -1 to $+1$). On the same way, the global confidence in Eq. 2 is computed from the corresponding width of the global confidence interval estimated from the average of both confidence intervals of valence and EEGstate, $w_v = L \cdot (1 - c_v)$ and $w_s = L \cdot (1 - c_s)$, and then corrected to account for the relative separation of values, $w_g = \frac{1}{L}\hat{w}_g \cdot (L - |v - s|) + |v - s|$, where $\hat{w}_g = \frac{1}{2}(w_v + w_s)$, so that $c_g = 1 - \frac{1}{L}w_g$.

The proposed merge of valence from robot ALMood estimation and the state signal from the EEG system has the advantage to provide a mean value as a global reaction, if both systems have similar confidence, but on the other hand, it will give more importance to one of them if the other has a lower confidence. In this way, each system can supply the information that is missing from the other, depending on the expressiveness of the person being monitored. Specially, in the case of ASD patients, for whom sometimes it is difficult to asses an emotion state only from visual clues (face gesture, gaze attention, head position, etc.) that is mainly used by the Pepper robot.

5   Conclusions

The idea of using robots as therapist tools in care assistance, specially for ASD patients, has been growing in the last decade. Research in this field has been increasing, thus providing in both ways, a better understanding on the set of diseases known as ASD and the developing on interaction between humans and robots.

The detection of emotions has been a large challenge during last decades, and many different approaches has been tested, where the EEG systems is only one of them, but it promises to have better results than many others. Our aim is to improve the emotional detections capabilities of robots with the EEG system to decrease the level of uncertainty of emotion detections. For such objective, we have proposed a first approach to extend the information data structure provided by the ALMood module in the Pepper robot emotional system by including the emotional state estimated from an EEG system, and the merge of both information sources to estimate a global reaction for the person in front of the robot.

In future works, we will merge our system with a set of other physiological signal monitors (electrocardiogram, electrooculogram, galvanic skin response, etc.), to provide even more reliability to the emotional state of ASD affected persons and hence to improve the results in the use of robots for the care assistance of such patients.

Acknowledgements. We want to acknowledge Programa de Ayudas a Grupos de Excelencia de la Región de Murcia, from Fundación Séneca, Agencia de Ciencia y Tecnología de la Región de Murcia.

References

1. Diehl, J.J., Schmitt, L.M., Villano, M., Crowell, C.R.: The clinical use of robots for individuals with autism spectrum disorders: a critical review. Res. Autism Spectr. Disord. **6**(1), 249–262 (2012)
2. Scassellati, B.: How social robots will help us to diagnose, treat, and understand autism. Robot. Res. **28**, 552–63 (2007)
3. Jeong, S., Dos Santos, K., Breazeal, C., et al.: Designing a socially assistive robot for pediatric care. In: Proceedings of the 14th International Conference on Interaction Design and Children, pp. 387–390. ACM, New York (2015)
4. Breazeal, C., Scassellati, B.: A context-dependent attention system for a social robot. In: IJCAI 1999 Proceedings of the Sixteenth International Joint Conference on Artificial Intelligence, pp. 1146–1153 (1999)
5. Fong, T., Nourbakhsh, I., Dautenhahn, K.: A survey of socially interactive robots. Robot. Auton. Syst. **42**(3), 143–166 (2003)
6. Scassellati, B., Admoni, H., Matarić, M.: Robots for use in autism research. Annu. Rev. Biomed. Eng. **14**, 275–294 (2012)
7. Ismail, L.I., Shamsudin, S., Yussof, H., Hanapiah, F.A., Zahari, N.I.: Estimation of concentration by eye contact measurement in robot- based intervention program with autistic children. Procedia Eng. **41**, 1548–1552 (2012)
8. Feil-Seifer, D., Mataric, M.J.: Defining socially assistive robotics. In: Proceedings of IEEE 9th International Conference on Rehabilitation Robotics (ICORR 2005), 28 June–1 July, Chicago, pp. 465–68. IEEE, Piscataway (2005)
9. Tapus, A., Mataric, M.J., Scassellati, B.: The grand challenges in socially assistive robotics. IEEE Robot. Autom. Mag. Spec. Issue Grand Challenges Robot **14**(1), 35–42 (2007)
10. Senju, A., Johnson, M.H.: Atypical eye contact in autism: models, mechanisms and development. Neurosci. Biobehav. Rev. **33**, 1204–1214 (2009)
11. Jeong, S., Logan, D.E., Goodwin, M.S., Graca, S., O'Connell, B., Goodenough, H., Plummer, L.: A social robot to mitigate stress, anxiety, and pain in hospital pediatric care. In: Proceedings of the Tenth Annual ACM/IEEE International Conference on Human-Robot Interaction Extended Abstracts pp. 103–104. ACM (2015)
12. Laufs, H., et al.: EEG-correlated fMRI of human alpha activity. Neuroimage **19**(4), 1463–1476 (2003)
13. Nunez, P.L.: Toward a quantitative description of large-scale neocortical dynamic function and EEG. Behav. Brain Sci. **23**(3), 371–398 (2000)
14. Gable, P.A., Poole, B.D.: Influence of trait behavioral inhibition and behavioral approach motivation systems on the LPP and frontal asymmetry to anger pictures. Soc. Cogn. Affect. Neurosci. **9**(2), 182–190 (2014)
15. Knyazev, G.G., Slobodskoj-Plusnin, J.Y., Bocharov, A.V.: Event-related delta and theta synchronization during explicit and implicit emotion processing. Neuroscience **164**(4), 1588–1600 (2009)
16. Leite, J., Carvalho, S., Galdo-Alvarez, S., Alves, J., Sampaio, A., Gonçalves, Ó.F.: Affective picture modulation: valence, arousal, attention allocation and motivational significance. Int. J. Psychophysiol. **83**(3), 375–381 (2012)

17. Liu, Y.-H., Wu, C.-T., Cheng, W.-T., Hsiao, Y.-T., Chen, P.-M., Teng, J.-T.: Emotion recognition from single-trial EEG based on Kernel Fisher's emotion pattern and imbalanced quasiconformal kernel support vector machine. Sensors **14**(8), 13361–13388 (2014)
18. Fanselow, M.S.: Neural organization of the defensive behavior system responsible for fear. Psychon. Bull. Rev. **1**(4), 429–438 (1994)
19. Centers for Disease Control and Prevention (CDC). Autism spectrum disorders (2011). http://www.cdc.gov/ncbddd/autism/index.html
20. Jeong, S., Logan, D., Goodwin, M., et al.: Challenges conducting child-robot interaction research in a pediatric inpatient care context. In: The First Workshop on Evaluating Child-Robot Interaction Held in Conjunction with the Seventh International Conference on Social Robotics (2015)
21. DiSalvo, C., et al.: All robots are not equal: The design and perception of humanoid robot heads. In: Proceedings of the Conference on Designing Interactive Systems (2002)
22. Wada, K., Shibata, T., Asada, T., Musha, T.: Robot therapy for prevention of dementia at home. Journal of Robotics and Mechatronics 19(6), 691(2007)
23. SoftBank Robotics Europe: ALMood API. NAOqi Documentation Center. http://doc.aldebaran.com/2-5/naoqi/core/almood.html

Signal Processing and Machine Learning Applied to Biomedical and Neuroscience Applications

Preliminary Study on Unilateral Sensorineural Hearing Loss Identification via Dual-Tree Complex Wavelet Transform and Multinomial Logistic Regression

Shuihua Wang[1], Yudong Zhang[1(✉)], Ming Yang[2(✉)], Bin Liu[3],
Javier Ramirez[4(✉)], and Juan Manuel Gorriz[4(✉)]

[1] School of Computer Science and Technology, Nanjing Normal University,
Nanjing 210023, Jiangsu, People's Republic of China
zhangyudong@njnu.edu.cn
[2] Department of Radiology, Childrens Hospital of Nanjing Medical University,
Nanjing 210008, People's Republic of China
yangming19710217@163.com
[3] Department of Radiology, Zhong-Da Hospital of Southeast University,
Nanjing 210009, China
[4] Department of Signal Theory, Networking and Communications,
University of Granada, Granada, Spain
{javierrp,gorriz}@ugr.es

Abstract. (Aim) Unilateral sensorineural hearing loss is a brain disease, which causes slight morphology within brain structure. Traditional manual method can ignore this change. (Method) First, we used dual-tree complex wavelet transform to extract features. Afterwards, we used kernel principal component analysis to reduce feature dimensionalities. Finally, multinomial logistic regression was employed to be the classifier. (Result) The 10 times of 10-fold stratified cross validation showed our method achieved an overall accuracy of $96.17 \pm 2.49\%$. The sensitivities of detecting left-sided sensorineural hearing loss, right-sided sensorineural hearing loss, and healthy controls were $96.00 \pm 2.58\%$, $96.50 \pm 2.42\%$, and $96.00 \pm 3.16\%$, respectively. (Conclusion) Our method performed better than five state-of-the-art methods.

Keywords: Unilateral sensorineural hearing loss · Dual-tree complex wavelet transform · Kernel principal component analysis · Multinomial logistic regression · Magnetic resonance imaging

1 Introduction

Hearing loss is a partial or even inability to hear. It is caused by a massive of different problems, such as birth complication, infection, medications, ageing, genetics, noise, trauma, toxins, etc. A hearing loss is determined by tests when the subject cannot hear 25 decibels for more than one year. Until 2013, there

© Springer International Publishing AG 2017
J.M. Ferrández Vicente et al. (Eds.): IWINAC 2017, Part I, LNCS 10337, pp. 289–297, 2017.
DOI: 10.1007/978-3-319-59740-9_28

are more than one billion people suffering from hearing loss [1]. Sensorineural hearing loss is a type of hearing loss [2]. It may occur in one or both ears. In this study, we aim to detect unilateral sensorineural hearing loss (USHL) into two types: left-sided and right-sided.

Magnetic resonance imaging (MRI) is an efficient tool to help diagnose USHL, because the USHL patients have a distinct difference with healthy controls from the view of brain structures, such as left superior/middle/inferior temporal gyrus, bilateral posterior cingulate gyrus and precuneus, lingual gyrus, and right parahippocampal gyrus [3]. Nevertheless, these differences are slight and subtle especially in the prodromal stage in USHL disease. Therefore, computer vision techniques are essential to help neuroradiologist to find those minor alterations.

In the last decade, Li [4] used fractional Fourier transform (FRFT) to detect left-sided and right-sided hearing loss. Chen [5] used wavelet packet decomposition (WPD) technique and least-square support vector machine (LSSVM). Wang et al. [6] combined wavelet entropy (WE) and directed acyclic graph support vector machine (DAG-SVM). Chen and Chen [7] employed three successful techniques: discrete wavelet transform (DWT), principal component analysis (PCA), and generalized eigenvalue proximal support vector machine (GEPSVM). Sun [8] employed wavelet energy, and proposed a quantum-behaved particle swarm optimization method. Wu [9] used contrast-limited adaptive histogram equalization approach. Lu [10] used radial basis function neural network. Chen [11] used fractal dimension based on Minkowski-Bouligand method to detect pathological brains.

After studying above literatures, we found they were confronted with three common problems: (i) Their datasets are imbalanced. This is because healthy controls are easily enrolled, while hearing loss patients are usually with other brain diseases, and hence those patients are not obedient for MRI scanning. (ii) They used wavelet or its variant as the feature, but wavelet decomposition can only detect textures along horizontal, vertical and diagonal directions. (iii) The performance of these detector systems are not satisfying and can be improved.

To solve these problems above, we enrolled more USHL patients so that the numbers of each class are equal. Besides, we proposed to use dual-tree complex wavelet transform, which has more accurate directional selectivity than standard wavelet transform. We also introduced kernel principal component analysis to reduce the features. The multinomial logistic regression was chosen as the classifier. Finally, the experiment shows our proposed method was better than the state-of-the-art methods.

2   Subjects

This study employed the 49 subjects in Reference [7], and then enrolled 11 new patients. Finally, we have 20 healthy controls (HC), 20 left-sided sensorineural hearing loss (LSHL) patients, and 20 right-sided sensorineural hearing loss (RSHL) patients. The dataset is now balanced. The inclusion and exclusion criteria, the pure tone audiometry implementation, the imaging parameters are all the same as in Reference [7]. Ethics Committee of Southeast University approved this research. The updated demographic data of all subjects are listed in Table 1, which clearly shows that all three classes are well matched with regards to gender, age, and education level.

Table 1. Demographic data of all subjects

	LSHL	RSHL	HC
Number	20	20	20
Age (year)	51.3 ± 9.8	53.5 ± 8.2	53.6 ± 5.4
Gender (m/f)	10/10	9/11	8/12
Education level (year)	12.4 ± 1.8	12.2 ± 2.2	11.5 ± 3.2
Disease duration (year)	17.5 ± 17.2	14.4 ± 15.0	-
PTA of left ear (dB)	78.2 ± 17.6	21.9 ± 3.4	22.2 ± 2.1
PTA of right ear (dB)	20.6 ± 4.1	80.7 ± 17.7	21.3 ± 2.2

(Data are mean ± SD, PTA = pure tone average, m = male, f = female)

Image preprocessing follows the standard steps. First, the brain extraction tool v2.1 software [12] was employed to extract brain tissues. All the brain images of 60 subjects were normalized to the Montreal neurologic institute (abbreviated as MNI) template. Then, we resampled them to 2 mm isotropic voxels, and smoothed them by a Gaussian kernel. Three experienced otologists were instructed to select the optimal slice for each subject that covers his/her majority tissues related to hearing. The selected slice was at $Z = 88$ (i.e., 16 mm) in MNI coordinate space. Figure 1(a) shows original image. Figure 1(b) shows the BET result. Figure 1(c) shows the selected brain image.

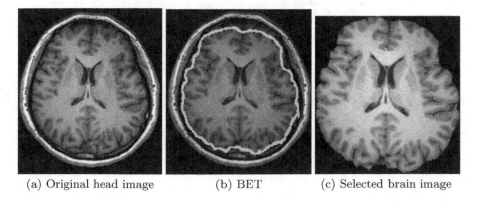

(a) Original head image   (b) BET   (c) Selected brain image

Fig. 1. Brain extraction result (The yellow line marks the brain region) (Color figure online)

3   Dual-Tree Complex Wavelet Transform

The physical structures of the brain are similar to fingerprints, which can be analyzed by wavelet successfully [13,14]. Hence, brain structure can also be analyzed by wavelet. The dual-tree complex wavelet transform (DTCWT) is an improvement of wavelet approach, based on the use of two separate two-channel filter banks, in order to improve the directional selectivity [15]. In the implementation, we need to design two separate DWT decompositions (tree a and tree b) [16]. Thus, the wavelet and scaling filters of tree a can produce both scaling and wavelet function [17], which are approximate Hilbert transforms of tree b. Figure 2 shows the two trees (a and b) used in a DTCWT, here $g_a(k)$ and $h_a(k)$ are the low-pass and high-pass filters for tree a, respectively. $g_b(k)$ and $h_b(k)$ are the low-pass and high-pass filters for tree b, respectively.

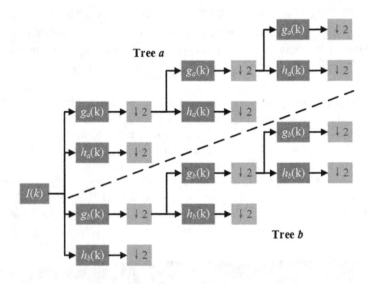

Fig. 2. Diagram of a 2-level DTCWT

For a 2D DTCWT, it produces at each decomposition level 6 directionally selective subbands [18] with six different rotation angles for both real ($\mathcal{R}$) and imaginary ($\mathcal{I}$) components. The real and imaginary components can form the magnitude $\mathcal{M}$ by the following formula

$$\mathcal{M} = \sqrt{\mathcal{R}^2 + \mathcal{I}^2} \tag{1}$$

4   Kernel PCA

From the view point of computer scientist, each pixel of the subband coefficients of DTCWT can be regarded as a feature, the size of which is too large and needs to be reduced. The shortcoming of principal component analysis (PCA) is it only deals well with dataset with linear structure. For nonlinear structure dataset, PCA performs not satisfying. The kernel principal component analysis [19] extends standard PCA, and it implements the same procedure but transforms the dataset into a higher dimensional space. Two important kernel PCAs are introduced below: One is polynomial kernel PCA (shorted as PKPCA):

$$z_p(x, y) = (a_1 \times (x \times y) + a_2)^{a_3} \tag{2}$$

The other is radial basis function kernel PCA (shorted as RKPCA):

$$z_r(x, y) = \exp\left(-\frac{\|x - y\|^2}{a_4^2}\right) \tag{3}$$

Note z_p and z_r represents the polynomial kernel and radial basis function kernel, respectively. Here a_1, a_2, a_3, and a_4 are hyper-parameters. Their optimal values can be obtained by grid searching approach. Note that KPCA is an important feature reduction method. In the future, we shall test feature selection method, which are also efficient in reducing dimensionality of features.

5   Classifier

5.1   Logistic Regression Model

Logistic regression (LR) [20] extends traditional regression analysis to the binary situation. Assume we have M independent variable as

$$x = [x_1, x_2, \ldots, x_M] \tag{4}$$

and assume there is one dependent variable y with value of either 0 or 1. In this way, the decision can be regarded as in following way:

$$y = \begin{cases} 1 & \beta_0 + \beta_1 x_1 + \beta_2 x_2 + \ldots + \beta_M x_M + \varepsilon > 0 \\ 0 & \text{o.w.} \end{cases} \tag{5}$$

where the values of the parameter vector $\beta = [\beta_0, \beta_1, \beta_2, \ldots, \beta_M]$ should be optimized, and β_0 is the intercept [21]. Besides, ε represents the unobservable Bayesian error.

To create the LR model, we create a latent variable z as

$$z = \beta_0 + \beta_1 x_1 + \beta_2 x_2 + \ldots + \beta_M x_M \tag{6}$$

Obviously z is a linear combination of x. By mimicking the logistic sigmoid function (z) defined by

$$\mu(z) = \frac{1}{1 + \exp(-z)} \tag{7}$$

We can finally define the binary LR model as

$$F(x) = \frac{1}{1 + \exp\left[-(\beta_0 + \beta_1 x_1 + \beta_2 x_2 + \ldots + \beta_M x_M)\right]} \tag{8}$$

where $F(x)$ represents the probability of dependent variable $y = 1$ [22].

5.2 Multinomial LR

Traditional LR can only handles binary class problem. The multinomial logistic regression (MLR) generalizes traditional LR to multiclass problem [23], and it is widely used in academic and industrial fields, such as credit evaluation [24], item detection [25], etc. The idea of MLR is simple. Suppose we have C different classes,

$$
y = \begin{cases} 1 & \text{Class 1} \\ 2 & \text{Class 2} \\ \dots & \dots \\ C & \text{Class } C \end{cases} \tag{9}
$$

then we can generate (C-1) LR regression models. Usually, the last class is chosen as the pivot [26], and the other (C-1) classes are regressed against the pivot class in sequence. In mathematical way, we have

$$
\begin{aligned}
\ln \frac{P(Y=1)}{P(Y=C)} &= \beta_{1,0} + \beta_{1,1}x_1 + \beta_{1,2}x_2 + \dots + \beta_{1,M}x_M \\
\ln \frac{P(Y=2)}{P(Y=C)} &= \beta_{2,0} + \beta_{2,1}x_1 + \beta_{2,2}x_2 + \dots + \beta_{2,M}x_M \\
\dots \\
\ln \frac{P(Y=C-1)}{P(Y=C)} &= \beta_{C-1,0} + \beta_{C-1,1}x_1 + \beta_{C-1,2}x_2 + \dots + \beta_{C-1,M}x_M
\end{aligned} \tag{10}
$$

In this study, since we need to handle a 3-class problem (LSHL, RSHL, and HC), the multinomial logistic regression was employed. Some other classifiers can also handle the multi-class problem, such as perceptron, feedforward neural network, decision tree, support vector machine (SVM) [27], fuzzy SVM [28], kernel SVM [29], twin SVM [30], etc. Nevertheless, the MLR has several advantages. It is one of the simplest classifiers, and it is fast to implement. Therefore, we chose MLR in this work.

6 Experiments and Discussions

Except the low-pass coefficients, every decomposition yields 12 coefficient sub-bands (six direction and each has a real and an imaginary component). We let the decomposition level vary from 1 to 4 with increment of 1. The results are pictured in Fig. 3.

Figure 3 shows the indicators change with the decomposition level. As is seen, all indicators achieve their highest when the decomposition level is three. The reason may be two fold: On one hand, more decomposition level will give better analysis of the brain image. On the other hand, too large decomposition level will introduce calculation error, thus decreasing the performance. Therefore, we believe three-level is the optimal for the DTCWT.

Table 2 offers our proposed method with five methods: FRFT + PCA + SFN [4], WPD + LS-SVM [5], WE + DAG-SVM [6], DWT + PCA + SVM [7], and DWT + PCA + GEPSVM [7]. The 10-fold stratified cross validation, we segment the entire dataset into ten folds randomly with equal distribution of each fold. Remember we have 60 subjects: 20 LSHLs, 20 RSHLs, and 20 HCs. Then each fold will contains 2 LSHLs, 2 RSHLs, and 2 HCs. In each trial, nine folds were

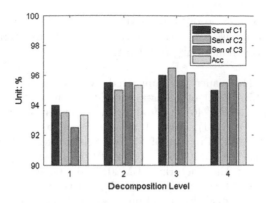

Fig. 3. Decomposition level comparison (Sen = Sensitivity; Acc = Accuracy)

used as training, and the rest for test. This procedure repeated such that each fold was used once for test. To further reduce the randomness, we repeat the 10-fold stratified cross validation ten times.

Table 2. Algorithm comparison

Method	Accuracy	Rank
FRFT + PCA + SFN [4]	95.10%	3
WPD + LS-SVM [5]	95.51%	2
WE + DAG-SVM [6]	95.10%	3
DWT + PCA + SVM [7]	94.08%	5
DWT +PCA + GEPSVM [7]	92.24%	6
DTCWT + KPCA + MLR (Proposed)	96.17%	1

The comparison results in Table 2 show that our proposed DTCWT + KPCA + MLR method yielded the largest accuracy of 96.17%. Next is the WPD + LS-SVM [5] algorithm that yielded an accuracy of 95.51%. Both FRFT + PCA + SFN [4] and WE + DAG-SVM [6] ranked third with an accuracy of 95.10%. The DWT + PCA + SVM [7] ranked firth with an accuracy of 94.08%. Finally, DWT + PCA + GEPSVM [7] performed the worst. Its accuracy only achieved 92.24%.

7   Conclusion

In this study, we proposed a novel unilateral sensorineural hearing loss detection method, which can identify left-sided hearing loss and right-sided hearing loss from healthy controls. Our method is based on three successful techniques: dual-tree complex wavelet transform, kernel principal component analysis, and multinomial logistic regression. The results showed our method is superior to five state-of-the-art approaches.

In the future, we may apply our method to other brain disease detection, such as Alzheimers disease [31], etc. Another research direction is to use class separation ability to validate our pre-selection slice.

Acknowledgment. This paper was supported by Leading Initiative for Excellent Young Researcher (LEADER) of Ministry of Education, Culture, Sports, Science and Technology-Japan (16809746), Natural Science Foundation of China (61602250, 61503188, 61562041, 61271231), Natural Science Foundation of Jiangsu Province (BK20150983, BK20150982), Program of Natural Science Research of Jiangsu Higher Education Institutions (16KJB520025, 15KJB470010), Jiangsu Key Laboratory of 3D Printing Equipment and Manufacturing (BM2013006), Open fund for Jiangsu Key Laboratory of Advanced Manufacturing Technology (HGAMTL1601), Open Program of Jiangsu Key Laboratory of 3D Printing Equipment and Manufacturing (3DL201602).

References

1. Vos, T., et al.: Global, regional, and national incidence, prevalence, and years lived with disability for 301 acute and chronic diseases and injuries in 188 countries, 1990–2013: a systematic analysis for the global burden of disease study 2013. Lancet **386**, 743–800 (2015)
2. Parker, M.A.: Biotechnology in the treatment of sensorineural hearing loss: foundations and future of hair cell regeneration. J. Speech Lang. Hear. Res. **54**, 1709–1731 (2011)
3. Yang, M., et al.: Brain structural and functional alterations in patients with unilateral hearing loss. Hear. Res. **316**, 37–43 (2014)
4. Li, J.: Detection of left-sided and right-sided hearing loss via fractional fourier transform. Entropy **18** (2016). Article ID: 194
5. Chen, P.: Computer-aided detection of left and right sensorineural hearing loss by wavelet packet decomposition and least-square support vector machine. J. Am. Geriatr. Soc. **64** (2016). Article ID: S350
6. Wang, S., et al.: Wavelet entropy and directed acyclic graph support vector machine for detection of patients with unilateral hearing loss in MRI scanning. Front. Comput. Neurosci. **10** (2016). Article ID: 160
7. Chen, Y., Chen, X.-Q.: Sensorineural hearing loss detection via discrete wavelet transform and principal component analysis combined with generalized eigenvalue proximal support vector machine and Tikhonov regularization. Multimedia Tools Appl. (2016). doi:10.1007/s11042-016-4087-6
8. Sun, P.: Preliminary research on abnormal brain detection by wavelet-energy and quantum-behaved PSO. Technol. Health Care **24**, S641–S649 (2016)
9. Wu, X.: Smart detection on abnormal breasts in digital mammography based on contrast-limited adaptive histogram equalization and chaotic adaptive real-coded biogeography-based optimization. Simulation **92**, 873–885 (2016)
10. Lu, Z.: A pathological brain detection system based on radial basis function neural network. J. Med. Imaging Health Inform. **6**, 1218–1222 (2016)
11. Chen, X.-Q.: Fractal dimension estimation for developing pathological brain detection system based on Minkowski-Bouligand method. IEEE Access **4**, 5937–5947 (2016)
12. Jenkinson, M., et al.: BET2: MR-based estimation of brain, skull and scalp surfaces. In: Eleventh Annual Meeting of the Organization for Human Brain Mapping, pp. 151–158 (2005)

13. Khalil, M.S.: Reference point detection for camera-based fingerprint image based on wavelet transformation. Biomed. Eng. Online **14**, 23 (2015). Article ID: 40

14. Xu, C., Cheng, X.M.: An algorithm for fingerprint identification based on wavelet transform and gabor feature. In: Third International Conference on Genetic and Evolutionary Computing, pp. 827–831. IEEE Computer Society (2009)

15. Yasin, A.S., et al.: Speech signal filtration using double-density dual-tree complex wavelet transform. Tech. Phys. Lett. **42**, 865–867 (2016)

16. Serbes, G., et al.: Directional dual-tree complex wavelet packet transforms for processing quadrature signals. Med. Biol. Eng. Comput. **54**, 295–313 (2016)

17. Thenmozhi, S., Chandrasekaran, M.: Multilayered secure medical image transmission with high payload using double density dual tree discrete wavelet transform. J. Med. Imaging Health Inform. **6**, 822–827 (2016)

18. Hill, P., et al.: Contrast sensitivity of the wavelet, dual tree complex wavelet, curvelet, and steerable pyramid transforms. IEEE Trans. Image Process. **25**, 2739–2751 (2016)

19. Phinyomark, A., Osis, S.T., Hettinga, B.A., Ferber, R.: Kernel principal component analysis for identification of between-group differences and changes in running gait patterns. In: Kyriacou, E., Christofides, S., Pattichis, C.S. (eds.) XIV Mediterranean Conference on Medical and Biological Engineering and Computing 2016. IP, vol. 57, pp. 580–585. Springer, Cham (2016). doi:10.1007/978-3-319-32703-7_113

20. Aly, W.M.: A new approach for classifier model selection and tuning using logistic regression and genetic algorithms. Arab. J. Sci. Eng. **41**, 5195–5204 (2016)

21. Zaidi, N.A., et al.: ALR: accelerated higher-order logistic regression. Mach. Learn. **104**, 151–194 (2016)

22. Herndon, N., Caragea, D.: A study of domain adaptation classifiers derived from logistic regression for the task of splice site prediction. IEEE Trans. Nanobiosci. **15**, 77–85 (2016)

23. Jostins, L., McVean, G.: Trinculo: Bayesian and frequentist multinomial logistic regression for genome-wide association studies of multi-category phenotypes. Bioinformatics **32**, 1898–1900 (2016)

24. Sun, J., et al.: Use of logistics regression model in credit evaluation for mobile subscribers. In: Proceedings of the 2nd International Conference on Value Engineering and Value Management, pp. 148–152. Publishing House Electronics Industry (2009)

25. Lee, S.: Detecting differential item functioning using the logistic regression procedure in small samples. Appl. Psychol. Meas. **41**, 30–43 (2017)

26. Monyai, S., et al.: Application of multinomial logistic regression to educational factors of the 2009 general household survey in South Africa. J. Appl. Stat. **43**, 128–139 (2016)

27. Wu, L.: Classification of fruits using computer vision and a multiclass support vector machine. Sensors **12**, 12489–12505 (2012)

28. Hajiloo, M., et al.: Fuzzy support vector machine: an efficient rule-based classification technique for microarrays. BMC Bioinform. **14** (2013). Article ID: UNSP-S4

29. Dong, Z.: Classification of Alzheimer disease based on structural magnetic resonance imaging by kernel support vector machine decision tree. Prog. Electromagnet. Res. **144**, 171–184 (2014)

30. Chen, M.: Morphological analysis of dendrites and spines by hybridization of ridge detection with twin support vector machine. PeerJ **4** (2016). Article ID: e2207

31. Lpez, M.M., et al.: SVM-based CAD system for early detection of the Alzheimer's disease using kernel PCA and LDA. Neurosci. Lett. **464**, 233–238 (2009)

On a Heavy-Tailed Intensity Normalization of the Parkinson's Progression Markers Initiative Brain Database

Diego Castillo-Barnes[1], Carlos Arenas[1], Fermín Segovia[1],
Francisco J. Martínez-Murcia[1], Ignacio A. Illán[2], Juan M. Górriz[1],
Javier Ramírez[1], and Diego Salas-Gonzalez[1(✉)]

[1] Department of Signal Theory, Networking and Communications, ETSIIT-UGR,
University of Granada, 18071 Granada, Spain
dsalas@ugr.es
[2] Department of Scientific Computing, The Florida State University,
Tallahassee, FL, USA

Abstract. In this work, we normalize the intensity of 40 FP-CIT SPECT images from the Parkinson's Progression Markers Initiative assuming that the histogram of intensity values follows an α-stable distribution. Then, we study the normalized images. The interclass separation of the Parkinson's disease (PD) brain images and the healthy control (HC) are calculated by means of the Mann-Whitney-Wilcoxon U-test. The intensity transformed images present higher inter-class separation according to the estimation of the U-test.

1 Introduction

[123I]FP-CIT (DaTSCAN) single photon emission computerized tomography (SPECT) brain images is a modality which is currently used to assist in the diagnosis of Parkinsonism [1,2] and the differentiation of parkinsonism and essential tremor [3].

The typical pattern of an image with this modality is a noisy and non-informative image of the brain except in an specific region, the striatum where the image exhibits higher intensity level [4]. 123I-FP-CIT binds to the dopamine transporters in the striatum. A healthy normal control (HC) patient is expected to present higher intensity values in the striatum than an image from a subject with Parkinson disease (PD). Specific binding regions in the striatum (putamen and caudate nuclei) appear more intense in HC than in PD subjects.

For this reason, when FP-CIT SPECT brain images are used for Parkinson's diagnosis, the count per voxel or intensity level in the striatum are compared between different subjects [5].

Nevertheless, the count per voxels depends not only on the type of subject (NC or PD) but also on the dosis of radiotracer used. For this reason, it is crucial to perform the intensity normalization of the images before to perform inter or intra subject comparison [6]. This preprocessing step is usually performed

© Springer International Publishing AG 2017
J.M. Ferrández Vicente et al. (Eds.): IWINAC 2017, Part I, LNCS 10337, pp. 298–304, 2017.
DOI: 10.1007/978-3-319-59740-9_29

by the so-called 'binding ratio'. The ratio between the intensity values in a specific region and a non-specific region (commonly the occipital cortex). The occipital cortex is the usual choice as a reference because the density of dopamine transporters is negligible in this region.

In this work, we perform the intensity normalization of the images from the Parkinson's Progression Markers Initiative (PPMI) database using an α-stable distribution approach [7]. This method assumes that the histogram of intensity values of the FP-CIT SPECT images follows an α-stable distribution.

2 Material and Methods

2.1 PPMI Database

The Parkinson's Progression Markers Initiative is the top leading observational clinical study carried out nowadays for the study of Parkinson's disease. The goal of this international project is to comprehensively evaluate people with Parkinson's disease and those at greater risk of developing the disease, and their differences with healthy controls. In order to identify the biomarkers of Parkinson's disease progression.

Currently this longitudinal study, following over 1,000 participants for up to 8 years, is taking place at 33 clinical sites worldwide. In this work we have selected 40 images from the PPMI database (13 HC and 27 PD).

2.2 Stable Intensity Normalization

Assuming that the intensity values of the FP-CIT SPECT brain data is a random variable with α-stable distribution with parameters α, β, γ and μ (see Fig. 1). The distribution of random variables can be easily transformed to another α-stable distribution with parameters α, β, γ^* μ^* applying the following linear transformation [7]:

$$Y \sim aX + b \tag{1}$$

where $a = \frac{\gamma^*}{\gamma}$ and $b = \mu^* - \frac{\gamma^*}{\gamma}\mu$.

2.3 Mann-Whitney-Wilcoxon U-Test

We use the absolute value of the U-statistic of a two-sample unpaired Wilcoxon test to estimate the voxel separability between classes. The Mann-Whitney-Wilcoxon U-test is more robust to outliers in the data than the t-test and does not assume that the data is Gaussian [8,9].

In order to perform the U-test all the observations are arranged into a single ranked series. We add up the ranks for the observations which came from group 1 (PD images). The statistic U is then given by:

$$U_1 = R_1 - \frac{n_1(n_1 + 1)}{2} \tag{2}$$

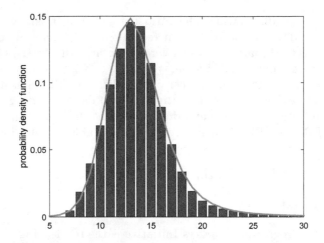

Fig. 1. Histogram of the brain intensity values for a sample image. Continuous line: predicted α-stable density.

where n_1 is the number of PD images, and R_1 is the sum of the ranks in sample 1.

Analogously we make the same calculation for sample 2 (or group 2, HC images):

$$U_2 = R_2 - \frac{n_2(n_2 + 1)}{2} \tag{3}$$

The distance U given by the Wilcoxon test is the smaller value of U_1 and U_2, $U = \min\{U_1, U_2\}$.

The U-test is a procedure that allows us to rank voxels of the brain FP-CIT SPECT images. Thus, this method let us to perform selection of regions of interest for later statistical classification. Voxels with highest U-test values present the greatest difference between HC and PD intensity values.

3   Results

Figure 2 depicts a montage showing a transaxial slice for each of the 40 original images selected from the PPMI database. This image depicts clearly the difference in intensity values between the images.

Figure 3 shows the same transaxial slice as in Fig. 2 after the application of the α-stable intensity normalization approach. The intensity normalization renders more homogeneous the visual aspect of the brain images.

Figure 4 depicts the histogram of the intensity values for the original images (left) and the histogram of stable transformed images (right). This Figure shows that the variability of the original images is reduced considerably after the normalization.

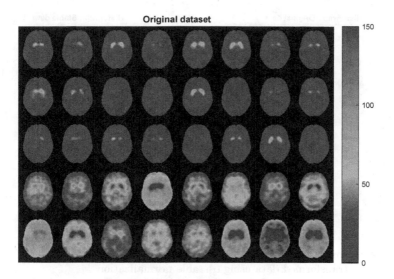

Fig. 2. 40 transaxial original brain images.

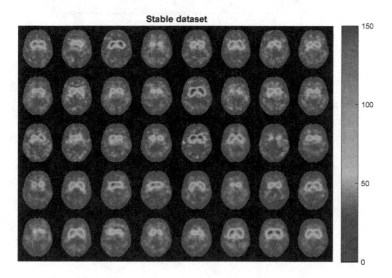

Fig. 3. 40 transaxial stable brain images.

Figure 5 shows the Mann-Whitney-Wilcoxon U-test calculated for the striatum region for 'original dataset' and the 'stable dataset'. The U-test values are ranked in descending order. This figure shows that the intensity values of the striatum in the HC and PD classes are more separated after intensity normalization.

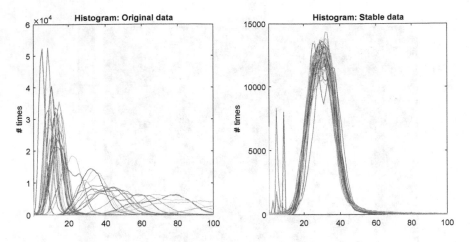

Fig. 4. Histogram of intensity values of the 40 images under study. Left: original dataset. Right: transformed data using α-stable normalization

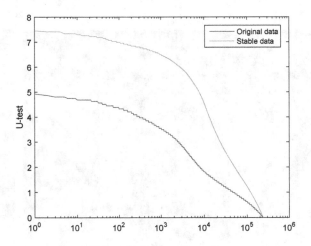

Fig. 5. Ranked U-test in descending order for voxels in striatum

Figure 6 shows the boxplot with the intensity values in the striatum for original and stable brain images. On each box, the central mark is the median. The edges of the box are the 25th and 75th percentiles, the whiskers extend to the most extreme data points not considered outliers, and outliers are plotted individually.

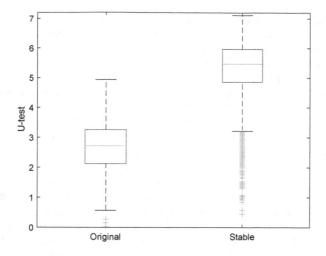

Fig. 6. Boxplot considering the intensity values in the striatum.

4 Conclusion and Future Work

In this work, we have applied a linear intensity normalization method to 40 images from the PPMI dataset. This method assumes that the intensity of a FP-CIT SPECT image is a random variable with α-stable distribution. The interclass distance between PD and HC images has been measured using the Mann-Whitney-Wilcoxon U-test. The intensity variability between images is decreased after normalization. Moreover, we have proven that the separation between intensity values in PD and HC images increases, specially in the striatum. In the future, the proposed methodology will be extended to the whole PPMI database. In addition, the results included in this contribution will be used as a preprocessing step of a feature selection procedure for statistical classification purposes.

Acknowledgements. This work was supported by MINECO/FEDER under the TEC2015-64718-R project and Junta de Andalucía under the P11-TIC-7103 Excellence Project.

References

1. Booij, J., Habraken, J.B.A., Bergmans, P., Tissingh, G., Winogrodzka, A., Wolters, E.C., Janssen, A.G.M., Stoof, J.C., Van Royen, E.A.: Imaging of dopamine transporters with iodine-123-FP-CIT spect in healthy controls and patients with Parkinson's disease. J. Nuclear Med. **39**(11), 1879–1884 (1998)
2. Booij, J., Tissingh, G., Boer, G.J., Speelman, J.D., Stoof, J.C., Janssen, A.G.M., Wolters, E.C.: [123i]-FP-CIT spect shows a pronounced decline of striatal dopamine transporter labelling in early and advanced Parkinson's disease. J. Neurol. Neurosurg. Psychiatry **62**(2), 133–140 (1997)

3. Benamer, H.T.S., Patterson, J., Grosset, D.G., Booij, J., De Bruin, K., Van Royen, E., Speelman, J.D., Horstink, M.H.I.M., Sips, H.J.W.A., Dierckx, R.A., Versijpt, J., Decoo, D., Van Der Linden, C., Hadley, D.M., Doder, M., Lees, A.J., Costa, D.C., Gacinovic, S., Oertel, W.H., Pogarell, O., Hoeffken, H., Joseph, K., Tatsch, K., Schwarz, J., Ries, V.: Accurate differentiation of Parkinsonism and essential tremor using visual assessment of [123i]-FP-CIT spect imaging: the [123i]-FP-CIT study group. Mov. Disord. 15(3), 503–510 (2000)
4. Salas-Gonzalez, D., Górriz, J.M., Ramírez, J., Illán, I.A., Padilla, P., Martínez-Murcia, F.J., Lang, E.W.: Building a FP-CIT spect brain template using a posterization approach. Neuroinformatics 13(4), 391–402 (2015)
5. Segovia, F., Górriz, J.M., Ramírez, J., Salas-Gonzalez, D.: Multiclass classification of 18F-DMFP-PET data to assist the diagnosis of Parkinsonism. In: PRNI 2016–6th International Workshop on Pattern Recognition in Neuroimaging (2016)
6. Brahim, A., Ramírez, J., Górriz, J.M., Khedher, L., Salas-Gonzalez, D.: Comparison between different intensity normalization methods in 123I-Ioflupane imaging for the automatic detection of Parkinsonism. PLoS ONE 10(6), e0130274 (2015)
7. Salas-Gonzalez, D., Górriz, J.M., Ramírez, J., Illán, I.A., Lang, E.W.: Linear intensity normalization of FP-CIT SPECT brain images using the-stable distribution. NeuroImage 65, 449–455 (2013)
8. Martínez-Murcia, F.J., Górriz, J.M., Ramírez, J., Puntonet, C.G., Salas-González, D.: Computer aided diagnosis tool for Alzheimer's disease based on Mann-Whitney-Wilcoxon U-test. Expert Syst. Appl. 39(10), 9676–9685 (2012)
9. Salas-Gonzalez, D., Górriz, J.M., Ramírez, J., Segovia, F., Chaves, R., López, M., Illán, I.A., Padilla, P.: Selecting regions of interest in SPECT images using Wilcoxon test for the diagnosis of Alzheimer's disease. In: Graña Romay, M., Corchado, E., Garcia Sebastian, M.T. (eds.) HAIS 2010. LNCS, vol. 6076, pp. 446–451. Springer, Heidelberg (2010). doi:10.1007/978-3-642-13769-3_54

Case-Based Statistical Learning:
A Non Parametric Implementation Applied
to SPECT Images

J.M. Górriz[1(✉)], J. Ramírez[1], F.J. Martinez-Murcia[1], I.A. Illán[3], F. Segovia[1],
D. Salas-González[1], and A. Ortiz[2]

[1] Department of Signal Theory and Communications, University of Granada,
Granada, Spain
[2] Department of Communications Engineering, Universidad de Malaga,
Málaga, Spain
[3] Department of Scientific Computing, The Florida State University,
Tallahassee, USA

Abstract. In the theory of semi-supervised learning, we have a train-ing set and a unlabeled data that are employed to fit a prediction model or *learner* with the help of an iterative algorithm such as the expectation-maximization (EM) algorithm. In this paper a novel non-parametric approach of the so called *case-based statistical learning* in a low-dimensional classification problem is proposed. This supervised model selection scheme analyzes the discrete set of outcomes in the clas-sification problem by hypothesis-testing and makes assumptions on these outcome values to obtain the most likely prediction model at the train-ing stage. A novel prediction model is described in terms of the output scores of a confidence-based support vector machine classifier under class-hypothesis testing. The estimation of the error rates from a well-trained SVM allows us to propose a non-parametric approach avoiding the use of Gaussian density function-based models in the likelihood ratio test.

Keywords: Statistical learning and decision theory · Support vector machines (SVM) · Hypothesis testing · Partial least squares · Conditional-error rate

1 Introduction

Machine learning has been successfully applied to many areas of science and engineering [11]. Some examples include time series prediction [2], optical char-acter recognition [18], signal and image classification in biomedical applications for diagnosis and prognosis [19,20], etc. The support vector machine (SVM) is a recently developed paradigm in machine learning [18] with applications to brain image processing and classification [1,4,6,10]. In this scenario, the purpose of these techniques is to provide objective clinical decisions and an early detection of abnormal perfussion/metabolic patterns [19].

© Springer International Publishing AG 2017
J.M. Ferrández Vicente et al. (Eds.): IWINAC 2017, Part I, LNCS 10337, pp. 305–313, 2017.
DOI: 10.1007/978-3-319-59740-9_30

The performance control of a SVM is a major requirement in any classi-fication problem [3], i.e. the development of computer-aided diagnosis (CAD) systems [5]. Typically, it is specified in terms of minimum error rate or overall accuracy [8,15] although many factors including noise, the inherent complexity of the classification task, computational constraints, etc. may inhibit the system from achieving the performance requirements for an specific application [14]. Fortunately, other solutions based on the optimal classification theory proposed in [3], i.e. the ones based on controlled error rates [14], have been analyzed and demonstrated their reliability and efficiency as methodologies for the classifier design. On the other hand, *decision theory* [12], that is, the application of sta-tistical hypothesis testing to the detection problem, is a well-known statistical technique that allows model/feature selection in the cross-validation (CV) loop [5]. The so-called case-based learning (CSL) employs a model selection algo-rithm in order to select the optimal classifier that minimizes the CV error (see Fig. 1) in a semi-supervised fashion. In a nutshell, this method consists in per-forming hypothesis testing on the set of unlabeled responses by the extraction of extended datasets under null & alternative hypotheses. The method results in a relabeling process for those patterns whose labels are rejected by the test. Other approaches for model/feature selection are based on Information Theory, filter methods, embedded and wrapper methods, etc. [9]. Unlike the latter methods CSL evaluates a *likelihood ratio test* on the class-dependent features and selects the most probable model among them. In particular, *supervised* feature extrac-tion (SFE) allows to obtain different datasets of features by hypothesizing on the unknown outcomes or responses of the processed pattern.

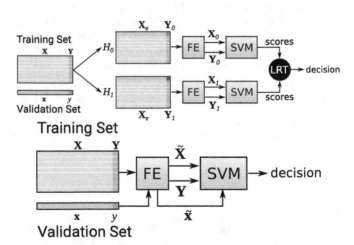

Fig. 1. Diagram of the non-parametric CSL model selection approach vs. baseline

2   Bayes Formulation of the Classification Problem

Consider a set of patterns $\mathbf{Z} = \{\mathbf{X} \in \mathbb{R}^p, Y \in \mathbb{R}\}$, represented by a set of vectors $\mathbf{X}$ in a d-dimensional Euclidean space and admissible classes $Y \in \{w_0, w_1\}$. The *evidence* of the feature vector can be written as:

$$p(\mathbf{x}) = p(\mathbf{x}|w_0)p(w_0) + p(\mathbf{x}|w_1)p(w_1) \tag{1}$$

where $p(w_i)$ is the prior probability of class w_i and, accordingly to Bayes' formula, the posterior probability is defined as:

$$p(w_i|\mathbf{x}) = p(\mathbf{x}|w_i)p(w_i)/p(\mathbf{x}) \tag{2}$$

Given the ideal learner or mapping $\tilde{f} : \mathbb{R}^d \mapsto \{w_0, w_1\}$ that assigns each feature vector to its real class, the classification problem can be tackled by minimizing the sample conditional error with respect to the set of mappings $\{f\}$:

$$\min_f p(w_i|\mathbf{x}) \quad \text{when} \quad \tilde{f}(\mathbf{x}) = w_j, i \neq j \tag{3}$$

The classifier f naturally divides the feature space $\mathbb{R}^d$ into two regions named R_0 and R_1, at least, assigning any new pattern to the category lying on the same side of the decision surface. The error rates E_i can be computed by integrating on these subspaces the conditional probabilities:

$$E_i = \int_{R_i} p(w_j|\mathbf{x})p(\mathbf{x})d\mathbf{x} \tag{4}$$

3   Case-Based Learning on the Conditional Error

Under the CSL approach [5], a class is considered as an hypothesis on a Neyman-Pearson hypothesis testing framework, that is, $H_i = w_i$ for $i = \{0,1\}$. Thus we try to maximize the probability of detection $P_D = P(w_i; w_i)$ of one of the hypotheses (classes) when it is true for a given significance level or probability of false alarm $P_{FA}(w_i; w_j)$, for $i \neq j$. In particular, w_1 is decided if the LRT holds:

$$L(\mathbf{x}) = \frac{p(\mathbf{x}; w_1)}{p(\mathbf{x}; w_0)} > \gamma \tag{5}$$

where γ is a constant threshold. Although this ratio is equivalent, in terms of ability to classify, to having the class posteriors for optimal classification [11], class posteriors allows us to introduce a non-parametric approach in this framework by formulating an overall error-rate ratio test from the integrated version of the conditional probability in Eq. 3 as:

$$\mathfrak{L}(\mathbf{x}) = \frac{E_0(w_1) + E_1(w_1)}{E_0(w_0) + E_1(w_0)} > \gamma \tag{6}$$

where $E_j(w_k) = \int_{R_j} p(w_i|\mathbf{x}; w_k)p(\mathbf{x})d\mathbf{x}$ is the error rate under w_k hypothesis in region R_j for $i \neq j$ and $k = \{0,1\}$. The precision in that regions can be defined as $P_j = E_j / \int_{R_j} p(\mathbf{x})d\mathbf{x}$. The hypothesis w_0 is decided if the LRT in Eq. 6 holds, that is, the one with minimum error rate in regions R_0 and R_1. In the CSL approach the sample realizations $\mathbf{x} = (x_1, \ldots, x_d)$ of the processed pattern under the class-hypotheses w_k, denoted by $(\mathbf{x}; w_k)$, are obtained by using a SFE scheme

[5]. In this case, Eq. 6 allows us to select the class whose conditional-error rate is minimum when one of the two class-hypotheses is true.

Given a pattern $\mathbf{x}$, the admissible classes $\{w_0, w_1\}$ and the training set $\mathbf{X} = [\mathbf{x}_1^T, \ldots, \mathbf{x}_N^T]^T$, two extended training sets are built for SFE as:

$$\begin{aligned} \mathbf{X}_e &= [\mathbf{x}^T, \mathbf{x}_1^T, \ldots, \mathbf{x}_N^T]^T \\ \mathbf{Y}_k &= [w_k, \mathbf{Y}^T]^T \end{aligned} \tag{7}$$

where $\mathbf{Y} = [y_1, \ldots, y_N]^T$, is the training label vector. Performing FE on these novel datasets, i.e. by LS or PLS approaches [5] we finally achieve the pre-processed extended datasets as $\mathbf{Z}_k = (\mathbf{X}_k, \mathbf{Y}_k)$ for $k = \{0, 1\}$, where $\mathbf{X}_k = T(\mathbf{X}_e)$ where T is the selected feature extractor, i.e. in LS estimate the projection operator $P_{\mathbf{w}}$.

3.1   An Implementation Using SVM

The effectiveness of the proposed methodology is demonstrated using SVM as the baseline classifier. The non-parametric method used here, in order to implement Eq. 6, is based on the empirical cumulative density (ECD) function for a trained SVM as defined in [14]. Many works have been reported on transforming output scores to probabilities [16] therefore the probabilities detailed throughout the paper can be estimated by them. The score output by the SVM for each feature indicates the likelihood that the input pattern belongs to a class thus it ranks input samples from the most likely members to the most unlikely members of a class [14]. Given a extended training dataset $\mathbf{X}_k$ with N samples, consisting of N_i samples of class w_i, the ECD function for class w_j under hypothesis w_k is defined in the output-score space of the SVM as:

$$F_j(t; w_k) = \frac{card(f(\mathbf{x}) < t, \mathbf{x} \subset R_j; w_k)}{N_j} \tag{8}$$

Following Eq. 4 the error rate function E_i in the region $R_i = \{\mathbf{x} \subset \mathbf{X}_e; t_1 < f(\mathbf{x}) \mapsto w_i < t_2\}$ can be approximated as:

$$\begin{aligned} E_i(t_1, t_2; w_k) &= \int_{R_i} p(w_j | \mathbf{x}; w_k) p(\mathbf{x}) d\mathbf{x} \\ &= p(w_j) \int_{R_i} p(\mathbf{x} | w_j; w_k) \simeq \frac{card(f(\mathbf{x}) < t_2, \mathbf{x} \subset R_j; w_k) - card(f(\mathbf{x}) < t_1, \mathbf{x} \subset R_j; w_k)}{N} \end{aligned} \tag{9}$$

where $\int_{R_i} p(\mathbf{x} | w_j; w_k) \simeq p(w_j)(F_j(t_2; w_k) - F_j(t_1; w_k))$ and $p(w_j) = N_j/N$. The selection of the limits t_1, t_2 under the confidence based-classifier design theory [14] allows to define a negative/positive bound below/above which the error rate is smaller than a targeted error and therefore, a decision on the input pattern can be achieved ($\mathbf{x} \subset R_0/R_1$). On the contrary, the samples are rejected ($\mathbf{x} \subset R_r$) because the decision is too risky.

In order to be conservative we need to include all the available samples of the dataset in the computation of error rates, thus these magnitudes are computed by locating the limits t_1 and t_2 on the boundaries of the regions. Thus, we select the decision surface of the SVM ($f(\mathbf{x}) = 0$) and the minimum f_{min} (maximum f_{max}) output-score value for class w_1 (w_0) in the previously defined region R_0 (R_1). In other words, R_r is assumed to be negligible or the targeted error to be huge. Finally, taking into account the definition of the error-rate and its correspondent ratio test, the decision rule can be formulated in terms of precision in regions R_0 and R_1 as:

$$\mathfrak{L}(\mathbf{x}) = \frac{P_0(w_1) + P_1(w_1)}{P_0(w_0) + P_1(w_0)} \tag{10}$$

where the precision functions are defined as:

$$P_0(w_k) = \frac{card(f(\mathbf{x}) < 0, \mathbf{x} \subset R_0; w_k) - card(f(\mathbf{x}) < f_{min}, \mathbf{x} \subset R_0; w_k)}{card(f_{min} < f(\mathbf{x}) < 0; w_k)}$$

and

$$P_1(w_k) = \frac{card(f(\mathbf{x}) < f_{max}, \mathbf{x} \subset R_1; w_k) - card(0 < f(\mathbf{x}), \mathbf{x} \subset R_1; w_k)}{card(0 < f(\mathbf{x}) < f_{max}; w_k)}$$

As a conclusion, we take advantage of the misclassified support vectors and rank them according to their output scores from the minimum/maximum value to zero. All the samples with scores included in these regions allows us to compute an approximation for the error rates as shown in Eq. 10. Once the most probable model is selected by this procedure, the set of training patterns are re-labeled accordingly and the resulting knowledge can be applied to new unseen patterns. The novelty of this approach is based on the correction in the degree of uncertainty of the labeling process using biomedical image databases, i.e. it is usually performed by visual assessment with the corresponding subjective bias. Nowadays, visual inspection of the neuroimages obtained by SPECT [17] or Magnetic Resonance Imaging (MRI) [13] is no longer acceptable for diagnostic purposes since it often misses crucial information and therefore can be misleading, thus learning from these examples could degrade the performance of any pattern recognition system.

4   Experiments

A set of experiments are carried out on synthetic and image databases where the small sample size problem is typically an issue, i.e. a SPECT image database [7]. To this purpose, a fair comparison using the same FE and statistical validation schemes for the proposed non-parametric approach and the baseline methods is performed. In both cases the error estimation is obtained by LOO-CV and a linear SVM classifier to avoid over-fitting. The number of extracted components for the FE methods should be small to proper estimate the error rate in the output score space. Firstly, we evaluate the posterior probability-based decision on a 2D experiment with known distributions. Two hundred samples are randomly drawn from two Gaussian distributions with means $\mu_0 = (0,0)$ and $\mu_1 = (1,1)$ and covariance matrices $S_0 = [1.4; .41]$ and $S_1 = [1 - .1; -.11]$. At the FE stage of the proposed method LS is applied to the input data to obtain the extended datasets. Under the class-hypotheses the extended datasets and the different SV configurations are obtained as shown in Fig. 2, where the same processed-pattern is considered. A zoom on these figures reveals an increase in the number of support vectors in the wrong subspace, that is, the conditional probability $p(w_i|x)$ for the computation of the error rate on this subspace R_j, for $i \neq j$, is increased. As shown in these figures, the processed sample (close to the margin) used to describe the operation of the proposed method is relevant [5] in the sense that a substantial change between the extended datasets and their SV configuration is obtained. The SVM-based classification stage on the selected dataset would benefit from the right assumption (the *real* pattern class) following a good performance of the SVM classifier (see Table 1). By increasing the number of input patterns up to 500 samples, a smoothed histogram of the SVM output scores, for each class, can be obtained in order to compare the regions R_i under class-hypotheses when one of them is true. The overlap of the output scores between training classes decreases on average when the correct assumption is considered, i.e. Kullback-Leibler distances d_c^r among distributions assuming class c with real class r, is $d_-^+ = 0.1030$, $d_+^+ = 0.0278$; $d_+^- = 0.0813$, $d_-^- = 0.0278$.

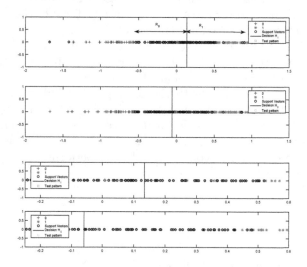

Fig. 2. SVM decision surfaces of extended datasets and support vector configuration for a processed-pattern with class w_0. Down: zoom on upper figures

Baseline SPECT data from 96 participants were collected including controls and AD subjects [7]. The SPECT images were reconstructed, preprocessed (intensity and spatially normalization) and labeled following the criteria as detailed in [7], where the demographic details are also shown. Overall, the database consists of 41 NOR, 29 AD1, 22 AD2 and 4 AD3 patients.

Table 1. Confusion matrix on training set (500 samples) using linear SVM for Gaussian data

		Prediction		Acc (%)
		Positive	Negative	
Nonp CSL	Positive	200	50	75.2
	Negative	74	176	
Baseline	Positive	202	48	70.4
	Negative	100	150	

Additionally, the SPECT images are converted into feature vectors, prior to classification, by means of two masking procedures. Firstly, all the brain-volume voxels are consider as features in the classification task. Secondly, several standardized brain regions in MNI space (Brodmann areas) are extracted from subjects and then classified, separately. Only the first PLS-component is considered (highest variance) transforming a complex task into a one-dimensional classification problem, as shown in the previous examples with Gaussian pdfs and the classical LS. The statistical measures to assess the performance of the CSL approach on the SPECT dataset are summarized in Table 2, where a linear SVM classifier in a CV loop is used for classification. This table shows how even using a small-sample size the improvement on the baseline, under the same experimental framework, is substantial. The PLS-based CSL method outperforms in 18 out of 20 BA the baseline although this improvement consist only in 4 positive samples and 14 negative samples. This performance yields an accuracy rate higher than the baseline in one point, as shown in Table 2.

Table 2. Statistical measures of performance for the proposed PLS-based method and the baseline approach on the SPECT database

	PLS	C-PLS		PLS	C-PLS	
Acc (%)	0.8130 ± 0.0340	**0.8228 ± 0.0273**	BAs	0.8333	**0.8545**	Brain volume
Spe (%)	0.7478 ± 0.0444	**0.7597 ± 0.0370**		0.7778	**0.8000**	
Sen (%)	0.8765 ± 0.0232	**0.8830 ± 0.0201**		0.8824	**0.9020**	
PL	3.47	**3.67**		3.97	**4.50**	
NL	0.16	**0.15**		0.15	**0.12**	
ConfM	[699 238]	**[703 224]**		[35 10]	**[36 9]**	
	[121 862]	**[116 876]**		[6 45]	**[5 46]**	

5 Conclusions

In this paper, the application of the non-parametric CSL method to a neuroimaging dataset and some connections with previous approaches are presented. The non-parametric CSL approach is evaluated on synthetic/SPECT image datasets

[7]. The CSL approach combines FE, hypothesis testing on a discrete set of expected outcomes and a cross-validated classification stage. This methodology provides extended datasets (one per class-hypothesis) by means of FE methods, which are scored probabilistically using the output scores of a properly trained SVM inside a CV loop. Our results demonstrate that, although the method can only be applied to the low-dimensional problem, due to the poor estimate of the conditional-error probability for a low ratio N/d, the resulting system provides a CV error estimate that outperforms the one obtained by baseline methods that do not consider such FE optimization.

Acknowledgement. This work was partly supported by the MINECO under the TEC2015-64718-R project and the Consejería de Economía, Inno- vación, Ciencia y Empleo (Junta de Andalucía, Spain) under the Excellence Project P11-TIC-7103.

References

1. Álvarez, I., Górriz, J.M., Ramírez, J., Salas, D., López, M., Puntonet, C.G., Segovia, F.: Alzheimer's diagnosis using eigenbrains and support vector machines. IET Electron. Lett. **45**(1), 165–167 (2009)
2. Cao, L.J., Tay, F.E.: Support vector machine with adaptive parameters in financial time series forecasting. Trans. Neural Netw. **14**(6), 1506–1518 (2003). http://dx.doi.org/10.1109/TNN.2003.820556
3. Chow, C.: On optimum recognition error and reject tradeoff. IEEE Trans. Inf. Theory **16**(1), 41–46 (1970)
4. Górriz, J.M., Lassl, A., Ramírez, J., Salas-Gonzalez, D., Puntonet, C., Lang, E.: Automatic selection of ROIs in functional imaging using Gaussian mixture models. Neurosci. Lett. **460**(2), 108–111 (2009)
5. Gorriz, J.M., Ramirez, J., Illan, I.A., Martinez-Murcia, F.J., Segovia, F., Salas-Gonzalez, D.: Case-based statistical learning applied to SPECT image classification. In: SPIE Medical Imaging Computer-Aided Diagnosis, vol. 78, pp. 1–4, February 2017
6. Gorriz, J.M., Ramirez, J., Lang, E.W., Puntonet, C.G.: Jointly Gaussian PDF-based likelihood ratio test for voice activity detection. IEEE Trans. Audio Speech Lang. Process. **16**(8), 1565–1578 (2008)
7. Górriz, J.M., Segovia, F., Ramírez, J., Lassl, A., Salas-Gonzalez, D.: Gmm based SPECT image classification for the diagnosis of Alzheimer's disease. Appl. Soft Comput. **11**(2), 2313–2325 (2011). http://dx.doi.org/10.1016/j.asoc.2010.08.012
8. Gorriz, J., Ramirez, J., Lassl, A., Salas-Gonzalez, D., Lang, E., Puntonet, C., Alvarez, I., Lopez, M., Gomez-Rio, M.: Automatic computer aided diagnosis tool using component-based SVM. In: IEEE Nuclear Science Symposium Conference Record, NSS 2008, pp. 4392–4395. IEEE (2008)
9. Guyon, I.M., Gunn, S.R., Nikravesh, M., Zadeh, L. (eds.): Feature Extraction, Foundations and Applications. Springer, Heidelberg (2006)
10. Illán, I., Górriz, J.M., Ramírez, J., Salas-González, D., López, M., Segovia, F., Chaves, R., Gómez-Rio, M., Puntonet, C.: 18F-FDG PET imaging analysis for computer aided Alzheimer's diagnosis. Inf. Sci. **181**(4), 903–916 (2011)
11. James, G., Witten, D., Hastie, T., Tibshirani, R.: An Introduction to Statistical Learning with Applications in R. Springer, Heidelberg (2013)

12. Kay, S.M.: Fundamentals of Statistical Signal Processing: Detection Theory. Prentice Hall Signal Processing Series, vol. II. Prentice Hall, Upper Saddle River (1993)
13. Khedher, L., Ramirez, J., Gorriz, J.M., Brahim, A., Segovia, F., Alzheimer's Disease Neuroimaging Initiative, et al.: Early diagnosis of Alzheimer's disease based on partial least squares, principal component analysis and support vector machine using segmented MRI images. Neurocomputing **151**, 139–150 (2015)
14. Li, M., Sethi, I.K.: Confidence-based classifier design. Pattern Recogn. **39**(7), 1230–1240 (2006)
15. Ortiz, A., Gorriz, J.M., Ramirez, J., Martinez-Murcia, F.J., Initiative, A.D.N., et al.: LVQ-SVM based CAD tool applied to structural MRI for the diagnosis of the Alzheimer's disease. Pattern Recogn. Lett. **34**(14), 1725–1733 (2013)
16. Platt, J.C.: Probabilistic outputs for support vector machines and comparisons to regularized likelihood methods. In: Advances in Large Margin Classifiers, pp. 61–74. MIT Press, Cambridge (1999)
17. Segovia, F., Gorriz, J., Ramirez, J., Alvarez, I., Jimenez-Hoyuela, J., Ortega, S.: Improved Parkinsonism diagnosis using a partial least squares based approach. Med. Phys. **39**(7), 4395–4403 (2012)
18. Vapnik, V.N.: Statistical Learning Theory. Wiley, New York (1998)
19. Weiner, M.W., Górriz, J.M., Ramírez, J., Castiglioni, I.: Statistical signal processing in the analysis, characterization and detection of Alzheimer's disease. Curr. Alzheimer Res. **13**(5), 466–468 (2016)
20. Wernick, M.N., Yang, Y., Brankov, J.G., Yourganov, G., Strother, S.C.: Machine learning in medical imaging. IEEE Sig. Process. Mag. **27**(4), 25–38 (2010)

PET Image Classification Using HHT-Based Features Through Fractal Sampling

A. Ortiz[1]([✉]), F. Lozano[1], A. Peinado[1], M.J. Garía-Tarifa[2], J.M. Górriz[3], J. Ramírez[3], and for the Alzheimer's Disease Neuroimaging Initiative

[1] Communications Engineering Department, University of Málaga,
29004 Málaga, Spain
aortiz@ic.uma.es
[2] Department of Pharmacology and Pediatrics, University of Málaga,
29004 Málaga, Spain
[3] Department of Signal Theory, Communications and Networking,
University of Granada, 18060 Granada, Spain

Abstract. Medical image classification is currently a challenging task that can be used to aid the diagnosis of different brain diseases. Thus, exploratory and discriminative analysis techniques aiming to obtain representative features from the images, play a decisive role in the design of effective Computer Aided Diagnosis (CAD) systems, which is specially important in the early diagnosis of dementias. In this work we present a technique that allows extracting discriminative features from Positron Emission Tomography (PET) by means of an Empirical Mode Decomposition-based (EMD) method. This requires to transform the 3D PET image into a time series which is addressed by sampling the image using a fractal-based method which allows to preserve the spatial relationship among voxels. The devised technique has been used to classify images from the Alzheimer's Disease Neuroimaging Initiative (ADNI) achieving up to a 92% accuracy in a differential diagnosis task (AD vs. controls), which proves that the information retrieved by our methodology is significantly related to the disease.

Keywords: Hilbert curve · EEMD · SVM · PET · Alzheimer's Disease

1 Introduction

Currently, computer-based medical image analysis methods have attracted considerable research attention, as they usually determine the performance of the Computer Aided Diagnosis tools. These techniques are especially important in

Data used in preparation of this article were obtained from the Alzheimer's Disease Neuroimaging Initiative (ADNI) database (adni.loni.ucla.edu). As such, the investigators within the ADNI contributed to the design and implementation of ADNI and/or provided data but did not participate in analysis or writing of this report. A complete listing of ADNI investigators can be found at: http://adni.loni.ucla.edu/wpcontent/uploads/how_to_apply/ADNI_Acknowledgement_List.pdf.

J.M. Ferrández Vicente et al. (Eds.): IWINAC 2017, Part I, LNCS 10337, pp. 314–323, 2017.
DOI: 10.1007/978-3-319-59740-9_31

neuroimaging techniques for the diagnosis of dementias, as three-dimensional and high resolution images are often available. This is the case of neuroimaging modalities for the diagnosis of neurodegenerative diseases such as the Alzheimer Disease, the most common type of dementia with more than 35.6 million people affected, and 7.7 million new cases every year (according to the World Health Organization). In this case, techniques such as Magnetic Resonance Imaging (MRI), Single Photon Emission Computed Tomography (SPECT) or Positron Emission Tomography using the 18F-fluorodeoxyglucose (FDG) radiotracer (18F-FDG PET) are being intensively used. These allow not only the manual processing of the images to obtain helpful data related to the neurodegeneration that occurs, but the early diagnosis of the disease by predicting the conversion from prodromal stages (Mild Cognitive Impairment, or MCI) to AD [18]. However, the large amount of data provided by these images, makes necessary to develop specific processing techniques. In fact, feature extraction in medical image processing still remains a challenge, as in real-world data the expected number of available samples is considerably lower than the dimension of the feature space. Thus, the development of effective techniques to reduce the number of features while preserving the information plays a decisive role, as they avoid the use of raw data (eg. VAF technique [19]) sidestepping the *curse of dimensionality* problem [4]. There are two alternative and complementary ways to reduce the dimensionality of the feature space. The first consist on selecting the most discriminative features which can be addressed by filter or wrapper techniques [3,7,13,20]. The second consist on the computation of a reduced set of new features from the raw data (i.e. the original feature space), obtaining a new, low-dimensional feature space [11,15,21]. These techniques has been previously used in functional PET imaging [12,14,16,17] to build CAD systems. This is, however, a challenging task since structural and functional changes in the early stages of AD are similar to those that appear due to the ageing natural process.

In this paper we propose the extraction of representative features from image data with a different approach. These features are computed in the time and frequency domains, but instead of using raw 3D image data, we first convert the images into a time series by sampling them using space-filling fractal curves that preserves the neighbourhood to avoid the spatial information loss in the vicinity of a voxel. As a result, a time series of voxel intensities is obtained for each image, and then, temporal and spectral features are computed from the components obtained by Empirical Mode Decomposition (EMD). A similar approach has been used in [2] to avoid the bidimensional extension of EMD which is computationally expensive.

Temporal (mean, variance and skewness) and spectral (centroid, variation coefficient, skewness and kurtosis) features computed over 6 Intrinsic Mode Functions (IMFs) (i.e. components) extracted in this work have demonstrated their discriminative ability, showing a classification accuracy of 90% and AUC of 0.91, beating the results obtained by VAF but using a reduced number of features.

The article is organised as follows. First, in Sect. 2 the methodology is presented, and the fractal curve-based sampling method used is explained. Later, in Sect. 2.3, the database and the results are presented and analysed. Finally, some conclusions are drawn in Sect. 3.

2   Methodology

2.1   Fractal Sampling Using 3D Homogeneous Hilbert Curves

A Hilbert curve is a continuous fractal space-filling curve geometrically described by Hilbert [8]. It can be defined as a continuous function whose domain is the unit interval $[0, 1]$ and its rang is in a 2D euclidean space, formally: $f : [0, 1] \longrightarrow [0, 1]^2$. Thus, for any point t on the unit line segment $[0, 1]$, this function assigns the corresponding point x, y in the unit square $[0, 1]^2$. However, the range of the Hilbert curves can be extended to n-dimensions. The $\mathbb{R} \longrightarrow \mathbb{R}^n$ mapping provided by Hilbert curves have the following properties [5] (for simplicity, $n = 2$):

- Continuity is preserved: values close in the $[0, 1]$ line have similar values in the $[0, 1]^2$ unit square (adjacency condition).
- The mapping is quasi-invertible: the conversion of similar (x, y) points into t values might not guarantee similar values of t. However, the construction of Hilbert curves tends to correspond similar values of (x, y) coordinates to similar t values. This is especially
- The curve is uniquely defined by fixing the mapping of the initial and final subintervals, as well as a rotation matrix.
- They can be generated by the iterative application of affine transformations to a starting mapping and can be implemented by recursive algorithms.

Figure 1 show an example of Hilbert curves in 2D and 3D.

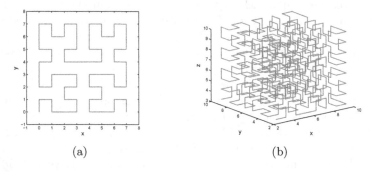

(a)   (b)

Fig. 1. Example of 2D (a) and 3D (b) Hilbert curves

Hilbert Huang Transform. The Hilbert-Huang transform [9] is an empirically-based method to analyze nonlinear and non-stationary time series. The method proposed by Huang et al. consist on decompose the signal into a number of components (namely, Intrinsic Mode functions, IMF hereafter) by means of Empirical mode Decomposition (EMD). Unlike other decomposition methods such as Fourier decomposition or wavelet decomposition, EMD does not use a priori basis to represent the original signal but it is adaptive in order to produce physically meaningful representations of data. Subsequently, Hilbert Spectral Analysis allow to explore the frequency-time distribution of signal amplitude. These two steps are described in the following as well as the way they are used in this work to extract features from the images.

Empirical Mode Decomposition (EMD). The EMD algorithm decomposes a signal $x(t)$ as a sum of oscillatory components, namely Intrinsic Mode Functions (IMF) using the *sifting* process [9]. Although there are many ways to descompose a signal into components (e.g. Fourier analysis or Wavelet decomposition), EMD does not make any assumption about the stationarity or linearity of the data and stays in the time domain. Moreover, the decomposition performed by EMD implies *completeness*, it is, the original signal can be exactly recovered by summing up the components.

The basic idea behind EMD decomposition is to consider a signal as a superposition of high frequency oscillations $dt_i(t)$ and low frequency oscillations $r_i(t)$. Thus, the method iterates on the slow oscillations component considered as a new signal to be decomposed:

$$x(t) = \sum_{i=1}^{N} d_i(t) + r_N(t) \tag{1}$$

where d_i are called Intrinsic Mode Functions (IMFs) and r_N is the residual signal that represents the overall trend.

In this work we used the Ensemble EMD (EEMD) method [6,22], which is an improved version of EMD that makes it more robust for noisy signals. The core idea of EEMD is to add white noise to the signal original, composing a number n of trials

$$x_i(t) = x(t) + w_i(t), \quad i = \{1, ..., n\} \tag{2}$$

Then, EMD decomposition is applied to $x_i(t)$, obtaining a set of n *noisy* IMFs. Finally, the (ensemble) means of corresponding *noisy* IMFs of the decompositions is computed and used as final IMFs. The use of EEMD in this work aims to deal with the intra-class inherent variability in real PET image data.

2.2   Feature Extraction by Hilbert Transform

After EEMD decomposition of the time series representing the subimages corresponding to each brain region, features are extracted from each IMF. These are obtained by means of the *Hilbert Transform*, which allows to obtain the analytic signal $z_i(t)$ from the $i - th$ IMF. Specifically, the analytic IMF $x_i(t)$ can be obtained as

$$z_i(t) = x_i(t) + j\mathcal{H}\{x_i(t)\} \qquad (3)$$

From $z_i(t)$ it is straightforward to compute the instantaneous amplitude as

$$a(t) = \sqrt{re(z_i(t))^2 + im(z_i(t))^2} \qquad (4)$$

and the instantaneous phase

$$\phi(t) = tan^{-1}\frac{im(z_i(t))}{re(z_i(t))} \qquad (5)$$

A visual analysis of the IMFs obtained from healthy and epilepsy patients during interictal and ictal periods after Hilbert transform (Fig. 2) reveals that they are quite different from one another.

Visually exploration of the real and imaginary parts for different IMFs obtained for CN and AD subject figures out differences between classes. Consequently, real and imaginary parts of $z_i(t)$ are used as features instead of computing more complex descriptors. Figure 2 show the real and imaginary parts for CN and AD subjects (blue and red line, respectively).

2.3   Experimental Results

2.4   Database

The database used in this work contains multimodal PET/MRI image data from 138 subjects, comprising 68 Controls (CN), 70 AD and 111 MCI patients from the ADNI database [1]. This repository was created to study the advance of the Alzheimer disease, collecting a vast amount of MRI and Positron Emission Tomography (PET) images as well as blood biomarkers and cerebrospinal fluid analyses. The main goal of this database is to provide a way to the early diagnose of the Alzheimer disease. Patient's demographics are shown in Table 1. However, in this work only MRI data is used.

Table 1. Patient demographics

Evaluation	Sex (M/F)	Mean age ± Std	Mean MMSE ± Std
NC	43/25	75.81 ± 4.93	29.06 ± 1.08
AD	46/24	75.33 ± 7.17	22.84 ± 2.91

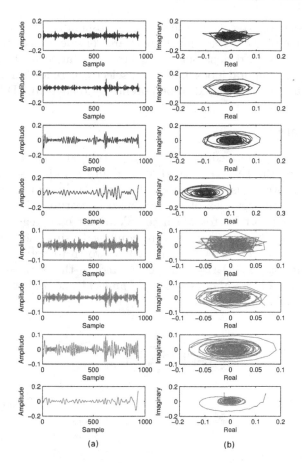

Fig. 2. First four IMFs (a) for AAL region 37 (Left Hippocampus) and their corresponding trajectory in the complex plane (b) for CN (blue) and AD (red) subjects. (Color figure online)

2.5   Image Preprocessing

PET images from the ADNI database have been spatially normalized according to the PET template, ensuring that each image voxel corresponds to the same anatomical position. After image registration, all the PET images were resized to $79 \times 95 \times 68$ voxels with voxel-size of 3 mm (Sagittal) $\times$ 3 mm (Coronal) $\times$ 3 mm (Axial). Subsequently, PET images are also normalized in intensity in order to compute comparable levels among the images. Intensity normalization is performed by means of the mean image, which is used as a normalization template. Specifically, the normalization value applied to each image is calculated as the mean of the 1% of the voxels with a higher activation level in the template. This helps to homogenize the activation levels, using the same scale and making them comparable. Moreover, we used the 116-regions Automated Anatomical

Labelling Atlas (AAL) to extract the voxels corresponding to these areas. Voxels on the outside of the atlas-defined areas are considered as background. On the other hand, only 42 regions out of the 116, distributed in the frontal, parietal, occipital and temporal lobes, have been selected here for brain connectivity modelling, as they are considered to be potentially related to AD [10].

2.6   Classification

In the experiments performed, 6 IMFs were extracted from each brain region using 20 stages in the EEMD method and adding 1% of noise. Subsequently, the Hilbert transform is used to compute the analytic version of each IMF and the coordinates in the complex plane were used as features. These features are used to train a Support Vector Machine (SVM) for each region. These SVM classifiers act as *weak classifiers* that are combined using the majority voting rule. The whole process is shown in Fig. 3. It is worth to note that a Principal Component Analysis (PCA) stage is used to reduce the dimensionality of the features to avoid the *curse of dimensionality problem* since only 138 subjects are available in the PET image database.

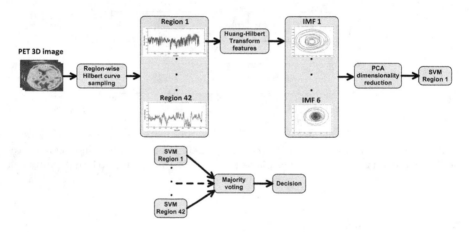

Fig. 3. Block diagram of the HHT-based method.

Classification results are summarized in Figs. 4 and 5 and Table 2. Specifically, Fig. 4 show the accuracy, sensitivity and specificity values obtained varying the number of principal components in the PCA stage. Moreover, these figures compare the performance obtained using the VAF approach, PCA over VAF values and HHT-based method presented in this paper. As these figures show, HHT-method provides a higher performance and a smaller dependence with the number of principal components used to reduce the dimensionality of the feature space. On the other hand, the ROC curves obtained for the three alternatives previously mentioned are provided in Fig. 5.

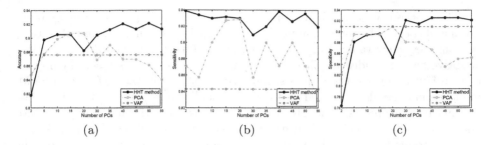

(a)   (b)   (c)

Fig. 4. Accuracy (a), Sensitivity (b) and Specificity (c) values obtained in the classification experiments for VAF, PCA and HHT-method.

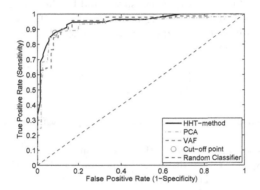

Fig. 5. ROC curves for VAF, PCA over VAF and HHT-method.

Table 2. Classification results for VAF, PCA and HHT-based method.

Method	Accuracy	Sensitivity	Specificity	AUC
VAF	0.87 ± 0.08	0.84 ± 0.12	0.90 ± 0.10	0.92
PCA (all regions)	0.90 ± 0.09	0.90 ± 0.11	0.89 ± 0.12	0.93
HHT method (42 regions)	$\mathbf{0.92 \pm 0.09}$	$\mathbf{0.93 \pm 0.10}$	$\mathbf{0.92 \pm 0.11}$	**0.95**

3   Conclusions and Future Work

In this paper, we propose a method to process 3D images using time-series data analysis techniques. This is addressed by converting the 3D image data into a time series by sampling the voxels using a fractal curve-based method which preserves the spatial relationship. The Huang-Hilbert Transform is then used to extract features from each brain region. The individual SVM classifiers acting over each region are combined as an ensemble to leverage the classification performance, and allowing to obtain up to 92% of accuracy and an AUC of 0.95 for the CN vs. AD classification task, which is close to the limit imposed by the ADNI clinical labels and outperforming the results obtained by VAF and PCA.

The method presented here can be improved and new proposals using temporal and spectral features computed from the IMFs, as well as the use of instantaneous frequency values will be explored in the future. On the other hand, the adaptive basis provided by EMD have clear advantages in this case, in comparison to Fourier or Wavelet analysis. Moreover, the use of sparse, ℓ_1-based SVM models could be also explored as they are usually more efficient to select discriminative features. Additionally, experiments using MRI data to explore GM and WM profiles by means of the extracted features could provide an interesting new way to model changes in brain tissues associated to the evolution of specific neurological diseases.

Acknowledments. This work was partly supported by the MINECO/FEDER under TEC2015-64718-R and PSI2015-65848-R projects and the Consejería de Innovación, Ciencia y Empresa (Junta de Andalucía, Spain) under the Excellence Project P11-TIC-7103.

References

1. Alzheimer's Disease Neuroimaging Initiative. http://adni.loni.ucla.edu/. Accessed 10 Mar 2014
2. Costa, P., Barroso, J., Fernandes, H., Hadjileontiadis, L.J.: Using Peano-hilbert space filling curves for fast bidimensional ensemble EMD realization. EURASIP J. Adv. Sig. Process. **2012**(1), 181 (2012)
3. de la Hoz, E., de la Hoz, E., Ortiz, A., Ortega, J., Martínez-Álvarez, A.: Feature selection by multi-objective optimisation: application to network anomaly detection by hierarchical self-organising maps. Knowl.-Based Syst. **71**, 322–338 (2014)
4. Duin, R.P.W.: Classifiers in almost empty spaces. In: Proceedings 15th International Conference on Pattern Recognition, vol. 2, pp. 1–7 (2000)
5. Estevez-Rams, E., Brito-Reyes, I.: Arithmetic properties of homogeneous Hilbert curves. ArXiv e-prints, pp. 1–14, November 2013
6. Gallix, A., GóRriz, J.M., RamíRez, J., IlláN, I.A., Lang, E.W.: On the empirical mode decomposition applied to the analysis of brain spect images. Expert Syst. Appl. **39**(18), 13451–13461 (2012)
7. Górriz, J.M., Lassl, A., Ramírez, J., Salas-Gonzalez, D., Puntonet, C.G., Lang, E.W.: Automatic selection of ROIs in functional imaging using Gaussian mixture models. Neurosci. Lett. **460**(2), 108–111 (2009)
8. Hilbert, D.: über die stetige abbildung einer linie auf ein flächenstück. Math. Ann. **38**(1), 459–460 (1891)
9. Huang, N.E., Shen, Z., Long, S.R., Wu, M.C., Shih, H.H., Zheng, Q., Yen, N.-C., Tung, C.C., Liu, H.H.: The empirical mode decomposition, the Hilbert spectrum for nonlinear, non-stationary time series analysis. In: Proceedings of the Royal Society of London A: Mathematical, Physical and Engineering Sciences, vol. 454, no. 1971, pp. 903–995 (1998)
10. Huang, S., Li, J., Sun, L., Liu, J., Wu, T., Chen, K., Fleisher, A., Reiman, E., Ye, J.: Learning brain connectivity of Alzheimer's disease from neuroimaging data. In: Bengio, Y., Schuurmans, D., Lafferty, J.D., Williams, C.K.I., Culotta, A. (eds.) Advances in Neural Information Processing Systems, vol. 22, pp. 808–816. Curran Associates Inc (2009)

11. Álvarez Illán, I., Górriz, J.M., Ramírez, J., Salas-Gonzalez, D., López, M., Puntonet, C.G., Segovia, F.: Alzheimer's diagnosis using eigenbrains and support vector machines. IET Electron. Lett. **45**(7), 342–343 (2009)

12. Martinez-Murcia, F.J., Górriz, J.M., Ramírez, J., Ortiz, A., s Disease Neuroimaging Initiative, et al.: A spherical brain mapping of MR images for the detection of Alzheimer's disease. Curr. Alzheimer Res. **13**(5), 575–588 (2016)

13. Kimovski, D., Ortega, J., Ortiz, A., Baños, R.: Parallel alternatives for evolutionary multi-objective optimization in unsupervised feature selection. Expert Syst. Appl. **42**(9), 4239–4252 (2015)

14. Martinez-Murcia, F.J., Górriz, J.M., Ramírez, J., Ortiz, A.: A structural parametrization of the brain using hidden Markov models-based paths in Alzheimer's disease. Int. J. Neural Syst. **26**(07), 1650024 (2016). PMID: 27354189

15. Ortiz, A., Górriz, J.M., Ramírez, J., Martinez-Murcia, F.J., Initiative, A.D.N., et al.: Automatic ROI selection in structural brain MRI using SOM 3D projection. PLOS One **9**(4), e93851 (2014)

16. Ortiz, A., Martínez-Murcia, F.J., García-Tarifa, M.J., Lozano, F., Górriz, J.M., Ramírez, J.: Automated diagnosis of Parkinsonian syndromes by deep sparse filtering-based features. In: Chen, Y.-W., Tanaka, S., Howlett, R.J., Jain, L.C. (eds.) Innovation in Medicine and Healthcare 2016. SIST, vol. 60, pp. 249–258. Springer, Cham (2016). doi:10.1007/978-3-319-39687-3_24

17. Plant, C., Sorg, C., Riedl, V., Wohlschläger, A.: Homogeneity-based feature extraction for classification of early-stage Alzheimer's disease from functional magnetic resonance images. In: Proceedings of the Workshop on Data Mining for Medicine and Healthcare, DMMH 2011, pp. 33–41. ACM, New York (2011)

18. Schroeter, M.L., Stein, T., Maslowski, N., Neumann, J.: Neural correlates of Alzheimer's disease and mild cognitive impairment: a systematic and quantitative meta-analysis involving 1351 patients. Neuroimage **47**(4), 1196–1206 (2009)

19. Stoeckel, J., Fung, G.: SVM feature selection for classification of SPECT images of Alzheimer's disease using spatial information. In: Proceedings of Fifth IEEE International Data Mining Conference (2005)

20. Theodoridis, S., Koutroumbas, K.: Pattern Recognition. Academic Press, Cambridge (2009)

21. Turk, M., Pentland, A.: Eigenfaces for recognition. J. Cogn. Neurosci. **3**(1), 71–86 (1991)

22. Zhaohua, W., Huang, N.E.: Ensemble empirical mode decomposition: a noise-assisted data analysis method. Adv. Adapt. Data Anal. **01**(01), 1–41 (2009)

A 3D Convolutional Neural Network Approach for the Diagnosis of Parkinson's Disease

Francisco Jesús Martinez-Murcia[1]([⊠]), Andres Ortiz[2], Juan Manuel Górriz[1], Javier Ramírez[1], Fermin Segovia[1], Diego Salas-Gonzalez[1], Diego Castillo-Barnes[1], and Ignacio A. Illán[3]

[1] Department of Signal Theory, Networking and Communications, University of Granada, 18071 Granada, Spain
fjesusmartinez@ugr.es
[2] Department of Communications Engineering, University of Málaga, 29071 Málaga, Spain
[3] Department of Scientific Computing, The Florida State University, Tallahassee, FL 32306-4120, USA

Abstract. Parkinsonism is the second most common neurodegenerative disease, originated by a dopamine decrease in the striatum. Single Photon Emission Computed Tomography (SPECT) images acquired using the DaTSCAN drug are a widely extended tool in the diagnosis of Parkinson's Disease (PD), since they can measure the amount of dopamine transporters in the striatum. Many automatic systems have been developed to aid in the diagnosis of PD, using traditional feature extraction methods. In this paper, we propose a novel system based on three-dimensional Convolutional Neural Networks (CNNs), that aims to differenciate between PD-affected patients and unaffected subjects. The proposed system achieves up to a 95.5% accuracy and 96.2% sensitivity in the diagnosis of PD.

1 Introduction

Parkinsonism is the second most common neurodegenerative disease, surpassed only by the prevalence of Alzheimer's Disease [11]. The most common cause of Parkinsonism is Parkinson's Disease (PD), a disease originated due to the progressive loss of dopamine transporters (DaT) of the nigrostriatal pathway, which leads to a decrease in the dopamine content of the striatum [5,6].

Currently nuclear imaging is being used consistently to assist the diagnosis of PD. The most common drug is ^{123}I-ioflupane (also known as DaTSCAN), a tracer that binds to the DaT in the striatum [3] emitting photons that can be detected using Single Photon Emission Computed Tomography (SPECT) equipment.

DaTSCAN images have been widely used in Computer Aided Diagnosis (CAD) systems, that aim at differentiating between PD affected subjects and normal controls (CTL) [2,13–15,18,20,24], or even differentiate between other diseases that lead to parkinsonism, such as multiple system athropy (MSA) or

© Springer International Publishing AG 2017
J.M. Ferrández Vicente et al. (Eds.): IWINAC 2017, Part I, LNCS 10337, pp. 324–333, 2017.
DOI: 10.1007/978-3-319-59740-9_32

progressive supranuclear palsy (PSP) [21,22]. These methods use feature extraction techniques, such as moments [18], Independent Component Analysis (ICA) [14], Partial Least Squares (PLS) [20] or Texture analysis [13] to correctly classify PD affected subjects.

Convolutional Neural Networks (CNN) are a particular type of Artificial Neural Networks (ANN) which are becoming increasingly popular in image analysis [10,15,22], given their adaptability to many types of projects. They have been used in medical imaging previously [15,22] with great success. Therefore, we propose that the use of a three-dimensional CNN based on Tensorflow [1] can be of great help to assist in the diagnosis of PD and provide useful information about the variability contained within.

In this work, we present an application of CNNs to the diagnosis of PD and SWEDD subjects. In Sect. 2 we present the methodology used to build the convolutional neural network and the evaluation methodology. In Sect. 3 we present and discuss the performance of the system under two different experiments, and finally, at Sect. 4, we draw some conclusions about this and propose future work.

2   Methodology

2.1   Volume Selection

DaTSCAN binds mainly to dopamine transporters at the striatum. Therefore, most of the space contained within these images is not relevant for diagnosis. Without loss of generality, we can extract the volumes of interest containing the striatum and obviate the rest, thus obtaining an significant feature reduction.

The procedure used here consist of a simple thresholding that has been previously used in PD [13,15], by which we binarize the average of all images in the dataset:

$$I_{BW} = I_{mean} > I_{th} \tag{1}$$

For which the intensity threshold I_{th} is computed as a percentage T of the maximum value of the average image. That is:

$$I_{th} = T \times I_{max} \tag{2}$$

Once we obtained I_{BW}, we use the minimum and maximum indices in all directions where any of the voxels of I_{mean} is greater than the threshold to define a box. Finally, the portion of any image that falls between these coordinates is taken as the input image I_{cut}. Figure 1 shows the final box using $T = 0.35$ superimposed on a sample subject.

2.2   Convolutional Neural Networks

Convolutional Neural Networks (CNNs) are a specific type of Artificial Neural Network (ANN) that is becoming increasingly important in the Machine Learning community [4,10,15,22]. They are a bioinspired variant of Multilayer Perceptrons (MLPs), in which the response of a neuron is approximated by a convolution operation. Since 2012, when an ensemble of CNNs [10] achieved lowest

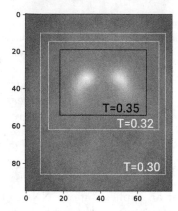

Fig. 1. Example of selected area for different threshold values.

error on the ImageNet classification benchmark [19], CNNs prevail over any other pattern recognition algorithm in the literature.

The architecture of CNNs usually comprises many types of layers, of which the most important are: convolution layers, max pooling layers and fully connected layers. Many combinations of these can be found throughout literature [1,4,10,15,16,22]. All CNNs share these properties: a local connectivity of the hidden units, use of pooling to introduce translation invariance, and parameter sharing. A 1-layer typical approach would include convolution of the input image with a set of filters and applying its corresponding activation function, downsmapling of the resulting signal by max-pooling and an output MLP that transform the activation signal into probability of classes (Fig. 2).

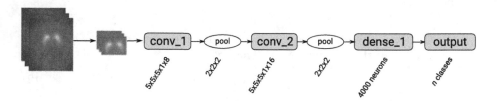

Fig. 2. Schema of our system.

Convolutional Layer. CNNs owe their name to the convolutional layer. The operation at a convolutional layer can be defined as follows. Let $\mathbf{V}_{i-1}$ be a tensor the activation map of the $(i-1)$-th layer (in the case of $i = 1$, it is the input volume). Let $\mathbf{W}_i$ be the set of K filters of the i-th layer, and $\mathbf{b}_i$ a bias term, a vector of length K. Then, the mathematical operation performed at the convolutional layer is:

$$\mathbf{V}_i = f_a \left(\mathbf{W}_i * \mathbf{V}_{i-1} + \mathbf{b}_i \right) \tag{3}$$

with $f_a(*)$ being the activation function, that we will detail later.

In the case of two-dimensional convolutions, $\mathbf{V}_{i-1}$ is a tensor of size $H \times W \times C$ (height, width and number of channels), and $\mathbf{W}_i$ a tensor of size $P \times Q \times R \times K$, containing K filters of size $P \times Q \times R$, with $R_i = K_{i-1}$ and $R_1 = 1$ for the first layer. With this definitions, the k-th convolution term for the k-th filter is:

$$\mathbf{W}_{ik} * \mathbf{V}_{i-1} = \sum_{u=0}^{P-1} \sum_{v=0}^{Q-1} \mathbf{W}_{ik}(P-u, Q-v)\mathbf{V}_{i-1}(x+u, y+v) \qquad (4)$$

which, extended to a three-dimensional environment, with a $\mathbf{V}_{i-1}$ of size $H \times W \times D \times C$, and a $\mathbf{W}_i$ of size $P \times Q \times R \times S \times K$ would result in:

$$\mathbf{W}_{ik} * \mathbf{V}_{i-1} = \sum_{u=0}^{P-1} \sum_{v=0}^{Q-1} \sum_{w=0}^{R-1} \mathbf{W}_{ik}(P-u, Q-v, R-w)\mathbf{V}_{i-1}(x+u, y+v, z+w) \quad (5)$$

After the convolution, the activations for each of the K filters are stacked, and passed to the following layer, usually a max-pooling layer.

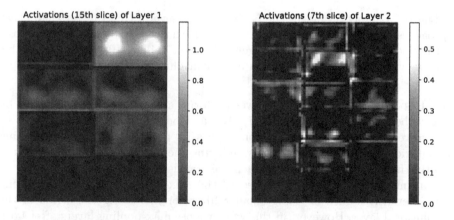

Fig. 3. Summary of the activations in the first and second layers, after feeding a normal control patient with a threshold $T = 0.35$.

The filter size $P \times Q \times R$ is an hyperparameter that is usually set a priori, often making $P = Q = R$ to create a cube, taking values of 3, 5 or even 7 in the literature. In this work we will use a value of $P = Q = R = 5$, with a structure of 2 layers with $K_1 = 8$ and $K_2 = 16$ filters respectively. In Fig. 3 we display the activation of the filters at the first and second layers after inputting a normal control patient.

The other two hyperparameters that control the output size of the activation layers are stride and zero-padding. Stride controls the step at which the convolution is computed, or in other words, how much overlapping there is between convolutions. That defines the receptive field of a neuron in the convolution layer, which is the part of the image to which each convolution filter is connected to.

Using a stride of 1, the convolution is performed at each voxel of the input. With a higher stride, there is less overlapping between receptive fields, and the output volumes will be smaller.

The zero-padding is a convenient technique that provides control of the output volume by padding the input volume with zeros. That way, after the convolution, the output volume can have the same size as the input volume, which in some cases is desirable. In this work we use a stride of 1 and zero-padding of 2 so that the output volume is the same size as the input volume.

Activation. The activation function is common to all types of ANNs. It is applied to the output of all the operations performed at the network, and provides an activation of the operations. Many different types of activation functions exist, among them the traditional sigmoid, although in the context of CNN the Rectified Linear Unit (ReLU) has gained a lot of popularity. The function itself is a non-saturating activation function:

$$f(x) = \max(0, x) \tag{6}$$

The ReLU function makes the CNN training several times faster than other approaches, since the calculation of its derivative has a lower computational cost. And it does so without losing any generalization ability [10]. Throughout this work, we will use the ReLU function in all convolutional layers.

Max Pooling. The max pooling layer performs a non-linear downsampling by keeping the maximum value over a $M \times M \times M$ block of the activation layer. This layer prevents the following layers from processing non-maximal values, reducing computational load. Furthermore, by reducing the input space and keeping the receptive field of the filters, we can achieve translational invariance.

Currently, there is a trend to discard the max-pooling layer [23], favouring other alternatives such as using smaller filters or increasing the stride of the convolutional layer. However, in this work we use max-pooling layers after both 1st and 2nd convolutional layers, all with a block size of $2 \times 2 \times 2$.

Dense Layers. At the end of a series of convolutional and max pooling layers, there is always a fully connected layer, also known as dense layers, in which all neurons all connected to all outputs from the last max pooling step. The structure of this part usually mimic a multilayer perceptron (MLP) in which the input layer is the output of the last max pooling layer, with one or several hidden layers and an output layer with as many neurons as classes. If we consider the convolution and max pooling layers a sophisticated feature extraction system, this can be considered the high-level reasoning part of the CNN. The activation here is computed by a matrix multiplication and a softmax activation function.

$$\sigma(\mathbf{z})_j = \frac{e^{z_j}}{\sum_{k=1}^{K} e^{z_k}} \quad \text{for } j = 1, \dots K \tag{7}$$

Dropout. A popular method for reducing overfitting in fully connected layers is Dropout [19]. It works by "turning off" some neurons at with a probability $1 - p$, and using only the reduced network. After this step, the "off" neurons are turned on again with their last weight matrix. This procedure is repeated in every training iteration. At testing time, all neurons are active, so their outputs are weighted by a factor of p, an approximation of using all possible 2^n networks. In this work we have used a dropout probability of 0.5.

2.3   Dataset

Data used in the preparation of this article were obtained from the Parkinson's Progression Markers Initiative (PPMI) database (www.ppmi-info.org/data). For up-to-date information on the study, visit www.ppmi-info.org. The images in this database were imaged $4 + 0.5$ h after the injection of between 111 and 185 MBq of DaTSCAN. Raw projection data are acquired into a 128×128 matrix stepping each 3 degrees for a total of 120 projection into two 20% symmetric photopeak windows centered on 159 KeV and 122 KeV with a total scan duration of approximately 30–45 min [8].

Afterwards, the images were registered to a custom template [17] using SPM-8 [7], resulting in $91 \times 109 \times 91$ images. A total of $N = 301$ DaTSCAN images from this database were used in the preparation of the article, 158 suffering from PD, 32 SWEDD and 111 normal controls.

Data Augmentation. To reduce overfitting and increase the generalization capabilities of our neural network, we have performed a simple data augmentation procedure, by feeding the neural network with the training set and a mirrored (over the sagital plane) version of this set.

2.4   Evaluation

We have performed a stratified 10-fold cross-validation evaluation of our proposed neural network [9]. In each fold, a confusion matrix has been estimated, from which parameters such as accuracy, sensitivity and specificity can be estimated. However, when using more than 2 classes, sensitivity and specificity cannot be computed. Instead, the accuracy and full confusion matrix are given.

To evaluate the performance of our system, we tested our system under two different experiments:

- **Experiment 1:** We tested the performance of the system under the same conditions, but varying the intensity threshold T, as proposed in Sect. 2.1 (note that due to memory restrictions on the GPU used, the minimum T used was 0.32).
- **Experiment 2:** We tested the system including and excluding the SWEDD subjects from the dataset, to see if there was any difference at all.

3   Results and Discussion

3.1   Experiment 1

In this experiment we show how the performance of our system evolves when varying the threshold T, in a PD vs CTL scheme. Results show that our system achieves high performance in the detection of PD in the PPMI dataset, obtaining up to a 0.955 ± 0.044 of accuracy and 0.962 ± 0.051 sensitivity for a threshold $T = 0.34$. Due to memory restrictions, we could not test the system for $T < 0.32$. However, a global tendency can be seen, in which the performance decreases with the threshold.

In Fig. 4 we compare the accuracy obtained with the histogram of the mean image (from which the threshold T and selection area is computed). We can see that most of the voxels are contained in for a threshold $T < 0.3$, and, is in this transition range (between 0.3 and 0.4) where more performance differences are obtained. Afterwards, the performance decreases slowly, at the same pace that the selection box size. This relation is easily seen when compared with the histogram, since the distribution of voxel intensities is concentrated in the lower intensities (background and internals of the brain) and there is a higher variability at the striatum.

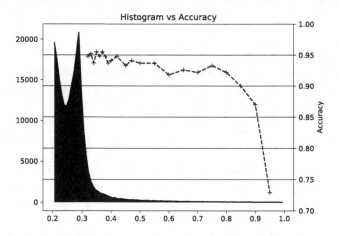

Fig. 4. Accuracy obtained at each threshold, compared with the histogram of the image.

3.2   Experiment 2

In this experiment we test the ability of our convolutional model to detect subjects labelled with SWEDD. SWEDD subjects display no evidence of dopaminergic deficit, whilst showing symptoms of Parkinsonism. Since there is no evidence of a decline in dopamine transporters, their images are extremely similar to controls, and current attempts have been unable to differenciate between them [6, 12, 15].

In this test, we use a selection threshold $T = 0.35$ for the images, and perform the same analysis as the previous one, obtaining an accuracy of 0.820 ± 0.068, and the following confusion matrix:

$$\begin{pmatrix} 94 & 27 & 4 \\ 13 & 1 & 2 \\ 4 & 4 & 152 \end{pmatrix} \tag{8}$$

Compared to accuracies obtained excluding SWEDD subjects (0.955 ± 0.044), we can see that the performance of our system degrades. Looking at the confusion matrix, it is easy to conclude that SWEDD subjects are extremely difficult to classify, since all but one were misclassified. The inclusion of the SWEDD class only meant a source of additional noise in the control class, and by extension, in our classification scheme.

4   Conclusions and Future Work

In this work we have demonstrated the ability of deep learning and convolutional neural networks in the diagnosis of Parkinson's Disease (PD). Particularly, we have applied a three-dimensional approach to convolutional layers that has never been tried before in DaTSCAN images. The high performance obtained in PD detection is an indication of our system's ability to detect patterns in DaTSCAN images. Furthermore, it demonstrates the utility of using 3D convolutional layers in the analysis of three-dimensional medical imaging. The CNN architecture proposed in this work was small, compared to large CNN such as LeNET or GoogLeNET, among others. That, together with the insignificant differences in dopamine transporters, may have had an impact on the smaller ability to differentiate SWEDD patients from controls. In the future, we plan to go deeper on this architecture in order to differentiate these a priori indistinguishable subjects, and obtain a higher performance.

Acknowledgements. This work was partly supported by the MINECO/FEDER under the TEC2015-64718-R project and the Consejera de Economía, Innovación, Ciencia y Empleo (Junta de Andalucía, Spain) under the Excellence Project P11-TIC-7103.

References

1. Abadi, M., Agarwal, A., Barham, P., Brevdo, E., Chen, Z., Citro, C., Corrado, G.S., Davis, A., Dean, J., Devin, M., Ghemawat, S., Goodfellow, I., Harp, A., Irving, G., Isard, M., Jia, Y., Jozefowicz, R., Kaiser, L., Kudlur, M., Levenberg, J., Mané, D., Monga, R., Moore, S., Murray, D., Olah, C., Schuster, M., Shlens, J., Steiner, B., Sutskever, I., Talwar, K., Tucker, P., Vanhoucke, V., Vasudevan, V., Viégas, F., Vinyals, O., Warden, P., Wattenberg, M., Wicke, M., Yu, Y., Zheng, X.: TensorFlow: large-scale machine learning on heterogeneous systems (2015). http://tensorflow.org/, software available from tensorflow.org

2. Benamer, T.S., Patterson, J., Grosset, D.G., Booij, J., Bruin, K., Royen, E., Speel-man, J.D., Horstink, M.H., Sips, H.J., Dierckx, R.A., Versijpt, J., Decoo, D., Linden, C., Hadley, D.M., Doder, M., Lees, A.J., Costa, D.C., Gacinovic, S., Oertel, W.H., Pogarell, O., Hoeffken, H., Joseph, K., Tatsch, K., Schwarz, J., Ries, V.: Accurate differentiation of Parkinsonism and essential tremor using visual assessment of [123I]-FP-CIT SPECT imaging: the [123I]-FP-CIT study group. Mov. Disord.: Official J. Mov. Disord. Soc. **15**(3), 503–510 (2000). PMID: 10830416

3. Booij, J., Habraken, J.B., Bergmans, P., Tissingh, G., Winogrodzka, A., Wolters, E.C., Janssen, A.G., Stoof, J.C., Royen, E.A.: Imaging of dopamine transporters with iodine-123-FP-CIT SPECT in healthy controls and patients with Parkinson's disease. J. Nucl. Med. **39**(11), 1879–1884 (1998)

4. Ciresan, D.C., Meier, U., Masci, J., Maria Gambardella, L., Schmidhuber, J.: Flexible, high performance convolutional neural networks for image classification. In: IJCAI Proceedings-International Joint Conference on Artificial Intelligence, Barcelona, Spain, vol. 22, p. 1237 (2011)

5. Eckert, T., Edwards, C.: The application of network mapping in differential diagnosis of Parkinsonian disorders. Clin. Neurosci. Res. **6**(6), 359–366 (2007). http://www.sciencedirect.com/science/article/pii/S1566277207000023. Neural Networks in the Imaging of Neuropsychiatric Diseases

6. Erro, R., Schneider, S.A., Stamelou, M., et al.: What do patients with scans without evidence of dopaminergic deficit (SWEDD) have? New evidence and continuing controversies. J. Neurol. Neurosurg. Psychiatry **87**, 319–323 (2016)

7. Friston, K., Ashburner, J., Kiebel, S., Nichols, T., Penny, W.: Statistical Parametric Mapping: The Analysis of Functional Brain Images. Academic Press, Cambridge (2007)

8. Initiative, T.P.P.M.: PPMI: Imaging Technical Operations Manual, 2nd edn, June 2010

9. Kohavi, R.: A study of cross-validation and bootstrap for accuracy estimation and model selection. In: Proceedings of International Joint Conference on AI, pp. 1137–1145 (1995). http://citeseer.ist.psu.edu/kohavi95study.html

10. Krizhevsky, A., Sutskever, I., Hinton, G.E.: Imagenet classification with deep convolutional neural networks. In: Advances in Neural Information Processing Systems, pp. 1097–1105 (2012)

11. Lau, L.M.L., Breteler, M.M.B.: Epidemiology of Parkinson's disease. Lancet Neurol. **5**, 525–535 (2006)

12. Marshall, V.L., Reininger, C.B., Marquardt, M., Patterson, J., Hadley, D.M., Oertel, W.H., Benamer, H.T., Kemp, P., Burn, D., Tolosa, E., et al.: Parkinson's disease is overdiagnosed clinically at baseline in diagnostically uncertain cases: a 3-year European multicenter study with repeat [123i] FP-CIT SPECT. Mov. Disord. **24**(4), 500–508 (2009)

13. Martinez-Murcia, F., Górriz, J., Ramírez, J., Moreno-Caballero, M., Gómez-Río, M., Initiative, P.P.M., et al.: Parametrization of textural patterns in 123i-ioflupane imaging for the automatic detection of Parkinsonism. Med. Phys. **41**(1), 012502 (2014)

14. Martínez-Murcia, F.J., Górriz, J.M., Ramírez, J., Illán, I., Ortiz, A.: Automatic detection of Parkinsonism using significance measures and component analysis in datscan imaging. Neurocomputing **126**, 58–70 (2014)

15. Ortiz, A., Martínez-Murcia, F.J., García-Tarifa, M.J., Lozano, F., Górriz, J.M., Ramírez, J.: Automated diagnosis of Parkinsonian syndromes by deep sparse filtering-based features. In: Chen, Y.-W., Tanaka, S., Howlett, R.J., Jain, L.C. (eds.) Innovation in Medicine and Healthcare 2016. SIST, vol. 60, pp. 249–258. Springer, Cham (2016). doi:10.1007/978-3-319-39687-3_24
16. Payan, A., Montana, G.: Predicting Alzheimer's disease: a neuroimaging study with 3D convolutional neural networks. arXiv preprint arXiv:1502.02506 (2015)
17. Salas-Gonzalez, D., Górriz, J.M., Ramírez, J., Illán, I.A., Padilla, P., Martínez-Murcia, F.J., Lang, E.W.: Building a FP-CIT SPECT brain template using a posterization approach. Neuroinformatics 13(4), 391–402 (2015)
18. Salas-Gonzalez, D., Górriz, J.M., Ramírez, J., López, M., Illan, I.A., Segovia, F., Puntonet, C.G., Gómez-Río, M.: Analysis of SPECT brain images for the diagnosis of Alzheimer's disease using moments and support vector machines. Neurosci. Lett. 461, 60–64 (2009)
19. Schmidhuber, J.: Deep learning in neural networks: an overview. Neural Netw. 61, 85–117 (2015)
20. Segovia, F., Górriz, J.M., Ramírez, J., Álvarez, I., Jiménez-Hoyuela, J.M., Ortega, S.J.: Improved Parkinsonism diagnosis using a partial least squares based approach. Med. Phys. 39(7), 4395–4403 (2012)
21. Segovia, F., Gorriz, J., Ramírez, J., Salas-Gonzalez, D.: Multiclass classification of 18 F-DMFP-PET data to assist the diagnosis of Parkinsonism. In: 2016 International Workshop on Pattern Recognition in Neuroimaging (PRNI), pp. 1–4. IEEE (2016)
22. Segovia, F., García-Pérez, M., Górriz, J.M., Ramírez, J., Martínez-Murcia, F.J.: Assisting the diagnosis of neurodegenerative disorders using principal component analysis and tensorflow. In: Graña, M., López-Guede, J.M., Etxaniz, O., Herrero, Á., Quintián, H., Corchado, E. (eds.) ICEUTE/SOCO/CISIS -2016. AISC, vol. 527, pp. 43–52. Springer, Cham (2017). doi:10.1007/978-3-319-47364-2_5
23. Springenberg, J.T., Dosovitskiy, A., Brox, T., Riedmiller, M.: Striving for simplicity: the all convolutional net. arXiv preprint arXiv:1412.6806 (2014)
24. Towey, D.J., Bain, P.G., Nijran, K.S.: Automatic classification of 123I-FP-CIT (DaTSCAN) SPECT images. Nucl. Med. Commun. 32(8), 699–707 (2011). http://www.ncbi.nlm.nih.gov/pubmed/21659911. PMID: 21659911

Non-linear Covariance Estimation for Reconstructing Neural Activity with MEG/EEG Data

L. Duque-Muñoz[1]($\boxtimes$), J.D Martinez-Vargas[2], G. Castellanos-Dominguez[2],
J.F Vargas-Bonilla[1], and J.D López[1]

[1] SISTEMIC, Engineering Faculty, Universidad de Antioquia UDEA,
Calle 70 No. 52-21, Medellín, Colombia
leonardo.duquem@udea.edu.co
[2] Signal Processing and Recognition Group, Universidad Nacional de Colombia,
Manizales, Colombia

Abstract. MEG/EEG brain imaging approaches are commonly based on linear covariance matrices that contain the prior information needed to solve the inverse problem. We expect that non-linear covariance matrices (or kernel matrices) provide more information than the widely used smoothers (Loreta, MSP) or data-based matrices (beamformers). Data-based covariance matrices have shortcomings such as being prone to be singular, having limited capability in modeling, complicated relationships in the data, and having a fixed form of representation. The multiple sparse priors (MSP) algorithm provides flexibility but in its original form it only contains smoothers. In this work, we propose to modify both MSP and beamformers by introducing a Gaussian kernel matrix with the objective of enhancing the reconstruction of neural activity. The proposed approach was tested with two well-known simulation benchmarks: Haufe's and SPM. Simulation results showed improvements in the ROIs recognition with Haufe's benchmark, and smaller localization error with SPM benchmark. A real data validation (MEG and EEG) was performed with the faces-scrambled dataset. The expected active sources were obtained, but their strength presented slight variations.

Keywords: MEG/EEG brain imaging · Kernel matrix · Beamformers · MSP

1 Introduction

Electroencephalography (EEG) and magnetoencephalography (MEG) are used in a wide number of applications, and range from clinical testing to cognitive Neuroscience. One aim in using EEG and MEG is to reconstruct the sources of

This work was partially supported by COLCIENCIAS (research projects 122266140116 and 111974455497).

J.M. Ferrández Vicente et al. (Eds.): IWINAC 2017, Part I, LNCS 10337, pp. 334–344, 2017.
DOI: 10.1007/978-3-319-59740-9_33

brain activity by means of non-invasive measurements of the associated bio-electromagnetic fields. Estimating the source distribution of brain electrical activity based on MEG/EEG measurements is an ill-posed and mathematically under-determined inverse problem, where a unique solution can only be obtained by making additional assumptions [1]. It can be computed by introducing prior beliefs on the structure of possible source configurations in a Bayesian inference framework [9].

There are numerous methods for solving the EEG/MEG inverse problem, each involving different prior assumption sets and cost functions [2]. They range from the minimum-norm estimation (MNE), in which the assumption is that all sources are active but with minimum energy. Weighted MNE [14] where a set of weights are estimated in such a way to produce the source distribution with the minimum power that fits the measurements in a least-square-error sense. Low resolution brain electromagnetic tomography (LORETA) and standardized low resolution brain electromagnetic tomography (sLORETA) [17] that include assumptions about smoothness on the cortical surface. Beamformers, which makes a direct estimate of source covariance from the data and is projected into the source space with the lead field matrix [4]. In order to generalize these approaches, this fixed prior covariance can be replaced by weighted sum of a set of possible covariance components. Each component might for example, describe the sensor-level covariance. The Multiple Sparse Priors algorithm [7,15] is a good example of this solution. All these approaches require the definition of a distributed source model and the estimation of spatial covariance matrices. However, these covariance matrices have shortcomings such as being prone to be singular, limited capability in modeling non-linear relationships, and they only evaluate linear relations among channels. Finally, these covariance matrices have fixed form of representation, and they cannot be altered to model different feature relationships [6].

To address these issues, we propose to use the kernel matrix in order to elucidate non-linear relationships in the channels and non-stationary behavior in the data. On each of its entries, the kernel matrix evaluates a Gaussian kernel function between a pair of channels [16]. The kernel function allows learning methods to represent and make use of objects similarities. Moreover, the kernel matrix is guaranteed to be non-singular even if samples are scarce. Kernel methods involve the use of positive definite matrices as suitable object descriptors, providing a solid framework for representing many types of data, as vectors in $\mathbb{R}^d$, strings, trees, graphs, and functional data, among others [8,18]. The kernel function is a flexible container for expressing knowledge about the problem as well as to capture the meaningful relations on input space [3].

The proposed approach was compared with the traditional covariance matrices. They were tested as prior information in the Beamformer and MSP approaches. We used two well-known benchmarks for simulating MEG/EEG activity: SPM and Haufe's [10]. In SPM benchmark we simulated MEG activity with 274 channels and different levels of noise. We then reconstructed the simulated sources and determined the noise effects. The Haufe's benchmark allowed us to simulate EEG activity with synchronous sources. In this case, we analyzed the regions of interest (ROIs) and evaluated their connectivity (interaction between these ROI's). Finally, we validated our approach with the faces-scrambled dataset [12]. We focused on the visual activity paradigm (early potentials) and compared all tested methods over glass brains.

2   Methods

2.1   M/EEG Inverse Problem

Given a set of MEG/EEG signals, the inverse problem involves the estimation of the location and waveform of the sources of neural activity (represented as current dipoles) within the brain. The relation between these sources and the MEG/EEG data can be expressed with the general linear model [5]:

$$Y = LJ + \epsilon \tag{1}$$

where $Y \in \mathbb{R}^{N_c \times N_t}$ are the measured MEG/EEG data with N_c channels and N_t samples, $J \in \mathbb{R}^{N_d \times N_t}$ is the amplitude of neural activity that propagates the energy of N_d current dipoles distributed across the cortical surface (assumed as fixed and normal to it). The gain matrix $L \in \mathbb{R}^{N_c \times N_d}$, commonly known as the lead-field matrix, describes the current flow from each dipolar source to each channel. The fixed location of the dipoles guarantees a linear propagation model. Finally, the measurements are affected by measurement noise ϵ, commonly assumed Gaussian with zero mean and covariance Q_ϵ.

Estimating the source distribution of brain electrical activity based on MEG/EEG measurements is an ill-posed and mathematically under-determined inverse problem, where a unique solution can only be obtained by making additional assumptions. The Bayesian framework is the most widely used approach to solve this problem. It is based on the a priori assumption that J is a zero mean Gaussian process with covariance Q (see [9] for a review on the field).

The prior probability density function (PDF) of the source activity $p(J)$, based on prior knowledge, is weighted by the likelihood $p(Y|J)$, allowing us to estimate the posterior source distribution using Bayes' theorem:

$$p(J|Y) = \frac{p(Y|J)p(J)}{p(Y)} \tag{2}$$

Within this approach, source estimation can be expressed as the expected value of the posterior distribution of the source activity given the data: $\widehat{J} = \mathrm{E}[p(J \mid Y)]$. Typically, MEG/EEG measurement noise is considered to be white Gaussian $p(\epsilon) = \mathcal{N}(\epsilon; 0, Q_\epsilon)$, with $Q_\epsilon \in \mathbb{R}^{N_c \times N_c}$ being the posterior covariance of the measurement. Making similar assumptions on the distribution of the likelihood and the prior probabilistic model $p(J) = \mathcal{N}(J; 0, Q)$, with $Q \in \mathbb{R}^{N_d \times N_d}$ being the prior covariance of the neural activity. For uninformative priors, this reduces to:

$$\widehat{J} = QL^T(Q_\epsilon + LQL^T)^{-1}Y \tag{3}$$

Equation (3) is used in most distributed algorithms based on Gaussian assumptions. Since Y is known and the lead field L can be computed based on a physical model of the head, the problem is focused on finding an estimate of the two covariance matrices Q and Q_ϵ.

2.2   Inversion Approaches

Multiple constraints can be used as source covariance matrix Q. One of them is the Beamformers algorithm that uses the data as prior information. It makes a direct estimate of the source covariance based on the assumption that there are no zero-lag correlated sources. It is computed as a single covariance diagonal matrix formed directly from the data:

$$Q = \text{diag}(\boldsymbol{\sigma}); \qquad \boldsymbol{\sigma}(i) = \frac{1}{\delta_i}(L_i^T(YY^T)^{-1}L_i)^{-1}, \qquad \forall i = 1,\ldots,N_d \quad (4)$$

where $\boldsymbol{\sigma}(i)$ is the i-th diagonal element of Q, L_i the i-th column of L, and the parameters δ_i are defined as:

$$\delta_i = \frac{1}{L_i^T L_i}; \qquad \forall i = 1,\ldots,N_d \quad (5)$$

The Beamformer approach is single prior-based. Other approaches such as the MSP consider the prior source covariance as the weighted sum of multiple prior components:

$$Q = \sum_j h_j C_j \quad (6)$$

Each $C_j \in \mathbb{R}^{N_d \times N_d}$ is a prior source covariance matrix that can take any form. The hyperparameters h_j weight these covariance components. These matrices may have different informative priors, for example, different smoothing functions, medical knowledge, fMRI priors as well as beamforming priors, and the proposed kernel matrices.

2.3   Non-linear Kernel

We propose to use the kernel matrix as prior information in the beamformers and MSP approaches. We introduce the estimation of the Non-Linear Covariance matrix to highlight the complex relations in the data $Y = \{y_j : \forall j \in [1,N]\}$. Each of its entries evaluates a Gaussian kernel function between a pair of channels to build the non-linear matrix [16].

Although there are many feasible functions, the Gaussian kernel defined as $\kappa\{y,\theta\} = g\{y,\sigma^2\} = (2\pi\sigma^2)^{-1/2}exp(-y^Ty/(2\sigma^2))$ is preferred since it aims finding a Reproducing Kernel Hilbert Space (RKHS) [19] with universal approximating capability, and with a single bandwidth parameter $\sigma \in \mathbb{R}^+$.

Two important facts must be highlighted. On one hand, given that Y is fixed and the factor $(y_i - y_j)$ points towards y_i, all directions are also fixed and attracting-nature. On the other hand, the kernel function is dependent on the free parameter σ (the Gaussian kernel bandwidth). The Information potential (IP) magnitudes become functions of the Gaussian kernel bandwidth. Actually, the IP follows a monotonically decreasing behavior over σ (see Fig. 1(a)). Hence, the importance of an adequate Gaussian kernel bandwidth becomes clear.

In this sense, we estimated the bandwidth of the kernel function as proposed in [16]. The procedure consists on estimating the bandwidth parameter from the observed data Y using the Gaussian Parzen estimate. It looks for a RKHS, by maximizing the overall IP variability with respect to the kernel bandwidth parameter. To this end, the variability of the estimated PDF $p_Y(y|\sigma)$ is maximized in terms of the kernel bandwidth parameter in the form:

$$\sigma^* = \arg\max_{\sigma} \mathrm{var}\{p_Y(y|\sigma)\} \tag{7}$$

where $\mathrm{var}\{p_Y(y|\sigma)\} = E\{(p_Y(y|\sigma) - E\{p_Y(y|\sigma)\})^2\} : \forall y \in Y$. However, we introduced a variation in this approach since the maximum point in the IP function does not reach the highest localization accuracy, as shown in Fig. 1(a) (Red point, maximum in the IP function). To this end, we look for the σ that minimizes the localization error (maximizes the accuracy of the reconstruction). We proposed the L-curve optimization since the value obtained in the corner reaches the highest accuracy with the non-linear kernel function (Fig. 1(b) black point, L-curve optimization).

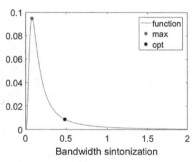
(a) Kernel bandwidth optimization

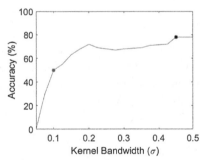
(b) Accuracy of the reconstruction with different optimization points

Fig. 1. Optimization of the kernel bandwidth σ, and the accuracy of the reconstruction with different values of σ. The maximum accuracy was reached with the value obtained with the L-curve optimizatio (Color figure online)

Figure 2 shows the covariance matrix (Fig. 2(a)) and the kernel matrix (Fig. 2(b)) computed for the beamforming approach. The kernel matrix, estimated with the Gaussian kernel, elucidates complex relations in the data while the simple covariance matrix does not.

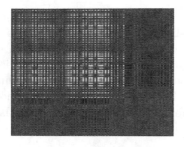

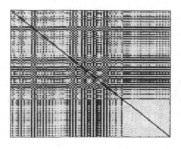

(a) Covariance matrix   (b) Kernel matrix

Fig. 2. Covariance matrices for beamforming priors. Note the complex relations shown in the kernel matrix (b) computed with the Gaussian kernel.

The key of this approach is the prior matrix used in the inversion scheme: beamformers or MSP (the standard covariance matrix or the kernel matrix). The coherence prior for beamformers proposed by Haufe [10] was also included here to compare our approach in their own benchmark. Table 1 describes the three data-based prior matrices compared here.

Table 1. Data-based priors compared in this work

Covariance	Direct estimation of source space covariance based on the assumption that there are no zero-lag correlated sources
Coherence	Estimation of surrogate MEG/EEG using a linear inversion P, with $LP = I$. Potential interactions among sources are neglected while maintaining other statistical properties of the data such as their power spectrum. This rises to quasi-independent sources. Then, using the lead-field matrix L, the quasi-independent time series are mapped back to sensor space to obtain surrogate sensor-space data. These surrogates possess the spatio-spectral correlation structure of the data, but by construction they do not contain interactions
Kernel	Estimation of the Non-Linear Covariance matrix in order to highlight non stationarities in the data

2.4   Simulation Set-Up

We used the benchmark of Haufe [10] for simulating the active sources. The simulations were performed with a realistic head model called the New York Head [13]. The New York Head model presents a detailed segmentation of six tissue types (scalp, skull, CSF, gray matter, white matter, air cavities) with an MRI resolution of $0.5\,\mathrm{mm}^3$. Based on this segmentation, a finite element model (FEM) was solved to generate the lead-field matrix. For conducting the simulations, subsets of 108 electrodes and 2000 cortical locations were selected. The dynamics of all background brain sources are modeled by pink noise process, whereas the interacting sources are generated as band-limited linear auto-regressive (AR) processes. The pseudo-EEG data obtained is close to real EEG data in terms of power spectra and spatial correlation structure. We used the eight regions of interest (ROIs) identical to the octants of the brain defined in this benchmark. We performed 100 simulation of two active ROIs that could be synchronous or not, evaluated the capability of the algorithms to determine the active ROIs, and used the imaginary part of the coherence to evaluate the connectivity between the ROI's.

Additionally, the software package SPM12 (http://www.fil.ion.ucl.ac.uk/ spm) was used for simulating single trial MEG datasets using realistic head models. The trials had $N_c = 274$ channels and 1 s time windows. They were simulated projecting one to five sources randomly located in the brain cortex. A sinusoidal signal of 20 Hz was used for simulating the synchronous neural activity. A number of 100 simulations were performed adding random white noise to the data with different signal to noise ratios: $SNR = \{-20, -5, 0, 5, 20\}$ dB. For both benchmarks, Haufe and SPM, the active regions were estimated with beamformers and MSP for comparison purposes. The beamforming priors used were the common covariance matrix (Cov), coherence [10] (Coh), and the Non-Linear kernel matrix (NL). The MSP was computed with the greedy search implementation (see [15] for details).

3   Results

3.1   Estimation Results with SPM Benchmark

In the SPM benchmark (Fig. 3), for one and two simulated sources the behavior of the algorithms were the expected, as the noise diminished together with the localization error. For one active source (Fig. 3(a)), the beamformers (both Cov and NL) and GS (with NL prior) were the algorithms with the lower localization error (around 5 mm with $SNR = 0$). However, the beamformers were affected when the simulations were performed with more than one source (and the error increased with correlated sources). With two active sources (Fig. 3(b)), the evaluated GS algorithms (both Cov and NL) presented the lower localization error (around 10 mm with $SNR = 0$ dB). Comparing the evaluated beamforming priors, the EBB-NL presented lower localization error (15 mm with $SNR = 0$ dB). In summary, the algorithms that included the kernel matrix as prior presented lower localization error compared with the well-known covariance matrix.

In Fig. 4(a), the temporal correlation criteria was evaluated from one to five active sources. The temporal correlation diminished as the number of active sources increased. The algorithms based on Greedy search (with both Cov an NL priors) remained with lower error than those based on Beamformers. Moreover, the algorithms that used the kernel prior from three to five sources presented higher correlation than those with the covariance prior.

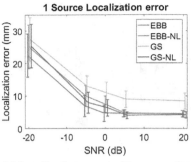
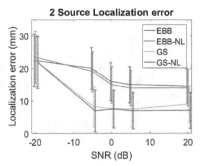

(a) Localization error with one active source

(b) Localization error with two active sources

Fig. 3. Evaluation of the SPM benchmark with one and two active sources. In both simulations the error goes down when the SNR decreases. In both simulations the NL-prior improved the localization of the active sources.

3.2   Estimation Results with Haufe's Benchmark

Table 2 presents the results obtained when evaluating beamformers and MSP (and its variants) in the Haufe's benchmark. The Haufe's approach evaluated the beamformers with coherence prior. With that approach, we found the active sources and summed the power in each ROI. The accuracy obtained with the Haufe's approach was 52%. However, the mean of the power in each ROI considerably increased the accuracy with all tested methods (at least 15%). Compared to the Haufe's approach, the kernel matrix with beamformers reached 75% of accuracy, and 85% with GS. Additionally, the connectivity analysis suggests that the non-linear kernel improves the accuracy with Beamformers and GS.

Table 2. Accuracy of the ROIs selection and connectivity in the Haufe's benchmark

Method	Beamformers [%]			MSP [%]	
	Coh	Cov	NL	GS	GS-NL
Sum of power in ROIs	52	58	56	60	62
Mean of power in ROIs	69	73	75	85	85
Connectivity	60	65	68	68	70

In Table 2, we observe that the Non-linear Kernel presented similar accuracy results compared with the simple covariance prior. However, the correlation among the estimated source time series were improved as seen in Fig. 4(b). The temporal correlation criteria is higher in the strongest source. The improvement with the Non-linear kernel was observed in the second source, were the temporal correlation increased in comparison to the other methods.

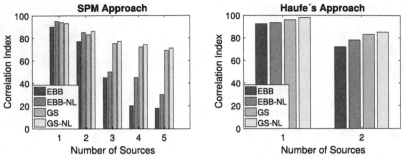

(a) Temporal Correlation SPM benchmark (b) Temporal Correlation Haufe's benchmark

Fig. 4. (a) The temporal correlation index was estimated from one to five active sources. The correlation was higher in the algorithms that used the kernel prior. (b) The temporal correlation criteria is higher in the strongest source, being the GS-NL the algorithm with higher correlation in both sources.

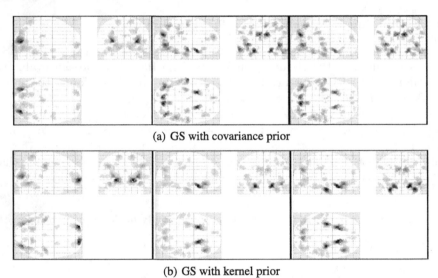

(a) GS with covariance prior

(b) GS with kernel prior

Fig. 5. (a) Estimation of the neural activity around P100 with GS and the simple covariance prior. EEG occipital activity, MEG, and fused information between EEG and MEG. (b) Estimation of the neural activity in P100 with GS and the non-linear kernel, EEG with occipital activity, MEG, and fused information between EEG and MEG. The highlighted activity between both priors is the same; however, the kernel prior gave priority to the activity in the frontal lobe.

3.3   Real Data Applications

EEG data acquired in a visual attention task [11] were used to observe the behavior of the covariance prior in MSP (Fig. 5(a)) compared to the kernel prior

(Fig. 5(b)). Averaged single subject data with the unfamiliar condition were used to establish the active region reference (Fig. 5). In both cases the visual activity was present (which is expected due to the characteristics of the experiments). However, the stronger estimated active sources are different in both cases. With the kernel prior, additionally to the visual activity, there is a highlighted frontal activity related to the early potentials. This would be desirable for posterior connectivity analysis, helping with the definition of the ROIs.

4 Conclusions

In this work, we proposed to use Gaussian kernel matrices as priors in the beamformer and MSP brain imaging approaches. With these kernel matrices we were able to model complex relationships in the data, obtaining improvements in source localization and connectivity analysis for two evaluated benchmarks: Haufe's and SPM. For real data applications, the kernel prior elucidated the expected occipital activity in the visual attention task. However, the kernel prior also highlighted other sources that the traditional covariance matrices did not show. Further research on introducing the non-stationary behavior of the MEG/EEG will be needed.

References

1. Babadi, B., Obregon-Henao, G., Lamus, C., Hamalainen, M.: A subspace pursuit-based iterative greedy hierarchical solution to the neuromagnetic inverse problem. Neuroimage **87**, 427–443 (2014)
2. Baillet, S., Mosher, J., Leahy, R.: Electromagnetic brain mapping. IEEE Signal Process. Mag. **18**(6), 14–30 (2001)
3. Belanche, L.: Developments in kernel design. In: European Symposium on Artificial Neural Networks, Computational Intelligence and Machine Learning, ESANN, pp. 369–378 (2013)
4. Belardinelli, P., Ortiz, E., Barnes, G., Noppeney, U., Preissl, H.: Source reconstruction accuracy of MEG and EEG Bayesian inversion approaches. Plos One **7**(12), e51985 (2012)
5. Dale, A.M., Sereno, M.: Improved localization of cortical activity by combining EEG and MEG with MRI cortical surface reconstruction: a linear approach. J. Cognit. Neurosci. **5**, 162–176 (1993)
6. Engemann, D.A., Gramfort, A.: Automated model selection in covariance estimation and spatial whitening of MEG and EEG signals. Neuroimage **108**, 328–342 (2015)
7. Friston, K., Harrison, L., Daunizeau, J., Kiebel, S., Phillips, C., Trujillo-Barreto, N., Henson, R., Flandin, G., Mattout, J.: Multiple sparse priors for the M/EEG inverse problem. NeuroImage **39**, 1104–1120 (2008)
8. Gartner, T.: A survey of kernels for structured data. ACM SIGKDD Explor. Newsl. **5**(1), 49–58 (2003)
9. Grech, R., Cassar, T., Muscat, J., Camilleri, K., Fabri, S., Zervakis, M., Xanthopoulos, P., Sakkalis, V., Vanrumste, B.: Review on solving the inverse problem in EEG source analysis. J. Neuro Eng. Rehabil. **5**(1), 25 (2008)

10. Haufe, S., Ewald, A.: A simulation framework for benchmarking EEG-based brain connectivity estimation methodologies. Brain Topogr. **2016**, 1–18 (2016)
11. Henson, R., Mouchlianitis, E., Friston, K.: MEG and EEG data fusion: simultaneous localisation of face-evoked responses. NeuroImage **47**(2), 581–589 (2009)
12. Henson, R.N., Wakeman, D.G., Litvak, V., Friston, K.J.: A parametric empirical bayesian framework for the EEG/MEG inverse problem: generative models for multi-subject and multi-modal integration. Front. Hum. Neurosci. **5**, 16 (2011)
13. Huang, Y., Parra, L.C., Haufe, S.: The New York head- a precise standardized volume conductor model for EEG source localization and tES targeting. Neuroimage **140**, 150–162 (2015)
14. Lin, F.H., Belliveau, J.W., Dale, A.M., Hamalainen, M.S.: Distributed current estimates using cortical orientation constraints. Hum. Brain Mapp. **29**, 1–13 (2006)
15. López, J.D., Litvak, V., Espinosa, J., Friston, K., Barnes, G.: Algorithmic procedures for bayesian MEG/EEG source reconstruction in SPM. NeuroImage **84**, 476–487 (2014)
16. Álvarez-Meza, A.M., Cárdenas-Peña, D., Castellanos-Dominguez, G.: Unsupervised kernel function building using maximization of information potential variability. In: Bayro-Corrochano, E., Hancock, E. (eds.) CIARP 2014. LNCS, vol. 8827, pp. 335–342. Springer, Cham (2014). doi:10.1007/978-3-319-12568-8_41
17. Pascual-Marqui, R.: Standardized low resolution brain electromagnetic tomography (sLORETA): technical details. Methods Find. Exp. Clin. Pharmacol. **24**, 5–24 (2002)
18. Shawe-Taylor, J., Cristianini, N.: Kernel Methods for Pattern Analysis. Cambridge University Press, Cambridge (2004)
19. Wahba, G.: Support Vector Machines, Reproducing Kernel Hilbert Spaces and the Randomized GACV. University of Winsconsin (1998)

Automatic Separation of Parkinsonian Patients and Control Subjects Based on the Striatal Morphology

Fermín Segovia[1]([✉]), Juan M. Górriz[1], Javier Ramírez[1],
Francisco J. Martínez-Murcia[1], Diego Castillo-Barnes[1],
Ignacio A. Illán[2], Andres Ortiz[3], and Diego Salas-Gonzalez[1]

[1] Department of Signal Theory, Networking and Communications,
University of Granada, Granada, Spain
fsegovia@ugr.es
[2] The Florida State University, Florida, USA
[3] Department of Communications Engineering, University of Málaga, Málaga, Spain

Abstract. Parkinsonism is the second more common neurological disease and affects around 1%–2% of people over 65 years, being around 20%–24% of them incorrectly diagnosed. The disorder is associated to a progressive loss of dopaminergic neurons of the striatum. Thus, its diagnosis is usually corroborated by analyzing neuroimaging data of this region. In this work, we propose a novel computer system to automatically distinguish between parkinsonian patients and neurologically healthy subjects using ^{123}I-FP-CIT SPECT data, a neuroimaging modality widely used to assist the diagnosis of Parkinsonism. First, the voxels of the striatum were selected using an intensity threshold. These voxels were then projected over the axial plane, resulting in a two-dimensional image with the striatum shape. Subsequently, the size and shape of the left and right sides of the striatum were characterized by 5 features: area, eccentricity, orientation and length of the major and minor axes. Finally, the extracted features were used along with a Support Vector Machine classifier to separate patients and controls. An accuracy rate of 91.53% ($p < 0.001$) was estimated using a k-fold cross-validation scheme and a database with 189 ^{123}I-FP-CIT SPECT neuroimages. This rate outperformed the ones achieved by previous approaches when using the same data.

Keywords: Morphological features · DaTSCAN · ^{123}I-FP-CIT SPECT · Striatum · Machine learning · Parkinson's disease · Support Vector Machine

1 Introduction

Parkinsonism is a clinical syndrome characterized by the presence of hypokinesia, tremor, rigidity, and postural instability [9]. The most common form of Parkinsonism is Parkinson's disease (PD), a neurological disorder that affects about

© Springer International Publishing AG 2017
J.M. Ferrández Vicente et al. (Eds.): IWINAC 2017, Part I, LNCS 10337, pp. 345–352, 2017.
DOI: 10.1007/978-3-319-59740-9_34

1%–2% people over 65 years and whose prevalence is increasing in developed nations due to the grow of the older population.

One of the neurological hallmark of Parkinsonism is a substantial decrease in the dopamine content of the striatum. For that reason, the diagnosis of this disorder is usually corroborated by means of neuroimaging data that allow visualizing that dopamine deficiency. Several neuroimaging modalities are frequently used for this purpose. For example, ^{123}I-ioflupane or ^{123}I-FP-CIT (also known by the trademark name DaTSCAN) is a radiopharmaceutical used along with a SPECT scanner to model the dopamine transporters in the striatum [2,21]. Recent studies have shown that this neuroimaging modality provides useful information to separate parkinsonian patients and neurologically healthy subjects [10,16,19]. ^{18}F-DOPA PET, ^{123}I-IBZM SPECT and ^{18}F-DMFP PET are other modalities widely used to assist the diagnosis of Parkinsonism [1,6,7,12,17,18].

Traditionally, experienced clinicians visually examined the neuroimages looking for low signal patterns in the striatum that corroborate the loss of dopamine content. However this procedure is subjective and prone to error since small differences in the neuroimaging data can be overlooked by the human eye. This can be noted in Fig. 1. It shows the axial slices containing the striatum of a control subject and two parkinsonian patients. Observe that differences between the control subject and the patient at advance stage are clearly visible however differences between the control subject and the patient at early stage are not so evident.

During the last decade, several computer systems have been proposed to assist the diagnosis of Parkinsonism. These systems analyze the neuroimaging data by means of statistical techniques that allow to automatically separate patients and controls with high accuracy. For example, in [5], the authors used the two-sample t-test implemented in Statistical Parametric Mapping (SPM) [8] to assess the group differences between control subjects and PD patients (and other dementias) using ^{123}I-FP-CIT SPECT data. A multivariate approach based on machine learning was proposed in [10] to the same purpose. And more sophisticated approaches based on principal component analysis and partial least squares were presented in [19] and [16] respectively. Finally, in [11] the authors proposed a multivariate system based on three different significance measures (the well-known Student's t-Test, the Mann–Whitney–Wilcoxon U-Test and the Relative Entropy) that was able to accurately separate parkinsonian patients and controls.

In this work we propose a novel approach to automatically distinguish between neurologically healthy subjects and parkinsonian patients using ^{123}I-FP-CIT SPECT data. Specifically we propose to use 10 features (5 per cerebral hemisphere) characterizing the size and shape of the striatum. Then, a Support Vector Machine (SVM) classifier [20] is used to separate control subjects and patients. This approach was evaluated using a dataset with 189 neuroimages acquired during a recent study carried out in the "Virgen de la Victoria" hospital (Málaga, Spain). An estimation of the classification accuracy was calculated by means of a cross-validation scheme. The obtained accuracy rate outperformed the one achieved by previous approaches.

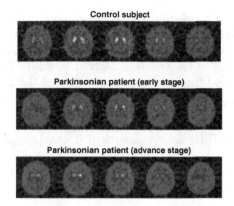

Fig. 1. Axial slices containing the striatum in ^{123}I-FP-CIT SPECT data from a control subject (top), a parkinsonian patient at early stage (middle) and a parkinsonian patient at advance stage (bottom).

Table 1. Group composition and demographic details of the data used in this work. μ and σ stand for the average and the standard deviation respectively.

	#	Sex		Age		
		M	F	μ	σ	Range
Controls	94	49	45	69.26	10.16	33–89
Patients	95	54	41	68.29	9.62	30–87

2   Materials and Methods

2.1   Dataset

A dataset consisting on 189 ^{123}I-FP-CIT SPECT neuroimages was used in order to evaluate the proposed methodology (demographic details are given in Table 1). The data were acquired during a recent study carried out in the "Virgen de la Victoria" hospital (Málaga, Spain). Subjects on treatment with drugs which have an effect, known or suspected, by a direct competitive mechanism at the level of dopaminergic transporters were excluded. The neuroimaging data were acquired 3 hours after the radiopharmaceutical injection (185 MBq of ^{123}I-ioflupane) using a SPECT gamma camera (Millennium model from General Electric) equipped with a dual head and general purpose collimator. The neuroimages were reconstructed by means of filtered back-projection algorithms without attenuation correction. A Hanning filter of frequency 0.7 was also applied.

After the reconstruction, the neuroimages were preprocessed in order to make them comparable. This procedure consisted on two steps: spatial registration and intensity normalization. The former was performed using the template matching algorithm implemented in the SPM toolbox (version 8). To this end, an *ad-hoc* template was computed [14] as follows: First the control neuroimages were spatially registered to a randomly selected one. Then, these neuroimages were averaged and made symmetrical. The intensity normalization [3,4,15] was carried out by dividing the intensity level of each voxel by a I_{max} value computed as the average of the 1% of the voxels of highest intensity (per neuroimage).

The data were labeled through visual inspection of the neuroimages by three experienced clinicians from the Nuclear Medicine service of the hospital. Two groups were defined:

- **Control subjects.** Bilateral, symmetrical uptake appeared in caudate and putamen nuclei.
- **Parkinsonian patients.** There were areas of significant reduced uptake in any of the striatal structures.

2.2 Feature Extraction Based on the Striatum Morphology

First, the striatum of each subject was parceled by applying an intensity threshold, I_x, computed as the 75% of the maximum intensity of the neuroimage. The threshold is therefore specific to each patient. Then, the axial slices of each image were projected over the axial plane resulting in a two-dimension image per subject. Finally, each resulting image was divided in two, containing respectively left and right striatum, i.e. the striatum area belonging to the left and the right cerebral hemispheres.

Once the ^{123}I-FP-CIT SPECT data corresponding to each subject were reduced to two binary two-dimensional images, 5 morphological features were extracted to characterize the size and shape of each part of the striatum. They are as follows:

- **Area.** Number of pixels in the left/right striatum. In practice is was computed as the number of pixels with intensity greater than 0 (because of the thresholding procedure).
- **Eccentricity.** Ratio of the distance between the foci of a conic section and its major axis length. It can be seen as a measure of how much an ellipse deviates from a circle.
- **Orientation.** Angle (measured in degrees and given in the range [−90, 90]) between the major axis of the ellipse and the x axis.
- **Length of the major axis.** Length (in pixels) of the major axis of the ellipse that has the same normalized second central moments as the region.
- **Length of the minor axis.** Length (in pixels) of the minor axis of the ellipse that has the same normalized second central moments as the region.

For last 4 metrics we supposed that left and right striatum have elliptical shape. As shown in Fig. 1, the shape of these regions is not regular however they can be satisfactorily approximated by an ellipse.

After this procedure, each subject was represented by 10 measures (5 per cerebral hemisphere) that were used as feature in the subsequent classification procedure. Figure 2 shows these measures (normalized so that they are in range [0, 1]) grouped by hemisphere and subject label.

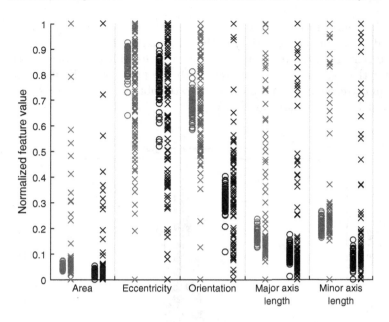

Fig. 2. Morphological features extracted for left striatum (blue) and right striatum (black). The features for control subjects are represented by circles whereas the features for parkinsonian patients are represented by crosses. (Color figure online)

3   Experiments and Results

A SVM classifier was used to separate controls and parkinsonian patients. The cost parameter, C, was set to the commonly used value of 1. The accuracy and other classification measures were estimated using a k-fold cross-validation approach ($k = 10$). Table 2 shows the results obtained by the proposed approach and by other baseline approaches (for comparison purposes). These baseline approaches used the intensity of the voxels in the striatum as feature. The first one used an intensity threshold to select those voxels whereas the second approach used an atlas to this purpose.

Table 2. Accuracy, sensitivity and specificity obtained by the proposed approach and other baseline approaches.

	Accuracy	Sensitivity	Specificity
Proposed method	91.53%	86.32%	96.81%
Striatum voxels (threshold)	87.30%	84.21%	90.43%
Striatum voxels (atlas)	89.42%	88.42%	90.43%

The significance of the accuracy rate obtained by the proposed method was estimated using a permutation test [13] and resulted on $p < 0.001$. In this test the classification procedure was repeated 1000 times using different label sets generated as random permutations of the original one. The p-value was estimated as the percentage of these classification procedures which accuracy was equal to or greater than the accuracy obtained with the true labels. Figure 3 shows the histogram corresponding to the accuracy rates obtained in all the classifications carried out for the permutation test.

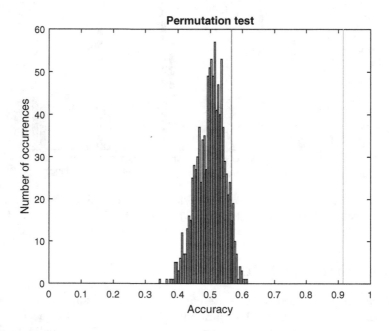

Fig. 3. Histogram of the accuracy rates achieved by using randomly generated label sets (1000 repetitions) and the proposed method. Red and blue lines are respectively the accuracy associated with a p-value of 0.05 and the accuracy obtained when using the true labels (91.53%). (Color figure online)

4   Conclusion and Future Work

A novel approach to distinguish between parkinsonian patients and control subjects using ^{123}I-FP-CIT data has been demonstrated. The procedure was performed in two steps. First, each neuroimage was summarized as a set of 10 features (5 per each cerebral hemisphere), which characterized the size and shape of the striatum. Then, a SVM classifier was used to separate patients and controls using the feature sets previously computed. The performance of this approach was evaluated using a datasets with 189 ^{123}I-FP-CIT neuroimages along with a k-fold cross-validation scheme. An accuracy rate of 91.53% ($p < 0.001$) was obtained, outperforming previous approaches based on using the intensity values of the voxels in the striatum as features.

As future work, we plan to evaluate other morphological features (as the gradient) and additional classification algorithms. We hypothesize that the advantages of the feature extraction method proposed in this work will be more evident with classical classifiers which are more affected by the small sample size problem.

Acknowledgment. The authors are grateful to MD. J.M. Jiménez-Hoyuela and MD. S.J. Ortega from "Virgen de la Victoria" hospital (Málaga, Spain) for their help in data management. This work was supported by the MINECO/FEDER under the TEC2015-64718-R project and the Ministry of Economy, Innovation, Science and Employment of the Junta de Andalucía under the Excellence Project P11-TIC-7103 and a Talent Hub project approved by the Andalucía Talent Hub Program launched by the Andalusian Knowledge Agency, co-funded by the European Union's Seventh Framework Program, Marie Sklodowska-Curie actions (COFUND Grant Agreement no. 291780) and the Ministry of Economy, Innovation, Science and Employment of the Junta de Andalucía.

References

1. Berding, G., Gratz, K.F., Kolbe, H., Meyer, G.J., Dengler, R., Knoop, B.O., Hundeshagen, H.: 123I-IBZM SPECT: reconstruction methodology and results in parkinsonism and dystonia. Nuklearmedizin. Nucl. Med. **33**(5), 194–199 (1994)
2. Booij, J., Tissingh, G., Boer, G.J., Speelman, J.D., Stoof, J.C., Janssen, A.G., Wolters, E.C., van Royen, E.A.: [123I]FP-CIT SPECT shows a pronounced decline of striatal dopamine transporter labelling in early and advanced Parkinson's disease. J. Neurol. Neurosurg. Psychiatry **62**(2), 133–140 (1997)
3. Brahim, A., Górriz, J.M., Ramírez, J., Khedher, L.: Intensity normalization of DaTSCAN SPECT imaging using a model-based clustering approach. Appl. Soft Comput. **37**, 234–244 (2015)
4. Brahim, A., Ramírez, J., Górriz, J.M., Khedher, L., Salas-Gonzalez, D.: Comparison between different intensity normalization methods in 123I-ioflupane imaging for the automatic detection of parkinsonism. PLOS ONE **10**(6), e0130274 (2015)
5. Colloby, S.J., O'Brien, J.T., Fenwick, J.D., Firbank, M.J., Burn, D.J., McKeith, I.G., Williams, E.D.: The application of statistical parametric mapping to 123I-FP-CIT SPECT in dementia with Lewy bodies, Alzheimer's disease and Parkinson's disease. NeuroImage **23**(3), 956–966 (2004)
6. Eshuis, S.A., Jager, P.L., Maguire, R.P., Jonkman, S., Dierckx, R.A., Leenders, K.L.: Direct comparison of FP-CIT SPECT and F-DOPA PET in patients with Parkinson's disease and healthy controls. Eur. J. Nucl. Med. Mol. Imaging **36**(3), 454 (2009)
7. la Fougère, C., Pöpperl, G., Levin, J., Wängler, B., Böning, G., Uebleis, C., Cumming, P., Bartenstein, P., Bötzel, K., Tatsch, K.: The value of the dopamine D2/3 receptor ligand 18F-desmethoxyfallypride for the differentiation of idiopathic and nonidiopathic Parkinsonian syndromes. J. Nucl. Med. **51**(4), 581–587 (2010)
8. Friston, K.J., Ashburner, J.T., Kiebel, S.J., Nichols, T.E., Penny, W.D.: Statistical Parametric Mapping: The Analysis of Functional Brain Images, 1st edn. Academic Press, Amsterdam, Boston (2006)
9. Greenberg, D., Aminoff, M., Simon, R.: Clinical Neurology, 8th edn. McGraw-Hill Professional, New York (2012)

10. Illán, I.A., Górriz, J.M., Ramírez, J., Segovia, F., Jiménez-Hoyuela, J.M., Lozano, S.J.O.: Automatic assistance to Parkinson's disease diagnosis in DaTSCAN SPECT imaging. Med. Phys. **39**(10), 5971–5980 (2012)
11. Martínez-Murcia, F.J., Górriz, J.M., Ramírez, J., Illán, I.A., Ortiz, A.: Automatic detection of Parkinsonism using significance measures and component analysis in DaTSCAN imaging. Neurocomputing **126**, 58–70 (2014)
12. Martinez-Murcia, F.J., Górriz, J.M., Ramírez, J., Moreno-Caballero, M., Gómez-Río, M.: The Parkinson's progression markers initiative: parametrization of textural patterns in 123i-ioflupane imaging for the automatic detection of Parkinsonism. Med. Phys. **41**(1) (2014)
13. Pereira, F., Mitchell, T., Botvinick, M.: Machine learning classifiers and fMRI: a tutorial overview. NeuroImage **45**(Suppl. 1), S199–S209 (2009)
14. Salas-Gonzalez, D., Górriz, J.M., Ramírez, J., Illán, I.A., Padilla, P., Martínez-Murcia, F.J., Lang, E.W.: Building a FP-CIT SPECT brain template using a posterization approach. Neuroinformatics **13**(4), 391–402 (2015)
15. Salas-Gonzalez, D., Górriz, J.M., Ramírez, J., Illán, I.A., Lang, E.W.: Linear intensity normalization of FP-CIT SPECT brain images using the α-stable distribution. NeuroImage **65**, 449–455 (2013)
16. Segovia, F., Górriz, J.M., Ramírez, J., Álvarez, I., Jiménez-Hoyuela, J.M., Ortega, S.J.: Improved Parkinsonism diagnosis using a partial least squares based approach. Med. Phys. **39**(7), 4395–4403 (2012)
17. Segovia, F., Górriz, J.M., Ramírez, J., Martínez-Murcia, F.J., Levin, J., Schuberth, M., Brendel, M., Rominger, A., Bötzel, K., Garraux, G., Phillips, C.: Multivariate analysis of 18F-DMFP PET data to assist the diagnosis of Parkinsonism. Front. Neuroinf. **11**, 1–9 (2017)
18. Segovia, F., Illán, I.A., Górriz, J.M., Ramírez, J., Rominger, A., Levin, J.: Distinguishing Parkinson's disease from atypical Parkinsonian syndromes using PET data and a computer system based on support vector machines and Bayesian networks. Front. Comput. Neurosci., 1–8 (2015)
19. Towey, D.J., Bain, P.G., Nijran, K.S.: Automatic classification of 123I-FP-CIT (DaTSCAN) SPECT images. Nucl. Med. Commun. **32**(8), 699–707 (2011)
20. Vapnik, V.N.: The Nature of Statistical Learning Theory. Springer, New York (2000)
21. Winogrodzka, A., Bergmans, P., Booij, J., van Royen, E.A., Janssen, A.G., Wolters, E.C.: [123I]FP-CIT SPECT is a useful method to monitor the rate of dopaminergic degeneration in early-stage Parkinson's disease. J. Neural Trans. (Vienna, Austria: 1996) **108**(8–9), 1011–1019 (2001)

Emotion Assessment Based on Functional Connectivity Variability and Relevance Analysis

C. Torres-Valencia$^{(\boxtimes)}$, A. Alvarez-Meza, and A. Orozco-Gutierrez

Automatics Research Group, Universidad Tecnológica de Pereira,
Pereira - Risaralda, Colombia
{cristian.torres,andres.alvarez1,aaog}@utp.edu.co

Abstract. The evaluation of emotional states has relevance in the development of systems that can automatically interact with human beings. The use of brain mapping techniques, e.g., electroencephalogram (EEG), improves the robustness of the emotion assessment methodologies in comparison to those schemes that use only audiovisual information. However, the high amount of data derived from EEG and the complex spatiotemporal relationships among channels impose several signal processing issues. Recently, functional connectivity (FC) approaches have emerged as an alternative to estimate brain connectivity patterns from EEG. Thereby, FC allows depicting the cognitive processes inside the human brain to support further brain activity discrimination stages. In this work, we propose an FC-based strategy to classify emotional states from EEG data. Our approach comprises a variability-based representation from three different FC measures, i.e., correlation, coherence, and mutual information, and a supervised kernel-based scheme to quantify the relevance of each measure. Thus, our proposal codes the inter-subject brain activity variability regarding FC representations. Obtained results on a public dataset show that the introduced strategy is competitive in comparison to state-of-the-art methods classifying arousal and valence emotional dimensional spaces.

Keywords: Emotion assessment · Functional connectivity · Variability · Relevance analysis

1 Introduction

Emotional states highly influence both human interaction and human computer/machine interaction. In fact, analyzing emotions has attracted enormous interest in the development of systems that can interact automatically with the user, e.g., brain-computer interfaces (BCI) [5]. Regarding this, emotion representation is divided into two broad categories: discrete and dimensional. The former includes basic emotions such as: anger, joy, surprise, disgust, fear, and sadness. The latter comprises the analysis of few subtle dimensions that can define an emotional stimulus from a more physiological point of view [8]. In particular, the emotions under dimensional category employs the arousal vs.

© Springer International Publishing AG 2017
J.M. Ferrández Vicente et al. (Eds.): IWINAC 2017, Part I, LNCS 10337, pp. 353–362, 2017.
DOI: 10.1007/978-3-319-59740-9_35

valence space characterization to describe the active/passive and the positiveness/negativeness responses, respectively, against a given emotional stimulus. Thereby, a wider range of emotions can be analyzed and quantified than in the discrete representation case [6,13].

Concerning the emotion assessment approaches, initial attempts included audiovisual data. This type of data allows the detection of few basic emotions (discrete representation), however, the analysis of facial expressions and speech proves a challenging task due to the inter-subject variability of discriminant emotion patterns [3]. Namely, visual emotion responses derived from body movements and facial expressions are regulated by the subject, that is why the audiovisual information lacks sort of robustness in this particular task. On the other hand, recent approaches use physiological data to support the assessment [13]. Physiological data allows studying different biological responses in the human body related to the central nervous system, which includes more accurate and detailed emotion patterns than audiovisual ones [10]. Although capturing physiological data poses an invasive sensing, recent efforts to improve the acquisition technology have been made. In particular, the electroencephalogram (EEG) provides a set of time series that allows the analysis of neural activity in different brain regions that can be easily related to cognitive processes, i.e., emotions [1,6]. Recent studies demonstrated that the EEG data and some cortical and subcortical regions of the brain could be used effectively for the discrimination of emotion responses [11]. Indeed, the EEG is preferred instead of other brain mapping technologies as functional magnetic resonance imaging (fMRI), because of its non-invasive scheme and improved time resolution. Nonetheless, some issues associated with the use of EEG include the low space resolution and the complex spatiotemporal relationships among channels.

Some works have tried to recognize emotions from EEG data by extracting a set of static features under constrained frequency bands, namely: theta, gamma, alpha, and beta rythms [12]. Besides, more elaborate feature extraction approaches, i.e., Dual-Tree Complex Wavelet Packet Transform (DT-CWPT), have been introduced to highlight emotion patterns from EEG recordings [3]. However, their results are still far from being satisfactory [1,13]. Recent techniques employ functional connectivity (FC) representations to support emotion assessment by the computation of statistical dependencies among EEG time series [4]. Such dependencies aim to code the relations of neurophysiological events characterized by generalized synchronization (GS), phase synchronization (PS), and information theory (IT) measures [9]. In this sense, authors in [6] employ a PS measure to detect the reactive band and relevant synchronized regions of the brain related to different emotions. Moreover, authors in [10] used a mapping technique to group a region of interest from EEG time series that gives an improved location of the brain areas related to emotional states. Similarly, authors in [7] exploited the correlation and the coherence measures within a graph theory scheme for emotion assessment. Though algorithms based on FC seem to be promising, the variability of the inter-channel dependencies and the selection of the FC measure still pose an open issue. Besides, the assessment success highly depends on the subject at hand that is related to the particular form in which the brain of each person works.

In this work, we introduce an FC variability (FCV) representation strategy to classify emotional states from EEG data. Our proposal codes FC variations from three different measures: correlation, coherence, and mutual information. Moreover, a supervised kernel-based relevance analysis is used to quantify each FC measure significance. Thus, the inter-subject dependency regarding the emotion assessment is addressed as a feature relevance analysis task concerning the employed measure. Our approach is tested using a publicly-available database known as *Database for Emotion Assessment using Physiological Data* (DEAP). In particular, a bi-class problem is built for both arousal and valence dimensions. The obtained results show competitive performances in comparison to state-of-the-art methods for subject-dependent emotion recognition. The rest of the paper is organized as follows: In Sect. 2, we present the theoretical background of FCV representation with relevance analysis. Section 3 describes the experimental set-up for emotion assessment, Sect. 4 discusses the obtained results, and the concluding remarks are outlined finally in Sect. 5.

2   Materials and Methods

2.1   Functional Connectivity Using a Variability-Based Representation

Let $u, v \in \mathbb{R}^L$ be a pair of EEG records of size L, a FC measure $\xi : \mathbb{R}^L \times \mathbb{R}^L \rightarrow \mathbb{R}$ between u and v can be defined in terms of their statistical interdependence. Following some well-known FC measures are briefly described.

Correlation-(COR). The linear correlation $\xi_{COR}(u, v) \in [-1, 1]$ between u and v in the time domain is computed by the Pearson's correlation coefficient as:

$$\xi_{COR}(u, v) = \frac{1}{\sigma_u \sigma_v} \sum_{L=1}^{l} (u_l - \bar{u})(v_l - \bar{u}), \tag{1}$$

where $\sigma_u, \sigma_v \in \mathbb{R}^+$ and $\bar{u}, \bar{v} \in \mathbb{R}$ are the standard deviation and the mean values of u and v, respectively.

Coherence-(COH). The linear time-invariant relationship between u and v at frequency range $[f_{\min}, f_{\max}]$ is calculated trough the coherence measure as:

$$\xi_{COH}(u, v) = \frac{1}{f_{\max} - f_{\min}} \sum_{f = f_{\min}}^{f_{\max}} \frac{|\zeta_{uv}(f)|^2}{\zeta_{uu}(f)\zeta_{vv}(f)}, \tag{2}$$

where $\xi_{COH}(u, v) \in [0, 1]$, $\zeta_{uv}(f) \in \mathbb{C}$ is the cross-spectrum of u and v, and $\zeta_{uu}(f), \zeta_{vv}(f) \in \mathbb{C}$ are the power spectrum of u and v, respectively.

Mutual Information-(MI). The MI between $\boldsymbol{u}$ and $\boldsymbol{v}$ allows revealing the uncertainty amount of one time series by observing the other. So, high-order correlations can be computed utilizing probability density estimators as follows:

$$\xi_{MI}\left(\boldsymbol{u}, \boldsymbol{v}\right) = \sum_{l=1}^{L} \hat{p}(u_l, v_l) \log\left(\frac{\hat{p}(u_l, v_l)}{\hat{p}(u_l)\hat{p}(v_l)}\right), \tag{3}$$

where $\hat{p}(u_l, v_l) \in [0, 1]$ is an estimation of the joint probability density function and $\hat{p}(u_l), \hat{p}(v_l) \in [0, 1]$ are the marginal density function approximations of u_l and v_l.

In practice, an emotion assessment framework includes a set of EEG data trials denoted as $\Psi = \{\boldsymbol{X}_n \in \mathbb{R}^{C \times T} : n = 1, 2, \ldots, N\}$, where $\boldsymbol{X}_n$ is the n-th observed trial with C channels and T time instants. Furthermore, let $\Gamma = \{b_n\}$ be the class label set, termed the emotion dimension class, where $b_n \in \{-1, +1\}$. Given the channel $\boldsymbol{x}_c \in \mathbb{R}^T$ of an observed EEG trial $\boldsymbol{X}$, we initially estimate a set of overlapped segments $\{\boldsymbol{z}_c^j \in \mathbb{R}^L : j = 1, 2, \ldots, Q\}$ which are split from $\boldsymbol{x}_c$, being $\boldsymbol{z}_c^j$ the c-th channel at the j-th window. To model time-variant dependencies among EEG channels, we compute the above-described FC measures between channel segments by building the set $\{\boldsymbol{A}^j \in \mathbb{R}^{C \times C}\}$, where matrix $\boldsymbol{A}^j$ holds elements:

$$a_{cc'}^j = \xi_m\left(\boldsymbol{z}_c^j, \boldsymbol{z}_{c'}^j\right), \tag{4}$$

with $a_{cc'}^j = a_{c'c}^j$, $m = \{\text{COR}, \text{COH}, \text{MI}\}$, and $c, c' = 1, 2, \ldots, C$. Afterwards, both the mean and the variance of each provided measure along segments are stored in matrices $\boldsymbol{\Delta} \in \mathbb{R}^{C \times C}$ and $\boldsymbol{\Omega} \in \mathbb{R}^{C \times C}$, holding elements:

$$\Delta_{cc'} = \frac{1}{Q} \sum_{j=1}^{Q} a_{cc'}^j, \tag{5}$$

$$\Omega_{cc'} = \frac{1}{Q} \sum_{j=1}^{Q} \left(a_{cc'}^j - \Delta_{cc'}\right)^2. \tag{6}$$

Finally, the feature vector $\boldsymbol{y} \in \mathbb{R}^{C(C-1)}$, coding the FC variability (FCV), is built after vector concatenation of $\boldsymbol{\Delta}$ and $\boldsymbol{\Omega}$ matrices ($\Delta_{cc'} = \Delta_{c'c}$ and $\Omega_{cc'} = \Omega_{c'c}$).

2.2   Relevance Analysis of Extracted FCV

Given a provided EEG set, a feature matrix $\boldsymbol{Y}_m \in \mathbb{R}^{N \times C(C-1)}$ can be obtained from Eqs. (5) and (6) by extracting FCV patterns based on the m-th measure, i.e., COR, COH, and MI. So, to highlight the most relevant connectivity measure regarding the set (subject) at hand, here, we employ a supervised kernel-based relevance analysis to take advantage of the available joint information, associating FCV variations to a given emotion dimension value. Namely, the FCV similarities among EEG trials $y_n, y_{n'} \in Y_m$ are coded by estimating a Gaussian kernel matrix $K_m \in \mathbb{R}^{N \times N}$ on Y_m, as follows:

$$k_{nn'} = \exp\left(-\|y_n - y_{n'}\|/2\sigma^2\right), \tag{7}$$

where $n, n' \in N$ and $\sigma \in \mathbb{R}^+$ is termed the kernel bandwidth. Further, on the emotion dimension space, we also estimate a kernel matrix $L \in \mathbb{R}^{N \times N}$ as follows:

$$l_{nn'} = \delta\left(b_n - b_{n'}\right), \tag{8}$$

where $\delta(\cdot)$ is the delta function. It is worth noting that each defined kernel reflects a different notion of similarity (FCV vs. labels). Therefore, we must still evaluate how well the kernel-based similarity matrix K_m matches with the target matrix L. To this end, a Centered Kernel Alignment (CKA) functional is used to appraise such a match as the inner product of both kernels to estimate the dependence $\mu_m \in [0, 1]$ between the jointly sampled data as follows [2]:

$$\mu_m = \frac{\langle \bar{K}_m, \bar{L} \rangle_F}{\sqrt{\langle \bar{K}_m, \bar{K}_m \rangle_F \langle \bar{L}, \bar{L} \rangle_F}}, \tag{9}$$

where $\langle \cdot, \cdot \rangle_F$ is the matrix-based Frobenius inner product. $\bar{K}$ stands for the centered kernel matrix $\bar{K} = \tilde{I} K \tilde{I}$, $\tilde{I} = I - 1^\top 1/N$, $I \in \mathbb{R}^{N \times N}$ is the identity matrix, and $1 \in \mathbb{R}^N$ is the all-ones vector. In this sense, μ_m weights allow ranking the relevance of an FCV, that is, the higher μ_m value the better the m-th FCV representation regarding the emotion labels. So, the highstest weigth value is employed to select the most relevant FCV (RFCV) for a given EEG set.

3   Experimental Set-Up

Testing Dataset and Preprocessing. The well-known *Database for Emotion Assessment using Physiological Data* (DEAP) is used to test the introduced FCV approach. The DEAP is publicly available and contains physiological recordings from 40 emotion elicitation experiments of 32 subjects. Each subject was requested to watch a one minute portion of a video that induces a particular emotion, then, an auto-tagging system captured the arousal, valence, dominance, and liking level of each video within the range 1 to 9. The collected data includes the following signals: EEG, electrooculogram, galvanic skin response, temperature, among others. The EEG data were acquired using a 32 channel biosemi configuration at 128 Hz and filtered by an artifact removal stage [8].

FCV Training. The proposed FCV approach is tested as feature extraction tool for emotion assessment. Thus, each DEAP subject dataset is configured as a biclass problem for both arousal and valence dimensions. The first class corresponds to arousal/valence levels between 1 and 5, meanwhile, the second one holds levels between 5 and 9. Furthermore, a window of 9 s with 25% overlapping is employed to compute the inter-channel dependencies based on FCV. The fixed window size aims to highlight channel dependencies under alpha, beta, gamma, and theta rhythms along time. Likewise, the configuration of the frequencies bands for the coherence measure are related to the aforementioned rythms ($f_{min} = 4\,\mathrm{Hz}$ and $f_{max} = 47\,\mathrm{Hz}$). Here, the FC measures are computed using the HERMES MatLab toolbox [9]. Subsequently, the FCV-COR, FCV-COH, FCV-MI, and RFCV are computed as in Sects. 2.1 and 2.2, yielding a feature extraction matrix $Y \in \mathbb{R}^{N \times P}$ with $N = 40$ emotion elicitation videos and $P = 992$ features for each considered representation. Finally, the discrimination between emotion classes is carried out based on a k-nearest neighbor classifier under a Gaussian similarity criteria. A nested 10-fold cross-validation strategy is used to test the system performance, where the number of nearest neighbors of the applied classifier is fixed as the one reaching the best accuracy within the following testing range $\{1, 3, 5, 7, 9, 11\}$.

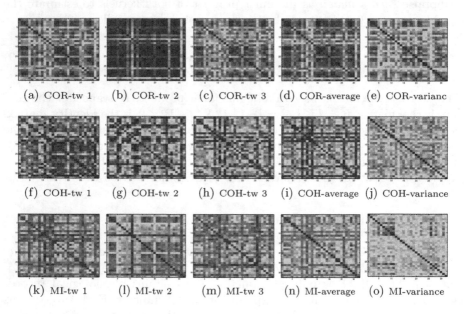

(a) COR-tw 1   (b) COR-tw 2   (c) COR-tw 3   (d) COR-average (e) COR-varianc

(f) COH-tw 1   (g) COH-tw 2   (h) COH-tw 3   (i) COH-average (j) COH-variance

(k) MI-tw 1   (l) MI-tw 2   (m) MI-tw 3   (n) MI-average   (o) MI-variance

Fig. 1. FC measures for the 32 EEG array in different time window (TW). Top row - COR measure, middle row - COH measure and bottom row - MI measure. Columns 1–3 from left to right corresponds to each measure in different (non-subsequently) TW. Column 4 is the average and column 5 the variance for all the time windows.

4   Results and Discussion

The FC scheme detailed in Sect. 2.1 allows the visualization of the variability in the connectivity patterns between EEG channels. Figure 1 shows an example of some time windows from the three measures over the subject 13 in a experiment with arousal and valence ratings of 8.09 and 6.15 respectively. It can be seen in Fig. 1 the variations in the dependences of channels from the EEG array for few time windows. As seen, the relationships on different channels from the EEG array varies in time, and some strong interdependences could be found according each FC measure. For this particular subject/experiment, the COR measure exhibit a strong interdependences between the majority of channels with a small degree of variability among all the time windows (Figs. 1(a)–(c)). On the other hand, for the COH (Figs. 1(f)–(h)) and MI measures (Figs. 1(k)–(m)), there is a higher degree of variability among time windows. The discussed variability for each measure is consequently summed up in the average and variance figures (columns 4–5 from Fig. 1). The average FC allows to observe the channels with strong interdependences as well as the channels with weak interdependences in the whole experiment. Likewise, the FC variance shows the channels interdependence variability across the experiment, with a higher degree of variability for the majority of channels in the COH (Fig. 1(j)) and the MI (Fig. 1(o)) measures.

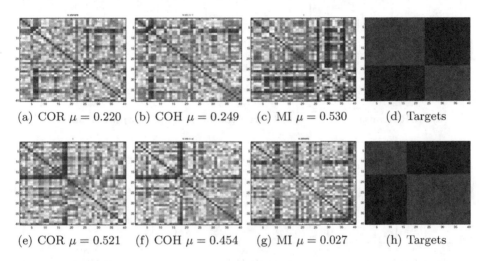

(a) COR $\mu = 0.220$ (b) COH $\mu = 0.249$ (c) MI $\mu = 0.530$ (d) Targets

(e) COR $\mu = 0.521$ (f) COH $\mu = 0.454$ (g) MI $\mu = 0.027$ (h) Targets

Fig. 2. Gaussian kernel transformation applied to the three FC connectivity measures and the targets matrix for two subjects 13 and 18

On the other hand, in Fig. 2, the FCV-based representation and emotion label similarities for each considered measure (see Sect. 2.2) can be analyzed. In this particular case, the FCV corresponds to the subjects 13 and 18 and the set of 40 emotion elicitation experiments. We can infer by visual inspection that exist a higher similarity between the FCV-MI approach and the target matrix for the subject 13 (Figs. 2(a)–(d)), which is also coded by the computation of the weights μ in the RFCV representation. In the other case, for the subject 18 there is a higher relation in the FCV-COR with the targets representation than for the FCV-COH and the FCV-MI (Figs. 2(e)–(h)). For both cases the RFCV allows to code the measure that seems to present the highest correlation with the targets.

FCV is used for classification purposes as stated in the experimental setup. A graphical description of those results can be found in Fig. 3, where the classification accuracy (CA) for each subject and each dimension are presented. Figures 3(a), (b), and (c) show CA for the 32 subjects in arousal dimension using the FCV-COR, FCV-COH and FCV-MI representation respectively. Likewise, Figs. 3(d), (e), and (f) present the CA for all subjects in the valence dimension. From the figures it can be noticed the differences in CA among subjects that evidences the subject-dependency of the FC measures. Also, a summary for each FCV measure is included in Fig. 3(g) for the arousal dimension and Fig. 3(h) for the valence dimension. From those figures, small differences in the CA when the FCV scheme is applied could be noticed and there is no evidence of one of the FCV schemes to present a superior performance in comparison to the others.

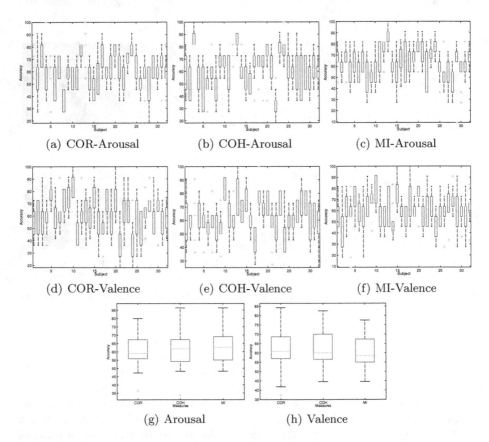

Fig. 3. Boxplots of classification accuracy (CA) per subject in each FC measure. Top row - arousal, middle row - valence and the bottom row, average CA for both dimensions

Finally, a summary of the results of CA for all the subjects is presented in Table 1 for the FCV and RFCV schemes. In this table the results of the proposed

Table 1. Mean emotion classification results [%] for all considered DEAP subjects.

Reference	Approach	Arousal	Valence
Koelstra et al. [8]	Linear features, power spectral - SVM	62.00	57.50
Soleymani et al. [12]	Power spectral - SVM	50.00	62.00
Gupta et al. [7]	Power spectral - HJORT - SVM	60.00	60.00
Padilla-Buritica et al. [10]	MSP - ROI signal - SVM	58.6	55.76
Daimi et al. [3]	Wavelet packet - SVM	67.00	65.00
This work	FCV-COR - KNN	61.93	63.35
This work	FCV-COH - KNN	63.45	61.62
This work	FCV-MI - KNN	62.48	60.78
This work	**RFCV - KNN**	66.00	65.73

methodology are compared against state-of-art works that have been developed in a similar framework using EEG data and the same database (DEAP). It can be seen that for all the works using the DEAP dataset, there is still room for improvement, since the higher results are around 67.00%. Our RFCV approach proves to obtain the higher CA for the valence dimension with 65.73% and the second higher CA for arousal dimension with 66.00%.

5   Conclusions

We introduced a novel FC representation approach for feature extraction to enhance automatic emotion assessment from EEG data. To this end, the proposed strategy incorporates three well-known FC measures: coherence, correlation, and mutual information, to code the temporal variability of EEG inter-channel dependencies. Moreover, a supervised kernel-based relevance analysis based on CKA is used to evaluate the significance of each FC variability regarding the considered measures. Our approach learns both important temporal inter-channel variations and relevant FC measures to deal with inter-subject dependency in emotion classification. Validation of the proposed feature extraction, termed RFCV, is carried out in a public dataset (DEAP). Attained results demonstrate that RFCV is a reliable methodology for emotion assessment in comparison to the state-of-art works. As future work authors plan to couple RFCV with a space state strategy to deal appropriately with the intrinsic EEG nonstationarity. Besides, information theory measures could be employed to reveal connectivity variations among EEG channels.

Acknowledgments. This work is supported by COLCIENCIAS grant 111074455778: "Desarrollo de un sistema de apoyo al diagnóstico no invasivo de pacientes con epilepsia fármaco-resistente asociada a displasias corticales cerebrales: método costo-efectivo basado en procesamiento de imágenes de resonancia magnética". Author C.A. Torres-Valencia was funded by the program "Formación de alto nivel para la ciencia, la tecnología y la innovación, Doctorado Nacional - Convoctoria 647 de 2014", funded by Colciencias.

References

1. Bajaj, V., Pachori, R.B.: Detection of human emotions using features based on the multiwavelet transform of EEG signals. In: Hassanien, A.E., Azar, A.T. (eds.) Brain-Computer Interfaces. ISRL, vol. 74, pp. 215–240. Springer, Cham (2015). doi:10.1007/978-3-319-10978-7_8
2. Cortes, C., Mohri, M., Rostamizadeh, A.: Algorithms for learning kernels based on centered alignment. J. Mach. Learn. Res. **13**, 795–828 (2012)
3. Daimi, S.N., Saha, G.: Classification of emotions induced by music videos and correlation with participants' rating. Expert Syst. Appl. **41**(13), 6057–6065 (2014)
4. Friston, K.J.: Functional and effective connectivity: a review. Brain Connect. **1**(1), 13–36 (2011)
5. Garcia-Molina, G., Tsoneva, T., Nijholt, A.: Emotional brain-computer interfaces. Int. J. Auton. Adapt. Commun. Syst. **6**(1), 9–25 (2013)
6. Gonuguntla, V., Mallipeddi, R., Veluvolu, K.C.: Identification of emotion associated brain functional network with phase locking value. In: 2016 IEEE 38th Annual International Conference of the Engineering in Medicine and Biology Society (EMBC), pp. 4515–4518. IEEE (2016)
7. Gupta, R., Laghari, K.U.R., Falk, T.H.: Relevance vector classifier decision fusion and EEG graph-theoretic features for automatic affective state characterization. Neurocomputing **174**(PB), 875–884 (2016)
8. Koelstra, S., Muhl, C., Soleymani, M., Lee, J.-S., Yazdani, A., Ebrahimi, T., Pun, T., Nijholt, A., Patras, I.: Deap: a database for emotion analysis; using physiological signals. IEEE Trans. Affect. Comput. **3**(1), 18–31 (2012)
9. Niso, G., Bruña, R., Pereda, E., Gutiérrez, R., Bajo, R., Maestú, F., del Pozo, F.: HERMES: towards an integrated toolbox to characterize functional and effective brain connectivity. Neuroinformatics **11**(4), 405–434 (2013)
10. Padilla-Buritica, J.I., Martinez-Vargas, J.D., Castellanos-Dominguez, G.: Emotion discrimination using spatially compact regions of interest extracted from imaging EEG activity. Front. Comput. Neurosci. **10**, 55 (2016)
11. Silva, C.S., Hazrati, M.K., Keil, A., Principe, J.C.: Quantification of neural functional connectivity during an active avoidance task. In: 2016 38th Annual International Conference of the IEEE Engineering in Medicine and Biology Society (EMBC), pp. 708–711, August 2016
12. Soleymani, M., Pantic, M., Pun, T.: Multimodal emotion recognition in response to videos. IEEE Trans. Affect. Comput. **3**(2), 211–223 (2012)
13. Torres-Valencia, C., Álvarez-López, M., Orozco-Gutiérrez, A.: SVM-based feature selection methods for emotion recognition from multimodal data. J. Multimodal User Interfaces **11**, 1–15 (2016)

MRI-Based Feature Extraction Using Supervised General Stochastic Networks in Dementia Diagnosis

D. Collazos-Huertas[✉], A. Tobar-Rodriguez, D. Cárdenas-Peña, and G. Castellanos-Dominguez

Signal Processing and Recognition Group, Universidad Nacional de Colombia, Manizales, Colombia
dfcollazosh@unal.edu.co

Abstract. One of the major research fields in medical applications is Computer-aided dementia diagnosis since it progressively declines the cognitive function and afflicts millions of people worldwide, becoming a leading cause of mortality and morbidity of elder people. Pattern recognition methods, applied to dementia diagnosis, improve either the feature extraction or the classifier stage. Particularly, deep learning machines have raised attention to clinical applications since they work in both stages to enhance the system performance. However, the architecture of these machines is highly complex, making hard their training procedures. In this work, we propose a deep supervised feature extraction approach using General Stochastic Networks through a supervised layer-wise non-linear mapping learning. To this end, we maximize the centered kernel alignment function, which accounts for the provided discriminative information regarding the projection of each layer of the network. Our proposal improves the classifier performance by highlighting the class discrimination during the training stage. Besides, we provide a non-linear relevance measure assessing the contribution of the input feature set to build each latent space which is related to the clinical knowledge. Comparison against other automated diagnosis approaches using different features and classification machines is presented for multi-class and bi-class scenarios on the widely-known ADNI database. As a result, our proposal outperforms the compared approaches, reduces the class biasing, and enhances clinical interpretability.

1 Introduction

Dementia is a chronic and progressive decline in cognitive function that afflicts almost 35.6 million people worldwide with this figure nearly doubling every 20 years because of population aging, resulting in a leading cause of mortality and morbidity of older people (approximately 5–7% of the population). Due to easing the visual inspection of histological changes, structural brain images became a critical support for the diagnosis of dementia and screening of its causes. Thus, the computer-aided diagnosis of dementia based on structural magnetic resonance imaging (MRI) allows classifying areas of visible brain atrophy or ischemia.

© Springer International Publishing AG 2017
J.M. Ferrández Vicente et al. (Eds.): IWINAC 2017, Part I, LNCS 10337, pp. 363–373, 2017.
DOI: 10.1007/978-3-319-59740-9_36

However, the automatic dementia identification model remains a key issue, whose outcome is influenced by many factors, such as feature extraction and/or selection, validation approach, quality image acquisition, training subject database, and clinical diagnosis criteria [1].

In pattern classification, the vast majority of MRI-based approaches for dementia identification consist of two major stages: feature extraction and classification. Despite the impact of the tool considered for the latter stage in the performance, its choice is less critical than the method for image measurements in the former stage [2]. In turn, the feature extraction stage aims at build informative and non-redundant sets of real-valued parameters, yielding to linear and nonlinear analyses. As an approach to the first case of analysis, the linear discriminant analysis (LDA) is used to select the most discriminating features feeding conventional classification machines [3]. Likewise, dimension reduction based on the independent component analysis (ICA) has been performed over high-dimensional voxel-wise features, improving the SVM classifier accuracy [4]. Nonetheless, LDA and ICA eliminate relationships between the dependent features, which may hold discriminating information, and constraint the dimensionality of the resulting feature set to the number of involved classes, hampering the complexity of classification machine. In the nonlinear case of analysis, projection matrices from principal component analysis (PCA) and logistic regressors have been stacked in a multi-layer architecture [5]. Since the model captures the input data variability and an elastic-net term regularizes the cost function, the generative properties of the resulting machine are preferred over the discriminating ones. Another non-linear approach implements an extreme learning machine with a high-dimensional hidden layer from region-of-interest features [6]. Despite allowing to find the most relevant anatomical structures for Alzheimer's diagnosis, demanded high-dimensional mappings increase the system uncertainty. Recently, deep learning architectures, seen as stacked non-linear mappings, have raised attention to clinical applications since they can simplify complex data distributions at each level of abstraction. Such a property allows capturing the tangled relationship among the variables representing the brain images, making possible to improve the dementia classification [7]. In the particular case of mild cognitive impairment, an intermediate neurological disease, non-linear modeling capabilities are expected to deal with its widely heterogeneous distribution. However, propagating input patterns through nonlinear mappings hinders the contribution of each input feature for the classification stage [8].

A supervised feature extraction approach is discussed within the framework of deep networks for supporting the dementia diagnosis. Firstly, we make use of the Center Kernel Alignment (CKA) criterion to compute layer-wise discriminative feature projections, aiming to improve the training of a discriminative General Stochastic Network (GSN). Secondly, we estimate the relevance of the input features, making use of the *tied weight* property of the GSN topology, so that the deep architecture enhances the data interpretability. Our approach is evaluated on two scenarios of dementia diagnosis from structural MRIs. To this end, we use morphological measurements (volume, area, and thickness) computed from FreeSurfer suite, which has shown suitable reliability under various acquisition conditions and has been widely tested in the field of neuroimaging. Attained classification results of several performance measures show that our proposal, mostly, improves baseline approaches, with the additional benefit of reducing the class biasing and enhancing the clinical interpretability.

2   Materials and Methods

2.1   General Stochastic Networks for Supervised Learning

General Stochastic Networks (GSN) indirectly estimate data distribution by solving a supervised function approximation problem using a Markov chain transition framework. An L-layered GSN Markov chain, illustrated in Fig. 1, propagates an input matrix $\boldsymbol{X}_t \in \mathbb{R}^{N \times D}$ upwards and downwards to the l-th matrix of latent states $\boldsymbol{H}_t^l \in \mathbb{R}^{N \times m_l}$ during T steps, with $l \in [1, \ldots, L]$, $t \in [1, \ldots, T]$, and $T > L$. The latent states build higher-order representations following:

$$
\begin{cases}
\boldsymbol{H}_t^l &= \left(\phi^l(\boldsymbol{b}^l + \boldsymbol{H}_{t-1}^{l+1} \left(\boldsymbol{W}^l \right)^\top + \varsigma_{in}) \right) \\
&\quad + \left(\phi^l(\boldsymbol{a}^l + \boldsymbol{H}_{t-1}^{l-1} \left(\boldsymbol{W}^l \right) + \varsigma_{in}) \right) + \varsigma_{out} \\
\boldsymbol{H}_t^0 &= \boldsymbol{X}_t
\end{cases}
\tag{1}
$$

where $\boldsymbol{b}^l \in \mathbb{R}^{m_l}$ and $\boldsymbol{a}^l \in \mathbb{R}^{m_{l-1}}$ are the bias vectors, $\boldsymbol{W}^l \in \mathbb{R}^{m_{l-1} \times m_l}$ encodes the l-th linear projection, vectors $\varsigma_{out} \in \mathbb{R}^{N \times m_l}$ and $\varsigma_{in} \in \mathbb{R}^{N \times m_{l-1}}$ are independent noise sources, the function $\phi^l(\cdot) \in \mathbb{R}$ implements the saturating, non-linear, element-wise operations, and $m_l \in \mathbb{N}$ stands for the dimension of the l-th latent state.

For classification tasks, supervised output information is introduced to the GSN graph, yielding to a discriminative-GSN (dGSN) with the following cost function: $\tilde{v} = \zeta \mathbb{E}\{\nu\left(\boldsymbol{X}_t, \boldsymbol{X}_0\right)\} + (1 - \zeta)\mathbb{E}\{\nu\left(\boldsymbol{H}_t^L, \boldsymbol{Y}\right)\}$, $\tilde{v} \in \mathbb{R}^+$, being $\nu(\cdot, \cdot)$ the assumed loss-function, $\mathbb{E}\{\cdot\}$ stands for the expectation operator, and the real-valued parameter $\zeta \in [0, 1]$ balances the compromise between the generative and discriminative terms. Matrix $\boldsymbol{Y} \in [0, 1]^{N \times C}$ contains N output vectors $\boldsymbol{y}_i \in [0, 1]^C : i \in [1, N]$, representing C mutually exclusive classes, so that the last layer is tied to the output dimension $(m_L = C)$.

2.2   Kernel-Based Feature Extraction for dGSN

In this sense, a layer-by-layer dGSN learning can enable the dimensionality reduction by properly transforming from the inputs to a reduced latent variable set so that it encodes the most salient attributes of the available MRI set. To this purpose, we estimate the initial dGSN parameters in such a way that the network learning starts with a pre-training procedure implemented by a set of linear projections at different layers of abstraction. Therefore, we define a matrix $\boldsymbol{Z}^l \in \mathbb{R}^{N \times m_l}$ that holds every l-th linear projection from the input data $\boldsymbol{X}$ along with the set of hidden layer sizes $\mathcal{M} = \{m_1, \ldots, m_{L-1}\}$, assuming $\boldsymbol{Z}^0 = \boldsymbol{X}$.

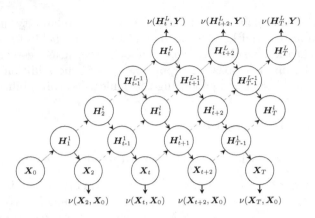

Fig. 1. Schematic design of a discriminative GSN Markov chain with back-probable stochastic units. − Upward step. − Downward step. (Color figure online)

Further, we gather all pair-wise similarities among feature samples into a kernel matrix $\boldsymbol{K}_{\mathcal{Z}}^l \in \mathbb{R}^{N \times N}$ with elements computed at layer as $k_{\mathcal{Z}}^l(ij) = \kappa_{\mathcal{Z}}^l\left(\mathrm{d}\left(\boldsymbol{z}_i^l, \boldsymbol{z}_j^l\right)\right)$, being $\mathrm{d} : \mathbb{R}^{m_l} \times \mathbb{R}^{m_l} \to \mathbb{R}^+$ a distance operator that, upon the assumption of linearity between the layer transitions, is the multi-dimensional Mahalanobis distance defined as $\mathrm{d}\left(\boldsymbol{z}_i^l, \boldsymbol{z}_j^l\right) = \left(\boldsymbol{z}_i^l - \boldsymbol{z}_j^l\right)\left(\boldsymbol{z}_i^l - \boldsymbol{z}_j^l\right)^\top$, $i, j \in [1, N]$. Each $\boldsymbol{z}_i^l \in \mathbb{R}^{m_l}$ holds each linear projection that we choose of a saturated class, that is, $\boldsymbol{z}_i^l = \phi(\boldsymbol{z}_i^{l-1}\boldsymbol{W}^l)$.

Aiming to improve the data interpretability and classification accuracy, we also incorporate the available supervised knowledge into the pre-training stage. So, we gather the output similarities into a matrix $\boldsymbol{K}_{\mathcal{Y}}$ with elements computed as $k_{\mathcal{Y}}(ij) = \kappa_{\mathcal{Y}}\left(\boldsymbol{y}_i, \boldsymbol{y}_j\right)$, in order to encode the discriminative information to get a suitable $\boldsymbol{W}^l$. Hence, we propose each matrix $\boldsymbol{W}^l$ to be learned by maximizing the similarity between $\boldsymbol{K}_{\mathcal{Z}}^l$ and $\boldsymbol{K}_{\mathcal{Y}}$ through the real-valued function that evaluates the alignment between both kernels (*Centered Kernel Alignment* − CKA) [9]:

$$\rho^l\left(\boldsymbol{K}_{\mathcal{Z}}^l, \boldsymbol{K}_{\mathcal{Y}}\right) = \frac{\langle \tilde{\boldsymbol{I}} \boldsymbol{K}_{\mathcal{Z}}^l \tilde{\boldsymbol{I}}, \tilde{\boldsymbol{I}} \boldsymbol{K}_{\mathcal{Y}} \tilde{\boldsymbol{I}} \rangle_F}{\|\tilde{\boldsymbol{I}} \boldsymbol{K}_{\mathcal{Z}}^l \tilde{\boldsymbol{I}}\|_F \|\tilde{\boldsymbol{I}} \boldsymbol{K}_{\mathcal{Y}} \tilde{\boldsymbol{I}}\|_F}, \quad \rho^l \in [0, 1] \tag{2}$$

where $\tilde{\boldsymbol{I}} = \boldsymbol{I} - N^{-1}\boldsymbol{1}\boldsymbol{1}^\top$ (with $\tilde{\boldsymbol{I}} \in \mathbb{R}^{N \times N}$) is a centering matrix, $\boldsymbol{I}$ is the identity matrix, $\boldsymbol{1} \in \mathbb{R}^N$ is an all-ones vector, and notations $\langle \cdot, \cdot \rangle_F$ and $\|\cdot, \cdot\|_F$ stand for the Frobenius inner product and norm, respectively. Thereby, we devise the optimization problem to compute the set of projection matrices $\widehat{\boldsymbol{W}}^l$ that maximize the alignment between $\boldsymbol{K}_{\mathcal{Z}}^l$ and $\boldsymbol{K}_{\mathcal{Y}}$. Thus, the pre-trained $\widehat{\boldsymbol{W}}^l$ initializes each l-th network layer. As a result, each CKA maximization score, ρ^l, provides an assembly of discriminative linear projections $\boldsymbol{W}^l$ that matches the most the relationships between the projected data $\boldsymbol{Z}^l$ and target information $\boldsymbol{Y}$.

Since the dGSN training back-propagates the discriminating information through the *tied weights* from the latent spaces to the input data, we propose to assess the relevance of input features relying on the matrix $\widehat{\boldsymbol{W}}^l \in \mathbb{R}^{m_l \times D}$. Such a relevance matrix holds D row-vectors $\widehat{\boldsymbol{w}}_d^l \in \mathbb{R}^{m_l}$, computed by the reverse mapping of the l-th nested projection into d-th feature as $\widehat{\boldsymbol{w}}_d^l = \boldsymbol{w}_d^1 \phi(\boldsymbol{W}^2 \phi(\boldsymbol{W}^3 \cdots \phi(\boldsymbol{W}^l)))$, $\forall d \in [1, D]$. Based on the fact that each $\widehat{\boldsymbol{w}}_d^l$ measures the contribution of the input features to build the latent space l, we propose to assess the relevance of the d-th feature as the generalized mean of its corresponding reverse projection vector, that is $\varrho_d^l = \left\| \widehat{\boldsymbol{w}}_d^l \right\|_p$, $\varrho_d^l \in \mathbb{R}^+$ where notation $\| \cdot \|_p$ stands for the ℓ_p-norm.

3   Experimental Setup and Results

We present a feature extraction methodology using General Stochastic Networks to classify structural MRI scans by the following three neurological categories of patient diagnosis: Alzheimer's Disease (AD), Mild Cognitive Impairment (MCI), and Healthy Control (HC). The methodological development of the proposed approach appraises the following stages: (*i*) Preprocessing including the segmentation and feature extraction procedures, (*ii*) Feature learning using kernel alignment to learn a projection matrix and relevance analysis, and (*iii*) Training of the dGSN-based classifier using a cross-validation scheme.

3.1   ADNI Database and Preprocessing

Validation of the developed methodology is carried out using the Alzheimer's Disease Neuroimaging Initiative (ADNI) collection[1], aimed at measuring the progression of MCI and early AD by combining several biological markers and clinical assessment. From the whole ADNI collection, we chose all subjects with processed structural MRI and diagnosed into one of the three class labels described above ($C = 3$), yielding to 694 subjects and $N = 1377$ images ($\sim$ two images per subject) distributed as: 379 into HC (48% male, 72.9 ± 6.2 y/o), 726 into MCI (55% male, 71.4 ± 7.4 y/o), and 272 into AD (59% male, 73.2 ± 7.5 y/o).

The preprocessing stage is carried out fully automatic using the `FreeSurfer` pipeline tool[2] that processes the structural brain MRI scans to calculate morphological measurements with suitable test-retest reliability across scanner manufacturers and field strengths. The main preprocessing pipeline contains: intensity normalization and bias field correction, tessellation of gray/white matter boundaries, parcellation of the brain cortex, and segmentation of white matter from the rest of the brain. Besides, `FreeSurfer` computes structure-specific volume, area, and thickness measurements, where the cortical and subcortical volumes are normalized to each subject's Total Intracranial Volume [10]. As a result, the feature

---

[1] www.adni-info.org.
[2] freesurfer.nmr.mgh.harvard.edu.

sets extracted for each subject are concatenated into a single feature matrix $\boldsymbol{X}$ with size $N = 1377$ and $D = 311$. Namely, 69 features of Cortical Volumes (CV), 38 features of Subcortical Volumes (SV), and 68 features of Thickness Average (TA), Thickness Std (TS) and Surface Area (SA) set.

3.2 Optimization of Network Parameters

In the optimization stage, each layer is firstly initialized using the Glorot uniform sampling. Then, the walkback training algorithm jointly optimizes the network weights and biases during $T = 4$ steps [11]. At each walkback step, the Stochastic Gradient Descent (SGD) minimizes the Mean Squared Error as the loss function. SGD parameters are empirically fixed as 0.05, 0.9, and 0.99 for the learning rate, the momentum weight, and the multiplicative annealing factor, respectively. All simulations are executed on a GPU using the computation library `Theano`[3].

With respect to dGSN topology, the hyperbolic tangent `tanh` and `softmax` functions are applied as non-linear mappings at hidden and output layers, respectively. Besides, we use a two equally-sized hidden layers (i.e. $m_1 = m_2 = m$) with the number of hidden units tuned by an exhaustive search for the highest classification accuracy a_c within the framed range of $m \in [5, D]$ and the trade-off fixed to the unbiased value $\zeta = 0.5$. According to the results of a 5-fold cross-validation strategy shown in Fig. 2(a), the performance improves as the layer size increases, meaning that the enhancement of the system complexity promotes the class unwrapping. Therefore, we make the optimal value $m_{\mathrm{opt}} = 300$, when the dGSN model performs $a_c = 76.3\%$.

3.3 Relevance Analysis of the dGSN-Based Feature Learning

The initialization procedure using the CKA principle is carried out implementing each one of the needed kernels, learning the discriminative feature set at each hidden layer in Sect. 2.2. In particular, we use a Gaussian kernel for the hidden layers, $\kappa_{\mathcal{Z}}^l \left(\mathrm{d} \left(\boldsymbol{z}_{ti}^l, \boldsymbol{z}_{tj}^l \right) \right) = \exp \left(- \mathrm{d}^2 \left(\boldsymbol{z}_{ti}^l, \boldsymbol{z}_{tj}^l \right) / 2\sigma_l^2 \right)$ with bandwidth $\sigma_l \in \mathbb{R}^+$, and the Delta function implementing the output kernel, $\kappa_{\mathcal{Y}} \left(\boldsymbol{y}_i, \boldsymbol{y}_j \right) = \delta \left(\boldsymbol{y}_i - \boldsymbol{y}_j \right)$. Thus, the dGSN learning machine is initialized with the estimated matrices $\boldsymbol{W}^1 \in \mathbb{R}^{D \times m_{\mathrm{opt}}}$, $\boldsymbol{W}^2 \in \mathbb{R}^{m_{\mathrm{opt}} \times m_{\mathrm{opt}}}$, and $\boldsymbol{W}^3 \in \mathbb{R}^{m_{\mathrm{opt}} \times C}$, where m_{opt} is tuned as above explained.

For the sake of comparison, we also carry out the conventional random initialization approach testing the ζ parameter within the range $\{0.1, 0.2, \ldots, 0.9\}$. Figure 2(b) displays the classification accuracy performed by dGSN in either initialization case, random and CKA-based. Note that low values of ζ emphasize the discriminative term of the objective function, while large values favor the generative term. Therefore, the optimal trade-off (i.e., $\zeta = 0.3$ for random and 0.2 for CKA) allows the discriminative term contributing the most to the objective function. Nonetheless, the supervised features extracted by CKA obtain an overall accuracy that outperforms the baseline random initialization.

---

[3] http://deeplearning.net/software/theano/.

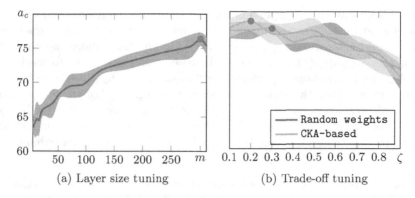

(a) Layer size tuning   (b) Trade-off tuning

Fig. 2. Mean and standard deviation of the accuracy performed by dGSN within the tested layer sizes and trade off values, where the red dot marks the best-reached value. (Color figure online)

Regarding to the feature relevance analysis, we measure the contribution of the D input features on building the latent spaces using the CKA-based learning as defined in Sect. 2.2. Aiming to provide a visual representation of the resulted relevance, we average this assessed contribution according to the corresponding anatomical structure as illustrated in Fig. 3. Thus, Fig. 3(a) and (b) hold the relevance at the first layer, so that the temporal, sensorimotor, and frontal lobes stand out as the most salient brain areas in terms of building the latent space. Figure 3(c) and (d) present the relevance change when moving from the first to the second layer and the second to the third layer, respectively. Note that deeper the abstraction layer, the more evident the structure contribution.

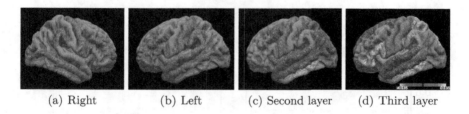

(a) Right   (b) Left   (c) Second layer   (d) Third layer

Fig. 3. Visual inspection of the obtained relevance for the brain areas. From left to right: contribution of the right and left hemispheres, relevance difference from the second to the first layer and third to the second layer.

3.4 Achieved Performance of Dementia Diagnosis

Here, we consider two scenarios of diagnosis, namely, multi-class and bi-class. Compared approaches, validated in the same scenarios, include regularized LDA (rLDA) [3], sparse logistic regression (SLR) [12], neural networks (NN-based) [13], and support vector machines (SVM-based) [14] classifiers. In either scenario of comparison, all algorithms are evaluated in terms of their classification performance: accuracy (a_c), area under the receiver-operating-characteristic curve (β), and class-wise true positive rate (τ). The area under the curve β is the weighted average of the area under the ROC curve calculated for each class.

Tables 1 and 2 display the performance measures accomplished by each classification approach in both diagnosis scenarios, respectively. For the first scenario, despite achieving lower τ and β values for the HC's, proposed dGSN-CKA outperforms the neural network-based and the generalized linear model concerning the remaining measures. For the second scenario, dGSN-CKA enhances the

Table 1. Classification performance on the testing groups for considered algorithms under evaluation criteria. *Results reported in the 2014 CADDementia challenge [1].

	a_c	τ^{HC}	τ^{MCI}	τ^{AD}	β	β^{HC}	β^{MCI}	β^{AD}
rLDA*	63.0	**96.9**	28.7	61.2	78.8	86.3	63.1	87.5
NN-based	70.9	78.4	66.6	68.3	85.3	**91.7**	78.4	88.3
GSN-CKA	**79.4**	78.0	**81.1**	**76.6**	**89.1**	89.7	**84.4**	**92.9**

Table 2. Classification performance on the pair-wise groups for considered algorithms under evaluation criteria. ($-$) Values not provided for the MCI vs. AD problem.

	HC vs MCI		HC vs AD		MCI vs AD		Average	
	a_c	β	a_c	β	a_c	β	a_c	β
SVM-based	–	73.5	–	92.0	–	68.6	–	78.0
SLR	57.3	61.0	71.2	78.0	68.9	65.2	65.8	68.0
GSN-CKA	**80.5**	**82.2**	**93.2**	**96.5**	**83.6**	**85.7**	85.7	88.1

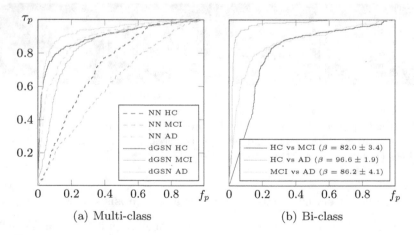

(a) Multi-class   (b) Bi-class

Fig. 4. ROC curves achieved by the best setup of NN and dGSN methods for both considered scenarios of diagnosis.

classification when compared to the baselines in the three tasks, namely, HC vs. MCI, HC vs. AD, and MCI vs. AD. Moreover, the most significant result is shown for MCI vs. AD, where the accuracy raises ∼14.7% point and the area under the curve ∼17.1% points, in comparison with the other algorithms. Besides, Fig. 4(a) compares the ROC curves for NN and dGSN classifiers tuned with the optimum parameter set. As seen, the dGSN performance betters the NN one in about ∼14.3%. Another aspect derived from the ROC curves is that the MCI class is the most complex to identify. Besides, the ROC curves in Fig. 4(b) show that classification tasks involving MCI are the most complex to solve, while HC subjects are easier to distinguish from Alzheimer's.

4   Discussion and Concluding Remarks

This work introduces a supervised feature extraction approach using a dGSN as a deep learning machine for automatic MRI-based dementia diagnosis. Aiming to improve the data interpretability and classification accuracy, we incorporate the available supervised knowledge into the dGSN initialization, employing the CKA principle.

In the parameter setting stage, the network layer size and the trade-off parameter prove to be the critical parameters that most influences the dGSN performance. Results obtained show that small or excessively large layer sizes lack the complexity to build a suitable discriminating model or tend to over-fit the data, so reducing the classifier performance. As regards the trade-off parameter, it is tuned by an exhaustive search procedure, reaching the best compromise between the generative and discriminative terms of the cost function.

Regarding the dGSN-based feature learning, the CKA principle is applied to initialize the network training aiming to introduce the supervised information of labels. Thus, the proposed feature extraction fosters the supervised discriminant information during the training stage improving the classifier performance. Besides, a relevance analysis is carried out by the downward dGSN mappings that back-propagate the projection information through the tied weights from the latent variables to the input data. As a result, the relevance analysis provided by dGSN highlights the most discriminating features, enhancing also the interpretation of the extracted deep feature set according to the clinical knowledge.

Finally, the trained dGSN-based classifier is evaluated in multi-class and bi-class scenarios of diagnosis. Obtained results show that the proposed dGSN-CKA allows modeling complex data relationships between the extracted features set improving the classification performance, with the additional benefit of reducing the class biasing. Physiologically, the relevance averaging over the anatomical structure turns out to be symmetrically distributed relating to the brain hemispheres, as well the structures that commonly are associated with dementia become more salient as the data is deeper projected. Therefore, the relevance of supervised deep features extracted provides useful clinical insights about the studied phenomenon. From both classification scenarios of dementia diagnosis,

MCI emerges as the class with the largest errors. Hence, discriminating the MCI remains challenging because of its widely heterogeneous distribution, the conversion to multiple neurological diseases, and the eventual turn back to HC.

As a future research direction, we will evaluate dGSN properties for predicting conversion from mild cognitive impairment to Alzheimer's disease, which is of particular interest in the medical field. We will also benefit from the discriminative properties of the CKA by introducing it in the cost function of the walkback training.

Acknowledgments. This work was supported by the research project 111974455497 founded by COLCIENCIAS.

References

1. Bron, E.E., Smits, M., et al.: Standardized evaluation of algorithms for computer-aided diagnosis of dementia based on structural MRI: the CADDementia challenge. NeuroImage **111**, 562–579 (2015)
2. Sabuncu, M.R., Konukoglu, E.: Clinical prediction from structural brain MRI scans: a large-scale empirical study. Neuroinformatics **13**(1), 31–46 (2015)
3. Sørensen, L., Pai, A., et al.: Dementia diagnosis using MRI cortical thickness, shape, texture, and volumetry. In: Proceedings of MICCAI Workshop Challenge on Computer-Aided Diagnosis of Dementia Based on Structural MRI Data, pp. 111–118 (2014)
4. Khedher, L., Ramírez, J., Górriz, J.M., Brahim, A., Illán, I.A.: Independent component analysis-based classification of Alzheimer's disease from segmented MRI data. In: Ferrández Vicente, J., Álvarez-Sánchez, J., de la Paz López, F., Toledo-Moreo, F., Adeli, H. (eds.) IWINAC 2015. LNCS, vol. 9107, pp. 78–87. Springer, Cham (2015). doi:10.1007/978-3-319-18914-7_9
5. Wachinger, C., Reuter, M., et al.: Domain adaptation for Alzheimer's disease diagnostics. NeuroImage **139**, 470–479 (2016)
6. Termenon, M., Graña, M., et al.: Brain MRI morphological patterns extraction tool based on extreme learning machine and majority vote classification. Neurocomputing **174**, 344–351 (2016)
7. Liu, S., Liu, S., et al.: Multimodal neuroimaging feature learning for multiclass diagnosis of Alzheimer's disease. IEEE Trans. Biomed. Eng. **62**(4), 1132–1140 (2015)
8. Suk, H.-I., Lee, S.-W., et al.: Hierarchical feature representation and multimodal fusion with deep learning for AD/MCI diagnosis. NeuroImage **101**, 569–582 (2014)
9. Brockmeier, A., Choi, J., et al.: Neural decoding with kernel-based metric learning. Neural Comput. **26**, 1080–1107 (2014)
10. Buckner, R.L., Head, D., et al.: A unified approach for morphometric and functional data analysis in young, old, and demented adults using automated atlas-based head size normalization: reliability and validation against manual measurement of total intracranial volume. NeuroImage **23**(2), 724–738 (2004)
11. Zöhrer, M., Pernkopf, F.: General stochastic networks for classification. In: Advances in Neural Information Processing Systems, vol. 27, pp. 2015–2023. Curran Associates Inc. (2014)

12. Zhan, L., Liu, Y., Alzheimer's Disease Neuroimaging Initiative ADNI, et al.: Boosting brain connectome classification accuracy in Alzheimer's disease using higher-order singular value decomposition. Front. Neurosci. **9**, 257 (2015)
13. Cárdenas-Peña, D., Collazos-Huertas, D., Castellanos-Dominguez, G.: Centered kernel alignment enhancing neural network pretraining for MRI-based dementia diagnosis. Comput. Math. Methods Med. **2016**, 10 p. (2016). doi:10.1155/2016/9523849. Article no. 9523849
14. Bron, E.E., Smits, M., et al.: Feature selection based on the SVM weight vector for classification of dementia. IEEE J. Biomed. Health Inform. **19**(5), 1617–1626 (2015)

Influence of Population Dependent Forward Models on Distributed EEG Source Reconstruction

E. Cuartas-Morales$^{(\boxtimes)}$, Y.R. Céspedes-Villar, J.D. Martínez-Vargas, L.F. Arteaga-Daza, and C. Castellanos-Dominguez

Signal Processing and Recognition Group, Universidad Nacional de Colombia, Manizales, Colombia
{ecuartasmo,yrcespedesv,jdmartinezv,lufarteagada, cgcastellanosd}@unal.edu.co

Abstract. In this study, we analyze how the forward model dependence on the study population influences the reconstruction of brain activity based on electroencephalographic (EEG) recordings. To this, we compare the source localization accuracy using generic and atlas-based head models, constructed with the Finite Difference Reciprocity method (FDRM). Additionally, we analyze the influence of including several tissues, as skull, scalp, gray matter, white matter, and cerebrospinal fluid. Comparison is carried out under a parametric empirical Bayesian (PEB) framework, that allows contrasting different forward modeling approaches using real data. Obtained results, based on event-related potentials (ERPs) of 31 subjects, show that the more realistic and more dependent on the study population the used head model, the better the ESI estimation.

Keywords: Forward model · Finite difference reciprocity method · EEG/ERP source imaging

1 Introduction

In the last years, multiple techniques for Electroencephalography (EEG) Source Imaging (ESI) solution have been developed for estimating, in a noninvasive way, the neural sources of electrical activity measured on the scalp. In this regard, these techniques require a volumetric conduction model (commonly known as EEG Forward Model), including information about the physical and geometrical properties of the head, and describing the electromagnetic field propagation of the neuronal activity throughout the head tissues to reach the scalp [9]. Hence,

E. Cuartas-Morales—This work was supported by *Prog. Nal. de Formación de Investigadores Generación del Bicentenario, 2012, Conv 528*, program *Jóvenes Investigadores e Innovadores, 2015, Conv 706*, and by the research project 111956933522 founded by COLCIENCIAS.

J.M. Ferrández Vicente et al. (Eds.): IWINAC 2017, Part I, LNCS 10337, pp. 374–383, 2017.
DOI: 10.1007/978-3-319-59740-9_37

the accuracy of ESI solutions is bounded on the capabilities of the forward model to properly describe the structural information provided by the individual Magnetic Resonance Image (MRI).

Nevertheless, acquiring MRIs for generating personalized head models is expensive, and in some cases unpractical. Consequently, head models are commonly constructed based on the anatomy of an arbitrary subject (generic head models), or the average of individual MRIs coregistered to a common space (atlas head models) [10]. As a result, in the absence of individual MRIs, an accurate representation of the brain geometry and conductivity of a subject inside a target population, may reduce localization errors in ESI.

Regarding the Forward Model computation, a 3-Tissues template head volume modeled with boundary element method (BEM) is often used, including scalp, skull and brain compartments [9]. However, these models do not usually include cerebrospinal fluid (CSF) and white matter (WM), which clearly affect the current-flow between sources and electrodes.

Consequently, for suitable EEG source reconstruction with Atlas-based head models, it is necessary to describe as accurately as possible the head geometry and conductivity of the target population, including age ranks, sociocultural levels, among others, and modeling the different conductive compartments in the human head in a realistic way [11].

In this work, we investigate whether the forward solution dependence on the study population, influence or not the source reconstruction based on EEG. In this regard, we create volumetric conductivity head models: (i) based on a Generic MRI, and (ii) based on a target population Atlas, using the Finite Difference Reciprocity Method (FDRM). Moreover, the forward models include from three (scalp, skull, and GM), to five (adding CSF and WM) tissues. Comparison is done regarding the achieved ESI precision. Obtained results prove that using realistic head models, based on the studied population, improves the performance of the ESI solution.

2   Methods

2.1   Forward Problem Framework

In the EEG source imaging (ESI), the forward problem estimates the electrode potential field, V, over the scalp that is generated due to current sources in the brain. Sources are modeled as current dipoles positioned inside the brain $r \in \mathbb{R}^{3 \times 1}$ with orientation $d \in \mathbb{R}^{3 \times 1}$. The scalar-valued potential $V(x, y, z) \subset V$ on the surface of a conductive volume x, y, z is defined by the Poisson equation as follows:

$$\nabla \left(\Sigma(x, y, z) \nabla V(x, y, z) \right) = I\delta(r - r_1) - I\delta(r - r_2), \tag{1}$$

where $I \in \mathbb{R}$ represents the current dipole magnitude, $\Sigma \in \mathbb{R}^{3 \times 3}$ is the conductivity tensor, and r_1 and r_2 are two coordinates positions determining the dipole direction. Notation $\delta(\cdot)$ stands for the delta function.

In case of the isotropic volumes, the conductivity $\Sigma(x, y, z)$ is scalar-valued. In this work we only use isotropic conductivities.

2.2 Forward Solution

For the numerical case, Eq. (1) is solved using FDRM for a 18-stencil representation as proposed in [3]:

$$\sum_{i=1}^{18} a_i \phi_i - \left(\sum_{i=1}^{18} a_i\right) \phi_0 = I\delta(\boldsymbol{r} - \boldsymbol{r}_1) - I\delta(\boldsymbol{r} - \boldsymbol{r}_2), \tag{2}$$

where the coefficient set $\{a_i \in \mathbb{R}\}$ holds the conductivity values and ensures the Dirichlet and Neumann boundary conditions [8], $\phi_i \in \mathbb{R}^{1 \times N_Z}$ is each discrete potential, being N_Z the non zero voxels where head tissues are present, ϕ_0 is the potential at the neighborhood origin.

Generally speaking, Eq. (2) results in a linear system that is solved using *BiCG stabilized* solver with *iLU* preconditioning [1]. However, the system implementation requires a high computational burden. To overcome this drawback, precalculated reciprocity potentials are employed to speed up the computation of the inverse solutions. As a result, we calculate a lead field matrix $\boldsymbol{L}_m \in \mathbb{R}^{N_c \times N_d}$ for a given electrode disposition with N_c channels, and source space with N_d sources (dipoles) located on the cortical surface with fixed orientation perpendicular to it.

2.3 Source Reconstruction

Given a $\boldsymbol{L}_m$ lead field matrix from a forward model, a distributed solution $\boldsymbol{Y} = \boldsymbol{L}_m \boldsymbol{J}_m + \boldsymbol{\varXi}$ is considered, with the aim of estimating brain activity. Here, $\boldsymbol{Y} \in \mathbb{R}^{N_c \times N_t}$ is the EEG data measured at N_t time samples, and $\boldsymbol{J}_m \in \mathbb{R}^{N_d \times N_t}$ is the amplitude of the N_d current dipoles. We assume that the EEG measured data are affected by zero mean Gaussian noise $\boldsymbol{\varXi} \in \mathbb{R}^{N_c \times N_t}$, with covariance $\boldsymbol{Q}_{\varXi} = \exp(\lambda_{\varXi}) \boldsymbol{I}_{N_c}$, being $\boldsymbol{I}_{N_c} \in \mathbb{R}^{N_c \times N_c}$ an identity matrix, and $\exp(\lambda_{\varXi}) \in \mathbb{R}$ an hyperparameter modulating the sensor noise variance. Furthermore, by assuming that $\boldsymbol{J}_m$ is a zero mean Gaussian process with prior covariance $\boldsymbol{Q} \in \mathbb{R}^{N_d \times N_d}$, brain activity estimation can be carried out in the form $\widehat{\boldsymbol{J}}_m = \boldsymbol{Q} \boldsymbol{L}_m^\top (\boldsymbol{Q}_{\varXi} + \boldsymbol{L}_m \boldsymbol{Q} \boldsymbol{L}_m^\top)^{-1} \boldsymbol{Y}$. We use two different alternatives to supply the source covariance matrix $\boldsymbol{Q}$:

Empirical Bayesian Beamformer (EBB): that assumes one global prior for the source covariance main diagonal (the off-diagonal elements are zero, i.e., no correlations assumed). The prior source variance $\boldsymbol{q} = [q_1, \ldots, q_d, \ldots, q_{Nd}] \in \mathbb{R}^{N_d \times 1}, \forall q_d \in \mathbb{R}^+$ is computed for every dipole in the following way:

$$q_d = (\boldsymbol{l}_d^\top \boldsymbol{Y} \boldsymbol{Y}^\top \boldsymbol{l}_d)^{-1} / \delta_d, \quad \forall d = 1, \ldots, N_d, \tag{3}$$

where $\boldsymbol{l}_d \in \mathbb{R}^{N_d \times 1}$ is the d–th column of $\boldsymbol{L}_m$, and $\delta_d = 1/\boldsymbol{l}_d^\top \boldsymbol{l}_d$ is a normalization parameter. At the end, the source covariance matrix is calculated as $\boldsymbol{Q} = \exp(\lambda_p) \operatorname{diag}(\boldsymbol{q})$.

Multiple Sparse Priors (MSP): where the source covariance matrix is constructed as a sum of a set of P patches $\{Q_p, p = 1, \ldots, P\}$ each one reflecting one potentially activated region of cortex, weighted by the respective hyperparameter λ_p, as follows [2]:

$$Q = \sum_{p=1}^{P} \exp(\lambda_p) Q_p \tag{4}$$

2.4   Assessment Quality Measure of Source Estimation Solutions

To estimate the hyperparameter set, we use the so termed free energy [12]. In this regard, for a given EEG recording and a certain forward model m, the free energy can be expressed as [5]:

$$F(m) = -\frac{N_t}{2} Tr(\boldsymbol{\Delta}^{-1} \boldsymbol{C}) - \frac{N_t}{2} ln\,|\boldsymbol{\Delta}| - \frac{N_c N_t}{2} ln 2\pi - \frac{1}{2}(\boldsymbol{\mu} - \boldsymbol{\eta})^T \boldsymbol{\Omega}^{-1}(\boldsymbol{\mu} - \boldsymbol{\eta})$$
$$+ \frac{1}{2} ln\,|\boldsymbol{\Upsilon}\boldsymbol{\Omega}^{-1}|, \tag{5}$$

where $\boldsymbol{\Delta} \in \mathbb{R}^{N_c \times N_c}$ is the estimated model covariance, computed as $\boldsymbol{\Delta} = \boldsymbol{LQL}^T + \boldsymbol{Q}_\Xi$; $\boldsymbol{C} \in \mathbb{R}^{N_c \times N_c}$ is the measured data covariance, $\boldsymbol{\mu}, \boldsymbol{\eta} \in \mathbb{R}^{N_p \times 1}$ are the prior and posteriors means of the hyperparameters $\{\lambda_\Xi, \lambda_p\}$. Likewise, $\boldsymbol{\Upsilon}, \boldsymbol{\Omega} \in \mathbb{R}^{P \times P}$ are the posterior and prior hyperparameter covariances. $|\cdot|$ represent the matrix determinant operator. Therefore, the Free Energy estimated in Eq. (5) can be considered as the difference between the model accuracy (the first two terms) and the model complexity (the last two terms). The Free Energy can be maximized using standard variational schemes [12].

Moreover, the values corresponding with different forward models m can be used to compare source reconstructions using Bayesian model selection [4]. In turn, the individual log Bayes factor between two models is defined as:

$$\log(\psi_{(m_1, m_2)}) = \frac{p(Y|m_1)}{p(Y|m_2)} = F(m_1) - F(m_2). \tag{6}$$

Here, Bayesian model selection is used to validate the influence of patient dependent forward models on the sources reconstruction task. This is carried out by calculating the log group Bayes factor which is the sum over subjects of individual log Bayes factors:

$$\log(\Psi) = \sum_{n=1}^{N} \log(\psi_{(m_i, m_j)}^n), \tag{7}$$

where, the subscripts i,j refer to the models being compared, and N is the number of subjects. According to [7], a model can be chosen in favor of other when there is a difference larger than 3 units.

3 Experiments

We investigate a key aspect of the forward model for distributed solutions to the EEG inverse problem, namely, the influence of the lead field matrix in source localization due to forward models that are dependent or not from the study population. In this regard, we consider two different scenarios: (i) Lead-field matrix from a Generic template, (ii) Lead-field matrix derived from an MRI Atlas of the study population. Consequently, we analyze, in the absence of a subject specific MR image, whether the inclusion of demographic structural information to create the forward model improves or not the EEG source reconstruction. In both cases (Generic and Atlas), we construct FDRM head models including five different tissues, and they are compared within the context of two various types of source priors, EBB, and MSP. The resulting models are compared based on ERP data of 31 subjects using Bayesian model selection for group studies. The testing outline is shown in Fig. 1.

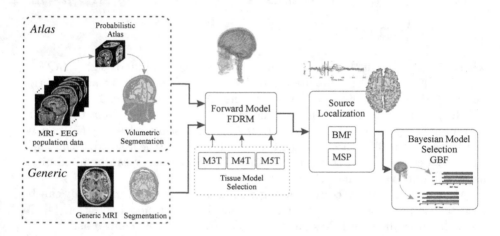

Fig. 1. Schematic representation of the tested methodology.

3.1 Database

EEG/ERP Data Description: The data are collected from 31 children within an age range from 5 to 6 years old, and two socio-cultural levels (high medium and low medium). The sample is randomly selected from preschool, elementary, and secondary courses at private and public schools in the Manizales city. For legal purposes, the children's parents agreed their participation in research through written permission. According to the historical data supplied by the children's parents, exclusion criteria is established for mental retardation, neurological antecedents (history of head trauma, epilepsy, and related) and psychiatric (psychiatric hospitalizations history, autism, and related).

The experimental protocol consists of a stimulation interface (individually auditive or visual) designed following the oddball paradigm with 20% target and

80% non-target stimulus. Simultaneously, Electroencephalogram (EEG) acquisition with stimulus marker signal is carried out. EEG recordings are performed with a single *Easy III EEG amplifier* provided by *Cadwell*, taken symmetrically from 19 electrodes with standard international system positions 10–20. Here, we center the analysis of ERPs extracted from EEG using an average process for target stimulus supported on the marker signal.

Magnetic Resonance Imaging (MRI) Data Description: With the purpose of obtaining a single structural head model for the EEG database, including the particular demographic dependence, we build a structural atlas from 10 of the 31 patients. In this study, 1.5 T MRIs are recorded by a General Electric OPTIMA MR 360 scanner with the following parameters: 1 mm × 1 mm pixel size, $T_R = 6$, $T_E = 1.8$, $T_I = 450$, and sagittal slices of 256×256 size and 1 mm spacing. Three 1.5 T MRIs are acquired for each subject and further averaged using the free surfer suite for enhancing the signal-to-noise ratio. Moreover, the Diffeomorphic Anatomical Registration Exponentiated Lie Algebra (DARTEL) algorithm generates the customized templates for the considered anatomical structures. DARTEL nonlinearly transforms individual probabilistic segmentations, initially provided by SPM, and merges them into a single template. Such a procedure is repeated a fixed number of iterations increasing the template crispness. DARTEL is applied using the default parameters: Linear elastic energy regularization, Levenberg-Marquardt optimization, and six outer iterations to construct the atlas from the 10 different patients, including the scalp, skull, cerebrospinal fluid (CSF), gray matter (GM) and white matter (WM) tissues.

First row of Fig. 2 shows the $3D$ surface of the skull, GM, and WM for the Atlas segmentation. Moreover, second and third rows show the axial, sagittal and coronal views for segmentations of three and five tissues.

In order to compare, a Generic model is created from a single MRI data of a healthy male patient [1], where the same five tissues are segmented using free surfer. In both cases (Atlas and Generic), the 19 EEG electrodes are coregistered to the scalp surface using field trip.

3.2   Forward and Inverse Problem Solution

From the segmentation with 5 tissues, three different forward models are defined for both, the Generic, and the Atlas MRI. The first model (M3T) contains three tissues, scalp, skull and GM. The second model (M4T) also holds CSF, while the third model (M5T) includes all the five tissues. The conductivities are set to $scalp = 0.33\,\mathrm{S/m}$, $skull = 0.02\,\mathrm{S/m}$, $CSF = 1.54\,\mathrm{S/m}$, $GM = 0.33\,\mathrm{S/m}$, and $WM = 0.14\,\mathrm{S/m}$, as recommended in [6]. Additionally, the volumetric forward models are calculated using the FDRM technique (see Sect. 2.2) in a $1 \times 1 \times 1$ mm volumetric space for both, the Generic and the Atlas MRI data. In addition, we use reciprocity potential precalculations for the 10–20 EEG system of the database, in order to speed up the inverse calculations.

With the aim of reconstructing the source space, we employ two ESI solutions, EBB and MSP. The source reconstruction is carried out to the ERPs

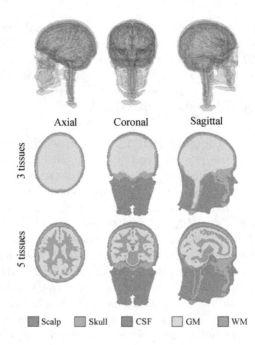

Fig. 2. Segmented head model: top: 3D surface of the skull, GM and WM. Segmentations including three and five tissues in the middle, and bottom, respectively.

extracted from each subject in each stimulation condition, i.e., a visual target, visual non-target, auditory target and auditory non-target. For MSP, the priors used to form the set of covariance components are those implemented in the Statistical Parametric Mapping (SPM12) software package. That is, we use 512 covariance components with selected columns of a Greens function covering the entire cortical surface. In order to perform this optimization scheme, we use a greedy search (GS) algorithm. Later, in both inverse solutions (EBB and MSP), the hyperparameters are tuned by maximizing the Free energy through the Restricted Maximum Likelihood (ReML) algorithm.

3.3   Group Studies for Model Selection

To compare the different models considered in this study, i.e., M3T, M4T and M5T for *Generic* and *Atlas* structural data, and each of the inverse solutions, we apply Bayesian model selection for group studies. In this regard, we compare the Free energy values of the inverse solutions over subjects, corresponding with the ERPs elicited by each stimulation condition. Then, the log group Bayes factor (Ψ) is computed, as explained in Sect. 2.4.

3.4   Results

Figure 3 shows an overview of the log group Bayes factor (Ψ) for each of the stimulus conditions and tested models. Here, the closer to zero the Ψ value, the better the reconstruction of a particular model. As seen, the difference between log group Bayes factors of Atlas and Generic models is greater than three, corresponding with substantial evidence for the Atlas based head models.

In the one hand, for the generic head models, there are small differences regarding the number of tissues used to create the lead field matrix. In turn, with the generic models, Ψ values for M3T, M4T, and M5T remain almost the same within each stimulation condition. On the other hand, for the atlas-based head models, M3T obtain the worst performance. This behavior is more noticeable with MSP as ESI solution. Furthermore, as expected, the performance improves when CSF tissue is included in the lead field matrix construction (M4T), since it yields a more realistic model. Nevertheless, the performance remains almost the same when WM tissue is included (M5T), producing a small improvement (less than three units in the Ψ value). This result can be explained given the lack of anisotropic conductivity values for some tissues, as WM and the skull.

Moreover, regarding the ESI solution, for all the tested models and stimuli, EBB overcomes MSP. This situation can be explained as ERPs produce distributed source activity, which can be better explained if source covariance components are independent, as in EBB, unlike the sparse covariance components pursued by MSP.

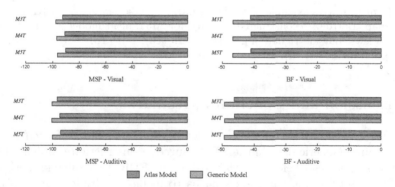

Fig. 3. Log GBF for: visual and auditive stimulation, BMF and MSP brainmapping method.

Figure 4 shows a representative example of the analyzed data. At the top, the ERP and topographic map calculated for the interval from 227 to 383 ms (black vertical lines) is shown, where the P300 wave appears. This wave is an ERP component elicited in the process of decision making. As expected, in the channel space, most energy components appear in the electrodes covering the parietal lobe. Likewise, in the source space, most activity in the P300 component also appears in the parietal lobe. This activity is highly expected in oddball paradigm experiments because it is related to decision-making processes. Moreover, some activity in the parietal lobe and cingulate gyrus, which are related to attention and working memory processes.

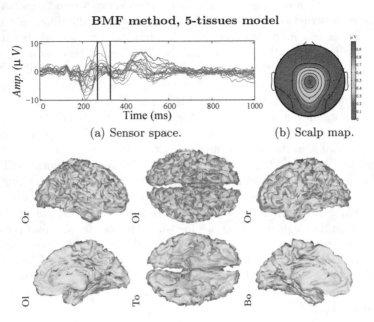

Fig. 4. Representative example of analyzed data. Top: sensor space - ERP and topographic map. Bottom: reconstructed activity for M5T head model and EBB as ESI solution. Views: outside right (Or), outside left (Ol), top (To), bottom (Bo), inside right (Ir) and inside left (Il).

4   Discussion and Concluding Remarks

In this work, we study the influence of demographic dependent forward models (Atlas) against Generic data in the EEG source reconstruction problem. To this end, we calculate lead field potentials using the FDRM volumetric method for both, Atlas and Generic data, allowing us to include multiple tissues. Namely, our first M3T tissue model includes scalp, skull and GM areas, similar to the standard Boundary Finite Elements Method that approximates surface potentials as a forward solution. Additionally, the second tissue model includes CSF (M4T), and the last one also includes GM (M5T). We used the MSP and EBB techniques as source reconstruction methods together with Group Bayes Factor, as a measure to analyze the quality of the reconstructed activity with different lead fields.

Analyzing the study population influence, we find strong log group Bayes Factor evidence (mayor than three units) for lead fields potentials from structural data that depends on the EEG study population using with both source estimation techniques (MSP and EBB). Is important to note that our Generic models are not in the age range of our demographic dependent Atlas. However, the results clearly favor the Atlas even in the case of different tissue spaces.

By assuming a 3-layered isotropic conducting approximation of the head (M3T), the results show that it is a strong simplification of reality. Regarding this fact, we find that including the CSF tissue improves the log group Bayes factor (Ψ) when we deal with demographic dependent forward models. Also, the results show little improvement with the inclusion of the WM area. This result can be explained because we are not considering the anisotropic behavior of this tissue, as it is difficult to obtain and has a high patient dependent distribution [13]. Therefore, we recommend as future work, the inclusion of anisotropic conductivities for a more realistic analysis.

References

1. Cuartas-Morales, E., Daniel-Acosta, C., Castellanos-Dominguez, G.: iLU preconditioning of the anisotropic-finite-difference based solution for the EEG forward problem. In: Ferrández Vicente, J.M., Álvarez-Sánchez, J.R., de la Paz López, F., Toledo-Moreo, F.J., Adeli, H. (eds.) IWINAC 2015. LNCS, vol. 9107, pp. 408–418. Springer, Cham (2015). doi:10.1007/978-3-319-18914-7_43
2. Friston, K., Harrison, L., et al.: Multiple sparse priors for the M/EEG inverse problem. NeuroImage **39**(3), 1104–1120 (2008)
3. Hallez, H., Vanrumste, B., et al.: Dipole estimation errors in EEG source localization due to not incorporating anisotropic conductivities of white matter in realistic head models, October 2007
4. Henson, R.N., Mattout, J., et al.: Selecting forward models for MEG source-reconstruction using model-evidence. NeuroImage **46**(1), 168–176 (2009)
5. Martínez-Vargas, J.D., López, J.D., Baker, A., Castellanos-Dominguez, G., Woolrich, M.W., Barnes, G.: Non-linear parameter estimates from non-stationary MEG data. Front. Neurosci. **10**, 366 (2016). PMC. Web. 11 May 2017
6. Montes, V., van Mierlo, P., et al.: Influence of skull modeling approaches on EEG source localization. Brain Topogr. **27**(1), 95–111 (2013)
7. Penny, W.D., Stephan, K.E., et al.: Comparing dynamic causal models. NeuroImage **22**(3), 1157–1172 (2004)
8. Saleheen, H.I., Ng, K.T.: New finite difference formulations for general inhomogeneous anisotropic bioelectric problems. IEEE Trans. Biomed. Eng. **44**(9), 800–809 (1997)
9. Strobbe, G., van Mierlo, P., et al.: Bayesian model selection of template forward models for EEG source reconstruction. NeuroImage **93**, 11–22 (2014)
10. Valdés-Hernández, P.A., Von Ellenrieder, N., et al.: Approximate average head models for EEG source imaging. J. Neurosci. Methods **185**(1), 125–132 (2009)
11. Vorwerk, J., Cho, J.-H., et al.: A guideline for head volume conductor modeling in EEG and MEG. NeuroImage **100**, 590–607 (2014)
12. Wipf, D.P., Owen, J.P., et al.: Robust Bayesian estimation of the location, orientation, and time course of multiple correlated neural sources using MEG. NeuroImage **49**(1), 641–655 (2010)
13. Wolters, C.H., Anwander, A., et al.: Influence of tissue conductivity anisotropy on EEG/MEG field and return current computation in a realistic head model: a simulation and visualization study using high-resolution finite element modeling. NeuroImage **30**, 813–826 (2006)

Influence of Anisotropic Blood Vessels Modeling on EEG Source Localization

E. Cuartas-Morales[1(✉)], Angel Torrado-Carvajal[2],
Juan Antonio Hernandez-Tamames[2], Norberto Malpica[2],
and G. Castellanos-Dominguez[1]

[1] Signal Processing and Recognition Group, Universidad Nacional de Colombia,
Manizales, Colombia
{ecuartasmo,cgcastellanosd}@unal.edu.co
[2] Medical Image Analysis and Biometry Lab, Universidad Rey Juan Carlos,
Madrid, Spain
{angel.torrado,juan.tamames,norberto.malpica}@urjc.es

Abstract. Reconstruction of source neural activity has an increasing importance due to its high time resolution, promoting its application in diagnosis of neurodegenerative and cognitive tasks. To improve the accuracy of reconstruction, we study the influence of anisotropic blood vessels in the EEG-based source localization solution, including several tissues. To this end, we develop a model that reflects physical properties of the head volume based on collected angiographic data. From obtained results of real data, we find that omission of the anisotropic blood vessels within the forward modeling may result in potential discrepancies larger than $35\,\mu V$ and dipole localization errors greater than 15 mm, especially, in deep brain areas.

1 Introduction

There are several neuroimaging techniques for monitoring and extracting more accurate information from the human brain, improving their impact on clinical applications like the medical treatment, surgery planning, or other customary brain research tasks [1]. To date, the Magnetic Resonance Imaging (MRI) or Computed Tomography (CT) has widely shown that their joint action along with functional analysis techniques (particularly, ElectroEncephaloGraphy – EEG) allows overcoming the often reported weakness in the single modality analysis. Thus, the combination of multi-modal information (incorporating patient-oriented models) become a useful tool in diagnosis and brain surgery planning, being in most cases the only suitable examination tool due to the high risk of alternative surgical interventions [2].

E. Cuartas-Morales—This work was supported by *Prog. Nal. de Formación de Investigadores Generación del Bicentenario, 2012, Conv 528*, program *Jóvenes Investigadores e Innovadores, 2015, Conv 706*, and by the research project 111974455497 founded by COLCIENCIAS.

© Springer International Publishing AG 2017
J.M. Ferrández Vicente et al. (Eds.): IWINAC 2017, Part I, LNCS 10337, pp. 384–393, 2017.
DOI: 10.1007/978-3-319-59740-9_38

Construction of the forward brain models for neural activity estimation from EEG faces several issues, being two the most challenging: (i) Accurate segmentation of the high amount of tissues inherent to the head volume, (ii) Development of anisotropic models to reflect the relevant physical properties of the human head adequately, influencing the propagation of brain electrical activity. Towards the former goal, the tissue segmentation is usually carried out based on the extracted information from a large series of two-dimensional slices of either MRI or CT, yielding the suitable head volume. Still, this task must be performed so that every slice must be registered within a single coordinate system to obtain a coherent three-dimensional volume, producing a gray scale dataset demarcating each one of the considered tissues [3]. In practice, the areas that are more likely to be segmented are the scalp (where the EEG electrodes are placed), skull, cerebro-spinal fluid, gray and white matter. Yet, this list of tissues is not enough to achieve the realistic and accurate forward models. Therefore, there is a need for incorporating a higher number of the brain structures.

Regarding the anisotropic behavior of head tissues, few works address the forward model calculation with a large number or tissues or even with anisotropy. However, the inclusion of anisotropy requires the use of volumetric techniques, like Finite Difference Method (FDM), rather than the well-known Boundary Finite Method. Here, we use the FDM reciprocity method (FDRM) to incorporate, not only volumetric information of the head tissues but also anisotropy in the forward solution. Therefore, we analyze the influence of introducing several tissues, namely, fat, muscle, eyeballs, and blood vessels. We also build an anisotropic model for blood vessels based on the contribution of blood-flow-induced conductivity [4]. Blood vessels are considered for measuring their influence as an essential head tissue within the EEG source localization problem.

For the purpose of evaluation, we perform testing on four different subjects who underwent an MRI study of patient-specific tissue model generation. Information about anisotropic areas of the white matter is extracted from Diffusion Weighted Imaging (DWI) data [5]. Besides, a segmentation mask of arteries obtained from a T2 angiogram is processed to estimate the direction of blood flow. From the results obtained on real data, we prove that the omission of the anisotropic blood vessels may result in potential discrepancies larger than $35\,\mu V$ in the forward solution and dipole localization errors greater than $15\,mm$, especially, in deep brain areas.

2   Material and Methods

2.1   Data Preprocessing

Construction of the Tissue Model. We carry out the tissue models based on the information extracted from T1-weighted, IDEAL, and TOF volumes by using the pipeline outlined in Fig. 1.

Image preprocessing was carried out using 3D Slicer built-in modules. The preprocessing steps included: MRI bias correction (N4 ITK MRI bias correction), and Registration (BRAINS) for movement correction. Cortical Segmentation,

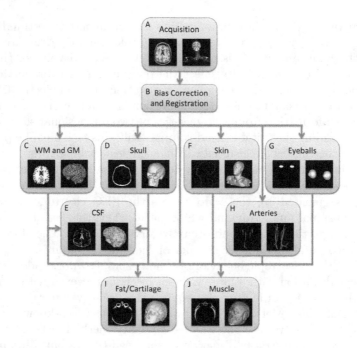

Fig. 1. Automatic segmentation pipeline for patient-specific MRI tissue models. Images are acquired with our MRI protocol (A). Bias correction and registration step (B). Freesurfer cortical segmentation (C). Cross-modality multi-atlas label-fusion skull segmentation (D). Residual and ventricular CSF segmentation (E). Skin segmentation (F). Eyeballs extraction (G). Approximation of the arteries (H). Remaining tissues are classified as fat (I) and muscle (J).

including brain white matter (WM) gray matter (GM), and cerebro-spinal fluid (CSF), was performed in the T1-weighted volume using FreeSurfer [6]. The skull was estimated using a multi-atlas and label fusion-based approach [7]. To this end, we applied to a CT database the Simultaneous Truth and Performance Level Estimation (STAPLE) algorithm [8]. The remaining CSF was computed as the residual of the skull and the FreeSurfer segmentation using a GNU Octave script. To segment the skin we developed an algorithm to calculate the background noise variance and thresholds of the anisotropically filtered volume. Then, Gaussian smoothing was applied to reduce aliasing artifacts in the skin surface. The eyeballs were segmented by applying a threshold and edge detection algorithm to the IDEAL in-phase head sequences. We also performed a smooth approximation of the main arteries by using an expectation-maximization algorithm to the median filtered TOF images. The remaining tissue was classified in muscle and fat/cartilage, using the expectation-maximization algorithm on the IDEAL fat and water images.

Modeling Anisotropic Blood Vessels. To perform segmentation of the arteries, we apply a mask that is extracted from a T2 angiogram and enables estimation of the blood flow direction. Then, a kernel with six directions is convolved with the mask to produce a normalized vector map that describes the eigenvectors inside all arteries. Further, we adjust the anisotropic blood vessel model to the anisotropic finite difference reciprocity method (AFDRM) algorithm [9], setting a local affine transformation A that points out towards the local eigenvector of the found gradient of the vessels. As in [4], the anisotropic blood conductivity at the maximum movement is defined as $\hat{\sigma} = \text{diag}(\sigma_b, \sigma_a, \sigma_b)$, where a $\sigma_a = 0.21\,\text{S/m}$, and $\sigma_b = 0.49\,\text{S/m}$. We fix $\sigma = A\hat{\sigma}A^\top$ for the local to global transformation.

DWI Tensor Calculation. Though MRI-T1 data is employed to build the structural head models, there is no information about anisotropic conductivity at each voxel. On the other hand, anisotropic conductivity shares a set of common eigenvectors with DWI diffusion tensors. Therefore, symmetrical diffusion tensors, $D \in \mathbb{R}^{3\times3}$, have eigenvalues that hold the voxel molecular mobility along the local directions, (x, y, z), where the ratio in each voxel between the largest eigenvalue and the average of the two other eigenvalues of the diffusion tensor is a fixed value [5]. Further, each DWI is corrected for eddy currents using FSL, and the Diffusion Tensor Images (DTI) are reconstructed applying the Diffusion-Toolkit [10]. Finally, we perform registration of DTI to the anatomical T1 image space by employing the FLIRT tool, using the preprocessed DWI $b0$ image.

2.2   Forward Problem Framework

As regards the EEG source reconstruction, the forward problem estimates an electrode potential field, V, at a specific point, (x, y, z), on the scalp, which is generated due to dipole sources inside the brain. Sources are modeled as current dipoles placed at position $r \in \mathbb{R}^3$ with orientation $d \in \mathbb{R}^3$. The scalar-valued potential $V(x, y, z) \subset V$ on the surface of a conductive volume x, y, z is defined by the Poisson equation as below:

$$\nabla\left(\Sigma(x, y, z)\nabla V(x, y, z)\right) = I\delta(r - r_1) - I\delta(r - r_2) \tag{1}$$

where $I \in \mathbb{R}$ is the current dipole magnitude, $\Sigma \in \mathbb{R}^{3\times3}$ is the conductivity tensor, and r_1 and r_2 are the two concrete coordinates determining the dipole direction, respectively. Notation $\delta(\cdot)$ stands for the delta function.

In the case of isotropic volumes, the conductivity $\Sigma(x, y, z)$ is scalar-valued, while the conductivity becomes a tensor in anisotropic volumes as below:

$$\Sigma_h^{(j)} = T^{(j)\top}\Sigma_s^{(j)}T^{(j)} \tag{2}$$

where Σ_h^j is the conductivity head matrix defined upon the uniform Cartesian coordinate system at the element j; $T \in \mathbb{R}^{3\times3}$ is a rotation transfer matrix defined by the orthogonal unit eigenvectors from the local to the global coordinate system; $\boldsymbol{\Sigma}_s^{(j)} = \mathrm{diag}(\sigma_{rad}^{(j)}, \sigma_{\tan}^{(j)}, \sigma_{\tan}^{(j)})$ is a diagonal matrix holding the local conductivity values in the tangential, $\sigma_{\tan}^{(j)}$, and radial directions, $\sigma_{rad}^{(j)}$, respectively. Additionally, we use the volume constrain introduced by [11].

2.3   Implemented EEG Forward Solution

We solve Eq. (1) numerically through the anisotropic finite difference methodology that is based on a 18-neighborhood representation as follows:

$$\sum_{i=1}^{18} a_i \phi_i - \left(\sum_{i=1}^{18} a_i \right) \phi_0 = I\delta(\boldsymbol{r} - \boldsymbol{r}_1) - I\delta(\boldsymbol{r} - \boldsymbol{r}_2) \tag{3}$$

where the $a_i \in \mathbb{R}$ coefficients hold the conductivity values and ensure the Dirichlet and Neumann boundary conditions, $\phi_i \in \mathbb{R}^{1 \times N_Z}$ are the discrete potentials, being N_Z the non-zero voxels, and ϕ_0 is the potential placed at the neighborhood center. Consequently, Eq. (3) results in a linear system $\boldsymbol{A}\phi = \boldsymbol{I}$ with unknown terms ϕ, that is solved using incomplete LU preconditioning and the BiCG-Stabilized solver as discussed in detail in [9]. However, due to the demanded high computational burden, precalculated reciprocity potentials are employed to speed up the computation of the inverse solution.

2.4   EEG Dipole Source Estimation

Within the inverse problem framework, we estimate the pairwise dipole parameters $(\hat{\boldsymbol{r}}, \hat{\boldsymbol{d}})$ by calculating the best electrode potentials, $\boldsymbol{v}_m$, that we minimize as follows:

$$(\hat{\boldsymbol{r}}, \hat{\boldsymbol{d}}) = \min_{r,d} \left\{ \frac{\|\boldsymbol{v}_e - \boldsymbol{v}_m(\boldsymbol{r}, \boldsymbol{d})\|_2^2}{\|\boldsymbol{v}_e\|_2^2} + c(\boldsymbol{r}) \right\} \tag{4}$$

where $\boldsymbol{v}_e \in \mathbb{R}^{N_d \times 1}$ are the vector of electrode potentials of the analytical reference model, $\boldsymbol{v}_m \in \mathbb{R}^{N_d \times 1}$ are the electrode potential vector estimated by the numerical test models, N_d the number of considered dipoles, and the term $c(\boldsymbol{r}) \in \mathbb{R}^+$ is a penalization parameter that is set to zero for dipole positions inside the gray matter, otherwise it is very large. Notation $\| \cdot \|_2$ stands for the Euclidean norm.

The procedure includes both the *reference* and *test* models to estimate the dipole error. Therefore, we initially compute the electrode potentials $\boldsymbol{v}_e$ and then the dipole parameters, $(\hat{\boldsymbol{r}}, \hat{\boldsymbol{d}})$. Namely, we introduce the following dipole localization error (DLE):

$$\varepsilon_L = \|\hat{\boldsymbol{r}} - \boldsymbol{r}\|_2 \tag{5}$$

3   Experimental Setup

3.1   DWI and Structural MRI Database

We validate the influence of anisotropic blood vessels modeling on EEG source localization, using data acquired from four healthy volunteers (three males and one female, mean age 35.00 ± 6.68 y, range: 28 y–44 y). Written informed consent was obtained from all subjects participating in this study. Images of the head were acquired on a General Electric Signa HDxt 3.0T MR scanner using the body coil for excitation and an 8-channel quadrature brain coil for reception. Imaging was performed using an isotropic 3DT1w SPGR sequence with $TR = 8.7$ ms, $TE = 3.2$ ms, $TI = 400$ ms, $NEX = 1$, acquisition $FOV = 260$ mm, matrix $= 320 \times 160$, resolution $= 1 \times 1 \times 1$ mm, flip angle $= 12$; an IDEAL T2 sequence with $TR = 3000$ ms, $TE = 81.9$ ms, $NEX = 6$, $FOV = 260$ mm, acquisition matrix $= 320 \times 160$, flip angle $= 90$, a Time of Flight (TOF) sequence consisting of 8 volumes with 6 slices overlap and $TR = 20$ ms, $TE = 2.1$ ms, $NEX = 1$, acquisition $FOV = 224$ mm, matrix $= 224 \times 224$, resolution $= 1 \times 1 \times 1$ mm, flip angle $= 15$, and a DWI sequence with $TR = 9200$ ms, $TE = 83.8$ ms, $TI = 0$ ms, $NEX = 1$, acquisition $FOV = 240$ mm, matrix $= 100 \times 100$, flip angle $= 90$, directions $= 45$, thickness $= 2$ mm.

All tested data (T1, IDEAL, and *DWI*) are aligned with a voxel similarity-based affine registration procedure in order to correct subject orientation and geometrical distortions. The registered *DWI* data were re-sampled to $1 \times 1 \times 1$ *mm* using the *FSL* toolbox. We used the AFDRM numerical algorithm to get the forward calculations in a normalized model with $1 \times 1 \times 1$ *mm* voxel partition, and the registered *DWI* data were used to approximate the anisotropic conductivity tensors in the white matter. Figure 2 shows the image segmentation for 9-tissues (left) and 5-tissues (right) distribution.

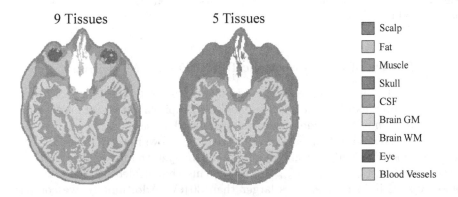

Fig. 2. Tissue segmentation.

In all described simulations, we test all considered models and patient data sets using the *10–20* EEG standard system with 23 electrodes and 22 lead pairs in a reciprocity approach with at least 3 million non-zero potentials using the AFDRM algorithm described in [9]. We carry out a separate test with two different relative residuals limit (10^{-6} and 10^{-13}) for the iLU preconditioning BiCG-Stabilized solver, finding that the differences are not relevant to forward calculations for $1 \times 1 \times 1$ mm resolutions. Regarding this, the algorithm takes about 1 min for a single lead pair calculation using 10^{-6} relative residual limit in an Intel Xeon 3.4 GHz processor with 64 Gb RAM.

In order to estimate the Dipole localization errors, we compare the four different patients, choosing the most complex head model as the reference that contains 9-tissues (anisotropic skull, white matter and blood vessels) against a simple 5-tissues model (only scalp, skull, CSF, grey and white brain, including also anisotropic skull and white matters). Results show a *DLE* larger than 30 mm in the deeper zones of the brain, and also a *DLE* larger than 20 mm in intercortical areas of the grey matter. Figure 3 shows the *DLE* for a single patient in 3 different planes.

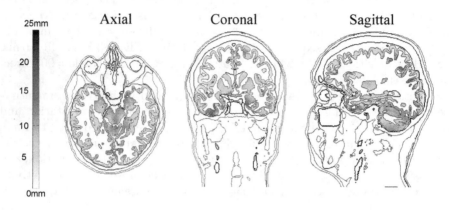

Fig. 3. Dipole localization errors for a 9-tissues segmentation against a simplify 5-tissues head model.

3.2   Influence of the Anisotropic Blood Vessels Modeling

We analyze the influence of anisotropic blood vessels in the four head models patients, chosen as *reference* the 9-tissues anisotropic blood vessel model against an 8-tissues *simplified* model neglecting the blood vessels.

Figure 4 shows the four patients (P1 trough P4 rows) in three different views (frontal, posterior and bottom columns). We analyze the forward potential difference norm ($\|V_{reference} - V_{simplify}\|$) showing that neglecting the anisotropic blood vessels induce differences larger than $30\,\mu V$. Additionally, we compared a reference head model with anisotropic blood vessels, against the same model neglecting the vessel segmentation obtaining *DLE* larger than 67 mm in zones near to the Willis polygon (deep brain areas), with a mean error of 4 mm for the *GM* area.

3.3   Computational Considerations

For the above-described simulations, we test all considered models and patient data sets using the *10–20* EEG standard system with 23 electrodes and 22 leaders in a reciprocity approach with at least 3 million non-zero potentials using the AFDRM algorithm described in the Sect. 2.3. We carry out a separate test with

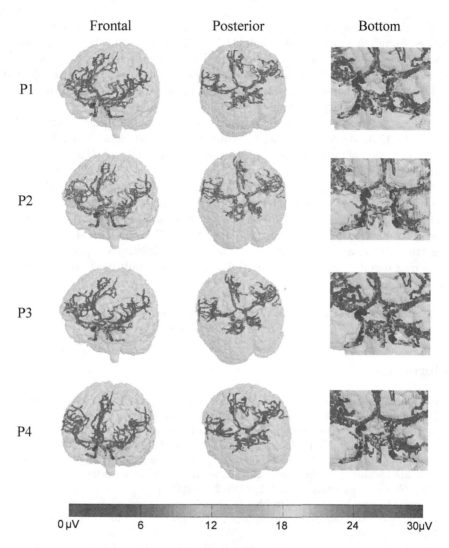

Fig. 4. Potential differences in the forward modeling.

two different relative residuals limit (10^{-6} and 10^{-13}) for the iLU preconditioning BiCG-Stabilized solver, finding that the differences are not relevant in the forward calculations for $1 \times 1 \times 1$ mm resolutions. Regarding this, the algorithm takes about 4 min for a single leadpair calculation using 10^{-6} relative residual limit in an Intel Xeon 3.4 GHz processor with 64 Gb RAM.

4 Discussion and Concluding Remarks

Forward modeling impacts directly in the EEG source localization, for this reason, the realistic head modeling with anisotropic capacity is needed for more accurate detection of activity sources. The AFDRM technique allows a faster calculation, supporting anisotropic conductivities [9]. The results show that neglecting some relevant tissues of the human head, like eyes, muscle, fat and anisotropic vessels directly influence the dipole estimations with errors larger than 30 mm. On the other hand, considering an anisotropic blood vessel modeling is necessary for a deep brain activity analysis.

Tissue segmentation in the forward realistic head models has a direct influence in the EEG dipole localization. Anisotropic blood vessel modeling shows that the inclusion of multiple tissues (fat, eyes, muscle, etc.) may affect the dipole estimation, especially in deep brain areas. For instance, not including anisotropic blood vessels yields DLE errors larger than 15 mm. Also, we find out that temporal and inferior behavior is affected concerning the potential accuracy and it could be a significant drawback for source localization in focal temporal epilepsy.

As a future research, we plan to analyze the EEG source localization errors using state of the art inverse solutions such as multiple sparse priors approach considering blood vessels and conductivity models for multiple-tissue segmentation of this work.

Acknowledgments. This work is carried out under grants: *Prog. Nal. de Formacion de Investigadores GENERACION DEL BICENTENARIO, Conv 528.*

References

1. Castaño-Candamil, S., Höhne, J., Martínez-Vargas, J.D., An, X.W., Castellanos-Domínguez, G., Haufe, S.: Solving the EEG inverse problem based on space-time-frequency structured sparsity constraints. NeuroImage **118**, 598–612 (2015)
2. Irimia, A., Goh, S.-Y.M., Torgerson, C.M., Stein, N.R., Chambers, M.C., Vespa, P.M., Van Horn, J.D.: Electroencephalographic inverse localization of brain activity in acute traumatic brain injury as a guide to surgery, monitoring and treatment. Clin. Neurol. Neurosurg. **115**(10), 2159–2165 (2013)
3. Montes, V., van Mierlo, P., Strobbe, G., Staelens, S., Vandenberghe, S., Hallez, H.: Influence of skull modeling approaches on EEG source localization. Brain Topogr. **27**, 95–111 (2013)
4. Wtorek, J., Polin, A.: The contribution of blood-flow-induced conductivity changes to measured impedance **52**(1), 41–49 (2005)
5. Cuartas-Morales, E., Cardenas-Pena, D., Castellanos-Dominguez, G.: Influence of anisotropic white matter modeling on EEG source localization, pp. 4920–4923, August 2014
6. Fischl, B., Salat, D.H., Busa, E., Albert, M., Dieterich, M., Haselgrove, C., Van Der Kouwe, A., Killiany, R., Kennedy, D., Klaveness, S., et al.: Whole brain segmentation: automated labeling of neuroanatomical structures in the human brain. Neuron **33**(3), 341–355 (2002)
7. Torrado-Carvajal, A., Herraiz, J.L., Hernandez-Tamames, J.A., Jose-Estepar, R.S., Eryaman, Y., Rozenholc, Y., Adalsteinsson, E., Wald, L.L., Malpica, N.: Multi-atlas and label fusion approach for patient-specific MRI based skull estimation. Magn. Reson. Med. (2015, in press)

8. Warfield, S.K., Zou, K.H., Wells, W.M.: Simultaneous truth, performance level estimation (staple): an algorithm for the validation of image segmentation. IEEE Trans. Med. Imaging **23**(7), 903–921 (2004)

9. Cuartas-Morales, E., Daniel-Acosta, C., Castellanos-Dominguez, G.: iLU preconditioning of the anisotropic-finite-difference based solution for the EEG forward problem. In: Ferrández Vicente, J.M., Álvarez-Sánchez, J.R., de la Paz López, F., Toledo-Moreo, F.J., Adeli, H. (eds.) IWINAC 2015. LNCS, vol. 9107, pp. 408–418. Springer, Cham (2015). doi:10.1007/978-3-319-18914-7_43

10. Wang, P., Wang, H.: A modified FCM algorithm for MRI brain image segmentation. In: 2008 International Seminar on Future BioMedical Information Engineering, vol. 3, pp. 26–29 (2008)

11. Wolters, C.H., Anwander, A., Tricoche, X., Weinstein, D., Koch, M.A., Macleod, R.S.: Influence of tissue conductivity anisotropy on EEG/MEG field and return current computation in a realistic head model: a simulation and visualization study using high-resolution finite element modeling. NeuroImage **30**, 813–826 (2006)

Brain White Matter Lesion Segmentation with 2D/3D CNN

A. López-Zorrilla[1], M. de Velasco-Vázquez[1], O. Serradilla-Casado[1],
L. Roa-Barco[1], M. Graña[1,2(✉)], D. Chyzhyk[2], and C.C. Price[3]

[1] Computational Intelligence Group, UPV/EHU, San Sebastian, Spain
manuel.grana@ehu.es
[2] ACPySS, San Sebastian, Spain
[3] McKnight Brain Institute, University of Florida, Gainesville, USA

Abstract. Automated detection of white matter hyperintensities (WHM) may have a broad clinical use, because WHM appear in several brain diseases. Deep learning architectures have been recently very successful for the segmentation of brain lesions, such as ictus or tumour lesions. We propose a Convolutional Neural Network composed of four parallel data paths whose input is a mixture of 2D/3D windows extracted from multimodal magnetic resonance imaging of the brain. The architecture is lighter than others proposed in the literature for lesion detection so its training is faster. We carry out computational experiments on a dataset of multimodal imaging from 18 subjects, achieving competitive results with state of the art approaches.

1 Introduction

White matter hyperintensities (WMH) can be caused by a variety of factors including ischemia, micro-hemorrhages, gliosis, damage to small blood vessel walls. Many patients showing WMH are idiopathic, however WMH have a strong relationship with age, arterial hypertension, demographic parameters such as gender, and some disease, such as diabetes, and biomarkers such as cholesterol [15]. It has been found associated with progressive cognitive impairment [5]. WMH are small size lesions compared with tumours and stroke lesions, lacking their structure of necrotic and inflamed tissues. They are mostly periventricular lesions,which primarily appear at the top of the horns of the lateral ventricles progressing around the ventricles. They may also appear as subcortical lesions [9,25]. Several magnetic resonance image (MRI) modalities may be used used for WMH detection and segmentation. They appear as hypointense in T1-weighted and as hyperintense in T2-weighted images [23]. The best modality is the fluid attenuated inversion recovery (FLAIR) imaging, where the lesions appear as hyperintense and with greater contrast, allowing to differentiate between periventricular and subcortical lesions. Recent studies [17,21] also consider diffusion tensor imaging (DTI), specifically the scalar coefficients such as fractional anisotropy (FA), radial diffusivity (RD), and mean diffusivity (MD), which give the information about privileged directions of water diffusion, so they are sensitive to microstructural changes in white matter.

© Springer International Publishing AG 2017
J.M. Ferrández Vicente et al. (Eds.): IWINAC 2017, Part I, LNCS 10337, pp. 394–403, 2017.
DOI: 10.1007/978-3-319-59740-9_39

In the last years, the interest in brain lesion image segmentation has increased, for example, public challenges have been carried out BRATS http:// braintumorsegmentation.org/ and ISLES http://www.isles-challenge.org/ to advance the field. Most research on small lesion detection has been carried out for multiple sclerosis (MS) patients. Early approaches consisted in semiautomatic labellings in structural images [16] and FLAIR [11]. Early multimodal approaches applied voxelwise fuzzy expert systems [1] and Markov random fields (MRF) [20]. Machine learning supervised approaches have been also applied, such as Random Forest [8] and MRF regularized versions [22]. Unsupervised approaches have made advantage of the brain symmetry for big lesion detection [6]. Recently, Deep Learning approaches report great success in the segmentation of brain tumours, specifically Convolutional Neural Networks (CNN) [18, 26] which is the approach that we are following in our own proposal.

Processing 3D medical images by the CNNs can be done in 3 ways: (a) Considering each 2D slice of the 3D volume in some direction (sagittal, coronal or axial) as an independent input image that is feed to the CNN [18, 26]. (b) Considering 3D windows of the volumetric image as input. (c) Considering hybrid 2D/3D inputs, i.e. feeding 2D slices and 3D windows of the volumetric image. This decision carries some implications in the CNN design, because a 3D input forces that hidden layers resulting of the filters have 3D structure [2, 24]. This additional structural complexity has been found cumbersome to deal with large datasets, because the number of operations scalate cubically instead of quadratically. So the intended advantage of preserving 3D spatial relation information, is countered by convergence issues and computational time, so that the 3D windows are small, loosing information of long distance spatial relations. Finally, the use of hybrid 2D and 3D input information [4, 7] allows a good balance between the preservation of 3D spatial relations and the long distance relations that can be analysed in 2D data. In our architecture, we have used an hybrid 2D/3D NN where we use a small 3D cube and three different 2D windows, one for each of the 3 dimensional axis. The paper contents is as follows: first we present the dataset used for the experiments. Secondly, we discuss our architecture and the others used for comparison. Then we present our experimental results and, finally, some conclusions and future work.

2   Materials

The experimental evaluation of the proposed CNN architecture has been carried out in a set of 18 subjects MRI images corresponding to a previous study [19] where WHM was performed manually, thus providing the ground truth segmentation for the present work as 3D lesion masks. Each subject image includes a 3D T1-weighted, FLAIR image, and diffusion weighted images from which DTI images, and subsequent FA coefficients, were computed using FSL software. T1-weighted volumes have been registered to 1 mm MNI template. The FLAIR and FA images have been corregisted to the MNI space by affine registration to normalized T1-weighted images. The lesion masks are also corregistered to MNI space. All the image intensities are normalized to the [0,1] interval.

3 CNN Architectures

Throughout the last years, Convolutional Neural Networks (CNNs) [13] have achieved excellent performance in many computer vision tasks. Several advances have solved convergence issues, and the advent of easy to exploit powerful Graphics Processing Units (GPUs) has speed up the training times by several orders of magnitude [3]. A CNN is a shared-weight neural network: all the neurons in a hidden layer share the same weights and bias. In fact, each layer implements a linear convolution filter whose kernel is learnt by gradient descent. Therefore, the output of the successive layers is a series of filtered/subsampled images which are interpreted as progressively higher level abstract features. Most CNN are applied to 2D signals, i.e. images, however in the medical image domain they are increasingly applied to 3D signals, i.e. volumetric imaging information. Specifically, two recent instances of CNNs have been succesfully applied to brain lesion segmentation [10,12] achieving remarkable succes in the BraTs competition. Another recent segmentation example using a 2D/3D input data is [7], where authors trained two separate CNNs for each input dimensionality, performing a combination of their outputs by averaging.

3.1 Our Proposal: MPCNN

Our proposal is a Mixed Parallel CNN (MPCNN), which takes four inputs: three orthogonal big 2D windows on 3D image slices (one per spatial dimension) centered at the same voxel of the brain, and a 3D window, a cube whose sides are smaller than that of the 2D windows. Therefore, 2D data carry farther away spatial relations, while the 3D window carries 3D spatial relations. The MPCNN architecture consists of four parallel CNN, three dedicated to process the 2D window, and the fourth processing the 3D window. Furthermore, we use multimodal MRI data, specifically T1, FLAIR and FA volumes, so that each voxel is in fact a three dimensional vector, much like an RGB image. In this sense, independent CNN filters at each layer are learnt for each image modality. The output is a couple of binary units that provide an estimation of the probability that the central pixel of the 2D and 3D windows is a WMH lesion voxel.

Figure 1 shows a diagram of the MPCNN architecture. Each parallel subnetwork is a CNN, composed of a sequence of convolutional layers and max-pooling layers which reduce the reduce the dimensionality of the feature space after each convolution. In the version of the network tested in this paper the dimension of each of the input 2D windows is 35×35, whereas the dimension of the input 3D cube is $11 \times 11 \times 11$. The activation function used to compute the output of each neuron of the CNN is the Rectified Linear Unit (ReLU) [13,14] due to both its efficient computation and the fact that it solves the vanishing gradient problem. The architectures of the three 2D CNNs are identical, they are composed of three convolutions with kernels of size 3×3. The number of convolutions increases along the layers, increasing the number of features accordingly.

Moreover, a dimensionality reduction max-pooling layer with pool size of 2×2 is applied to the output of the second and third layers. The dimensions of

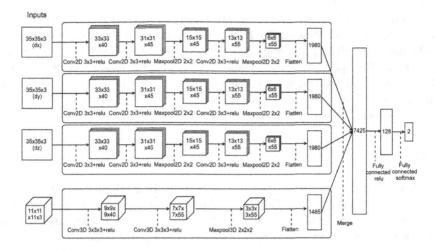

Fig. 1. The structure of the proposed for WMH lesion detection

the output of each layer are shown in Fig. 1. Thus, each 2D subnetwork's output layer has $6 \times 6 \times 55 = 1980$ neurons. The 3D CNN is composed only of two 3D convolutions (with kernel size of $3 \times 3 \times 3$), and one 3D max-pooling (with pool size of $2 \times 2 \times 2$) after the second convolution. Finally, all the subnetworks are merged (this results in $1980 \times 3 + 1485 = 7425$ nodes) and fully connected to the next layer, composed of 128 neurons. Finally, these 128 outputs are used to compute the final output of the network via the Softmax function. Hence, the two outputs will always be bounded between 0 and 1, and they will sum 1. This facilitates a probabilistic interpretation of the network output as a probability of lesion at the central voxel.

3.2 DeepMedic

The other architecture tested for comparison is the DeepMedic [12], whose architecture has two main components; a 3D CNN and a fully connected 3D Conditional Random Field (CRF), which performs a postprocessing of the CNN output removing false positives. The CNN consists of four layers with $5 \times 5 \times 5$ kernels for feature extraction, and the classification layer is implemented as a convolutional layer with kernel of size $1 \times 1 \times 1$, allowing efficient dense-inference. The 3D CNN network has two pathways; one processes local information and the other processes larger contextual information, hence carrying out multi-scale processing of the data. Moreover, BN (Batch Normalization) is also applied to all the hidden layers, so that all Feature Maps obtained after each layer are normalized, preserving the signal, and avoiding sourious weight convergence. After that, there are two hidden layers for combining the multi-scale parallel pathways. The full network is trained patch-by-patch and the size of the batches is selected automatically according to the neighborhood of the voxel in the input. The batches are built by extracting segments from the training images with

50% probability of being centered on a foreground or background voxel, which corrrects the class-imbalance. The DeepMedic network training implementation downloaded from github was originally prepared for the ISLES and BraTS challenges, reporting state-of-the-art results on both performance on brain tumor and stroke lesion. However, since in our problem we only have 2 outputs not 5 as in the segmentation problems, in order to work with this network the last layer output has been reduced from 5 to 2 outputs.

4   Results

The MPCNN architecture has been implemented in Python using Keras with Tensorflow as backend. The DeepMedic implementation has been dowloaded from github (https://github.com/Kamnitsask/deepmedic). The training and validation scripts have been executed in a desktop computer with RAM of 16 GB, and GPU NVIDIA GTX 1070 which has been used to speed up training. For

Table 1. Results of the networks using leave one out validation. Each row is the TPR (True Positive Rate) on the test image, DM DeepMedic, MPCNN Mixed Parallel CNN. cte/lin/log = constant/linear/log increase of imbalance ratio. Bold highgligh maximum per row.

#image	DM	MPCNN cte			MPCNN lin		MPCNN log	
		Th = 0.35	0.45	0.5	0.2	0.15	0.2	0.15
#1	0.642	0.583	0.515	0.483	0.640	0.687	0.659	**0.709**
#2	0.591	**0.761**	0.703	0.679	0.589	0.625	0.614	0.652
#3	0.572	**0.830**	0.785	0.760	0.617	0.666	0.637	0.684
#4	**0.659**	0.649	0.592	0.564	0.608	0.650	0.587	0.640
#5	0.715	0.673	0.628	0.599	0.621	0.684	0.662	**0.722**
#6	0.600	**0.829**	0.803	0.791	0.562	0.608	0.583	0.626
#7	0.616	0.504	0.595	0.572	0.628	**0.669**	0.574	0.620
#8	0.310	**0.504**	0.437	0.405	0.280	0.323	0.268	0.309
#9	0.331	0.577	0.533	0.512	0.537	**0.583**	0.466	0.514
#10	0.564	**0.711**	0.656	0.630	0.561	0.607	0.561	0.598
#11	0.641	0.611	0.569	0.548	0.643	**0.677**	0.581	0.631
#12	0.657	**0.715**	0.671	0.646	0.568	0.614	0.582	0.626
#13	0.617	**0.705**	0.649	0.620	0.504	0.559	0.615	0.661
#14	0.564	0.591	0.516	0.479	0.476	0.530	0.544	**0.595**
#15	0.716	**0.796**	0.762	0.746	0.726	0.756	0.716	0.755
#16	0.781	0.730	0.670	0.642	0.724	0.768	0.753	**0.787**
#17	0.638	**0.717**	0.665	0.639	0.570	0.612	0.511	0.554
#18	0.432	**0.596**	0.531	0.501	0.127	0.153	0.385	0.454
Mean	0.591	**0.671**	0.627	0.601	0.554	0.598	0.572	0.619

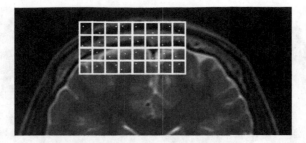

Fig. 2. Brain image subsampling to obtain the training dataset

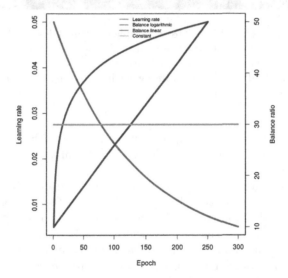

Fig. 3. Schedule of learning parameters: learning rate (red) ratio of imbalance in the training set. (Color figure online)

validation, we apply leave one out over the 18 available subject datasets. To carry out the training in a limited reasonable time, we have subsampled the brain images as shown in Fig. 2 to obtain the training dataset. The brain image is decomposed in regular non-overlapping windows and a random voxel is picked from this window as the center for the 2D/3D windows that conform the inputs. This process ensures a rather regular sampling interval and that the whole brain volume is sampled. Testing is carried out evaluating all the brain voxels in the test datasets. The problem is naturally imbalanced, i.e. there are many more healthy than lesion voxels, therefore we need to respect this imbalance in the training dataset. We have tried an strategy that starts training with balanced datasets (i.e. 1:1 imbalance ratio) and ends up with an imbalanced training dataset, varying the composition of the training dataset at each epoch. Figure 3 shows the evolution of the training imbalance, we have a constant imbalance

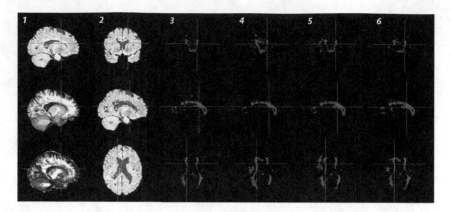

Fig. 4. Data and results of subject #18. 1-Sample sagittal slides of T1, FA and FLAIR volumes. 2-WMH ground truth lesion manually labeled overlaid on FLAIR slices 3, 4, 5, 6-prediction (green) and ground truth lesion (red), 3 for DeepMedic, 4 MPCNN standard training, 5 and 6 MPCNN training with increasing imbalance ratios, linear and logarithmic. (Color figure online)

30:1, a linear increase from 10:1 up to 50:1, and a logarithmic increase in the same range. We report True Positive Ratio (TPR) values, measuring how well the lesion is detected.

Accuracy results for each test images are presented in Table 1. The second row corresponds to the decision threshold applied to the network output unit to decide if the voxel is a lesion voxel. We have found empirically that reducing the threshold for normal tissue class decision (thus increasing the threshold for lesion) we obtain some improvement. This asimetry in the decision threshold may be related to the imbalance of the dataset, but we do not know for sure. Remaining rows correspond to the test result of each image, the last row corresponds to the average over all tests. We have found the best average results with the constant imbalance and a decision threshold 0.35. In all experiment instances our proposal is competitive or outperforms the DeepMedic results. Looking at the result per each image, there is a wide variability in results, in some cases reaching very low values. Our proposed MPCNN is faster to train than DeepMedic (a ratio 7:1). If we consider the maximum TPR achieved, we conclude that the architectures need to be improved, and that the success in tumour segmentation does not ensure success in WMH lesion detection.

Figure 4 presents visual results of the experiment. From left to right, the first column shows images of the three modalities as an ilustration of the dataset. The second column shows the lesion detected manually in three slices of brain #18 overlaid on the FLAIR image. Next columns illustrate the detection by DeepMedic (3), and the three imbalance strategies for MPCNN (4, 5, 6). It can be appreciated that all of them leave some lesion clusters undetected, and overestimate others. DeepMedic seems to create spurious lesion detection clusters, while our proposal MPCNN false alarms are more of the kind of cluster extensions, or conections between clusters. So, some qualitative differences of the response of the architectures can be appreciated which deserver further analysis and experimentation. One artifact that is common in all detections: all approaches find spurious detections along the boundaries of the ventricles.

5   Conclusions and Future Work

We have proposed and tested a new 2D/3D CNN architecture for the detection of WMH lesions, which are smaller than other brain lesions (tumours and stroke lesions), lacking the necrotic and inflammation structures. We compare results with two other architectures published in the literature achieving competitive results. Qualitative assessment of the results, shows some advantage of our approach, which is closer to the manual segmentation in the sense that follows more closely the delineated voxel clusters, and creates less spurious detection clusters. The combination of 2D and 3D input windows allows to process the long distance spatial relations, while reducing the computational burden.

Ongoing work improves the validation process computing a more complete cross-validation procedure, and more datasets will be included in the experiment. Our proposal may be also subject to changes in kernel parameters and other features of the CNN. Notice that no postprocessing to remove false alarms is done, contrary to DeepMedic, so additional work in postprocessing MPCNN results may provide enhanced results. In order to go ahead in this research area, we made the code available in github so that everyone can contribute to it.

References

1. Admiraal-Behloul, F., van den Heuvel, D.M.J., Olofsen, H., van Osch, M.J.P., van der Grond, J., van Buchem, M.A., Reiber, J.H.C.: Fully automatic segmentation of white matter hyperintensities in MR images of the elderly. NeuroImage **28**(3), 607–617 (2005)
2. Brosch, T., Yoo, Y., Tang, L.Y.W., Li, D.K.B., Traboulsee, A., Tam, R.: Deep convolutional encoder networks for multiple sclerosis lesion segmentation. In: Navab, N., Hornegger, J., Wells, W.M., Frangi, A.F. (eds.) MICCAI 2015. LNCS, vol. 9351, pp. 3–11. Springer, Cham (2015). doi:10.1007/978-3-319-24574-4_1
3. Ciresan, D., Giusti, A., Gambardella, L.M., Schmidhuber, J.: Deep neural networks segment neuronal membranes in electron microscopy images. In: Advances in Neural Information Processing Systems, pp. 2843–2851 (2012)
4. de Brébisson, A., Montana, G.: Deep neural networks for anatomical brain segmentation. In: 2015 IEEE Conference on Computer Vision and Pattern Recognition Workshops (CVPRW), pp. 20–28, June 2015
5. Debette, S., Markus, H.S.: The clinical importance of white matter hyperintensities on brain magnetic resonance imaging: systematic review and meta-analysis. BMJ **341**, c3666 (2010)
6. Erihov, M., Alpert, S., Kisilev, P., Hashoul, S.: A Cross saliency approach to asymmetry-based tumor detection. In: Navab, N., Hornegger, J., Wells, W.M., Frangi, A.F. (eds.) MICCAI 2015. LNCS, vol. 9351, pp. 636–643. Springer, Cham (2015). doi:10.1007/978-3-319-24574-4_76

7. Gao, X.W., Hui, R., Tian, Z.: Classification of CT brain images based on deep learning networks. Comput. Methods Programs Biomed. **138**, 49–56 (2017)
8. Geremia, E., Clatz, O., Menze, B.H., Konukoglu, E., Criminisi, A., Ayache, N.: Spatial decision forests for MS lesion segmentation in multi-channel magnetic resonance images. NeuroImage **57**(2), 378–390 (2011)
9. Schulz, U.G., Grueter, B.E.: Age-related cerebral white matter disease (Leukoaraiosis): a review. Postgrad. Med. J. **88**, 79–87 (2012)
10. Havaei, M., Davy, A., Warde-Farley, D., Biard, A., Courville, A., Bengio, Y., Pal, C., Jodoin, P.-M., Larochelle, H.: Brain tumor segmentation with deep neural networks. Med. Image Anal. **35**, 18–31 (2017)
11. Iorio, M., Spalletta, G., Chiapponi, C., Luccichenti, G., Cacciari, C., Orfei, M.D., Caltagirone, C., Piras, F.: White matter hyperintensities segmentation: a new semi-automated method. Front. Aging Neurosci. **5**, 76 (2013)
12. Kamnitsas, K., Ledig, C., Newcombe, V.F.J., Simpson, J.P., Kane, A.D., Menon, D.K., Rueckert, D., Glocker, B.: Efficient multi-scale 3D CNN with fully connected CRF for accurate brain lesion segmentation. Med. Image Anal. **36**, 61–78 (2017)
13. Lecun, Y., Bottou, L., Bengio, Y., Haffner, P.: Gradient-based learning applied to document recognition. Proc. IEEE **86**(11), 2278–2324 (1998)
14. LeCun, Y., Bengio, Y., Hinton, G.: Deep learning. Nature **521**(7553), 436–444 (2015)
15. Murray, A.D., Staff, R.T., Shenkin, S.D., Deary, I.J., Starr, J.M., Whalley, L.J.: Brain white matter hyperintensities: relative importance of vascular risk factors in nondemented elderly people. Radiology **237**, 251–257 (2005)
16. Payne, M.E., et al.: Development of a semi-automated method for quantification of MRI gray and white matter lesions in geriatric subjects. Psychiatry Res.: Neuroimaging **115**(1), 63–77 (2002)
17. Pelletier, A., Periot, O., Dilharreguy, B., Hiba, B., Bordessoules, M., Chanraud, S., Pérés, K., Amieva, H., Dartigues, J., Allard, M., Catheline, G.: Age-related modifications of diffusion tensor imaging parameters and white matter hyperintensities as inter-dependent processes. Front. Aging Neurosci. **7**(255) (2016)
18. Pereira, S., Pinto, A., Alves, V., Silva, C.A.: Deep convolutional neural networks for the segmentation of gliomas in multi-sequence MRI. In: Crimi, A., Menze, B., Maier, O., Reyes, M., Handels, H. (eds.) BrainLes 2015. LNCS, vol. 9556, pp. 131–143. Springer, Cham (2016). doi:10.1007/978-3-319-30858-6_12
19. Price, C.C., Mitchell, S.M., Brumback, B., Tanner, J.J., Schmalfuss, I., Lamar, M., Giovannetti, T., Heilman, K.M., Libon, D.J.: MRI-Leukoaraiosis thresholds and the phenotypic expression of dementia. Neurology **79**(8), 734–740 (2012)
20. Schwarz, C., Fletcher, E., DeCarli, C., Carmichael, O.: Fully-automated white matter hyperintensity detection with anatomical prior knowledge and without FLAIR. In: Prince, J.L., Pham, D.L., Myers, K.J. (eds.) IPMI 2009. LNCS, vol. 5636, pp. 239–251. Springer, Heidelberg (2009). doi:10.1007/978-3-642-02498-6_20
21. Tuladhar, A.M., van Dijk, E., Zwiers, M.P., van Norden, A.G.W., de Laat, K.F., Shumskaya, E., Norris, D.G., de Leeuw, F.-E.: Structural network connectivity and cognition in cerebral small vessel disease. Hum. Brain Mapp. **37**(1), 300–310 (2016)
22. Tustison, N., Wintermark, M., Durst, C., Avants, B.: Miccai society, ants and árboles. In: MICCAI BraTS Workshop, Nagoya (2013)
23. Uchiyama, Y., Kunieda, T., Hara, T., Fujita, H., Ando, H., Yamakawa, H., Asano, T., Kato, H., Iwama, T., Kanematsu, M., Hoshi, H.: Automatic segmentation of different-sized Leukoaraiosis regions in brain MR images. In: Proceedings of SPIE, vol. 6915, pp. 69151S–69151S-8 (2008)

24. Urban, G., Bendszus, M., Hamprecht, F., Kleesiek, J.: Multi-modal brain tumor segmentation using deep convolutional neural networks. In: MICCAI BraTS (Brain Tumor Segmentation) Challenge: Proceedings, Winning Contribution, pp. 31–35 (2014)
25. Yoshita, M., Fletcher, E., Harvey, D., Ortega, M., Martinez, O., Mungas, D.M., Reed, B.R., DeCarli, C.S.: Extent and distribution of white matter hyperintensities in normal aging, MCI, and AD. Neurology **67**(12), 2192–2198 (2006)
26. Zikic, D., Ioannou, Y., Brown, M., Criminisi, A.: Segmentation of brain tumor tissues with convolutional neural networks. In: Proceedings MICCAI-BRATS, pp. 36–39 (2014)

Circadian Modulation of Sleep-Wake Dynamics Evaluated by Transition Probabilities

L.F. Perez-Atencio[2], Nicolas Garcia-Aracil[1], Eduardo Fernandez[1],
Luis C. Barrio[2], and Juan A. Barios[1(✉)]

[1] Biomedical Neuroengineering Research Group (nBio),
Department of Systems Engineering and Automation,
Miguel Hernandez University, Avda. de la Universidad s/n,
03202 Elche, Spain
jbarios@umh.es

[2] Unit of Experimental Neurology, Ramn y Cajal Hospital-IRYCIS,
Carretera de Colmenar km 9, 28034 Madrid, Spain
http://nbio.umh.es/, http://www.hryc.es

Abstract. Behavioral states in rodents and other mammalian species alternate between wakefulness (WK), rapid eye movement (REM) and non-REM (NREM) sleep at time scale of hours (i.e., circadian and ultradian periodicties) and from several tens of minutes to seconds (i.e., brief awakenings during sleep). Quantified and statistical analysis of bout durations and transition probability analysis of sleep-wake dynamics constitute a powerful method for evaluating endogenous sleep control mechanisms and sleep disturbances. Here we studied the circadian influence over sleep-wake activity in mouse model by analyzing as a function of lightdark (LD) cycle, the Kaplan-Meier (KM) survival curves and the transition probability (TP) of Markov chains. Survival curves of WK showed a bimodal statistical distribution. Circadian rhythm modulated specifically WK bouts increasing its duration during activedark period. In contrast, NREM and REM KM curves did not change significantly along LD cycle. Circadian modulation of TP was found only for state-maintenance-probability in WK and for $p_{\text{WK}\to\text{NREM}}$ transitions which increased and decreased respectively during activedark period. In conclusion, Markov modelling of sleep stages adequately evaluate the circadian and ultradian modulation of sleep-wake dynamics during dark and light phases.

Keywords: Markov chains · Survival curves · Transition matrices · Sleep-wake cycle · Circadian rhythmicity · Ultradian rhythms · Mouse model

1 Introduction

The sleep-wake cycle (SWC) is a dynamic phenomenon, resulting from the complex alternating activity of sleep-wake neural networks of basal forebrain,

© Springer International Publishing AG 2017
J.M. Ferrández Vicente et al. (Eds.): IWINAC 2017, Part I, LNCS 10337, pp. 404–415, 2017.
DOI: 10.1007/978-3-319-59740-9_40

hypothalamus and brainstem. Appropriate control of this brain activity permits behavioral state transitions between WK, REM and NREM sleep [1,2]. Cycling between sleep and WK is regulated at time scales of seconds to several tens of minutes by the intrinsic activity of sleep-wake neuronal networks [3] and of hours under control of circadian and ultradian rhythms [4,5]. Main circadian oscillator regulating the brain arousal system is located in the suprachiasmatic nucleus [6].

Although presence of circadian and ultradian rhythms along the SWC is a clear indication of the existence of time-dependent variations in sleep architecture, transitions between sleep-wake states occur at unpredictable moments and in unpredictable directions, so that statistical tools are a useful way for studying sleep dynamics. It is therefore important to understand the bout-to-bout dynamics at short- and long-term in the context of ultradian and circadian modulation. Markov chains represent a class of stochastic processes of great interest for a wide spectrum of practical applications. In particular, discrete time Markov chains permit to model the transition probabilities between discrete states [7], allowing to model the dynamics of SWC in mammals. Markov chains have also been used for studying physiology of human sleep [9], and some clinical applications of these methods have also been reported [2,10]. For example, Markov chains have been used for studying the sleep of patients with narcolepsy, where a deficit of orexin produces a sleep with normal amounts of sleep and wake, but very brief states with increased transitions between them [2], while in the knockout-orexin mouse model there is no evidence of disordered circadian control [8]. Given the stochastic nature of state transitions along the SWC under normal and pathological conditions, SWC are well suited to be modeled by discrete time Markov chains. Markov analysis provides accurate information of the probability of staying in one state (i.e., state stability), closely related to state duration), and of the transition probabilities from and to that state (i.e., rates), that cannot be obtained by other existing methods.

Bout duration of sleep stages can be studied by survival curve analysis. Lo et al. [3] introduced the use of bout duration survival analysis for characterizing the distribution of brief awakenings during sleep. This technique measures the probability that a given bout will survive long enough to reach a given duration, and the resulting survival curves can be statistically analyzed to evaluate the sleep structure and underlying mechanisms, e.g. in rats [11] or humans [12].

The current study was designed to investigate using this methodology the effect of dark/light circadian modulation over short- and long-term sleep-wake patterns.

2   Materials and Methods

2.1   Animals

Male wild-type mouse (C57Bl/6) of three-month age were used in this study (N = 10). All experimental procedures were approved by Institutional Animal Care and Use Committee of Ramón y Cajal Hospital (Madrid, Spain).

2.2   Surgery and EEG/EMG Recordings

Animals were implanted under anesthesia with an electrode of nickel-chromium (140 microns) in prefrontal cortex (1.5 mm rostral, 1.5 mm lateral and 1 mm ventral to bregma), a second electrode in the CA1 region of hippocampus (-2.4 mm rostral, 1.5 mm lateral, 1.5 mm ventral), two stainless steel screws in the prefrontal region, for ground and indifferent references, and a silver plate in the muscles of the neck for EMG recording. Nine days after surgery, mice were transferred to a circular cage and the implanted cap fixed to a rotating anti-gravitational connector allowing free movements; after period of habituation of 72 h in the sound attenuated chamber with a 12 h light/dark cycle, a constant temperature (22–24 °C), and ad libitum access to food and water, 24 h of uninterrupted recording were acquired. EEG of the cortex, hippocampus and EMG signals were filtered from 0.5 Hz to 500 Hz, amplified (x5000-10,000) (Cyberamp 380, Axon Instruments) and digitized at 1 kHz (Axon CNS Digidata 1440).

2.3   Sleep-Wake Staging

Sleep scoring was accomplished using an offline automated sleep scoring system, based on custom scripts (MATLAB 2008, Mathworks, USA). For automated staging, z-score of rms of band filtered EEG/EMG signals was calculated from cortex; δ_{cx} (1–4 Hz), σ_{cx} (10–15 Hz), β_{cx} (15–25 Hz); hippocampus, θ_{hc} (7–10 Hz), γ_{hc}^1 (25–55 Hz); γ_{hc}^2 (55–125 Hz); and EMG (55–90 Hz). θ_{hc}/δ_{cx} and β_{cx}/γ_{hc}^1 indexes were calculated. Initially, epochs with low β_{cx}/γ_{hc}^1, high θ_{hc}/δ_{cx} and high EMG are assigned to WK, epochs with low θ_{hc}/δ_{cx}, high β_{cx}/γ_{hc}^1 and low EMG to NREM, and epochs with high θ_{hc}/δ_{cx} and low EMG to REM, using a fixed threshold, and non-assigned epochs were classified in a first pass of MATLAB K-*means* algorithm. Then, thresholds were recalculated and a second pass of the algorithm determined the definitive staging.

Automated scoring was finely tuned through validation with a semiautomated visual staging of the wake-sleep epochs performed by two expert scorers. This analysis classified every 5 s epochs in WK, NREM and REM states. For helping in the analysis, quantified indexes of EEG/EMG recordings were used by the scorers as an aid in ambiguous scoring epochs.

In order to evaluate staging, spectral analysis of staged epochs was performed. NREM epochs shown a predominance of low frequency (1–4 Hz). In cortex and hippocampus, REM epochs had a predominance of hippocampal theta (7–10 Hz) activity and a desynchronization between cortex and hippocampus that is evidenced by the distinctive behavior of the spectral curves between the regions of the brain previously described. After staging, the corresponding polysomnograms are constructed for each mouse recording, and mean durations and total amount of each state for 12 h of dark and light periods were calculated. For the visual analysis of the signals we used the software SPIKE 2 (V 6.18, CED, UK).

2.4 Data Analysis

After staging, analysis of recordings was performed using two complementary approaches: (1) for each state, bout durations (measured to the nearest 5-sec epoch) were evaluated using survival curves. (2) state-to-state transition probabilities were quantified using a Markov analysis.

Survival Curves: Bout durations (min) of each recording were processed by Kaplan-Meier survival curve analysis using 5-sec (i.e. single epoch) time bins: $S_{(ti)} = S_{(ti-1)} * ((r_i - d_i)/r_i)$ where $S_{(ti)}$ is the proportion of the original number of bouts surviving at the end of time bin ti, $S_{(ti-1)}$ is the proportion of the original number of bouts remaining one time bin before ti, r_i is the number of bouts remaining at the start of time bin ti, and d_i is the number of bouts that terminate during time bin ti. Initially, the analysis was performed without reference to time-dependent factors (i.e., in each animal, all data were pooled; 24-h pooled). To evaluate circadian modulation, light and dark epochs were then examined separately.

Markov Chains: A discrete time Markov chain is a sequence of random variables characterized by the Markov property, by which the state S at any time $t + 1$ depends on the state at time t but not on previous history. State transition probabilities describe the probability of going from stage i to stage j in a discrete time step (n) of 5 s: $P_{ij} = P_r(X_n = j | X_o = i)$. The transition probabilities of Markov chains between the 3 WK-sleep states (WK, NREM andREM) were arranged in a matrix with the form

$$\begin{bmatrix} P_{\text{WK}\to\text{WK}} & P_{\text{WK}\to\text{REM}} & P_{\text{WK}\to\text{NREM}} \\ P_{\text{REM}\to\text{WK}} & P_{\text{REM}\to\text{REM}} & P_{\text{REM}\to\text{NREM}} \\ P_{\text{NREM}\to\text{WK}} & P_{\text{NREM}\to\text{REM}} & P_{\text{NREM}\to\text{NREM}} \end{bmatrix}.$$

where each element of position (i, j) represents the transition probability $P_{i\to j}$: e.g., probability of transition from NREM state to REM state is denoted as $P_{\text{NREM}\to\text{REM}}$. State maintenance probabilities, (p_{ii}) that describe the probability of remaining in one state, are denoted as P_{WK}, P_{NREM}, P_{REM}. Markov chains have been already validated as a model for sleep dynamics in mouse and rat [11], so we did not perform specific tests to validate prior Markov analysis assumptions. Markov analysis was performed using the markovchain package (R environment, ver. 0.6.5.1) [7].

2.5 Statistical Analysis

Data were presented as mean value or percentage of total value±SE. Differences between the groups were evaluated using the Student's t-test, Mann-Whitney test, and Bonfferoni test (Anova), depending on the compliance with the normality hypothesis of the data using Sigmaplot (San Rafael, Hearne Scientific Software, 2006) and R statistical software [13].

3   Results

The complex dynamics of transitions between all behavioral states in adult mouse (WK and NREM and REM sleep) along a dark/light cycle is illustrated in Fig. 1. Inspection of hypnograms shows a clear influence of circadian rhythm over

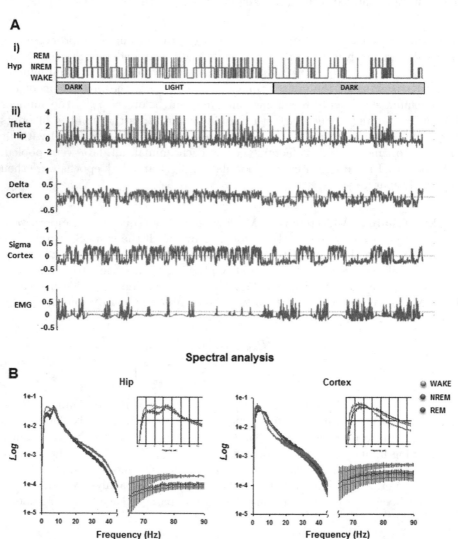

Fig. 1. Circadian modulation of the wake-sleep cycle in mouse C57Bl/6. (A) The hypnogram (i) to determine the WK, NREM and REM states was generated automatically through the RED thresholds, based on the frequency pattern of the EEG activity of the cortex and hippocampus. Longer episodes of wakefulness were observed in the cycle of darkness and shorter in light, the duration of the periods is of 12 h. (B) to determine the veracity of the swords the power spectrum of the signal was realized in all the WK, NREM and REM.

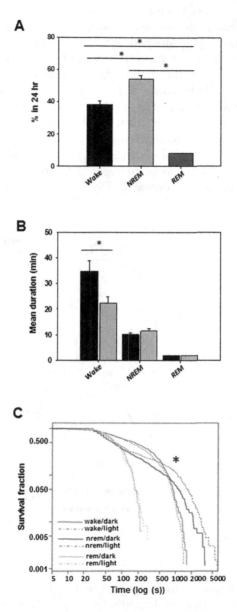

Fig. 2. (A) Percentage of epoch WK, NREM and REM indicating that WK > NREM > REM ($p < 0.05$), (B) Total duration of wakefulness and NREM increased and decreased respectively during darkness compared to phase light. (C) The cumulative wake shown by the Kaplan-Meyer survival curves showed a biexponential distribution with a significant increase in dark-phase wakefulness (*Anova, $p < 0.05$).

SWC: during dark (active) period, long lasting WKs alternate with NREM-REM sleep cycles that contain brief and frequent awakenings, while in light (resting) phase the brief awakenings dominate over long WKs (Fig. 1Ai).

In (Fig. 2A) shows the percentage of total sleep times in 24 h of recording, it is observed that NREM > WK > REM ($p < 0.05$) Quantitative analysis of state durations showed that mean duration of WK epochs increased significantly in dark in comparison with light phase, while NREM and REM show no differences ($p < 0.05$) (Fig. 2B). Accordingly, the survival curve of WK exhibited a biexponential distribution, while REM and NREM survival curves were monoexponential (Fig. 2C). However, only the cumulative distribution corresponding to the longer WK durations during dark period of circadian rhythm. Thus, data clearly indicate that two types of wakes can be segregated by its bout duration, and that only wake are under of circadian control (Fig. 3).

SLEEP BEHAVIOR IN DARK/LIGHT

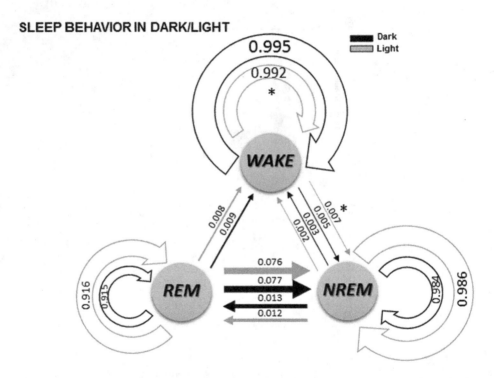

Fig. 3. Markov chain diagram, which explains the dynamics of wake-sleep through the cycle of darkness/light. Circular cycles indicate the probability of state maintenance and the arrows show transitions between states; In black and gray the periods of darkness and light respectively are represented. WK and NREM states were more stable than REM, whereas $p_{REM \rightarrow NREM}$ and $p_{NREM \rightarrow REM}$ state transitions were the most likely. Circadian modulation increased the stability of WK mainly by reducing the transitions from WK to NREM during the dark active period ($p < 0.05$).

Transition probabilities matrix derived from Markov analysis revealed high probabilities for staying in one state and much lower probabilities of transition between different states. The order of state maintenance probabilities, which correlated with the corresponding values of bout-duration, was $P_{WK} > P_{NREM} > P_{REM}$ with statistically significant differences between all states ($p < 0.001$). The sequence of transition probabilities (i.e., the rate) was as followed: $p_{REM \to NREM} \gg p_{NREM \to REM} \gg p_{REM \to WK} \approx p_{WK \to NREM} \gg p_{NREM \to WK}$, revealing that there are important differences in the transitions probability depending on the involved states and its direction. Transitions from REM to NREM were the most frequent and statistically different each other and with the rest of state transitions ($p < 0.001$), while transitions of $p_{NREM \to REM}$, were more frequent than the transitions of $p_{REM \to WK}$, $p_{WK \to NREM}$, and $p_{NREM \to WK}$, ($p < 0.05$). Regarding to circadian modulation, only the stability of WK state varied significantly with circadian rhythm ($p < 0.01$), increasing and decreasing respectively in dark and light phase, and only the probability of state transitions from WK to NREM decreased significantly in the dark phase in comparison with light period ($p < 0.05$), while $p_{WK \to NREM}$, was higher than $p_{NREM \to WK}$ during the light period ($p < 0.01$).

4   Discussion

The regulation of SWC in mammals is still a research topic [15]. Classical 2-process model of sleep states that an homeostatic process (process S) interacts with a circadian pacemaker (process C) to regulate the SWC [4,14]. Main master clock of C is the suprachiasmatic nucleus, a small group of neurons located at the hypothalamus, influencing on orexin-containing wake-promoting neurons in lateral hypothalamus, that are the main responsibles of regulating sleep and arousal. S process increases sleep pressure after long wake periods. Evidence now suggests that adenosine, a small inhibitory aminoacide, is the main candidate to be the physiological signal of S. Brain levels of adenosine increase with prolonged wakefulness, initially in the basal forebrain and then throughout the cortex, and decrease during sleep. Delta power of EEG in NREM sleep represents the principal marker of S during sleep; theta activity in waking is a marker of the rising limb of S. Core body temperature and melatonin rhythms are markers of C [14]. After this classical 2-process model proposed by Borberly [4,14], the advances in neurophysiology have led to a proliferation of models of SWC trying to extend it to a more physiological setting, e.g. the PR model [5]. Although classical models of SWC have been usually based on differential equations, discrete-time Markov chains have also demonstrated to be an adequate tool for modelling the cyclical dynamics of sleep and WK [2,7–10]. Markov analysis provides accurate information of the probability of staying in one state (i.e., the state stability, closely related to state duration), and of the transition probabilities from and to that state (i.e., rates).

Normal sleep is characterized by the periodic alternance of NREM and REM sleep (i.e., NREM-REM sleep cycle). In monophasic sleep, as in humans, after a first NREM-REM period, two to seven ultradian cycle follow until waking up.

In polyphasic species, such as rodents, sleep is distributed across 24 h in hundreds of short bouts, including variable proportions of the two states, while apparently mostly beginning with NREM. In addition to the regular sleep-wake pattern, humans and animals often exhibit brief awakenings from sleep [3]; brief awakenings are commonly observed across species and appear to occur randomly throughout the sleeping period, with a not fully understood dynamics. Because they exhibit robust scale-invariant features across different mammalian species [3], may reflect intrinsic aspects of the endogenous sleep control mechanism [citar 3].

We present a detailed analysis of WK bout durations in the mouse model. Brief-WK represented the majority of all WK bouts., but they were only slightly affected by circadian and ultradian rythms, as was previously reported in rat [11]. In contrast, the long WK bouts were strongly modulated by circadian influences. The concept that short and long WK bouts differ in terms of their underlying mechanism and functional significance is not new [3,11,16–18] and differing statistical approaches have converged to this concept. Detailed studies, using survival curves, conclude that the two type of WK are present in rats [11,17]. Simasko et al. showed that sleep was more fragmented than previously recognized by using a cut-off interval of 5-min to separate brief and long WK. We have used in mice 150 s as the temporal window, a value comparable having in account species-dependent differences, even although our methodology for sleep staging is different (they used a commercial software, with visual confirmation). We are not aware of any previous work reporting, in mice, an objective criteria to differentiate between brief and long WK. Circadian modulation was not explored in [3], because they only used rodent data from light period.

The analysis of the TP markov matrix reflects some interesting results. First, all of the states had different state maintenance probabilities ($p < 0.01$), although only WK shown significant circadian modulation. Second, during dark period, increased wake stability and $p_{WK \to NREM}$ transitions, and during light period, increased wake/NREM transitions. In summary, circadian modulation mainly affects to sleep-wake cyclicity rather to NREM-REM sleep cycle.

Moreover, our data suggest three levels of probability importance: first, state maintenance probabilities. Second, transition probabilities going to NREM sleep ($p_{WKB/ \to NREM}$, $p_{REM \to NREM}$ and of $p_{WKL \to NREM}$). The rest of transitions have less probabilistic relevance. These values indicate that quantitative probabilistic relevance of NREM sleep parallels its functional relevance. NREM produces slow oscillations generated intracortically, which, far from being epiphenomena, produce synaptic plasticity in cortical neurons and resonant activity in the corticothalamic loops, particularly during sleep spindles, with the consequence that the inputs of environment are inhibited and the cerebral cortex is deprived of signals (22). Circadian modulation of TP matrix also reveals the existence of two subsets of probabilities: one group that is modulated by the light (p_{WKL} and $p_{WKL \to NREM}$ probabilities, that increase in darkness) and another one (the rest) that is not modulated by light (NREM-REM-brief WK).

The question of the regulation of REM sleep, the intrasleep awakening dynamics, and the role of awakenings in the resetting of sleep regulation are still matters of debate [19]. Bennington et al. have proposed that the need for REM increases exclusively during NREM, thus suggesting a somehow subservient function of REM [20]. Work related to wakening paradigms also support this view, so that awakenings reset the NREM/REM ultradian process [21]. Other authors have postulated long-term and short-term homeostatic regulation of REM independent of NREM sleep with an accumulation in the absence of REM during both WK and NREM sleep [22]. Our data seem to support the first of the hipothesis, in the sense that we did not found modifications of probabilities for going to REM sleep along the circadian cycle (at least in the conditions of this experiment, where no deprivation or any experimental manipulation of sleep was performed), suggesting that every modification in REM amounts along the recordings are related to NREM changes. We also found that WKB-related probabilities were not modulated by circadian influences, so that WKB might be considered as an intrinsic part of the classic cycle NREM-REM, that maybe should be reclassified as NREM-REM-WKB cycle.

The analysis of the TP markov matrix provides some interesting insights about the properties of the SWC. First, all behavioral states show a distinct intrinsic stability, quantified by their state maintenance probabilities, but they can be grouped into highly stable states (WKL and NREM), and very instable states (WKB and REM). The most frequent transitions took place from the instable states to the stable NREM i.e., while the probability of transitions between the most stable states (i.e., between WKL and NREM) or of REM to WKL and WKB are significantly less frequent; the rest of transitions, from WKL and WKB to REM or from NREM to WKB were rare or inexistent. Second, that only the stability of long WK state and its transitions to NREM are modulated by circadian rhythms: longer lasting WKL bouts are generated more during active-dark than inactive-light phases due to the reduction of transitions from WKL to NREM; during the resting light phase, the probability of transitions from WKL to NREM is significantly higher than those in the opposite direction, i.e., from NREM to WKL. It indicates that circadian modulation affects to WKL-NREM cyclicity but not to NREM-REM-WKB sleep cycle.

The transitions values to input from the other states in NREM sleep indicate that quantitative probabilistic relevance of NREM sleep parallels its functional relevance. NREM produces slow oscillations generated intracortically, which, far from being epiphenomena, produce synaptic plasticity in cortical neurons and resonant activity in the corticothalamic loops, particularly during sleep spindles, with the consequence that the inputs of environment are inhibited and the cerebral cortex is deprived of peripheral signals [23]. The input transitions to rem also deserves a short commentary. Bennington et al. have proposed that the need for REM increases exclusively during NREM, thus suggesting a somehow subservient function of REM [20]. Other authors have postulated long-term and short-term homeostatic regulation of REM independent of NREM sleep with an accumulation in the absence of REM during both WK and NREM sleep [22].

Our data seem to support the first of the hypothesis, in the sense that we did not found significant modifications of probabilities along the circadian cycle for going from and to REM sleep (at least in the conditions of this experiment, where no deprivation or any experimental manipulation of sleep was performed), suggesting that every modification in REM amounts along the recordings are related to NREM changes. We also found that WKB-related probabilitiy transitions were not modulated by circadian influences, so that they might also be considered an intrinsic part of the classic cycle NREM-REM, that maybe should be reclassified as NREM-REM-WKB cycle.

5 Conclusions

In the mouse model, the application of quantified analysis of state bout durations in combination with transition probability analysis of sleep stages with discrete-time Markov chains constitute a powerful method for evaluating the probabilistic and statistical parameters of WK, NREM and REM sleep mechanisms, and for extension of sleep disorders. We found a bimodal distribution for duration of WK bouts (brief and long WK) with a temporal breakpoint of 150 s, having a differential circadian modulation. Of all state transitions, only those between long WK and NREM stages are controlled by circadian rhythms, favoring the hypothesis of the participation of brief WK into NREM-REM intrinsic sleep cycle.

Acknowledgements. This work was supported by a grant from the Spanish Ministry of Economy and Competitiveness (BUF2015-71078P) to L.C.B.

References

1. Jones, B.E.: The neural basis of consciousness across the sleep-waking cycle (1998)
2. Ferri, R., Pizza, F., Vandi, S., Iloti, M., Plazzi, G.: Decreased sleep stage transition pattern complexity in narcolepsy type 1. Clin. Neurophysiol. **127**, 2812–2819 (2016)
3. Lo, C.C., Chou, T., Penzel, T., Scammell, T.E., Strecker, R.E., Stanley, H.E., Ivanov, P.C.: Common scale-invariant patterns of sleep-wake transitions across mammalian species. Proc. Natl. Acad. Sci. U.S.A. **101**, 17545–17548 (2004)
4. Borbély, A.A.: A two process model of sleep regulation. Hum. Neurobiol. (1982)
5. Phillips, A., Robinson, P.: A quantitative model of sleep-wake dynamics based on the physiology of the brainstem ascending arousal system. J. Biol. Rhythms **22**, 167–179 (2007)
6. Aston-Jones, G., Chen, S., Zhu, Y., Oshinsky, M.L.: A neural circuit for circadian regulation of arousal. Nat. Neurosci. **4**, 732–738 (2001)
7. Spedicato, G.: Markovchain: an R package to easily handle discrete Markov chains. R package version 0.2 **2** (2015)
8. Mochizuki, T., Crocker, A., McCormack, S., Yanagisawa, M., Sakurai, T., Scammell, T.E.: Behavioral state instability in orexin knock-out mice. J. Neurosci. **24**, 6291–6300 (2004)
9. Kemp, B., Kamphuisen, H.: Simulation of human hypnograms using a Markov chain model. Sleep **9**, 405–414 (1986)

10. Kim, J., Lee, J.S., Robinson, P., Jeong, D.U.: Markov analysis of sleep dynamics. Phys. Rev. Lett. **102**, 178104 (2009)
11. Stephenson, R., Famina, S., Caron, A.M., Lim, J.: Statistical properties of sleep-wake behavior in the rat and their relation to circadian and ultradian phases. Sleep **36**, 1377 (2013)
12. Klerman, E.B., Wang, W., Duffy, J.F., Dijk, D.J., Czeisler, C.A., Kronauer, R.E.: Survival analysis indicates that age-related decline in sleep continuity occurs exclusively during NREM sleep. Neurobiol. Aging **34**, 309–318 (2013)
13. R Development Core Team: R: A Language and Environment for Statistical Computing. R Foundation for Statistical Computing, Vienna, Austria (2008). ISBN 3-900051-07-0
14. Borbély, A.A., Daan, S., Wirz-Justice, A., Deboer, T.: The two-process model of sleep regulation: a reappraisal. J. Sleep Res. (2016)
15. Brown, R.E., Basheer, R., McKenna, J.T., Strecker, R.E., McCarley, R.W.: Control of sleep and wakefulness. Physiol. Rev. **92**, 1087–1187 (2012)
16. McShane, B.B., Galante, R.J., Jensen, S.T., Naidoo, N., Pack, A.I., Wyner, A.: Characterization of the bout durations of sleep and wakefulness. J. Neurosci. Methods **193**, 321–333 (2010)
17. Simasko, S.M., Mukherjee, S.: Novel analysis of sleep patterns in rats separates periods of vigilance cycling from long-duration wake events. Behav. Brain Res. **196**, 228–236 (2009)
18. Behn, C.G.D., Brown, E.N., Scammell, T.E., Kopell, N.J.: Mathematical model of network dynamics governing mouse sleep-wake behavior. J. Neurophysiol. **97**, 3828–3840 (2007)
19. Le Bon, O.: Which theories on sleep ultradian cycling are favored by the positive links found between the number of cycles and rems? Biol. Rhythm Res. **44**, 675–685 (2013)
20. Benington, J.H., Heller, H.C.: REM-sleep timing is controlled homeostatically by accumulation of REM-sleep propensity in non-REM sleep. Am. J. Physiol.-Regul. Integr. Comp. Physiol. **266**, R1992–R2000 (1994)
21. Grözinger, M., Beersma, D.G., Fell, J., Röschke, J.: Is the nonREM-REM sleep cycle reset by forced awakenings from REM sleep? Physiol. Behav. **77**, 341–347 (2002)
22. Ocampo-Garcés, A., Vivaldi, E.A.: Short-term homeostasis of REM sleep assessed in an intermittent REM sleep deprivation protocol in the rat. J. Sleep Res. **11**, 81–89 (2002)
23. Steriade, M.: The corticothalamic system in sleep. Front. Biosci. **8**, d878–d899 (2003)

EEG Source Imaging Based on Dynamic Sparse Coding as ADHD Biomarker

F.M. Grisales-Franco[1], J.M. Medina-Salcedo[2], D.M. Ovalle-Martínez[3],
J.D. Martínez-Vargas[1(✉)], D.G. García-Murillo[1],
and G. Castellanos-Dominguez[1]

[1] Signal Processing and Recognition Group,
Universidad Nacional de Colombia, Bogotá, Colombia
{fmgrisalesl,cgcastellanosd,jmartinezv}@unal.edu.co
[2] Universidad Autnoma de Manizales, Manizales, Colombia
[3] Universidad Distrital Francisco José de Caldas, Bogotá, Colombia

Abstract. The study of the psychiatric disorder denominated Attention-deficit hyperactivity disorder (ADHD) demands the assessment of specific behavior, measured and evaluated through biomarkers like the neuroimaging that is applied due to the assumed association between with changes in the structure and function of the ADHD brain. Because of the provided time resolution, Electroencephalographic (EEG) signals and derived versions have recently gained increased attention for studying event-related potentials (ERPs). Moreover, relate to the ADHD diagnosis, techniques of EEG/ERP source imaging (ESI) are effective to locate brain areas related to attention task and analyze spatiotemporal patterns of the P300 wave. Therefore, with the aim to accurately determine the spatial location and temporal patterns involved in attention task, there is a need for implementing an adequate ERP marker able to incorporate the spatial and temporal prior information to the ESI solution. In this paper, the influence of the source reconstruction is evaluated on visual and auditory evoked potentials through an ESI solution, namely, Dynamic Sparse Coding that is based on physiological motivated spatio-temporal constraints over the source representation. As a result, the DSC-based approach improves the characterization of the spatio-temporal dynamics of the attentional evoked potentials processes, including reduced amplitudes in the P300 components of the ERPs in the ADHD group.

Keywords: ADHD Biomarker · EEG/ERP source imaging · Dynamic Sparse Coding · P300

1 Introduction

Attention-deficit hyperactivity disorder (ADHD) is a psychiatric disorder characterized by symptoms like inappropriate levels of inattention or lack of focus, hyperactivity, and impulsivity [1]. ADHD is considered a childhood disorder

© Springer International Publishing AG 2017
J.M. Ferrández Vicente et al. (Eds.): IWINAC 2017, Part I, LNCS 10337, pp. 416–425, 2017.
DOI: 10.1007/978-3-319-59740-9_41

that can persist into adolescence, even in adulthood with symptomatic differences across the age groups, carrying a high financial cost, familiar and interpersonal relationship difficulties, and adverse academic and vocational outcomes. So, ADHD has become a public health concern, and understanding the biologic nature of the disorder is a scientific and clinical increasing focus.

By the type of information provided for their implementation, biomarkers for ADHD can be classified based on the following principles: clinical, biochemical, genetic, proteomic or neuroimaging. This last marker is employed because ADHD has been related to differences in the structure and function of the brain, as well as changes in its neurotransmission [2]. Consequently, functional imaging methods and neurophysiological techniques have been used to provide the ADHD biological foundation, by characterizing spatial and temporal brain activation patterns related to this disorder. Between neuroimaging techniques, the functional magnetic resonance imaging (fMRI) has been used in several studies because of its high spatial resolution [3]. Nevertheless, such method is expensive and do not offer a good temporal resolution. On the other hand, the Electroencephalography (EEG) and its derivations, as the event-related potentials (ERPs), which provide high temporal resolution, and low implementation cost compared to other options, have become in potential techniques for application in ADHD diagnosis [4]. Specifically, ERPs reflect the phasic activity of cortical neurons to an internal or external stimulus and provide excellent temporal resolution to pinpoint when demanding attentional processes occur. By instance, for attention studies using oddball paradigms, the ERPs are used to analyze the P300, which is a positive wave that appears around of 300 ms after stimuli presentation. As the P300 wave only appears when the subject is engaged in the task of detecting a specific stimulation, its analysis has been widely used to diagnose ADHD [5]. In turn, children with ADHD have difficulties attending task-related events, which has been consistently associated with reductions in the P300 wave amplitude.

Furthermore, some works have focused on finding the brain areas related to attention tasks, to locate an accurate ADHD marker by analyzing spatiotemporal patterns of the P300 wave. In this regard, EEG/ERP source imaging (ESI) methods have been employed to examine the location and distribution of the current sources involved in oddball paradigms, and to elucidate differences between the activation patterns in control and ADHD subjects [6]. However, reconstruction of electrophysiological activity in the cortex based on scalp measurements is not straightforward because of a well known ill-posed inverse problem. This means that due to the large number of unknown parameters (possible active sources over the brain cortex), compared to the low number of EEG/ERP electrodes, the spatial location of the neural sources of the scalp-recorded activity cannot be conclusively determined, i.e., the inverse problem has no unique solution [7]. Consequently, for accurately determining the spatial location and temporal patterns involved in attention tasks, that could be used as an ADHD marker, a proper inclusion of spatial and temporal prior information must be included to solve the ill-posed inverse ESI solution [8].

In this paper, we reconstruct the brain activity recorded during oddball experiments, elucidating the generators of visual and auditory evoked potentials, to gain insights about the relation between the spatial and temporal characteristics of the P300 related neural activity and the ADHD disorder. For the ESI solution, we use a Dynamic Sparse Coding (DSC) method previously proposed in [9], that is based on physiologically motivated spatio-temporal constraints over the source representation, and it is suited to reconstruct the nonstationary brain activity, as the case of ERPs. Subsequently, we search significant differences between ADHD and control groups using statistical analysis. As a result, we obtain a better characterization of the spatio-temporal dynamics involved in the attentional evoked potentials processes, including reduced amplitudes in the P300 components of the ERPs in the ADHD group.

2   Methods

2.1   Visual and Auditory Evoked Potentials

Database Description: The real EEG data used in this study were selected from 30 children aging within ranges from 5 to 16 years, belonging to two socio-cultural levels (high medium and low medium). The sample was randomly selected from preschool, elementary, and secondary courses at private and public schools in the city of Manizales. Also, written permission was requested from the child's parents for participation in the research.

The following exclusion criteria were used: mental retardation, neurological antecedents (history of head trauma, epilepsy, and related) and psychiatric (psychiatric hospitalizations history, autism, and related) of importance according to the historical data supplied by the children's parents. Besides, the *Neuropsychological Assessment of Children (NAC)* was applied to each child in two sessions of about an hour and a half. Sections of NAC were randomly altered to monitor the effects of fatigue and order in the application of the subtests. Also, the Wechsler Intelligence Scale for Children was applied, to calculate the validity of the NAC. Finally, experts rated the results in different cognitive and academic abilities and then a systematized database was created, including the results of children in the various tests. As a result, twenty children in the ADHD group and ten children in the control group were grouped for further analysis.

Experimental Paradigm of Cognitive Evoked Potentials: After the neuropsychological test, we proceeded to take EEG data from all participants using an oddball paradigm, consisting of two stages, the first with visual stimuli and the second with auditory stimuli. In each condition, the stimulus lasts 130 ms, while the waiting time between two consecutive stimuli is 1 s. Within each stage, the subjects had to pay attention to a pre-defined (target) stimulus and count their occurrence, ignoring the presentation of other stimuli (non-targets). The non-target stimulus was presented by 80% of the trials, while the target occurred for the 20% remaining, resulting in approximately 160 non-target stimuli and 40 target stimuli.

EEG recordings were taken symmetrically using 19 electrodes with standard international system positions 10–20. Data were sub-sampled at 250 Hz and segmented in 1 s epochs. The resulting epochs were averaged separately for each subject, stimulation condition targets, and non-targets.

2.2   Source Space Reconstruction

With the purpose of locating the visual and auditory evoked potentials-related brain activity, we consider the *Dynamic Sparse Coding* (DSC). The principal idea behind this method is to estimate the cortical source activity, encouraging spatial sparsity and temporal homogeneity. For this, we assume the following linear model that represents the electromagnetic field magnitude measured by the scalp [10]: $Y = LJ + \Xi$,, where $Y \in \mathbb{R}^{C \times T}$ is the EEG data measured by $C \in \mathbb{N}$ sensors at $T \in \mathbb{N}$ time samples, $L \in \mathbb{R}^{C \times D}$ is the *lead field matrix* that represents the relationship between D distributed sources inside the brain and the sensor EEG activity, $J \in \mathbb{R}^{D \times T}$ is the cortical source activity, and $\Xi \in \mathbb{R}^{C \times T}$ is the observation noise measured with spatial covariance $Q_{\Xi} \in \mathbb{R}^{C \times C}$.

Under this model, the maximum a-posteriori (MAP) estimate of J can be determined by minimizing a particular cost function [11]. In the case of DSC, the current density is expressed as a linear combination of locally smooth, but confined spatial basis function: $J = \Phi H$,, where $\Phi_s \in \mathbb{R}^{D \times S}$ holds S spatial basis functions, and $H \in \mathbb{R}^{S \times T}$ is a matrix of weighting coefficients to be estimated. In order to enforce sparsity and temporal homogeneity, two regularization penalties are introduced so that the cost function of DSC takes the form:

$$\widehat{H} = \operatorname*{argmin}_{H} \{||Y - L\Phi H||_F^2 + \lambda_s ||H||_1 + \lambda_t \sum_{t \in T-1} ||h_{t+1} - h_t||_1\}, \quad (1)$$

where $\lambda_s \in \mathbb{R}^+$ and $\lambda_t \in \mathbb{R}^+$ are the spatial and temporal regularization parameters, respectively, and vector $h_t \in \mathbb{R}^{C \times 1}$ holds the t-th column of H. Notation $|| \cdot ||_p$ stands for the L_p-norm. Finally, the estimation of the neural activity is accomplished by the following linear mapping: $J = \Phi\widehat{H}$.

The DSC method considered in this work is applied to the ERPs obtained from each subject and experimental condition, namely visual target, visual non-target, auditory target and auditory non-target stimuli, as follows:

Head Model Implementation: With the aim of modeling the source space, we employ a tessellated surface in the gray-white matter interface with $D = 8196$ vertices (i.e., the number of available source locations), having the source orientations fixed orthogonally to the surface. Also, the lead fields are computed using a standardized volume conductor model (specifically, we employ the boundary element method) with a mean distance between neighboring vertices adjusted to 5 mm. The employed spatial basis Φ.

Statistical Analysis: Once the source activity is estimated, the dipole-wise source power is calculated and averaged in the time range from 227 to 383 ms, which corresponds to the ERP P300 component [12]. Afterward, we compare the response to target stimuli between groups (ADHD vs. Control). In this regard, the power difference is evaluated between two cases: visual target ADHD group vs. visual target control group, and auditory target ADHD group vs auditory target control group. The comparison is carried out using a two-sided pairwise Student-t test. Significant differences in power are assumed for brain areas achieving t-scores with absolute values greater than 2.0639, corresponding to alpha levels $p < 0.05$, uncorrected.

3   Results

Figure 1 shows the sensor-space data, as well as the results of the source reconstruction using DSC for the visual (Fig. 1(a) to (d)) and auditory (Fig. 1(e) to (h)) evoked potentials elicited by the target stimuli for representative subjects. Likewise, Fig. 2 shows the corresponding results for the non target stimuli. Panels ((a) and (e)) show the trial-wise stimulus-locked EEG time series, with red vertical lines at 227 ms and 383 ms. In panels ((b) and (f)) the average scalp topography from 227 ms to 383 ms is shown. Panels ((c) and (g)) depict the time series of the reconstructed activity, and panels ((d) and (h)) show the corresponding source reconstruction in the same time range. The time ranges from 227 ms to 383 ms is chosen since it corresponds to the P300 component of ERP. For both visual and auditory stimulation, DSC localizes components of the P300 in the prefrontal cortex coinciding with studies suggesting that deficits or dysregulation in subregions of the prefrontal cortex may carry to the spectrum of ADHD symptoms [13]. Namely, the dorsolateral prefrontal cortex regulates attention, and its impairment may lead to symptoms of inattention and distraction. Furthermore, the right inferior prefrontal cortex regulates behavior, and its impairment may carry to symptoms of impulsivity and hyperactivity. Moreover, the ventromedial prefrontal cortex regulates emotions responses. Particularly, in the case of visual stimulation, active areas appear in the occipital cortex neighborhood, being consistent with the stimulation produced. In the case of auditory stimulation, there are active areas near to the superior parietal lobule, which is associated with working and visuospatial memory. This finding coincides with types of ADHD and its association with spatial working memory deficits [14]. Besides, there are minimum actives areas in the temporal lobe associated with the stimulus.

In all cases, the reconstructed time series draws a clear representation of the dynamics found in the original ERP responses, and the cortical reconstruction shows actives areas proximate to the active zones in the scalp map. Generally, we observe that target stimuli lead to more local regions of estimated brain activity, while non-target stimuli the activity seems to be more dispersed.

Statistical Analysis: Figure 3 shows the results of the dipole-wise Student-t test for differences in power between groups (ADHD vs. Control) for visual and

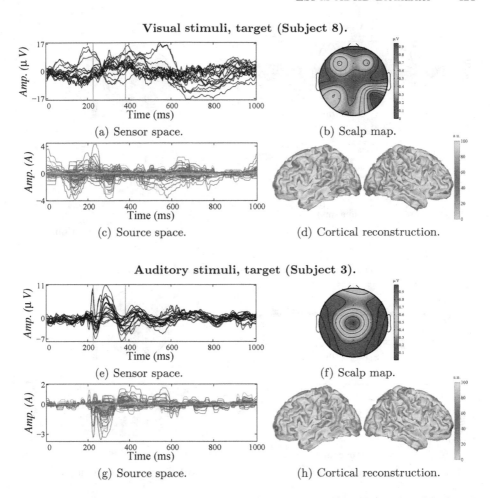

Fig. 1. Sensor-space EEG data and DSC source reconstruction of visual and auditory evoked potentials elicited by *target* stimuli for representative subjects.

auditory target stimuli, respectively. Here, dark blue color denotes higher amplitudes in the P300 for the ADHD group, while dark red color denotes higher activity in the control group. In both cases, significant differences (red areas of higher intensity) are found nearby to the ventral and dorsal attention networks. This finding is consistent with studies that have found reduced activity in these attention networks in children with ADHD [15]. Particularly, with the visual stimuli, there are active areas near to the posterior cingulate gyrus associated with topographic and topokinetic memory. Moreover, this area is related to the high-demand visual processing. The posterior inferior temporal gyrus (associated with the visual fixation and sustained attention to color and shape) also presents significant differences between the control and ADHD groups under the visual stimulation. For the auditory stimuli, we found actives areas in the gyrus rectus

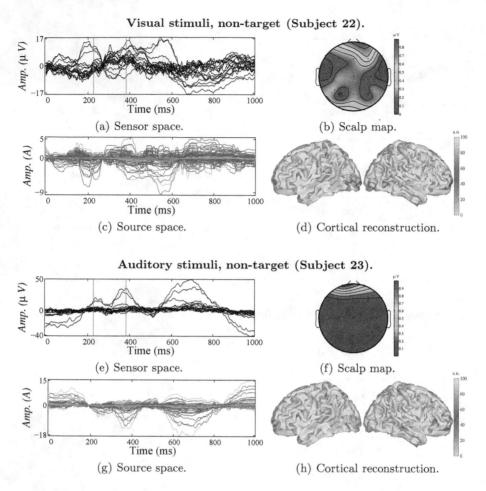

Fig. 2. Sensor-space EEG data and DSC source reconstruction of visual and auditory evoked potentials elicited by *non-target* stimuli for representative subjects.

involved in auditory non-speech processing, the temporal pole that response to auditory stimulation, and the middle temporal gyrus related to processing complex sounds. Also, it is noted that in both conditions of stimulation, the significant differences are given only for positive values. This situation means that the amplitude of the activity related to P300 has a greater amplitude in control subjects than in ADHD subjects. In both stimuli, these differences are seen in the network of frontoparietal attention. The results are consistent with recent studies that show reductions in the amplitude of P300 in areas surrounding this region in children with ADHD.

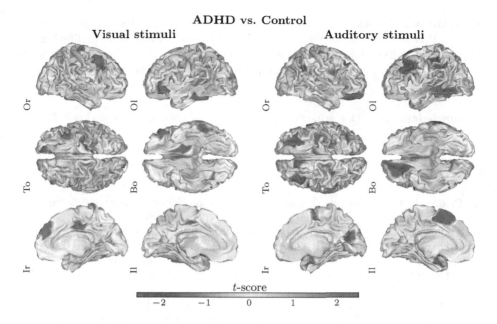

Fig. 3. Examples of t-score maps computed for differences in dipole-wise power for ERPs analysis with visual and auditory stimuli between groups (ADHD vs. Control). Views: Outside right (Or), Outside left (Ol), Top (To), Bottom (Bo), Inside right (Ir) and Inside left (Il). (Color figure online)

4   Discussion and Concluding Remarks

In this work, we have analyzed differences in the neural generators of the P300 component during an oddball task in control and ADHD children. The source estimation is carried out through a regularized method for neural activity reconstruction named Dynamic Sparse Coding (DSC). This method explicitly includes both (space and time) constraints on the solution of the EEG inverse problem to reach a suitable trade-off between the corresponding space and time resolutions. As a result, DSC improves the estimation of the active sources with powerful non-stationary brain activity like ERPs, and it describes in a suitable way the space-time structure of the visual and auditory stimuli responses.

The active areas under the oddball paradigm are highly related to the used stimuli. For instance, more active areas are found in the neighborhood of the occipital cortex in visual stimuli, and the temporal lobe in the auditory stimuli. Furthermore, we found actives areas near to zones specialized for regulating attention, behavior, and emotions, and near to zones with functions related to memory. All these functions are related to the oddball paradigm, and therefore with the ERPs. Finally, the results show significant differences near to the ventral and dorsal attention networks. These differences show, for both types of simulation, greater amplitudes in the control group than in the ADHD group.

As the future work, we plan to find the networks related to each of the components P3a and P3b of the P300 differentiated on the state-of-the-art literature. Also, we would like to investigate whether, in addition to the reduced amplitudes in the P300 component, the connections related to the attention processes are also affected.

Acknowledgments. This work was supported by the research project 111956933522 founded by COLCIENCIAS.

References

1. Prince, J.: Catecholamine dysfunction in attention-deficit/hyperactivity disorder: an update. J. Clin. Psychopharmacol. **28**(3), S39–S45 (2008)
2. Thome, J., Ehlis, A.-C., Fallgatter, A.J., Krauel, K., Lange, K.W., Riederer, P., Romanos, M., Taurines, R., Tucha, O., Uzbekov, M., et al.: Biomarkers for attention-deficit/hyperactivity disorder (ADHD). A consensus report of the WFSBP task force on biological markers and the world federation of ADHD. World J. Biol. Psychiatry **13**(5), 379–400 (2012)
3. Cortese, S., Kelly, C., Chabernaud, C., Proal, E., Di Martino, A., Milham, M.P., Castellanos, F.X.: Toward systems neuroscience of ADHD: a meta-analysis of 55 fMRI studies. Am. J. Psychiatry (2012)
4. Johnstone, S.J., Barry, R.J., Clarke, A.R.: Ten years on: a follow-up review of ERP research in attention-deficit/hyperactivity disorder. Clin. Neurophysiol. **124**(4), 644–657 (2013)
5. Szuromi, B., Czobor, P., Komlósi, S., Bitter, I.: P300 deficits in adults with attention deficit hyperactivity disorder: a meta-analysis. Psychol. Med. **41**(07), 1529–1538 (2011)
6. Janssen, T.W.P., Geladé, K., van Mourik, R., Maras, A., Oosterlaan, J.: An ERP source imaging study of the oddball task in children with attention deficit/hyperactivity disorder. Clin. Neurophysiol. **127**(2), 1351–1357 (2016)
7. Xu, L., Wu, T., Valdes-Sosa, P.A.: Incorporating priors for EEG source imaging and connectivity analysis. Front. Neurosci. **9** (2015)
8. Giraldo, E., Martinez-Vargas, J.D., Castellanos-Dominguez, G.: Reconstruction of neural activity from EEG data using dynamic spatio-temporal constraints. Int. J. Neural Syst. **26**, 1650026 (2016)
9. Martínez-Vargas, J.D., Grisales-Franco, F.M., Castellanos-Dominguez, G.: Estimation of M/EEG non-stationary brain activity using spatio-temporal sparse constraints. In: Ferrández Vicente, J.M., Álvarez-Sánchez, J.R., de la Paz López, F., Toledo-Moreo, F.J., Adeli, H. (eds.) IWINAC 2015. LNCS, vol. 9107, pp. 429–438. Springer, Cham (2015). doi:10.1007/978-3-319-18914-7_45
10. Baillet, S., Mosher, J.C., Leahy, R.M.: Electromagnetic brain mapping. IEEE Sig. Process. Mag. **18**, 14–30 (2001)
11. Grech, R., Cassar, T., Muscat, J., Camilleri, K., Fabri, S., Zervakis, M., Xanthopoulos, P., Sakkalis, V., Vanrumste, B.: Review on solving the inverse problem in EEG source analysis. J. NeuroEng. Rehabil. **5**(25), 792–800 (2008)
12. Volpe, U., Mucci, A., Bucci, P., Merlotti, E., Galderisi, S., Maj, M.: The cortical generators of P3a and P3b: a loreta study. Brain Res. Bull. **73**(4), 220–230 (2007)
13. Arnsten, A.F.T.: The use of α-2a adrenergic agonists for the treatment of attention-deficit/hyperactivity disorder. Expert Rev. Neurother. **10**(10), 1595–1605 (2010)

14. Vance, A., Silk, T.J., Casey, M., Rinehart, N.J., Bradshaw, J.L., Bellgrove, M.A., Cunnington, R.: Right parietal dysfunction in children with attention deficit hyperactivity disorder, combined type: a functional MRI study. Mol. Psychiatry **12**(9), 826–832 (2007)
15. Hart, H., Radua, J., Nakao, T., Mataix-Cols, D., Rubia, K.: Meta-analysis of functional magnetic resonance imaging studies of inhibition and attention in attention-deficit/hyperactivity disorder: exploring task-specific, stimulant medication, and age effects. JAMA Psychiatry **70**(2), 185–198 (2013)

Identification of Nonstationary Brain Networks Using Time-Variant Autoregressive Models

Juan David Martinez-Vargas[1]([✉]), Jose David Lopez[2],
Felipe Rendón-Castrillón[1], Gregor Strobbe[3], Pieter van Mierlo[3],
German Castellanos-Dominguez[1], and Diana Ovalle-Martínez[4]

[1] Signal Processing and Recognition Group,
Universidad Nacional de Colombia, Bogotá, Colombia
jmartinezv@unal.edu.co
[2] SISTEMIC, Facultad de Ingeniería, Universidad de Antioquia, Medellín, Colombia
[3] Medical Image and Signal Processing Group, Ghent University, IBBT, Ghent,
Belgium
[4] Universidad Distrital Francisco José de Caldas, Bogotá, Colombia
dmovalle@gmail.com

Abstract. Electroencephalographic (EEG) data provide a direct, non-invasive measurement of neural brain activity. Nevertheless, the common assumption of EEG stationarity (i.e., time-invariant process) neglects information about the underlying neural networks connectivity. We present an approach for finding networks of brain regions, which are connected by effective associations varying over time (*effective connectivity*). Aiming to improve the performed connectivity analysis, brain source activity is initially reconstructed from EEG recordings, applying an inverse EEG solution with enhanced spatial resolution. Further, a time-variant effective connectivity measure is used to investigate the information flow over some predefined regions of interest. For testing purposes, validation is carried out simulated and real EEG data, promoting non-stationary dynamics. The obtained results of performance prove that inherent interpretability provided by the time-variant processes can be useful to describe the underlying neural networks flow.

1 Introduction

To date, the importance of measuring connectivity between spatially separate, but functionally related brain regions has become of a big interest in the study of human neural functions. Though most of the related work is designed for functional magnetic resonance imaging, Electroencephalography (EEG), which non-invasively monitors the electrical brain activity, is increasingly used because of the provided high temporal resolution at a low cost. Moreover, EEG data analysis allows exploring the dynamics and adaptability of different cognitive processes, yielding reliable connectivity estimates between the brain regions [1].

Generally speaking, EEG source connectivity analysis comprises two stages: (*i*) EEG signals are mapped into a source space, employing a given inversion solution method, (*ii*) modeling of spatio-temporal dynamics of activation patterns is performed using the predefined Regions of Interest (ROI) set [7]. In the

© Springer International Publishing AG 2017
J.M. Ferrández Vicente et al. (Eds.): IWINAC 2017, Part I, LNCS 10337, pp. 426–434, 2017.
DOI: 10.1007/978-3-319-59740-9_42

first stage, the accuracy of brain mapping profoundly limits the interpretability of the connectivity measurements [4]. Also, the resulted connectivity measure tends to show fake connections among regions, if the mapped brain regions are not the true brain activity generators. Another aspect to consider is the static nature of most inversion solution methods that may lead to inaccurate temporal patterns of the mapped activity generators, resulting in the estimation of false connections. In the second stage, the functional or effective connections between brain regions, which mainly differ in the inclusion (effective) or not (functional) of the information flow direction, can be investigated by applying measurements of connectivity or information flow to the regions of interest [5]. Specifically, Effective connectivity is defined as the influence that one neural system exerts over another, either directly or indirectly. In contrast to functional connectivity, that is, the temporal correlations between remote neurophysiology events, the effective connectivity describes the direction of interactions between brain regions. Consequently, several measures have been proposed, commonly including space, time, and frequency domains [3]. Although most of the connectivity approaches assume that connectivity patterns remain constant at the time, there is growing evidence that brain dynamics are non-stationary [9]. As a result, there is a clear need to quantify dynamic changes in the network structure through the time [6].

With the aim to improve identification of nonstationary brain networks, this work comprises two processing stages: Initially, brain activity is represented as a set of small spatial basis functions or patches, enforcing a compact and sparse support through the well-known approach (termed *Multiple Sparse Priors*). Further, some regions of interest are selected based on the recovered sources with the highest energy. Then, to accurately encode the temporal dynamics of underlying neural networks, a time variant effective connectivity measure is employed, quantifying the information flow changes over the selected regions through time. Obtained results on simulated and real EEG databases show that the proposed approach enables identifying with increased accuracy the brain activity information flow when non-stationary data is analyzed.

2   Methods

2.1   Brain Source Estimation

For estimating the brain activity, we consider the following distributed solution:

$$Y = LJ + \Xi, \tag{1}$$

where $Y \in \mathbb{R}^{C \times T}$ is the EEG data measured by C sensors at T time samples, $J \in \mathbb{R}^{D \times T}$ is the amplitude of the D current dipoles in each three-dimensional dimension distributed through cortical surface, and $L \in \mathbb{R}^{C \times D}$, commonly named lead field matrix, is the gain matrix representing the relationship between sources and EEG data. Besides, EEG measurements are assumed to be affected by zero mean Gaussian noise $\boldsymbol{\Xi} \in \mathbb{R}^{C \times T}$, having a matrix covariance $\boldsymbol{Q_{\Xi}} = \lambda_{\boldsymbol{\Xi}} \boldsymbol{I}_C$, where $\boldsymbol{I}_C \in \mathbb{R}^{C \times C}$ is an identity matrix, and $\lambda_{\boldsymbol{\Xi}} \in \mathbb{R}^+$ is the noise variance. Under these constraints, the brain source activity can be estimated as:

$$\hat{\boldsymbol{J}} = \boldsymbol{Q} \boldsymbol{L}^\top (\boldsymbol{Q_\Xi} + \boldsymbol{L} \boldsymbol{Q} \boldsymbol{L}^\top)^{-1} \boldsymbol{Y}, \tag{2}$$

where $\boldsymbol{Q} \in \mathbb{R}^{D \times D}$ stands for the source covariance, constructed as a weighted sum of P available spatial solutions (or *patches*) $\{\boldsymbol{Q}_p, p = 1, \ldots, P\}$, each regarding one potentially activated cortex region weighted by its respective hyperparameter $\lambda_p \in \mathbb{R}^+$, as follows (termed *Multiple Sparse Priors* – MSP) [2]:

$$\boldsymbol{Q} = \sum_{p \in P} \exp(\lambda_p) \boldsymbol{Q}_p.$$

In practice, optimization of noise variance and source covariance hyperparameters $\{\lambda_{\boldsymbol{\Xi}}, \lambda_p\}$ is done using standard variational schemes as detailed in [8].

3   Time-Varying Effective Connectivity

In order to estimate the causal relation among all current dipoles, a time-variant connectivity measure, namely, *full frequency adaptive directed transfer function* (*ffADTF*), can be calculated from the coefficients of a *Time-variant Autoregressive* (TVAR) model, as proposed in [5]:

$$\rho_{ij}(t) = \frac{\sum_{f=f_1}^{f_2} |H_{ij}(f,t)|^2}{\sum_{d=1}^{D} \sum_{f'=f_1}^{f_2} |H_{id}(f',t)|^2},$$

where $H_{ij}(f,t)$ is the time-variant transfer matrix of the system, that describes the information flow from source j to source i, $\forall i, j = 1, \ldots, D$, at frequency f and time t. As $H_{ij}(f,t)$ may increase when there is no power in the spectrum of dipole j at that frequency and time, each term should be weighted by the autospectrum of the sending source. Thus, the modified effective connectivity measure, or *spectrum-weighted adaptive directed transfer function (swADTF)*, is computed as follows:

$$\varrho_{ij}(t) = \frac{\sum_{f=f_1}^{f_2} |H_{ij}(f,t)|^2 \sum_{d=1}^{D} |H_{jd}(f,t)|^2}{\sum_{d'=1}^{D} \sum_{f'=f_1}^{f_2} |H_{id'}(f',t)|^2 \sum_{d''=1}^{D} |H_{d'd''}(f',t)|^2}.$$

As a result, the swADTF value allows analyzing the causal relation among all signals at a predefined frequency band over time.

4   Experimental Set-Up

4.1   Validation on Simulated Activity

Simulated Data Description. The simulation is designed to test whether the swADTF measure can describe the directional flow that occurs during the onset of an evoked activity. Thus, two active dipoles are simulated that promote a similar behavior to an evoked-response potential, generating the corresponding non-stationary time series by real Morlet wavelets of 1.5 s length, sampled at 200 Hz. The random central frequency of the Morlet wavelet is sampled from a Gaussian distribution with a mean of 9 Hz and standard deviation of 2 Hz. The stimulus started at $t = 0$ and the activity propagates from simulated active dipole #1 to dipole #2 at $t = 0.1$ s. Besides, the background noise of the dipole signals is set to have a $1/f$ spectral behavior. Therefore, each EEG is calculated by multiplying the simulated brain activity by the lead field matrix (see Eq. (1)).

For the source space modeling, we employ a tessellated surface of the gray-white matter interface with 8196 vertices (suitable source placements), having orientations fixed orthogonally to the surface. Also, the lead fields are computed using a volume conductor (calculated by boundary element method) with a mean distance between neighboring vertices adjusted to 5 mm. Thus, a synthetic EEG is generated under 128-channels configuration.

Three experimental setups, holding 100 simulations each, are performed to test the sensibility to the noise of the proposed connectivity based approach. To this end, a measurement noise is added to get signal-to-noise-ratio (SNR) levels of 0, 5, 20 dB. Location of active dipoles is randomly selected for each simulation. Figure 1 shows a schematic representation of the proposed testing for the simulated EEG data.

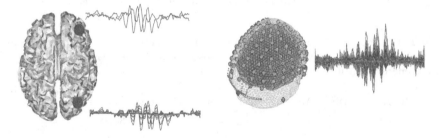

Fig. 1. Simulation set-up. Left panel: source level activity that spreads from the blue to the green location (time series of the simulated activity is shown with the same colors). The entire source activity is depicted. Right panel: generated sensor level (EEG) activity. (Color figure online)

Source Level Effective Connectivity Analysis. Neural activity reconstruction is obtained by the MSP approach, using a greedy search optimization method. Then, to avoid the computation of D × D connectivity values, the regions of interest (ROIs) are determined. To this end, a region with approximated ratio of 20 mm in the cortical surface around the dipoles with the highest energy is drawn. Consequently, the closest active dipoles are defined as the same ROI, avoiding spurious connectivity. Afterward, the averaged time series of each ROI and the connectivity measure for all the regions are extracted. Calculation the involved connectivity measure is performed under the following parameters: order of the time variant auto-regression model is set at $p = 15$, update coefficient of the Kalman filter is fixed as 0.001, and the smoother parameter is empirically adjusted to 100. Also, the connectivity is computed within the frequency interval, ranging from 0 to 30 Hz.

Due to the swADTF value is a time-variant measure, the averaged value over time is estimated to compare among several connectivity values directly. Besides, we describe the directional flow of the brain activity by the first two ROIs that have the highest averaged swADTF value, and that are assumed as the source and sink regions, respectively. For the subsequent analysis, the remaining ROIs are discarded. For the sake of comparison, the source and sink regions are also selected based on the energy of the reconstructed activity over each ROI (first two regions with the highest energy).

Results of Assessed Performance. As the assessment measure, the minimum Euclidean distance is computed between all dipoles of the selected ROIs and the simulated source and sink dipoles. Also, we employ as performance measure the percentage of times when the real connectivity direction is correct. Table 1 shows the error distances estimated for SNR = 0, 5, and 20 dB. As seen, the mean localization error of the connectivity-based approach is consistently lower that reduces when the SNR value increases. In the same way, the proposed method reproduces the connectivity direction in up to 88% of the times, unlike the energy-based approach that only obtain an accuracy of 50%.

Table 1. Connectivity direction error and mean localization error for different signal to noise ratios, simulated with both the proposed connectivity based approach (con) and the energy measure (en).

SNR	Acc (con)[%]	Acc (en)[%]	Loc. error (con) mm	Loc. error (en) mm
0	64	46	24.66	30.18
5	83	49	9.83	30.86
20	88	54	10.48	26.4

Figure 2(a) presents the localization error for each of the two simulated sources assessed by both tested algorithms: connectivity (con), and energy based (en) for a fixed SNR = 5. As can be seen, the variation among simulations is significantly higher with the energy-based algorithm. This result is expected due to the different accuracy in connectivity direction provided by each algorithm. Note that the solution is robust to both kinds of simulated noise conditions, namely, neural background activity and sensor level activity, as shown by the error box-plot in Fig. 2(a), fixing SNR = 20.

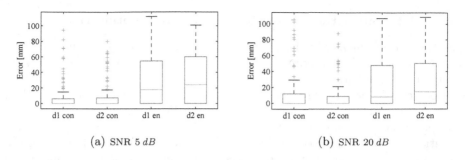

(a) SNR 5 *dB*   (b) SNR 20 *dB*

Fig. 2. Error box-plot showing the euclidean distance between the first active source and its estimation (d1), and the second active source and its estimation (d2), for both the connectivity measure (con) and the energy based measure (en), in 100 experiments with SNR 5 and 20 dB respectively.

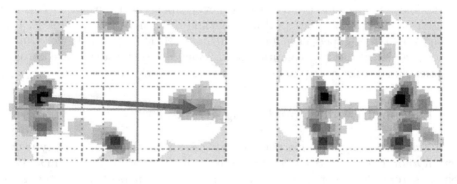

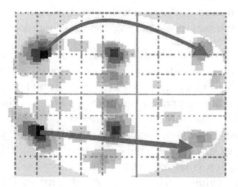

Fig. 3. Connectivity map obtained over the EEG brain image of the faces condition from the faces-scrambled paradigm. Note how the connectivity does not follow the higher energy sources and instead focused the temporal lobe, suggesting expectation of recognizing the face. (Color figure online)

4.2   Validation on Faces-Scrambled Paradigm Identification

Database Description. This EEG data collection was acquired from a subject who participated in a multimodal study of face perception[1]. The data were recorded while making symmetry judgments of faces and scrambled faces. Either type of faces was presented for 600 ms, every 3600 ms while data were acquired on a 128-channel Active-Two system, sampled at 2048 Hz. After artifact rejection, the epochs were baseline-corrected from −200 ms to 0 ms, averaged over each condition and down-sampled to 200 Hz. For modeling of the source space, the same tessellated surface with 8196 vertices, and the same model, calculated by boundary element method, was applied to build the lead fields.

Results for Faces Conditions. As observed in Fig. 3 that displays the source reconstruction for faces condition of the faces-scrambled paradigm, the proposed methodology managed to avoid the high energy dipoles in the fusiform gyrus and focused in the frontal cortex (red lines outline the connectivity assessed). Due to the attitude of expectancy for recognizing each face, this behavior can be anticipated since the face condition study suggests that there is a controlled response besides the perceptual one.

5   Discussion and Concluding Remarks

In this work, we propose a methodology for measuring the nonstationary neural activity flow in the case of evoked response potentials. To this end, brain activity extracts from EEG recordings by solving the Multiple-Sparse-Priors inverse solution, and then, a time variant effective connectivity is used for analysis in more detail the information flow over some predefined regions of interest. However, based on the results obtained from simulated and real EEG data, the following aspects should be considered for implementation of the proposed methodology:

- Due to the fact that the connectivity exhibits a high sensibility to the source reconstruction, the MSP-based source reconstruction is incorporated with the purpose of avoiding loss of quality of the performed accuracy. In fact, the higher the demanded localization quality of spatial-temporal patterns – the larger the needed accuracy provided by the source reconstruction solution.
- For the sake of validation, the proposed approach is contrasted with an energy based strategy, yielding a connectivity direction that is enhanced up to 88% of the times. Also, the source localization is improved, reaching a localization error of approximately 10 mm for the values SNR = 5 and 20. Regarding the noise rejection, the proposed approach shows a stable behavior.
- The considered nonstationarity of the underlying networks in the EEG recordings is clearly affecting the performance achieved by the proposed and comparison approaches. Thus, Table 1 shows that the energy-based methodology (that does not take connectivity into account) fails in detecting the real

---

[1] freely available at http://www.fil.ion.ucl.ac.uk/spm/data/mmfaces/.

connectivity flow accurately. Consequently, even the brain activity sources have been rightly identified by the mapping algorithm, the temporal dynamic analysis must be incorporated to improve the activity flow detection.

- Since the location accuracy is improved, a better interpretability of results may be supplied. Thus, in the case of tested faces-scrambled database, the connectivity avoids the hippocampus and points out to the frontal lobe, suggesting that there is a controlled response due to the attitude of expectancy for recognizing each face.

As a concluding remark, the performed validation on real and simulated data prove that the proposed approach enables identification of the information flow over regions of interest drawn over the brain cortex. To this end, we discuss a more detailed analysis of the temporal patterns, extracted from EEG recordings, in a predefined frequency band. Consequently, even all experiments are carried out for the case of evoked response potentials, the methodology can be readily extrapolated to other types of brain dynamics, such as epileptic activity. Also, the inclusion of a brain mapping method that encourages a set of temporal constraints will be considered as future work, attempting to improve the accuracy of the connectivity analysis.

Acknowledgments. This work was supported by the research project 11974454838 founded by COLCIENCIAS.

References

1. Brookes, M.J., O'Neill, G.C., Hall, E.L., Woolrich, M.W., Baker, A., Corner, S.P., Robson, S.E., Morris, P.G., Barnes, G.R.: Measuring temporal, spectral and spatial changes in electrophysiological brain network connectivity. NeuroImage **91**, 282–299 (2014)
2. Friston, K., Harrison, L., Daunizeau, J., Kiebel, S., Phillips, C., Trujillo-Barreto, N., Henson, R., Flandin, G., Mattout, J.: Multiple sparse priors for the M/EEG inverse problem. NeuroImage **39**(3), 1104–1120 (2008)
3. Greenblatt, R., Pflieger, M., Ossadtchi, A.: Connectivity measures applied to human brain electrophysiological data. J. Neurosci. Methods **207**(1), 1–16 (2012)
4. Grosse-wentrup, M.: Understanding brain connectivity patterns during motor imagery for brain-computer interfacing. In: Koller, D., Schuurmans, D., Bengio, Y., Bottou, L. (eds.) Advances in Neural Information Processing Systems 21, pp. 561–568. Curran Associates, Inc (2009)
5. van Mierlo, P., Carrette, E., Hallez, H., Raedt, R., Meurs, A., Vandenberghe, S., Van Roost, D., Boon, P., Staelens, S., Vonck, K.: Ictal-onset localization through connectivity analysis of intracranial EEG signals in patients with refractory epilepsy. Epilepsia **54**(8), 1409–1418 (2013)
6. Monti, R.P., Hellyer, P., Sharp, D., Leech, R., Anagnostopoulos, C., Montana, G.: Estimating time-varying brain connectivity networks from functional MRI time series. NeuroImage **103**, 427–443 (2014)
7. Schoffelen, J.M., Gross, J.: Source connectivity analysis with MEG and EEG. Hum. Brain Mapp. **30**(6), 1857–1865 (2009)

8. Wipf, D., Nagarajan, S.: A unified bayesian framework for MEG/EEG source imaging. NeuroImage **44**(3), 947–966 (2009)
9. Woolrich, M.W., Baker, A., Luckhoo, H., Mohseni, H., Barnes, G., Brookes, M., Rezek, I.: Dynamic state allocation for MEG source reconstruction. NeuroImage **77**, 77–92 (2013)

Detection of EEG Dynamic Changes Due to Stimulus-Related Activity in Motor Imagery Recordings

L.F. Velasquez-Martinez[1]([⊠]), A. Alvarez-Meza[2],
and G. Castellanos-Dominguez[1]

[1] Signal Processing and Recognition Group, Universidad Nacional de Colombia,
Manizales, Colombia
lfvelasquezma@unal.edu.co
[2] Automatics Research Group, Universidad Tecnologica de Pereira,
Perereira, Colombia

Abstract. Brain-computer Interfaces aims to assess brain activity patterns by analyzing multichannel time series extracted from electrical recordings, as a result of neuron interactions, e.g., Electroencephalography (EEG) that is a record of the neuronal electrical activity measured in the cerebral cortex having a high temporal resolution. Generally, BCI systems are based on the cognitive neuroscience paradigm termed as Motor Imagery (brain activity patterns of the imagination of a motor action, e.g., the imagination of hand movements). Nevertheless, the designing an MI-based BCI system requires an appropriate EEG data analysis to reach the needed performance for real-world BCI applications. Particularly, the selection of the active segment or the segment with the informative signals related to a determinate MI task is determinant for the possible performance. Hence, to select the window signal stimulus-related, detecting temporal changes in data are necessary to understand how a cognitive process unfolds in response to a stimulus. For this purpose, a non-stationary degree estimation based on the first Statistical moments (mean and covariance) is assessed. The results show that the changes in the non-stationary measure are directly related to executed stimulus during the EEG MI recording. The findings could be used to select the active analysis window and consequently, improving the MI classification tasks.

Keywords: EEG · Motor Imagery · Non-stationarity measure · BCI

1 Introduction

The EEG signal is a record of the neuronal electrical activity along of scalp measuring the currents that flow during synaptic neurons excitations in the cerebral cortex. Due to high temporal resolution present on the EEG recordings, they have been useful for studying the brain dynamics and used in several applications

© Springer International Publishing AG 2017
J.M. Ferrández Vicente et al. (Eds.): IWINAC 2017, Part I, LNCS 10337, pp. 435–443, 2017.
DOI: 10.1007/978-3-319-59740-9_43

such as testing afferent pathways (evoked potentials), investigate epilepsy and locating the seizure origin, game controlling, Brain Computer Interfaces (BCI) applications, among others [1,2]. The main BCI assumption is that the neural activity generated by the brain is independent of its normal output pathways of peripheral nerve techniques. Thus, the electrical activity of brain function might provide a new non-muscular channel for sending messages and commands to the external world. Usually, BCI systems are based on the cognitive neuroscience paradigm termed as Motor Imagery (MI), that is, the brain activity patterns of the imagination of a motor action, e.g., imagination of the hand movements [3,4].

To date, EEG-based BCI has received increased attention and enlarge the number of applications and uses, mainly due to the development of both portable EEG acquisition systems and dry electrodes which not need conductive gel for the preparation of EEG recording. However, the designing an MI-based BCI system requires an appropriate EEG data analysis to reach the required performance for real-world BCI applications [5]. Particularly, the selection of the active segment or the segment with the informative signals related to a determinate MI task is determinant for the possible performance as is shown in [6]. It allows selecting just the interesting brain activity stimulus-related without information that would be unrelated to brain responses decreasing the classification performance. Thus, to select the window signal stimulus-related, detecting temporal changes in data are necessary to understand how a cognitive process unfolds in response to a stimulus.

We aim to detect EEG dynamic changes due to stimulus-related activity in MI recordings, a non-stationary degree estimation based on the first Statistical moments (mean and covariance) is assessed. The obtained results experimentally show that the changes in the non-stationary measure are directly related to executed stimulus during the EEG MI recording. Besides, the findings could be used to select the active analysis window and consequently, improving the MI classification tasks. The paper is organized as follow: Sect. 2 describes the theoretical background of the proposed approach. Section 3 provides an overview of the experiments and results from tested methods. Lastly, Sect. 4, outlines the work discussion, conclusions and future work.

2   Non-stationary Degree Estimation

Let a time series $X = \{x(t) \in \mathbb{R}^D; t = 1, \ldots, T\}$, with mean $\bar{\mu} \in \mathbb{R}^D$ and covariance $\bar{\Sigma} \in \mathbb{R}^{D \times D}$ computed as:

$$\bar{\mu} = \mathbb{E}_{\mathscr{T}} \{x(t)\}, \tag{1}$$

$$\bar{\Sigma} = \mathbb{E}_{\mathscr{T}} \{x(t)x(t)^{\top}\}, \tag{2}$$

being $\mathbb{E}_{\mathscr{T}} \{x(t)\} = \frac{1}{|\mathscr{T}|} \int_{\mathscr{T}} x(t)dt$ the averaging operator and $\mathscr{T} \subset \mathbb{R}$ the analysis interval.

By extracting M overlapped segments from the time series using a window $\mathscr{W} \subset \mathscr{T}$ ($|\mathscr{W}| = L$ and $L \ll |\mathscr{T}|$), we obtain a set of segments

$\mathscr{X} = \{\boldsymbol{X}_m \in \mathbb{R}^{L \times D} : m = 1, \ldots, M\}$ with $\boldsymbol{X}_m = \{\boldsymbol{x}(t) : t \in [(m-1)\lambda + 1,$ $(m-1)\lambda + L]\}$ where $\lambda \in \mathbb{R}^+$ is the window overlap. Besides, the corresponding means and covariance values of the segments build the sets $\mathscr{U} = \{\boldsymbol{\mu}_m \in \mathbb{R}^D :$ $m = 1, \ldots, M\}$ and $\mathscr{S} = \{\boldsymbol{\Sigma}_m \in \mathbb{R}^{D \times D} : m = 1, \ldots, M\}$.

Then, the time series is said to be second order stationary if its first two moments remain constant over the time, that is, for all $t, \tau \in \mathbb{R}$ the following conditions hold

$$\mathbb{E}_{\mathscr{S}} \{\boldsymbol{x}(t)\} = \mathbb{E}_{\mathscr{W}} \{\boldsymbol{x}(t+\tau)\} , \tag{3}$$

$$\mathbb{E}_{\mathscr{S}} \left\{\boldsymbol{x}(t)\boldsymbol{x}(t)^\top\right\} = \mathbb{E}_{\mathscr{W}} \left\{\boldsymbol{x}(t+\tau)\boldsymbol{x}(t+\tau)^\top\right\} , \tag{4}$$

Since above conditions are strongly restrictive, we propose to account for the temporal changes in the time series $\boldsymbol{X}$ by comparing each segment $\boldsymbol{X}_m$ and the whole series $\boldsymbol{X}$ using the Kullback-Leibler divergence (D_{KL}). Such a divergence is a measure of dissimilarity between probability distributions P and Q defined as $D_{KL}(P\|Q) = \sum_i P(i) \log \left(\frac{P(i)}{Q(i)}\right)$. In this work, we consider the analytical expression of D_{KL} for two Gaussian distributions, since such a distribution is the maximum-entropy one consistent with the moments specified in (1) and (2), besides it holds the least restrictive distributional assumptions [7]. It is worth noting that measuring D_{KL} using the moments of two Gaussian distributions implies that means and covariances encode the non-stationarity, not that data are normally distributed [8]. The divergence between $\boldsymbol{X}_m$ and $\boldsymbol{X}$ is then defined as:

$$\xi_m = D_{KL} \{\mathcal{N}(\boldsymbol{\mu}_m, \boldsymbol{\Sigma}_m), \mathcal{N}(\bar{\boldsymbol{\mu}}, \bar{\boldsymbol{\Sigma}})\} , \tag{5}$$

yielding to the following analytically simplified non-stationarity measure [9],

$$\xi_m = T_r \left\{\{\boldsymbol{\mu}_m \boldsymbol{\mu}_m^\top + 2\boldsymbol{\Sigma}_m \bar{\boldsymbol{\Sigma}} \boldsymbol{\Sigma}_m\} - \bar{\boldsymbol{\mu}}\bar{\boldsymbol{\mu}}^\top - 2\bar{\boldsymbol{\Sigma}}\right\} ,$$

where $T_r\{\cdot\}$ stands for the trace operator. Thus, widely varying values of ξ_m indicate less stationary time series along the time domain.

3   Experiments and Results

3.1   EEG Database

The experimental test was developed using the well-known EEG Motor Imagery (MI) database *Dataset IIIa* provided by Laboratory of Brain-Computer Interfaces (BCI-Lab) from Graz University of Technology[1]. The database consists of EEG signals recorded from three subjects while were sitting in a comfortable chair in front of a computer screen. From each subject, the recordings were measured at 60 electrode positions, using the left mastoid for reference and the right mastoid as ground. The EEG signals were sampled at 250 Hz, and lastly, filtered between 1 and 50 Hz with a Notch filter on. For this data set, the cue-based BCI paradigm consisted of four different MI task, namely the imagination of

---

[1] http://bbci.de/competition/iii.

movement of the left hand (class 1 - $C1$), right hand (class 2 - $C2$), both feet (class 3 - $C3$), and tongue (class 4 - $C4$). Particularly, the experiment included several runs, at least 6, with 30 trials each-each. As is shown in Fig. 1, after a trial begun, in the first 2 s was presented a blank screen. Then, an acoustic stimulus was performed at 2 s, indicating the beginning of the trial and a cross + was displayed between 2–3 s. In addition, at 3 s the cue was shown as an arrow to the left, right, up or down for 1 s indicating to imagine a left hand, right hand, tongue or foot movement, respectively, until the cross disappeared at 7 s. Each of the 4 cues was displayed 10 times within each run in a randomized order.

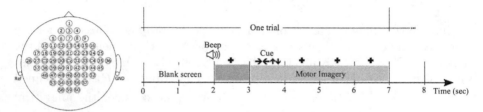

Fig. 1. Left: EEG electrode positions. **Right**: trial timing of the motor imagery database (Cue MI: left hand, right hand, feet, and tongue.)

3.2 Parameters Setting

For the database, a set of EEG signals $\Psi = \{X^{(r)} : r = 1, \ldots, R\}$ with $X^{(r)} \in \mathbb{R}^{C \times T}$ was acquired for each subject going under evaluation, being $R = 30$ trials, $C = 60$ channels, and $T = 1750$ time samples. For illustrative purposes, in this work, all the analysis are presented for the third subject ($S3$). According to [10,11] the signals are filtered between 8–30 Hz using a Butterworth filter (order 5) to take out for the concrete information related to MI activities, particularly, both the μ (8–13 Hz) and β (13-30 Hz) bands (rhythms) are widely-known for contributing the most to the motor activity classification, because these rhythms are associated with those cortical areas directly connected to the brain's normal motor output channels.

The non-stationary measure ξ_m^r is computed by each EEG trial (X^r). However, the analysis is developed in two ways: *(i)* ξ_m^r is performed considering the trial as a multivariate signal $X^r \in \mathbb{R}^{60 \times 1750}$ where the estimation of means and covariances will be $\bar{\mu} \in \mathbb{R}^{60}$ and $\bar{\Sigma} \in \mathbb{R}^{60 \times 60}$ and consequently $\mu \in \mathbb{R}^{60}$ and $\Sigma \in \mathbb{R}^{60 \times 60}$. *(ii)* We considerate a univariate signal $X^r \in \mathbb{R}^{1750}$ for the ξ_m^r evaluation, by mean of selecting an interesting channel, as a result, the empirical computation of both means and covariances will be $\bar{\mu}, \bar{\Sigma}, \mu, \Sigma \in \mathbb{R}$. Furthermore, the signal is windowed with 90% of overlap, obtaining $M = 283$ overlapped segments. Based on the same band of interest and the Nyquist theorem, the segment length value $L = 60$ needed during calculation was adjusted as $L \geq 2f_m$, being $f_m = 30$ Hz the biggest considered frequency. Finally, we obtain for each trial a $\xi^r = \{\xi_m^r : m = 1, \ldots, 283\}$ containing the estimated non-stationary measures for each window. Computation of the non-stationary index ξ_m^r is showed in details in Algorithm 1.

Algorithm 1. $-\ \boldsymbol{\xi}^r$ computation

Inputs: A EEG trial $\boldsymbol{X}^r$
Outputs: $\boldsymbol{\xi}^r = \{\xi^r_m : m = 1, \ldots, 283\}$
    Computing both empirical $\bar{\boldsymbol{\mu}}$ and $\bar{\boldsymbol{\Sigma}}$ over trial
    Choosing multivariate or univariate analysis
    Extracting the set $\mathscr{X}$ of overlapped M segments
        for $<m = 1 : 283>$
            Computing both empirical $\boldsymbol{\mu}_m$ and $\boldsymbol{\Sigma}_m$ over each $\boldsymbol{X}_m$
            $\xi^r_m = T_r \left\{ \{\mu_m \mu^\top_m + 2\Sigma_m \bar{\Sigma} \Sigma_m\} - \bar{\mu}\bar{\mu}^\top - 2\bar{\Sigma} \right\}$
        end

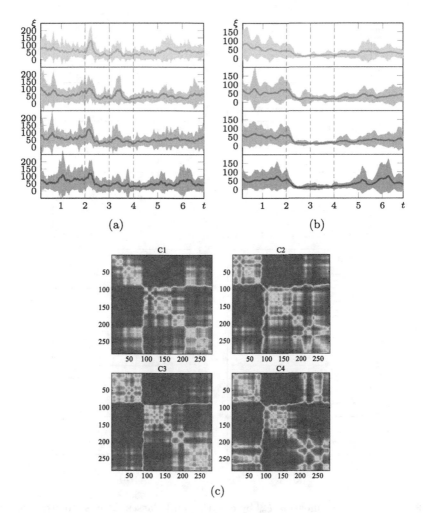

Fig. 2. Multivariate analysis by class. (a) ξ_m computed using raw data, (b) ξ_m computed using filtered signals (8–30 Hz), ($-$C1, $-$C2, $-$C3 and $-$C4). (c) Estimated $p-values$ by class.

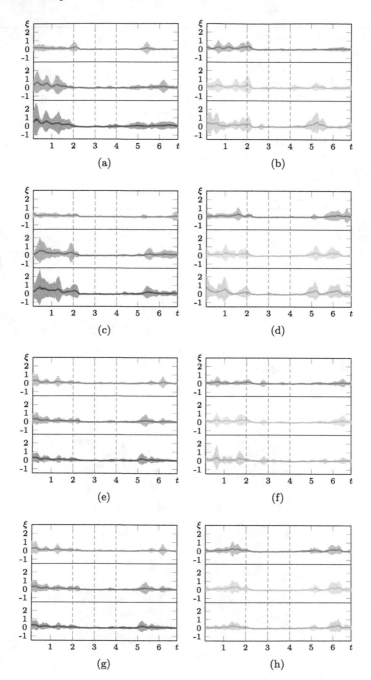

Fig. 3. Non-stationary measure ξ_m^r by channels and classes. **Rows:** Representing the classes Cl_1, Cl_2, Cl_3, and Cl_4, consecutively. (Color figure online)**Columns:** *Left:* ξ_m^r estimated over MI paradigm related channels, $-C3$, $-Cz$, $-C4$. *Rigth:* Non-stationary measure ξ computed over MI paradigm non-related channels $-$Ch1, $-$Ch46, $-$Ch60. (Color figure online)

Additionally, with the purpose of assessing the distribution differences between non-stationary measures ξ_m^r a two-sample t-test is carry out ($\mathscr{F}\{\cdot\}$), where the obtained $p-values$ will be $\rho = \mathscr{F}(\xi_n, \xi_m) \in [0,1]$ being $\boldsymbol{\xi}_m = \{\xi_m^r : r = 1, \ldots, 30\}$, and $\boldsymbol{P} = \{\rho_{nm} : n, m = 1, \ldots, 283\}$.

3.3 Obtained Results

Figure 2 shows the achieved results for the multivariate analysis. Figures 2a and b present the mean and standard deviation values of the ξ_m computed for both, raw data in Fig. 2a and filtered signals in Fig. 2b. Moreover, the obtained $p-values$ for the filtered data in $\boldsymbol{P}$ by class from the assessed two-sample t-test are showed in Fig. 2c.

The univariate analysis results are shown in Fig. 3. The Non-stationary measure assessing are presented by channels and classes. Each row represents one class from $C1$, $C2$, $C3$, and $C4$, consecutively. The columns show the obtained results between the non-stationary measure estimated in both, MI paradigm related channels $ChC3$, $ChCz$, and $ChC4$ (*left*: Figs. 3a, c, e, g) and MI paradigm non-related channels $Ch1$, $Ch46$, and $Ch60$ (*right*: Figs. 3b, d, f, h). For all non-stationary measure figures the doted red lines indicate the time markers for the stimulus, accordingly, at $t = 2$ s a beep and a cross are executed, at $t = 3$ s the cue is shown by 1 s and at $t = 4$ s a cross is shown newly until the trial is over.

4   Discussion and Concluding Remarks

According to the considered window, w for the non-stationary measure ξ_m^r estimation, the length $L = 60$ was chosen taking into account the maximum frequency of analysis. However, the overlap directly influences on the smoothness non-stationary wave related to the time resolution changes of this measure.

On the other hand, from the multivariate analysis in Fig. 2, we could see that the measure computed using the raw data Fig. 2a, in general, has high values of non-stationary for all time comparatively with the measure estimated using the filtered data in Fig. 2b. However, there are some high values shown in Fig. 2a for all classes between $t = 3$ s and $t = 4$ s (time where the cue is presented) that are removed after the filtering process as is shown in Fig. 2b. This information, that is more non-stationary could be related to brain process due to they are not linked to MI tasks, e.g. θ (4–8 Hz) band may occur in emotional or cognitive states [12] or γ (26–44 Hz) band that modulates perception and consciousness [13]. Particularly, movement or preparation for movement typically leads to decreasing activity of μ and β rhythms on the brain side contralateral to the movement.

In addition, from the obtained $p-values$ for the filtered data (see Fig. 2c), the results show three different dynamics for all the analyzed classes. The first 80 windows ($t \approx 0$–2 s) have a similar dynamic. Nevertheless, these $p-values$ are similar with the obtained $p-values$ for the last windows (windows 210–283 corresponding approximately to $t \approx 5$, 12–7 s). Undoubtedly, for all the classes the dynamics present in these windows are different to the dynamics present in the windows 125–175 related to $t \approx 3$–4, 28 s due to the lowest assessed $p - values$. Indeed, the dyna mic is similar in this window interval and should be associated with MI tasks. Furthermore, there is a particular dynamic presented from windows 80–100 ($t \approx 2, 3$–2,5 s) that has a similar dynamic over all the windows, it should be linked with the visual stimuli present during all trial executions from $t \approx 2$–7 s (cross, cue, cross).

In case of the univariate analysis showed in Fig. 3, there is no significant difference between the analysis related channels and those unrelated to the stimulus was presented. Nonetheless, for all the classes the non-stationary measure have a similar behavior. In fact, for all channels, during the first $t = 2$ s where a blank screen is presented, we assessed high non-stationary values for this time interval. That could be explained by activity shown in the EEG signal while the subject is seeing the blank screen, although we have filtered the signals in the band 7–30 Hz, there are some brain process related to other activities as stress and anxiety that could be performed on 23–30 Hz frequency band. Subsequently, at $t = 2$ s become a diminution of the ξ computed values just after the beep and the cross are executed, whereby, the subject started to be focused on the coming task. At $t = 3$ s the cue is presented and the non-stationary values continue being smaller until at some time point after $t = 4$ s, where the cue is replaced by a cross, the estimated non-stationary values started to increase; indicating that this last dynamic change could be related with a weary-trial-subject.

Generally, the considered non-stationary measure detecting the different dynamics from the non-stationary point of view. However, the EEG signals could have temporal changes that do not find out in the first two Statistical moments, in that way, it could be appropriate using measures that take into account higher order Statistical moments that could improve the non-stationary estimation also add information in the analysis by channels, where no significant differences were finding.

In this work, we have tested and discussed a non-stationarity measure based on the two first Statistical moments to detect EEG dynamic changes due to stimulus-related activity in MI tasks. Due to the imagination and execution of tracking movements are associated with neural rhythm power changes in the μ and β bands, we filtered the signal between 7–30 Hz enhancing the non-stationary estimation. The analysis was assessed in two ways, as multivariate and univariate processes. The obtained results show that the changes in the non-stationary measure are directly related to executed stimulus during the EEG recording, as well as, at some time point after the cue is taken out the subject appears to lose the attention on the cue-experiment and consequently the non-stationary measure increase. The achieved results could be helpful to select the active window time where the subject is developing a determined MI task, and we can use this information to improve the MI classification task.

As future work, it could be interesting to test others non-stationary measures that include higher Statistical moments to describe the time series behavior, tuning the overlap parameter with the purpose of taking into account the each trial dynamics. Also, for the MI classification task, we could use the results discussed in this work on the selection of active time segment in the covariance estimation of Common Spatial Patterns (CSP) technique.

Acknowledgment. This work was supported by Under grants provided by a PhD. scholarship funded by COLCIENCIAS (covocatoria No. 727) and the project *Sistema de realidad aumentada para la proyeccin de conexiones cerebrales producidas por estmulos afectivos a partir de seales de EEG*, (cdigo 36075).

References

1. Velásquez-Martínez, L.F., Álvarez-Meza, A.M., Castellanos-Domínguez, C.G.: Motor imagery classification for BCI using common spatial patterns and feature relevance analysis. In: Ferrández Vicente, J.M., Álvarez Sánchez, J.R., Paz López, F., Toledo Moreo, F.J. (eds.) IWINAC 2013. LNCS, vol. 7931, pp. 365–374. Springer, Heidelberg (2013). doi:10.1007/978-3-642-38622-0_38
2. Guerrero-Mosquera, C., Navia-Vázquez, A.: Automatic removal of ocular artefacts using adaptive filtering and independent component analysis for electroencephalogram data. IET Sig. Process. **6**(2), 99–106 (2012)
3. Wolpaw, W.R., Birbaumer, N., McFarland, D.J., Pfurtscheller, G., Vaughan, T.M.: Brain-computer interfaces for communication and control. Clin. Neurophysiol. **113**(6), 767–791 (2002)
4. Allison, B.Z., Wolpaw, E.W., Wolpaw, J.R.: Brain-computer interface systems: progress and prospects. Exp. Rev. of Med. Dev. **4**(4), 463–474 (2007)
5. Alvarez-Meza, A.M., Velasquez-Martinez, L.F., Castellanos-Dominguez, G.: Feature relevance analysis supporting automatic motor imagery discrimination in EEG based BCI systems. In: 35th Annual International Conference of the IEEE Engineering in Medicine and Biology Society (EMBC), pp. 7068–7071. IEEE (2013)
6. Hsu, W.-Y.: EEG-based motor imagery classification using enhanced active segment selection and adaptive classifier. Comput. Biol. Med. **41**(8), 633–639 (2011)
7. Von Bünau, P., Meinecke, F.C., Scholler, S., Müller, K.-R.: Finding stationary brain sources in EEG data. In: Annual International Conference of the IEEE Engineering in Medicine and Biology Society (EMBC), pp. 2810–2813. IEEE (2010)
8. Castaño-Candamil, S., Höhne, J., Martínez-Vargas, J.-D., An, X.-W., Castellanos-Domínguez, G., Haufe, S.: Solving the EEG inverse problem based on space-time-frequency structured sparsity constraints. NeuroImage **118**, 598–612 (2015)
9. Hara, S., Kawahara, Y., Washio, T., BüNau, P., Tokunaga, T., Yumoto, K.: Separation of stationary and non-stationary sources with a generalized eigenvalue problem. Neural networks **33**, 7–20 (2012)
10. Rodríguez, G., García, P.J.: Automatic and adaptive classification of electroencephalographic signals for brain computer interfaces. Med. Syst. **36**(1), 51–63 (2012)
11. Zhang, H., Guan, C., Bci competition iv-data set i, et al.: learning discriminative patterns for self-paced EEG-based motor imagery detection. Front. Neurosci. **6** (2012)
12. Álvarez-Meza, A.M., Velásquez-Martínez, L.F., Castellanos-Dominguez, G.: Time-series discrimination using feature relevance analysis in motor imagery classification. Neurocomputing **151**, 122–129 (2015)
13. Baars, B.J., Gage, N.M.: Fundamentals of Cognitive Neuroscience: A Beginner's Guide. Academic Press, Cambridge (2012)

Sleep Stages Clustering Using Time and Spectral Features of EEG Signals

An Unsupervised Approach

J.L. Rodríguez-Sotelo[1]([✉]), A. Osorio-Forero[2], A. Jiménez-Rodríguez[3],
F. Restrepo-de-Mejía[1], D.H. Peluffo-Ordoñez[4], and J. Serrano[5]

[1] Universidad Autónoma de Manizales, Manizales, Colombia
jlrodriguez@autonoma.edu.co
[2] Universidad de los Andes, Bogotá, Colombia
[3] University of Freiburg, Freiburg im Breisgau, Germany
[4] Universidad Técnica del Norte, Ibarra, Ecuador
[5] Universidad de Yachay, San Miguel de Urcuqui Canton, Ecuador

Abstract. Sleep stage classification is a highly addressed issue in polysomnography; It is considered a tedious and time-consuming task if done manually by the specialist; therefore, from the engineering point of view, several methods have been proposed to perform an automatic sleep stage classification. In this paper an unsupervised approach to automatic sleep stage clustering of EEG signals is proposed which uses spectral features related to signal power, coherences, asymmetries, and Wavelet coefficients; the set of features is classified using a clustering algorithm that optimizes a cost function of minimum sum of squares. Accuracy and kappa coefficients are comparable to those of the current literature as well as individual stage classification results. Methods and results are discussed in the light of the current literature, as well as the utility of the groups of features to differentiate the states of sleep. Finally, clustering techniques are recommended for implementation in support systems for sleep stage scoring.

1 Introduction

Polysomnography (PSG) is the main diagnostic tool for sleep disorders [23]. Among the signals recorded throughout this process is the electroencephalography (EEG) signals. The EEG has been widely used to assess cognitive functions and to differentiate sleep stages within the clinical practice. Sleep architecture is usually divided into stages regarding to the patterns proposed by Rechtschaffen and Kales (R & K) [25], or a modification of those patterns published by the American Academy of Sleep Medicine (AASM) [3]. Such patterns mainly correspond to 5 stages: first, is the lightest stage of sleep, the transition phase, where the person feel drifting off. Second stage of sleep is still considered light sleep and occurs when the brain activity starts to slow down. Stage 3 sleep is the start of deep sleep, also known as slow wave sleep. Of the five stages of sleep, the four is the one when is experienced a deepest sleep of the night. The brain only shows

© Springer International Publishing AG 2017
J.M. Ferrández Vicente et al. (Eds.): IWINAC 2017, Part I, LNCS 10337, pp. 444–455, 2017.
DOI: 10.1007/978-3-319-59740-9_44

delta-wave activity. The stage 5 is when there is dream. It is also referred to as active sleep or REM sleep.

Indeed, the classification of such stages throughout the PSG recordings is one of the most investigated problems in the field [2] due to the time and expertise required to achieve the task. Besides, this task is performed under certain criteria that may be considered ambiguous; and even, interrater reliability of visual inspection of sleep stages is between 76.8% and 80.6% [6]. This implies a great difficulty in the visual assessment of the stages in their association with diseases and sleep disorders, and in understanding their functions. For over 40 years, automatic classification of sleep stages from the quantitative characteristics of the EEG signals has been available [26], with results of around 84% of accuracy when compared to the clinicians [20]. Some studies also have greater results (of up to 97% of accuracy) but only when automatic detection of SWS (Slow-Wave Sleep) [28], or combining S1 and REM stages in a single stage [1]. Nevertheless, a new study that used a complex-valued neural network achieve a 94% and 95% of accuracy when R&k and AASM rules were used respectively [24].

The difficulty with these methods is that they do not always provide the same results in the clinical practice [26], largely due to the lack of agreement among evaluators in qualifying sleep stage transitions, which is not always taken into account when designing automatic systems. In addition, most studies in the area have included supervised algorithms, which by their nature do not have a good generalization ability [8]. Authors such as [12] have studied the feasibility of clustering methods based on centroids; in those studies, EEG spectral characteristics were used and they reported classification efficiencies of about 80%. The proposed methodology combines EEG signals in different sleep stages; this for different sets of features corresponding to the absolute powers of the different EEG rhythms, relative powers and ratios among rhythms, coherences and interhemispheric asymmetries, and coefficients of the Wavelet Transform (WT). The clustering algorithm is the J-means+; which uses a criterion jump over regions that improves the cluster with respect to a cost function. This article aims to evaluate the performance of different set of features in clustering sleep stages.

2 Materials and Methods

2.1 Notation

Given a set of EEG recording channels $\mathbf{X} = \{\mathbf{x}_1, \ldots, \mathbf{x}_8\}$, each cannel $\mathbf{x}_i$, can be divided in n signal segments called epochs, $\mathbf{x}_i = \{\mathbf{x}_i^1, \ldots, \mathbf{x}_i^n\}$, each one of 30 s; $\xi_i^j = \left(\xi_{i_1}^j, \xi_{i_2}^j, \ldots, \xi_{i_q}^j\right)$ corresponds to the set q-dimensional of features obtained of the i-th channel of the j-th epoch.

It is defined Z as a collection of subintervals $Z = \{z_D, z_T, z_A, z_B, z_{G_a}, z_{G_b}\}$, that correspond to the signals in different frequency bands, where $0 < z_D \leq 4$ Hz corresponds to the Delta rhythm, $4 < z_T \leq 8$ Hz to Theta rhythm, $8 < z_A \leq 13$ Hz to Alfa rhythm, $13 < z_B \leq 30$ Hz to Beta rhythm [3], $30 < z_{G_a} \leq 45$ to low Gamma rhythm and $45 < z_{G_b} \leq 58$ to high Gamma rhythm [5].

2.2 Methodology

The methodology consists of 4 stages (1); the first one is the data recording, the second one the feature extraction, the third one the process of unsupervised classification and the last one the validation process and results evaluation (Fig. 1).

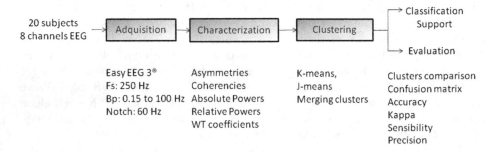

Fig. 1. Methodology used for the unsupervised analysis of EEG signals

2.3 Data Collection

20 polysomnographic recordings during an 8-hour period were taken on 20 young adults (13 women and 7 men) with a mean age of 21.9 ± 1.99 with no sleep disorders. They were students from the Autonoma University of Manizales (UAM®). These recordings were taken in the laboratory of Neurophysiology Oscar Moscoso Arisa UAM®. Acquisition parameters correspond to a sampling frequency of 250 Hz, an analog band pass filter of 0.15 to 100 Hz and a digital Notch filter of 60 Hz. Of the total polysomnography recordings, 8 mono-polar channels of EEG signals were selected for the clustering stage. The entire sample was collected with the Polysomnograph Easy 3 Easy Cadwell® and EEG 3® software. For each participant, a 3-hour sleep period was selected in order to ensure at least one complete sleep cycle. EEG data were exported in European Data Format (.edf) and loaded with EEGLAB [7] library. The sleep stage annotation for validation of results was performed by an expert using the parameters of [25]. Stability criteria were used for the transition among stages. A transition to a new stage is performed if and only if three consecutive epochs belong to the new one.

Features

Absolute powers $\{\zeta_1, \ldots, \zeta_{704}\}$ Absolute powers correspond to the mean power of each of the rhythms described above in the Notation section; These are calculated by using a spectrogram.

$$Y_i(t, f) = \int_{-\infty}^{\infty} \mathbf{x}_i(\tau) g(\tau - t) e^{-j2\pi f t} d\tau, \tag{1}$$

where $\mathbf{x}_i(\tau)$ is the i-th EEG channel and $g(\tau - t)$ is Hamming window of the same size of the epochs with a sliding of 20% and therefore an overlapping of 80%. Afterwards power spectral density is obtained,

$$P_i^{(z)}(t, f_z) = |Y_i(t, f_z)|^2,\qquad(2)$$

where f_z belongs to an interval $\left(z_k^L, z_k^H\right]$ of frequency of each rhythm Z with k in $\{D, T, A, B, G_a, G_b\}$.

Besides, it was considered low amplitude, mixed frequency rhythms (4–7 Hz), vertex waves (0–2 Hz) of central channels, slow waves (SWS) (0.5–2 Hz) of frontal channels, and sawtooth waves (2–6 Hz) with frequency ranges proposed in the AASM manual [3], for the absolute power features.

For the distribution $P_i^{(z)}(t, f_z)$, the following features were calculated: mean power $P_\mu^{(z)}(t) = \mu\left(P_i^{(z)}(t, f_z)\right)$, the power of the median frequency of each rhythm $P_{Me}^{(z)}(t) = P_i^{(z)}(t, f_{Me})$, the power of the frequency with greater variance $P_{MaxVar}^{(z)}(t) = P_i^{(z)}(t, f_{MaxVar})$, and the power of the frequency with greater Shannon entropy $P_{MaxEnt}^{(z)}(t) = P_i^{(z)}(t, f_{MaxEnt})$.

Relative powers and ratio among EEG rhythms $\{\zeta_{705}, \ldots, \zeta_{824}\}$: Relative powers (P_R) were calculated as the ratio between the mean power of each *Delta, Theta, Alfa, Beta* and *Gamma* rhythm regarding the sum of the total EEG rhythm as,

$$P_R = P_{z_k}/P_T = (1/P_T) \sum_{i=z_k^L}^{z_k^H} P\left(f_{z_k^i}\right),\qquad(3)$$

where P_{z_k} is the power of the frequency band of interest and P_T is the total power of all rhythms Z. Besides, among this group of features there are also power ratios among pairs of rhythms as,

$$P_{z_k/z_m} = P_{z_k}/P_{z_m} = \sum_{i=z_k^L}^{z_k^H} P\left(f_{z_k^i}\right) \Bigg/ \sum_{j=z_m^L}^{z_m^H} P\left(f_{z_m^j}\right),\qquad m \neq k,\qquad(4)$$

where P_{z_k} is the power of the frequency band of interest and P_{z_m} is the power of a second frequency band of interest; both belong to the rhythms Z .

Asymmetries $\{\zeta_{825}, \ldots, \zeta_{844}\}$ In the EEG, asymmetry has been used as a measure of the hemispheric difference of emotional processing [14]. In this study, 4 logarithmic asymmetries were calculated for each rhythm *Delta* $\{\zeta_{825}, \ldots, \zeta_{828}\}$, *Theta* $\{\zeta_{829}, \ldots, \zeta_{832}\}$, *Alfa* $\{\zeta_{833}, \ldots, \zeta_{836}\}$, *Beta* $\{\zeta_{837}, \ldots, \zeta_{840}\}$ and *Gamma* $\{\zeta_{841}, \ldots, \zeta_{844}\}$, which correspond to the channel pairs of frontal (F3-A2, F4-A1), central (C3-A2, C4-A1), parietal (P3-A2, P4-A1) and occipital channels (O1-A2, O2-A1). Asymmetries were calculated by using laterality coefficient, that is an indirect measure understood as $CL = \ln(P_L) - \ln(P_R)$, where P corresponds to the absolute power of a frequency range.

Coherences $\{\zeta_{845}, \ldots, \zeta_{864}\}$ Interhemispheric coherences are calculated for pairs of the aforementioned channels and for each of the EEG rhythms. This is understood as the estimate of the smoothed power and cross power spectral density as:

$$\gamma_{xy}^2 = \frac{|S_{xy}^2(f_z)|^2}{S_{xx}^2(f_z)S_{yy}^2(f_z)} \tag{5}$$

Where $S_{xy}^2(f_z)$ is the cross power spectral density, that is the transform of the cross correlation of signals to the frequency space $S_{xy}^2(f_z) = \int_{-T}^{T} R_{xy}(\tau)e^{-j2\pi f_z t d\tau}$ with $R_\tau = \lim_{T \to \infty} \int_0^T x(t)y(t+\tau)d\tau$ and f_z belongs to interval aforementioned. The coherence feature corresponds to the mean of Eq. 5.

Wavelet Transform (WT) $\{\zeta_{865}, \ldots, \zeta_{960}\}$ La WT corresponds to the representation of the signal from $WT(f(a,b)) = \int_{-\infty}^{infty} f(t)\psi_{a,b}(t)dt$, where $\psi_{a,b}(t)$ are the named Wavelet scalar functions subjected to a parameter "a", and moved given a parameter "b" of a function $\psi(t)$, as shown below:

$$\psi_{a,b}(t) = \frac{1}{\sqrt{|a|}} \psi\left(\frac{t-b}{a}\right) \tag{6}$$

These parameters for discrete Wavelets functions are usually given by $a = a_0^j$ and $b = kb_0 a_0^j$ with complete j and k, $a > 1$ and $b > 0$. Therefore the bases of the Discrete Wavelet Transform (DWT), are defined as follows:

$$\psi_{j,k}(t) = \frac{1}{\sqrt{a^j}} \psi\left(\frac{t}{a_0^j} - kb_0\right) \tag{7}$$

In the practice, values as $a_0 = 2$ and $b_0 = 1$ are taken. Solution behaves as a Multiresolution analysis [21]; in

such case DWT can be observed as the implementation of scalar functions (associated with a low pass filter $h(n)$) and Wavelet functions (associated with a high pass filter $g(n)$) related in a way as $g[n] = (-1)^n h(1-n), \sum g[n] = 0$ and $\sum h[n] = \sqrt{2}$. For this, the original signal is passed through a high pass filter to the half of the specified frequency, that in signal processing, it is generally used the sampling frequency (F_s), followed by a low pass filter to the maximum allowed by the signal ($F_s/2$). Subsequently, half of the samples can be eliminated since the signal maximum frequency is ($F_s/2$); then, the signal is subsampled by a factor of 2 (which may be well performed by removing a point via the signal). This process can be as iterative as required, depending on the level to which you want to perform the decomposition. For this study the decomposition procedure was up to an 8-th level [21].

The filter $g[.]$ is the original Wavelet that behaves as a high-pass filter, and the low pass filter $h[.]$ is its mirror version. The subsampled signal filter $g[.]$ corresponds to detail signals (D_i). Similarly, the filter output h is known as the approximation A_i , where i corresponds to the level at which the decomposition is found. The Wavelet function used in this study corresponds to Daubechies function to the order 20; which has been previously used in the analysis of EEG signals [21]. This decomposition features were selected because the frequency ranges containing information of important EEG for classifying sleep stages, are in the lowest levels of decomposition feature of maxima and minimum of the details D_6, D_7 and D_8, and A_8 approximation.

Clustering Algorithm. The set of features of the EEG recordings X of all patients with N observations and q features, are grouped into M clusters.

The algorithm corresponds to a new form of heuristic search for a neighbors of a partial solution that leads to a local optimum. This method is a proposal to solve the problem of Minimum Sum-of-Squares Clustering (MSSC), improving the final partition to classical methods such as k-means or h-means partition; when having a relatively high set of clusters; this method is called J-means [13].

Additionally, after completing the searching phase of the local optimum, partition is improved, including the k-means algorithm. Thus, the clustering algorithm used in this study corresponds to a two-step algorithm, the first one is the local optimum search from J-means and, after such search, the k-means algorithm is applied. The algorithm is called J-means + [13]. The problem with the MSSC can be expressed as follows.

$$\min_{P_M \in \Omega_M} \sum_{i=1}^{M} \sum_{x_l \in C_i} \|x_l - \bar{x}_i\|^2 \tag{8}$$

where x_l corresponds to a sub-cluster q-dimensional of the complete cluster of data, belonging to the i-th cluster C_i, M is the amount of clusters, P_M is the found partition of the Ω_M possible partitions, $\|.\|$ is the Euclidean norm and $\bar{x}_i$ is the cluster centroid C_i, calculated as, $\bar{x}_i = (1/|C_i|) \sum_{l:x_l \in C_i} x_l$.

With the above definitions, we can express the J-means algorithm in the following steps [13].

Step 1. Initialization M centroids of the initial cluster of features are selected at random, and an intial partition is performed by using the Eq. 8 criteria, this provides the following partition $P_M = \{C_i\}(i = 1, \ldots, M)$, with its respective centroids and the calculation of the objective function f_{opt}.

Step 2. Occupied and unoccupied elements Unoccupied points that are outside a q-dimensional sphere of radius ε about the centroid of each cluster are selected.

Step 3. Jump to the neighbors The best partition P'_M and its corresponding target function f'_{opt} in the jump of neighbors regarding the current solution P_M are found. To achieve this step it is necessary: (a) Explore the neighborhoods. (b) For each $j(j = 1, \ldots, N)$ repeat the following steps: - *Relocation*: Add a new cluster with centroid $\bar{x}_{M+1}$ of an occupied element x_j and find the index i associated to the best suppression of one of the current centroids; indicate with the change in the value of the target function by using the Eq. 9. -*Preserve the best combination*: maintain the pair of indices i and j, where v_{ij} is minimum. (c) Replace the centroid $\bar{x}_i$ for $\bar{x}_j$ and update the allocation when obtaining a new partition P'_M and the target function as follows, $f'_{opt} = f_{opt} + v_{ij}$.

$$v_{ij} = \frac{n_i}{n_i + 1} \left\| \bar{x}_i - x_j \right\|^2 - \frac{n_l}{n_l - 1} \left\| \bar{x}_l - x_j \right\|^2, \quad x_j \in C_l \qquad (9)$$

Step 4. Ending or movement If $f'_{opt} > f_{opt}$, stops, since a local minimum was found in the previous iteration, on the contrary, replace the current solution P_M for P'_M and f_{opt} for f'_{opt} and go back to *Step 2*.

Once finishing the stage of J-means algorithm, k-means algorithm is developed as an initialization by using centroids from the previous partition. The k-means algorithm can be implemented as described in [17].

Clusters Comparison. To evaluate the performance of a set of cluster, it is required a cluster comparison of epochs that experts classify in sleep stages. Five "expected centroids" (EC) as the mean of each of the features of the clusters formed by the expert's evaluation. The Euclidean distance of each of the centroids formed by the clustering was calculated (calculated centroids CC); finally, CC is considered as belonging to the sleep stage for which the distance is minimum.

Evaluation and Validation. For this study, evaluation measures that require data labels were used. With this information and with the epochs clustering results, a confusion matrix ($\mathbf{C}$) is created in order to measure the performance of the proposed methodology. Performance was evaluated by using measures such as, sensitivity (Se), precision (P) and efficiency (Accuracy (Acc)); this is also done to compare the obtained results with other research studies.

Kappa of Cohen (k) coefficient was also calculated [4] on the confusion matrix in order to compare the results between the clustering epochs and the expert's classification.

3   Results and Discussion

Table 1 shows the results of the sleep stage clustering of EEG signals with respect to the manual scoring. These results represent the mean and standard deviation of the accuracy and Cohen Kappa coefficient for the 19 participants. Results were calculated for five groups of features; the best results were obtained with relative powers and power ratios among EEG rhythms.

Efficiency results of this study are comparable with those found in previous studies using supervised learning methods for automatic classification of sleep stages; for example in [19] results of up to 81% of agreement when compared to experts scoring were obtained, by using sets of four features and supervised classification methods. The results with the features of relative powers and power

Table 1. Comparison of the automatic classification of sleep stages to the manual scoring. (SD: standard deviation).

Set of features	Asimmetries	Coherences	Relative powers	Absolute powers	Wavelet coefficients
Accuracy (SD)	0,55 (0,08)	0,57 (0,11)	0,73 (0,09)	0,64 (0,09)	0,58 (0,09)
Kappa (SD)	0,39 (0,1)	0,43 (0,12)	0,64 (0,11)	0,51 (0,11)	0,43 (0,1)

ratios among EEG rhythms (*Acc*: 0.73 *Kappa*: 0.64) are comparable to those results with a similar set of features in a study of artificial neural networks by [27]. In such study, a 74% of accuracy for the classification of four groups of stages (Awake, Steps 1 and 2, Stages 3 and 4 and REM sleep) was reported. In this study, the fact that the relative powers and power ratios showed better results than the absolute powers for classifying stages suggests that the relationships among EEG rhythms are more useful to discriminate sleep stages. The asymmetry and coherences features, including the coherence among channels exhibited the lowest results in the classification of sleep stages.

Some authors have still reported differences in the gamma coherences values [5] when compared among the different sleep stages. The results of the maximum and minimum coefficients of WT for the latter approximation (A_8) and the last three details (D_8, D_7 and D_6) are lower than those reported in studies that include these features. In [10], for example, results were about 90% of efficiency, using the mean, standard deviation, the power and kurtosis of these coefficients. A WT with a resolution of 4 levels was performed in that study. In [22], an efficiency of 77.6% was found using the mean square value of the coefficients of the discrete WT of 8 levels as features. Nevertheless, these studies used supervised learning techniques for the classification. For further research studies, the implementation of other WT features may improve the outcomes.

Table 2 shows the values of Sensibility (*Se*) and Precision (*P*) of the classification system for each sleep stage. The calculation of the results was performed for 5 epochs that represent the waking (*W*), somnolence (N_1), light sleep (N_2), deep sleep (N_3), and REM sleep. Another epoch that represents the artifacts was also used. The rows represent the mean and standard deviation of the results obtained for the 19 participants, where the comparison between the final partition and the manual scoring regarding the mean of each cluster was performed. This was done for the five set of features.

The results for the five stages are similar to those reported in the literature. The stages with lower sensitivity and precision were for the *W*, as well as for N_1 and N_2 stages; Also, other studies have reported that N_1, N_2 stages show lower performance for automatic classification [10,30]. By contrast, the N_3 and *REM* stages exhibited the best performance clustering, for all sets of features. This contrasts with current studies that reported low scores for REM in relation to the other stages [15].

Table 2. Sensitivity and precision results of unsupervised clustering for sleep stages. (mean (SD), Arts: Epochs with artifact.)

Stages	Asymmetries		Coherences		Relative power	
	Se	P	Se	P	Se	P
W	0,31 (0,33)	0,31 (0,34)	0,53 (0,32)	0,4 (0,26)	0,57 (0,4)	0,51 (0,39)
N1	0,26 (0,31)	0,15 (0,18)	0,22 (0,33)	0,16 (0,24)	0,45 (0,44)	0,27 (0,28)
N2	0,39 (0,32)	0,4 (0,31)	0,29 (0,33)	0,3 (0,29)	0,58 (0,35)	0,59 (0,34)
N3	0,66 (0,3)	0,54 (0,23)	0,69 (0,28)	0,52 (0,23)	0,83 (0,15)	0,87 (0,1)
REM	0,68 (0,25)	0,53 (0,24)	0,68 (0,21)	0,61 (0,24)	0,92 (0,09)	0,79 (0,21)
Arts	0,22 (0,3)	0,28 (0,41)	0,43 (0,4)	0,4 (0,38)	0,05 (0,22)	0,02 (0,07)
	Absolute powers		Wavelet Transform			
	Se	P	Se	P		
W	0,27 (0,35)	0,29 (0,37)	0,30 (0,39)	0,18 (0,25)		
N1	0,28 (0,35)	0,20 (0,26)	0,23 (0,3)	0,15 (0,22)		
N2	0,47 (0,35)	0,43 (0,31)	0,43 (0,26)	0,46 (0,28)		
N3	0,80 (0,17)	0,75 (0,19)	0,76 (0,2)	0,64 (0,19)		
REM	0,72 (0,34)	0,52 (0,29)	0,54 (0,43)	0,47 (0,31)		
Arts	0,36 (0,37)	0,51 (0,46)	0,23 (0,31)	0,37 (0,43)		

Since the interest in this study is the clustering of the sleep stages, artifacts were considered as a single cluster. However, some artifact detection methods could be used to explore in depth this issue, as the ones proposed in [9].

Other approaches such as fractal and multifractal measures are used to classify sleep stages in a supervised schema. For example [30] reported total kappa coefficients between 0.77 and 0.84. However, such approaches were not considered in this study due to the main interest in spectral features that provide a similar performance and low computational cost.

A well-known problem in sleep staging is the transition among stages which have been proposed as a possible source of staging discrepancies; a recent methodology to improve automatic classification is the so called classification smoothing [20]. This method consists in the implementation of certain rules that consider the temporal contextual information to enhance continuity between stages; for example a contiguos block of REM→S1→REM epochs would be changed to REM→REM→REM.

Another promising alternative for sleep stage classification that could be beneficiated by the use of clustering techniques is the combination of multiple classifiers that "vote for a class membership" to improve the classification, method that has been recently applied by [16] with supervised algorithms. Automatic sleep stages classification is still a current problem in up-to-date literature; for instance, there are studies that have reported accuracies ranging from 57% to 69% [29] to accuracies higher than 90% [1,15,18,24,28]. Nevertheless, all the latter approaches used supervised learning to deal with the mentioned problem.

Clustering techniques have been previously proposed as a good alternative to classify [13] or improve [12] automatic classification. Even from late eighties [11], clustering analysis in using features from EEG signals have shown to have some relevant utility in sleep stage classification and could even help to better understand the dynamics of sleep stages.

Finally, the proposed methodology have some advantages for being unsupervised; mainly in terms of training and labelling by the specialist. This results in generalization capacity and in time saving. However, the performance of the algorithms is less than those observed in the literature regarding supervised approaches. These algorithms are useful to provide specialists with support regarding the sleep scoring problem.

4 Conclusion

The proposed methodology is a favorable alternative when designing systems of automatic classification of sleep stages to provide support to specialists. One of the advantages is that it requires no training and is not limited to particular databases; besides, the computational cost of clustering algorithm is relatively low, similar to k-means algorithm. The most significant results were identified with relative powers and power-ratios among rhythms; on the contrary, the asymmetry features and interhemispheric coherence exhibited a low classification performance compared to the expert's perspective. A new method is proposed to evaluate the clusters obtained with expert's labels in order to compare the results with previous studies. This procedure can be extended to other clustering algorithms and other data clusters with labels. For further research studies, it would be important to assess the usefulness of nonlinear features for clustering sleep stages that lead to evaluate the signal complexity and dynamics. The relevance of the features regarding the representation of the data is to be studied.

Acknowledgments. This study is part of the "classification of sleep stages polysomnographic recordings from feature selection methods and unsupervised clustering" coded 328-038 in 2013 at the Autonoma University of Manizales. The research groups involved are Neuroaprendizaje and Automática research groups. The translation process was in charge of the Translation Center of the Autónoma University of Manizales.

References

1. Aboalayon, K.A.I., Almuhammadi, W.S., Faezipour, M.: A comparison of different machine learning algorithms using single channel EEG signal for classifying human sleep stages. In: 2015 Long Island Systems, Applications and Technology, pp. 1–6 (2015). http://ieeexplore.ieee.org/lpdocs/epic03/wrapper.htm?arnumber=7160185
2. Agarwal, R., Gotman, J.: Digital tools in polysomnography. J. Clin. Neurophys. Off. Publ. Am. Electroencephalogr. Soc. **19**(2), 136–143 (2002). http://www.ncbi.nlm.nih.gov/pubmed/11997724
3. Berry, R.B., Budhiraja, R., Gottlieb, D.J., Gozal, D., Iber, C., Kapur, V.K., Marcus, C.L., Mehra, R., Parthasarathy, S., Quan, S.F., Redline, S., Strohl, K.P., Ward, S.L.D., Tangredi, M.M.: Rules for scoring respiratory events in sleep: update of the 2007 AASM manual for the scoring of sleep and associated events. J. Clin. Sleep Med. **8**(5), 597–619 (2012)
4. Brennan, R.L., Prediger, D.J.: Coefficient kappa: some uses, misuses, and alternatives. Educ. Psychol. Meas. **41**(3), 687–699 (1981)

5. Cantero, J.L., Atienza, M., Madsen, J.R., Stickgold, R.: Gamma EEG dynamics in neocortex and hippocampus during human wakefulness and sleep. NeuroImage **22**(3), 1271–1280 (2004)
6. Danker-Hopfe, H., Anderer, P., Zeitlhofer, J., Boeck, M., Dorn, H., Gruber, G., Heller, E., Loretz, E., Moser, D., Parapatics, S., Saletu, B., Schmidt, A., Dorffner, G.: Interrater reliability for sleep scoring according to the Rechtschaffen & Kales and the new AASM standard. J. Sleep Res. **18**(1), 74–84 (2009)
7. Delorme, A., Makeig, S.: EEGLAB: an open source toolbox for analysis of single-trial EEG dynamics including independent component analysis. J. Neurosci. Methods **134**(1), 9–21 (2004)
8. Duda, R.O., Hart, P.E., Stork, D.G.: Pattern Classification. Wiley, Hoboken (2000)
9. Durka, P.J., Klekowicz, H., Blinowska, K.J., Szelenberger, W., Niemcewicz, S.: A simple system for detection of EEG artifacts in polysomnographic recordings. IEEE Trans. Biomed. Eng. **50**(4), 526–528 (2003)
10. Fraiwan, L., Lweesy, K., Khasawneh, N., Wenz, H., Dickhaus, H.: Automated sleep stage identification system based on time-frequency analysis of a single EEG channel and random forest classifier. Comput. Methods Programs Biomed. **108**(1), 10–19 (2012)
11. Gath, I., Geva, A.B.: Unsupervised optimal fuzzy clustering. IEEE Trans. Pattern Anal. Mach. Intell. **11**(7), 773–780 (1989)
12. Gunes, S., Polat, K., Yosunkaya, Ş.: Efficient sleep stage recognition system based on EEG signal using k-means clustering based feature weighting. Expert Systems with Applications **37**(12), 7922–7928 (2010)
13. Hansen, P., Mladenović, N.: Variable neighborhood search: principles and applications. Eur. J. Oper. Res. **130**(3), 449–467 (2001)
14. Harmon-Jones, E.: Unilateral right-hand contractions cause contralateral alpha power suppression and approach motivational affective experience. Psychophysiology **43**(6), 598–603 (2006)
15. Hassan, A.R., Bhuiyan, M.I.H.: Computer-aided sleep staging using complete ensemble empirical mode decomposition with adaptive noise and bootstrap aggregating. Biomed. Signal Process. Control **24**, 1–10 (2016)
16. Zhang, J., Wu, Y., Bai, J., Chen, F.: Automatic sleep stage classification based on sparse deep belief net and combination of multiple classifiers. Trans. Inst. Meas. Control **38**, 435–451 (2015)
17. Jain, K., Murty, M.N., Flynn, P.J.: Data clustering a review. ACM Comput. Surv. **31**(3), 264–323 (1999). http://portal.acm.org/citation.cfm?doid=331499.331504
18. Kouchaki, S., Sanei, S., Arbon, E., Dijk, D.J.: Tensor based singular spectrum analysis for automatic scoring of sleep EEG. IEEE Trans. Neural Syst. Rehabil. Eng. **23**(1), 1–9 (2015). http://ieeexplore.ieee.org/ielx7/7333/7001725/06834801. pdf?tp=&arnumber=6834801&isnumber=7001725$$nhttp://ieeexplore.ieee.org/ xpls/abs_all.jsp?arnumber=6834801&tag=1
19. Krakovská, A., Mezeiová, K.: Automatic sleep scoring: a search for an optimal combination of measures. Artif. Intell. Med. **53**(1), 25–33 (2011)
20. Lan, K.C., Chang, D.W., Kuo, C.E., Wei, M.Z., Li, Y.H., Shaw, F.Z., Liang, S.F.: Using off-the-shelf lossy compression for wireless home sleep staging. J. Neurosci. Methods **246**, 142–152 (2015)
21. Mallat, S.G.: A theory for multiresolution signal decomposition: the wavelet representation. IEEE Trans. Pattern Anal. Mach. Intell. **11**(7), 674–693 (1989)

22. Oropesa, E., Cycon, H., Jobert, M.: Sleep stage classification using wavelet transform and neural network, International computer science institute (1999). http://citeseerx.ist.psu.edu/viewdoc/download?doi=10.1.1.45.6844&rep=rep1&type=pdf

23. Pastor, J., Fernández-Lorente, J., Ortega, B., Galán, J.M.: Comparative analysis of the clinical history and polysomnography in sleep disorders. Diagnostic relevance of polysomnography. Revista De Neurologia **32**(1), 22–29 (2001). http://www.ncbi.nlm.nih.gov/pubmed/11293094

24. Peker, M.: A new approach for automatic sleep scoring: combining Taguchi based complex-valued neural network and complex wavelet transform. Comput. Methods Programs Biomed. **129**, 203–216 (2016)

25. Rechtschaffen, A., Kales, A.: A Manual of Standardised Terminology, Techniques, and Scoring System for Sleep stages of Human Subjects. UCLA Brain Information Service, Los Angelos (1968)

26. Robert, C., Guilpin, C., Limoge, A.: Review of neural network applications in sleep research. J. Neurosci. Methods **79**(2), 187–193 (1998)

27. Ronzhina, M., Janoušek, O., Kolárová, J., Nováková, M., Honzík, P., Provazník, I.: Sleep scoring using artificial neural networks. Sleep Med. Rev. **16**(3), 251–263 (2012)

28. Su, B.L., Luo, Y., Hong, C.Y., Nagurka, M.L., Yen, C.W.: Detecting slow wave sleep using a single EEG signal channel. J. Neurosci. Methods **243**, 47–52 (2015)

29. Wang, Y., Loparo, K.A., Kelly, M.R., Kaplan, R.F.: Evaluation of an automated single-channel sleep staging algorithm. Nat. Sci. Sleep **7**, 101–111 (2015)

30. Weiss, B., Clemens, Z., Bódizs, R., Halász, P.: Comparison of fractal and power spectral EEG features: effects of topography and sleep stages. Brain Res. Bull. **84**(6), 359–375 (2011)

Segment Clustering for Holter Recordings Analysis

J.L. Rodríguez-Sotelo[1]([⊠]), D.H. Peluffo-Ordoñez[2],
D. López-Londoño[1], and A. Castro-Ospina[3]

[1] Universidad Autónoma de Manizales, Manizales, Colombia
jlrodriguez@autonoma.edu.co
[2] Universidad Técnica del Norte, Ibarra, Ecuador
[3] Instituto Tecnológico Metropolitano, Medellín, Colombia

Abstract. In this work, an efficient non-supervised algorithm for clustering of ECG signals is presented. The method is assessed over a set of records from MIT/BIH arrhythmia database with different types of heartbeats, including normal (N) heartbeats, as well as the arrhythmia heartbeats recommended by the AAMI, usually found in Holter recordings: ventricular extra systoles (VE), left and right branch bundles blocks (LBBB and RBBB) and atrial premature beats (APB). The results are assessed by means the sensitivity and specificity measures, taking advantage of the database labels. Also, unsupervised performance measures are used. Finally, the performance of the algorithm is in average 95%, improving results reported by previous works of the literature.

1 Introduction

For outpatient electrocardiographic test there exist Holter recordings which are recorded for long time and allow assessing the heart condition without altering the patient daily activities. Thus, they are useful to detect transitory and irregular pathologies that are hard to diagnose in short-time ECG (12 leads). The problem of this kind of test is the wide amount of heartbeats which complicates its visual inspection. For this reason, computer analysis systems have been developed and are commonly used as a diagnostic support. In general, these systems work off-line taking into account some factors that add variability, such as: signal length, artifacts, EMG noise and different dynamic behavior and morphology (different patient and/or pathology). Then, it is necessary to analyze each heartbeat, in detail, to detect a specific heartbeat. Therefore, unsupervised classification is preferred in this approach, being clustering the most frequently used technique for unsupervised analysis of ECG signals. In addition, given the wide amount of heartbeats and the highly transitory nature of pathologies, processing time and unbalanced classes are other important issues to be taken into consideration.

In this work, a full methodology for segment unsupervised grouping is presented that improves the computational cost and sensitivity to unbalanced

J.M. Ferrández Vicente et al. (Eds.): IWINAC 2017, Part I, LNCS 10337, pp. 456–463, 2017.
DOI: 10.1007/978-3-319-59740-9_45

classes in comparison with traditional analysis scheme [1,2,5]. Proposed method includes proper stages for characterization, feature selection, initial parameters estimation and partitional clustering. All these stages are developed in a sequential scheme, where similar clusters are grouped into new clusters per couple of segments taking into account exclusion and merger criteria based on dissimilarities. Signals are characterized using techniques recommended by scientific literature, including: heart rate variability (RR period), Hermite coefficients and wavelet detail and approximation coefficients (db2). Feature selection stage is carried out through the Q-alpha algorithm, which employs spectral information and cluster coherence analysis to determine the relevance features and the estimate number of clusters. For unsupervised grouping, the estimation of the number groups employing spectral techniques is first performed. Next, to avoid the problem of convergence into a local minimum distant from optimal value, JH-means criterion, which is based on minimum sum of squares and dynamic assignment of centers, is applied to determine the initial partition. Finally, clustering stage is done by using a general iterative model for center-based clustering with soft membership functions; in particular, density-based clustering with nonparametric estimation is considered.

2   Materials and Methods

2.1   Clustering

Clustering is the assignment of a set of observations into subsets so that observations in the same cluster are considered similar with regard to employed features. Because of expensive computational cost that is inherent to clustering analysis when having a large data set, methods based on heuristic searches are commonly used, which basically follow the next steps [3].

Cluster Initialization. Since the need of computational stability and a proper initial partition, a convenient number of subsets over the studied recording data might be fixed, providing an stable initial partition of grouping stage. In particular, a trivial form of subset number, k, is achieved if adjusting this amount equal to the number of unity eigenvalues of next normalized affinity matrix [6]:

$$\mathbf{A}^* = \mathbf{D}^{-1/2}\mathbf{A}\mathbf{D}^{-1/2}, \ \mathbf{A} = \mathbf{Y}\mathbf{Y}^\top,$$

where $\mathbf{D} = \mathrm{diag}(\mathbf{A}\mathbf{1}_n)$ is the grade of matrix $\mathbf{A}$, and $\mathbf{1}_d$ is a d–dimensional unity vector and $\mathbf{Y}$ is a linear weighted projection of the data matrix $\mathbf{X}$.

Matrix $\mathbf{Y} = \widetilde{\mathbf{X}}\mathbf{V}$, where $\mathbf{V}$ corresponds to the principal components of $\widetilde{\mathbf{X}}$ and $\widetilde{\mathbf{X}} = \mathbf{X}\mathbf{W}$, represents the weighted data matrix. A detailed analysis of the weighting matrix $\mathbf{W}$ is discussed in [4].

Once a group number is fixed, initial centers are fixed by using JH–means algorithm, which avoids clustering solution falls into a local minima, is based on iteratively searching of optimal local space solution, as discussed in [7].

Grouping. To make sure that individual class distributions are of Gaussian class the well known expectation maximization procedure is used, when the next expression is minimized:

$$E = -\sum_{i=1}^{n} \log \left(\sum_{j=1}^{k} p(\mathbf{x}_i \mid \mathbf{q}_j) p(\mathbf{q}_j) \right) \qquad (1)$$

where $p(q_j)$ is the prior probability for a cluster with centroid q_j, and $p(x_i \mid q_j)$ is the conditional probability between data and different centroids, which is estimated by Parzen's window approach, as described in [8]. In this case, optimization task is achieved by a general iterative model for clustering that allows an actualization of centroids by introducing a soft membership function as well as fixed weights. This method is well-described in [7].

Performance Measures. As a cluster validity measure the *clustering index* $\gamma = E_1/E_2$ is proposed that expresses the relation between the expected value of the objective function (1), assessed if considering an ideal partition E_1, and the value E_2 estimated for the final partition. Since $E_2 \geq E_1$ one might infer that index is regarded to a proper clustering if its value lies some close to 1. It must be quoted that the measure proposed above is no sensitive to the number of clusters.

On the other hand, as another cluster validity measure to be considered, clustering quality is assessed that is based on spectral graph partitioning [9], when a good clustering desires both tight connections within partitions and loose connections between partitions. Thus, the cluster coherence is calcules as follows:

$$\epsilon_M = \frac{1}{k} \sum_{l=1}^{k} \frac{\mathbf{M}_l^\top \mathbf{A} \mathbf{M}_l}{\mathbf{M}_l^\top \mathbf{D} \mathbf{M}_l}$$

where $\mathbf{M}$ is the matrix formed by the membership values of all elements to each cluster: $M_{ij} = m(\mathbf{q}_j/\mathbf{x}_i)$, $\mathbf{M}_l$, denotes a membership submatrix associated with the cluster l.

The matrix $\mathbf{M}$ is binary, then, when smooth clustering is implemented, the following conversion must be performed, $m_{ij} = \langle \max \arg m(\mathbf{q}_j/\mathbf{x}_i) \rangle$, $j = 1, \ldots, k_r$, where $\langle \cdot \rangle$ is 1 if its argument is true and 0 otherwise. Due to normalization with respect to the affinity matrix, the maximum value of ε_M is 1, therefore, it indicates a good clustering if its value is near 1. Furthermore, because of the nature of the function, a large set of groups is penalized.

Nonetheless, this work takes advantage of the fact that studied database is labeled and supervised measures are accomplished. Thus, performance outcomes can be contrasted with another similar works.

The sensibility and specificity quantify the proportion of beatings from OC and the MC that are correctly classified, respectively. Both indexes measure the partition quality with respect to ideal case, when the quantity of clusters equates to the number of classes, but each cluster holding just one class beatings. Nonetheless, there is no ideal partition, i.e., one should expect more clusters than classes. Besides, some clusters may contain majority and minority beatings from another classes. Therefore, the partition might be penalized when holding a relatively large number of groups, as discussed in [4].

2.2 Segment Analysis

In this work, a segment-based approach is introduced to decrease the computational cost. The general idea of this approach is to divide input recordings into segments to be independently processed and clustered, and at the end formed clusters for each segment are merged according to union and exclusion criteria. Then, the first step is fixing a proper number of segments. This parameter is estimated for each recording and chosen as one that its validity measures provide equivalent or better performance than the analysis of full length processing of input recordings. The proper selection of number of localized clustering segments is constrained by following restrictions: twice of number of features must exceed the amount of heartbeats per segment, and the minimum of computational cost should be reached. All segments are to have the same length.

After grouping all data points belonging to each segment as described in Sect. 2.1, the second step is segment merger. To this end, some criteria based on estimation of the proximities between each cluster and the remaining clusters are considered. Merger process is carried out in a sequential scheme where segment are merged per couples as follows. Clusters corresponding to the two first contiguos segments are merged, resultant partition from such merger is then joined with the clusters of immediately next segment and so on. Lastly, clusters are merged or conserved as independent ones according to a dissimilarity measure among heartbeats related to the set of centroids. In this connection, DTW algorithm, denoted as $\mathrm{dtw}(\cdot, \cdot)$, is used, as detailed in [1].

The segment analysis procedure is explained in Algorithm 1. The number of groups k^l is estimated for each segment as described in Sect. 2.1.

With segment clustering algorithm proposed here, incorrect clustering of minority classes is avoid as well as computational load is decreased.

2.3 Proposed Method

Figure 1 depicts a methodology for Holter arrhythmia analysis that appraises the next stages: (a) Preprocessing, (b) Feature estimation, (c) Analysis of relevance, and (d) Clustering. Recordings are preprocessed and segmented based on calculation of QRS complex.

Heartbeat features, which are calculated using variability, prematurity, morphology and representation measurements of the heart rate variability, are extracted by weighted linear projection. Lastly, projected data is grouped by soft clustering algorithm. Because of restrictions for reducing computational load, the methodology is complemented by framing along the time axis the input data into N_s successive divisions of Holter recordings, where each frame is separately

---

Algorithm 1. Segment clustering

Given the input data set $\mathbf{X} \in \mathbb{R}^{n \times p}$, the number of segments N_s and a constraint parameter ϵ

1. Divide the set of data into N_s segments: $\mathbf{X} = \{\mathbf{X}_1, \ldots, \mathbf{X}_{N_s}\}$, where $\mathbf{X}_l$ is a $n_l \times p$ sub-matrix and $n_l = \mathrm{round}(n/N_s)$

2.   Cluster data points of each segment in k^l groups, i.e., form partitions $\mathbf{P}^l = \{\mathbf{C}_1^l, \ldots, \mathbf{C}_{k^l}^l\}$ and compute their respective centroids $\mathbf{Q}^l = \{\mathbf{q}_1^l, \ldots, \mathbf{q}_{k^l}^l\}$

For $l = 2$ **until** N_s **do**

   3. Compare centroids: $\vartheta = \mathrm{dtw}\left(\mathbf{b}(\mathbf{q}_a^l), \mathbf{b}(\mathbf{q}_b^{l-1})\right)$,

   where $\mathbf{b}(\mathbf{q})$ denotes the pattern vector corresponding to centroid $\mathbf{q}$ and $a = 1, \ldots, k^l; b = 1, \ldots, k^{l-1}$

   if $\vartheta < \epsilon$

   4. Cluster $\mathbf{C}_a^l$ is merged with $\mathbf{C}_b^{l-1}$: $\mathbf{C}_a^l \leftarrow \mathbf{C}_a^l \bigcup \mathbf{C}_b^{l-1}$

   otherwise

   Cluster $\mathbf{C}_a^l$ is considered to be an independent cluster for the next segment analysis

   End If

End For

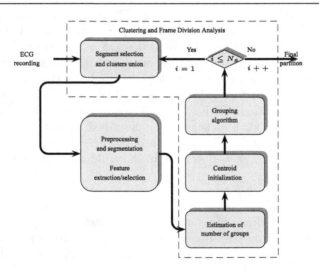

Fig. 1. Block diagram of proposed unsupervised methodology for Holter monitoring of cardiac arrhythmias.

processed. Therefore, according to the assumed criterium of homogeneity between two given consecutive frame divisions, resulting clusters can be either merged or split.

3 Results

The results of clustering are accomplished by framing each recording into $N_s = 6$ divisions and the resulting clusters are merged as described in Sect. 2.1. The number of segments is achieved experimentally, improving the trade–off among the number of segments, computational cost and quality of partition. Thus, the segment analysis enhances the performance if comparing to the whole data clustering. In fact, it reduces the probability that a minority class heartbeat might be clustered wrongly. Furthermore, in most cases, the sum of processing times over all segments turns to be considerably shorter than the time of analysis of whole recording data for one iteration. Therefore, the introduced framing approach significantly reduces the computational cost.

The Fig. 2 shows a comparison of the system performance using the sensibility measure described in Sect. 2.1. This test was carried out by varying the number of segments (N_s) from 1 to 10 and using as input data the complete feature set and the processed data with the relevance analysis methods discussed above. It can also see that sensibility increases as N_s increases.

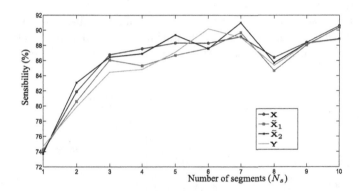

Fig. 2. Comparison between proposed method and the reference methods using error bars, which measure processing time and performance

Figure 3 depicts the behavior of computational cost of the proposed method by varying N_s from 1 to 10. When $N_s = 1$, the methods spend more time to carry out the process, but when N_s increases, the processing time decreases.

Defining the unit time (TU) as the time necessary to process the whole record in one iteration $(N_s = 1)$ using only the initial vector of features, resultant performance can be expressed as multiples or fractions of TU. Figure 4 shows some error bars where it is noted that computational cost improve as N_s increase. This test was carried out using all the relevance analysis methods and the initial data set, however, in Fig. 4 are shown the most relevant results making a comparison between Q-α and reference methods, i.e., by analyzing all variables, the relevant ones and PCA. When $N_s = 1$, WPCA and PCA methods spend more time to carry out the process regarding the reference methods, but when N_s

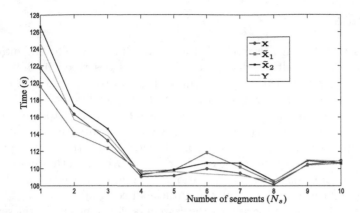

Fig. 3. Comparison between proposed method and the reference methods using error bars, which measures processing time and performance

increases, the processing time decreases. It can also see that error bar calculated as $1 - Se/100$, decreases as N_s increases.

In Fig. 4 can be seen that after some number of segments, the computational cost increases again. This is because the initialization and feature selection routines that are performed for each segment, increase processing time.

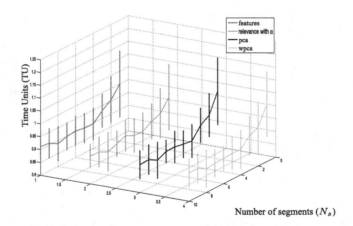

Fig. 4. Comparison between proposed method and the reference methods using error bars, which measure processing time and performance

4   Conclusions

The proposed methodology includes the segment analysis that compensates the high computational cost employed in Holter analysis, being possible its implementation for real time applications. Besides, the assumed grouping an initialization stage, which includes estimation of number of groups and center initialization, is based on spectral techniques and soft partitional clustering and generates a proper final partition.

The methodology provides an useful tool to analyze cardiac arrhythmias with suitable quality since it is based on non-supervised training, that is, there is no need for labelling of recordings, which mostly is not feasible for Holter monitoring.

Testing of considered methodology by using introduced cluster validity measures shows a comparable performance in comparison to another referenced works, based on either supervised or unsupervised training and carried out for the MIT/BIH database.

As future work, additional spectral clustering stages should be explored with the possibility of unifying the stages of feature selection and clustering, in order to improve further the accuracy and the computational load for the system.

Acknowledgements. This work is part of project number 249-028, funded by the Universidad Autónoma de Manizales.

References

1. Cuesta, D., Biagetti, M., Quinteiro, R., Mico-Tormos, P., Aboy, M.: Unsupervised classification of ventricular extrasystoles using bounded clustering algorithms and morphology matching. Med. Biol. Eng. Comput. **45**(3), 229–239 (2007)
2. De-Chazal, P., O'Dwyer, M., Reilly, R.: Automatic classification of heartbeats using ECG morphology and heartbeat interval features. IEEE Trans. Biomed. Eng. **51**(7), 1196–1206 (2004)
3. Jain, A., Murty, M., Flynn, P.: Data clustering: a review. ACM Comput. Surv. **31**(3), 265–323 (1999)
4. Rodríguez-Sotelo, J.L., Delgado-Trejos, E., Peluffo-Ordoñez, D., Cuesta-Frau, D., Castellanos-Domínguez, G.: Weighted-PCA for unsupervised classification of cardiac arrhythmias. In: Conference proceedings of the IEEE Engineering in Medicine and Biology Society, pp. 1906–1909 (2010). http://www.sciencedirect.com/science/article/B6WDJ-4NX2NHW-4/2/bcd26d87922d1691141f30adfbaab88b
5. Lagerholm, M., Peterson, C., Braccini, G., Edenbrandt, L., Sörnmo, L.: Clustering ECG complexes using hermite functions and self-organising maps. IEEE Trans. Biomed. **48**, 838–847 (2000)
6. Ng, A.Y., Jordan, M.I., Weiss, Y.: On spectral clustering: analysis and an algorithm. In: Advances in Neural Information Processing Systems 14, pp. 849–856. MIT Press (2001)
7. Rodríguez-Sotelo, J.L., Peluffo, D., Frau, D.C., Ordónez, D.P., Domínguez, G.C.: Non-parametric density-based clustering for cardiac arrhythmia analysis. In: Computers in Cardiology, CINC (2009)
8. Sotelo, J.L.R., Peluffo, D., Frau, D.C., Ordónez, D.P., Domínguez, G.C.: Non-parametric density-based clustering for cardiac arrhythmia analysis. In: Computers in cardiology, CINC (2009)
9. Yu, S.X., Shi, J.: Multiclass spectral clustering. In: Proceedings of the Ninth IEEE International Conference on Computer Vision ICCV 2003, p. 313. IEEE Computer Society, Washington, DC (2003)

Towards a Deep Learning Model of Retina: Retinal Neural Encoding of Color Flash Patterns

Antonio Lozano[1], Javier Garrigós[1]($\boxtimes$), J. Javier Martínez[1],
J. Manuel Ferrández[1], and Eduardo Fernández[2]

[1] Dpto. Electrónica, Tecnología de Computadoras y Proyectos,
Universidad Politécnica de Cartagena, Cartagena, Spain
javier.garrigos@upct.es
[2] Instituto de Bioingeniería, Universidad Miguel Hernández, Alicante, Spain

Abstract. The retina is the first stage of visual neural information coding on the visual system, and several challenges remain on its functioning. Overcoming these challenges would suppose both a step further in the general understanding of the biological neural systems and a potential way to enhance millions of people's lives that suffer from visual degeneration or impairment. In this work, a data-driven deep learning approach is applied to learn the behavior of mice's retinal ganglion cells in response to light, as a step towards the development of a system able to mimic a real retina in terms of neural coding of visual stimuli.

Keywords: Retina modeling · Neural coding · Deep learning · Convolutional neural networks

1 Introduction

Neurosensory systems still remain as a big challenge to scientists, although great achievements have been done until now. Combined efforts from several scientific and engineering disciplines contributed to the knowledge and technology that allows us to prevent, treat and hopefully overcome some of the human diseases and limitations by building the knowledge corpus, diagnostic systems, rehabilitation treatments and prosthesis for the disabled among others. In this work, a deep learning data-driven approach is proposed to tackle one of this early neurosensory pathways challenges: the modeling of a mammal's retina in response to light patterns. In this first approach retinal neural recordings from homogeneous color flash patterns are taken, processed and fed into a supervised machine learning system -a 3D Convolutional Neural Network (CNN)- able to process spatio-temporal visual stimulus and reproduce the retinal behavior to this kind of patterns, with the aim of being able to mimic more complex responses in the future and to compare results with similar researches on the field.

In the past, several retinal ganglion cell's models have been proposed. Some of them are used as general models of early neurosensory pathaways, like Linear-Nonlinear [1], Generalized Linear Models [2] or Integrate and Fire [3], and their

J.M. Ferrández Vicente et al. (Eds.): IWINAC 2017, Part I, LNCS 10337, pp. 464–472, 2017.
DOI: 10.1007/978-3-319-59740-9_46

application provided different results as its shown on [4]. Recent works have proposed hybrid systems as fine tuning physiological models with Genetic Algorithms [4] and the use of Deep Learning techniques [4–6].

In the last few years, the field of machine learning witnessed the raise of new deep artificial neural networks architectures -CNNs, LSTMs, GRUs, hybrid architectures, GANs- with a series of features like dropout [7] for regularization purposes, parameter sharing that decreased the computational cost per layer and the wide use of alternatives to the sigmoid and hyperbolic tangent activation functions -ReLU, LeakyRELU, PRelu, ELU- that helped to handle the vanishing gradient problem and performed better in some situations [8]. In addition, the high computational charge that this machine learning systems entails has been notably tackled by the use of GPUs.

Recently, Convolutional Neural Networks have been proved to be a great tool for visual recognition problems, outperforming other traditional machine learning techniques [9] like SVMs, with the significant advantage of being able to perform end-to-end learning, this is, the absence of a necessity for hand-craft features. This, and the structural analogy between CNNs and the visual LGN-V1-V2-V4-IT pathaway [10], following the way of Fukushima's Neocognitron [11], makes CNNs to be a likely suitable solution for the bio-inspired vision encoding task.

This kind of CNN, data-driven methodology has been recently used for modeling tiger salamander retina ganglion cells [4], and it is also the methodology on which our modeling is driven. In [4], convolutional neural networks were proved to be able to model more accurately retinal responses to both natural and artificial stimuli than the previous techniques and generalize better across stimuli types when modeling a tiger salamander's retina. In our approach, a deep convolutional neural network is trained to mimic the spike trains obtained after stimulating real mice retina with simple color patterns.

The rest of this paper is organized as follows. Section 2 presents the methods for retinal response recording and the proposed modeling approach. Section 3 shows and discusses the results obtained with our experimental setup and the 3D-CNN model architecture implemented. Finally, Sect. 4 summarizes the main contributions of our research and the remaining challenges.

2 Proposed Methodology

2.1 Materials and Methods: Retinal Recordings and Pre-processing

Retinas were extracted from wild-type mice bred within a local mice colony following the same preparation setup as in [12]. Extracellular recordings were obtained from the retinal ganglion cell layer in the isolated mouse retina using an array of 100 electrodes with 400 μm inter–electrode distances [13].

The data obtained from each channel was digitized with 16-bit resolution and 30 kHz sampling rate and stored together with the visual stimulus provided to the retina. The recorded spike events were characterized using Nev2lkit, a free open source software for spike sorting [14].

The retina was then stimulated with several repetitions of a 500 ms color flash followed by darkness for 1500 ms, as it is shown in Fig. 1.

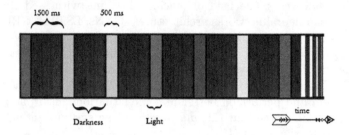

Fig. 1. Temporal representation of the stimulus, consisting in homogeneous color flases presented periodically. (Color figure online)

The detected spike trains for every one of the 26 retinal ganglion cells that provided useful information attending standard deviation significance and noise levels, together with the corresponding stimulus were considered valid data to develop our retina model. The model's training input will consist on batches of 40 frames taken from the stimuli, each frame of 50×50 pixels representing one hundred of second of video, this is, 400 ms of temporal stimuli, (Fig. 1), and the output will be a spiking probability function for each of the 26 neurons recorded that provided insightful data. This function comes from the convolution of spike trains with a Gaussian function which transforms this discrete spike events into a virtually continuous objective to fit, so it transforms a classification problem -discrete classes corresponding to number of spikes in a bin- into a regression one -analog firing function-.

2.2 Proposed Modeling Approach

In this work, a data-driven approach is proposed for the model, in contrast with the usual physiological models of retina. Our goal is to build a system that is able to learn by itself the necessary computations to produce a response similar to the recorded behavior of a biological retina.

The architecture of the proposed model (Fig. 2) consists on a series of 3-dimensional convolutions of volumes of data coming from the stimulus video frames followed by a fully connected -dense- layer that will provide the desired output. Each convolutional layer is followed by an nonlinear activation function (ReLU, PReLU) and a Maxpooling layer in some cases to reduce the dimensionality of the output volume of the convolution layers and promote feature spatio-temporal invariance. An empirical, trial-and-error process was carried out to adjust the size and several parameters of the different layers. The selected values frequently represent a trade off between several tendencies. For example, it should be noted that applying pooling to the temporal axis would mean more robustness to pattern shifts on this dimension and less computational charge on the consequent layers, but certain temporary dependence was desirable to model the behavior of the retina, so an excess of temporal pooling would undermine temporal resolution and therefore, model prediction ability of the temporal dynamics.

After these stages, the resultant tensor is flattened and it inputs a fully connected layer, called also a dense layer, followed with another nonlinear activation function that will output the firing probability prediction for each neuron every hundredth of second.

The actual spikes were then generated by simulating a Poisson process with a millisecond resolution for each firing probability estimate. The number and size of the filters was varied to achieve the best results. As expected, the temporal dimension of the kernels was the most relevant set of parameters, given that in this experiment, the spatial dimensions of the network's didn't provide more information than flash's color (RGB values of the pixels). The network showed robustness to a wide range of values on the search space for the number and dimensions of the filters, probably indicating that this network exceeded the computational power to map the input with the desired output. While this could be seen as a waste of resources in usual applications, its to be noticed that here we were developing a prototype that should be able to fit high spatio-temporal complex patterns in the near future.

For the weight initialization, a Lecun uniform function was used, which takes samples from an uniform distribution parametrized in relation to the number of inputs to that layer [15]. Both L1 and L2, and eventually activity regularizers were also included among the parameters for every layer. The network building and training was performed using the widely adopted deep learning frameworks Tensorflow [16] and Keras [17].

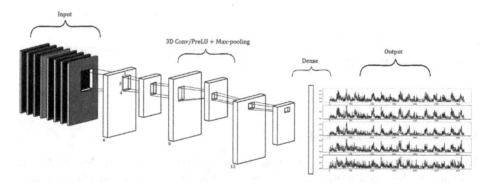

Fig. 2. Illustration of one of the 3D CNN's architectures tested, with 6, 8 and 12 filters respectively in the convolutional layers and $3 \times 3 \times 4$ kernels. (Color figure online)

3   Results

3.1   Training

Training was performed over 90% of 360000 data samples (obtained from 360 s of stimulus-response recording of sliding volumes of frames) and the correspondent probability of spikes for the 26 neurons, with a standard 70–30% split for training/validation, while the remaining 10% of the recorded data was used as held-out data for testing. Different dropout percentages were used in the layers of the network to prevent overfitting and several optimizers like ADAM, Stochastic Gradient Descend and RMSprop were tested. The loss functions that achieved better performance were Poisson and Mean Squared Logarithmic Error (MSLE), which lead to slightly different characteristic shaping of the objective function.

Figure 3 shows the evolution of Poisson loss objective function for training and validation sets as training was performed. In addition, other indicators as Mean Absolute Error (MAE) and Mean Squared Error (MSE) were used for monitoring. Finally, early stopping was used, this is, the training stopped when the validation set error started to have a positive tendency, this is, when the model starts to overfit.

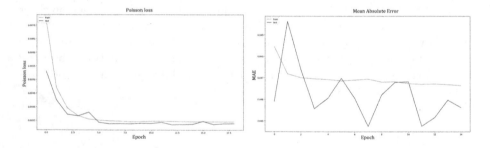

Fig. 3. Several indicators were monitored during training. In the image: minimizing Poisson cost function (left) and MAE (right).

3.2   Results and Discussion

To measure the goodness of the fitting, several metrics were used. Among them: Poisson loss between model predictions and unseen data (related with the log-likelihood of two variables under Poisson distribution assumption), Pearson's correlation coefficient between spiking probability functions and Pearson's coefficient between PSTH (Peri-Stimulus Time Histogram) generated from 29 trials of the same stimulus (6 color flashes) for every of the 26 neurons on the network's output (Fig. 4).

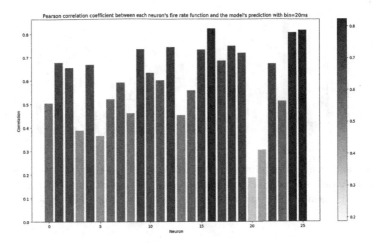

Fig. 4. Correlation coefficient between neuron's firing rate and model's prediction for the 26 neurons that were simulated. (Color figure online)

The results were encouraging, showing high correlations. As an example, Fig. 5 illustrates a PSTH from both model and biological neuron responses measured within 20 ms bins, with an 84% correlation coefficient and a qualitatively coherent behavior.

As Fig. 6 shows, the model responds with a different characteristic firing probability waveform to each of the stimuli, with a rising of the fire rate with a slightly different delay for each neuron when the light is showed and with a depression or rising of the spiking probability when the light faded out or after some hundredths of second of darkness. In brief, ON and ON/OFF behaviors

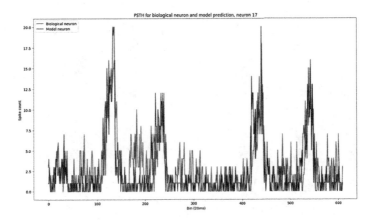

Fig. 5. Peri-stimulus Time Histogram (PSTH) of both real (blue) and model (black) neuron 17. (Color figure online)

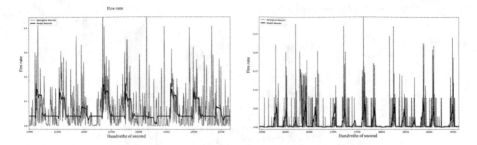

Fig. 6. Dynamic firing probability function of a real neuron (blue) versus model neuron (black). The model is able to fit different types of neurons at once, with different base firing rate and characteristic shapes. On the figure, neurons 17 -left- and 4 -right-. (Color figure online)

were observed both in the real retinal recordings and the model predictions, and the CNN was able to model at the same time a variety of neuronal behaviors to the same stimulus, with different qualitative responses and different fire rate baselines. This kind of adaptation can be observed in Fig. 6, where a comparison between a biological neuron's firing probability function and the CNN model's prediction is shown, for two neurons with significant different behavior.

It is also noticeable that the CNN was very sensitive to the gaussian smoothing of the actual spike train, changing the way of fitting depending on the standard deviation used on the gaussian, predicting poorly a mean fire rate when the standard deviation was too low and therefore, unable to compensate the neuron's variability on the response.

Figure 7 illustrates raster plots for both biological and model ganglion cell's responses to 29 repeated trials of the same light pattern (neuron 17 in this

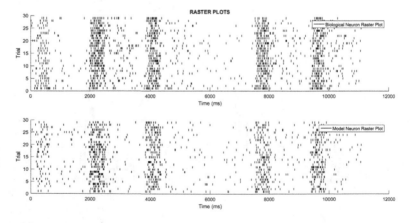

Fig. 7. Comparison between recordings and model generated raster plots for neuron 17.

case). Its noticeable that the CNN's neuron is predicting a qualitatively similar response than the real ganglion cell, with a concentrated firing activity after the light flashes and similar temporal dynamics.

4   Conclusions and Future Work

In this paper, a data-driven methodology for modeling retinal ganglion cell responses to color light flash patterns has been discussed and applied to the case of mice retina with positive results, showing high correlation with the spiking probabilities obtained from biological spike train responses. In addition, the Peri-Stimulus Time Histogram built from Poisson-simulated spike trains showed a similar behavior in both, the model and the real retina. On the way to achieving these good results, several structural and parametric decisions were taken for the model, resulting in a CNN model that showed high sensitivity to the activity and parametric regularizers on the dense layers on one side, and to the variance of the gaussian with which the spike trains were filtered on the other. These facts revealed that the retinal spiking variability handling will play an important role in future developments.

Among our proposals for future works, are the use of recurrent layers that take into account the spiking history of each neuron, the change in the spike generation to more advanced and flexible models like inhomogeneous Gamma and inverse Gaussian proposed in [18], the exploration of the inner activations and learned filters as done in [4,9], that may help in the understanding of retinal computations and, finally, the use of highly-complex and realistic visual stimulus that allows us to build a powerful and more generalizing retinal model.

Acknowledgements. We want to acknowledge Programa de Ayudas a Grupos de Excelencia de la Región de Murcia, from Fundación Séneca, Agencia de Ciencia y Tecnología de la Región de Murcia.

References

1. Pillow, J.W., Shlens, J., Paninski, L., Sher, A., Litke, A.M., Chichilnisky, E.J., Simoncelli, E.P.: Spatio-temporal correlations and visual signalling in a complete neuronal population. Nature **454**, 995–999 (2008)
2. Burkitt, A.: A review of the integrate-and-fire neuron model. Biol. Cybern. **95**(1–19), 97–112 (2006)
3. Chichilnisky, E.J.: A simple white noise analysis of neuronal light responses. Comput. Neural Syst. **12**, 199–213 (2001)
4. Mcintosh, L., Maheswaranathan, N., Nayebi, A., Ganguli, S., Stephen, A.: Deep learning models of the retinal response to natural scenes. Adv. Neural Inf. Process. Syst. **29**, 1369–1377 (2016)
5. Crespo-Cano, R., Martínez-Álvarez, A., Díaz-Tahoces, A., Cuenca-Asensi, S., Ferrández, J.M., Fernández, E.: On the automatic tuning of a retina model by using a multi-objective optimization genetic algorithm. In: Ferrández Vicente, J.M., Álvarez-Sánchez, J.R., de la Paz López, F., Toledo-Moreo, F.J., Adeli, H. (eds.) IWINAC 2015 Part I. LNCS, vol. 9107, pp. 108–118. Springer, Cham (2015). doi:10.1007/978-3-319-18914-7_12

6. Turcsany, D., Bargiela, A., Maul, T.: Modelling retinal feature detection with deep belief networks in a simulated enviroment. In: Proceedings of the ECMS 2014 (2014)
7. Srivastava, N., Hinton, G., Krizhevsky, A., Sutskever, I., Salakhutdinov, R.: Dropout: a simple way to prevent neural networks from overfitting. J. Mach. Learn. Res. **15**, 1929–1958 (2014)
8. He, K., Zhang, X., Ren, S., Sun, J.: Delving deep into rectifiers: surpassing human-level performance on imagenet classification. In: Proceedings of the 2015 IEEE International Conference on Computer Vision, pp. 1026–1034 (2015)
9. Krizhevsky, A., Sutskever, I., Geoffrey, E.: Imagenet classification with deep convolutional neural networks. In: 25th Proceedings of the Advances in Neural Information Processing Systems, pp. 1097–1105 (2012)
10. Lecun, Y., Bengio, Y., Hinton, G.: Deep learning. Nature **521**(7553), 436–444 (2015)
11. Fukushima, K.: Neocognitron: a self-organizing neural network model for a mechanism of pattern recognition unaffected by shift in position. Biol. Cybern. **34**(4), 193–202 (1980)
12. Díaz-Tahoces, A., Martínez-Álvarez, A., García-Moll, A., Humphreys, L., Bolea, J.Á., Fernández, E.: Towards the reconstruction of moving images by populations of retinal ganglion cells. In: Ferrández Vicente, J.M., Álvarez-Sánchez, J.R., de la Paz López, F., Toledo-Moreo, F.J., Adeli, H. (eds.) IWINAC 2015. LNCS, vol. 9107, pp. 220–227. Springer, Cham (2015). doi:10.1007/978-3-319-18914-7_23
13. Fernández, E., Ferrández, J.M., Ammermuller, J., Normann, R.: Population coding in spike trains of simultaneously recorded retinal ganglion cells. Brain Res. **887**(1), 222–229 (2000)
14. Bongard, M., Micol, D., Fernández, E.: NEV2lkit: a new open source tool for handling neural event files from multi-electrode recordings. Int. J. Neural Syst. **24**(04) (2014)
15. LeCun, Y., Bottou, L., Orr, G.B., Müller, K.-R.: Efficient backprop. In: Orr, G.B., Müller, K.-R. (eds.) Neural Networks: Tricks of the Trade. LNCS, vol. 1524, pp. 9–50. Springer, Heidelberg (1998). doi:10.1007/3-540-49430-8_2
16. Abadi, M., Agarwal, A., Barham, P., Brevdo, E., Chen, Z., Citro, C., Corrado, G., Davis, A., Dean, J., Devin, S., Ghemawat, S., Goodfellow, I., Harp, A., Irving, G., Isard, M., Jia, Józefowicz, R., Kaiser, L., Kudlur, M., Levenberg, J., Mané, D., Monga, R., Moore, S., Murray, D., Olah, C., Schuster, M., Shlens, J., Steiner, B., Sutskever, I., Talwar, K., Tucker, P., Vanhoucke, V., Vasudevan, V., Viégas, F., Vinyals, O., Warden, P., Wattenberg, M., Wicke, M., Yu, Y., Zheng, X.: TensorFlow: large-scale machine learning on heterogeneous distributed systems. In: Computer Science - Distributed, Parallel, and Cluster Computing, Computer Science - Learning (2016)
17. Chollet, F.: Keras 2015. https://github.com/fchollet/keras. Accessed March 2017
18. Barbieri, R., Quirk, C.M., Frank, L.M., Wilson, M.A., Brown, E.N.: Construction and analysis of non-poisson stimulus-response models of neural spiking activity. J. Neurosci. Methods **105**(1), 25–37 (2001)

Author Index

Printed in the United States
By Bookmasters